THE PATRICIAN TRIBUNE

STUDIES IN THE HISTORY OF GREECE AND ROME

P. J. Rhodes and Richard J. A. Talbert, editors

W. JEFFREY TATUM

The Patrician Tribune

Publius Clodius Pulcher

THE UNIVERSITY OF NORTH CAROLINA PRESS

CHAPEL HILL AND LONDON

© 1999 The University of North Carolina Press

All rights reserved

Designed by April Leidig-Higgins

Set in Minion by Keystone Typesetting, Inc.

Manufactured in the United States of America

Library of Congress Cataloging-in-Publication Data

Tatum, W. Jeffrey. The patrician tribune : Publius Clodius

Pulcher / by W. Jeffrey Tatum.

p. cm. — (Studies in the history of Greece and Rome)

Includes bibliographical references and index.

ISBN 978-0-8078-7206-2 (pbk: alk. paper)

1. Clodius, Publius, ca. 93–52 B.C. 2. Politicians—Rome—Biography.

3. Rome—Politics and government—265–30 B.C. I. Title. II. Series.

DG260.C63T37 1999   937'.06'092 [B]—DC21   98-37096 CIP

Portions of this work were previously published, in somewhat
different form, in "Cicero's Opposition to the *Lex Clodia de Collegiis*,"
Classical Quarterly 40 (1990): 187–94, and "The Poverty of the Claudii
Pulchri: Varro, *De Re Rustica* 3.16.1–2," *Classical Quarterly* 42 (1992):
190–200, and are reproduced here by permission of
Oxford University Press.

TO JANELLE MARIE TATUM

CONTENTS

This, however, is not painting a portrait; but gauging the length
and breadth of several features, and jotting down their dimensions
in arithmetical ciphers.—CARLYLE

Clodius Pulcher has always been deemed important, in varying guises. He attracts the attention of the critic of Catullus and of the student of Cicero. His transition from patrician to plebeian status alerts the historian of early Rome. His participation in and legislation on constitutional and religious matters, as well as his mobilization of popular demonstrations and violence, are topics that in themselves and in their connections impinge upon significant aspects of Roman legal and cultural history. And his political career, in the final decade of the republic, looms too large for anyone to overlook it. Nevertheless, for far too long scholars were disposed to regard Clodius, if not actually as something of a bizarre and awful prodigy, then rather narrowly as "the enemy" (of Cicero, of the *optimates*, of the state, of the prevailing social order) or as a virtual cipher (for Crassus, for Caesar, for the dynasts). The inclination to reduce Clodius to someone's foil or fill-in had the effect of tending to eliminate Clodius himself from consideration as a factor in as well as a product of the events of the fifties. Nor was the study of Clodian legislation, or of other issues associated with Clodius, unaffected by this habitual simplification.

Everything was transformed in 1966, when Erich Gruen, in a seminal article, rejected past depictions of Clodius as a mere "instrument." On the contrary, Gruen insisted, it was necessary to view Clodius as an "independent agent," an argument he advanced with compelling clarity and conciseness. Incisive and penetrating—and revisionist—studies followed immediately, the best of which remain those of Lintott and Rundell. Gruen's article has done so much to reinvigorate and to advance our appreciation of Clodius that one fears the accusation of ingratitude if one ventures to criticize it. But it must be said that Gruen, and perhaps too many of his successors, go too far in their revisionism. Gruen's Clodius, simply but I think fairly put, possesses such consistent and extraordinary independence as neither Cicero nor even Caesar could display. In other words, the pendulum swung too far to the other extreme. The problem lies in the radical polarity imposed upon our estimation of Clodius's performance in political life. The treatment of Clodius offered here, though far closer on this point to Gruen than to his predecessors, strives to achieve a more balanced view. It will be for others, of course, to adjudicate its success. In any case, there is more to Clodius's politics than his relationship with the dynasts, and the pages that follow attempt to cover, sometimes in necessarily technical detail, other dimensions of Clodius's political triumphs and failures.

Biographical studies of Clodius have not been plentiful. The brisk survey by Lacour-Gayet, while not without value, reads (more transparently than most accounts of late republican history) as a pastiche of Ciceronian excerpts, filled in with odd bits of Plutarch and Dio. Far more valuable, indeed still worthwhile on its own terms, is the monograph-length article in volume two of Drumann and Groebe's *Geschichte Roms*, the faults of which are due mostly to its being so outdated. The present book represents the first biography of Clodius Pulcher in English and, so far as I know, the first modern biography in any language.

Which is not to say that there has been a shortage of scholarship devoted to Clodius. In recent years Clodius's life and career have been illuminated, from a variety of perspectives, by numerous books and articles. To offer a doxography is to invite *invidia*, but there can be no overlooking the technical contributions of Linderski and Flambard, the flood of publications by Loposzko, the careful and elegant researches of Moreau, or the sociological advances made by Nippel. My debts to these scholars, and to many others, I have endeavored to document in my notes. They will be obvious in the text in any case. Two fairly recent works require specific comment. Frequent reference will be made in the following passages, often in dissent, to P. J. J. Vanderbroeck's *Popular Leadership and Collective Behavior in the Late Roman Republic (ca. 80–50 B.C.)* and to H. Benner's *Die Politik des P. Clodius Pulcher*. This should not be taken as a negative commentary on the usefulness of either volume, especially of the former. And their abundant presence in my notes attests to the seriousness with which I take both studies. But I cannot deny that my premises, my approaches, and, consequently, my conclusions are frequently (and frequently notably) different from either Vanderbroeck's or Benner's.

Because varying premises about the nature of political and social life in the late republic can lead to divergent interpretations of the same events, I have thought it best to state my prepossessions plainly and from the start. Hence the opening chapter, which is my own synthetic representation of the nature of Roman politics and some of the main problems affecting its study. I do not aver that the chapter is markedly original, only that it serves to indicate the understanding of Roman politics and society that will subtend my investigation of Clodius's career. At the very least, I hope that it will clarify for the reader what is here meant by, say, *popularis*, or what I take to be some of the central complexities that confronted all Roman statesmen. Thereafter the shape of the book is one natural to a biographical approach: it is chronological, though with excursions into constitutional, religious, and legal matters embedded in the narrative. These excursions are not by any means digressions; quite the contrary: in my view they are every bit as important to a proper understanding of Clodius's significance to the late republic as is the narrative of Clodius's trials, campaigns for office, political violence, and public posturing. No apologies, I trust, are required for a discussion of the late republic which takes Clodius as its emphasis and unifying principle. I hope that I will not be charged with having succumbed to any "great man" philosophy of history.

I come now to the acknowledgments, the part of the book I have most looked forward to writing. The research on which this study is based was funded in part by grants from the Council on Faculty Research of The Florida State University, whose assistance I happily recognize. My gratitude to those who have read and criticized my work, in toto or in part, by letter or viva voce, as well as to those who have throughout this project helped and encouraged me, is immeasurable. Which makes it a pleasure for me to express my thanks to the late A. E. Astin, Ernst Badian, Tom Hillard, Allan Kershaw, Christoph Konrad, T. Loposzko, Philippe Moreau, and Christopher Ratté. I have benefited enormously from the kindness and the erudition of Jerzy Linderski and Robin Seager, each of whom has gone far beyond anyone's conception of the requirements of friendship. Of my colleagues at The Florida State University, my greatest debts, gladly recalled, are to Hans-Friedrich Mueller, John Kelsay, Jeff Knapp, David Levenson, and Tim Stover. Though I have enjoyed so many benefactors, I am nonetheless especially grateful to Tessa Bartholomeusz, whose support, advice, and friendship have been invaluable. Two notices remain: All that a student can owe to his teacher, that and so much more I owe to M. Gwyn Morgan. And what I owe to Janelle Tatum, who was once my wife and who has endured everything involved in the writing of this book, I need not reduce to words. This book is dedicated to her.

THE PATRICIAN TRIBUNE

CHAPTER ONE

Politics and Popularity
in the Late Roman Republic

1

Sallust insists that the *res publica* was ultimately torn apart when the dignity of the nobility and the liberty of the people were corrupted into rapacity and predaciousness.[1] Rabble-rousing tribunes inveighed against the senate, whose members found specious pretexts for defending their own privileged position. During the late republic, Sallust laments, "all those who disturbed the commonwealth put forward worthy motives, some claiming to protect the rights of the people, others that they were strengthening the senate's authority. But it was all pretense. Every man was fighting for his own power" (*Cat.* 38). *Libertas populi* and *senatus auctoritas* were traditional principles of political authority whose inevitable tension reverberated through the history of the republic. For a time, when Hannibal's menace taught the senate and people of Rome the value of harmony and so long as the Romans' conquests could sustain the lesson, the unnatural chord of popular liberty and senatorial authority remained unbroken.[2] But the tribunate of Tiberius Gracchus, in the opinion of Cicero's Laelius, split a single people into two parts (*Rep.* 1.31), thereby initiating the much discussed conflict between *populares* and *optimates*.[3]

Our own treatment of this conflict must begin with the apparently straightforward question: who were the *populares*—or, perhaps better, what was a *popularis*, the singular form being the commoner?[4] The locus classicus for this inquiry is Cicero's *Pro Sestio*, in which speech the orator responds to the prosecution's emphatic designation of Sestius's associates—who, of course, included Cicero—as *natio optimatium* ("a race of superior men," *Sest.* 96): "There have always been two categories of men in this city who have endeavored to participate in public affairs and in doing so to distinguish themselves. Of these two categories, one desired to be deemed—and actually to be—*populares*; the other, *optimates*. Those who wished their words and deeds to be agreeable to the masses were considered *populares*; however, those who conducted themselves so that their policies might win the approval of the best citizens were considered *optimates*." Cicero's transparently biased formulation reveals the basic opposition: *populares* appeal to the masses, *optimates* to the "best men," a division of the citizenry that, by a bold twist, Cicero makes out to be wider in its embrace than even the *multitudo*: "Who, you may ask, is 'the best citizen'? They are uncountable in number (for otherwise the state could not exist). They are the principal men of the senate, and those who follow their lead; they are the men of the grandest orders, to whom a senatorial career is open; they are Romans living in municipalities and in the countryside; they are businessmen. Even freedmen are among the *optimates*. The numbers of the *optimates* are spread far and wide—and at various levels of society. To avoid misunderstanding, the whole category can be characterized and defined in brief: all are *optimates* who are neither criminal nor evil by nature, nor mad nor weighed down by private debt." The *optimates*, Cicero then concludes, are the healthy, the wealthy, and the wise (*et integri et sani et bene de rebus domesticis*).

Cicero's comments are obviously partisan; the *Pro Sestio* is not an analytical treatise. Nonetheless, it demonstrates the difficulty of recovering the true nature of *popularis* politics: Cicero, our principal informant, nearly always casts the *popularis* in the role of demagogue, while the optimate opponent stands for all that is best for the *res publica*.[5] Yet, because he hoped to be convincing, certain general truths had to be respected. As Cicero must concede, the *popularis* was not a recent phenomenon. However late it was before the term actually entered political discourse, such politicians had in a sense always been in Rome, which means that they hardly represented a radical departure from *mos maiorum*.[6] What, then, rendered the *popularis* objectionable? The good man and the bad alike, Sallust declaims, seek glory, office, and power; what distinguishes them are their approaches: one is honest, the other, lacking in *bonae artes*, must rely on duplicity (*Cat.* 11.2). Cicero's censure of the *popularis* is not dissimilar: Cicero detests his attachment to the mob— and his opposition to the senatorial elite. Such behavior the worldly consular could explain only as deriving from a flaw in character.[7]

The *optimates*, according to Cicero, sought *otium cum dignitate*, honorable and dignified peace, a blessed state that relied upon venerable foundations: "religious scruple, the auspices, the powers of the magistrates, the authority of the senate, the law, tradition, the courts, the rule of law, good faith and credit, the provinces, the allies, the glory of the empire, the army, the treasury" (religiones, auspicia, potestates magistratuum, senatus auctoritas, leges, mos maiorum, iudicia, iuris dictio, fides, provinciae, socii, imperi laus, res militaris, aerarium, *Sest.* 98). Now of course no Roman could object to Cicero's reverence for religion, tradition, or *fides*; these laudable elements are present in Cicero's catalog primarily in order to create the appropriate climate for Cicero's exaltation of *senatus auctoritas* and *aerarium*, terms whose significance is more sharply felt once one perceives the absence from the list of *libertas* or *populi iura*.[8] P. A. Brunt has rightly emphasized that whatever decency is implied or indicated by Cicero's description of the *optimates*, it is solvency that makes for the genuine good man. The *popularis*, however, in his appeal to the masses linked himself to the very stratum that posed the most serious threat to men of means. The urban poor were "wretched, half-starved, ready to drain the treasury dry" (*Phil.* 13.16); the rural poor "have never appreciated this state nor wished to see it stable" (*Cat.* 4.19). In short, Cicero would have agreed wholeheartedly with Sallust's assertion that "men without means of their own are always envious of the good and raise up the bad. In their hatred of their own circumstances they are eager to turn everything upside down" (*Cat.* 37). For Cicero, the *popularis* was inevitably a threat to the senate's authority and to the state's stability.[9]

Because the various techniques of the *popularis* politician and the issues he typically espoused have been collected and studied in detail, a fuller picture than the one offered by Cicero can be provided.[10] With one notable exception, it is senators who are designated *populares*, most of them tribunes of the *plebs*.[11] The basis for the designation, in Meier's oft-repeated view, is a certain political style—one that enacts an opposition between people and senate and seeks to employ the legislative authority of the people rather than the prestige of the senate to meet its ends.[12] But what ends? The Gracchi sought agrarian reforms, at least initially, as well as certain material benefits for the urban *plebs*, such as grain subsidies. Legislation that curbed the arbitrary power of the senate and magistrates earned the *popularis* label, as did any bill that explicitly promoted popular sovereignty. Finally, and most intriguingly, there was a fair amount of *popularis* legislation that, while demanded in the people's name, was clearly a matter of importance only to a very limited and privileged portion of the *populus*; this was especially the case with legislation that promoted the interests of the equestrian order at the expense of the senate, the most obvious example being the various attempts at jury reform.[13] Consequently, the historian must take great care to shun the natural temptation to treat the *populares* exclusively or even primarily as champions of the poor and oppressed.

What emerges is an image of *optimates*, itself a collective that resists neat definition,[14] defending the status quo against the attacks of reformists, each side persuaded of its own correctness. That there was a need for reform, especially social reform, in the late republic is undeniable. The decay of the peasantry that sparked the Gracchan reforms is a familiar if vexing problem.[15] Equally well recognized are the misery and squalor that plagued the lives of the urban poor, who lived cramped, uncomfortable, and undernourished—ravaged by diseases born of Rome's grossly unhygienic conditions—in appalling tenement houses owned by insensitive landlords.[16] Nor can one ignore the discontents of the *equites* in Rome or of the Italian aristocracy, who after the Social War constituted a small but powerful portion of the *populus Romanus*.[17] The armies, and to be sure their generals, represented a threat to the republic of a completely different order.[18] And finally, and perhaps most importantly, Rome required reform at the institutional level; that most successful of city-states, so we are told, stood in need of reconceptualizing its political order, its constitution, in response to its international empire.[19] No *popularis*, however, ever sought to reform the political system in any genuinely radical sense.[20] Each reform proposal, insofar as it embodied an honest attempt to resolve a crisis, sought in its own way to maintain the integrity of the pristine *res publica*, which was nostalgically remembered with fondness, however faint or distorted the actual recollection. In other words, there was a conservative dimension to the innovations of the *populares* that renders epithets like "progressive" not merely anachronistic but inaccurate.[21] Similarly with *Fürsorgegesetze*: although many *popularis* proposals addressed the needs of the lower orders, it would be inaccurate to characterize the body of known *popularis* legislation as primarily oriented toward either welfare measures or social reform in general. And one hastens to point out that, whencesoever the original impulse for most social reforms, proposals were often successfully passed into law only through the influence of politicians who are not easily classified as *populares*.[22]

This is why it is misleading to attempt to define the *populares* as reformists devoted to particular ends. At least two further impediments arise. For one, the political concerns of *populares* varied over time. Crude divisions can be—and have been—made: the Gracchan reforms seem aimed at preventing the erosion of the peasantry and at the preservation of the traditional citizenry; in the aftermath of the Gracchi, *popularis* legislation focused on the requirements of the *equites*; in the post-Sulla period a significant quantity of *popularis* legislation directed itself toward enhancing the careers of political grandees, like Pompey or Caesar.[23] That this diverse body of proposals and legislation was *popularis* is vouchsafed by Cicero and other sources; its very variety, however, defies neat definition.

A second obstacle to describing a *popularis* in terms of his specific political program is the brief extension of the typical *popularis* career. Notwithstanding the qualification our limited sources inevitably impose on such observations, it remains the case that most *populares* were tribunes and that their *popularis* activity terminated with their office. Only Caesar and Clodius succeeded in maintaining themselves in lengthy and constant *popularis* careers.[24] Now there exists a natural and obvious relationship between the functions of the tribunate—whose principal duty, at least in theory, was to protect the *iura populi*—and the *popularis* stance; it is one, however, that should not be pressed too hard, since a review of tribunician activity during the late as well as the middle republic will reveal how few tribunes were in fact *popularis* in orientation.[25] At all events, because Roman politicians and Roman politics dealt principally with immediate and relatively short-term objectives, the lack of constancy on the part of identifiable *populares* is perhaps unsurprising. Nonetheless, its implications for a manageable conception of the *popularis* are inescapable. The condition of being a *popularis* was not necessarily expected to be permanent or irremediable (depending on one's point of view). As seems characteristic of Roman politics, the designation focused on the particular stance adopted in a particular situation.[26]

Consequently, scholars ordinarily resort to a definition based on political style: a *popularis* was one who—in opposition to the senatorial majority—pursued his political goals by appealing to the people.[27] This approach brings with it several advantages. It allows one to acknowledge the makeshift particularity, the tendency to converge into ad hoc conformations—the *Gegenstandsabhängigkeit*—of Roman political behavior.[28] It also explains very nicely not only why it is wrong to imagine that the *populares* formed anything resembling a modern political party but even why there was no necessary affinity among any collection of *popularis* politicians.[29] Indeed, nothing significant regarding the essential nature of a Roman politician's personal agenda, his intentions, or the type and particulars of his various connections follows necessarily from the mere fact that he is designated a *popularis* by the sources. After all, the institutions of popular legislation lay open to any magistrate with the proper power to exploit them. And unless one was willing to resort to military intervention, only one alternative was available to the politician stymied in the senate—though without question the example of C. Laelius (cos. 140), who so wisely and celebratedly relented in the face of senatorial opposition, represented what was from the optimate perspective the conduct ideally desired (Plut. *Ti. Gracch.* 8.3–4).

If the quintessence of *popularis* politics resides in technique, it must still be emphasized that *populares* were judged not solely by their methods but also by their motives. To take an easy example, Marcus Porcius Cato, while tribune in 62, passed a law that considerably expanded the scope of Roman grain subsidies; moreover, in 58 he benefited from the passage of an *imperium extraordinarium* that had been proposed by Clodius Pulcher.[30] The grain dole and extraordinary commands represent the most characteristic forms of *popularis* legislation in the final decades of the republic. Yet there was no question of Cato's being an enemy of the senatorial establishment. In 62 it served the interests of the senate to respect the welfare of the urban *plebs*; the demands of Cato's competitive dignity and the political exigencies of the moment prompted his acceptance of a special command in Cyprus.[31] In short, Cato's activities lack the attitude toward the senate and people that would lead a Roman of Cicero's leanings to condemn them. More embrangled cases might be adduced. The reformist tribune of 91, M. Livius Drusus was praised by Cicero as the bulwark of the senate and its virtual patron.[32] Significantly, Drusus's techniques and legislation were typically *popularis* in form, the critical difference residing in his powerful senatorial support, men like M. Aemilius Scaurus (cos. 115) and L. Licinius Crassus (cos. 95).[33] Before his term was out, however, Drusus, whose personal arrogance and burgeoning importance incited suspicion among his peers and whose reasonable proposals brought vigorous opposition from various forceful constituencies, lost the senate's backing, with catastrophic consequences. The details and difficulties of Drusus's tribunate need not detain us.[34] What emerges distinctly from his and Cato's career is the importance of personality and motive in the establishment and evaluation of a *popularis* political career. *Animorum disiunctio dissensionem facit.*[35]

To seek a strict and precise definition of the *popularis*, then, is probably a mistake. It seems better to conclude that there obtained a broad (but not indeterminable) notion of what it meant to be a *popularis*. Certain politicians claimed the designation, Cicero at times attempted to usurp it.[36] And some politicians will have had it foisted on them in the heat of disagreement and debate. Clearly, there were measures that had a *popularis* association, and certain political techniques likewise carried a *popularis* connotation. Not actions merely, but a distinct and recognizable attitude, one demonstrating support for popular *libertas* even in the face of senatorial infringement, indeed especially in the face of such opposition, must have been a factor of great importance in the challenging task of winning *popularitas*.[37] This opposition, if not pushed too far, need not have alienated the senatorial establishment invariably or irrevocably. Herein lies an insurmountable difficulty. Although we (like the Romans) can operate only in the domain of perceptions, it must nonetheless be admitted that the Romans sought to discern in the *popularis* his particular motivations. Sincerity is notoriously resistant to proof whereas results are both more conspicuous and more marked, but for the Roman *popularis* it was vital that he convince his constituency that the *via popularis* stood for something more to him than mere political manipulation—at least if he hoped to enjoy enduring popularity—while perhaps at the same time assuring his senatorial colleagues that he represented no menace to the republic (unless of course he was willing to hazard the senate's hostility). We must, then, incorporate into our definition of a *popularis* an element that—it being impossible to peer into the souls of our fellow human beings—is frustrating in its elusiveness. But there can be no avoiding the fact that it mattered a great deal that the *popularis* convince others of the honesty of his motives.

2

This brings us to the question of whether there existed in Rome a *popularis* ideology.[38] Granted that Roman culture did not stress the establishment or observance of well-articulated, systematic ideologies, it is apparent, just the same, that Romans held basic principles that were strongly enough felt that they often governed or influenced their political actions to a greater extent than did mere expediency. Romans may not have been consistent in the application of their principles, nor does coherence of a philosophical type emerge from our record of the past as a paramount Roman concern. Still, their various principles were rarely completely haphazard, and if we are willing to respect a syndrome of principles—a code—in lieu of a detailed manifesto as the basis for certain kinds of political decisions, then we may inquire into the question of a *popularis* ideology without straying from the character of Roman politics.

Roman politics was, from one perspective, the exercise of *virtus* for the sake of the common good in order to earn glory and praise from one's fellow citizens; from another, it was the competition among the elite for power and prestige, fierce and incessant strife for supremacy within a community of aristocrats whose membership was unable to tolerate a superior. The purpose of political life, from the former view, was the preservation and betterment of the *res publica*, a goal that all Romans professed to be the highest and one to which every individual ambition ought to be subordinated. The struggle for political preeminence, however, meant winning popular acclaim, securing election to the curule magistracies, and garnering the prestige to sway legislative assemblies and meetings of the senate. These two aspects of public life, though certain at times to promote discord and cross-purposes, were hardly incompatible, and to a large extent they define the warp and woof of the Roman political fabric. In the swirl of this activity, the government was charged with maintaining order and resolving crises. The grammar of Roman politics comprised many parts: birth, wealth, family ties, political friendships, and *clientela*, items whose relative importance—complicated by the distinctly varying circumstances of routine and exceptional political moments—continues to spark disagreement. It will be sufficient to observe that the rapid pace and evident complexity of Roman politics render it impossible to seize upon any one component as *the* key to understanding the whole, nor can we forget how many and conflicting were the demands simultaneously imposing themselves on the individual politician. As the individual sought to promote his interests in politics, he was confronted with the task of accommodating his own agenda with that of his colleagues and supporters even while he endeavored to ease the tension between the demands of his own *dignitas* and the loftier values sanctioned by tradition.[39]

This is clearest in the career of Cicero. Of all Romans, Cicero's are the best-known political sentiments, familiar not only from his numerous speeches and letters, but also from his political treatises, in which, inspired by the model of Greek philosophy, he felt the need to impose order and organization on his political instincts and ideals. Cicero's treatises required explication of a more serious nature than the persuasive and sometimes misleading disquisitions of his oratory. All of which provides us with not only a deep and detailed knowledge of Cicero's political beliefs, but also a possible means of measuring his honesty and his fealty to his own convictions. This is not the place to appraise Cicero's career in detail, but one must observe that, for all his *studium laudis* and despite the frequent criticism that Cicero was a political weathervane, he was in fact over his long career reasonably faithful to certain basic tenets. And when Cicero lapsed from his convictions, as he did in the aftermath of the conference at Luca, his letters manifest pangs of guilt and embarrassment.[40] At the outbreak of the civil war, though Cicero was dilatory in joining the Pompeians, his letters display unequivocally his strong resolution to stand with Pompey, notwithstanding that the faults of the man and his party—as well as the odds against them—were sorely plain.[41] The letters of Caelius Rufus contrast starkly: Cicero's cynical correspondent could readily admit that Caesar's cause was the worse, but because it was the stronger he intended to offer his full devotion to the invading proconsul.[42] The point of this is simply that, however natural it is for us to construe Roman politics exclusively in terms of powerful egos in constant competition for personal glory—and we are by no means wrong to do so in the proper measure—we should never ignore the fact that the Romans themselves, who were capable of remarkable openness in describing their motives,[43] viewed their actions in somewhat loftier terms, and at least some of them strove to be true to the *mos maiorum* as they understood it. For Cicero, the optimate ideology, which valued the primacy of the senate, the harmony of the orders, and the maintenance of property rights, lay at the root of many of his political choices and constantly served as the measure of his own political virtue.[44] It is not unreasonable to wonder if there existed senators of a *popularis* stamp who were similarly inspired by the concepts of popular liberty and the rights of the *plebs*.

That there existed principles to support an oppositional stance, at least one in favor of the *plebs*, cannot be doubted. The Conflict of the Orders that characterized the early republic and that drew to its peaceful conclusion with the passage of the *lex Hortensia* of 287, while it most notably brought about the amalgamation of the patrician and the plebeian aristocracy, also generated the tribunate, whose function throughout the republic was, through its wide-ranging powers, to protect plebeians from originally patrician but soon simply aristocratic magistrates. Furthermore, by making *plebiscita* binding on the entire populace, the *lex Hortensia* secured in principle and in fact the independent political power of the *plebs*. J. von Ungern-Sternberg has underscored how lasting the disaffection and disunion between humbler plebeians and the new nobility actually were.[45] The *plebs* continued to exist as a separate political entity; lowly plebeians remained aware of their inferiority in the face of the senate. And the tribunate, for all its incorporation into the aristocratic agenda, by virtue of the *auxilium* that it must surely have continued to offer to those in need (especially in usual, ordinary affairs), remained intrinsically an office of opposition. That is, the tribune, in his exercise of his regular duties, embodied the abiding possibility of conflict between magistrate and citizen, especially the humble citizen. All of which points to an ever present sense of popular estrangement from the dominant aristocracy.[46] Hence the success of a politician like C. Flaminius, who was able to capitalize on discontents still deeply felt despite the concessions that had been made by patricians to aristocratic plebeians.

One need not seek out aberrations: all politicians, regardless of their natural inclination, were obliged to court popular favor through public munificence, further indication of a traditional awareness of the need to conciliate the masses.[47] The extent to which the ancient record of the Conflict has been contaminated by the events of the late republic remains a controversial subject over which formidable authorities continue to wrangle.[48] What is incontestable is that certain ideas, such as *ius auxilii* (the tribune's right to offer his assistance to a citizen in jeopardy) and, more crucial yet, *ius provocationis* (the right of each citizen to make an appeal to the people in capital cases)—each predicated on potential opposition between commoner and magistrate, indeed, each based on the fear of victimization—emerged during the Conflict to remain constant themes in Roman politics, even if they were somewhat less prominent during and in the aftermath of the Second Punic War.[49] When in 121 Gaius Gracchus and his followers sought to secede to the Aventine, the message was clear: for Gaius, his *popularis* agenda was founded in the rights of the *plebs* that had been earned during the Conflict; it was sanctioned by *mos maiorum*.[50] Like *senatus auctoritas*, the *iura populi* were essential elements of the Roman constitution.

Nor can we afford to underestimate the significance of the theoretical sovereignty of the Roman people. "It is fitting that all powers, all commands, all commissions are granted by the Roman people" (Cic. *Leg. Agr.* 2.17). As Fergus Millar has stressed, the power of the Roman people was not merely a formal nicety to be alluded to in speeches and decrees, but was reflected in the nature of political conduct and even in the physical construction of the city.[51] If we need not exaggerate unduly the populist element in Roman political life that Millar claims to detect—and it is perverse to question the aristocratic locus of political initiative and activity in Rome—we must nonetheless appreciate how Millar's arguments vigorously remind us that popular *libertas* was sanctioned by law and by custom.[52] The constitution was neither a screen nor a sham. *Res publica*, Cicero informs us, meant *res populi*, and, while some parts of the *populus* clearly counted for more than other parts, its protection and even its admittedly limited participation in government were recognized as essential to the Roman constitution by Polybius and by Cicero, if more grudgingly by the latter.[53] Democracy did not inform the Roman conception of good statecraft. Yet that is no reason to think that all Roman aristocrats shared Cicero's disdain for the office of tribune, the *telum libertatis*, whose sworn duty was to preserve the rights of the *plebs*, a task that might even be felt to require the conferring of *beneficia* on the people.[54] Daily political practice demanded that all Roman politicians to some degree cultivate the people—or some component of the people—in manifold ways, whether descending to the forum, speaking from the Rostra, campaigning for office, or proposing and arguing legislation before an assembly. Respect for *libertas* obtruded even more strikingly upon the conduct of the ten tribunes, whose constant residence in Rome was obligatory and the very doors of whose homes had to remain open to the public they served.[55]

All of which is to say that there was ample material for the construction of senatorial principles that were sensitive to the rights of the people. It is frustrating that no political credo exists representing this perspective so fully as Cicero does the optimate point of view, but we can, I think, be fairly certain that it existed. Not that it will have mattered until the late second century. Again, as Millar has observed, we can with fairness describe the classical republic as a time when "popular rights become quite well established, and popular demands, for victories, booty and land, were quite easily met."[56] Perhaps we should be more explicit: there must have been senators who, motivated by principles analogous to (though rather different from) those that inspired Cicero, felt a deep obligation to preserving the *iura populi* and even to providing *commoda populi* (so long as it was responsible to do so).[57] Nor can this have been objectionable, however tasteless, to a senator of divergent sentiments, it being recognized that no one could deny the legitimacy either of *populi iura* or *senatus auctoritas*.

3

For us, given the nature of our sources, the *popularis* exists in the exercise of his opposition to the senatorial leadership, usually in a conflict brought to an extreme pitch. Such incidents, inherently remarkable (hence their survival in the record) and frequently obscure in detail, inevitably give rise to estimations of intentions, of motivation. However difficult to uncover, motives are a natural and necessary object of historical inquiry—so long as the historian and his reader bear in mind the tentative nature of whatever conclusions are reached. This problem confronts the study of *optimates* and *populares* alike. Owing to the sheer bulk of our data, we feel confidence in our capacity to recuperate Cicero's motives, at least often enough. Most would assume the same was true of M. Cato, especially in view of Cicero's exasperated letters to Atticus complaining of Cato's excessive devotion to principle in moments when expedience demanded compromise; however, one finds a far less flattering view of Cato in Caesar's *Bellum Civile*, and one shudders to imagine what Cato's image would be if the notoriously vituperative *Anticato* were our only extant source for his career.[58] Plainly, the impulses driving political acts were controversial and of vital interest to the Romans themselves, and the contradictory signals that have made their way to us are often confounding. Appian, for example, considered Caesar's lavish expenses a token of his demagoguery; Sallust, on the other hand, attributed Caesar's openhandedness to finer motives.[59] And Caesar's is the one lengthy and successful *popularis* career susceptible of anything like adequate scrutiny. One seeking after what we might consider a genuine commitment to *iura populi* must be disappointed, however: once Caesar attained to absolute power—itself a situation so abnormal that one estimating Caesar's overall career hesitates to ascribe too much significance to the acts of his final days—he abandoned the *causa popularis* entirely.[60] Matters are equally equivocal for other, even other well-known, figures. The explosive careers of the Gracchi, for instance, truncated and inconclusive, lent and lend themselves to varying interpretations.

One difficulty is the modern tendency to see the choice of the *via popularis* either as mere politicism or as an expression of social altruism, as if this dichotomy were inevitable or even natural. Charity and unselfishness, however, were not conspicuous Roman virtues, and such evidence as we possess points to entirely different impulses. We may ignore the numerous disreputable incentives for *popularis* conduct adduced by Cicero: fear of punishment (*metus poenae*) and financial embarrassment (*implicatio rei familiaris*) (*Sest.* 99) can be paralleled in Caesar's attacks on his optimate opponents and are merely characteristic terms of Roman invective (though one cannot safely conclude that, simply because an accusation finds many parallels, it is ipso facto untrue).[61] More frequently the orator invoked *furor*, a ubiquitous optimate charge, whose tenor is so extremely hostile that discussion is unnecessary: the cry of *furor* is the imputation of demagoguery, a characteristic response to *popularis* politics but not a very informative one.[62] More helpful to us is the common assertion on Cicero's part that certain politicians, men like the Gracchi or Saturninus, turned to the *via popularis* only when they had been confronted with obstruction so severe that they perceived their public image, their *dignitas*, to have been damaged. At *De Haruspicum Responso* 46, in his effort to ascribe P. Clodius's political behavior to perversity rather than to any motive comprehensible to a Roman audience, Cicero takes pains to describe the crucial events that drove the great *populares* of the past to depart from the proper policy of respect for the senate's authority: the senate's repudiation of Mancinus's Numantine treaty filled Tiberius Gracchus with *dolor* and *timor*; Gaius, his brother, was inspired by *pietas, dolor,* and *magnitudo animi*; for Saturninus, who was superseded in his position as overseer of the grain supply, *dolor* was the responsible agent in his defection to the *popularis* cause; and finally Sulpicius, for whom *dolor* is not mentioned as an explicit cause (instead, a *popularis aura* blew him from the moderate course of his justified opposition to Julius Caesar Strabo). Clodius, Cicero will go on to argue, had no comparable excuse. Ample discussion of these familiar events may be found elsewhere, and Cicero's criticism of Clodius will be examined later in this book. What is relevant to our present discussion is Cicero's assertion that these eminent *populares* were driven by aristocratic virtues—especially by *dolor*—to persist in their opposition to the senatorial majority.[63] Now it is all too obvious that, in this passage, Cicero's rhetorical strategy is to deny such aristocratic tendencies to his noble enemy; however, the strategy itself is inconceivable unless it was actually the case that Romans, particularly senators and equestrians, expected patterns of behavior like the ones Cicero outlines. The requirements of Roman *dignitas* are well known: Catiline and Caesar demonstrated the extremes to which wounded dignity might drive a man.

Examples proliferate, not all so notorious as the Gracchi or Saturninus. Cn. Domitius Ahenobarbus (cos. 96), when tribune in 104, was angered because he was not co-opted into the college of augurs (or, less likely, of pontiffs; the evidence is uncertain).[64] He retaliated in the fashion of the nobility by prosecuting the man responsible for his exclusion, M. Scaurus, but unsuccessfully. He then proposed—and passed—a law that transferred sacerdotal elections to the people, *popularis* legislation that resulted in Domitius's being elected pontifex maximus in the following year.[65] Moreover, his son, the consul of 54, believed that he had inherited *urbana gratia* from his father as a consequence of this legislation.[66] Domitius's law undeniably advanced the political importance of the *populus*, and that he did so under the influence of *dolor* (though this is nowhere explicitly attested) may have appealed to whatever *invidia senatus* existed among the lower classes. This, however, was the extent of Domitius's *popularis* career, and one is hard pressed to detect anything but aristocratic pique underlying his legislation. Once his ambitions were accommodated, Domitius engaged in no further agitation for popular privileges. As Cicero saw it, the tribune went just so far as he legitimately could go ("quoad posset, quoad fas esset, quoad liceret," *Leg. Agr.* 2.19). Nothing prevents us from viewing Domitius's conduct as springing solely from his personal ambition or from regarding his recourse to the people in the face of perceived aristocratic opposition as a sort of pis aller necessary for the maintenance of his pride and the furtherance of his career. But his success shows that the people were satisfied as to his worthiness to receive their support in the regular elections for pontifex maximus. Nor did Domitius's actions render him a pariah within the walls of the curia. Whatever motives resided in Domitius's deepest soul, when matters came to an embarrassing pass, he was able to resort to the *popularis ratio* not only because it was a familiar political technique, but also because it was based in traditional principles that were at the very least susceptible to aristocratic employment.

This isolates one important qualification that must be joined to our discussion of *popularis* ideology. The ideological background that supported popular rights was by no means alien or hostile to the aristocratic perspective. Because it aimed at the preservation of the traditional *res publica*, *popularis* ideology was absolutely not incompatible with the primacy of the senatorial class in ordinary politics. We catch a glimpse of this in Cicero's *popularis* oration against the bill of P. Servilius Rullus (tr. pl. 63), which proposed to establish a commission to raise funds in order to buy land for distribution to the poor. Near the start of this speech (*Leg. Agr.* 2.9), Cicero asks the public: "What is so popular with the people as peace? . . . What is so popular as freedom? . . . What is so popular as tranquillity?" (quid enim est tam populare quam pax? . . . quid enim est tam populare quam libertas? . . . quid enim est tam populare quam otium?). These, in the consul's view, represent the finest goals of the *popularis*. What Cicero—and others of his ilk—balked at in the controversial *rogatio* was the redistribution of property, something the bill's proponents clearly claimed to be its single most *popularis* feature but which Cicero, by rather tortuous reasoning, tried to depict as hostile to the interests of a free people. *Commoda populi* were difficult for many aristocrats to stomach (a reality that spotlights Cato's *lex frumentaria* all the more brightly). As for *libertas*, Cicero cannot approve of unrestrained and irresponsible freedom. Yet even a *popularis* could share Cicero's view that *libertas* should not become *licentia*—even while he insisted that *auctoritas* should not become *regnum*.

We would be wise to bear in mind the aristocratic orientation even of the most ardent champions of liberty. Roman society was infused with the notion of quid pro quo. Friendship and religion no less than politics recognized that *beneficia* earned *gratia*. Publilius Syrus put it succinctly: "only knaves and fools believe that *beneficia* come for free."[67] Which explains the appeal of the *popularis ratio*, at least when not taken to dangerous extremes. Popular support was a precious commodity, especially in a society so intensely oriented toward public demonstrations of honor and prestige. The approval of the crowd brought support to the candidate for office and a favorable audience at legislative assemblies. At trials, which were public affairs at Rome, the influence of the *corona* was undeniable.[68] Generally speaking, popularity was sought by all politicians. In his correspondence Cicero seems almost embarrassed to report to Atticus his delight at being cheered by the crowd at the games.[69] Pompey the Great felt no such qualms: in his famous dream on the eve of Pharsalus, he pictured his triumph in terms of thunderous applause received in his own theater.[70] Gaius Gracchus, in an excerpt preserved by Gellius, insists that no one appears before the people unless he wants something from them. He himself, so he claimed, sought *bona existimatio* and *honos*.[71] Such motives the Roman people expected of their leaders, and admired.[72] Consequently we must adjust our notions of political commitment and political sincerity. The successful *popularis* persuaded the people of his genuineness and did so in terms corresponding to their expectations. The *populus Romanus* did not expect selflessness (though they might demand sacrifice) from any of its senators, and whereas certain gestures of solidarity with the lower orders could prove advantageous to the aspiring *popularis*, this in no way implies that the Roman people expected their champions to be commoners or to have the common touch.[73]

No one expected constant political activity on the part of a *popularis*. Nor did the *popularis*—any more than any other politician—make or pretend to make specific and enduring commitments to the *plebs* or to any portion of the *populus*. The candidate for office at Rome was well advised not to resort to political or statesmanlike declarations while on the stump or in the senate (*Comm. Pet.* 33, 53). The basis of a successful canvass, so we are told, distilled itself into the following parts (21): benefits actually bestowed on various constituencies, the expectation of future benefits (*spes*), and personal attachment (*adiunctio animi ac voluntas*). *Spes* was vital, easy to inspire, and too easily overextended (44, warning against the making of promises that cannot be kept). Here it must be underlined that the *Commentariolum Petitionis* does not refer to promises of a purely political nature but to personal favors. Even at *Comm. Pet.* 53, where the author urges "videndum est ut spes rei publicae bona de te sit et honesta opinio," the context concerns the value of maintaining a splendid public image in order to advertise one's good prospects.[74] It may well be that an active tribunate was enough to win lasting popular favor (Domitius Ahenobarbus *filius* apparently thought so)—and we should remind ourselves that all politicians could foresee an end to their activism, whether it took the form of Cicero's unrealized vision of *otium cum dignitate* or the luxurious retirement enjoyed, even relished, by the *piscinarii*.[75] The Roman people had a long memory, especially when it was prodded by their leaders, a fact that lent potential and lasting significance to every episode. They were also pragmatic, or fickle.[76] Their expectations and their reactions cannot be made to conform precisely to modern prejudices.

4

Which brings us to the necessity of better understanding social stratification in Rome, by which we shall mean social stratification in the city of Rome (despite the necessity of occasionally looking beyond the city's confines for sources and data).[77] Students of Roman culture, and not only those of Marxist inclination, have tended to analyze the structure of Roman society in terms of economic criteria.[78] For sensible reasons. The most summary consultation of our literary sources reveals the enormous emphasis that Romans of the upper classes placed on wealth, and on poverty—an emphasis reflected in evaluative judgments and institutionalized in the timocratic nature of the Roman constitution.[79] The Roman census located each individual in a class defined by wealth, or more accurately by worth, since character as well as cash was a determinant.[80]

This wrinkle, the calculation of status on the basis of noneconomic factors, is what makes the identification of strata so problematic—in any society, not only in ancient Rome. For it is clear that, among the wealthy, further subdivisions, often quite minute, were readily drawn: in the senate one distinguished consulars from praetorians, categories of importance that existed alongside species of pedigree such as noble and patrician. Senators respected the splendor of the equestrian order, itself rather heterogeneous, yet it is also clear that, depending on the circumstance, they could feel conspicuously superior—remarkable when one observes that, apart from *honores*, senators and (at least some) *equites* were indistinguishable (or so it seems from our perspective).[81] *Tribunii aerarii* were for whatever reason separated out from the rest of the *equites*, evidently as inferiors to *equites equo publico*, and the *apparitores*, for all their wealth and importance (and their prestige in the eyes of those occupying the lower strata), could be and often were openly despised by senatorial types.[82]

For the elite elements in Rome, then, it is clear that differentiation was not predicated solely on finances. Other factors, different from though not necessarily unrelated to economic ones, played an important role in the creation of groups. One thinks immediately of Max Weber's three-dimensional analysis of stratification (and its subsequent revisions and refinements at the hands of social theorists), thereby implicating differences in power and prestige in addition to property as constituents of stratification.[83] Such criteria, however, are markedly subjective, difficult to measure, especially for the extraneous observer of Roman society. Notwithstanding the obstacle of identifying and articulating the various noneconomic determinants in stratification, it is undeniable that these multifarious factors represent the bases upon which groups were formed both in an objective sense and also in the sense of a collective self-awareness and the potential for common action.

Matters become more difficult when one turns to the lower classes. The ancients, like many sociologists since, generally distinguished only three wide classes: the rich, the poor, and those falling somewhere between, who, in Appian's opinion, would identify themselves with either the upper or the lower class.[84] Efforts to refine this crude system must rely in the first instance on the terminology employed by the Romans themselves. Yet this has not proven wholly satisfactory: the Latin term *ordo*, used by the Romans to describe certain civic groups, most often (though here the fragmentary nature of our evidence may be chiefly responsible) indicates elite *ordines* like senators, *publicani*, or *aerarii*. For the rest, despite the appearance of orders like *proletarii*, we more often find only indeterminate expressions like *tenues homines*. The distinctions signified by *ordo* are useful, but not exhaustive of social stratification in Rome.[85] Categories like slave (*servus*), freedman (*libertinus*), and freeborn (*ingenuus*), to name the most obvious, were by no means of trifling consequence. In any case, the *ordines* do not shed much light on the bulk of the population, who were frequently lumped together under the heading *ceteri ordines*. Unfortunately, there is little else to illuminate the common strata. Exploration can begin by dividing the *plebs rustica* from the *plebs urbana*, a reasonable separation so long as its tentative nature is also recognized.[86]

To speak of the poor, wealthy Romans on the whole employed the most depressingly disparaging vocabulary—and one frustrating in its lack of precision.[87] Occupational nomenclature offers another route to the situation of ordinary Romans.[88] Thus we can isolate *opifices* (craftsmen) and *tabernarii* (shopkeepers), terms that, because many shopkeepers made their products only when they were ordered, overlapped in regular usage. The craftsmen and shopkeepers whose names subsist were evidently men of modest means but by no means destitute; the same cannot be said for their employees. We also know of *mercenarii*, who were day laborers, as were *conducticii*.[89] And some Romans, though not many, will have been idlers.[90]

Not a few historians of Rome, especially those on the continent, have attached special economic and (consequently) political significance to these designations.[91] Matters are, as always, more complicated. A term like *opifex* was hardly specific: its sense could range from a prosperous owner of a shop (or several shops) to a modest but independent craftsman to a mere hireling or apprentice.[92] Thus there need not be any social or political unity among groups described as *opifices* in our literary sources, since few Romans of the upper classes showed themselves keenly interested in representing craftsmen and shopkeepers in discriminating detail. Nor do designations like *opifex* or *tabernarius* in and of themselves tell us whether we have to do with freedmen or *ingenui*. Not all *opifices* and *tabernarii* were freedman, nor does reason dictate that *libertini* completely dominated the ranks of craftsmen, though it must be admitted that freedmen do dominate the surviving epigraphical record.[93] Nor does it follow that *mercenarii* were predominantly *ingenui*, though they may have been. This classification must have included, along with common, unskilled laborers, anyone incapable of maintaining himself in an agricultural career as well as those who failed as shopkeepers.[94] Given the independence of so many freedmen, which obtained for a variety of reasons, it should not be assumed that the unskilled or failed *libertinus* had any advantages over a failed farmer, an uprooted veteran, or an untrained *ingenuus* of any sort.[95]

The attitudes of the upper classes toward various occupations are quite familiar. Agriculture, war, and politics were the only forms of employment fit for men of quality. Trade was sordid, except when conducted on a grand scale (Cic. *Off.* 1.150f.). *Publicani* and *negotiatores* could be *splendidi*; *mercatores* were less respectable. Craftsmen and laborers, whatever distinctions might be drawn among themselves, were contemptible.[96] But this is not the whole story, and one must take care not to ignore the attitudes of humbler Romans themselves, insofar as they can be known. The ordinary Roman, predictably, resented being despised—or perhaps one should merely observe that upper-class Romans thought they did.[97] More important is the apprehension that lowly Romans did not share in the aristocratic disdain for skilled work, a truth evidenced by the very epigraphical evidence that affords us our knowledge of Roman occupations and by numerous texts.[98]

This awareness points to a commonsensical distinction that ought perhaps to be made explicit: until now we have considered the stratification of Rome either from an elitist perspective or from an external one. Equally important for understanding Roman culture, and especially if we hope to employ stratification as a means to elucidating particular political events, is what might be called local or proximate stratification: that is, how did a particular Roman or a particular Roman group from the lower classes view its own position in society? All Romans could think of themselves with pride as part of the *universus populus Romanus*—as such they were *omnium gentium domini* (Cic. *Leg. Agr.* 2.22)—but there was more to their self-consciousness than its grandest scale; other, narrower means of self-definition were available. The *Commentariolum Petitionis*, perhaps the only Republican source in which a Roman writer scrutinizes the different grades of Roman society without the purpose of passing either sweeping or elitist judgments, isolates the various constituencies that a candidate for the consulship had to solicit if he hoped to succeed at the polls: the nobility, senators and *equites*, *publicani*, *municipia*, men of every *ordo*, men with influence in the various centuries, tribes, *sodalitates*, *collegia*, *pagi*, *vicinitates*.[99] If a man could have influence within a tribe or neighborhood, this implies that these associations possessed some self-awareness, some identity. Success within such an organization, and the success of the organization itself, one may suppose, were matters of crucial importance to an individual Roman's local significance, an aspect of daily (and political) life that can hardly be deemed inconsequential. In other words, winning or maintaining the favor of the officers of one's *collegium* may have in certain situations mattered more to a member of that *collegium* than any competing motivation. This is the most intelligible context for the *homines in suis vicinitatibus gratiosi* and the *principes conlegiorum, pagorum, vicinitatum* of the *Commentariolum Petitionis*, men whose political clout, though minor in the grand scheme of things, was significant enough to be worthwhile acquiring for the ambitious candidate.[100] Little wonder Cicero could count as an asset his representation of the interests of various *collegia* in court.[101] In the final analysis, Romans may have made choices and estimations in terms of proximate stratification much more often than we realize or are capable of recovering.

Certain configurations are more manifest to us than others are. Perhaps the most obvious illustration of collective deference, wherein identifiable groups were brought together for the express purpose of exhibiting their own status and of conferring status upon others, were the voting assemblies.[102] This is most apparent in the centuriate assembly, in which the *populus Romanus* was divided into classes and centuries, each of whose membership was decided by wealth and character (though mainly by wealth, one presumes) and, except for the *equites* and the five lowest classes (the noncombatants), was further divided by age (whether senior or junior). The organization and operation of this assembly accorded greater political power to the elite than to the commons, yet even while the superiority of the rich was upheld, so nonetheless was the integration of Rome's various strata enacted. Less finely delineated were the tribal assemblies, the *comitia tributa* and the *concilium plebis*. Both labored under inequities, though of a sort quite different from that obtaining in the centuriate assembly. For instance, the population was not evenly distributed over the thirty-five tribes: all freedmen, who represented a huge proportion of the city's inhabitants, were enrolled into the four urban tribes.[103] In addition, the tribes' geographical distribution throughout Italy created a state of affairs in which the actual voters of rural tribes enjoyed de facto superiority over those from the urban tribes, whose greater frequency and closer proximity to the polling place had the effect of diluting their votes. The *concilium plebis*, by its very definition, excluded patricians, and as an assembly it symbolized not so much the functional dimension of stratification (i.e., the tendency of society's parts to work toward integration) as Rome's potential for conflict.

The assemblies both arranged the people into their various grades and provided a context for the politician's interaction with the articulated populace. A similar context was presented by the Roman spectacles, whose audiences were arranged in such a way that Rome's social stratification was to some degree represented.[104] There the politician might measure his popularity with the various elements of his countrymen. As Cicero put it: "The expression of popular opinion that we see at elections and public meetings is sometimes spurious and rehearsed; and while it may be possible to raise a thin smattering of cheers at the theaters or gladiatorial shows with a rented crowd, nonetheless it is easy enough to see how it is done and who is behind it—and how the majority of honest citizens react" (*Sest.* 115). The shows were crucial tests of one's public esteem, frightening because, contrary to a recent thesis, they were beyond anyone's control.[105] More important, though, were elections, inasmuch as every politician's goal was not only to be appreciated by the people in general terms, but more specifically to attain to the *summa laus*, thereby unequivocally to bask in popular approval and to excel his peers. All of which demanded the cultivation of the various components of the Roman people: "We senators, tossed upon the stormy waves of popular favor, must modestly bear the fluctuations of the people's will. We must win it, keep it, or assuage it when it is angered. If *honores*—which only the people dispenses—are important to us, we must never weary of courting the people's favor. For the people always desires to be asked, always desires that candidates appear in the guise of suppliants. The people bestows *honores* upon those candidates by whom it is most vigorously canvassed" (*Planc.* 11–12).

Stratification suggests vertical relationships, an awkward expression that will suffice to bring us to the much discussed matter of patronage.[106] A technical definition of *patrocinium* does not survive from antiquity. Patronage, the formal dependency of the disadvantaged on certain members of the elite, a voluntary relationship founded upon *fides*, was said to have been instituted by Romulus himself.[107] Whatever the nature of that earliest form of patronage, the outlines of patronage are certainly more distinct (though by no means entirely clear) in the late republic. Patronage, as Richard Saller defines it, was a social relationship primarily between individuals (though collectives may also have had their patron) that was reciprocal and asymmetrical. In what might be called its classic form, the *patronus* protected his *cliens* at law and looked after his basic welfare; in return he could expect deference and he might hope for his client's devotion. Furthermore, their tie was voluntary, a point that distinguishes the patron-client relationship from that of the patron and his freedman.[108] That there were areas of gray—the most controversial being the vague distinction between *amicus inferior* and client—and that the various levels of society produced individuals who were both patron and client are all to be expected and in fact can be found in our ancient records.

The social importance of *clientela* is indubitable. In a world without welfare or safety nets, patronage was essential for the survival of the humblest Romans. And Wallace-Hadrill has argued impressively that the very scarcity of resources in the ancient world must have bolstered the influence of patrons, who offered a poor man his only hope for even a slender share from society's scrimptions.[109] The position of the patron was based on his superiority in *auctoritas, dignitas,* and *vires.*[110] It follows from this that the proliferation of clients and grand displays might be taken as emblems of authority and power, which represents only one of several reasons why the houses of great men were ordinarily open to *all* citizens and not merely their (traditional or hereditary) clients.[111] Clients, presented in bulk for public consumption, implied clout. Thus clients mattered not only for their votes, which will have been inconsequential for the most part anyway, nor for the protection or (conversely) the physical menace they might offer, though this aspect should not be underestimated by any means.[112] But it was the public image and that image's capacity for intimidating others—commoner and senator alike—

that lent so much urgency to the possession of large bands of clients in Roman public life.

But to what extent did *clientela* matter politically? A survey of modern scholarship might well give the impression that *clientela* was the single most powerful dynamic in the physics of Roman politics.[113] In a simplified (but not, I think, inaccurate) formulation, the commonly held paradigm runs rather like this: senators possessed clients, at Rome or in the countryside or even abroad, whose loyalty and votes they controlled; the most powerful politician would be the one who could manipulate the most voters by forging political combines among the elite, associations usually assumed to be organized by marriage ties and the traditional bonds that existed between certain family groups (i.e., factions). On this argument, the equilibrium of the classic republic was largely owed to the strength of *clientela*, which, it is argued, began to disintegrate during the late republic under the assault first of the *populares* and finally the *duces*.[114] Yet there are compelling arguments against this estimation of *clientela's* centrality. In the first place, however strongly Romans felt that clients should limit their devotion to a single patron, the evidence is abundant that clients claimed several patrons.[115] One can infer from this sensible practice that many clients would not have felt compelled to obey their patron's will if a better deal presented itself.[116] Whether the supporters of Tiberius Gracchus were clients or partisans or both, the opportunity to earn daily wages in the countryside preempted Gracchus's claims on their participation in the disturbances attending his attempt to win reelection.[117] More important, as Brunt has argued at length, is the conclusion that, since all political grandees counted clients among their resources, success at the polls, while it surely benefited from endorsements from fellow members of the aristocracy, must in the end have depended on other advantages: a superior reputation based on birth or merit, greater and recent personal accomplishments, and, a facet of public life that was certainly discussed by the Romans far more than *clientela*, electioneering practices. In short, while one ought to respect the social importance of *clientela* in the late republic, its political significance, while considerable, has been exaggerated.[118] Especially when matters came to crises, clients were only one resource to which the Roman magnate turned for strength.

5

The diversity of possible political bases in Rome becomes apparent from an examination of electoral practices. During the late republic a candidate for office was required to submit his *professio* at least a *trinundinum* before the actual polling.[119] Once accepted as a candidate, he was expected to canvass for support (*petitio*), a demanding process that entailed at the very least a good deal of circulating (*ambitus*) and glad-handing (*prensatio*). During the late republic, few candidates waited so late to begin their campaigns.[120] Cicero, as we learn from a letter to Atticus (*Att.* 1.1.1–2), initiated his campaign for the consulship of 63 on 17 July 65. The *Commentariolum Petitionis* (16–17) makes the obvious recommendation that a candidate should guarantee himself the backing of his truest friends and his family circle, the latter group extending through fellow tribesmen (*tribules*), neighbors (*vicini*), clients (who in view of their placement in the list are here apparently thought of as dependents), freedmen, and even slaves. For display, the candidate should take pains to be seen with *homines inlustres honore ac nomine*, whether or not they actually participated in the canvassing; to secure his rights, the candidate needed the friendship of magistrates, especially the consuls and tribunes; and, finally, in order actually to carry the vote, he must be able to count among his friends *homines excellenti gratia*, men with clout (18). To garner so wide a circle of friendships, the *Commentariolum Petitionis* concedes, one must grant the word *amicus* a broader definition than it carries in ordinary usage (17). The accuracy of the *Commentariolum Petitionis* is well evidenced by Cicero's letters to Atticus (*Att.* 1.1, 1.2), themselves clear testimony to Cicero's efforts to shore up the support of a genuine and valuable friend: Cicero relates to Atticus his plans to focus his attentions on the voters of Cisalpine Gaul and his efforts to keep the friendship of powerful nobles, in this instance L. Domitius Ahenobarbus (cos. 54); furthermore, he urges the equestrian Atticus to bring his own influence to bear on the nobility so that they will support Cicero's canvass.

The requirements of a successful *petitio* are treated in yet fuller detail in the *Commentariolum Petitionis*. The obvious necessity of winning over nobles, rich *equites*, and *publicani* is stressed repeatedly. Cicero is also pressed to forge friendships with influential citizens, ambitious men who are able to work their will over their tribes. The favor of these men should be won by whatever means possible (*quibuscumque poteris rationibus*), an oblique expression made clearer by the author's subsequent reference to *sodalitates*. This imprecise Latin word possesses several meanings, one of which denotes an organization whose purpose was to distribute donatives—and bribes—throughout the tribes.[121] But bribery is not a recommendation of the *Commentariolum Petitionis* (we shall return to bribery below, however), and the author represents the relationship to be sought by the candidate in unexceptionable terms: "they will be spurred to enthusiastic support both by the expectation of your sense of responsibility in the future and by your recent good services" (19). These men, whose industry was to be motivated by the expectation of access to a consul, derived their influence both in the tribes and in the centuries (18) by establishing themselves as intermediaries between powerful politicians, to whom they could promise to deliver votes, and the voters themselves, over whom they could exercise influence by dint of their reputation as well-connected types. This is a familiar—and risky—political posture, and, as the *Commentariolum Petitionis* implies (22, 24), these individuals had to contend with rivals. The distribution of donatives was only one form of mediation, though, as our sources demonstrate in abundance, it was a form both traditional and pervasive.

The reference to both tribes and centuries suggests that we have to do with the centuries of the first class in the *comitia centuriata*, membership in which was assigned on the basis of tribe as well as wealth.[122] Which would mean that the *Commentariolum Petitionis* is here recommending that the candidate bolster his support among the politically active members of the first class, some of whom will surely have been the tribal *curatores*. Each of Rome's tribes maintained common property in the city, which was used as a central headquarters. It was to these offices that candidates or their representatives went to solicit support (*circumire tribus*). The tribal officials, *curatores*, who presumably were themselves elected by their tribe, were the vital contacts to be acquired. They in turn were assisted by *divisores*, whose job it was to distribute the legitimate gifts that a candidate could proffer to his own tribe. *Curatores* were men of substance, *equites*, as may have been the *divisores* as well.[123]

Members of this first class were of course also to be located throughout Italy, and, as the author of the *Commentariolum Petitionis* observes (31f.), these men were eager for the friendship of the mighty in Rome, for they saw in such connections some measure of protection for themselves. Though the municipal gentry had to be convinced that the candidate's friendship was genuine, nonetheless we have here a clear illustration of the kind of patronage, formulated in the language of friendship, that Saller has elucidated in detail for the society of the early empire.[124] For these *rustici*, though they were clearly subordinate to the likes of Cicero, were at the same time men of some means, members of the first class, and capable of influencing an election's outcome: "and so, when you have made into your own supporters in the centuriate assembly those men who have, on account of their own ambitions at election time, gained for themselves the most influence with their fellow tribesmen, and when you have won over the rest of those who have some clout in their tribes on account of their hometown or their neighborhood or their *collegium*, then you ought to have high hopes" (*Comm. Pet.* 32).

Support was to be sought outside the confines of the well-to-do. Again the *Commentariolum Petitionis* advised Cicero to embrace men possessed of influence from the remaining classes: "multi homines urbani industrii, multi libertini in foro gratiosi navique versantur" (29). These might be approached directly or through contacts. They were men whose influence derived not from their substance but from their placement in the organizations of the city, the *collegia*, the *pagi*, the *vicinitates*.[125] *Collegia*, religious and social organizations based principally on occupation or neighborhood, were for the ordinary Roman a precious source of recreation, security, and dignity.[126] It may be possible to distinguish occupational colleges (*collegia opificum*) from the neighborhood clubs that cultivated the Lares Compitales (the so-called *collegia compitalicia*), but it is far from clear, given the regionalized distribution of many Roman crafts as well as the upper classes' unwillingness to display detailed familiarity with the arrangements of the lowest orders, how scrupulously distinctions are maintained in our sources.[127] Epigraphic evidence, originating from the colleges themselves, does little to clarify the various types of *collegia* (occupational, religious, regional).[128] Moreover, Roman districts, the *montes*, *pagi*, and *vici*, were all organized along the lines of the *collegia opificum*, and in the late republic the *vici* were especially significant units; these associations cannot always be easily distinguished from *collegia*.[129] As Flambard rightly observes, Roman *collegia* defy the sort of neat and tidy taxonomy modern scholars long for.[130]

So far as our sources inform us, *collegia* ranged in size from around one hundred members to over a thousand (*vici*, by comparison, seem to have averaged about three thousand members).[131] They held regular meetings and suppers, they celebrated sacred festivals, and they formed corporations to provide for members' funerals, a detail which points to the *collegium*'s pursuit of honor, however cheap.[132] Membership in a *collegium* was wholly voluntary.[133] Assemblies were held, at which officers, bearing titles like *sacerdos* and *flamen*, *curator*, *notarius*, *scriba* and *viator*, even *quaestor*, were elected. The chief official of a college was its *magister*, whose authority, lacking any civil status, was vested entirely in the consent of the membership.[134] No one in the typical *collegium* was well-to-do, yet there were distinctions both of relative wealth and of status—*collegia* were open to free, freed, and slave alike—that had to be observed.[135] Comparison with municipal *collegia* would suggest that the *collegia* of Rome had a quasi-military organization, with their members divided into *centuriae* or (more commonly) *decuriae*, which would hardly be surprising in view of the limited formal models available to any Roman association.[136] The overall structure of the *collegium*, it appears, reflected the biases and prejudices of Roman society at large. Nonetheless, *collegia*, it must be underlined, provided simple Romans with their best opportunity for local prestige and a rare chance to excel and to matter (albeit in a modest way) in a state whose economic opportunities and political power were not at all distributed in their favor.

The political potential of *collegia*, especially for winning popular support, was no secret in Rome.[137] These organizations published statements that made their sentiments unmistakable, often in the form of honorific decrees for leading statesmen.[138] A *collegium* could enjoy the favors of a *patronus*.[139] The politician who established ties with the leadership of the *collegia*, whom the *Commentariolum Petitionis* designates as their *principes*, might well hope to win the support of the masses: "if you establish a friendship with the leading men of the *collegia*, then, through them, you will easily secure the remainder of the masses" (30). This approach, one notices immediately, was not merely efficient for the senator, but lent greater prestige to the local *magister*, who might boast of his connection, however tenuous in reality, to a Roman senator (or his agent).

There is another dimension to elections, alluded to but disapproved of in the *Commentariolum Petitionis*—namely, electioneering: "I see that no election is so polluted with bribery [*largitio*] that some centuries do not return, without bribes, the candidates with whom they have a special connection" (56). However distasteful to the author of the *Commentariolum Petitionis*, there can be no question but that electoral corruption was rampant in the late republic. Respectable donatives, such as gifts to one's own clients or even to one's own tribe, like lavish expenses for public games or civic construction, were, as we have seen, entirely unobjectionable, and in fact the occupation of *divisor*, who on behalf of a busy politician distributed largess to his *tribules*, was quite honest (if never from an aristocratic point of view exactly prestigious).[140] But in time, as candidates felt unable to live within the constraints of traditional practices, they expanded the scope of their donatives in the hope of winning the votes of every tribe. By the late republic, the term *divisor* had come to indicate professional bribery agents, men who accepted funds for disbursement from a candidate or, more usually, the candidate's associate (so as to avoid too blatant an appearance of impropriety), who was referred to as a *sequester* or *interpres*. *Sodalitates*, companies whose chief functions were bribery and intimidation, arose to provide these essential services to candidates. Techniques for electoral corruption kept well in advance of legal remedies; hence it was that, despite the legion of *leges de ambitu* in the late republic, electoral malpractice remained a constant feature of political life.[141]

All of which should suffice to demonstrate that the candidate for office at Rome, however separate the senatorial class to which he belonged, was obliged to rely on elaborate contacts—assiduously sought after and maintained—at all levels and of all colors, some rather sordid. Every candidate was the center of an intricate network of variegated complexity, nor was any politician's base of support uniquely his. It seems evident from the account of the *Commentariolum Petitionis* that *homines gratiosi* were cultivated by numerous politicians and that their loyalty could hardly be regarded as beyond question. *Sodalitates*, even if they masqueraded as friends, were essentially hirelings, which meant that they could not afford to reject a customer. Elections were particular moments toward which immense effort and wealth were expended by anxious candidates and their associates. The coalitions that boosted candidates into the consulship (or whatever office) were not assumed to be permanent or lasting. The constituencies from which each coalition was assembled were too diverse, as we have seen. Their common interest, so it appears, was their desire to have a friend in high places, and, for reasons that need only have been coincidental, each constituency placed its hopes in the same prospective friend.

For the candidate on the make it was necessary to display the range and depth of his support during his visits to the forum. This daily exercise can be divided into three parts, as can the ensemble of a candidate's supporters in each particular phase: there were greeters in the morning (*salutatores*), those who accompanied the candidate on his march to the forum (*deductores*), and those who followed the candidate through his public transactions (*adsectatores*).[142] It would be a mistake to conclude that each phase was dominated by a different sector of the populace.[143] Although most *salutatores* were humble clients for whom it was an *officium* to attend the morning *salutatio* (an *officium* they sometimes fulfilled for more than one patron), men of standing sometimes paid calls too and they were greeted with appropriate dignity.[144] In the opinion of the *Commentariolum Petitionis*, it was crucial to have an ostentatious assembly for the *deductio* (36, 53). Consequently, *deductores* should be met at a regular time and not kept waiting. Now while it is unquestionable that senators and *equites* took part in the *deductio* of candidates, it does not follow that men of this rank dominated the ranks of *deductores*.[145] After all, the advice of the *Commentariolum Petitionis* suggests that quantity and not quality was the principal desideratum of the *deductio*, which implies that no one should have been turned away. Both *equites* and *tabernarii* will have had business to attend to later in the day, which might explain some of the emphasis on punctuality, but it seems unlikely that anyone will have been keen to cool his heels for a tardy candidate—especially when there was no shortage of rival candidates from whom one might expect one's attendance to be rewarded. In the same way *adsectatores* could be recruited from a variety of ranks. Some might attend voluntarily—noble youths for instance, who were handsome ornaments for candidates and who may well have meant to curry favor for themselves—while others might thereby satisfy an obligation.[146] Prospective *adsectatores* might find themselves busy at times regardless of their intentions, which is why their dutifulness had to be cultivated, and in any case the personnel, except for the neediest of dependents, probably fluctuated from day to day.

Those who acted as *deductores* and *adsectatores* were politically active Roman citizens. So, too, were the inhabitants of the countryside who made their way to the city to vote. One must add as well those denizens of the forum who made it their business to attend public assemblies. Not all Roman citizens, it seems, were politically active. Ramsay MacMullen, for instance, has argued on the basis of the dimensions of Rome's polling places and of the techniques of Roman voting that during the late republic as few as 2 percent of Rome's citizens actually cast ballots in the elections.[147] Fewer yet will have participated in legislative assemblies. While MacMullen's method is hardly incontestable, his results seem to look generally in the right direction, and we shall not err by much if we conceive of popular political participation in Rome in fairly minimal terms.

Once it is recognized that in absolute numbers not many citizens actually participated in politics, the question then arises as to which citizens, from which classes, participated. This, I think, is a query that does not admit of a single answer. Various issues—and various personalities—inspired various constituencies. Under typical circumstances the poorest citizens would merely have wasted their time had they elected to attend the *comitia centuriata*.[148] Not so the tribal assemblies (and especially legislative assemblies). Presumably at all elections the greatest numbers comprised city dwellers. But Tiberius Gracchus, his brother, and Gaius Marius were all able to attract large numbers of *rustici* to the city to vote, as Pompey, in his efforts to secure Cicero's recall, was able to mobilize supporters from throughout Italy. Likewise, one should not assume that the crowds attending *contiones* (the public addresses of magistrates) were always of the same composition. *Tabernarii* often closed their shops for issues they perceived, for whatever reason, to be vital, but it should be clear by now that an expression like *tabernarii*, in view of the various *collegia* and neighborhoods included under that rubric, does not necessarily refer to a single interest group (though it may do so, depending on the issue of course).[149] Different *tabernarii* may have been excited by different issues. A craftsman always had to make a choice whether or not to close his shop and, again as we have seen, matters of proximate importance may sometimes have taken priority over those of civic importance (as they regularly did for the majority of the citizens who chose not to participate at all). That is to say, on a particular political issue a humble Roman may have felt it more important to his life to satisfy the expectations of his college's *magister* than to respond to the exhortations of a distinguished senator. Similar considerations apply to *mercenarii*. On some days these men will have had ample time to assemble in the forum, but certainly not always: they were *non occupati* only when they could not help it. Nor can veterans or visiting rustics be excluded automatically.[150]

Christian Meier has coined the term *plebs contionalis* to refer to that portion of the urban population which he believes composed the regular core of those participating in *contiones* and tribal assemblies. This term has gained wide acceptance among Roman historians, who nonetheless disagree as to its exact designation.[151] In my opinion, the term is problematic precisely because it implies a consistency on the part of the active component of the citizenry that probably did not obtain. For one thing, few citizens can have had the time or resources to participate in *every* official activity, not to mention the additional demands of supporting a candidate standing for office. The calculations of Claude Nicolet are valuable in this regard: "A Roman citizen who wanted to play a full and effective part in political life would be summoned at least 20 times a year for operations which might last altogether 40 or 60 days. Much of his time was thus spent attending to public duties in the Campus Martius and the forum. It is hardly an exaggeration to say that being a citizen was a full-time profession."[152] In my view, few even of the politically active citizens participated on a "full-time" basis. There will have been exceptions, of course, and those whose residences or businesses put them near the forum (or the Campus Martius) will have have had readier access than others to assemblies, as a result of which they may have been politically active somewhat more consistently, but it seems far more likely that the number of active citizens was rather larger than the number actually represented in any particular event; it was only that each citizen with political inclinations actually involved himself only occasionally, when he felt it convenient or necessary to do so.[153]

6

It should by now be clear that ordinary Roman politics was as focused on local, proximate needs as on what we would call national issues. The Romans sought competent leadership able to manage whatever crisis might befall the state: it is to the credit of the aristocracy that it was regularly able to provide an ample supply of acceptable choices. To secure political support, if we may believe the evidence of the *Commentariolum Petitionis*, a candidate had to convince particular individuals and groups that—if he were elected—they could expect his personal, specific attention to their needs. *Spes*, not ideas or platforms, garnered support. And if *amicitia* failed, there was always bribery, which represented an even more blatant quid pro quo arrangement between politician and voters. The diversity of the electorate and the Roman inclination to view political relationships in personal, patronal (at least in its broadest sense) terms militated against the emergence of class consciousness and political programs.

This is not to say that a popular political ideology did not obtain among ordinary Romans.[154] The rhetoric of the forum did not ring hollow with the *plebs*, as Fergus Millar has reminded us. But nor should we assume that the beliefs and expatiations of the senatorial class corresponded precisely to the ideas flitting about in the mentalities of their audiences, since only a few issues can have commanded anything like universal interest with the lower classes. Bread and circuses—as C. Fannius demonstrated pointedly in 122—were widely regarded as entitlements by the city's populace, however fragmented it was with respect to other considerations. *Commoda populi* might be despised in some quarters, but the people's sights could also be set higher. *Libertas*, though it too had diverse significations, was paramount in the ideology of the *plebs*: *auxilium* and *provocatio* were two of its most precious manifestations. Rights of this sort, by dint of their broad appeal, became the common currency of any politician hoping to shape popular opinion— hence their exploitation in the representation of issues with no apparent relevance or real interest to the common people of Rome.[155]

The populace of Rome, even if we limit our concern to the politically active contingent, was too fragmentary and too fluid to allow us to see Roman politics simply in terms of the overarching conceptions of popular ideology. In the pejorative formulation of Pseudo-Sallust, the multitude was "scattered into different employments and ways of life, exhibiting absolutely no unity" (in artis vitasque varias dispalata, nullo modo inter se congruens, *Ep. ad Caes.* 5.6). Which is why, although political analysis must be sensitive to the claims of *libertas populi* and *senatus auctoritas* on individual statesmen and on various elements of the people, and no treatment of Roman history can ignore the potential for propaganda inherent in these concepts, it must nonetheless take special care not to reduce the history of the late republic into a schematic conflict between *populares* and *optimates* (or into any other simplistic dichotomy), as if that were the means to discerning the crucial essence of the historical events of that period. Patriotism mattered. Personal interests mattered. Roman politics was asnarl with varied and conflicting claims and ambitions, the perplexed and involuted nature of which we must endeavor to appreciate and unravel even while we resist either hastily resorting to single-minded methodological techniques—as if we were Alexander before the Gordian knot—or, in our bewilderment, succumbing to desperate confusion.

CHAPTER TWO

Handsome Arrogance

1

The patrician Claudii, removed to Rome from Sabine Regillum at the dawn of the Roman Republic, reached their first consulship in 495, when Attus Clausus held the office, the first of many illustrious and formidable Claudians: Ap. Claudius the Decemvir, the arrogant tyrant manqué of the annalists; Ap. Claudius Caecus, victor in war, tenacious censor, brilliant builder and—traditionally—an unsuccessful political reformer who hoped to adlect the sons of freedmen into the senate and to redistribute *humiles* throughout the (then) thirty-one tribes.[1] Two sons of the censor, Claudius Pulcher and Claudius Nero, originate the two patrician lines who served Rome with such distinction that, according to Suetonius, before the end of the republic the Claudian name held claim to twenty-eight consulships, seven censorships, six triumphs, and two ovations. "There was no epoch in Rome's history," as Ronald Syme has put it, "but could show a Claudius." The Pulchri constituted the senior line. Not many of Rome's noble families could rival them in splendor, and, unlike the Julii or Sergii or so many patrician houses that struggled during the first century to regain their past station, the Claudii Pulchri never suffered eclipse. The family collected magistracies, amassed wealth on an international scale, and became proverbial for its *clientela* and notorious, at least by the last century of the republic, for its arrogance.[2] Though averse to sullying their own house with adoption, the Claudii Pulchri cultivated extensive connections in order to magnify their influence. During the first century they enjoyed strong and valuable ties to the Caecilii Metelli and the Servilii, to name only two. Licinius Lucullus and M. Cato and Pompey the Great were to be numbered among their kin.[3] Even Cicero, for all his feuds with the Claudii Pulchri, could not deny their unsurpassed *claritas*: *amplissimum genus* he calls them, *nobilissimi et clarissimi*.[4] Nobility, though never beyond the reach of the ablest of Rome's aristocracy, was hard won nevertheless. And to maintain a place at the top with constancy was a feat very few families had the resources or talent to accomplish: the Claudii Pulchri were prominent for nearly half a millennium.

In 143 the consul Ap. Claudius Pulcher won a victory over the Salassi in Cisalpine Gaul. Despite the senate's opposition and a tribune's veto, Appius celebrated a triumph, shielded on his chariot by his daughter, a Vestal Virgin. Later, Appius was elected to the censorship in 136 and thereafter became *princeps senatus*. He was father-in-law to Tiberius Gracchus, whose reforms he supported, and he left two sons, Appius and Gaius. Of the latter we know little, rather surprisingly, since he was consul in 92 and half a century later Cicero remembered his "summam nobilitatem et singularem potentiam" (*Brut*. 166). Appius's career, less smooth, is better documented. Unwilling to acquiesce in the domination of Cinna, he removed himself from Rome in 87, shortly after his praetor-ship. Outlawed and consequently expelled from the senate, he returned to the city as a lieutenant of Sulla, under whose careful eye he was at long last elevated to the consulship for 79. Severe illness prevented him from assuming his proconsulship until 77, at which time Appius campaigned successfully in Macedonia against the Scordisci and other tribes. In the following year, however, he finally succumbed. The consul of 79 left three sons, the youngest of whom was Publius Claudius Ap. f. Ap. n. Pulcher Pal., known to his contemporaries and to us as Clodius.[5] On the evidence of his *cursus*, Clodius was born in 92. Thus he was but sixteen when he was left fatherless, an unfortunate but far from uncommon predicament among Roman youth.[6]

Clodius was born to a large family. His eldest brother, the supercilious and superstitious Appius, harbored in his nature an overweening ar-rogance that proved imperturbable even when he was caught out in the most shameless action.[7] His sensational career did nothing to denature his imperious mien: he was consul in 54, and in 50 he held the last patri-cian censorship of the Roman Republic, an office he exercised with Catonian severity.[8] Gaius, the remaining brother, failed to replicate the success of his namesake, the consul of 92. Though he merited the prae-torship in 56 and from 55 to 53 was proconsul of Asia, where he was honored at Pergamum, his career ground to a halt in 51 when he was condemned *de repetundis*. Cicero mentions his culture, perhaps with irony.[9]

In addition to three sons, the consul of 79 left three daughters. The

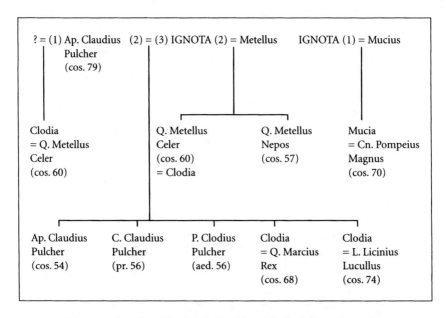

Figure 1. The Claudii Pulchri: Shackleton Bailey's Reconstruction

eldest, Clodia Metelli, is possibly the most notorious woman in all of Roman history after Cleopatra. We have the impression of knowing her well owing to the bulk of evidence in the verses of her jilted lover and in the letters and speeches of Cicero, who detested her. However, the enormity of the task of recuperating the historical Clodia from such oblique and partial testimony has been convincingly demonstrated.[10] Like too many Roman women, she remains a faint figure, the more so on account of her notoriety, which tends to obfuscate matters. Clodia Metelli was married before her father's death, probably in 79, was widowed in 59 and—despite the unrelentingly scandalous impression derived from our sources—may have died an *univira*.[11] The remaining Clodiae, also of scabrous repute, were likewise wed to consuls, one to Licinius Lucullus (cos. 74), the other, who bore the (for prosopographers) troublesome epithet Tertia, to Marcius Rex (cos. 68).[12]

The household of Appius, for all its grandeur and notoriety, eludes precise reconstruction. The once standard views of Drumann and Münzer, still to be found in the genealogical tables of Syme's *The Augustan Aristocracy*, have been discredited by Shackleton Bailey's demonstration that the relationship obtaining between the sons of the consul of 79 and the brothers Metellus, Celer (cos. 60), and Nepos (cos. 57), which Cicero designated by employing the term *fratres*, must be either that of *sons of*

HANDSOME ARROGANCE

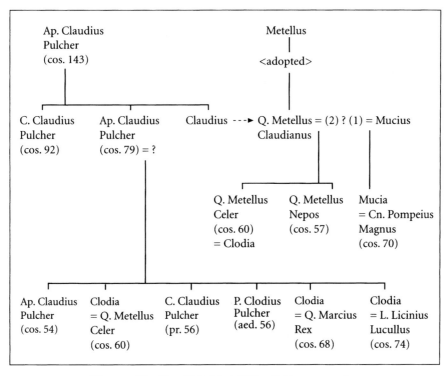

Figure 2. The Claudii Pulchri: Hillard's Reconstruction

brothers or that of *half brothers*.[13] The latter possibility is preferred by Shackleton Bailey, who is followed by T. P. Wiseman.[14] On that reconstruction the two Metelli and the brothers Claudius Pulcher were children of the same mother, and since Mucia, Pompey's bride, was *soror* to the Metelli, the same remarkably fertile woman will have been her mother as well (thus Mucia was half sister to the Claudii Pulchri). Now, since Clodia Metelli must have had a mother different from her husband's, she must (in this reconstruction) also have been a half sister to the remaining Claudii Pulchri (see figure 1). A different reconstruction, proposed by T. W. Hillard, M. Taverne, and C. Zawawi, is possible, however. This postulates that the father of the Metelli (who was tribune ca. 90) was by birth a son of the consul of 143 and subsequently adopted either by L. Metellus Diadematus (cos. 117) or M. Metellus (cos. 115).[15] This view would allow the Metelli to remain cousins to the Claudii Pulchri rather than half brothers, and it would allow Clodia Metelli to remain a full sister to the Claudii Pulchri (see figure 2). Although Shackleton Bailey's reconstruction is far better known, it possesses no claim to superior plausibility—unless as a prosopographer one holds an aversion to speculative adoptions. *Non liquet* must remain the unsatisfying judgment between the two hypotheses. In any case, because the Roman *familia* was, during the late republic, directed both in concept and in sentiment toward agnatic relationships, we should take care not to exaggerate the bond between the Metelli and the Claudii Pulchri, whatever its precise nature.[16]

After the demise of the consul of 79, his family came under the care of the eldest son, himself but nineteen years old. A passage in Varro has generated the belief that the Claudii Pulchri were left in embarrassed circumstances only to be rescued by the generosity of the notoriously stingy Licinius Lucullus, who took a Claudian bride without a dowry and relinquished a legacy in Appius's behalf, information that provoked the surprise of Ronald Syme but has otherwise been accepted by scholars with little demur.[17] Yet upon closer examination, both of the particular Varronian passage and of Varro's literary characterization throughout the *De Re Rustica*, one may safely conclude that the Claudian poverty represented in Varro is—and was intended to be recognized as—a humorous fiction.[18] Young Clodius may have labored under pressures heretofore too little appreciated, but poverty, even relative poverty by the standards of his class, was not among them.

2

Clodius's brilliant heritage and his splendid connections were wonderful assets, plainly, but the full significance of their effect upon the young patrician requires some expansion. Scholars have long focused attention on the difficult struggle in Roman politics faced by the *novus homo*.[19] Like unrequited love, it seems, political and social frustration are more immediately engaging and perhaps more universally accessible subjects than the plights of the privileged. Yet, for all the important advances and insights attained though our fascination with *novitas*, and they are many, an unfortunate ill effect is the pervading assumption that nobles who often represented the chief obstacle to talented newcomers were themselves guaranteed consulships by virtue of their birth alone (e.g., Cic. *Verr.* 2.5.180; *Pis.* 1–2). A locus classicus is Asconius 23 (C), a passage elucidating Cicero's remark in the *Pro Scauro* that it was the consul of 115 who inspired him to seek the consulship (*Scaur.* 4). Asconius's explanation of Cicero's admiration for and identification with Scaurus reveals an easy prejudice:

One might ask why Cicero said this [that Scaurus's example led him to believe that he might attain to a brilliant career, though he lacked high birth, by dint of hard work and determination], since Scaurus was a patrician. The splendor [*claritas*] of that class has brought even the laziest men to high office. But Scaurus, though patrician, belonged to a family whose fortunes had been low for three generations. For neither his father nor his grandfather nor even his great-grandfather had held office—I suspect this was due to their slender resources and their complete lack of industry. Consequently, Scaurus had to struggle just like a new man.

No one would question the advantage of inherited *claritas*, nor can it be denied that some *inertes homines* benefited thereby to the extent that they reached high offices. Yet Scaurus's own family's history reveals how misleading the assumption of automatic success can be. Financial difficulties and laziness, as well as early deaths and pure ineptitude, were among the several hazards to be overcome by many nobles. In fact, Keith Hopkins and G. P. Burton have demonstrated how difficult it was, and how rare, for a family to hold the *fasces* over several generations.[20] What appeared to *novi* to be inevitable success was very largely the result not only of good fortune but also of incessant and considerable industry. As Fergus Millar has observed (with respect to the second century B.C.), if Roman elections had operated with the simplistic predictability suggested by the complaints of new men and the suppositions of some scholars, there would have been far fewer new men and the *fasti* would have resembled the co-opted memberships of the priestly colleges much more closely than they do.[21]

The ambitious Roman aristocrat sought to win *gloria* through the demonstration of *virtus*, most conspicuously in war but also, and most necessarily for his advancement, by attaining political office.[22] Glory was the token of popular favor, which was evidenced at the polls; indeed, the quest for *gloria* has rightly been deemed the fundamental justification, for the aristocracy, of its own political labors, glory earned by reaching the praetorship and, most splendid of all, the consulship.[23] The attainment of *gloria* was a continual labor, vital to one's *dignitas* and the noble excellence that the Romans recognized with *laus*.[24] Every election placed the candidate's reputation at risk—hence the ubiquitous expression *contentio dignitatis*.[25] The *summa laus*, the ultimate objective, was the consulship.[26]

Roman notions of success engendered competition, while devotion to the *res publica* combined with personal jealousy to discourage excessive individual preeminence.[27] The Romans lauded outstanding—but not overshadowing—accomplishment. For them *gloria* was not an inexhaustible resource: there was a finite number of opportunities to be elected consul. One man's success was always another man's failure, out of which emerged *invidia*, an emotion that could sour relations even between the dearest of friends. The prominence of *invidia* in Roman society accents for us the darker aspect of their intense rivalries for distinction.[28]

In the scramble for honors, the scion of a great house possessed definite advantages. But no one inherited the consulship.[29] The noble strained under a burden different from, but no less weighty than, the new man's. Every young Roman was obliged to equal and if possible to surpass the achievements of his father, as many passages attest, though none perhaps so eloquently as the ancient epitaph of Cn. Cornelius Scipio.[30] From his youth the noble pursued *gloria* and *dignitas* with a zeal nourished by his fear of failure. The stoic M. Porcius Cato, for all his posturing, labored under *dolor repulsae*—or so Caesar could plausibly assert.[31] Catiline, though his family had long ago vacated the consulship, was ashamed to have suffered a *repulsa*, particularly when the people preferred a new man to himself. How much greater the pressure, then, that a consul's son must have felt as he entered upon his career, an ancestral burden many times heavier in a family that regularly attained the *summa laus*. Not only hunger for glory but also the terror of *ignominia* motivated the young Roman noble whose inherited *claritas* would render his failure a catastrophe visible to everyone.[32] This is why established families opposed intruders to the senate not when they competed for the relatively easily attainable quaestorship, but when they contested the praetorship and especially the consulship. The intensity of political competition was keenest in the post-Sullan decades. For reasons often discussed, the Romans of the late republic were afflicted by a longing for personal power and prestige that they could neither curb nor satisfy. Overpowered by ambition, the most determined politicians scrupled anything and everything in the struggle for ascendancy and superiority.[33] *Contentio dignitatis* was replaced by *certamen dominationis*. The aristocratic ideal that honored *res publica* before one's individual *gloria* quickly eroded and was finally trampled under foot by Caesar.

From the outset Clodius was compelled to reach the consulship. Anything less was failure, and only death could excuse that. Claudian greatness confronted Clodius at every turn, in the trophies and *imagines* of his family's atrium—and throughout the city. T. P. Wiseman has vividly described the impression that must have been made by the Claudian monuments of ancient Rome: the Appian Way, the Appian Aqueduct, and, perhaps most conspicuous of all, the temple of Bellona, which was decorated by Clodius's father "with shield-portraits of all his ancestors, thus turning it into a *monumentum* of the family as a whole."[34] Which is not to mention the pageantry of Roman funerals, so much admired by Polybius for their value in inculcating both family pride and honest ambition. The sons of the consul of 79 could not deny the demands of their heritage; little wonder that Clodius's eldest brother was frightening in his *Appietas*.[35]

Despite the demands of his past, the ambitious patrician faced particular hurdles in the *cursus honorum*: although entitled to stand early for the higher magistracies, he was barred from the tribunate, an office useful for acquiring popular or senatorial gratitude, and the plebeian aedileships.[36] Worst of all, while both consuls might be plebeian, only one could be patrician, thereby reducing further his opportunities to maintain his family's honor. *Dolor repulsae* drove Catiline to treason, *contentio dignitatis* brought the republic to civil war. Who can doubt that *timor ignominiae* haunted every Roman noble, and especially a Claudius Pulcher?[37]

3

But there is a danger in attempting to plumb too deeply the psychology of Publius Clodius. Motivations matter and interest, but one must avoid transgressing the lamentably narrow limits of our available evidence. In his *Life of Cowley* Dr. Johnson says of a predecessor that "he has given us the character not the life of Cowley." This is a peril to which the biographer of Clodius cannot, alas, be exposed. The problem of course lies in the paucity of our sources and their biases. Although the late republic was not without its historians, nor from 59 onward were the proceedings of the senate's deliberations undisclosed (in addition to which Clodius himself maintained a careful record of his career), nonetheless our knowledge of the political history of the fifties—the decade in which Clodius was most conspicuous—mostly depends on Cicero's version of events or on later, derivative historians who, while enjoying access to useful, independent witnesses, cannot always be trusted to have employed their sources with the greatest of care or competence.[38]

That Cicero's evidence constitutes an unfriendly account of Clodius's activities requires no argument; that the orator remains a vital but problematic source for Roman politics generally is increasingly appreciated by historians and constitutes one of the primary challenges in the study of the late republic. Yet he—like Sallust when he is relevant—has the capital merit of being an extant contemporary source. We are fortunate to possess as well the learned and reliable—though by no means infallible—commentary of Q. Asconius Pedianus, who annotated some of Cicero's speeches in the fifties of our era. He was a scholar whose admiration for Cicero commendably did not blunt his keen critical faculties; it is owing to Asconius, to draw a single if sensational example, that we are able to detect the misleading falsehoods in Cicero's account of Clodius's death in *Pro Milone*.[39] Otherwise for the study of Clodius we are compelled to turn to much later accounts, principally Plutarch, whose highly literary (and didactic) Roman biographies draw on authors like Sallust and Asinius Pollio but with inconsistent accuracy (and for purposes other than the relating of a detailed historical narrative), and Cassius Dio, suffect consul in A.D. 205 (or 206), a voracious reader and an industrious historian but one whose sources are so difficult to discern with precision or confidence that the current generation of historiographers has despaired altogether of doing it.[40] Nevertheless, Plutarch and Dio often provide crucial supplements—and precious correctives—to Cicero.

All of which highlights the tentative nature of any attempt to discuss the fifties or to examine the life of Clodius Pulcher. Qualifying reconstructions of events or other arguments with the obvious disclaimer that our exiguous resources must check our confidence is an all too frequent necessity. To do so regularly would be exceedingly tedious. And, inasmuch as uncertainty is far from alien to the classicist's experience, admissions of doubt and admonitions to caution will be deployed along the lines ordinarily observed by ancient historians. In the end, or so one hopes, the enterprise will not be wholly lacking in usefulness.

So far the impediments to constructing a life. The obstacles to our acquiring a sense of Clodius's character are greater yet. To be candid, they are insuperable. Had we a Plutarchan biography we might at least enjoy an ancient and thoughtful evaluation of Clodius's personal qualities. What actually emerges from the ancient sources—no doubt due mainly to the enduring influence of Cicero—is the employment of Clodius as a rhetorical type: his name became a by-word for baseness, to be contrasted with that of M. Cato or to be linked with Catiline's.[41] Whatever the true nature of the man, he must remain largely obfuscated by a tradition that was mostly interested in politics and tended to view its politicians in terms of great generals, defenders of the senate or *popu-*

lares—a schematic frame of reference that found quite satisfactory Cicero's characterization of Clodius as a wild and menacing demagogue.[42]

Little more can be said on the subject, and this account of the tribune's career will not pretend to offer the reader a portrait of the complete Clodius. But before proceeding further, it may be worthwhile to attempt to gauge the length and breadth of a few features, randomly reported and, one hopes, not interpreted in too far-fetched a fashion. Clodius's political exploitation of popular violence has propelled some modern scholars to diagnose in Clodius some sort of psychopathy, a mistaken reaction that in effect perpetuates the accusations of Cicero.[43] Despite Cicero's rhetoric, there is nothing to suggest that Clodius's contemporaries thought him mad or even (ultimately) unreasonable. His arrogance, excessive even by Roman standards, is documented, and the events of his career disclose a penchant for recklessness and audacity.[44] That Clodius was sometimes prone to exceed the boundaries of propriety, in his personal life as well as his public one, is difficult to deny—and Cicero was certainly able to find sympathetic listeners when he claimed, in the aftermath of his exile, of his enemy's *crudelitas*.[45]

But there is more to a man than his temper. Plutarch describes the young Clodius as eloquent, an estimation reflected in other sources—including Tacitus—even if the flamboyant tribune won no mention in the *Brutus*.[46] His success in rousing the *plebs* indicates Clodius's oratorical vigor, of which we can detect only traces in his invective formulations: Cicero is *hostis Capitolinus*, Cato *carnifex civium*.[47] We need not wonder whether Clodius was well educated: the cultivation and the philhellenism of his family are amply attested, and Clodius himself constantly kept the company of Greeks.[48] During the Bona Dea scandal, Clodius's cause attracted the enthusiastic support of the *barbatuli iuvenes*—to Cicero's disgust—and, at a later time, Clodius's followers hurled insulting epigrams at Pompey that had been composed by no less a figure than the poet and orator C. Licinius Calvus.[49] Calvus, like Clodius's sister, was an intimate of Catullus. Whatever the poet from Verona thought of Clodius upon their initial acquaintance, he eventually penned an epigram attacking the Claudian's arrogance, personal morality, and political behavior.[50] The point, however, is not that the two did not get along with one another but rather that one finds Clodius so well ensconced in the smart set of his day. Even Cicero describes him (without obvious irony) as *urbanissimus*.[51] Interestingly, the orator and the tribune shared the same personal architect, though Clodius was the preferred customer.[52]

The Bona Dea scandal coupled with rumors of incest with his sisters prohibits a high opinion of Clodius's personal morality. Indeed, Clodius's prurient curiosity about the Bona Dea's secret rituals—forbidden to male eyes and no doubt imagined by many Roman men to have been unbridled debauches—and his willingness to transgress Roman proprieties by resorting to transvestism may suggest a personality not merely fascinated by luridness but also fond of risk and wickedly excited by the opportunity to overstep societal boundaries.[53] If Clodius was such a man, ever attracted to the edge, he would hardly be unique in human history, though his elite origins could only increase his chances for indulging his penchant for hazard. Did Clodius's periculous proclivities lead him to incest? The smear was not an uncommon one in the late republic—even Cicero's fondness for his daughter became material for base imputation—but its topicality does not imply its inaccuracy in every case. And the fact of the matter is that Clodius does come in for more than his share of abuse: indeed, incest becomes a virtually obligatory ingredient in anti-Clodian invective.[54] But how can we go beyond that? I rather doubt that my capacities for lurid fantasy are superior to anyone else's, so I shall keep mine to myself. It is not irrelevant, though, that Clodius's contemporaries took so much evident pleasure in revisiting the nature of his affections for his sisters.

That Clodius was (at the very least) something of a roué does not distinguish Clodius from very many of his contemporaries. What is more remarkable, however, is that, in spite of the religious and sexual scandals dogging him, Clodius was very capable in the fifties of adopting a posture of strict religiosity and old-fashioned rectitude. To be sure, this pose invited Cicero's sarcasm, but his attitude was hardly universal. Valerius Maximus records the reconciliation of Clodius and a certain Lentulus, who had been one of Clodius's prosecutors during the Bona Dea affair: on trial for *ambitus*, this Lentulus was defended by his former enemy. During the trial, Clodius made a great display of invoking the goddess Vesta herself as witness to his desire for reconciliation and for justice, which would have been impossible had Clodius been considered by all or even by most to be the immoral and irreligious creature of Ciceronian invective.[55] Even Cicero, in defending Milo after Clodius's murder, tried to make an issue of the fact that, on that fateful day, Clodius had traveled without his wife—which he almost never did (*Mil.* 28); the prevailing assumption, or so Cicero clearly expected, was that Clodius had become quite the family man. Clodius's very assumption of such a traditional stance ought to complicate our conception of his public image. After all, why should Cicero attack—and why should Clodius attempt—what everyone recognized as ridiculous and utterly unrealistic? The answer must be that, after his tribunate, in the mid-fifties (the period in which this posturing becomes evident), not everyone in Rome shared Cicero's (or Catullus's) low opinion of Clodius's character.[56]

Finally, a comment on Clodius's looks. No physical representation survives, but Cicero's frequent sport with Clodius's cognomen perhaps opens the door to speculation. Cicero's habitual recourse to *pulchellus* in and of itself means nothing: the dashing Caelius Rufus was called *pulchellus Iason*; *pulchellus* was wielded in a different sense, by the famous orator, L. Crassus, against the cripple L. Aelius Lamia, in a cruel, humiliating barb that was much admired by Cicero.[57] Presumably Cicero meant the diminutive form to be demeaning to Clodius. Yet the orator's use of *pulcher* and *pulchellus*, while often belittling, never suggests that Clodius is lacking in the good looks and exquisite manners that his name implies—which is most striking when one considers the Roman proclivity (shared by Cicero and illustrated in Crassus's treatment of Aelius Lamia) for fleering at ugliness and physical defects generally.[58]

One will probably not err by much in picturing Clodius as a handsome, urbane, and proud (at times, indeed, obnoxious) noble, of violent temper and of somewhat dubious moral fiber—possessed of a fascination with adventure yet capable nonetheless of very traditional pretensions. Parallels in antiquity and in subsequent history are not hard to find, an observation that ought to prompt the concern that our Clodius is already too much a type (if one different from Cicero's representation) and too little a personality. It will have to suffice to conclude with the obvious statement that Clodius possessed virtues and vices enough to attract allies and to repel enemies. Neither a monster nor a saint, he entered upon the Roman scene a young aristocrat more than eager to hear and to answer to destiny's call.

4

Of Clodius's childhood we know nothing—except Cicero's malicious report that as a boy the young patrician was so frightened of the dark that he habitually slept with his older sister, a pattern of behavior that supposedly led to less innocent conduct when Clodius was less childlike.[59] Ancient biographers, unlike their modern counterparts, tended to be uninterested in an individual's development from child to adult; consequently, even well-known figures from the Roman Republic usually emerge into view not as boys but already as young men.[60] For Clodius the story of his youth can be recovered only in the most fragmentary condition. Isolated episodes, often recounted solely to portray his inferior character, supply glimpses of his life before his enmity with Cicero thrust him into the orator's preoccupations, at which time Clodius inspired a steady stream of worry and invective that at least provides us with something like a continuous account of his career.

Clodius first surfaces in the East, where he served in the Third Mithridatic War on the staff of his brother-in-law, L. Licinius Lucullus, who held the supreme command in this war from 73 until 67, when he was superseded by Pompey.[61] Clodius's eldest brother was an honored legate in Lucullus's camp. In 71 he represented Lucullus at the court of the Armenian king Tigranes, whither he had been sent to demand the surrender of Tigranes' father-in-law, Mithridates himself.[62] Appius's haughtiness while at Tigranocerta (which merely reflected Lucullus's own diplomatic style where Tigranes was concerned) and his willingness to intrigue in the internal affairs of Armenia have attracted wide notice, and Appius's assignment indicates the extent to which Lucullus was inclined to find appropriate offices for his patrician connection. In 74, when Lucullus departed Rome for the East, Clodius was in his eighteenth year, a traditional and appropriate age for beginning the military service that was certainly expected of a future magistrate.[63] Although Clodius cannot be detected in Lucullus's service until 67, he was without question on the general's staff before that time and there seems little reason to resist the idea that he left Rome in 74 along with his brother and brother-in-law.[64] The prospect of military service as Lucullus's *contubernalis* and in company with Appius in the period's most glamorous theater of war must have appeared extremely inviting to young Clodius, nor was there anything to keep him in Rome. The supposition that in 73 Clodius prosecuted Catiline for incest with the Vestal Virgin Fabia, though widespread even in recent scholarship, has been refuted by P. Moreau.[65] By 73 young Clodius, smitten by *cupido gloriae*, had begun his pursuit of *laus* in the most traditional and manly of Roman fashions.

But Clodius enjoyed less esteem than did his brother in the eyes of Lucullus, and the resentment of the young patrician led him to stage a mutiny of Lucullus's troops. The story of Clodius's mutiny suffers from confusion in the ancient sources and (some) controversy in modern accounts. Lucullus's eastern command, though unpopular with the *publicani* and an object of envy at Rome, was a brilliant success well into the year 69, when the proconsul won a sensational victory at Tigranocerta, in the aftermath of which he overran southern Armenia in search of the defeated but elusive Mithridates and wintered in the fabulously wealthy Gordyene. Subsequently, however, Lucullus's campaign, faced with opposition both from Mithridates and from Tigranes of Armenia, became bogged down, with the result that the proconsul found himself increasingly vulnerable to his political enemies, who set about dismantling his command. It was while the troops were wintering in the city of Nisibis (from late 68 to the spring of 67) that Clodius encouraged them to mutiny, an action that Plutarch—our most extensive source for this incident—represented as the turning point of Lucullus's military career (even though he mistakenly situated the rebellion in Gordyene instead of Nisibis).[66] Plutarch's account and the historical significance of the episode as well as Clodius's role and motives require closer examination.

What led to the mutiny at Nisibis? Although 69 had been a season of glorious triumphs for Lucullus, his failure to capture Mithridates prevented him from concluding the war. In 68 the Romans invaded northern Armenia, but this incursion led only to arduous fighting with dubious, unsatisfactory results. Mithridates and Tigranes constantly harassed the legions, menaced their supply lines, yet adroitly contrived to avoid a pitched battle. Stymied, Lucullus hoped that by marching further northward—so as to invest Artaxata, the old capital of Armenia—he might force the monarchs to come to the city's defense, thereby bringing matters to their final resolution. Unfortunately, unexpected cold weather hampered the army's progress and proved so unpleasant that at length the troops refused to go on. Frustrated once again, Lucullus turned south in the hope of salvaging the season's profitless campaign—and to restore his soldiers' flagging morale—by attacking Nisibis, a city guarded by a brother of the king and housing an imperial treasury. While Lucullus descended upon Nisibis, Tigranes recovered control of much of southern Armenia and Mithridates marched westward, where he defeated the legate Fabius Hadrianus and locked him up in Cabira, thereby threatening to regain control of Pontus.

So far the disappointments of 68, all of which should make clear that Plutarch's emphasis on the events at Nisibis as the turning point in Lucullus's fortunes is contrived. In fact, the inspiration for Plutarch's highlighting of Nisibis can be traced to the arrangement of Sallust's narrative of the Third Mithridatic War in his *Historiae* (the fourth book of which dealt with Lucullus's operations against the two monarchs and probably concluded with the capture of Nisibis, whereas the fifth book opened with Mithridates' recovery of Pontus and other reversals) as well as Plutarch's own fascination with the proconsul's inability to preserve the loyalty of his troops, a major theme of the *Lucullus*.[67] Hence the lavish treatment of Clodius's mutiny, "the event that most of all vitiated the undertakings of Lucullus" (*Luc.* 34.1).

While at Nisibis, Lucullus plotted an invasion into the remaining provinces of Tigranes' southern empire, into Adiabene, a sensible strategy for forcing the Armenian king to wage a pitched battle.[68] Lucullus's plan, however, was susceptible of gross misinterpretation by his enemies as a grandiose and utterly irresponsible expedition into Parthia.[69] In any event, this extension of Roman operations was hardly likely to win the enthusiasm of Lucullus's troops, who were already wearied and resentful of the Armenian campaign. They had proved recalcitrant often enough already and it seems inescapable that this proposed march into Adiabene constituted the immediate cause for Clodius's mutiny, a surmise supported by the contents of Clodius's speech as it is reported in Plutarch (*Luc.* 34.3–4):

> Consequently [the troops] received Clodius gladly and called him "the soldier's friend." For his part, he acted as if he were indignant on their behalf, if there was never to be an end to their many wars and labors, but instead they were spending their lives waging war with every nation and roaming over every land, getting for themselves no appropriate return for such military service, but instead escorting the wagons and camels of Lucullus, which were laden with golden vessels inlaid with gems—while Pompey's troops, who were now citizens, settled down with wives and children, had possession of fertile land and prosperous cities, their rewards, not for having driven Mithridates and Tigranes into uninhabited deserts, not for having demolished the royal palaces of Asia, but for having waged war with exiles in Spain and with runaway slaves in Italy. "Why then, if we are never to have an end to campaigning, why then do we not protect what is left of our bodies and our spirits for a general to whom the wealth of his soldiers is his fairest decoration?"

This oration, which probably derives from Sallust's *Historiae*, is somewhat at odds with Plutarch's own narrative.[70] Clodius complains that the soldiers are given no rest and are forced to fight against every nation and in every land. In the speech's framework, however, Plutarch makes a march back to Pontus the focus of the army's disobedience, which not only clashes with Clodius's oration but is also out of joint with the subsequent narrative, wherein the legions do in fact march to Pontus as ordered. In Sallust's account the mutiny was doubtless introduced so that Clodius could rail against Lucullus's "Parthian expedition"—though perhaps the historian was more accurate in describing the general's intentions—thereby providing a more appropriate context for the patrician's litany of objections. Even if it is agreed that Sallust is our primary source for the mutiny at Nisibis and that his account of its attendant circumstances offered a different perspective on the soldiers' resistance from the one found in Plutarch, other problems arise. The extent to which one can trust the historicity of Sallust's record of Clodius's speech can hardly be determined in such a way as to win consensus: Sallustian practice suffices to overcome serious doubts as to the actual occurrence of the mutiny (which is reported by Cicero and Dio as well as Sallust and Plutarch) and would indicate (as common sense suggests) that Clodius did indeed deliver a speech; the content of the preserved oration, however, so distinctly anti-Pompeian, strongly suggests that it represents the sentiments of Sallust as he composed his *Historiae* rather than those of Clodius as he instigated his mutiny.[71]

We may turn to the nature and historical significance of Clodius's actions at Nisibis. The older view that Clodius acted as Pompey's agent at Nisibis has recently (and rightly) been demolished, nor is there any reason to believe that Clodius's actions were intended to curry favor with Lucullus's enemies in Rome.[72] This is not to say that Lucullus's political difficulties did not influence the patrician's behavior, rather, it is simply that Clodius's mutiny was unnecessary for the undermining of Lucullus's position and so could not earn any real gratitude from those anxious to see the proconsul recalled. As early as 69 Asia had been withdrawn from Lucullus's province; the following year the praetor L. Quinctius worked for Lucullus's supersession so effectively that the skinflint proconsul, who was aware of his problems at home, was compelled to resort to bribery.[73] From the moment he invaded Armenia, Lucullus was in need of conspicuous victories and a speedy conclusion to the war if he hoped to overcome the inevitable criticism of his rivals.[74] Unfortunately, the campaign of 68 did nothing to settle matters, as we have seen. The proconsul was not recalled in that year, but Cilicia was removed from his command and assigned to Q. Marcius Rex. Moreover, the tension between the general and his troops became a political issue in the city, with the result that there was a movement to release from service some of Lucullus's soldiers. By the time Lucullus settled into winter quarters at Nisibis, political realities had rendered his continued command beyond hope. Nor was Lucullus's military situation impressive: it was at Nisibis that he learned of Fabius's defeat and the loss of Pontus.[75] In such circumstances, Clodius's mutiny can hardly be considered instrumental in Lucullus's fall—though by preventing the Adiabene expedition he may have robbed his general of any chance of repairing his dignity before his supersession.

Dio attributes Clodius's behavior to his "innate love of revolution" (νεωτεροποιία), a term reminiscent of Sallust's description of the mutineer as *ex insolentia avidus male faciendi*, but he offers nothing more specific (and Sallust's phrase, of course, is a disjoined fragment).[76] Plutarch, however, provides a fuller and different picture.[77] He does not stress the future tribune's rabble-rousing capacities—even his description of Clodius as "the soldiers' friend" (φιλοστρατιώτης), a term associated with demagoguery and in its own way unflattering to Clodius, serves primarily to make Clodius a foil to the unpopular Lucullus.[78] Instead the biographer underscores Clodius's patrician arrogance: resentful that he had not received from Lucullus the honor he felt he deserved, Clodius staged the mutiny in order to revenge himself upon his general.[79] Plutarch's interpretation of the mutiny's origin is plausible and, while not demonstrable beyond all doubt, certainly rings truer than modern attempts to infer from Clodius's actions either a conspiracy (with Pompey) or an early challenge to the Sullan order.[80] Clodius's mutiny, it seems safe to say, was a personal (if extravagant) expression of aristocratic rancor.

Clodius timed his vengeance well: the soldiers were securely garrisoned in a wealthy city; Lucullus was arranging an expedition that, whatever its strategic value, was certain to be unpopular and could fairly be deemed exceptionable in view of his imminent supersession. Inasmuch as Lucullus's sun had set, the ambitious Clodius could foresee little practical danger in offending his commander: despite the patent illegality of his conduct, Clodius no doubt felt safe in assuming that his rank and his brother's influence as well as Lucullus's crippling unpopularity would shield him from the proconsul's exacting any penalty; Roman mutinies often went unpunished, nor had Lucullus anything to gain from exacerbating his existing difficulties with his legions or with his opponents in Rome.[81] Furthermore, the new proconsul in Cilicia, Marcius Rex, was also Clodius's brother-in-law, nor were Lucullus and Marcius Rex on very good terms, or so one might gather form the latter's malicious jibe that, were he to send troops to assist Lucullus, they would surely mutiny.[82] Cilicia offered the disgruntled patrician a safe haven, whither he removed himself, unmolested by Lucullus, who would find other opportunities to satisfy his animus toward Clodius. The mutiny at Nisibis was a very personal affair, all very much *de haut en bas*: patrician insolence bred impertinent, even brazen, retaliation for what was perceived by Clodius to be an intolerable slight upon his status and his talents. His insurrection, however, had little historical significance—except insofar as Clodius alienated Lucullus, thereafter a formidable personal enemy. But in larger terms Clodius's mutiny made no difference to Lucullus's failure, nor did it excite the passions of Clodius's most vocal enemy: Gabinius's legislation, which was the beginning of the end for Lucullus's eastern command, was proposed early in 67, at nearly the same time as Clodius's mutiny, and the earliest (and only nearly contemporary) mention of the mutiny comes from Cicero, who makes very little of it.[83]

5

After the mutiny at Nisibis, Clodius left Lucullus's army, either by desertion or dismissal (in the event, the distinction was irrelevant), to join the staff of Marcius Rex, proconsul in Cilicia.[84] Marcius Rex has been the object of considerable disparagement from modern scholars, who take the silence of our sources for proof of Marcius's inactivity.[85] And in the grand scheme of things there can be no denying that Marcius Rex, like Acilius Glabrio, takes on the appearance of little more than a stopgap in the transition from Lucullus's Mithridatic command to Pompey's. But this is not entirely fair. Marcius's assignment was to quash brigandage in Cilicia, in addition to which he involved himself in Syrian affairs as a means of promoting Roman interests there as well as of maintaining the security of his province.[86] The province of Cilicia, originally established to fight piracy, had in the past provided a springboard to greater things and even in 67 it offered its share of opportunities.[87] In short, it was a plum. Presumably Marcius entertained hopes of winning his mead of glory and he was not wholly unsuccessful. Although his proconsulship was truncated by the *lex Manilia*, he was honored in Argos (or so it seems) and in 63 he was encamped outside Rome awaiting a justly deserved triumph.[88] Marcius's conduct during the Bellum Catilinae was scrupulously correct and *en bon aristocrate*.[89] If no colossus, Marcius enjoyed a distinguished and creditable career. It was this brother-in-law who gave Clodius his first documented opportunities for responsible action. And in view of Clodius's (disappointed) expectation of a legacy from Marcius in 61, we may safely assume that their relationship proved more cordial, to outward appearances at least, than that between the young Clodius and Lucullus.[90]

The problem of Mediterranean piracy is well known.[91] An unexpected result of Rome's overthrow of the Hellenistic monarchies, who had previously policed the seas, was the flourishing of piracy in the first century. No mere buccaneers, the pirates maintained large fleets efficiently organized for warfare. Mountainous Cilicia provided an ideal stronghold, difficult to reach by land by dint of the area's fierce tribesmen as well as its physical obstacles; in fact, neither Rome nor Byzantium would ever pacify the hill country completely. Marcius's campaign was no minor affair and required engaging the enemy at sea while battling on land the wild inhabitants of the Taurus range.[92]

Clodius played a major role in Marcius's campaign. He was set in charge of a fleet, probably as a naval prefect, with the task of engaging the pirates at sea.[93] This was a position of prestige, responsibility, and danger.[94] And, in the end, Lucullus's reservations about the young Clodius's military capacities found apparent if unfortunate vindication when the patrician was defeated and taken prisoner by the pirates. The captive Clodius appealed to Ptolemy, the king of Cyprus, to ransom him.[95] However, the monarch's stinginess led him to offer only two talents for Clodius, a pittance that amused the pirates and infuriated the patrician.[96] Nonetheless, Clodius was soon released by the pirates—at the cost of his chastity in Cicero's malign report, though it is more likely the Clodius was set free owing to the pirates' fear of Pompey, who was sweeping eastward toward Cilicia.[97] Pompey's war on piracy, begun in early spring, proved so successful that the terrorized outlaws quickly found it prudent to surrender to the Roman admiral, especially when his clemency had become known to them.[98] After regaining his freedom Clodius continued to serve in the war against the pirates, under Pompey's command even if technically Marcius's prefect.[99]

Pirates alone did not occupy Marcius's attention during his proconsulship. He also involved himself in Syrian politics. Because Clodius played a role as Marcius's operative in Syria, it will be well to review briefly the circumstances both men faced there. The kingdom of Syria was wealthy and, owing to its position as the common neighbor to Roman Cilicia, Egypt, and Parthia, of considerable strategic importance, all the more so on account of its political instability.[100] Constant dynastic strife had led to the removal of the Seleucid house; the throne had passed to Tigranes of Armenia, who alone seemed able to offer the realm security from foreign menace and from civil war. The details of Tigranes' acquisition of Syria are uncertain, but under his rule the country enjoyed fourteen years of relative peace and prosperity, marred only by the terrible earthquake of 69.[101] However beneficial Armenian suzerainty may have been to the Syrians, it became objectionable to the Romans when, in 72, Mithridates took refuge with his son-in-law Tigranes, who became implicated in the war with Rome.[102] After Lucullus invaded Armenia and forced Tigranes to relinquish his hold on Syria, the proconsul seized the opportunity to place on the throne a friendly king, Antiochus XIII Asiaticus.[103] This Antiochus, son of the formidable Cleopatra Selene and Antiochus X Eusebes, had come with his brother to Rome around 73 in order to claim the throne of Egypt; in this they failed, but the senate recognized them as the rightful rulers of Syria, endorsing them although not enthroning them.[104] So it was that in 69 Antiochus Asiaticus was to hand as an eminently suitable candidate for Lucullus to place on the Syrian throne: a legitimate Seleucid who had been approved by the senate. As a welcome bonus, Antiochus could also claim popular support.[105] Unfortunately, the Seleucid proved unable to maintain his grip on regal power. Though able to suppress open resistance, he failed to prevent his enemies from fleeing to his rival kinsman, Philip II Barypous, the son of Philip Epiphanes Philadelphus.[106] Philip was in Cilicia, whence he came to Antioch relying on the support of an Arab chieftain named Aziz. Antiochus likewise turned for aid to an Arab sheikh, Sampsigeramus. The two Arabs, however, conspired to do away with the kings and to divide Syria between themselves. But whereas Sampsigeramus captured and imprisoned Antiochus, Philip, apprised of the scheme, occupied Antioch and, to protect himself against Aziz's designs, appealed to the proconsul of Cilicia, at that juncture Marcius Rex.[107]

Marcius elected to assist Philip.[108] That the proconsul should be concerned with Philip's predicament was perfectly natural inasmuch as Roman governors were expected to secure their provinces and especially their frontier. An unstable Syria, potentially vulnerable to Tigranes' influence, was plainly inimical to Roman interests. Nor was it outside the scope of a promagistrate's office to recognize and support friendly kings.[109] Though independent action always entailed risk for a Roman promagistrate—especially when the conduct of foreign policy was so politically charged as it was during the sixties—it was nonetheless a normal requirement of the job.[110] In support of his decision to intervene in Philip's behalf, Marcius could refer to the immediate precedent of Lucullus's backing of Antiochus, point to Antiochus's hopeless position as Sampsigeramus's prisoner, and argue the need for a strong Syria in Rome's program to repress any resurgence of the pirates. In addition to such patriotic motives, considerations of personal advantage also prompted the proconsul's intervention: a grateful king was a generous friend, and royal gifts to Roman supporters had become normal.[111] Philip would not be the only one indebted to Marcius. The Italian business community in Antioch would also appreciate a resolution to Syrian civil war.[112] Finally, there was the prestige and status to be gained in Rome itself from attaching to oneself a friendly king and from winning popularity among foreign peoples.[113] Marcius succeeded, at least for the short term, in installing Philip, who in gratitude and deference designated himself φιλορώμαιος, an epithet frequently employed by mon-

archs whose thrones rested heavily on Roman favor.[114] In 67 the proconsul himself visited Antioch, a gesture of Roman support, at which time
he began the construction of a great circus and a palace. In the aftermath
of the earthquake of 69 Antioch was no doubt in serious need of public
building. Both a royal palace and especially a circus represented natural
and marked tokens of Rome's favor and Marcius's patronage.[115]

It was after completing his service with Pompey that Clodius himself
was sent by Marcius to Antioch.[116] Philip's throne was again in peril and
the young officer was dispatched to strengthen the king's resistance to his
Arab enemies.[117] Marcius's confidence in his brother-in-law was evidently unshaken by recent events, in addition to which the proconsul no
doubt hoped to profit from Clodius's substantial contacts in Syria—in
particular the political connections that Ap. Claudius had recently established there.[118] Dio reports that Clodius offered to defend the people of
Antioch from certain unspecified Arabs, presumably Aziz and Sampsigeramus. Although Aziz had failed in his attempt to carry out his part in
their joint conspiracy against the Seleucids by allowing Philip to escape
to Antioch, Sampsigeramus still had Antiochus in his power. It is not
unreasonable to conjecture that Sampsigeramus was endeavoring to undermine Philip's position by exploiting the rival claims of Antiochus. By
the end of 67 Pompey was active in Cilicia; thus there was the possibility
of a change in Roman policy (and in fact Antiochus did later make a
fruitless appeal to Pompey while still in the clutches of the Arab). Whatever the particulars of this penultimate episode in Syria's dynastic con-
vulsions, the one clear fact is that Clodius was unsuccessful in propping
up Philip—dramatically so if we can believe Dio's version of events.
Nothing more of Philip is heard in Syria, though at some point he fled to
Egypt. As for Clodius, he returned to Rome, perhaps in the company of
Marcius Rex.[119]

Clodius's eastern service is difficult to assess, not least because what
fragmentary knowledge of it we possess derives from hostile sources
intended to blacken Clodius's reputation. Even so, one is struck by the
very traditional nature of Clodius's initial career: the young patrician,
seeking military distinction, exploited to the hilt his family connections
in order to hasten his advancement. The only truly startling episode took
place at Nisibis when, insulted by Lucullus, Clodius resorted to an outrageous and illegal expedient for revenging himself. The incident at
Nisibis, however, was hardly nascent demagoguery; pique, not politics,
inspired Clodius's insubordination. Yet it was owing mainly to his elevated birth that Clodius's military career was unaffected by his excessive
and mutinous conduct. Quite the contrary, Marcius Rex, who was no

revolutionary, installed Clodius in positions of responsibility and trust. Not that Marcius's favor did much for Clodius's military reputation. His service with Pompey may have been unexceptionable, but his failures under Marcius, however understandable, remained uneclipsed by glorious deeds done in compensation. Once again it was Clodius's noble birth that shielded him from detractors. What Rosenstein has called the "myth of universal aristocratic competence" may not have excused every Roman commander's incompetence, but it most certainly applied to a *nobilis* like Clodius, whose hereditary *virtus* would continue to be assumed by the Romans—even in the presence of military setbacks (which the Romans were capable of explaining in terms that did not discredit their noble leadership).[120]

6

Upon his return from the East, Clodius introduced himself to public life by undertaking a prosecution. This was a time-honored means of securing a reputation—and other rewards—though a prosecutor naturally ran the risk of incurring lasting and dangerous enmities.[121] Still, the importance of a Roman politician was often measured by the stature of his enemies as well as of his friends (the important thing being that the balance, in terms both of quantity and quality, tilted in favor of one's friendships).[122] Furthermore, a case attracting considerable celebrity would offer a young orator an excellent opportunity to showcase his skill and, if the case were chosen well, his patriotism. At the same time, a young Roman's tender years might mitigate (at least somewhat) the potential for giving offense and would certainly diminish the likelihood of suffering disgrace if the prosecution should fail. Clodius, as we have seen, won a brilliant reputation as an orator, a profession from which he drew a perhaps excessive profit, though the record of Clodius's forensic career is lamentably thin.

In a sly remark Cicero claims that Clodius, when he returned to Rome, at first considered dragging his own relatives into court, but, electing otherwise upon maturer consideration, he entered into base collusion with the disreputable Catiline at the latter's trial for extortion in 65.[123] Unnecessary ingenuity has been expended in attempting to recognize a genuinely historical reference in Cicero's calumniation; a more sensible approach is to observe with Lenaghan that imputing to Clodius a discreditable (and unrealized) intention to prosecute his relations "was an easy charge to make, since it concerned something which did not happen."[124] Indeed, the disparagement appears to stand in Cicero's *De*

Haruspicum Responso not only as an independent insult but also to underscore the charge of *praevaricatio*: Clodius, Cicero implies, was so perverse that he nearly hauled his own kin into court, whereas a notorious miscreant like Catiline could claim his cooperation.[125] This was an effectual rhetorical stratagem—in 56, when *De Haruspicum Responso* was delivered. But the circumstances of 65 were otherwise, as Cicero well knew.

L. Sergius Catilina had been praetor in 68 and had subsequently served as governor of Africa. When he returned to Rome in 66 to stand for the consulship, his *professio* was rejected by the consul, L. Volcacius Tullus, though only after much consultation with other senators (a procedure that attests to the seriousness of crossing Catiline, at this juncture in any case).[126] Catiline's reversal represented Clodius's opportunity. Although Catiline could claim influential friends in the senate, men like Q. Catulus (cos. 78) and L. Manlius Torquatus (cos. 65), Volcacius's refusal to admit his candidature was a blow. The full complement of motives behind Volcacius's action, which was unquestionably a legitimate exercise of his prerogative, remains uncertain, but there can be no doubt than one factor was the report of Catiline's improprieties in Africa.[127] When a deputation from Africa formally presented its grievances against Catiline—in advance of the governor's return to the city—a great stir resulted in the senate.[128] Thus Catiline was at once significant enough and vulnerable enough to be worth prosecuting. Clodius leapt into the breach.

Or did he? In the aftermath of his exile Cicero regularly asserted that Clodius had actually been in collusion with Catiline, hence the latter's acquittal.[129] But by then Cicero had long been purveying his equation of Clodius and the revolutionary Catiline, so the slander was congenial to the orator's preferred representation of his archenemy and, no doubt, to his natural prejudices about Clodius's inherent character. Cicero's contemporary references to the trial are more equivocal. In a letter to Atticus (composed in July 65) that reviewed his likely competitors in the consular elections to be held in 64, Cicero mentions Catiline in such a way as to suggest that the patrician's condemnation was seen at the time as a virtual certainty: "Catiline—if his jury rules that there is no light at midday—will certainly be a candidate" (*Att.* 1.1.1). Yet shortly thereafter, in another letter to Atticus, Cicero relates that he is considering defending Catiline, a compromise encouraged among other things by the rumor that Cicero's bid for the consulship was to be opposed by the nobility. Furthermore, in spite of Catiline's obvious guilt, Cicero was hopeful of an acquittal: "we have the jury we want, owing to the complete compliance of the prosecution" (iudices habemus quos volumus, summa accusatoris voluntate, *Att.* 1.2.1). The phrase *summa accusatoris voluntate* has often been taken as proof of Clodius's collusion.[130] Yet Asconius was not convinced of Clodius's *praevaricatio*. According to Asconius, the belief that Clodius had engaged in collusion arose first from Catiline's actual acquittal and especially from Clodius's overly cooperative manner in the selection (*reiectio*) of the jury.[131] Clearly Asconius did not accept Cicero's later accusations as fact. As we can infer from Asconius's criticisms of the account of the trial given by the historian Fenestella (who belonged to the generation preceding Asconius's), the precise historical record of Catiline's trial became hazy rather early on.[132] Elsewhere Catiline's acquittal is attributed to bribery.[133] All of which makes it difficult to justify rejecting Asconius's uncertainty on the matter of Clodius's conduct in Catiline's trial. In the face of Asconius's unwillingness to agree with Cicero, it seems better to follow more recent historians who reject the charge of *praevaricatio* altogether.[134]

Few details of the actual trial are known.[135] Manlius Torquatus, who was consul at the time of the trial, stood up for Catiline, as did many men of consular rank. Although the influence of this collective *auctoritas* failed to persuade the senatorial jurors of Catiline's innocence, the *equites* and *tribuni aerarii* (if we may believe Asconius on this specific matter) voted for acquittal.[136] Perhaps such men were more susceptible to the impact of consular testimony, or to Catiline's (alleged) bribery. In any event, Catiline escaped conviction and Clodius failed in his first prosecution. Whether the infamy of collusion arose immediately or later it is impossible to determine, but in view of Catiline's manifest guilt there must have been a strong sense of an opportunity lost.

7

Undeterred by this setback, Clodius pursued yet another avenue to advancement, this time the cultivation of L. Licinius Murena as his personal friend and his political mentor. There had been ample opportunity for Clodius and Murena to develop an association during their service under Lucullus in the Mithridatic War, a war in which Murena (unlike the young patrician) had campaigned as one of Lucullus's principal and most effective legates.[137] Like Clodius, though, Murena and Lucullus had a falling out, ill feeling reflected in the negative and clearly distorted account of Murena's service preserved in Plutarch's *Lucullus*.[138] It has been plausibly argued that the denigration of Murena in Plutarch's narrative can be traced to the epic poem that Archias, Lucullus's client poet, composed for the sake of glorifying his patron.[139] If Archias depicted Lucullus's lieutenants as puny and ineffectual foils to the great man, then one may well believe that Murena's skin bristled at every recollection of the poet's lines in praise of the great general. There was also Lucullus's difficulty in maintaining good relations not merely with his troops but with his fellow officers (not only Clodius), a flaw of character mentioned by Plutarch.[140] Clodius's enmity with Lucullus, in addition to the assets of his estimable family name (and what can already be seen as considerable if not exactly effectual energy), may have gone a long way to recommend the young patrician to Murena, who, elected to a praetorship for 65, became proconsul in Transalpine Gaul in the following year.[141] Clodius became a member of Murena's staff.[142]

The nature of Clodius's duties while in Gaul are unknown; there is only the inevitable accusation of criminal conduct from section 42 of Cicero's *De Haruspicum Responso*, where Clodius's early career receives a summary and derogatory review. On the subject of Clodius's provincial service, Cicero asserts: "Then he went to Gaul with Murena. In this province he forged the wills of dead men, murdered young wards, and formed criminal alliances and associations with many." Clodius is elsewhere called a forger of wills, regular stock in the inventory of vituperative oratory, all intended (and no doubt often effective) in arousing *indignatio*, especially in view of the seriousness with which Romans viewed last wills and testaments.[143] Now prevailing Roman sensibilities regarding provincial administration unquestionably countenanced a good deal of corruption before allowing itself to become outraged, and it was expected that service on a governor's staff ought to be profitable.[144] So we should not be surprised if Clodius's tenure in Gaul worked to his advantage. But Cicero's invective in *De Haruspicum Responso* hardly jibes with his glowing report of Murena's governorship in *Pro Murena*, where inter alia it is observed that Murena won the praise of the *equites* through his exemplary administration, enforcing the payment of outstanding debts and generally advancing the interests of Rome's business class.[145] Clodius, who continued in Murena's good books, can scarcely have been a renegade under so upright a governor. In the matter of his Gallic service, there is no reason to take Cicero's charges against Clodius seriously.

Murena returned to Rome in 63 to stand for the consulship. The elections for 62 were remarkable for their extraordinary circumstances and their scandalous conduct. The field of candidates included, besides Murena, Ser. Sulpicius Rufus, D. Iunius Silanus, and Catiline, undaunted despite his past setbacks (which included a *repulsa* in the previous year's elections). Cicero, whose alarmist speech against Catiline in the senate succeeded in postponing the consular *comitia*, heightened election day tensions when he appeared melodramatically clad in a cuirass. While

Catiline contended with the hostile consul, Murena faced the menacing opposition of Sulpicius, who virulently threatened prosecution should he lose the election. Sulpicius's anxieties were well founded. Murena was a solid *bonus* from a respected praetorian family; his father had celebrated a triumph, glorious if undeserved; he himself enjoyed the reputation of a distinguished general—whatever the opinion of Archias's muse. Furthermore, as we have noted, Murena had recently made himself pleasing in the eyes of the equestrian order, and the city was teeming with Lucullus's veterans, home for their general's triumph but keen to support their past comrade-in-arms. Murena left little to chance, however, rounding off his canvass with generous electoral *largitio*.[146]

Clodius was Murena's ardent supporter. The presence of the young patrician in Murena's retinue would of course lend dignity to his campaign, and youthful nobles were noted for their zealous political efforts.[147] If we could narrow our aperture somewhat, we might expect to see Clodius playing a role in the management of Murena's veteran supporters, if Clodius was still regarded by the troops as "the soldiers' friend." But the only known, and no doubt the most important, of Clodius's activities in Murena's campaign consisted in his helping to implement the candidate's bribery scheme. Before we focus further, then, a few comments on *ambitus* may prove helpful.[148]

We have seen in the previous chapter how industriously a candidate was expected to labor in the winning of votes. Gifts of money—buying the vote—was a regular component of electoral success, legal and not wholly disreputable so long as the practice was constrained within traditional and (by the late republic) legally imposed limits. The post-Sullan aristocracy, however, proved unable to observe the prescribed boundaries. Hence the plethora of legislation designed to curb unacceptable electioneering practices—*ambitus*—and the crush of litigation in the last decades of the Roman Republic. Still, the practice of bribery continued unabated; in fact, it became increasingly commonplace in Roman elections and was quite well organized. Payments were dispensed through the agency of *divisores*: these were originally middlemen responsible for distributing gratuities among members of a candidate's own tribe, a traditional and legitimate form of patronage. But by the late republic the role of the *divisores* had been corrupted so that they supplied the network for the general disbursement of bribes. *Divisores* of this ilk were liable to be despised by senatorial types, but the performance of their job made them rich, and, owing to the necessity for candidates of participating in electoral bribery (if only to keep pace with their rivals), the *divisores* were an influential group. *Divisores* did not ordinarily receive their funds directly from the candidate (since it was patently illegal to distribute gifts in an alien tribe); instead, they were engaged and paid by a friend or ally of the office seeker, a role designated by the terms *sequester* or *interpres*. This, presumably, was Clodius's function in Murena's campaign: Clodius served as the necessary go-between entrusted with Murena's cash and responsible for recruiting the *divisores* who would put it to proper—or rather improper—use.[149]

It is sometimes suggested that Clodius's electioneering on Murena's behalf provided the germ of his later organization of the urban poor.[150] But this is exceedingly unlikely. Clodius's task involved nothing more than securing the services of the required *divisores*. Granted they were doubtless very much worth knowing for the young patrician, nonetheless Clodius's association with the *divisores* hardly constituted a grassroots connection. And it is important to note that bribery at consular elections was not primarily intended to corrupt the urban poor, whose votes carried no appreciable weight in the *comitia centuriata*.[151] Admittedly the lower classes had an important role to play in the pageantry of Roman elections, and they certainly benefited to some degree from the largess of the contending candidates, but the bulk of Murena's cash was earmarked for men of the upper classes, whose votes mattered most.[152] In supporting Murena, Clodius certainly became intimately acquainted with the techniques of waging an electoral campaign in Rome—that was largely the point—and he strengthened his connection with the consul of 62. But none of this was especially novel or in any way indicative of the direction of his later mastery of the *plebs urbana*.

Murena and Iunius Silanus were elected consuls for 62, in response to which unfavorable returns Catiline commenced his infamous conspiracy. Sulpicius elected to pursue a less radical tack: he charged Murena *de ambitu*.[153] The innocuous Silanus was spared prosecution, in no small measure because he was kin to Cato, who assisted in the case against the other consul-elect.[154] Murena was defended by no less a figure than Cicero, whose speech in Murena's behalf remains a splendid illustration of the orator's wit. Although Clodius was not actually accused, his name must surely have been mentioned in the course of the trial. Cicero informs us that C. Postumus, another of Murena's prosecutors, spoke "de divisorum indiciis et de deprehensis pecuniis" (*Mur.* 54). Unfortunately Postumus's oration does not survive, nor does Cicero's rebuttal; only the rubric DE POSTUMI CRIMINIBUS records the original placement of Cicero's response to Postumus's allegations. The absence of this portion of Cicero's speech is apparently the result of the orator's own editing, and Moreau has made the attractive suggestion that a prime motive for Cicero's expunging of this passage was its inclusion of a defense of Clodius's role as Murena's supporter.[155]

Postumus's defamatory rhetoric was not forgotten; in fact, Cicero himself resorted to like accusations once he had become Clodius's enemy. At the Bona Dea trial, which took place in 61, Clodius was denounced for bribing the masses.[156] And Cicero went so far as to cry shame on Clodius for cheating the *divisores* of their full payments.[157] Nor was Cicero's malice limited to recriminations of thieving: in the aftermath of his exile, the orator portrayed Clodius not merely as defrauding the *divisores* but actually as murdering them in his own home.[158] None of these charges carries much conviction, not because Clodius was incapable of dishonesty or brutality but because the *divisores* were collectively too important and too formidable to risk alienating—especially at this stage in Clodius's career.[159] In any case, the success of Clodius's candidate suffices to prove that the young patrician had secured a regular and satisfactory working relationship with the *divisores*, whatever the *mendaciuncula* promulgated by his enemies.

Murena's trial took place under the cloud of Catiline's conspiracy, a circumstance stressed by Cicero in his defense in order to stiffen the jury's resolve to support the position of the consul and of the accused, who was consul-elect (and whose disgrace could only serve the ends of the enemies of stability). Asconius informs us that Cicero often reproached Clodius for having been an adherent of Catiline. One rumor, no doubt traceable to Cicero himself, reported that, at the time when Catiline had removed himself from Rome to Etruria, Clodius gave serious consideration to joining him there, but in the end thought better of it.[160] This imputation, reminiscent of Cicero's reproach that Clodius had thought of prosecuting his kinsmen (but had not actually done so), can mean very little; an unrealized intention is an easy and irrefutable slander. Plutarch's account of Clodius's conduct is very different: "At the time of the Catilinarian conspiracy, Cicero found Clodius most anxious to help and to protect him" (*Cic.* 29.1). In the years following 63 many Romans had to defend themselves against slanders implicating them in Catiline's conspiracy. As Clodius became assimilated to Catiline in Cicero's rhetoric, it was inevitable that he suffer the same incrimination. Yet few scholars have accepted the rumor preserved by Asconius.[161] Such appeal as it has enjoyed derives from the belief that Clodius was guilty of *praevaricatio* at Catiline's trial, an idea that has been rejected in the preceding pages. And without that connection between the two men, there is nothing to connect Clodius with the conspiracy. In fact, one would not naturally expect an alliance to emerge from Clodius's prosecution of Catiline (if, as has been maintained here, Clodius's prosecution was an honest one). In 63 Clodius was intimately associated with Murena, who was staunch in his opposition to Catiline.[162] Clodius's exertions on Murena's behalf were nothing less than exertions against Catiline's candidacy, after all. Similarly, Clodius's brother-in-law and former commander, Marcius Rex, made a virtue of his delayed triumph by exercising his *imperium* to help to suppress Catilinarian troops.[163] Not that the behavior of Clodius's associates necessarily indicates the nature of Clodius's attitude at the time, but once it is recognized that Clodius had clearly placed himself in the camp of Catiline's opponents in the elections for 62, his actions manifest themselves as very much in accordance with the conduct of his friends. In any event, it is hard to find any incentive for a Claudius Pulcher—wealthy, propertied, and solidly establishment—to throw in his lot with a champion of *novae res*, a man who could not really match the Claudii in pedigree and had proved incapable even of beating a new man like Cicero at the polls. Despite Cicero's insinuations, then, it is infinitely more likely that in 63 Clodius stood beside the consul of Rome, loyal to his class and its interests, as Plutarch reports.[164]

The friendship between Murena and Clodius may have been strengthened by a nominal *affinitas*. In 58 Clodius was brother-in-law to the obscure patrician L. Pinarius Natta, the pontifex who in that year presided over the consecration of Cicero's Palatine property. By the year 63 this Natta was Murena's stepson.[165] Combining these two data, Lily Ross Taylor proposed that Clodius's relation to Natta was not owing to his marriage to some hypothetical Pinaria, but rather to Fulvia, the daughter of M. Fulvius Bambalio and Sempronia, and the woman who was certainly Clodius's wife by 58.[166] Natta's priestly assistance to Clodius was at the strong urging of his mother and sister, a combination recalling the behavior of Sempronia and Fulvia at Milo's trial in 52.[167] Now, if Fulvia was Natta's sister, then Sempronia must have had three husbands: a Pinarius Natta, M. Fulvius Bambalio, and, by 63, Murena. Consequently, Murena was Fulvia's as well as Natta's stepfather.

One cannot date Clodius's marriage to Fulvia with precision. Still, it was perfectly natural for a Roman aristocrat to marry in his late twenties.[168] The birth dates of Clodius's and Fulvia's known children offer little help: their daughter, Claudia, the future wife of the young Octavian, was probably born in 57.[169] P. Claudius Pulcher, their son, who was praetor apparently some time after Actium, is more difficult to place.[170] Q. Metellus Scipio, in a speech against Milo delivered after Clodius's murder in 52, referred to Claudius as *parvulus*, though clearly the diminutive was for pathetic effect. In 44 Claudius could still be described as *puer*.[171] Granted that the parameters of *pueritas* were flexible, a birth date around 62–59 would suit both references well, and young Claudius would then be too young to have become praetor until after 31.[172] All of which is at least suggestive of a marriage around the time of Murena's consulship, thereby establishing a nominal affinity between Clodius and Murena, which would certainly have been a suitable capstone to their mutually beneficial friendship. Yet it must be recalled that Fulvia, who was in addition to her other compelling qualities quite wealthy, will have been an attractive bride at any time on her own merits.[173] Moreover, since Fulvia's father, the puzzling Bambalio, outlived Clodius, it was he and not Murena who became Clodius's actual father-in-law, which ought to caution us against attaching too much political significance to Clodius's affinity with Murena.[174]

<h1 style="text-align:center">8</h1>

It is time for an assessment of Clodius's early career and his first steps in politics. What is most remarkable upon review is the orthodoxy of his methods to advance himself. Taking advantage of his family's connections to acquire promising positions, Clodius sought to garner foreign, especially military, accomplishments and to develop personal political contacts. The mutiny at Nisibis, though it would have its own nemesis, was patently an aberration, inspired by a perhaps exaggerated sense of *dignitas* but certainly not by innate revolutionary tendencies. Indeed, during the Catilinarian conspiracy, Clodius was among the *boni* who stood in defense of the *res publica*. Clodius's loyal service to Marcius Rex, to Pompey, and to Murena demonstrates that he was certainly willing to work—as he necessarily must—in a junior capacity, so long as his patron did not step on his pride. But the violent break with Lucullus reveals in Clodius an arrogance that would not let him see himself or permit others to treat him as a mere flunky: *vehementis ingenii vir*. It is perhaps dangerous to lay so much stress on a quality that seems to be part of the standard equipment of any Roman noble and especially of any Claudian. But arrogant Clodius was, despite his holding a resume containing no conspicuous successes and a few undeniable disasters. And arrogance is a trait that goes a long way to explain the stupidity of the Bona Dea scandal as well as the tribune so ready to take on Pompey the Great.

CHAPTER THREE

The Bona Dea Scandal

1

The Bona Dea scandal, through its own notoriety and especially as a result of the feud with Cicero that resulted from it, directs considerable attention on Clodius's senatorial career. Consequently, from 61 onward Clodian testimonia multiply dramatically. Before we turn to the sacrilege and the trial, however, it will be best to review the salient events of 62, a year of noteworthy activity in Rome capped by the return to Italy of Pompey the Great. Admittedly this brief excursus departs from Clodius temporarily, but it sets the scene, as it were, for the *fabula Clodiana*.

The Catilinarian conspiracy continued to dominate Roman politics as 62 began. The leading conspirators within the city had been detected, arrested, and executed without trial, this last a momentous act performed with the advice and consent of the senate. While Cicero carried out the actual execution, the day belonged to M. Cato, whose forceful oratory had countered Caesar's objections to the death sentence.[1] But Cato was not the only one to see in the conspiracy a vehicle for his career. Metellus Nepos, Clodius's *frater*, had recently returned from the East, where he had been legate to Pompey. Like Cato he was a tribune for 62.[2] Straight after entering office he displayed his loyalties by promulgating a bill to recall Pompey as a means of coping with Catiline's forces in Italy. Nepos's dignity and Pompey's distant remove from the city forbid our viewing the tribune as a mere cipher for the great man. Clearly, Nepos acted independently as Pompey's man on the spot. Unfortunately for both of them, however, Nepos's incompetence harmed rather than helped his general's interests.[3]

At the start of Nepos's tribunate it was still possible to put forward strong arguments for summoning Pompey from the East: Catiline's army was not to be despised, and, if not immediately suppressed, it threatened to rouse subversive elements throughout Italy.[4] There were already related uprisings and warning signs of further unrest.[5] And the ominous rumor that Catiline would arm the slaves evoked memories of Spartacus's revolt. Nepos hoped to exploit these circumstances, thereby providing Pompey with justification for returning to Italy with his army intact. Caesar, who also wanted to win Pompey's favor, gave Nepos his backing.[6] But the passing of time weakened Nepos's case: Catiline's military situation deteriorated so rapidly that by the beginning of January it was hopeless. Nepos, however, failed to appreciate how thoroughly Catiline's disintegration undermined the prospects for his own bill and doggedly attempted to force his bill through the assembly at the first possible moment.[7] Anticipating (though underestimating) opposition, he and Caesar recruited thugs to overawe any resistance. But the senate's reaction, spearheaded by Cato, squashed the violent tribune. Thereafter the *senatus consultum ultimum* was passed, its principal effect being the suspension from office of both Caesar and Nepos.[8] Caesar was shrewd enough to repent. But Nepos, whose stubbornness had provoked the debacle, fled to Pompey.[9]

This affair only exacerbated Rome's anxiety over Pompey's return. The fearful prospect of a second Sulla, the ruthless *adulescentulus carnifex* grown up, allowed Pompey's enemies to reassert themselves: Lucullus had finally been permitted, in 63, to celebrate his triumph; in 62, after four years of waiting, Q. Metellus Creticus entered the city in triumphal procession.[10] Nepos's riotous assembly, and especially his flight eastward, added grist to the mill. That consummate politician, M. Crassus, made a grand pageant of his feigned terror, gathering his family and wealth and fleeing Italy like a refugee.[11] Pompey, who recognized the state of things in Rome, dispatched letters to various senators in an effort to reassure them of his peaceful intentions.[12] He divorced Mucia, thus renouncing his connection with Nepos, an action that won general approval at the cost of offending the brothers Metellus.[13] Upon landing at Brundisium near the end of the year Pompey ostentatiously dismissed his troops and looked toward establishing proper and respectful relations with the senatorial aristocracy.[14] He initiated marriage negotiations, seeking brides for himself and his elder son from the family circle of Cato—but to no avail.[15]

We have no information concerning Clodius's conduct during the early months of 62. Presumably he was busy preparing for the elections at which he would stand for the quaestorship. There is no reason to think he cooperated with Nepos in his efforts to win Pompey's recall. Whereas

Nepos had begun his tribunate by condemning Cicero's execution of the Catilinarians, Clodius and Appius had both supported the consul during the crisis, and it was too early for them to ignore their previous roles. Furthermore, Nepos's actions were singularly ill advised. Winning Pompey's favor was an inviting motive, but if Clodius had participated in the riotous assembly of his *frater*, it seems likely that Cicero would have used it against him at one point or another. More probably Clodius sidestepped the issue altogether, and by the time the Catilinarian danger was over, at the summer elections, Clodius won his first magistracy, though we possess, not surprisingly, no details of his canvass or election to the quaestorship.[16] Nor do we know much of Clodius's time as quaestor-elect—until, that is, we come to the Bona Dea scandal.

2

The mysterious rites of the Bona Dea, which admitted only women as participants, were celebrated annually in early December. In 62 they were performed in the house of Caesar, the pontifex maximus.[17] During the night of the observance, when all male persons were forbidden to be present, Clodius, in the guise of a flute player, sneaked into the ladies' midst, allegedly seeking out Pompeia, Caesar's wife. He was discovered and barely escaped—and that was managed, so it was said, only with the timely assistance of a slave girl. The Vestals immediately repeated the ceremony, to maintain the *pax deorum*, and the *nobilissimae feminae* in attendance soon made the incident known to their husbands. The ensuing scandal dominated Roman politics throughout the first months of 61, largely eclipsing Pompey's homecoming, and it very nearly destroyed Clodius's career.[18]

As so often at Rome, religion and politics are inseparable in the Bona Dea affair. Nonetheless, for the sake of our analysis it will be necessary to distinguish the predominantly religious and the predominantly political aspects of the scandal, since motives of both kinds guided the senate's reaction. And before any consideration of the incident's repercussions can begin, Clodius's actual culpability must be decided. In a certain sense, it might be objected, the point is moot inasmuch as Clodius and no one else was blamed for the sacrilege. Yet an accurate appreciation of the course of events, especially of Clodius's ultimate acquittal, depends very much on whether he did or did not intrude upon the secret rites. If, as Balsdon suggested, Clodius's innocence is a strong possibility, then the senate's readiness to believe the worst and the jury's decision to acquit must be explained in terms entirely different from the sources' accounts.[19] Certainty is difficult. As Balsdon properly observed, extant versions of the incident not only fail to agree, but reveal considerable embellishment over time, some of it demonstrably false.[20] Still, the earliest attested reference to the sacrilege, which comes in a letter from Cicero to Atticus, mentions Clodius's deed without any doubt about his guilt, a datum that carries all the more weight when one observes that this letter was penned before the scandal became a political issue and, more important yet, before the rift between Cicero and Clodius occurred (which is not to say with Plutarch that the two were actually friends at the time of the scandal).[21] While later evidence against Clodius may be tainted with varying degrees of tendentiousness, this letter shows that— before Cicero's celebrated enmity with Clodius had developed and before Cicero believed he had anything to gain politically from striking a pose hostile to Clodius—*he* was convinced of Clodius's guilt.[22] The patrician's involvement must have been, in Cicero's opinion, painfully obvious. One might also adduce the witness of Caesar's mother and sister: although (as will be seen) it was plainly contrary to Caesar's interests and wishes, they persisted in their testimony, which asserted that Clodius had indeed profaned the mysteries.[23] The weight of credible evidence, then— such as there is—falls on the side of the prosecution in despite of the jury's verdict in the end.

Often enough, Clodius's violation of the Bona Dea sacrifice is not taken seriously per se (in contradistinction to the political controversy that soon supervened), as if his presence at the rites were no more than a minor matter whose circumstances made for an entertaining item of gossip.[24] Yet Cicero, in the very letter just referred to, evinced sincere concern over the scandal from its very beginning—before the matter was raised in the senate: "I believe that you have heard that P. Clodius, son of Appius, was caught—dressed as a woman—in Caesar's house while a sacrifice for the well-being of the republic was taking place, and that he made it out alive with the help of a slave girl; the affair is a signal scandal. I am sure that it distresses you" (*Att.* 1.12.3).[25] Modern scholars disagree over the tone of Cicero's remarks to Atticus, but there can be no reason for doubting that Cicero believed his friend would naturally be troubled by the involvement of one of Rome's noblest young men, an acquaintance—by then a Roman magistrate—in so reprehensible a situation.[26] Cicero could hardly have expected even his Epicurean correspondent to be amused at Clodius's religious offense, which was after all the heart of the matter.[27]

Because the Bona Dea admitted only women to her rites, Clodius's *delictum* consisted simply in being in Caesar's house on the night of the sacrifice.[28] He had, moreover, gazed upon the sacred objects forbidden to the eyes of men, or so Cicero later alleged.[29] Clodius's intrusion brought the service to a halt. Indeed, the sources report that pandemonium broke out when his deep voice signaled his gender. Since the worship of the Bona Dea was *pro populo*, Clodius's trespass ruptured the *pax deorum*, thereby endangering *salus publica*.[30] Now it is difficult even for the ever skeptical modern to describe such a situation as trivial or its creation as prankish. The notion that the Romans of the late republic were too jaded or cynical to take their religion seriously is by now thoroughly outdated, the product (as has been pointed out more than once) of the unwarranted imposition of Christianizing assumptions about the essential and necessary conditions of true religion.[31] This is not to say that there were neither skeptics in Rome nor opportunists who knew how to exploit *religio* for their own purposes, as indeed there were, nor is it to deny the extent to which Romans of the higher orders recognized in civic religion a medium of social control. But the former observation, being applicable to every society, is merely banal, and the latter actually underscores the significance of religious observance in a culture more than ordinarily concerned with the maintenance of order and whose religion was understood to serve functions different from but no less valuable (to its practitioners) than those of Christianity. Cicero's age displays ample evidence of religious feeling and of interest in religious issues. Even for those who did not actually place credence in Roman *religio*, its observance was a component of decorum and morality—in short, a civic duty. Cicero himself represents varying attitudes toward the topic of religion, from philosophical skepticism to a zealous concern for the preservation of tradition. As a matter of fact, our period accords us our first opportunity to observe the Romans ruminating on the subject of religion at all, activity that can hardly be deemed to reveal widespread uninterest or disbelief or cynicism among the elite.[32]

One should note as well that Clodius's action offended against basic Roman moral sensibilities. His invasion of Caesar's house besmirched the character of the Vestals, and he had surreptitiously approached the city's noblest matrons. Furthermore, the quaestor-elect had exchanged his toga for feminine attire, a most unsuitable practice from the Roman point of view.[33] By such sordid conduct Clodius had disgraced his magistracy (it is too easy to follow Plutarch in treating Clodius as if he were barely more than a boy when he penetrated the goddess's mysteries), thereby insulting the Roman people. Romans, as P. Veyne has demonstrated, were inclined to condemn any sort of excessive behavior, a category that must include posing as a woman in order to commit sacrilege.[34] The scandal could not but have aroused the Romans' throttling censoriousness. All of which renders Cicero's concern over the Bona Dea scandal perfectly natural. And we may be confident that Cicero expected Atticus to react as he himself did to the news of Clodius's disgrace.

But the point that must be made straightaway is that this disgrace, though a weighty burden in Roman society, is all that Clodius need have suffered. Once Clodius had been driven back into the night, the Vestals repeated the sacred rites. Any harm done to the *pax deorum* was remedied by this act of *instauratio*. If the Good Goddess was herself unsatisfied, "deus ipse vindex erit" (Cic. *Leg.* 2.19) encapsulated the prevailing Roman sentiment on such matters. Clodius had committed no crime, a consideration to which we shall revert, though he might reasonably have expected adverse personal judgments from his censorious peers (a prospect Clodius seems hitherto rarely to have feared) and there was of course always the possibility of a censorial *nota* in the next *lectio senatus* (whether Clodius's arrogance, already amply demonstrated, permitted him to recognize that as a real possibility can only be a matter for speculation).[35]

Whether there was to be any immediate punishment for his indiscretion rested with Caesar. As rumor had it, after all, Clodius had invaded Caesar's house in an effort to seduce his wife. While the prevailing religious temper may have had few avenues to pursue (if one hoped to punish the outrageous patrician), there were ways open to Caesar, whose personal rights had been trampled upon and who could legitimately have hauled Clodius into court.[36] Instead the pontifex maximus elected to do nothing, insisting later that he was innocent of any knowledge of his wife's corruption or of the particulars of the Bona Dea scandal.[37]

As for Caesar's wife, that Clodius was engaged—or aspired to be be engaged—in an adulterous affair with Pompeia cannot be proved, nor is it a necessary motivation for Clodius's escapade. The charge does not appear in Cicero's early letters, only in his later and less reliable invective.[38] Moreau incautiously asserts that the role of Habra (if that was in fact her name), the female slave who aided Clodius's escape, implies Pompeia's complicity.[39] But the details of the incident are so uncertain that it is perhaps best to dismiss such a colorful particular altogether. Another version, after all, represents Clodius as merely hiding in the poor girl's quarters, and no evidence suggests that she implicated her mistress, even under torture.[40] Caesar never acknowledged the affair.[41] Nor does his divorce from Pompeia signify recognition of her guilt.[42] The divorce came only after the Clodius business was raised in the senate and the *pontifices* had rendered their opinion.[43] The embarrassment of such a scandal was reason enough for Caesar to dissolve his marriage and thus unfetter himself from a wife whose reputation had already been tainted and would undoubtedly be stained further in the (by then) inevitable *quaestio*. A man whose *dignitas* was of greater importance to him than his life would hardly hesitate to divorce his wife under such circumstances. Besides, Caesar had problems of his own, none of which he can have wanted to advertise at this time. After the fiasco of his cooperation with Metellus Nepos, Caesar was more interested in making friends than enemies. The interruption of the Bona Dea's rites, which were conducted in his own house, can only have revived the resentment still felt by those chagrined in 63 by Caesar's unexpected election to the office of pontifex maximus: the Bona Dea episode, if exaggerated, was certain to sully Caesar's tenure as the high priest of Rome, an embarrassment he had no intention of suffering could he avoid it. Wracked by a turbulent praetorship, burdensome personal debts, and now scandal in his very home, Caesar was far too eager to remove himself to his province to let himself be further impeded by Clodius.[44]

Another reason for Caesar's benevolent attitude toward Clodius, one that has received considerable attention from recent scholars, can be found in the sources: Caesar respected Clodius's clout.[45] The Bobbio Scholiast describes Clodius in 61 as *potentissimus homo*; according to Dio his acquittal was vouchsafed by his ἑταιρεία. And both Plutarch and Appian emphasize Clodius's formidable popularity.[46] In view of the retrospective influence of Clodius's later career on the ancients who mention his earlier undertakings, a certain amount of skepticism is called for. Nonetheless, Clodius did possess *potentia*, as subsequent events demonstrated, and it is worth considering the nature of his influence.

First and foremost was the enormous prestige enjoyed by a Claudius Pulcher, a Clodian resource whose importance has already been stressed sufficiently. Now one might have reckoned that Clodius's line of Claudian credit had been exhausted by the time of the scandal—some in the senate clearly thought so, but wrongly. For the young patrician, as we have seen, had not been entirely indolent in recent months, and his successful campaign for the quaestorship had brought him and the luster of his family's name warmly before the public. The sources stress Clodius's popularity, and, although many historians incline to detect in this information the beginnings of Clodius's effective organization of the *plebs*, they have not adequately appreciated that Clodius's career hitherto had mostly been conducted outside Rome.[47] Moreau considers the presence of Pompey's legions in Rome at this time a potent source of Clodius's popularity, but this factor should perhaps not be unduly underlined.[48] In any case, it is unnecessary to seek after specific sources for Clodius's popularity in 61: after all, generations of consulships and proud accomplishments, memorialized in numerous *monumenta*, guaranteed his family's reputation.[49] The Roman people could and did feel strong loyalties to certain grand names. As Cicero said of Calpurnius Piso, the consul of 58: "When you were elected quaestor, even men who had never laid eyes on you entrusted that honor to your name. You were elected aedile, or rather, a Piso was elected aedile by the Roman people—not the Piso that you are. In the same way the praetorship was bestowed upon your ancestors" (*Pis.* 2). Cicero's sentiment is the resentful rhetoric of the *novus homo*, tendentious but not therefore without basis. As Cicero knew, members of the nobility were not ashamed to find a political silver spoon in their mouths; indeed, they gloried in it (when they had the chance). In view of the fact that the people had just elevated this Clodius to the quaestorship, his popularity in 61 ought to come as no surprise to anyone, so there is no need to seek its explanation in gangs or veterans. As for Clodius's religious delict, while it was probably offensive to senators, it was unlikely to count for quite so much to the man on the street— not because he was less pious, but because his familiarity with the Bona Dea's December rites was extremely meager, if not totally wanting. He remembered the Good Goddess on the first of May, when the dedication of her temple on the Aventine was celebrated.[50]

Clodius's popularity with the *plebs* was not perhaps of so much concern to Caesar as the young man's position within the aristocracy. Caesar certainly had no wish to offend Clodius's brothers, whatever he thought of Publius, and that fact alone may suffice to explain his clemency. Furthermore, though Clodius clearly had enemies in the senate (or he would never have been tried), his past service to men like Marcius Rex and Murena gave him important friends as well. One of the consuls for 61, Pupius Piso, was Clodius's *amicus*, as was, apparently, the elder Curio, *consularis* and *triumphator*.[51] Pompey was a factor in everyone's political calculus, even after his peaceful intentions became known. His attitude toward Clodius may have occasioned concern. Pompey's divorce from Mucia proclaimed his renunciation of Metellus Nepos; it also incurred for him the animosity of Nepos's brother, Celer. Did Pompey mean only to repudiate the disgraced tribune, or was he dissociating himself from the Metelli *and* the Claudii Pulchri? Cicero's correspondence reveals that *he*, at any rate, did not lump them all together.[52] There is no reason to believe Pompey did either. After all, Pompey and Clodius had served together during the Pirate War, and Clodius had done nothing to damage the great man (and in any case Pompey had no reason to offend the

Claudii even as he jettisoned the Metelli). Nor was it only among the elder statesmen that Clodius counted his friends. Some young senators, like the tribune Q. Fufius Calenus, and youthful nobles like the younger Curio, were devoted to Clodius.[53] It was from this latter group that Clodius derived his most conspicuous support during the actual trial. When Cicero later reported that *operae* were being assembled as the stage was being set for the trial, he did not mean that Clodius was organizing the gangs of thugs he would deploy in the fifties (though thugs may have been involved), rather that clubs of young aristocrats—the *sodalitates*—described by the orator as *barbatuli iuvenes* and *adulescentes nobiles* were mobilizing (along with their retainers).[54]

Some of Clodius's callow aristocratic supporters may be identifiable, at least tentatively. The central figure was clearly Curio.[55] His own youthful intimacy with the tender M. Antony was to become notorious. Antony himself was *intimus Clodi* in 58, though his active alliance with Clodius did not last much beyond that year. Later Antony actually threatened Clodius's life. Still, in the aftermath of Clodius's fatal encounter with Milo, the future triumvir emerged as a *subscriptor* to the prosecution and sometime later was married to Clodius's widow, the redoubtable Fulvia.[56] Other young notables forged a more durable relationship. Cn. (possibly, or Q.) Gellius Publicola, son of the consul of 72 and uncle of the consul of 36, was so ardent a champion of the downtrodden that he shunned the senate and married a freedwoman to hammer home his point (such was Cicero's construction of Gellius's marriage in any event). He was slightly older than Clodius, but not out of place among the *adulescentes nobiles*; in the fifties he appears as Clodius's strong ally: the wet nurse of all revolutionaries, as Cicero dubs him (*Vat.* 4).[57] Decimus Brutus, the future tyrannicide, only just beyond his teens in 61, was also closely linked to Clodius in the fifties.[58] Two other young men of prominent origins, each of whom aided Clodius before his ascension in 58, may also be included here: C. Herennius, allegedly the impecunious son of a *divisor*, was the tribune of 60 who endeavored to transfer Clodius to plebeian status and P. Fonteius, scion of an important Tusculan clan and soon to become Clodius's adoptive father.[59] With greater hesitation one might mention C. Porcius Cato (tr. pl. 56), but there is no good reason to assume a connection with Clodius before 58.[60] Uncertainty also attends Clodius's relationship with C. Licinius Calvus. Licinius Calvus undoubtedly belonged to the social world of Clodius, his sister, and (of course) Catullus. During the time of Clodius's enmity with Pompey, Calvus's invective epigrams provided the text for Clodius's followers when they taunted the great man.[61] It has been suggested that Calvus was among

Clodius's supporters at the time of the Bona Dea trial, a consideration to which we shall presently return. Nor should the possible presence of Caelius Rufus be overlooked, though his connection with Clodius (like that with his sister) was ultimately to turn bad.[62] But for now we must have done with names. The preceding provides a sufficient sense of Clodius's companions, who rallied round him during the scandal. They cannot all be identified with confidence, yet there can be no doubting that the *barbatuli iuvenes* were numerous and important enough to irk and to worry Cicero.

Young Clodius's resources, then, were ample. When the Bobbio Scholiast describes him as *potentissimus*, he is perhaps exaggerating, but he is not grossly in error. Clodius's *potentia* was grounded in family strength and his own political investments. Caesar's inaction, then, especially his polite discretion regarding his wife's reputation, would offend few men in the senate, while his tacit *beneficium* to Clodius might well have been expected to provide the basis for an alliance should Clodius survive the scandal.[63] The devotion and energy of Clodius's friends during the trial proved the wisdom of Caesar's reticence and the accuracy of his estimation of Clodius's clout.

3

Friends in high places certainly worked to Clodius's advantage at the start. In 62 the consuls were Iunius Silanus and Murena. The latter was Clodius's *amicus*, and, according to the principle that the senior consul presides over the senate in the odd numbered months only, Murena would have held the *fasces* in December. Predictably, he did not introduce the Bona Dea question.[64] Although each had a perfect right to do so, none of the consulars chose to press Murena to take up the matter, perhaps out of sympathy for his situation (knowing that *amicitia* demanded he look after Clodius's interests) or perhaps because it was normal at year's end to leave new business for the new consuls to handle. When the senate convened on the Kalends of January, another friend of Clodius, M. Pupius Piso, presided. Again, the consul ignored Clodius's violation of the Good Goddess's sacrifice, for reasons easily comprehended. Again the consulars were silent, although the senate's meeting on the Kalends of January was traditionally devoted to the discussion of religious affairs.[65] Perhaps in the time intervening between Clodius's sacrilege and the first of January they had given serious consideration to the hazards of attacking a Claudius Pulcher instead of directing their attention toward Pompey. In spite of the seriousness of Clodius's delict, after all, there was no obvious, scripted course of action for the senate to follow.[66] The *pax deorum* was intact. No disaster offered an avenue for civil prosecution. There was no penal code governing religious delicts other than *sacrilegium* (the theft of sacred objects) and *incestum* (the corruption of a Vestal Virgin). It could reasonably be hoped, even expected, that the censors to be elected in 61 would prevent Clodius from entering the ranks of the senate after his quaestorship expired, a suitable and appropriate punishment, but there was nothing else conveniently to hand.[67] For now the *consulares* remained judiciously quiet.

Their example, however, was not imitated by Q. Cornificius, as Cicero emphatically underscored for Atticus. He formally brought the matter before the senate.[68] Why Cicero does not say. Cornificius was very rich and a good, solid citizen.[69] Praetor in 67 (or 66), he had stood unsuccessfully for the consulship in 64. He played a responsible role during the Catilinarian conspiracy as Cethegus's custodian. In Cicero's oratory he is *severrimus* and *integerrimus*, hyperbole that finds more pedestrian confirmation in Cicero's correspondence with Cornificius's son and in the judgment of Asconius that he was *sobrius et sanctus vir*.[70] Though a presentable *bonus*, a comment by Cicero in another letter to Atticus suggests that something about Cornificius was not quite right. In discussing his rivals in the upcoming consular election, he remarks: "Of my rivals, those who seem certain are Galba, Antonius, and Q. Cornificius. At the mention of the last of these I think that you either laughed or groaned" (*Att.* 1.1.1). What precisely was wrong with Cornificius we do not know. What is certain is that Cicero regarded Cornificius, for all his probity, as something of a joke. That Cornificius rebelled against the consulars' lead and forced the senate to deal with Clodius's sacrilege is in complete accord with the source's portrayal of his strongly moral character and Cicero's opinion that he could sometimes stray out of his depth. Quite possibly Cornificius's religious sensibilities were played upon by Clodius's enemies or by discreet consulars hoping to send up a trial balloon. In any event, Cornificius's motion forced the senate's hand: by a *senatus consultum* the matter was referred to the *pontifices*.[71]

Cornificius's motion burst the dam. It was inevitable that the priestly college should declare the violation of the Bona Dea's rites *nefas*.[72] In religious matters the senate traditionally concurred with the opinion of the pontiffs—though what (if any) action was to be taken resided wholly in the senate's sphere of competence.[73] The college may also in this instance have called for a further repetition of the sacrifice, though this was unnecessary.[74] The pontiffs' decree, it must be stressed, was limited to a religious judgment and to a recommendation as to the expiation required by the delict. The *pontifices* could not demand anyone's prosecution. But once the issue had been raised in the senate and the senate had formally acknowledged it by a *consultum*, all hesitancy to act against Clodius vanished: the delict had become an official concern, which was odd in view of the fact that Roman *religio* was satisfied by *instauratio*. Once the *pax deorum* was reaffirmed the state had no obligation to seek out a guilty party. For confirmation of this we may satisfy ourselves with a single example from Livy, who reports of money stolen from the temple of Locrian Proserpina in 200, that is, during the classic republic.[75] This *sacrilegium* violated the *pax deorum*, as *prodigia* indicated, and expiatory sacrifices were duly offered. But no culprit was found, nor, apparently, did it matter. In Clodius's case, suddenly, there were senators willing to force the issue. A *senatus consultum* was passed requiring the consuls to promulgate a *rogatio* that would set up a special tribunal to try the young patrician for *incestum*. This decree evidently enjoyed strong senatorial support, since Pupius Piso, who in fact opposed the bill, felt compelled to propose it despite his friendship with Clodius.[76]

Whence this bill's backing among the senators? Religious outrage, as we have seen, cannot at this stage account for the senate's vote inasmuch as the requirements of Roman sensibilities had already been met. Moral outrage at Clodius's excesses—and Cicero does early on describe himself as a Lycurgus and the senate as an Areopagus—presents a backdrop against which the attitude of the silent majority of senators might become more discernible.[77] Yet even that will not sufficiently elucidate the senate's conduct. Nor have matters been clarified by those scholars who seek to represent Clodius's delict as an act of political symbolism (which, if true, might help to explain the senate's strong response, but would not explain the delay preceding its response).[78] Private feuds and schemes, not readily mentioned in our sources (even Cicero is reticent in this instance, for reasons that will soon emerge), must now be summoned to the stage of the *fabula Clodiana*.

As Balsdon demonstrated long ago, Clodius's enemies constituted a *factio* determined to ruin him.[79] He had attracted powerful enemies, none more redoubtable than his former commander and brother-in-law, Licinius Lucullus. After the mutiny at Nisibis, Lucullus had good reason to hate Clodius, and his desire for revenge was perfectly unexceptionable by Roman standards.[80] Upon his return to Italy he had divorced his Claudian wife, bitterly denouncing her for incestuous relations with Clodius. Still, three ignominious years had to pass before Lucullus was allowed his triumph.[81] Then, in 61, Cornificius's motion concerning the Bona Dea scandal afforded at long last a prime opportunity for vengeance, which Lucullus—not quite yet the rotting sponge represented in Plutarch's biography—seized upon greedily.[82] For this enterprise he enlisted his intimate friends Catulus and Hortensius, the former of whom would relish the prospect of embarrassing Caesar, on whose watch, so to speak, Clodius's breach occurred. Other enemies of the young patrician perceived a legitimate opening: the Cornelii Lentuli, who nursed a private grudge against Clodius, joined the fray.[83] The aggressively anti-Clodian stance of *principes* like Lucullus, Catulus, and Hortensius, once adopted, no doubt emboldened many who had remained hesitant, and the attitudes of Valerius Messalla, of C. Piso (cos. 67), another of Clodius's enemies, and even of Cicero himself may have been influenced by their leadership.[84] Clodius's enemies, unsurprisingly, were in a position to unleash Cato's energies as well.[85]

Against such a formidable array it is hardly astonishing that Pupius Piso yielded. Still, the overtly personal hostility of the anti-Clodius group, understandable though it was, made it easier for the patrician's adherents to justify their actions on his behalf. Clodius himself underscored the personal dimension of the issue by humbling himself in the senate: his ostentatiously repentant gestures had their effect on many *boni*, who must have recognized the enormity of establishing an extraordinary tribunal to deal with Clodius's actions.[86] In the end, the clash over Clodius's future had little to do with religion, as Balsdon rightly saw. The issue quickly gave way to private feuds which, lacking adequate heft, soon exaggerated their gravity by adding to themselves the rhetoric of political principle.

Before coming to that, however, we must revert to a technical matter: what charge could be laid against Clodius? The bill promulgated by the consuls, the *rogatio Pupia Valeria*, called for an extraordinary *quaestio* to try Clodius for *incestum*, though the legal situation of this prosecution remains enigmatic.[87] The term *incestum* (or *incestus*) refers to two distinct crimes: (1) sexual relations between relatives to whom such intimacy is forbidden, and (2) the failure of a Vestal to preserve her chastity intact. The two crimes were quite distinct in their mode of trial and of punishment.[88] Although accusations that Clodius had committed incest with his sister (Lucullus's ex-wife) surfaced during his trial, this was obviously not the accusation at issue.[89] Clodius's case was assimilated to incest in the other sense. This *crimen incesti* was a dreadful offense because the Vestals' chastity was essential to *salus publica*, and, because no expiation could restore what had been lost, *incestum* called for exceptional, even drastic, measures.[90] An accused Vestal was tried by the pontifex maximus and the pontifical college; if condemned, she was entombed alive and her paramour was to be beaten to death (though exile was the more common result).[91] But this process could hardly be adopted for prosecuting Clodius because there was never any suggestion that a Vestal had in fact been corrupted.[92] This is what makes Clodius's situation unique: though the Vestals' chastity was unquestioned, he was to be tried for incest nevertheless.

This feat was managed by proposing a law that defined a further, more specific aspect of *incestum*: henceforth anyone invading the secrets rits of the Bona Dea would be deemed to have committed *incestum*.[93] One might argue that the intrusion of a man into the exclusively feminine rites of the Good Goddess—a festival necessarily attended by the Vestals—was tantamount to an assault on the Vestals' *pudicitia* and posed a danger to their chastity. Such loosely syllogistic reasoning the Romans called *libera interpretatio* and, whatever its inadequacies as sound legal discourse, only a train of thought along such lines will explain the basis for Clodius's trial.[94] All of which indicates how misplaced are the efforts of scholars who try to make Clodius's incest trial fit with the other known incest trials.[95] The singularity of this case stems from the fact, already discussed, that the Romans did not have an extensive penal code governing *religio*: incest and *sacrilegium* were the only charges of a religious nature available to them, and yet it was apparently felt that Clodius's offense had to be regarded as a religious delict though it actually fitted the definition of neither.

There were distinct advantages in charging Clodius with *incestum*. Its solemnity opened every avenue of investigation. For example, slaves were expected to testify against their masters at incest trials.[96] Furthermore, quaestors were clearly not immune from prosecution *de incestu*.[97] Which left Clodius only one sure route of escape: to vacate Rome for a province in order to invoke the *lex Memmia* on the grounds of being *absens rei publicae causa*.[98] The senate soon blocked this avenue as well when it voted not to allocate provinces until a *lex de Clodii incestu* was brought to a vote, though this was not the sole motive behind the senate's action.[99]

4

Opposition to the *rogatio Pupia Valeria* was led by Pupius Piso himself with the support of the tribune Fufius Calenus, the future consul of 47. Their attack centered on one clause: the *rogatio* stipulated that the jurors be chosen not by lot, as was the usual procedure for *quaestiones perpetuae*, but by the urban praetor, who would preside over the case.[100] Why this particular feature of the bill became the bone of contention is not at all clear. Granted that such a procedure entailed the possibility of producing a packed jury—and this conceivability was stressed emphatically by Clodius's friends—the likelihood of that outcome was probably not so very great in fact.[101] Even with the passage of the bill, the jurors would still be selected from the *album iudicum*, and it is unthinkable that defense and prosecution would not have retained the right of *reiectio*. Nor could the urban praetor limit his choice to senators since, by the *lex Aurelia*, the jury was bound to consist of senators, knights, and *tribuni aerarii*.[102] Consequently, the intent of this clause was probably not to fix the jury. Rather, it was simply a typical feature of *quaestiones extra ordinem*.[103] Perhaps a jury recruited by the praetor instead of mere chance would be less susceptible to tampering. Even so, to hold that from the very first Clodius regarded bribery as his sole prospect for securing an acquittal is to work backward from Cicero's later complaints that Clodius corrupted the jury.[104] In fact, the challenge to the jury clause, which protracted matters considerably, underscored the extraordinary nature of the proceedings against Clodius and consequently made the claim of unfairness appear more plausible.

There was another reason for attacking the jury's proposed composition: Fufius Calenus could oppose the move as an attempt by the senate to usurp greater authority in *quaestiones* than was its due—that is, he could quite appropriately claim to challenge the *rogatio* in his role as champion of the people. Strict logic, it must be observed, is beside the point in circumstances of this sort. The sheer novelty of the senate's action in extending the scope of *incestum* in order to try one Roman could not help but electrify the atmosphere of the *rogatio*'s public reception. Legislation concerning juries had long been a focus of popular *invidia senatus*, and, although the issue in the *rogatio Pupia Valeria* was not the composition of the jury but the process of its selection, it is easy to see how Fufius could distort the bill so that it appeared an unfair extension of the senate's power and a threat to the liberty of a Roman citizen.[105] In this way a principle could be claimed as a legitimate basis on which to invoke popular opposition to the bill.

Fufius's strategy was revealed at a *contio* held outside the *pomerium* on the Campus Flaminius.[106] The site was chosen so that Pompey, who was now at Rome awaiting his triumph, could attend. Fufius, with Pupius Piso's encouragement, hoped to elicit Pompey's support, evidently on the assumption that the great man's loyalty to Pupius Piso (if not his past acquaintance with Clodius) would prompt a favorable opinion. Before he had left for the East, after all, Pompey had been opposed by the very men who were now pushing the *rogatio*: C. Piso, Hortensius, and Catulus.[107] And Pompey's feelings for Lucullus were well known.[108] Further-more, Pompey had himself criticized senatorial control of the courts in the past.[109] On this occasion, Fufius prudently avoided asking Pompey for his views on Clodius's delict or its actionable nature, but he did ask him if he thought it a good idea for jurors to be selected by a praetor.[110] Cicero recognized the *popularis* quality of Fufius's tactics: in his letter to Atticus in which he described this *contio*, he referred to Fufius as *levissimus tribunus*.[111] Pompey was likewise alert to the implications of the tribune's query and, more concerned with his own reputation in the Curia than with Clodius's problems, he spoke at length μάλ' ἀριστο-κρατικῶς in praise of the senate's *auctoritas*.[112]

After the *contio* was dismissed, the consul Valerius Messalla, encour-aged by Pompey's public oratory, convened the senate outside the city so that again Pompey could be present. Unlike the tribune, Messalla interro-gated Pompey in specific terms, making direct reference to the religious issue of Clodius's delict and to the bill that had been promulgated. Pom-pey continued in the same vein as before, putting his generic seal of approval on all decrees of the senate.[113] Part of that speech extolled Cic-ero's role in the Catilinarian conspiracy. Not to be outdone, Crassus, who, like Pompey, presumably spoke *de promulgata rogatione*, also heaped praises on Cicero's consulship. Clearly, Cicero's conduct during the Cati-linarian conspiracy was the exemplum of choice that day when defending the prerogative of the senate, a choice that Cicero helped to promote when he followed up Crassus's oration with a virtuoso rehearsal of his own favorite themes: the gravity of the senate, the harmony of the orders, the remnants of the conspiracy.[114]

Cicero's consulship was a natural topos: the events of 63 and the various trials stemming from the Catilinarian conspiracy established Cicero, at least for a time, as a vital symbol of *senatus auctoritas*. The introduction of the Catilinarian menace, however, and Cicero's public standing, while important for Cicero's reaction to the Bona Dea scandal, should not lead us into believing that genuinely revolutionary forces were at work. Rather, in 61 these items constituted the appropriate and necessary rhetorical elements in any argument in support of *senatus auctoritas*, which was the obvious and unavoidable principle to wield in response to Fufius's attack on the *rogatio Pupia Valeria*. Rhetoric and posturing were employed to influence public opinion at all levels outside the senate in an attempt to block the *rogatio Pupia Valeria*, a pointed example of *popularis* politics being more a method than a platform. But, for all Cicero's hue and cry, the stability of the republic was not at stake in the Bona Dea affair. Fufius—and the other supporters of Clodius—were simply struggling to transform his case into a cause. It was this move, with its various registers of engagement, that drew Cicero so strongly into the anti-Clodian faction. As the debate over the *rogatio* became more and more an argument over *senatus auctoritas*, Cicero, whose ardor had actually cooled since the matter of Clodius's scandal was broached in the senate, was drawn into the fray—both figuratively and as a figure of the argument. The rhetoric of the controversy encouraged the *Clodiani* to exploit *invidia Ciceronis*, just as it led Cicero to denounce Clodius's supporters as *grex Catilinae*. Cicero's emblematic status as the champion of the senate's prestige, a cause in which he genuinely believed, as well as the orator's natural desire to preserve and indeed to enhance his own *dignitas* within the senatorial elite, led him to join Clodius's enemies in an effort to squash any challenge to *senatus auctoritas* and to restore the republic's moral health.[115]

This may be an opportune moment to comment more fully on Cicero's portrayal of Clodius as Catiline's successor. As we have seen, Clodius opposed Catiline at the time of the latter's conspiracy. But from 61 onward, the orator refers frequently to Clodius and his followers as if they constituted a continuation of the Catilinarian plot. Now in the case of one of Clodius's associates, L. Sergius, who is mentioned in *De Domo* as the *armiger Catilinae* (*Dom.* 13), this assertion was true enough, whatever its real significance.[116] That Catiline left behind him a well-articulated network of followers remains unlikely, however, and there is no reason to think of Clodius as Catiline's heir in any sense at the time of the Bona Dea scandal. The *grex Catilinae* which championed Clodius was the invention of Cicero's rhetoric, inspired by the terms of the debate over the *rogatio Pupia Valeria*, and if the phrase had any specific reference it was merely to the *barbatuli iuvenes* (and other friends of the young patrician) who were hardly undertaking to overthrow the state. When in the fifties Clodius rose to become the most formidable of *popularis* politicians, driving Cicero into exile by championing the rights of the executed Catilinarians, the assimilation of Clodius into the image of Catiline that had begun in 61 was both natural and effective for Cicero's anti-Clodian invective. The appeal this rendering of his bitterest enemy held for Cicero is made clear by the orator's application of it to Antony when the future triumvir replaced Clodius as the orator's archenemy. Cicero's exclamations of Catilinarian menace throughout the fifties are best confronted with extreme skepticism and, ultimately, with disbelief.[117]

When the *rogatio Pupia Valeria* was finally brought before the people, its opponents were ready. Curio led a band of young nobles, who exhorted voters to reject the *rogatio*. Pupius Piso himself spoke against it. Then, after the *contio* was dismissed and the people had been assembled to vote, Clodius's supporters seized the voting gangways, handing out only *tabellae* marked A (*antiquo*).[118] So Cicero. Since the presiding consul had the right to choose his assistants in supervising the voting, it may well be the case, as Moreau has suggested, that the *operae Clodianae* of Cicero's account were simply the magistrate's helpers carrying out their appointed function.[119] That they dishonestly distributed only nay votes, however, cannot be doubted in view of Cato's response. When he recognized Pupius Piso's subterfuge, Cato, repeating his riotous conduct of 62, leapt to the Rostra to deliver an illegal harangue. He enjoyed the backing of Hortensius and M. Favonius and "many other good citizens." The assembly was broken up by this *concursus bonorum* and the senate immediately summoned.[120]

The spectacular illegality of the assembly's performance—on both sides—provoked a massive turnout.[121] Pupius Piso attempted to convince the senate to let the *rogatio* drop, a move Clodius seconded by pathetically and no doubt repentantly pleading with individual senators. At this time, if not before, C. Scribonius Curio (cos. 76), Curio's illustrious father, took Clodius's part: he formally moved the rejection of the senate's decree instructing the consuls to present the *rogatio*.[122] The motion failed, however, with the senate voting against it overwhelmingly, by 400 votes to 15, thus reaffirming its original *consultum*. The senate was adamant on this point, refusing to conduct any other official business until the *consultum* was carried into effect.[123] In the face of such unity Fufius dared not to interpose his veto.[124] He yielded to the senate's purpose.

After being defeated in the senate, Clodius and his allies took his cause to the streets: Clodius began holding *contiones* berating the senate for its obstinate stance.[125] To challenge the *rogatio* he continued to employ the *popularis* techniques Fufius had initiated, stirring up popular *invidia* against the senate, focusing particularly on *invidia Ciceronis*, which was easily linked to the people's resentment of expropriatory authority.[126] Clodius assaulted Cicero's role as Catiline's vanquisher and, more significantly, as the consul who, on the pretext of senatorial authority, had put Roman citizens to death without trial. Recalling a refrain from Cicero's *Catilinarians* Clodius derided the orator unstintingly: "me tantum 'comperisse' omnia criminabatur," a jibe that Caesar and others appropriated.[127] These speeches stung Cicero to precipitate response. To protect his *dignitas* he attacked not only Clodius, but also Pupius Piso and the

Curiones, indeed *totam illam manum*, delivering orations in whose ferocity he took special pride.[128]

Despite Cicero's invective, Hortensius came seriously to fear that Fufius would find enough backing to veto the *rogatio* without fear.[129] Whereas the tribune had not had the nerve to defy the senate when its anger united it, he could, with popular support, make an effective public stand. With the passing of time and of emotion, a confrontation with the people may well have seemed less desirable to many senators. And Hortensius may have sensed that the chance for cornering Clodius was fast slipping away. Furthermore, as the clash between the two sides persisted, important governmental business was delayed—to the dissatisfaction of many within and without the senate.[130] A compromise was needed.

While Clodius's supporters had originally hoped that by challenging the jury clause of the *rogatio* they could rout the opposition, Hortensius's solution wrecked their strategy. He accepted Fufius's complaint: Hortensius arranged to drop the bill's prescriptions for jury selection, so that Clodius could be tried on the very terms which he had demanded. The proposal could not be rejected by Fufius, since it removed his objection to the *rogatio*, nor by Clodius, for he had in his speeches continued the same argument against excessive senatorial authority (as epitomized by Cicero). This clever stratagem was a victory for Hortensius and his friends.[131] Cicero criticized it *post eventum*, and probably at the time too, since the senate's retreat on this point left him in a rather foolish and exposed position.[132] The parliamentary mechanics of all this have been explained by Balsdon.[133] Fufius asked for a new debate on the *rogatio* and insisted on a division of the issue into two parts: (1) that there should be a trial, and (2) that the praetor should select the jury. The first point passed, the second was defeated, and Fufius was entrusted with the task of submitting to the people a new bill, which differed from the *rogatio Pupia Valeria* only in the matter of the jury.[134] This bill was subsequently passed into law.

5

Curio *pater*, who had already advocated abandoning the attempt to try Clodius, now stood as his *patronus*.[135] There were others, but their names go unrecorded.[136] Better known are the prosecutors, chief of whom was L. Cornelius Lentulus Crus (cos. 49).[137] There existed a personal feud between the Cornelii Lentuli and Clodius; like Lucullus they viewed the Bona Dea scandal as an opportunity to work harm on an enemy.[138] Not only was Lentulus Crus Clodius's accuser, but two of his three *subscriptores* were Cornelii Lentuli: Cn. Lentulus Marcellinus (cos. 56) and L. Lentulus Niger, the *flamen Martialis*.[139] Moreover, P. Lentulus Spinther, the future consul of 57, sat as a juror and, with an ostentatious flourish, voted for condemnation.[140] The third *subscriptor*, rounding off the prosecution, was C. Fannius (tr. pl. 59), a close friend of Lucullus.[141]

Cicero describes the *reiectio* as a clamorous, brawling procedure. Its result, in his view, was a disaster.[142] Yet these same jurors, when Cicero was called as witness, showed themselves willing to offer their lives in his defense (or so he claimed) and, in so doing, paid him an honor far worthier (or so he claimed) than any to be found in the annals of Athenian or Roman history.[143] This silly discrepancy reveals that, on the topic of Clodius's jury, Cicero's reliability is less than total. After the debate over the manner of the jury's selection and especially after the verdict that acquitted the patrician, Cicero's contempt, whatever its justice, was inevitable.

Of the trial itself we are told very little. Although trials for *incestum* allowed the examination under torture of the defendant's slaves, Clodius had made this impossible by sending some abroad to his brother, the rest to properties he owned in Gaul.[144] An impressive array of witnesses was summoned by the prosecutor: Caesar's mother Aurelia, his sister Julia, Cato, Lucullus, and, most notably, Cicero.[145] There were no doubt others whose names are now lost to us, as are the names of all Clodius's witnesses save one. Cato's testimony is unknown.[146] Aurelia and Julia testified to the defendant's presence at the Bona Dea's rites. Lucullus's purpose was to blacken Clodius's character, thus demonstrating the probability of his guilt in the issue *sub judice*; to this end he recounted the mutiny at Nisibis and Clodius's incestuous relations with Clodia, Lucullus's former wife.

Curio denied Clodius's guilt and one of the proofs, though surely not the only one, was an alibi: the quaestor designate had been away from Rome the night of the crime, at Interamna.[147] A burgher of that town, C. Causinius Schola, an intimate friend of Clodius, testified that he had been the accused's host.[148] As Balsdon has noted, Cicero was only one of several witnesses—though unquestionably the most sensational—who contradicted Schola's evidence.[149] One wonders what Cicero's testimony actually was or was meant to be. He claims to have said very little and nothing of special import.[150] Yet when he was called there was an uproar and the entire jury acted as his bodyguard, a gesture that devastated Clodius and his counsels. The morning following his testimony, he was greeted by crowds.[151] Ciceronian amplification may be at work in the latter account, but in view of Cicero's previous anti-Clodian oratory it is likely that all sides expected a virulent denunciation. This will explain the strong reaction of Clodius's forces to the jury's behavior. However, if Cicero reported his testimony to Atticus truthfully, he must have been a major disappointment to the prosecution.[152]

Signs of possible violence, perhaps bands of youths or family retainers, led the jury to seek protection before it would render its verdict. Such caution was taken by some as a bad sign for the indicted quaestor. With only one negative vote the senate passed a decree commending the jury and instructing the magistrates to attend to its protection. The *iudices* then voted 31 to 25 for acquittal.[153] Clodius had narrowly escaped conviction.

6

Clodius's enemies condemned the jury's verdict as purchased, a natural explanation under the circumstances but not for that reason necessarily an incorrect one.[154] Clearly many factors and motives influenced Clodius's judges; on the other hand, Clodius's situation was critical, and many other senators, including members of his own family, had employed and would continue to employ bribery as a means of obtaining acquittal.[155] Catulus's bon mot, wondering if the jurors had requested a *praesidium* to guard their illicit gains, and the gleeful response to Cicero's insinuations about Clodius's bribery indicate that the senate was at least suspicious.[156] The attempt by Cato to punish the corrupted jurors of the lower orders, who had, evidently, provided the votes favorable to Clodius, reveals his own opinion, and the fact that it passed the senate (although it failed to become law) implies that that body's members were more than merely suspicious: they were willing to alienate the *equites* to punish the dishonest jury.[157] None of this, however, compels us to accept Cicero's version of the affair simply as it stands. But it would be very helpful to us to know just exactly how it does stand, as there remain difficulties of interpretation which must delay us. Here is the relevant text, as reconstituted by Shackleton Bailey (Cic. *Att.* 1.16.5):

> Nosti Calvum ex Nanneianis illum, illum laudatorem meum, de cuius oratione erga me honorifica ad te scripseram. biduo per unum servum, et eum ex ludo gladiatorio, confecit totum negotium. arcessivit ad se, promisit, intercessit, dedit. iam vero (o di boni, rem perditam!) etiam noctes certarum mulierum atque adulescentulorum nobilium introductiones non nullis iudicibus pro mercedis cumulo fuerunt.

You know that *Calvus ex Nanneianis*, the one who praised me, about whose complimentary speech regarding myself I wrote you. Within a couple of days, by means of a single slave, and one from the gladiatorial barracks at that, he settled the whole business. He called them to his house, made promises, offered guarantees, made gifts. On top of that (good god what a sordid affair!) to some jurors, in addition to their profits, came evenings with certain women and introductions to boys from noble families.

The sensational and sordid particulars are embellishments on, not documentation for, the corruption of the whole court. That Cicero's testimony had gone uncredited was reason enough for him to believe the worst. What is of capital importance in this passage is the identification of *Calvus ex Nanneianis ille*, a topic that has long engaged scholarly attention. There are two proposed identifications: was Clodius's bagman M. Crassus, the powerful consular and former censor, or C. Licinius Calvus, the orator and poet? The problem is mired in speculative guesswork and a heavy burden of *Wissenschaft*. Gruen and Seager have prudently judged the issue a *non liquet*.[158] Yet the matter cannot simply be ignored. The belief that Crassus rescued Clodius from conviction has had an important influence on modern interpretations of Clodius's (and Crassus's) politics in subsequent years.[159] After all, if Crassus, by saving the young patrician, placed him under so heavy a burden of gratitude in 61, it would be fair to look for Crassan influence throughout Clodius's subsequent career (however difficult it may be actually to prove such influence). And scholars adopting this line of thought have at some times used Clodius's actions to infer Crassus's schemes, at other times interpreted Crassus's actions as indicative of Clodian policies. Consequently, a review of the proper sense of Cicero's phrase is essential.

As remarked above, it is reasonably certain that bribery played some role in Clodius's acquittal, though it does not follow from this that every one of the thirty-one jurors who voted to absolve the quaestor had been bought off. Cicero, of course, does not distinguish various motives in his condemnation of the trial's outcome, nor did Clodius's enemies, men like Catulus. Rumor had it that the corrupted jurors had received as much as HS 400,000 each to secure their vote, a staggering sum that ought to be viewed with heavy skepticism.[160] *Fama volat*, and the immensity of Clodius's bribe was soon so well circulated that Cicero could assume his audience's full familiarity; hence his witticisms in the *In Clodium et Curionem* and his quips in the senate.[161]

Whatever the actual figures, one point is certain: Clodius himself supplied the money. Nothing in Cicero's description of *Calvus ex Nanneianis* requires one to conclude that this person operated with his own funds: whoever Calvus was, he merely did the legwork, or rather, his slave did. In his invective against Clodius, Cicero makes it clear that Clodius spent his own fortune; indeed, he claims that corrupting the jury ruined the young noble: "he emerged from that trial completely naked, as if from a shipwreck!"[162] Allusions in this same speech to anxious creditors are meant to prove Clodius's general financial embarrassment, not to implicate Clodius's sponsors in illicit payoffs.[163] Clodius, Cicero alleges, even considered reneging on his pledges to the corrupted jury.[164] Since Clodius used his own funds to bribe the jury, there is no reason to pursue the identification of Calvus with Crassus. Cicero informs us that Clodius used *sequestres*—middlemen—to disburse his money, a detail that explains the role played by *Calvus ex Nanneianis*, whoever he was.

Why, then, the persistent identification of this figure with Crassus? Speculation that Crassus profited in the Sullan proscriptions from the property of a certain Nannius (mentioned at *Comm. Pet.* 9), which is a name quite distinct from Nanneius, and, further, that Crassus did so under the assumed name of Licinius Calvus must count for little.[165] Nor, despite its frequent surfacing, is there any basis for the assumption that Crassus was bald (hence *calvus*). The only potential connection of *Calvus ex Nanneianis* to Crassus is Cicero's depiction of the former as *illum laudatorem meum*, which can be taken as an allusion to Crassus's flattering oration mentioned by Cicero at *Att.* 1.14.3. But, as Tenny Frank recognized long ago, this allusion only seems obvious in Cicero's correspondence owing to its present form, a selection from which numerous letters written to Atticus at this time have clearly been omitted.[166] Which leaves little to recommend the identification with M. Crassus.

Does anything recommend Licinius Calvus? His role in the circle of Clodius and his sister makes him available to be of service to Clodius. And the task assigned him in Cicero's letter fits his youthful station. We do not know of Calvus flattering Cicero before 61, yet at the same time there is nothing to suggest that Calvus was Cicero's enemy either, at least not at this time. In general, then, a good though not compelling case can be put for identifying *Calvus ex Nanneianis* with young Licinius Calvus.[167] Indeed, an ingenious (though by no means farfetched) proposal of Wiseman even makes sense of the otherwise incomprehensible *Nanneianis*: the word, he proposes, though corrupted in our texts, was originally Greek; in fact, Cicero's phrase was *ex νεανίαις* (one should recall that Cicero introduces his whole retelling of the Clodian trial with a quotation, in Greek, from the *Iliad*). Thus, in Wiseman's suggestion,

Cicero wrote: Nosti Calvum ex νεανίαις illum (you know that Calvus, so well known among the young men). Certainty, as usual, eludes, however, and it is important to bear in mind that *calvus* could be a coarse, abusive term in Latin. Along these very lines, Calvus appears to have been a stock character from mime.[168] The precise import of Cicero's phrase, then, must remain dubious. But if we feel in duty bound to find a particular reference, the more likely candidate must be Licinius Calvus. M. Crassus may safely be dismissed from consideration.

Since it cannot be shown that Crassus played a significant role in Clodius's trial, one may wonder to what extent Pompey involved himself after the initial debates over the *rogatio Pupia Valeria*. The vigorous efforts of Pompey's friend Pupius Piso on the accused's behalf have been taken as an indication of the great man's favor.[169] Cicero saw it otherwise (*Att.* 1.14.6). Cicero's only other comment on (and our only other evidence for) Pompey's involvement in the Bona Dea trial is a passage from *De Haruspicum Responso*, a speech delivered long after the event, from which contradictory conclusions have been drawn.[170] The troublesome bit is *illum reum non laudarat*, which is taken to mean either that Pompey refused to give a *laudatio* in Clodius's support or that Pompey disapproved of the prosecution of Clodius.[171] The rhetoric of the passage tends to support the latter interpretation, but the relevant phrase is so brief and is embedded in an argument so tendentious that it would be an unsound enterprise to attempt to make much of it. It seems likely enough that Pompey simply kept aloof from the trial, endorsing senatorial authority so long as he was pressed, but not assailing Clodius. His conduct, Cicero told Atticus, pleased no one, and for once, we may presume, Cicero and Clodius agreed on something.

7

It remains to speculate on Clodius's motives in perpetrating his offense against the rites of the Bona Dea. Several guesses have been advanced. J. Gagé ascribes Clodius's sacrilege to curiosity: it was the Claudian *gens* that first introduced the cult to Rome; young Clodius was merely investigating the legacy of his ancestors.[172] Curiosity of a different quality is suggested by Moreau, who rightly notes that, whereas we have no evidence that Caesar's wife was ever actually corrupted, this need not prevent our supposing that Clodius was hopeful when he invaded Caesar's house. Furthermore, Moreau observes, the enterprise involved numerous enticements: the *frisson* of the costume, the element of cunning subterfuge, the flouting of convention.[173] To this one might add the exhilarating risk of apprehension as well as the prurient fantasies of the Roman male, who tended to imagine that all women were promiscuous by nature. If Juvenal's lurid depiction of the utterly unrestrained goings on of the goddess's mysteries only approximates the salacious conjectures of Clodius's contemporaries, it becomes all the easier to comprehend how a young man of dissolute nature might have been tempted to snatch at least a peek.[174] What was so genuinely shocking to Clodius's seniors at least, and properly suggestive of the man's moral fiber, was that he was not at all deterred by the dictates of civic religion, by the dignity of his office, or even by anxiety over the senate's censoriousness.

The Bona Dea incident remains a remarkable specimen of ineptitude and pointless, unprofitable rashness. It suggests a dangerous combination of arrogance and immaturity. But if Clodius had originally viewed his adventure as little more than a lark, serious only to the most severe, he was soon made painfully aware of his own misapprehensions. The scandal very nearly ruined his career. And in any event it left his future prospects, if not in shambles, then certainly blighted by the disgrace of the past several months.

CHAPTER FOUR

From Patrician to Plebeian

1

Clodius secured his acquittal, but at severe cost. The embarrassment of the scandal was exacerbated by the humiliation of a trial, itself an affront to Clodian *dignitas*. The young patrician heard himself abused in speeches enumerating his every vice—and vices that he did not possess. He had been assailed as murderer, adulterer, and debaucher of his own sister, all before the people and all in the presence of a jury that came close to convicting him. Of greater significance for the future, Clodius's trial had revealed how little support he enjoyed in the senate, for all his illustrious lineage.[1]

After the trial, Clodius's enemies rushed to stigmatize the verdict as bought and paid for. Catulus and Cicero denounced the jury's venality. The rectitudinous Cato persuaded the senate to decree the promulgation of a bill whose provisions would require the punishment of nonsenatorial jurors proved guilty of accepting bribes, a proposal that, following so rapidly the verdict on Clodius, could hardly avoid being viewed as an expression of senatorial outrage over the outcome of the Bona Dea trial. The senate's disapproval was not limited to gestures of censure. Cicero roused the senate to deprive Pupius Piso of Syria, which had apparently been assigned to him as his proconsular province. In this way, the consul was punished for his support of Clodius, and Clodius, too, suffered a blow, since he had also expected to take up provincial responsibilities in Syria, evidently as Piso's quaestor. In his *In Clodium et Curionem*, Cicero portrayed his enemy as utterly bankrupted by his outlays for bribery—*ut illo iudicio tamquam e naufragio nudus emersit*—and, consequently, harassed by creditors.[2] Syria, in Cicero's version of events, represented Clodius's hope for solvency. These aspersions (whatever their veracity) were fitted to the senate's temper: the salient point is that Clodius expected to be sent to Syria, clearly a profitable appointment, but was disappointed. The senate's hostility was unmistakable.

And there seemed no end to Cicero's invective, much of which ultimately appeared in the form of the *In Clodium et Curionem*, a text that later circulated in Cicero's name but against his will, if it is to be identified with the poorly composed attack on Scribonius Curio that proved so keen an embarrassment during the orator's exile.[3] However that may be, the relationship between any specific performance by Cicero and the (fragmentary) text of the *In Clodium et Curionem* must remain problematic, and K. Geffcken may well be right in proposing that what came down to Quintilian and the Bobbio Scholiast as the *In Clodium et Curionem* was a miscellany of Ciceronian invective from the aftermath of the Bona Dea trial.[4] One notable Ciceronian assault came at a meeting of the senate on 15 May, when Cicero spoke at length on the health of the republic, by which he meant its ability to withstand Clodius's escape from justice.[5] Lentulus Sura, he reminded the *patres conscripti*, had twice been acquitted, as had Catiline: continuing a pattern of abuse begun during the conflicts that preceded the trial, Cicero cataloged Clodius as the third such menace to the state. The quaestor rose to respond; thereupon a slanging match ensued between the two during which the patrician jeered at the orator's origins and pretensions, but without scoring a hit. Cicero's wit won the day, and Clodius—upset—collapsed into silence ("magnis clamoribus adflictus conticuit et concidit").[6]

Under such circumstances, Clodius must surely have been plunged deeply into *dolor*, the predictable aristocratic response to insult and injury. Despite his pleas, Clodius had been unable to move the senate during the events leading to his trial—a trial that in his estimation should never have taken place. The loss of Syria and the constant contumely and disparagement cast upon him by Catulus, Cato, and especially Cicero— to the obvious glee of (too) many senators—must have underscored for him how precipitously his esteem among his peers had collapsed. Clodius's noble sensibilities leave *dolor* the only natural reaction, and it is worth noting how diligently Cicero endeavors in his inventory of demagogues in *De Haruspicum Responso* (delivered years after the event, to be sure) to deny *dolor* to Clodius in the aftermath of the Bona Dea scandal.[7] *Dolor*, as Cicero makes clear, might drive a politician to disreputable actions, but as a response to perceived setbacks it was very much a legitimate aristocratic reflex and therefore not, if the orator could have his way, one to be attributed to his enemy.[8]

Clodius tried to counter Cicero by holding *contiones* in which he savaged the orator, and not only the orator. All who had had a part in his prosecution came in for abuse, including the Vestals. Of these he singled out for special slander a relation of Cicero's wife, Fabia. Enter Cato, whose involvement was adequate to silence Clodius (and to earn Cicero's gratitude). A later tradition introduced the false embellishment that Cato drove Clodius from the city.[9] In fact, the patrician lingered in Rome longer than was expected.

When he delivered the *In Clodium et Curionem*, Cicero claimed that Clodius planned to be present at the consular elections.[10] In 61 these were postponed by the senate so that Aufidius Lucro could put forward his bill *de ambitu*. When the senate met to decide whether to accommodate Lucro's bill, Clodius again came in for a Ciceronian jibe, evidence, perhaps, of Clodius's attendance, though it cannot be known if he was able to stay in Rome until 27 July, when the elections were actually held.[11] The Bobbio Scholiast perceived an allusion to Clodius's electioneering in the reference to consular comitia in the *In Clodium et Curionem*, and Cicero's joke in the senate makes Clodius out to be a dishonest *divisor*. Cicero's pejorative perspective notwithstanding, it is far from unreasonable to surmise that Clodius intended to involve himself in the coming elections. After all, his half brother (and brother-in-law), Metellus Celer, was standing for office. Celer could certainly and legitimately call on his patrician kin to support his canvass. Other motives obtrude as well. The elections, it was clear by July, would be rife with bribery, not least because Pompey meant to purchase the consulship for his protégé, L. Afranius.[12] In this enterprise, Cicero reports, Pupius Piso was to lend his assistance by coordinating the *divisores*. Clodius, by now an old hand at such tactics, could, by working in Afranius's behalf, repay Piso for his past support and at the same time bestow a favor on both Afranius and Pompey. To be sure, there was money to be made in such activities as well. None of this, one hastens to point out, need be attributed solely to Clodius's initiative: a man in Clodius's circumstances could be presumed to be tractable.[13] Clodius, desperate to amplify his senatorial resources, may have sought to satisfy Celer and Piso alike.

Eventually it was necessary for Clodius to take up his province in Sicily.[14] The island was governed by a propraetor, C. Vergilius Balbus (pr. 62), an experienced administrator in Sicily, assisted by two quaestors, one of whom was stationed in Lilybaeum, the other at Syracuse.[15] Where Clodius was based and who was his colleague go unrecorded. In fact, nothing is known of Clodius's quaestorship. Not that the populace of

Rome was in the habit of taking a keen interest in the activities of Sicily's quaestors, a point hammered home to Cicero upon his own return from Lilybaeum, where he had been posted when quaestor.[16] By early June 60 Clodius had returned to Rome, his passage from Sicily having been exceptionally swift.[17] Vergilius Balbus stayed on as governor, but it was unremarkable for Clodius's service as quaestor to have terminated after a single year and before the conclusion of his commander's tenure.[18]

However tempting the prospect, it would be incautious to attempt to extract much significance from Cicero's report to Atticus of an exchange between himself and Clodius (cited in a letter from early June 60) that took place not long after the patrician's return as the two men were escorting a candidate for office to the forum.[19] During the *deductio*, Clodius asked Cicero if he (having served as quaestor in Sicily and having celebratedly represented himself in court as the island's champion) had been in the habit of providing Sicilians with seats at gladiatorial contests, a not very subtle dig at the new man's limitations as a traditional patron. When the orator replied that he had not, Clodius announced that, as Sicily's new patron, he would establish the practice. One difficulty, he remarked in feigned confidence, was Clodia Metelli's unwillingness to share more than a foot of the space at her disposal (as wife of the consul), an obvious boast on Clodius's part that displayed his rich family connections even if in the guise of a (simulated) complaint. Cicero's notorious return—a dirty joke about Clodius's alleged incest with Clodia—makes it very clear that he got the point of Clodius's remarks. Though amusing, this anecdote teaches us nothing about Clodius's quaestorship in Sicily save that he was willing to make the predictable claim to being the island's new patron, a banal bit of posturing that manifested itself in social gestures routine to someone of Clodius's class.

2

What principally attracts the attention of the sources during that time were Clodius's efforts, even while abroad, to arrange for his transfer from patrician to plebeian status. Indeed, during the year 60 Clodius made several reasonably well documented attempts to divest himself of his patrician rank (these are discussed below). This brings us to the oft-cited but rather murky matter of *transitio ad plebem*, a complicated issue that has long generated controversy.[20] The evidence is spotty and mostly inferential. That it was possible for patricians to become plebeian is beyond dispute, but the means by which such a transfer was executed remain unclear: Clodius's exertions constitute our only evidence for the operation—and, in the end, Clodius failed, largely on procedural grounds, to perform a successful *transitio*. Instead, he became plebeian through a form of adoption.[21]

The historical tradition of Rome, Cicero complained in writings both public and private, was too often contaminated by the false traditions of powerful families—*falsi triumphi, plures consulatus, genera etiam falsa et ad plebem transitiones*—lies likely to baffle the scholar and to stain the official record with a permanent, mendacious color.[22] The extent to which confusion and falsehood were possible can be illustrated from a coin minted in the very year of the Bona Dea scandal: as moneyer, L. Aemilius Lepidus Paullus, the future consul of 50, advanced his spurious claim to descend from the victor at Pydna by designing a denarius the reverse of which recalled the three occasions when L. Aemilius Paullus had been hailed as *imperator*, itself a completely fictitious tradition.[23] Similar examples could be multiplied, nor had the situation improved appreciatively when Livy undertook his labors.[24] The consequences of this predicament are several and serious, though for our purposes we need concentrate on the obvious concern, false transitions from patrician to plebeian status. The reasons why a plebeian family might allege patrician antecedents require no exposition. That there were plebeian families who could plausibly make such claims is the very essence of the difficulty. The pretense is ridiculed by Cicero in his *Brutus*: it would be a patent nonsense, he points out, were he to avow descent from Manius Tullius, the patrician who was consul in 500. The same might be said for M. Tullius Decula (cos. 81), a plebeian whose very existence has led some scholars to challenge Cicero's statement that Manius was a patrician.[25]

Therein lies the principal difficulty for the modern scholar. The early *fasti* of the Roman Republic came down to the late republic in competing versions, which were not always susceptible of reconciliation but were always liable to embellishment.[26] These *fasti* include rather a few holders of patrician magistracies possessing names that, in later and better documented periods, belong clearly to plebeian houses, a state of affairs that prompts one to wonder whether such magistracies could actually be held by plebeians before 366 (the traditional date of the first plebeian consulship) and, if so, with what frequency were they so held. The situation is made worse by our current inability to trace with any real accuracy the process by which (or the chronology according to which) the patriciate took its ultimate form.[27] Nor are matters improved by efforts expended on the part of many late republican aristocrats to blur (to their advantage) the precise lines of descent among those who held a common *gentilicium*.[28] All of which prevents any definitive solution to many of the questions complicating our efforts to understand *transitio ad plebem*. For we cannot as yet know, when we come to consider later plebeians whose name are homonymous with early consuls, whether we have to do with a family that was once patrician but underwent a *transitio*, or one that by some process unknown to us simply lost its patrician standing, or one that, though for a time it was competitive in the ranks of families which were then forming the patriciate, could not sustain its membership in their number. For whatever reason or reasons, some *gentes* apparently had collateral branches, one of which was patrician, the other plebeian (certainly there were patrician and plebeian families possessing the same *nomen gentilicium* during the same period).[29] Explanations proliferate, but none has yet unriddled the sphinx.

Let us return to the topic of false transitions. It was an easy matter for Cicero to indulge his aversion to false claims of patrician origins, especially since nobody would have tolerated such a boast from him. He could even go so far as to refer jokingly to Servius Tullius as his regal kinsman. But there was a tradition, current no doubt in Arpinum, that his family derived from a famous Volscian warrior king named Tullus Attius. Other families found themselves in a position to put forward grander affectations: the Octavii insisted that they had been elevated to patrician rank under the monarchy, only to revert *ad plebem* until Caesar restored their previous station.[30] This conceit commanded greater clout. But, between these extremes, there were *transitiones* that the Romans themselves queried. A single example will suffice. In his account of the foiling of Sp. Maelius's plot to seize power, Livy provides a critique of the report by some authorities that L. Minucius, who played a leading role in stopping Maelius, was transferred to the *plebs*.[31] Because in the early republic the Minucii appeared in positions that ought to be held by patricians, yet in later periods the family was clearly plebeian, a *transitio ad plebem* was naturally assumed to have taken place. And it is this Minucius who was deemed the transitional figure, for it was maintained that, in the aftermath of Maelius's execution, Minucius was co-opted as an eleventh tribune. This version of events is preserved in Pliny, and it was evidently inscribed on a *titulus* affixed to a well-known *imago* of Minucius.[32] Livy, however, rejects Minucius's tribunate as unthinkable. Livy does not specifically object to the possibility of Minucius's *transitio*, but, once his co-optation into the college of tribunes is eliminated, the rationale of his transfer to plebeian status vanishes as well. Still, it should be noticed that Livy rejects neither the procedure of *transitio* nor co-optation by the tribunes: it is the anomaly of an eleventh tribune that excites the historian's disbelief and consequently leads him to suspect the

FROM PATRICIAN TO PLEBEIAN

entire account of Minucius's tribunate. But all of this was obscure by Livy's time: the very arguments he advances make it plain that his was one opinion amid many.

The Romans' awareness of false *transitiones* implies their appreciation of genuine transfers. And there can be no question that it was once possible for patricians to surrender their status in order to become plebeians. In Mommsen's inventory of *transitiones*, he mentions the Octavii, Sp. Tarpeius and A. Aternius, the consuls of 454 who, though patricians (so Liv. 3.65.1), were co-opted into the college of tribunes in 449, and the aforementioned case of L. Minucius, admittedly with the sensible concession that these instances belong to a period whose historical record is less than satisfactory ("Diese Fälle gehören der halb historischen Zeit").[33] He insists, however, on the complete historicity of the *transitiones* of the Papirii Masones, the Sempronii Atratini, C. Servilius (pr. before 218), P. Sulpicius Rufus (tr. pl. 88), Clodius, and P. Cornelius Dolabella (cos. suff. 44).[34] Now the Papirii Masones and the Sempronii Atratini fall into the controversial category specified above: the relationship between the plebeian and patrician bearers of these names cannot be decisively determined.[35] But there can be no doubting the *transitio* of C. Servilius, although it is attested explicitly in no ancient source.

The father of this C. Servilius, P. Servilius (cos. I 252, II 248), was patrician, whereas Gaius's sons, C. Servilius Geminus (cos. 203) and M. Servilius Pulex Geminus (cos. 202), were plebeian, a condition evident from their holding of plebeian offices and their co-optation into plebeian vacancies in priestly colleges.[36] The only reasonable conclusion, long recognized, is that Gaius underwent a *transitio ad plebem* sometime before his praetorship (since he was captured by Gauls in 218 and not rescued until 203). Gaius represents the earliest indisputable instance of *transitio ad plebem* known to us, testimony to the enormous poverty of our information on the subject. It is singularly unfortunate that our sources are too scrappy for us to determine whether Gaius's *transitio* was at all remarkable. Why the son of a man twice consul should alter his status so radically is not immediately obvious. Gaius was not, to our knowledge, a tribune—or, if he was, he was not a controversial one. Perhaps, as has been propounded, Gaius believed that plebeian status would improve his odds at winning the consulship. One can but observe that his change of status did nothing to injure his sons' prospects. The case of C. Servilius certainly proves that *transitio* was possible and, it would seem, acceptable as late as the Second Punic War.

A brief summary may prove useful. By the late republic, Cicero and Livy make clear, Roman history had been at least somewhat confounded by the false attribution to individuals and family records of transitions to plebeian status, canards introduced by aristocrats motivated by anti-quarianism and social ambition. Nevertheless, the tradition of ancient *transitiones* and the example of Servilius make it plain that there was indeed such a thing as *transitio ad plebem*, however it was executed.[37] The annalistic tradition tends to associate *transitio ad plebem* with co-optation into the college of tribunes, although this may well be another instance of the Romans' tendency to view the emergence of the patriciate in terms of the conflict between tribunes and senate that subtended late republican thinking on such matters.[38]

After Servilius, however, no further specimens of *transitio* emerge from our sources until Clodius's (unsuccessful) efforts—with the possible and vexatious exception of P. Sulpicius Rufus, to whom we must now turn. The ill-fated tribune of 88 bore a patrician name, or so it appears, and the question of his *transitio* certainly bears on Clodius's various and fruitless attempts to become a plebeian. Consequently, the issue must delay us further.

In the fourth century, a Ser. Sulpicius Rufus was several times military tribune with consular powers.[39] Thereafter the Sulpicii Rufi vanish from their distinguished position, reemerging only in the first century, though hardly in conspicuous abundance. Best known to us is the eminent jurist and consul of 51, Ser. Sulpicius Q. f. Rufus, who, Cicero informs us, was inordinately proud of his patrician heritage (*Mur.* 15). Nevertheless, again on the evidence of Ciceronian speechifying, Sulpicius's nobility required a good deal of antiquarian research to appreciate: his father had remained equestrian, and his grandfather, though a senator (as Münzer rightly discerned), was a virtual unknown (*Mur.* 16). His son, an orator of signal repute, was father to Sulpicia, the remarkable poet. The pros-opographical calculations of G. V. Sumner have plausibly identified as the jurist's brother P. Sulpicius Q. f. Rufus, who was quaestor in 69 and proconsul in Bithynia and Pontus in 46–45.[40] So far the patrician Sulpicii Rufi. The ill-fated tribune of 88—obviously plebeian—was also a Rufus, as Valerius Maximus explicitly states.[41] If this is correct, it is quite possible that Sulpicius, or one of his direct forebears, underwent *transitio*. Other possibilities also present themselves, as we have already seen. The tribune may derive from a plebeian line of Sulpicii Rufi that was other-wise unattested, perhaps a line of Sulpicii who arrogated to themselves the venerable cognomen. The nature of the relationship obtaining be-tween the tribune of 88 and his son (Caesar's valiant legate and very possibly the censor of 42)[42] and the family of the patrician jurist are irre-trievable without more information. The absolute silence of the sources regarding Sulpicius's *transitio* has disposed some scholars to doubt that one actually took place.[43] If, on the other hand, one assumes that Sulpicius in fact underwent an unmentioned *transitio*, then one is required to conclude that the young man's *transitio* was in no way controversial. This is the inescapable implication of Cicero's *De Oratore*, the dramatic date of which is 91, when, according to Cicero, Sulpicius's future tribunate was anticipated with great favor. In the end, however, the silence of the sources is probably best explained by the assumption that Sulpicius was plebeian from the start (we may leave aside whether his line had always been plebeian or had in the past become so by *transitio*).

3

The important question of precisely when Clodius made up his mind to seek plebeian status must be addressed. M. Slagter has argued that the Bobbio Scholiast makes it clear that the decision was reached and made public during the events of the Bona Dea affair—or even before.[44] The sole item of evidence is fragment 14 (Crawford) of the *In Clodium et Curionem*, a text the difficulties of which have already been remarked upon. The fragment reads:

> Cum se ad plebem transire velle diceret, sed misere fretum transire cuperet.

> Although he claimed that he wished to cross over to the *plebs*, in fact he desperately desired to cross over the [Messinian] strait.

The Bobbio Scholiast, in his commentary, observes that a patrician is ineligible to be tribune, an office sought (in his opinion) by Clodius in the expectation of revenging himself upon his enemies; he goes on to explain the specific reference of the strait mentioned by Cicero and to inform the reader that Clodius was ultimately quaestor in Sicily.[45]

Because Clodius's comments regarding *transitio* must have been made in *contiones*, Slagter dates them to the period preceding Clodius's trial. But Clodian *contiones* were as much a feature of the trial's aftermath as its preliminaries.[46] A somewhat stronger case for the early dating of Clodius's plebeian plans is made by J. Crawford, who suggests that in fragment 14 Cicero is asserting that, whatever Clodius's public protestations, he lusted in his heart to remove himself to his province in Sicily, where he might escape prosecution.[47] Now this is by no means an impossible interpretation of the line. Admittedly it is evident that, by the time of the *In Clodium et Curionem*, Cicero had already succeeded in depriving

Pupius Piso of Syria, thereby dashing Clodius's dreams of an appointment there, and Clodius had by then drawn a Sicilian province. But that need not prohibit Cicero from launching an anachronistic slur intended to depict Clodius as cravenly hoping to flee Rome in order to save himself from prosecution. Nor, it must be said, is it unthinkable that, in the struggle over the *rogatio Pupia Valeria*, Clodius, joining in the attack on the excesses of *senatus auctoritas*, might have expressed a wish to defend the people as its tribune—if only it were possible. Rhetoric of this brand, however, even if it was actually employed, need not be confused with a political manifesto.[48]

This line of speculation need carry no conviction, however. Nothing in the fragment or in the exegesis of the Bobbio Scholiast locates Clodius's expressed intention of securing plebeian status before or during the Bona Dea scandal. A likelier interpretation of the line, one should suppose, takes as its point of departure the orator's mention of Sicily, the province allotted to Clodius *after* his acquittal (when Piso's provincial assignment was canceled). The point of Cicero's barb would then be that, whatever political aspirations voiced by Clodius during his recent *contiones* (be they plans to campaign for friends or to seek a *transitio ad plebem*), the disgrace of his trial and his purchased acquittal was such that the quaestor was in actuality anxious to leave the city in which he was so unwelcome (one recalls that the *In Clodium et Curionem* tends to portray the acquitted Clodius along the lines of a Catiline). Whatever force the line might possess would be unaffected by the fact that any pressure on Clodius to depart from Rome would in reality be owed to his responsibilities as quaestor. In any case, there exists no real evidence that Clodius showed any signs of seeking a *transitio ad plebem* until after the Bona Dea trial, by which time the young patrician believed that he had ample reason to consider turning to so drastic an undertaking.

4

Clodius, having publicized his decision to seek transition to plebeian status, made arrangements, either before his passage to Sicily or while abroad, with C. Herennius, a tribune for 60, for the latter to introduce legislation, the terms of which would require a competent magistrate to bring before the centuriate assembly a bill that would transfer Clodius to the *plebs*.[49] What influence Clodius had over Herennius goes unstated (the tribune seems a minor enough figure), but it was adequate to secure his quick and lasting loyalty. Already by 20 January 60 (the date of Cic. *Att.* 1.18), Herennius had been active in Clodius's behalf, though in vain owing to the vetoes imposed by some of his colleagues.[50] It is easier to see why Metellus Celer, by then consul, felt obliged to promulgate a *rogatio* for Clodius, itself a mere gesture in view of the inevitability of tribunician veto.[51] Still, in Cicero's opinion at least, Celer's courtesy to his *frater* diminished his *auctoritas*. Herennius, it appears, persisted in his exertions until Clodius's return.[52]

Whence the opposition to the bills promulgated by Herennius and Metellus Celer? Cicero viewed the proposals as deserving of veto, but not on account of any legal technicality or even because he did not believe that a *lex centuriata* was sufficient to change Clodius's status. At *Att.* 1.18.4 and especially at *Att.* 1.19.5, Cicero treats the matter as an unseemly triviality—indeed, he does not take Clodius's scheme to become tribune seriously until after the patrician's return from abroad.[53] Apart from Herennius and L. Flavius, no other tribunes are known in 60, which makes it impossible to decide the extent to which personal animosities in the college played a role. But, in light of the fact that, before this endeavor by Clodius, there is no record of opposition to a *transitio ad plebem*, the repeated vetoes require consideration.

Part of the answer may lie in the tribunate of Sulpicius, to which we have already referred. If Sulpicius did undergo a *transitio* in order to become tribune, then his disastrous tenure of the office might have engendered an elite prejudice against patrician transfers. This possibility cannot be eliminated, though it is worth noting that in none of the surviving record of Ciceronian disapproval of Clodius's transfer—or of his entire tribunate for the matter—is the baleful example of Sulpicius's reckless career adduced.[54] Nor is it clear why Clodius's first attempt to reinvigorate his career at Rome should have been to expose himself to assimilation to Sulpicius, if the memory of that *transitio* continued to excite hostility.

If the legislation proposed on Clodius's behalf was not impermissible and if there was no specific reason to oppose *transitio* in itself, the vetoes of the tribunes must have been a response to Clodius himself and to his circumstances. Clodius's desire to become plebeian signified his intention to stand for the tribunate. The nearly unanimous opinion of antiquity was that Clodius sought the tribunate in order to revenge himself on Cicero.[55] This explanation, which reflects the extent to which the orator's construction of Clodius's career dominated later authors, is true but too simple. Even in the wake of Clodius's return from Sicily, after all, Cicero himself believed that his exchanges with Clodius, though rough, were undertaken *familiariter*.[56] Clodius unquestionably held a grudge against Cicero, and the orator's invective could hardly improve their relationship. Clodius's designs upon the tribunate came hastily upon his acquittal, as we have seen, yet there existed other avenues open to a vengeful Clodius, such as a retaliatory prosecution, all of easier and more immediate access to the young patrician than the office of tribune. Naturally Clodius could be expected to do all he could, in whatever circumstances, to help his friends and to harm his enemies. Consequently, Cicero tended to keep a wary eye on Clodius, and it was predictable that he would view Clodius's machinations entirely in terms of their consequences for himself. But, for the community at large, other considerations supervened: Herennius's bill was not blocked in order to save the consular from the quaestor.[57]

It has been proposed that Clodius's decision to become plebeian is essentially unrelated to his specific circumstances after the Bona Dea trial.[58] Rather, so the hypothesis runs, because he was the third son in a patrician family, his prospects for attaining to a consulship were thereby diminished and so, recognizing this impediment, Clodius hoped to improve his chances for attaining a consulship by altering his status. It is a fact that there are few known instances of three brothers from a single family being elected consul, but surely this is more a reflection of demographic realities than political ones. As for political impediments, in the case of Clodius's own family, the failure of his brother Gaius to rise beyond the praetorship was due entirely to his own corruption, not to an unwillingness on the part of the people to see a second Claudius Pulcher reach the consulate. Nor, in the end, did Clodius's plebeian status guarantee him the highest office. To be sure, patricians were ineligible for the tribunate and the plebeian aedileship, nor did they enjoy unqualified access to the curule aedileship and consulship. Obviously any patrician could enhance his opportunities to stand for elected office and his statistical chances for elevation to the consulship if he underwent a *transitio*. Nevertheless, few patricians, in the late republic at least, availed themselves of the privilege of transfer. Clodius no doubt knew his odds, but there is no pressing reason to think that these matters counted heavily in his decision. Nor, if such were his primary considerations, were they the sort to provoke much resistance.

Clodius was not the first noble to be driven to the tribunate by a serious blow to his prestige and his prospects. The *dolor* of such an ordeal, which brought to the fore of a Roman's consciousness an awareness of his feeble condition even as it fired his ambition to acquire a station of undeniable superiority, excited the politician's ordinary appetite for conspicuous achievement to the extent that his contemporaries might regard him as simultaneously tractable and suspicious.[59] *Dolor*, as

FROM PATRICIAN TO PLEBEIAN

Cicero observes, thrust the Gracchi into the tribunate; Saturninus was similarly impelled.[60] The tribune's office offered a young man anxious to advance himself ample opportunities to do so, whether he elected to raise his stock with the senatorial establishment by imposing judicious vetoes and sponsoring responsible legislation or chose to curry favor with a powerful clique or individual or, finally, determined to make a name for himself by courting *popularitas*.[61] Nor need he limit his prospect to but a single course if, deficient in *gratia*, he intended to make the heaviest possible investment in *beneficia*.

Clodius's *dolor*, then, made him a man to watch. It has already been suggested that his involvement in the elections for 60 was to some degree a reflex of his dolorous state. The disclosure during his quaestorship of his plan to transfer to the *plebs* in order to become tribune, while neither illicit nor wholly alien to Roman traditions, nonetheless constituted an extreme response to the Bona Dea scandal, which his contemporaries could only interpret as dangerous insofar as it served to indicate the lengths to which Clodius might go in trying to repair his (exaggerated) sense of *dignitas*. Hence suspicion—and resistance.

Another element of the opposition to Clodius's *transitio* should also be considered, even if it must remain speculative. If Sulpicius Rufus in fact did not undergo a *transitio*, then there is no record of anyone's doing so from the time of the Second Punic War until Clodius's quaestorship. Now this may well be an accident of our exiguous sources, but it is worth pondering whether Clodius's announcement aroused not merely suspicion but also astonishment. After all, Cicero, as we have seen, did not actually take Clodius's efforts seriously until a strenuous senatorial debate on the subject took place, after Clodius's return from Sicily. If Clodius's scheme combined novelty with extremity, then opposition cannot have been entirely unforeseen.

5

Clodius must have been disappointed by Herennius's ineffectualness and Metellus Celer's lack of enthusiasm. But he would not be deterred, nor could he be induced at this point to contemplate surrendering his name with his status: Clodius steadfastly refused resorting to adoption in order to become plebeian. By June Celer was in staunch opposition to his kinsman.[62] This may well be due to Clodius's obstinate refusal to let the topic of his *transitio* fade, especially as there were other matters pressing the senate and the consul.[63] But we must now turn to the account of Clodius's *transitio* reported by Dio.[64] That Dio's version of events is in some measure garbled is generally recognized. The real issue, however, is whether he preserves any information of historical value. Mommsen believed that he did, a view that provoked a learned debate with Lange, who, worried by the abundant problems in the Greek account, was disposed to reject it altogether. A reconsideration here can hardly be escaped.[65]

According to Dio, Clodius persuaded some of the tribunes to propose a law that would allow patricians to be elected to the tribunate, but this plan failed. Thereafter Clodius abjured his patrician status and entered the plebeian assembly in order to be elected tribune. Metellus Celer, however, prevented the election on the grounds that Clodius was acting contrary to custom. Dio then explains—his opinion, as Lange recognized, not Celer's—that *transitio* was only possible by a *lex curiata*. Mommsen attempted to provide a thorough conflation of Cicero's evidence with Dio's account, a move to which Lange (and others) took exception on the grounds that Dio describes actions taken by Clodius after his return to Rome, whereas Cicero makes it clear that Herennius and Celer proposed their bills during Clodius's absence. Now Lange's criticism is only partly valid: although Clodius's abjuration can only be imagined taking place in the city, his (alleged) effort to persuade the tribunes to open the tribunate to patricians hardly required his physical presence in Rome—which is not to say that Dio is necessarily to be integrated with Cicero's record of events. In the end, his account may be too problematic to be of great use.

It is unthinkable that Clodius tried to persuade the tribunes to propose a bill that would open the office to the patriciate. In light of Herennius's failure, nobody could have been such a fool as to suggest a measure so open to objection (and so clearly doomed from the start). Unless he is engaging in free invention, Dio has misunderstood something in his sources. It is quite possible that Dio is providing a garbled version of Herennius's actual *rogatio*. A more speculative explanation (which again requires postulating a muddle on Dio's part) is also available. Perhaps while contemplating his options, Clodius ventilated the feasibility of his becoming a tribune and a plebeian by co-optation. We know very little about co-optation of tribunes. Livy mentions it only three times, all in very early books, but, as he presents it, *cooptatio* supplies one means whereby a *transitio* may take place.[66] The *lex Trebonia* of 448 forbade co-optation of tribunes, but Livy's criticism of the normal account of Minucius's tribunate in 438 (discussed above) reveals that many Roman historians were unaware of the law.[67] It does not matter that co-optation is unlikely ever actually to have occurred. By the late republic, it was an undeniable element of the tradition (Livy obviously took it seriously). Desperate to become tribune, even more so after the failures of Herennius and Celer, Clodius may have considered trying to resurrect the anachronism of co-optation, and his lucubrations on the subject may have made their way into a source that Dio subsequently failed to grasp satisfactorily.[68]

We must now turn to the remainder of Dio's entry. Mommsen identified Clodius's abjuration of his patrician rank (τήν τε εὐγένειαν ἐξωμόσατο) with *sacrorum detestatio*, another procedure about which we are poorly informed.[69] We know from Gellius (15.27.3) that *sacrorum detestatio* took place in the *comitia calata*, which apparently met twice a year: 24 March and 24 May.[70] If so, and if one accepts Mommsen's identification, then the *sacrorum detestatio* attributed by Dio to Clodius will have taken place on 24 May, immediately upon his return to the city. We may, then, take Dio's account to say that Clodius, after returning to the city, undertook a *sacrorum detestatio* on 24 May, on the basis of which he claimed to be a plebeian and attempted to stand for the tribunate. Mommsen took *sacrorum detestatio* to be equivalent to *transitio ad plebem*—clearly Clodius did as well—an equation objected to already by Lange, who pointed out the numerous difficulties plaguing Dio's account. Dio insists that a *lex curiata* was required for Clodius's transition, a transparent contamination from Clodius's ultimate adoption (which did require a *lex curiata*), a conflation reflected as well in Dio's use of the word ἐκποίησις ("adoption") at 37.51.2 to indicate Clodius's alleged *transitio*: the verb ἐκποιεῖν, used at Dio 38.12.2 to refer to Clodius's transfer to plebeian status, also regularly denotes adoption. But let us tolerate Dio's uncertain formulation for a moment. After all, his was a legitimate confusion. The purpose and nature of *sacrorum detestatio* were far from straightforward to Clodius's contemporaries, a state of affairs evidenced by Ser. Sulpicius Rufus's researches into the matter, efforts resulting in his learned treatise *De Sacris Detestandis*, which may well have been published by 63.[71] Clodius plainly felt that *sacrorum detestatio* was sufficient to render him a plebeian. Metellus Celer disagreed.

Hence the senatorial debate mentioned by Cicero at *Att.* 2.1.5 (written in early June). Clodius's improvisations over the past months had brought him to a position that was unclear at least to some, for there should have been no debate whatsoever if the whole of the senate immediately saw Clodius's actions along the lines asserted by Metellus Celer. Cicero's adulatory praise of Celer's resistance to his kinsman's designs makes plain the strenuous quality of the consul's opposition. Others will have expressed their views as well, including Clodius himself.[72] Cicero, now convinced that Clodius earnestly sought to become tribune and anxious over the consequences for himself, joined the fray. And, on this day, the orator was victorious: "I broke the man," he reported to Atticus. The attitude of the senate was enough to put a stop to Clodius's experimentation with *transitio ad plebem*. He had attempted to transfer by a *lex centuriata*, but had been blocked by tribunician veto. He had floated other procedural possibilities for becoming plebeian, settling finally on *sacrorum detestatio*, which Clodius believed sufficient for a valid *transitio*. However, the opposition of the consul was sustained in senatorial debate. All of which left Clodius in a worse condition than any he had previously suffered: he had by now alienated a powerful relation, he had offended by his stubbornness those in the senate who had suspected his motives, and, through his dramatic and drastic undertakings, he had advertised his political impotence.

6

Of course, 60 was a year for frustrated men, the most consequential of whom was Pompey the Great. The difficulties attending his return from the East are well known.[73] In 60, he had hoped, the energies of the reliable Afranius would secure the passage of his eastern *acta*, but this enterprise crumbled under the pressure of senatorial resistance. Changing flanks, the great man deployed a tribune, L. Flavius, who sponsored an agrarian law intended to provide benefits both for Pompey's veterans and for the urban *plebs*.[74] Again there was senatorial hostility. Lucullus and Cato took the lead, but it was Metellus Celer's opposition that proved decisive. When the tribune went so far as to imprison the refractory consul, who thereupon summoned an obedient senate to his cell, the matter degenerated into a farce. All of which was an embarrassment for Pompey, whose politics had failed yet again. At this time, understandably enough, Pompey began making a conspicuous shift toward Cicero.[75] But not only toward Cicero. In the aftermath of the Flavius debacle, Pompey began to cultivate Clodius.

Nothing is known of Pompey's advances toward Clodius but brief observations in two of Plutarch's *Lives*. Neither text is free of difficulties.[76] In each passage, Clodius is described as a leading demagogue, a thing he clearly was not in 60 for all his noises about becoming a tribune. But Plutarch, in order to depict Pompey's desperate straits, seeks to represent the Sullan general as reliant on the man who will soon emerge as his *popularis* foil (the disgrace of it all is amplified in the *Pompey*). The focus is not on Clodius, however, but on Pompey.[77] Moreover, in each passage,

Clodius serves principally to prefigure and to underscore Pompey's fateful move toward the *popularis* and Marian who would ultimately prove a more redoubtable foe, namely Caesar. In other words, as so often in Plutarch, literary concerns have taken priority over purely historical ones. But Plutarch need not have invented Pompey's overtures to Clodius. The great man had an eye for talent, however minor the figure, and he knew how to be amicable without making substantive commitments. Still, whatever relationship came to exist between Pompey and Clodius, it was unquestionably overshadowed from Pompey's perspective by the return of Caesar, his election to the consulship, and the formation of the coalition known as the First Triumvirate.

Clodius's activities subsequent to Caesar's return and during the first three months of his consulship are matters for conjecture.[78] He had few options but to pursue his connection with Pompey and to look hopefully toward Caesar, to whom the young patrician was already deeply obliged.[79] The powerful *factio*, however, was interested in recruiting at a higher level: in December 60 it appealed (unsuccessfully) to Cicero to join its company.[80] Clodius, by contrast, had little to offer, even in a junior capacity, except obedience. There was no motive for the triumvirs to cut Clodius loose, but nor is there any reason to assume that they did more than keep him waiting in the wings. Through the fall and winter, then, as perhaps at no other time in his life, Clodius was consigned to play the lackey, all the while anxious to steal the spotlight. His big break came in March 59.

The first months of Caesar's consulship proved utterly shocking. By resorting to intimidation and to outright violence, the coalition had quite suppressed the opposition of M. Calpurnius Bibulus, who was Caesar's colleague, Lucullus, and Cato.[81] Caesar's tactics were unabashedly *popularis* in character, a strategy that tended to intensify *invidia senatus* as the *plebs* rallied behind the dynasts. Cicero, who shared the senate's alarm and indignation over Caesar's methods, became anxious over his own position as well, a reaction that was natural enough inasmuch as he had become a target for antisenatorial sentiments.[82] Still, one should not overestimate the triumvirate's success: thanks to its own extreme methods, the coalition had to anticipate a backlash once its opposition became galvanized (a process hastened by their enormities) and once that opposition found an opportunity to strike back. One such moment seemed to come at the trial of C. Antonius, Cicero's unsavory fellow consul in 63.[83] Despite his distaste for the man, Cicero felt obliged to defend Antonius because, under current political conditions, he saw the prosecution as an attack upon himself. His defense of Antonius took the shape of a contumacious diatribe, exposing the threat posed to the republic by the triumvirs' violence and in particular denouncing Caesar virulently. Antonius was condemned, but Cicero's invective had hit its mark: Caesar was sorely wounded—and was outraged—while the coalition itself was thoroughly unnerved.[84] Within only a few hours of Cicero's speech, the triumvirs arranged for Clodius to become a plebeian, a response the immediacy and the extremity of which constitute ample evidence for the coalition's insecurity. Cicero was taken aback, and even Clodius may have been pleasantly surprised to find himself, at long last, a plebeian. But the circumstances of his transfer will not have escaped him, nor the indignity of having been shunted aside for months until he was required as a sort of bogey man to frighten Cicero. Nor will Clodius have failed to perceive the fragility of a coalition that was driven to such actions while believing itself to be his master.

7

But first the technicalities. Clodius finally became plebeian by adoption, the means he had striven in 60 to avoid.[85] Since he was *sui juris*, Clodius could only avail himself of the form of adoption called *adrogatio*, a procedure that, because it involved a drastic change in a citizen's status (viz. passing into the *potestas* of another), required public sanction in the form of a decree of the *comitia curiata* (for this reason Clodius was stalled in his every effort to become a plebeian, since even *adrogatio* required the formal assent of a public assembly).[86] Caesar, as consul, summoned the curiate assembly (i.e., the thirty lictors who represented the *curiae*) and promulgated the *rogatio de adrogatione*.[87] In his role as pontifex maximus, he sanctioned the propriety of the adoption, while Pompey, who attended as augur, made sure that no unfavorable omens were observed. The assembly then approved Clodius's adoption by P. Fonteius, a plebeian youth of some twenty years, who forthwith emancipated his new son.[88]

After his return from exile in 57, Cicero objected that Clodius's adoption had been invalid and so his tribunate had been illegal.[89] This claim comes in his speech *De Domo*, which was delivered before the pontiffs as part of Cicero's effort to recover his property on the Palatine Hill. The orator claimed that Clodius's adoption by Fonteius violated the spirit of *adrogatio* proceedings (which was doubtless true) and he absurdly prophesied the extinction of the patriciate were Clodius's precedent to be allowed to stand.[90] He also brought more specific criticism to bear on the matter: (1) Fonteius was too young to adopt Clodius, his senior by several years; (2) the pontifical college had not investigated the adoption before it was approved by the curiate assembly; (3) Clodius did not become Fonteius's heir, but instead continued to use his old name and to maintain Claudian *sacra*; (4) the transaction took place while Bibulus was watching the skies; and (5) in summoning the *comitia curiata*, Caesar failed to observe the *lex Caecilia et Didia*.[91]

Before we take up these points, it must be stressed that Cicero presses them in a case argued before the pontifical college in 57. Cicero did not question the legality of Clodius's *adrogatio* in his private correspondence in 59, although he had retired to his country estates owing to the menace presented by Clodius.[92] Only in the aftermath of his exile, and for obvious reasons, did Cicero impugn the legitimacy of Clodius's tribunate on the grounds that his adoption had been defective. But Cicero got very little purchase on his objection. The orator was forced to concede that few saw things his way, and in fact, when he was eventually constrained to defend Caesar's consular legislation, he actually adduced the universal opinion that Clodius's tribunate had been completely valid in order to demonstrate the legitimacy of Caesar's actions.[93] Consequently, whatever conviction Cicero may have hoped his arguments to carry, and however reliable they may seem to us, none of them convinced his contemporaries.

A natural societal concern underlies Cicero's objection to Fonteius's youth, and it must surely have been uncustomary for an older man to be adopted by a younger one. However, even under the empire it remained undecided whether a younger man could adopt an older, and it was not until the late empire that the practice was expressly forbidden.[94] As to the role of the pontiffs in *adrogatio* proceedings, this complaint is part of the orator's pose in *De Domo* of comprehensive deference to the competence of the college hearing his case. In his discussion of *adrogatio*, Gellius informs us that by his day, owing to the seriousness of the operation, pontiffs were present to make inquiry into the appropriateness of an adrogation and to supervise the administration of the oath formulated by Q. Mucius Scaevola (perhaps an element of the *sacrorum detestatio* that was part of the adrogation procedure).[95] It is reasonable to assume that a pontifical presence was always customary at adrogation proceedings, though whether, as Cicero implies at *Dom.* 38, a formal decree of the college was required seems less likely. Apparently it was Caesar's view that the supervision of the pontifex maximus was adequate for official purposes. Nor can we be sure, as Slagter has pointed out, that no other pontiffs attended the ceremony.[96] The problem posed by Bibulus's nonstop *spectio* throughout 59 was more serious and perhaps explains Pompey's authoritative presence as augur.[97] Bibulus's controversial obstruction will be discussed more fully in the next chapter. Here it will suffice to note that the objection went unvoiced in 59 until Caesar himself vainly attempted to repudiate Clodius's adoption (at a time when Clodius was threatening, if elected tribune, to rescind Caesar's legislation).[98] By 57 that was a dead issue.

Which brings us to two arguments of little obvious consequence to the legality of Clodius's *adrogatio* but which say much for his attitude toward the process. After his adoption, Clodius's name ought to have become P. Fonteius P. f. Pulcher (or, alternately, Clodianus), yet he retained his old name familiarly and officially.[99] Furthermore, his children continued to bear the Claudian name.[100] Habits of nomenclature in the late republic are problematic, but parallels for Clodius's practice exist, though all postdate Clodius's adrogation. From the eighty-three cases of adoption documented by Shackleton Bailey for the period 130–40,[101] we know of eight instances comparable to Clodius's, a sampling of which will demonstrate that Clodius, though diverging from common custom, was not acting illegally: D. Brutus (cos. desig. 42) preserved his name even after his adoption by a Postumius Albinus. In a situation somewhat closer to that of Clodius, P. Cornelius Lentulus Spinther, adopted in 57 by a Manlius Torquatus in order to enter the college of augurs, continued to style himself P. Lentulus P. f. in correspondence and on coinage. Finally, Dolabella, who with full presence of mind imitated Clodius in arranging to be adopted by a plebeian in order to stand for the tribunate, never took the name of his adoptive *gens*, though his son did.[102] Unless Clodius was a trendsetter, one must conclude that during the late republic Romans were not overly scrupulous about adoptive nomenclature. Still, Clodius certainly could have called himself Fonteius, and the evidence that we possess suggests that it would have been a normal practice for him to have done so. That he chose to do otherwise indicates his unwillingness to be severed from his Claudian station.

A further expression of his determination to retain his position as a Claudius Pulcher (albeit a plebeian one) was Clodius's refusal to exchange Claudian *sacra* for Fonteian, despite the formal *sacrorum detestatio*, which had been necessary for the *adrogatio*. Cicero can hardly be inventing Clodius's preservation of his native *sacra*, but that concession does not entail our accepting his assertion that such an action vitiated the adoption. Obviously neither Fonteius nor the remaining patrician Claudii Pulchri lodged protests, and in any event the policing of private *sacra* seems to have been a matter left to the jurisdiction of the censors: our entire evidence for such scrutiny comes from the strict census of the elder Cato, who applied the *nota censoria* to a L. Veturius for his neglect of family *sacra*.[103] Exceptionable though Clodius's obvious manipulation of the adrogation process may have been, that in itself did not constitute an invalidating illegality.

Cicero insists that the *lex curiata* which confirmed Clodius's adrogation was void on the ground that Caesar had not let a *trinum nundinum* elapse before the convocation of the *comitia curiata*, thereby violating the *lex Caecilia et Didia* of 98.[104] The suddenness with which Clodius was trundled out for transfer to the *plebs* seems to add heft to Cicero's brief, though the whole issue raises the question of why Cicero never raised so apparently straightforward and reasonable a legal objection in 59, a time when (as we shall see presently) he felt very threatened by Clodius. Nor, one must add, did anyone else object to Caesar's actions on this basis. The likeliest conclusion is that the *lex Caecilia et Didia* did not explicitly apply (and therefore was not construed as applying) to the *comitia curiata*. The innocuous legislation that ordinarily fell within its purview and the ease with which it was convened distinguished the curiate assembly from the important *comitia* (the *centuriata* and *tributa* as well as the *concilium plebis*) that came logically within the scope of the law. When Cicero invokes the *lex Caecilia et Didia* in *De Domo*, the only exemplum he adduces to illustrate the consequences of its violation is the annulment of M. Livius Drusus's tribunician acts, "quae contra legem Caeciliam et Didiam latae essent" (*Dom.* 41).[105] Now Drusus's legislation was in fact rescinded en bloc, but not (so far as we know) because it failed to comply with the stipulation demanding a *trinum nundinum*; rather, Drusus's laws seem to have been annulled because they were passed *per vim* or *contra auspicia* or, possibly, *per saturam*.[106] The introduction of Drusus is of course intended to remind the pontiffs of a relevant precedent for abrogating tribunician measures, but the effect of the reference is largely psychological: the requirement of a *trinum nundinum* is irrelevant to the validity of Drusus's program, which itself is irrelevant to the proceedings of the *comitia curiata*. Cicero, then, in claiming that the *lex Caecilia et Didia* was violated, was attempting through the misrepresentation of the law to prejudice the pontiffs against Clodius on the matter of the orator's recovery of his property. His reference to the law hardly constitutes reliable evidence for its application to Clodius's adoption. This is not the only instance in *De Domo* of Ciceronian distortion of particular pieces of legislation when they can be fitted to his argument.[107]

In summary, Cicero's critique of Clodius's adoption is a mixture of invention and biased reportage. Nevertheless, it is plain that Clodius's adrogation was a mere expedient that allowed the triumvirs to frighten

Cicero and permitted Clodius to become eligible for the tribunate. It was a remarkable occurrence, though not an illegal one. But, as Cicero does manage to demonstrate, Clodius's behavior was uncustomary in certain respects and therefore objectionable. His ultimate success in transferring to the *plebs* can only have stirred greater consternation in a year already marked by apprehensiveness.

8

Clodius's adoption was engineered and executed by Caesar and Pompey in order to silence Cicero.[108] The adoption surely had been discussed in advance, but its sudden actualization suggests that no definite plans had been developed by the dynasts or by Clodius. Cicero retired to his country estates, a response perfectly satisfactory to Caesar, where he endeavored to stay apprised of political events at Rome—and especially of Clodius's designs—through various informants, chief among them Atticus.[109] The accommodating equestrian enjoyed easy access to Clodia Metelli, who was intimate with her brother's schemes, and perhaps to Clodius himself.[110] The hypothetical transition having become a reality, Clodius's political situation was transformed. He had but to stand to become tribune, in which office he could certainly be expected to apply his full energies. But to what purpose? Cicero obviously feared for his own safety. The triumvirs must have felt fairly confident that they could count on Clodius's gratitude and consequently his obedience, but, if that was their estimation of Clodius, they were doomed to swift disappointment. The newly formed plebeian saw at once that his personal prospects did not count high among the coalition's priorities. And he soon came to appreciate that, the precise nature of his future tribunate being undetermined, he had something to dangle before all parties in the struggles of 59, dynasts and *optimates* alike. Despite the *popularis* pose of the Bona Dea affair, he was in a position to recreate himself now. That had largely been the point of his desire to become a plebeian in the first place.

At the start, Clodius appeared to cooperate with the coalition. He threw himself behind Vatinius's proposal to establish a Gallic command for Caesar, which was probably promulgated in April.[111] This effort should not be attributed purely to gratitude: Clodius was hopeful of being selected for the agrarian commission created by Caesar's earlier law regulating the distribution of Campanian land.[112] Other prizes for Clodius were floated: one was an enormously profitable embassy, perhaps to Alexandria as part of Rome's recognition of Ptolemy XII as the legitimate monarch of Egypt.[113] The fact that Clodius anticipated one or both of these honors makes it plain that he tended to view himself as someone whose support the coalition must cultivate. In the event, however, neither distinction materialized. Instead Clodius was pressed to undertake an embassy to the court of Tigranes, a signal honor to be sure, but not, apparently, a remuneration adequate to compensate him for postponing his tribunate, which probably would be necessary if he were to depart for the East this late in the year.[114] Offices sought, offices denied, and offices refused, the pattern indicates that Clodius and the triumvirs had not yet arrived at a mutually satisfactory collaboration. Clodius's willfulness must have made his coming tribunate appear too risky for the coalition to hazard, hence the effort to distract him by sending him to Tigranes. Still, their purpose was not to break with Clodius or even to forbid the possibility of his ever being tribune (which would cost them their hold over Cicero); rather, they wanted to make it clear that he was not a full partner with his seniors. Cicero, at least, could enjoy the dissension between Clodius and his benefactors, and he took special glee that Clodius was being treated so disgracefully, not so much like a tribune as a *tabellarius*.[115]

Cicero continued to count as an element in the calculus of April 59. Although Caesar would have appeared justified, after Antonius's trial, in turning Clodius loose on the orator, for Pompey it was a point of honor that he shield his friend from the man he chose to regard as his creature.[116] Consequently the means were contrived whereby Cicero might escape Clodius's menace, should it prove necessary and so long as the orator was willing to become indebted to the coalition. As for Clodius's ambition, intense after the past months of embarrassment and impotence, it was not to be slaked by an embassy to the East. Against the wishes of Caesar and Pompey, Clodius declared his determination to stand for the tribunate. The swelling unpopularity of the dynasts emboldened Clodius to challenge them openly—or at least to challenge one of them openly: he pronounced himself *inimicissimus Caesaris* and vowed, once tribune, to rescind his new enemy's legislation.[117] Caesar responded with a vain attempt to repudiate Clodius's adoption, but it carried no credibility.[118] Too many in the senate were keen to see the consul discomfited, and the threat to attack Caesar's legislation instantly rendered Clodius a prospective optimate. Though suspect and isolated since the Bona Dea scandal, he appeared no danger to the senate when set next to the triumvirate. Even his archenemy was impressed by Clodius's boldness: "let him, let him be elected tribune," wrote Cicero to Atticus, in a letter in which he disparaged Bibulus's efforts to resist the dynasts as noble but useless. Clodius's hostility to Caesar, Cicero hoped, would split the coalition.[119] However calculated this demonstration was on Clodius's part, his conspicuous willingness to oppose Caesar advertised the future tribune's independence and enhanced his own political importance.[120]

Still, one must not exaggerate Clodius's significance. The most strikingly popular symbol of anti-Caesarian sentiment was Clodius's friend, the younger Curio. He led the youthful opposition to the consul.[121] And others were stirred to express their animosity as well, such as Metellus Nepos and C. Memmius, to name but two.[122] However, though Nepos was a kinsman of Clodius and Curio an *amicus*, it goes too far to postulate a Clodian group beginning to form behind Clodius's interests.[123] It makes far more sense to see these men as fellow opportunists taking advantage of the coalition's unpopularity to express each his own dissatisfaction and to advance each his own position. Curio may well have been influenced by Clodius, but he did not need his friend's encouragement to resent Caesar (who was already the object of his father's hatred). As for Nepos, his animosities were directed at Pompey, and they were motivated by personal factors (the humiliating cut signaled by Pompey's divorce of Mucia).

By May, Pompey was increasingly sensitive to his loss of respectability, caused in his opinion by Caesar's methods. His public pronouncements indicated a drift from the consul, the very thing Cicero had longed for.[124] But Caesar reacted adroitly: he reinforced his alliance with Pompey by granting him the privilege of speaking first in the senate and, far more important, by arranging a marriage between his own daughter and the great man.[125] Clodius's activities in May fade from the record, but he must have recognized Caesar's success in repositioning himself. He certainly remained on good enough terms with Pompey that the latter could persist in his assurances to Cicero that Clodius was dependable.[126] The orator, whatever he thought of Pompey's guarantees, no longer believed that Clodius could break up the coalition (impossible now that Pompey had married Julia), nor, more significantly, did he entertain hope that Clodius would expend his energies opposing the dynasts.[127] For their part, the triumvirs seem to have become reconciled to the inevitability of Clodius's tribunate. By the end of the month, prospective candidates for offices in 58 were required by the terms of Caesar's second—and controversial—agrarian law (concerning Campania) to take an oath of allegiance to that measure before a *contio* summoned for the very purpose.[128] Only M. Iuventius Laterensis (pr. 51), who had intended to stand for the tribunate, refused to swear, which means that Clodius must have joined all the other possible candidates in binding themselves to the *execratio* of Caesar's law, a gesture that, if carried out in Caesar's presence (if, as seems likely, he convened the meeting),[129] must have given public definition to the two men's détente.

Tensions persisted, nevertheless. Clodius, for all his courtesy toward Pompey, would not relent from threatening Cicero.[130] Because Pompey was said to bear responsibility for the adoption, public opinion anticipated an open break between the orator and Pompey over Clodius.[131] But, though frustrated in so many particulars in his dealings with Clodius, Pompey refused to be embarrassed on this point: he demanded that Clodius and Appius Claudius give pledges for Cicero's security, and they acquiesced. Though he would not desist from harsh abuse, Clodius promised not to act against Pompey's wishes.[132] Yet Clodius's schemes remained unpredictable: one moment he attacked the triumvirs, the next he moved against the *boni*.[133] Doubtless he hoped to cut a truly independent path, to configure himself as a man to be taken seriously yet not one beyond the pale of negotiation. For a politician who lacked any real basis for power, this strategy perhaps represented the best way to remain a player. But the game was precarious, and Cicero, for one, hoped Clodius would falter in the attempt.[134]

9

In July or August, the tribunician elections for 58 were held, at which, predictably, Clodius was successful in his canvass.[135] Still, the tribune-elect remained something of an unknown quantity. Pompey may have felt confident in his grip on Clodius, but Caesar must have been less sanguine. The consular *comitia* had been postponed, after all, another significant variable to fret about, and Caesar, soon to take up an exacting province, cannot have been untroubled by the prospect of so ostensibly inconstant a figure as Clodius wielding the powers of a tribune in Rome with only Pompey, himself still hankering after senatorial respectability, there to restrain and direct him. Clodius, given his ambiguous signals regarding the *boni*, might actually yield to Pompey's insistence that he dismiss his hostilities toward Cicero, or so Caesar had to worry; indeed, Clodius might begin to reckon the optimate cause the stronger one (especially if the consular elections went against the coalition) and decide to place his tribunician resources at the disposal of the dynasts' enemies. How would Pompey conduct himself under such circumstances?

The Vettius affair eliminated all such doubts. The indisputable facts of the incident are few enough to stimulate, now as then, copious speculation.[136] A certain L. Vettius, who had been an informer for Cicero during the Catilinarian conspiracy, approached the younger Curio, whose acquaintance he had fostered, with information concerning a plot to assassinate Pompey. Curio at once reported the scheme to his father, who told Pompey and who introduced the matter to the senate. Vettius, summoned before the *patres*, was allowed, despite protests, to explain himself. He revealed that Curio, along with the noble youth of whom he was leader, and with support from Bibulus, had planned to murder Pompey. The allegations were refuted and rejected. Vettius was placed in chains. But, on the next day, Caesar produced the man before the people so that he might again retail his story. This time he offered a new supply of conspirators: Lucullus, C. Fannius, L. Domitius—and Cicero. Prosecutions were said to be in the air, but, before any action could be taken, Vettius was found dead. The incident was sensational and important, but its author resists discovery. Cicero believed that Caesar was the chief conniver behind the plot, and most scholars have inclined toward this view. But other candidates have been put forward as well, including Pompey himself.[137] The mystery persists.

One clear result of the Vettius affair was the estrangement of Pompey from Cicero, a consequence which has prompted the proposal that Clodius was the real mastermind of the incident.[138] But not a shred of evidence exists to implicate Clodius. His name is never associated with the affair even by Cicero—even in the aftermath of the orator's exile, when his anti-Clodian invective was at its most inventive. For Clodius to have eluded all gossip and all Ciceronian suspicion seems incredible—especially given the prominence of the Curiones—unless he was truly unconnected with the plot. In other words, nothing supports the theory that Clodius was behind the Vettius affair except the fact that its consequences were to some degree in his benefit, and that is no proof that he engineered them. The advantage Clodius took from the Vettius affair indicates rather the remarkable deftness that he was beginning to show on occasion. The threat against Pompey's life restored the great man—and his coalition—to popular favor.[139] The consular elections, long delayed, returned L. Calpurnius Piso, Caesar's father-in-law, and Aulus Gabinius, Pompey's longtime friend.[140] C. Cato attempted to prosecute Gabinius for *ambitus*, but the praetors denied him even a hearing. Outraged, he assailed Pompey as *privatus dictator*, whereupon he received a brutal thrashing, violence that punctuated the renewed clout of the triumvirate.[141] So Clodius pursued friendship with Pompey and rapprochement with Caesar.[142] Neither his association with Curio nor his past lack of cooperation could be used against him now that his loyal intentions were being made manifest. And he was better placed than ever to nurture in Pompey's mind the suspicions about Cicero that Vettius had planted.[143]

Clodius's solid shift toward the coalition was clear enough to Cicero: for the first time in 59 he began to expect the support of the *boni* should Clodius bring an indictment against him.[144] If there was any lingering uncertainty on anyone's part, it was removed when, at the end of the year, Clodius, now tribune, prevented Bibulus from speaking when he laid down his consulship.[145] Clodius, it had to be obvious to all, was the dynasts' new champion in the college of tribunes.[146] And, while he had displayed his characteristic willfulness and had tried to advertise his political independence, Clodius had in the end seen how much power could be created and exerted in a combination and how necessary it was to have one's own resources if one desired to play more than a bit part in any coalition. At the commencement of his tribunate, then, Clodius was seen as the triumvirs' man, formidable in energies and in arrogance, but hardly so powerful that he could not be managed. Indeed, by many in the senate it will have been assumed that Piso and Gabinius were the men to make their mark on 58. Few can have anticipated that Clodius had done far more to prepare for his office than merely flaunt its potential usefulness to the dynasts. In fact, he had formulated a dynamic and far-reaching legislative program that would mark him out as the ultimate *popularis*—and yet also something rather more.

CHAPTER FIVE

Popular Tribune

1

On 10 December 59, the day he entered his tribunate, Clodius Pulcher promulgated four bills, all of which subsequently passed into law without opposition, *quattuor leges perniciosae*, as Asconius dubs them.[1] These laws provided the foundation for Clodius's formidable tribunician career and helped to establish a basis for political power not only in 58 but well beyond. The legislation, as we shall see presently, was far-reaching, acutely relevant, and, what is perhaps less often observed, balanced enough to give Clodius the *popularis* credentials he sought without thoroughly alienating his senatorial contemporaries. Clodius did not suck these measures from his thumb: they represented the product of much thought, careful formulation, and a good deal of what we might call research. In drafting his legislative program, an activity that may have begun as early as July 59, Clodius must have entered into numerous consultations, though in circles apparently unvisited by Cicero. Still, while Clodius must have expected the obvious results of his four laws, one ought to hesitate before assuming that from the start Clodius foresaw all their ramifications. Clodius's legislative program won enormous popularity for its author and soon gave him the opportunity to devise novel means for the rapid and violent mobilization of the *plebs urbana*. The first benefit was anticipated by the tribune; the second advantage, however, can hardly have been calculated from the beginning.

This is perhaps the moment to remind ourselves of the fact that no Roman politician ever operated alone or in literal isolation, though it is normally convenient to speak as if that were the case. All aristocrats, and Clodius was no exception, enjoyed a wealth of retainers, freedmen, and clients, whose gratitude and services they could rely on in ordinary and extraordinary circumstances alike.[2] Consequently, it should occasion no surprise that, as Clodius's stature in Roman political affairs becomes more conspicuous, several of his subordinates begin to emerge into view. Scholars have collected their names, and they are frequently described as *Clodiani* (or referred to by Ciceronian rubrics like *duces operarum* or even *operae Clodianae*), all expressions of limited exactitude and therefore minor usefulness.[3] Some humble figures associated with Clodius's activities in 58 (and subsequently) will have been, as we shall see, shopkeepers and heads of *collegia*. As such, they constitute a remarkable constituency, which will require further discussion. But Clodius had not yet secured such loyalties at the commencement of his tribunate. More to the point at that moment were figures like Damio, a freedman of Clodius who participated in the political violence of 58, and obvious clients like C. Clodius and P. Clodius (both active in the courts) and possible ones like T. Claudius (Clodius's *subscriptor* in a prosecution in 56).[4] Other likely subordinates at this time (client may be too precise a term here) were a certain Titius from Reate, soon to be *dux et auctor* of gangs of *mercenarii*, L. Gavius, described by Cicero as *P. Clodi canis*, T. Patina, a certain Scato, and Pola Servius, *homo taeter et ferus*, another apparition of the courts.[5] Such men, though naturally defamed by Cicero, were useful and even necessary to Clodius. But he was hardly unique in possessing such associates.

Nor was Clodius the only tribune to have the services of a scribe, though the relationship that developed between himself and Sex. Cloelius, unless it antedated his year in office, was truly extraordinary. Indeed, it may be that Cloelius was not actually Clodius's *scriba tribunarius* and that the origin of their connection is to be found elsewhere. But in 58 and subsequently, Cloelius emerges as Clodius's right-hand man, the partner of his labors and the man chiefly responsible for the actual drafting of Clodius's legislation. Cloelius may have been a freedman (some scribes were), but again it seems more likely that he was an *ingenuus* stemming from an aspiring family in Terracina. As a scribe, he belonged to an order at which an eminent senator might sneer but one nevertheless whose members possessed ample wealth individually and formidable clout collectively. In the aftermath of Clodius's death in 52, Cloelius was condemned for violence and exiled. No less a figure than M. Antony, when consul, secured his return to the city.[6]

Clodius enjoyed notable supporters as well. D. Brutus Albinus has been suspected of having been a youthful adherent. M. Antony certainly was. One fascinating lieutenant was Gellius, the brother of L. Gellius Publicola (cos. 72) and the son of L. Marcius Philippus (cos. 91). Though of noble extraction, Gellius remained equestrian and, notoriously, married a freedwoman. On Cicero's hateful reckoning he cut a disgraceful and violent figure, *nutricula seditiosorum omnium*, but his caste, at least, was clearly superior to the orator's own.[7] Followers like these belong to a completely different category from the freedmen and clients whom we have met thus far. These were *amici*, which meant that they were *Clodiani* only so long as they cared to be. And in the course of events Gellius and Clodius had a temporary falling out, and Antony ultimately broke with Clodius—though he championed his memory.[8]

The point of this has been to make explicit the degree to which Clodius was, even when "on his own" so to speak, a consortium of interests and obligations. But none of this constitutes a Clodian party in any meaningful sense. Exact affiliations tend to resist a neat taxonomy in Rome in any case. Clodius had also to consider his partners and rivals in government during the coming year. L. Calpurnius Piso and A. Gabinius, the consuls for 58, were intimates of Caesar and Pompey. On the other hand, the dynasts, especially Caesar, who would possess no executive powers in Rome itself during 58, remained unpopular in the senate. Two praetors for the coming year, Domitius Ahenobarbus and C. Memmius, were vocal enemies of the coalition and were soon to attempt to overthrow Caesar's *acta*.[9] Clodius, who could count few friends among his tribunician colleagues, concluded that his best chances sat with the consuls, which meant that cooperation with the triumvirs had to constitute an important element of his tribunician strategy.[10] Hence his treatment of Bibulus as the latter left office. But matters were not quite so simple. Clodius had by this point learned the necessity of working in combination with those more powerful than himself, a hard lesson for the arrogant patrician, but one that made him, at this stage at least, keen to avoid provoking the utter hostility of the senatorial majority, as Caesar had done. Under these circumstances, with so many hazards to be negotiated by a tribune of such prodigious ambition, it becomes equally meaningless to speak of Clodius as an instrument or as an independent agent. From different perspectives he was both—or neither. Which simply meant that he had become a full participant in the continuing contest of Roman politics.

Between the promulgation of Clodius's four laws and their adoption, the tribune began to advertise the significance of his new program and had to contend with resistance from his most predictable opponent, Cicero. But, before turning to the politics of this *trinum nundinum*, it will be convenient to make a thorough examination of the *quattuor leges* themselves, after which we can return to the story of their introduction and enactment. Clodius's four laws were (1) the *lex de collegiis*, which rehabilitated the *collegia* suppressed by the *senatus consultum* of 64 and which allowed for the enrollment of new *collegia*; (2) a *lex frumentaria*, providing for the distribution of modest amounts of free grain; (3) the *lex de agendo cum populo* (frequently called the *lex Clodia de obnuntiatione* by modern scholars), which modified the *leges Aelia et Fufia*; and (4) the *lex de censoria notione*, which reformed the procedure by which censors conducted the *lectio senatus*.[11] Each of these laws will be described in turn and in detail.

2

Lex Clodius de collegiis. It has been remarked already how *collegia* played a role in Roman political life—prosperous professional *collegia* and *collegia tenuiorum* alike.[12] The latter were, for obvious reasons, perceived by the senate as vulnerable to political manipulation—an apprehension underscored by certain events during the sixties. At the time of the Ludi Compitalicii in 67, the tribune C. Manilius forced the passage of a law distributing the votes of freedmen throughout all the tribes (instead of containing them in the urban tribes); in late December 66 there was once again violent and subversive activity, subsequently obfuscated by the fiction of the First Catilinarian Conspiracy.[13] As a result of such incidents, the senate passed a decree in 64 that abolished *collegia* deemed hostile to the state and forbade the annual celebration of the Ludi Compitalicii.[14] Exactly which colleges were included in the senate's ban remains the subject of debate—and surely the senate's decree admitted the possibility of lengthening the list of subversive *collegia*—but it is no longer reasonable to conclude that all but a few *collegia* were made illegal at this time.[15] The fact that the senate outlawed the Ludi Compitalicii supplies a valuable clue: these *ludi* were observed after the Saturnalia in honor of the Lares Compitales, the deities of the crossroads who watched over Rome's neighborhoods.[16] The Lares Compitales and their festival appealed primarily to the lower classes, and at least since the days of Mommsen scholars have spoken of *collegia compitalia*, though attestation for the existence of such colleges, devoted to the cultivation of the Lares and constituting the basic unit of local urban organization, is exceedingly thin.[17] Indeed, quite cogent arguments have been adduced for attributing the "official" cultivation of the Lares Compitales and the celebration of the Ludi Compitalicii to the *magistri vicorum*, thereby removing the participation of the *collegia stricto sensu* to the private sphere altogether.[18] Confident conclusions face formidable obstacles, however:

the relationship between *vici* (and other regional associations) and the occupational and religious *collegia* has yet to be determined in such a way as to win scholarly consensus—a state of affairs for which the lack of clarity in our sources, both literary and epigraphic, is responsible. Consequently, overly schematic descriptions of these associations are hazardous in the present condition of our knowledge.[19] Still, it is certain that *collegia* participated in the Ludi Compitalicii, whatever their precise or officially sanctioned role, and it is reasonably certain that these *collegia* were for the most part *collegia tenuiorum*. There was, to be sure, popular resistance to the suppression of colleges by the senate: in 61 an unknown tribune lent his *auxilium* to the *collegia* who attempted to celebrate the Ludi Compitalicii, though the effort was frustrated by the consul-designate, Metellus Celer, whose redoubtable *auctoritas* overawed the tribune as well as the celebrants.[20]

The forbidden *collegia* were restored to legitimacy by Clodius's *lex de collegiis*.[21] Furthermore, Clodius's law allowed for the establishment of new *collegia*, the enrollment of which was part of an exhaustive recording, district by district, of the city's colleges, *tota urbe descriptio* as Cicero called it (*Dom.* 129). This *descriptio* was conducted at the Aurelian tribunal, where the tribune both compiled the lists of city's *collegiati* and divided them further into *centuriatae* and *decuriae*.[22] Cicero ridiculed the enterprise as a *dilectus servorum*, a criticism that raises the question of the participation of slaves in the *collegia*, especially in the newly formed *collegia*. In fact *servi* did enjoy membership in *collegia*; however, the prevailing social biases affecting slaves in Rome were replicated even in humble colleges.[23] Not slaves but freedmen composed the majority in Rome's *collegia*—in particular, one suspects, the occupational *collegia*.[24] Now it was Cicero's habit, again reflecting the prejudices of Roman society, to refer to *libertini* in servile terms when he meant to depict them unfavorably, as he regularly did when *collegia* supported the hateful tribune.[25] Thus it is impossible to take Cicero's descriptions of *collegia* literally. The same can be said for the orator's hostile reviews of Clodius's popular following: the statesman who frequently referred to Rome's regular citizenry as scum and sewage did not scruple to represent the *Clodiani* as slaves.[26]

At the same time, it must be admitted that the newly founded *collegia* were likely to comprise individuals who had previously been unable to obtain membership even in modest colleges, presumably because they were too impoverished to pay the most minimal dues, which suggests that the *nova collegia* enrolled Romans of the poorest stamp.[27] These *collegia* would require at least some patronage if they were to offer any of the benefits of ordinary colleges.[28] Which is not to say that such patronage came from Clodius; smaller fry, men like Clodius's associates Sex. Cloelius or C. Clodius, possessed substance enough to assist these lowly colleges. In any case, it was probably not common meals or burial insurance that made the *nova collegia* precious to their members: the granting of state recognition bestowed on their organizations a sense of importance and significance that held out a prospect, however slender, of honor that was new for the destitute Romans who enrolled. Like the members of the traditional *collegia* that were restored by the tribune, the new *collegiati* had ample reason to feel grateful to the tribune who had raised their stake in public life by enhancing and enriching their local prestige.[29]

3

Lex Clodia frumentaria. While outright famine was rare, shortages of food were distressingly common in the Greco-Roman world.[30] In Rome of the late republic, a populous city that relied primarily on the importation of grain to feed its multitudes, poor inhabitants were at constant hazard owing most commonly to a scarcity of available grain caused by prices having risen beyond the ordinary Roman's budget, a state of affairs that ensued not merely from natural catastrophes and accidents but also from inadequate storage facilities, administrative muddle, or price gouging by speculators. Sicily, Sardinia, and Africa fed the urban populace, inadequately perhaps, but with tolerable consistency by and large. Throughout the republic, individual crises, which for obvious reasons affected the poor rather than the rich, were alleviated by ad hoc remedies, primarily by the emergency distribution of discounted grain, acts of euergetism rather than of policy. For the government's part, it strove to ensure that Rome's private suppliers had adequate facilities at their disposal in the grain-producing provinces as well as at Puteoli, Ostia, and Rome; moreover, it took pains to be sure that merchants engaged in reasonably sound business practices. These responsibilities resided with the provincial magistrates, with the *quaestor Ostiensis*, and, chiefly, with the aediles, though no tidy allocation of duties is preserved for our benefit.[31]

An exceptional sequence of disasters in the 130s in conjunction with increased demands for military procurements supplied the economic background to Gaius Gracchus's controversial *lex Sempronia frumentaria*, which provided for the monthly sale of a ration of grain to citizens domiciled at Rome at the fixed rate of 6⅓ asses (1½ sesterces) per modius.[32] Gracchus seems also to have encouraged the building of granaries to increase Rome's storage capacity and possibly to provide sites for distribution.[33] The *lex Sempronia* entailed no means test, as the sensational presence of L. Calpurnius Piso Frugi (cos. 133) among its beneficiaries attests, nor should we overestimate its utility to Rome's poorest citizens. Recipients still had to meet the cost of the subsidized grain, in addition to which they faced milling and baking charges. Furthermore, on the likely assumption that the ration allowed for was not much (if at all) greater than the five modii which would eventually become the standard allotment, its inadequacy as a source of nourishment even for an individual much less a household meant that purchasing grain at market prices would still be necessary. Nonetheless, Gaius's measure may have helped to stabilize prices somewhat and it certainly introduced a modicum of predictability to the grain market.[34] As such, it was revolutionary—and welcome to the people, though in the senate it incurred complaints of a distressingly modern and familiar temperament: Gaius's law, it was objected, would destroy the ordinary Roman's incentive to industry even while it bankrupted the treasury. Neither objection was true, but the pervasive perception that the subsidy was exorbitantly expensive forced Gaius to seek special revenues—and the government's fear of this entitlement's cost in fact outlived the republic.[35]

Various revisionary measures governing grain distributions supervened, including (apparently) a complete Sullan elimination of the program from 81 until 73, when the *lex Terentia et Cassia* restored the subsidy (now five modii per month) for good.[36] In 62 the tribune M. Cato, acting in response to Catilinarian unrest and with senatorial approval, passed a law extending the benefits of the *lex Terentia et Cassia* with the express purpose of assisting "the poor and the landless *plebs*" (Plut. *Cat. Min.* 26.1). Whatever the details of the *lex Porcia*, it is clear that this measure raised the cost of *frumentationes* by at least thirty million sesterces— the most dramatic increase in Rome's history to that point.[37] The absence of jeremiads decrying impending bankruptcy is owed to Cato's senatorial endorsement.

Gracchan origin and Sullan hostility sufficed to render any *commodum populi*, like a *lex frumentaria*, a *popularis* measure, even one secured *ex patrum auctoritate*. But the fear of scarcity and of price fluctuations was strong enough to cause discontent, demonstrations, and even riot without instigation from above.[38] The inclination of any politician to take advantage of the *plebs*' apprehensions, it might have been felt in the aftermath of the *lex Porcia*, had been sufficiently checked—hence Caesar's efforts in 59 to remove some of Rome's poor to the *ager Campanus* along with Pompey's veterans, a gesture that inter alia reflected continued difficulties in provisioning the city in 59. Expanding the scope of the *frumentationes* apparently either did not occur to Caesar or seemed beyond the pale so soon after Cato's legislation. In fact, if we can believe a passing remark of Cicero, their increasing unpopularity in mid-59 led Caesar and Pompey actually to threaten to eradicate the grain dole.[39]

The *lex Clodia* provided Roman citizens, in all likelihood those aged ten and over, a free monthly ration of five modii of grain.[40] That the law was *summe popularis* can scarcely be doubted, nor does Asconius's judgment require amplification. This is not to say that the *plebs frumentaria* was now limited to the poor, which it certainly was not; rather, for the first time the very poor were able to take full advantage of the literal fruits of Rome's empire.[41] Clodius's law was welcome to all divisions of the *plebs urbana* and won him the people's lasting devotion. But it goes too far to assert that his measure eliminated (or was intended to eliminate) opportunities for patrons to display private munificence to clients (even the Principate could not do that). Clodius was not out to supplant *clientela* with state social services: such a mentality was probably beyond the capacities of any Roman aristocrat, and in any case there is no reason to believe that humble Romans were anxious to escape the advantages, such as they were, of *clientela*. In consideration of the limited potential of *clientela* to influence political decision making at moments of earnest conflict, *favor populi* possessed its own appeal to the tribune.

It has been suggested that, because his later political leverage rested so heavily in his *popularitas*, Clodius needed to continue to appear before the *plebs* as their principal benefactor, which means that the *lex frumentaria* was simply the first step in Clodius's design to monopolize the provision of *commoda populi* thereafter, a commitment that would require him to take long-term charge of the grain supply and to guard the office jealously. But this is not how *popularis* politics tended to operate: it was not normally the case that the *plebs* kept expecting continued good works from a *tribunus popularis* beyond his year in office. Popularity, though secured by benefactions, was often more enduring than that, the amplitude of a tribune's good work being sufficient to secure *gratia* over a long period of time.[42] Nor should one always assume that only the basest motives lie behind public favor.[43] Clodius's law was a sensational success, but it was not necessary for him, nor was it intended by him, to become the permanent overseer of grain distributions or of public largesse generally in order to exploit the gratitude of the *plebs*.[44]

The increased cost of this public largesse, whatever the reliability of Cicero's reactionary fulminations, rapidly eclipsed those of the *lex Porcia*, with the result that the senate was obliged to instruct the curule aediles to mint a special issue of coinage in 58 and, more significantly,

Clodius soon felt it advantageous to entrust Cato with the annexation of Cyprus, a revenue-enhancing measure that paralleled the reorganization of Asia's finances by Gaius Gracchus and the senate's exercise of the Cyrene bequest in 74.[45] Figures and costings for Clodius's law have been generated, all based on sources reporting statistics that are sometimes dubious and always of uncertain application. As Geoffrey Rickman has aptly appraised matters, "the whole thing becomes a game with only one dangerous result, the delusion of certainty." Nonetheless, we shall probably not err by much if we tentatively conclude that Clodius's law provided a monthly dole to around 300,000 recipients at an annual cost to the state of approximately 108 million sesterces (exclusively for the grain, if the price to the state, which surely fluctuated, averaged around six sesterces per modius).[46] The point is that Clodius's measure *was* expensive and was doubtless perceived by many in the senate to be excessively so—though no tribune dared to impose his veto.

Clodius's law is often declared an unprecedented intrusion by the Roman government into the business of provisioning the city. Under the terms of the *lex frumentaria*, so the argument runs, Clodius's scribe, Sex. Cloelius, assumed powers not unlike those of Pompey's *cura annonae* in 57: Cloelius had authority over all matters concerning public and private grain, over producers, contractors, and granaries. This view has often been accepted even by scholars astonished at this traffic so uncharacteristic of Roman practices. Two passages are adduced in support of the thesis, neither of which, in my opinion, contributes to sustaining it:

Asconius 8 (C): Diximus . . . P. Clodium . . . quattuor leges tulisse: annonariam, de qua Cicero mentionem hoc loco [*Pis.* 9] non facit—fuit enim summe popularis—ut frumentum populo . . . gratis daretur.

I have remarked that P. Clodius passed four laws: one of these was a grain law [*annonariam*], which law Cicero does not mention here owing to its extreme popularity, requiring that grain [*frumentum*] be distributed to the people at no cost.

Cic. *Dom.* 25: . . . Sex. Cloelio . . . omne frumentum privatum et publicum, omnis provincias frumentarias, omnis mancipes, omnis horrearum clavis lege tua tradidisti.

By the terms of your law you handed over to Sex. Cloelius all publicly and privately owned grain, all grain-producing provinces, all contracts, every key to the granaries.

J.-M. Flambard, noting that Asconius refers to Clodius's law with the adjective *annonaria* instead of *frumentaria*, infers from that detail that the measure included a comprehensive plan for provisioning Rome, which can be detected in Cicero's description of the activities of Clodius's scribe at *Dom.* 25, activities that are claimed to constitute a virtual *cura annonae* anticipating Pompey's in the subsequent year.[47]

Now, as Flambard admits, *annonarius* is a rare adjective found mostly in later legal and epigraphical texts; Asconius's usage here exhausts the occurrences of *lex annonaria* collected in the *Thesaurus Linguae Latinae* or to be found in the authors whose works are stored in the Packard Humanities Institute Disk (CD 5.3).[48] In view of the word's overall rarity as well as the fact that the office of *praefectus annonae* was well established by the time Asconius was writing his commentaries (a condition that offers a plausible source for the term's suggestion), it can only be deemed rash to attempt to substantiate so decisive a conclusion from Asconius's word choice in this context. The Bobbio Scholiast, after all, far the less original source, says of Clodius, "frumentariam legem tulit."[49] And Asconius's explication of the law's enactment goes no further than mentioning the distribution of free grain.

We may now turn to Cicero's comments in the *De Domo*. The passage in question forms part of the orator's defense of Pompey's *cura annonae*, which was proposed by Cicero himself in the wake of his return from exile and was vigorously attacked by Clodius. Pompey's post was itself controversial, the predictable objection being that once again too much power was being placed in one man's hands.[50] The very necessity of Cicero's defense of Pompey's *cura*—and nearly every extraordinary command created an uproar—is adequate to render the formal elevation of Clodius's scribe unthinkable.[51] It is far more likely that, having passed his *lex frumentaria*, it was the tribune's own responsibility to implement it.[52] Thus Clodius had at the very least to revisit the official protocols for the procurement, storage, and delivery of public grain to the appropriate recipients. Furthermore, Clodius would have a natural interest in attending to the adequate supplying of the city (at least under his watch). And it could hardly be cause for astonishment if Clodius delegated some or several of these chores to his scribe, thereby providing Cicero, who makes much of the tribune's dependency on Cloelius, with additional grist for his mill.[53] The *cura annonae* of Cloelius, then, should be credited to Ciceronian rhetoric, not Clodian legislation, nor should Clodius's pains over the successful implementation of his scheme be confused with a novel intrusion by the Roman state into private enterprise.[54]

It is in this light that one must interpret the provision of the *lex*

Gabinia of 58 exempting the island of Delos from the costs of storing state grain.[55] Given the obvious expense of Clodius's *lex frumentaria*, it was only natural to assume that the tribune, or in any event the state, would at some point feel compelled to seek revenues to support the new dole (which, of course, is exactly what came to pass when Clodius annexed Cyprus). Consequently, the *lex Gabinia*, the purpose of which was to declare sacred Delos exempt from Roman taxation (and which was evidently passed shortly after the Clodian law), made explicit reference to *pro custodia publici frumenti pecunia* for the sake of the island's unambiguous fiscal protection. In other words, the provision was redundant (given the island's general release from financial responsibilities) and so prophylactic. In no way can the *lex Gabinia* be interpreted as support for the contention that the *lex Clodia* formally interfered in the practical affairs of *provinciae frumentariae*.

We are surprisingly ignorant of the means by which grain was dispersed to the *plebs frumentaria* before the reorganization of the dole by Caesar at the conclusion of the civil war. Warehouses and porticoes may have served as distribution centers, and census lists may have provided a check against fraud by noncitizens, though by 58 such lists must have been woefully out of date (the censors of 61, whoever they were, did not complete their tasks) nor could they have done much to discriminate between resident and transient citizens.[56] Caesar's method was to revise his lists by district and to employ *domini insularum* to implement his retrenched scheme.[57] Now it has already been remarked that Clodius's enrollment of *collegia* was organized, naturally enough, by district (*vicatim*). This *descriptio* would also have provided the first opportunity to compile a current record of the most likely recipients of the grain distributions and may have suggested to Clodius an efficient mechanism for actually dispensing the free rations. After all, at least once before in the record of the republic, for the year 203, we find grain distributed to the citizenry by district, and it has even been suggested that this represented the normal mechanism.[58] However that may be, there is no reason to consider Caesar's method original to himself. When he assumed his *cura annonae*, Pompey, who had no desire to rely on Clodius's contributions, apparently resorted to census rolls that were in desperate need of revision if they were to accommodate the contemporary needs of the distributions (which suggests that census lists had not been used by Clodius).[59] In all likelihood, then, Clodius utilized the newly constituted *collegia* for the allocation of grain.[60] The benefits will have been several. Not only would such a move represent an economy of effort on Clodius's part, but, by adding the *frumentatio* to the traditional functions of the *collegia*, Clodius could reinforce dramatically in the minds of the *plebs* the munificence and magnitude of his legislation. Furthermore, by entrusting the officers of the *collegia* with the responsibility of carrying out the distribution, he simultaneously enhanced their local prestige and bound them more tightly in gratitude to himself. Small wonder, then, that in the food riots of 57 Clodius could count on leaders of *collegia*.[61]

This method of distribution also helps to shed light on the swelling number of grain recipients in the aftermath of Clodius's legislation. Now to some extent this was due to an increase in manumissions by slave owners keen to retain the *obsequium* of their (freed) slaves while relieving themselves of the cost of their maintenance, though this factor, attested in the sources, may have been exaggerated by modern scholars.[62] Another ground for the expansion of the dole was the immigration to the city of impoverished rural *plebs*, for whom the *frumentatio* offered hope of material advancement.[63] But still another cause can be cited: the liberality of Clodius and his agents, loath to reject any applicant, no doubt inflated the number of grain recipients; such liberality can only have been encouraged still further by Clodius's use of his *descriptio* of the restored *collegia*, whose membership included slaves as well as citizens.

4

Lex Clodia de agendo cum populo (lex Clodia de obnuntiatione). Another of Clodius's laws, which we may for our purposes call the *lex Clodia de agendo cum populo*, altered the existing regulations for limiting or prohibiting the gathering of public assemblies. Our only sources for this law are Cicero's angry denunciations of it as well as the reports of Asconius and Dio, each of whom may be said to do little more than repeat the orator (though in more banal language).[64] Because this is the most poorly understood of the *quattuor leges*, it will be useful to tabulate Cicero's charges and to examine the evidence for each in detail. Essentially, according to Cicero, this Clodian law enacted the following changes:

1. The *leges Aelia et Fufia* were abrogated.
2. It was now possible to pass legislation on all *dies fasti*.[65]
3. The *auspicia* were abolished.
4. *De caelo servasse* was no longer allowed during assemblies or at least during legislative assemblies.
5. *Intercessio* was abolished.

Explanations of these stipulations are in order (insofar as they can be adequately provided) before our discussion can proceed.

Let us begin with the *leges Aelia et Fufia*, two distinct (though related) laws.[66] Just when these laws were passed, which Cicero dates approximately one hundred years before his delivery of the *In Pisonem* (i.e., in 55), is contested; ordinarily scholars tend slavishly to follow Cicero and so reckon the date at around 158–150, although a few, seeing in the laws a reaction to the perturbation of Ti. Gracchus's tribunate, prefer to set their passage as late as 132.[67] The precise nature of their provisions remains uncertain. Both had to do with the circumstances under which *comitia* could be held. The Bobbio Scholiast informs us that these laws prohibited the carrying of legislation in the period between the announcement and the holding of elections.[68] And Asconius reports that the *lex Aelia* somehow strengthened or reinforced (*confirmaverat*) *obnuntiatio*. Cicero of course regarded the *leges Aelia et Fufia* as the bastion of sound government in Rome, a bulwark against tribunician insanity, but, as scholars have not been slow to notice, our information for these laws comes to us in the same unreliable form and context as do our testimonia for the *lex Clodia*.[69]

Still, with only this evidence to go on, we can make sense of Cicero's remarks about the Clodian law's effect on *dies fasti*. In the Roman calendar the fundamental distinction made between various types of days was that between *dies nefasti*, on which no public business could be transacted, and the remaining days, which were called *dies fasti*. These latter were further divided into two categories, *dies fasti et comitiales*, on which assemblies were permitted, and *dies fasti*, on which litigation was permitted but not the convening of assemblies.[70] Whether it was an innovation or simply the codification of custom, the *leges Aelia et Fufia* (probably the *lex Fufia*) had made the days between the announcement and holding of elections *dies non comitiales*, a requirement that was occasionally suspended by the senate. Clodius's law, said by Cicero to have made it possible to legislate on all *dies fasti*, evidently revoked this limitation—though without completely revoking the *lex Fufia*, a fact of which we can be certain since C. Porcius Cato (tr. pl. 56) was prosecuted (unsuccessfully) under the Fufian law in 54.[71] This provision of Clodius's law seems in itself harmless enough, though, if Sumner is correct in detecting in the *lex Fufia*'s restriction a reaction to Ti. Gracchus's attempt to win votes for a second tribunate by proposing legislation welcome to the multitude and equites, then there may have been at least some popular favor to have been earned in removing the restriction.[72]

We may now pass to the *lex Aelia*, which dealt with *obnuntiatio*, an augural procedure that the tribune is said to have abolished. The importance of augural law to Roman religion and Roman public life is too well known to require rehearsal: *augusto augurio postquam inclyta condita Roma est*. The pace of public life was regulated by the observance of good omens and bad.[73] Public assemblies convened by curule magistrates required the consultation of *auspicia impetrativa* (omens sought through *spectio*, the power, originally associated with patrician magistracies, to seek signs from the sky, from the flight of birds, and from the feeding of birds), and any assembly could be stopped by *auspicia oblativa* (unsought and unexpected bad omens, which any citizen could detect and report, though only the report of an augur required acknowledgment). Legislation passed or officers elected in an assembly conducted in defiance of unfavorable omens could be vitiated. Vitiated does not mean invalid, however; a consul who was *vitio creatus* was a consul nonetheless, though he would be expected to abdicate voluntarily.[74] Another means of regulating the augural soundness of public assemblies was *obnuntiatio*, a procedure that may best be understood by distinguishing its two components: an official possessing the right of *spectio* could announce by edict that he would spend the night preceding an assembly examining the sky for omens (the magistrate would proclaim that *se de caelo servasse*);[75] if the assembly convened in spite of the announced observation, the observing magistrate had to appear before the presiding officer, before the assembly commenced its proceedings, in order to announce the results of his *spectio* (*dico: fulmen vidisse*). *Obnuntiatio* could not be ignored by the presiding officer.[76] The right could be limited, however: according to Aulus Gellius, it was the custom for consuls to append to their edicts summoning the *comitia centuriata* the formula "ne quis magistratus minor de caelo servasse velit" (13.15).

Obnuntiatio was an ancient practice, and its extension to tribunes may have gone as far back as the fifth century.[77] What, then, was the purpose of the *lex Aelia*? Perhaps it again codified the *mos maiorum* at a time when clarity was needed, or perhaps it regulated who could obnuntiate against whom and under what circumstances.[78] By the time we reach Clodius's tribunate it is clear that magistrates (unless temporarily impeded by consular or senatorial injunction) could impede one another's actions. Tribunes could obnuntiate against magistrates, including censors, as well as against their tribunician colleagues.[79] But could magistrates obnuntiate against tribunes? The common assumption is that they could, but the existence of this right has been denied largely on th[e] grounds that it finds insufficient support in the record of consular o[p]position to tribunician legislation.[80] Yet the testimony of Cicero's *Sestio*—our sole evidence for magisterial obnuntiation of tribunician [leg]islation—cannot be ignored.[81] Remarking in 56 on the riot that ens[ued]

January 57 when Q. Fabricius attempted to pass a *plebiscitum* recalling the orator from exile, Cicero communicates the following (*Sest.* 78):

> victa igitur est causa rei publicae, et victa non auspiciis, non inter-
> cessione, non suffragiis, sed vi, manu, ferro. Nam si obnuntiasset
> Fabricio is *praetor* qui se servasse de caelo dixerat, accepisset res
> publica plagam, eam quam acceptam gemere posset; si intercessis-
> set conlega Fabricio, laesisset rem publicam, sed iure laesisset.

> Therefore the cause of the state was defeated, and defeated not by
> the auspices, not by veto, not by votes, but by violence, by force, by
> the sword. For if the *praetor* who had announced that he had ob-
> served the sky for omens had obnuntiated against Fabricius, the
> state would have received a blow which it could live to complain
> about; if a colleague had vetoed Fabricius, he would have wounded
> the state, but he would have inflicted the wound constitutionally.

The expansion of the codices' ·*P·R*· to *praetor*, though accepted by all principal editions, is admittedly not immune to criticism. Nevertheless, it remains the best reading so far advanced.[82] The contrary-to-fact nature of Cicero's statement is irrelevant to the point at issue: clearly Cicero was able to conceive of his restoration's being prevented by praetorian *obnuntiatio* of tribunician legislation (whereas in fact Fabricius's bill was derailed by violence). Only by rejecting the soundness of the text of *Sest.* 78 (viz. by rejecting *praetor* as the correct resolution of ·*P·R*·) is it possible to conclude that magistrates lacked the right to obnuntiate against tribunes. Whether this right was formally established by the *lex Aelia*, as it is sometimes argued, must remain in doubt.[83]

Asconius, following Cicero in sentiment but adding more detail, ·ims that *obnuntiatio* was important in the impeding of dangerous lation, by which he presumably means *popularis* or reformist legisla- "obnuntiatio enim qua perniciosis legibus resistebatur, quam Aelia firmaverat," Asc. 8 [C]). This remark echoes Cicero's asseveration Aelian and Fufian laws "often crippled and suppressed tribunes langerous politics" (saepe numero tribunicios furores debilita- resserunt, *Vat.* 18). Indeed, it is generally maintained that *ob-* as a mainstay of optimate strength in the factional strife of nd late republic. Yet there are good reasons to doubt this. senate could also be frustrated by searching the heavens, a lains the regular prohibition on *obnuntiatio* in consular e centuriate assembly mentioned earlier.[84] Moreover, it d that *obnuntiatio* was at best a delaying mechanism, weaker than the veto and more dependent upon *concordia* as a tool of political control (since vitiated legislation was not ipso facto invalid). As E. J. Weinrib rightly stresses and as we have seen, magisterial *obnuntiatio* is exceedingly rare in the record of Roman politics. Tribunician interference with other tribunes is somewhat better attested, reflecting the undeniable fact that the senatorial establishment tended to find ample support in the tribunician colleges both in the middle and in the late republic.[85] Although in the disintegration of political harmony that characterized the decline of the republic the tribunician veto perhaps became rather more vulnerable than it had been before the momentous events of 133, it nonetheless remained a more conspicuous resource than *obnuntiatio*.[86] This, of course, was not the case with the events of 59, which initiated a rancorous debate over augural and legislative proprieties that soon involved vociferous and frequent reproaches from Cicero, all of which has left its impression in Dio's excessive emphasis on the significance of Clodius's legislation affecting *obnuntiatio* (Dio believed that this law above all others paved the way to Cicero's exile) and, one might add, in the tendency of modern scholarship to be obedient to Dio's analysis.

Obnuntiatio came to the fore in the year 59. In the teeth of senatorial opposition—and the opposition of his colleague—Caesar turned to the people to carry his first agrarian law. Bibulus attempted to block Caesar's legislation through *obnuntiatio*, but was forcibly expelled from the forum: the *fasces* were shattered and the consul himself was bathed in filth. Thereafter Bibulus retired to his house, where he spent the remainder of the year searching the heavens—"per edicta obnuntiaret," as Suetonius (*Iul.* 20.1) puts it. He did not, however, announce the results of his *spectio* personally; instead, he sent lictors to do so, or at least this is the conclusion to be drawn from the Dio's admittedly not unclouded account. The consul was imitated in his continual *obnuntiatio* by three tribunes.[87]

Now it has long been recognized that, in order to be valid from a narrowly technical standpoint, the bad omen perceived by *spectio* must be announced in person.[88] The mere declaration *de caelo servasse*, while ordinarily sufficient to persuade a tribune or magistrate not to waste his time gathering an assembly only to have it dismissed because of *obnuntiatio*, was not per se a binding restriction: since the possibility, however slender, of a fruitless *spectio* had to be assumed, a determined or a rigidly scrupulous official might convene his assembly in any event. Hence the requirement to report the omen on the spot and in person.[89] So far the ineluctable logic of augural law. But the undeniable distinction between *de caelo servasse* and actual *obnuntiatio* may have been less clear to most Romans, even of the senatorial order, than it was to those learned in the augural discipline. After all, the conflict between Caesar and Bibulus, in which Bibulus's rights as a consul were denied even while augural law was technically observed, as well as Bibulus's recourse to nonstop *spectio*, were unprecedented—and owing to the long-standing tradition of respecting an announcement *de caelo servasse* there existed an equally undeniable body of opinion to the effect that it was *nefas* to hold an assembly while the heavens were being observed. Cicero, in the aftermath of his return from exile, insisted that the *libri reconditi* of the augurs forbid holding an assembly when an announcement *de caelo servasse* has been made (*Dom.* 39), and in a sensational *contio* conducted by Clodius later in his tribunate, the augurs, questioned as to the effect of Caesar's legislation having been passed in despite of Bibulus's *spectio*, answered that the consul's acts "vitio lata esse" (Cic. *Har. Resp.* 48).[90] Bibulus's edicts unmistakably made a powerful, if misleading, impression on his contemporaries. In view of the tremendous stir caused by Caesar's and Vatinius's neglect of their colleagues' edicts—which went on for more than a year—as well as the pronouncements of the augurs (even granting that these were made unofficially and *in contione* and so were not formal *responsa* of the college), one can only conclude that the augural rules governing *obnuntiatio* were imperfectly understood by most senators, a conclusion that obtains even if the misunderstanding was willful on the part of some. Out of which one can only draw the incontestable inference that the *leges Aelia et Fufia* were silent on such matters. Consequently, in 59 (and subsequently) *mos maiorum* had the effect of clouding and confounding *disciplina auguralis*. It was a state of affairs crying out for legislation.

Which brings us again to the *lex Clodia*, which law, Cicero claimed, eliminated the *auspicia*, *de caelo servasse*, and *intercessio*. This last item is either a patent absurdity or was meant to indicate *obnuntiando interecessio*.[91] The suggestion that Clodius did away with the *auspicia* is likewise ridiculous; it was clearly intended to add hyperbolic force to the orator's attack on Clodius's reform. Now it is generally accepted that Clodius modified the regulations governing *obnuntiatio*, although, owing to our incomplete understanding of the *lex Aelia*, it remains difficult to discern the exact nature of the change imposed by Clodius's law. Multiple hypotheses have been advanced and, although doxographies are ordinarily to be eschewed, the degree of uncertainty surrounding this law justifies a brief review of the most notable reconstructions of the *lex Clodia* hitherto proposed: (1) *obnuntiatio* was indeed abolished by Clodius but was shortly thereafter restored by the senate when Clodius's law was abrogated,[92] (2) Clodius's law allowed the assemblies to suspend *obnuntiatio* when it was thought necessary,[93] (3) the right of *obnuntiatio* was removed from curule magistrates,[94] (4) curule magistrates and tribunes could obnuntiate against electoral but not legislative assemblies,[95] and (5) curule magistrates could obnuntiate against electoral but not legislative assemblies.[96]

Hypothesis (1) is contradicted by Cicero himself (*Prov. Cons.* 46), nor is it likely that the orator would have failed to mention it had a Clodian law been annulled. As for hypothesis (2), it is difficult to imagine just how its implementation could itself overcome the obstruction it was designed to avoid (since a vote to suspend *obnuntiatio* could itself be delayed); in any case, the senate shielded the legislation recalling Cicero simply by decree (much as consuls were once entitled to do for bills destined for the centuriate assembly, as we have seen in Gellius). Consequently, there is nothing to recommend the second hypothesis. Curule magistrates certainly retained the right of *obnuntiatio* after 58 at electoral assemblies (Cic. *Phil.* 2.81). Whether they did so at legislative assemblies depends on the correct interpretation of *Sest.* 78, a text cited and examined earlier. In my view, the parallelism of *obnuntiatio* and *intercessio* in that passage requires that both be deemed to have been potential, if from Cicero's perspective lamentable, methods for obstructing the *rogatio Fabricia*. And on any fair reading of *Phil.* 1.25 it is incontestable that Cicero believed tribunes had the right to exercise *obnuntiatio* in the year 44.[97]

The evidence of *Sest.* 78 and *Phil.* 1.25 is crucial to facilitating the proper understanding of the explanation of the *lex Clodia* provided by Asconius (Asc. 8 [C]) and Dio (38.13.6), which is occasionally taken to show that the *lex Clodia* dealt exclusively with legislative assemblies. This is mistaken: Asconius's description of the law says only "eos dies quibus cum populo agi liceret," which is equivocal, and Dio explicitly states that Clodius introduced his legislation lest *obnuntiatio* be used to prevent his bringing Cicero to trial (φοβηθεὶς ὁ Κλώδιος μὴ γραψαμένου αὐτοῦ τὸν Κικέρωνα ἀναβολήν τέ τινες ἐκ τοῦ τοιούτου καὶ τριβὴν τῇ δίκῃ ἐμποιήσωσιν), an assertion that, although very likely to be Dio's own interpretation of events, must nonetheless indicate how the historian intended the rest of his sentence to be understood.[98]

Under the terms of the *lex Clodia*, edicts announcing observations of the heavens and *obnuntiatio* continued—or at least could legitimately continue—to be activities of all officials endowed with *spectio*; *obnuntiatio* remained possible for all assemblies, electoral, legislative, judicial, or censorial. What becomes remarkably obvious in the aftermath of Clodius's law is the absolute necessity for an obnuntiating official to deliver his announcement in person before the commencement of an assembly. This is illustrated unmistakably in the well-known episode of 57 in which the consul, Metellus Nepos, skulked along the back streets of Rome in an effort to make his way to the Campus Martius (so as to conduct aedilician elections) without allowing T. Annius Milo, a tribune who had spent the night in observation of the skies, from announcing the ill omens in person. C. Meier and T. N. Mitchell have independently made the very plausible suggestion that the substance of Clodius's law was an explicit requirement that edicts *de caelo servasse* must be followed by an actual announcement of the omens made in person before the initiation of an assembly's business.[99] Whatever opinions or sensibilities had prevailed previously, mere *servatio* could no longer be claimed to blight the legitimate convening of any assembly.

Legislation along these lines can only be regarded as moderate and sensible. Caesar's enemies had been quick to rally around Bibulus's edicts in 59. But for all its potential usefulness in menacing if not overthrowing Caesar's legislation, Bibulus's obstructionism set a precedent whose dangers must have been obvious even to Bibulus's staunchest supporters: the thought that a disgruntled magistrate or tribune could, without so much as leaving his house, paralyze the government for a year will not have been a prospect to please anyone. Hence the need for a reform, actually a clarification, of *obnuntiatio*. That Clodius's law only codified into public law what was in fact sound augural doctrine should occasion no surprise in view of the inclination of Roman legislation to settle conflicts arising from uncertain or vaguely defined prerogatives. Clodius's law incited no resistance in 58, just the opposite of what one would expect if its provisions represented a stark violation of Roman *religio* or if the bastion of sound government were indeed being breached. Quite the contrary: Clodius's law allowed the perpetrator of the Bona Dea delict to pose as the champion of correct *religio*. And because it was not retrospective, Clodius's law need not prejudice the outcome of the auspicial feud between Caesar and the *optimates*.

Only from the nontechnical point of view could Clodius's law be seen as an infringement upon the exercise of *obnuntiatio*—hence Cicero's (much later) appeals to the solemn significance of announcements *de caelo servasse*. But this Clodian law offered a welcome solution to a serious confusion. While one may rightly suspect that Clodius had no wish to encounter the remote control *obnuntiatio* faced by Caesar and Vatinius, it is nonetheless a mistake to view the *lex Clodia de agendo cum populo* as exclusively *popularis* in its appeal. This law, which extended the range of the *dies comitiales* and incorporated into civil law the correct procedure for *obnuntiatio*, was intended to win stature for its author, to show Clodius as something more than a mere *tribunus popularis*.[100]

5

Lex Clodia de censoria notione. Much the same can be said for the fourth of Clodius's measures, which dealt with a matter admittedly of general public interest but of particular relevance to the senatorial classes, to wit: the revision of the album of senators by the censors, the *lectio senatus*.[101]

The *lectio senatus* was not one of the original duties of the censors. It was the censors' responsibility, obviously enough, to conduct the official census, that is, to compile the lists that indicated each individual's property class and to perform the lustrum. One facet of the former task was the *cura morum*, since in Rome character (and not merely wealth) determined one's place in society. During the census, every citizen was subject to the censors' scrutiny, though in practice only the upper classes were affected. If the censors judged an individual morally wanting, they might satisfy themselves with a reprimand, or they might place a mark (*nota*) on the census list alongside the individual's name; they might even append a brief explanation of the their mark (*subscriptio censoria*). Furthermore, the censors could impose various sanctions on objectionable citizens.[102] An individual charged with an offense was customarily given an opportunity to present his side, pleading his own case or relying on the services of an advocate. Such defenses were often successful.[103] Only with the passage of the *lex Ovinia* sometime before 312 was the revision of the senate roll assigned to the censors.[104] But the *lectio*, though carried out by censors, was not thereafter an integral part of the census proper. It remained independent of the census and was usually completed before the census itself was begun. The *lectio*, unlike the censorial *cura morum*, was conducted privately by the censors. The revised roll of senators was simply read to the public. Disappointed senators could react as they chose, but, inasmuch as the revision was concluded when the list was promulgated, there was no opportunity to stage a defense, nor did an expelled senator have any appropriate recourse against his expulsion.[105]

We may now turn to the actual provisions of Clodius's law. According to Asconius, Clodius's law prevented the censors from excluding anyone from the *album senatorum*, or from punishing them with any sort of *ignominia*, unless both censors agreed on the punishment and only after the individual had been accused in their presence.[106] At least two innovations emerge from Asconius's description of the *lex Clodia*. Under the old procedure for conducting the *lectio* and the *cura morum*, the *nota* affixed by one senator took effect unless the other censor opposed it (that is why expulsions and sanctions were frequently attributed to one and not the other of a pair of censors). Clodius's law necessitated explicit condemnation by both censors. The second innovation, and it is an important one, has to do with the formalization of the *lectio senatus*. Already, as we have seen, it was customary for individuals to have an opportunity to defend themselves during the census proper (Clodius's law, it seems, rendered that custom a legal requirement of the *regimen morum*). Clodius, however, assimilated the procedure of the *lectio* to that which had been customary in the census proper: henceforth, senators would hear the charges against them and would be granted an opportunity to defend themselves before the censors could remove them from the senate. Such defenses, which transformed the revision of the *album senatorum* into a very public undertaking, were totally new to the *lectio*. In fact, formal proceedings (*iudicia*) would henceforth become a necessary part of any *lectio* that attempted to remove a senator.[107]

The background to this law is vital to appreciating its purpose. The recent history of the censorship was a source of senatorial anxiety by the fifties. It has been suggested, rightly in my view, that there existed among the elite a notion that the senate had a maximum capacity.[108] Unfortunately, because the Sullan constitution provided for the automatic adlection of quaestors and tribunes, there was likely to be a superabundance of members by the time each *lectio senatus* rolled around, a circumstance that invited the censors' *nota*. Moreover, the Romans' obsessive concern for personal *dignitas*, in combination with the intensification of political rivalries characteristic of the late republic, provided enormous temptation for the abuse of censorial powers, especially when such politicism could pose as diligence in preserving the senate's prestige. The censors of 70 purged the senate of sixty-four members, an astounding figure that included an ex-consul.[109] This unsparing census cast a long shadow. During the census of 64, the tribunes, fearing their own exclusion, contrived to obstruct the *lectio*, with the result that the censors finally resigned.[110] Schooled by the failure of their predecessors, the censors of 61 allowed the membership of the senate to swell to an unacceptable number.[111] However, following the course of least resistance was no solution, and the lenient census of 61 must have generated apprehensions about the conduct of the next one.

Such forebodings inform the drafting of Clodius's measure, which provided each senator a legal ground for challenging the censors should he feel, as indeed he must, that his removal from the senate would be unjust.[112] And, as we have noted earlier, defenses made before censors, which were public affairs, were often efficacious. Now it has often been asserted that this law was intended to shield its author from future efforts to expel him from the senate, which is possible at some level, I suppose, but hardly to the point (and, of course, such an explanation imports *parti pris* assumptions about Clodius's plans from the start of his tribunician career). Nor does it seem likely, though again it is not impossible, that the fate of Clodius's father, who was passed over by the censors of 86, influenced the tribune.[113] But clearly it was more important to Clodius at this time to establish some solid senatorial support, and, as we have seen, Clodius's law, with the safeguards it provided to all senators, must have held wide appeal, particularly among the *pedarii*, the senators most likely to be ejected in the event of a harsh *lectio*. Though unimportant individually, *pedarii* were important in bulk, a lesson Clodius had been bright enough to absorb from Crassus's political career.[114] Clodius's law, in other words, was a reform that safeguarded the individual and collective dignity of the senators by introducing what ostensibly were small innovations that tended to conform with custom.[115]

Cicero, naturally, wanted the matter to be seen differently. Clodius's law, he insisted after his return from exile, was tantamount to abolishing the censorship itself, an obvious exaggeration.[116] But Cicero was on the right track: Clodius's legislation, by blunting the effectiveness and efficiency of the *lectio senatus*, did in fact diminish the powers of the censors.[117] That, of course, was precisely what was so appealing about the law to many senators, and Clodius's law was at least an attempt to solve the problems attending the Roman census. In the end, however, it was unsuccessful. The hearings prescribed by the *lex Clodia* were so many and so protracted in 54, when the next census was attempted, that the prospect of a *lustrum* was made hopeless.[118] The political factors that in the event rendered Clodius's law impractical are not difficult to discern, and, after the failure of 54, the *lex Clodia* was abrogated in 52, after Clodius's death, by the consul Metellus Scipio.[119]

6

But that was far in the future. It is now time to return to the days between the promulgation of the *quattuor leges* and their ratification. Clodius's legislative program, as Dio rightly observed, aimed at winning over not only the *plebs* but the equites and senators as well.[120] Free grain and *collegia* certainly won the hearts of the common people. Clodius's clarification of the process of *obnuntiatio* earned respect as prudent and timely legislation. And the reform of the *lectio senatus* was plainly designed to garner senatorial appreciation. Few among the *boni* will have been thrilled by Clodius's *popularis* measures, obviously, but free grain was a proposal that could hardly be stopped and at least the remainder of Clodius's legislative package made it clear that he was no revolutionary in any sense of the word. In fact, the entire slate suggested balance. Consequently, there was no movement to block Clodius's legislation from passing, on the part of the dynasts or on the part of the *boni*. Only Cicero offered resistance, and he was persuaded to give way, not by the dynasts, interestingly enough, but by the very princes of the senate.

It is crucial, for all the balance of Clodius's legislative program, not to underestimate his *popularis* ambitions in 58: the principal target of Clodius's legislation was unquestionably the *plebs*. In order to focus attention on his *rogatio de collegiis*, that is to say, in order to sensationalize the benefit he intended to confer upon the people, the tribune engineered the celebration, on the Kalends of January 58, of the Ludi Compitalicii, an act that dramatically anticipated the effect of his bill.[121] A demonstration of this nature was not original. In December 61 an unknown tribune had tried the same thing, but had been frustrated by the consul-designate, Metellus Celer, whose personal prestige overawed him.[122] The failure of 61 could only enhance Clodius's reputation if he were successful. Consequently, he threw his full support behind the *magister* who actually conducted the celebration, no other than Sex. Cloelius.[123] It is at this juncture that the tribune L. Ninnius Quadratus makes his appearance, though his opposition to Clodius's plans to restore the *collegia* may have been known since their promulgation. Ninnius attempted to prevent the *ludi*. The episode calls for careful examination.[124]

According to Dio, Ninnius, together with Cicero, worked to block all of Clodius's legislation.[125] In view of Cicero's increasing reluctance to rely on the assurances of Pompey that Clodius meant him no harm, his recourse to the obscure tribune seems perfectly understandable, and it reminds us that Cicero was not the helpless figure he so often appears to be. Cicero recognized that Clodius's future lay in whatever acclaim he should win from his initial legislative package, and, with Ninnius's cooperation, Cicero meant to stall Clodius's momentum. Hence Ninnius's presence at the Ludi Compitalicii, where he could legitimately stand up for the senatorial decree of 64. If Clodius's celebration could be spoiled, that would constitute a damaging blow to Clodius's prestige. In the event, the tribune was not competent to disperse the celebrants, and, being no Metellus, he had lacked the stature to intimidate Clodius.[126] But his demonstration signaled trouble. After all, Ninnius was quite competent to veto Clodius's *rogatio*: he could invoke once again the *senatus consultum* of 64 and, since he was already on record as an adversary of *collegia*, he could justify his actions in terms of consistency and *dignitas* as well. None of this was lost on Clodius, who quickly cut a deal with Cicero: he promised to do the orator no harm if Cicero called off Ninnius. Cicero agreed, and the sole impediment to the passage of Clodius's package was thereby removed.[127]

Dio, as we have seen, claims that Cicero intended to bar *all* of Clodius's legislation, but this must be an error. After all, Cicero can hardly have expected Ninnius, or any other tribune, to interpose his veto against Clodius's *lex frumentaria*, nor was any tribune likely to incur senatorial resentment by obstructing the *lex de censoria notione*. And as for the *lex de agendo cum populo* (which Dio believed posed the most serious threat to Cicero's security), we have seen already that that law was a sound measure clarifying a genuine confusion and hiding no *popularis* sting.[128] Which leaves the *lex de collegiis*, and, in fact, when one looks to Cicero's only allusion to his active opposition to Clodius's legislation, which comes in a letter to Atticus composed in September 58 (after his departure from Rome), Cicero mentions no other law: "but if, now and in the past, you loved me as you ought, you would never have allowed me to go without the good advice in which you abound, you would never have allowed me to be persuaded that it was to my advantage that the *lex de collegiis* be passed" (*Att.* 3.15.4). That this tantalizing remark refers to the events described by Dio seems inescapable.[129] Otherwise Cicero never mentions the affair, but we cannot build on that, inasmuch as Cicero can hardly have wanted to admit that he had been outsmarted by Clodius. The glee with which Dio reports Cicero's deception is ample indication of how embarrassing the incident was for its victim.[130] Nor can Cicero's letter be used to support a reconstruction wherein the ex-consul had opposed all of Clodius's legislation but subsequently dropped his opposition only to the *lex de collegiis*, for the simple reason that none of Clodius's four laws was vetoed or carried amid controversy or violence: Cicero's opposition only mattered to Clodius because he could arrange for a loyal tribune to interpose a veto (Clodius was not especially concerned with winning Cicero's personal approbation), which means that for Cicero to lament that he was persuaded to *allow* the passage of the *lex de collegiis* when he was unable to stop the rest of Clodius's agenda would be ridiculous. Instead, Cicero and Ninnius had intelligently and effectively concentrated on one law, the most vulnerable in the package. Consequently, Clodius was compelled to make a bargain.

It remains to consider why Cicero took Clodius at his word. As his correspondence in 59 makes clear, Cicero was perceptive enough to doubt the sincerity of Clodius's pledge to Pompey, and he was soon skeptical of the dynasts themselves. Yet Clodius was not offering Cicero and Ninnius anything that he had not already promised the triumvirs. The agreement was crucial to Clodius, inasmuch as Cicero was in a position to do serious harm to the tribune's schemes. Whatever winning ways Clodius may have possessed, however, it is very hard to believe that on his own he was capable of charming Cicero. Which means that Clodius's offer must have been endorsed by a third party whom Cicero was inclined to trust solidly even in negotiations bearing so heavily on his own future. The dynasts are clearly excluded here. Nor is Atticus, though admittedly trustworthy and well connected, a likely candidate, since, even at his most bitter, Cicero criticized his friend only for his passivity in these matters. One is left only with speculations, but it seems reasonable to look for Clodius's intermediary among the *optimates*.[131] Clodius had flirted with them during the latter months of 59, after all, and his balanced legislative program may have given him a degree of credibility in representing himself to the *boni* as interested in matters other than personal vengeance. Clodius was in a position to persuade the *optimates* that he genuinely wanted a compromise with his enemy, a compromise that was mutually advantageous and one that he could portray as placing both himself and Cicero in the *optimates'* debt. That a Cato or Hortensius may have seen in this an opportunity to shift Clodius and Cicero away from Pompey requires no stretch of the imagination. Nor does one have to plumb the psychology of Cicero very deeply to understand why he would be more inclined to rely on the assurances of such figures. In the end, of course, Clodius betrayed them all, a subject to be taken up in detail in the next chapter. But we may note here that, when Cicero was attacked by Clodius later in 58, the *optimates*, far from rushing to the orator's assistance, actually advised him to capitulate, counsel that Cicero later regarded as having been not only unwise but malicious as well. But by then, as we shall see, Clodius had attained to unprecedented *popularitas*, had garnered the support of the consuls, and had elevated Cato to a special command. Cicero he had left with few resources. This suggestion cannot be regarded as proved beyond doubt, of course, but it seems the best explanation of Clodius's success in neutralizing Ninnius's opposition. And it reveals that, at the start of 58, Clodius sustained ties with the dynasts and with the senate (if stronger ties with the former than with the latter), a wide-reaching political configuration reflected in the varying constituencies of his four laws.

Clodius busied himself throughout January in implementing his legislation on *collegia* and the grain dole, activities discussed above in examining the various *leges Clodianae*. The undertaking of restoring the old and establishing the new *collegia* all the while devising adequate means for distributing free quantities of grain to the *plebs* must have proved a full-time occupation. Nevertheless, politics could not be overlooked. The enemies of the coalition concentrated their first attacks in 58 directly on Caesar. In the senate, the validity of the *acta* of the previous year was challenged by Domitius Ahenobarbus and Memmius.[132] Three days of acrimonious and inconclusive debate supervened. Of Clodius's contribution we hear nothing, and he may well have sat silent, but, however preoccupied with other matters, he can hardly have been disinterested, since his plebeian status was so thoroughly implicated in the legitimacy of Caesar's consulship. The agreement brokered between the tribune and Cicero did not place the former under so great an obligation to the *boni* that he could be expected to ignore his own interests or to trust in senatorial goodwill to the extent that he might believe Caesar's early downfall would not affect the ultimate fate of his own *popularis* legislation, however uneventful its passage. Still, there was much to be learned from merely observing the proceedings, and little to be gained by acting in advance of a real resolution on the part of the *patres*.

As for Caesar, after enduring three days of senatorial bickering, he removed himself outside the pomerium in order to assume his proconsular imperium. Court action followed, directed now not at Caesar, who was immune from prosecution under the terms of the *lex Memmia* protecting those absent from the city *rei publicae causa*, but instead at his ex-quaestor, whose identity remains unknown.[133] The purpose of this indictment was to pave the way for a serious legal challenge to Caesar: by condemning Caesar's quaestor for illegalities relating to the *acta* of 59, a sold basis (at least theoretically) for securing Caesar's ultimate condemnation would thereby be established. Unfortunately for the cause of Caesar's enemies, however, the case against the quaestor seems to have come to nothing.[134] The next move, in the view of some, was an attempt by a tribune, L. Antistius, to bring Caesar to trial, a rather pointless and pathetic action if indeed it took place in 58. Some question must remain, but the weight of the evidence (such as it is) favors the conclusion advanced by Badian that the fruitless attempt to try Caesar was undertaken in 56.[135] Caesar was clearly beyond reach in the opening months of

58, as two previous trial balloons (the senatorial debate and the indictment of Caesar's quaestor) had indicated. The dynast's enemies had to seek a different stratagem.

We come now to an episode of large significance in Clodius's career, though at first glance he appears a minor player.[136] This is because our principal source is Cicero's *In Vatinium*, where, naturally, the orator's focus is on his victim. Our other and more problematic source, the Bobbio Scholiast, is of course intent on elucidating Cicero, not recording the career of Clodius.[137] Nevertheless, in outline at least, events are clear enough. Early in 58—we cannot date the episode with precision but certainly before Caesar's departure in March and probably rather earlier— an accusation was brought against P. Vatinius for violating the *lex Licinia Iunia*, which regulated legislative procedures. That this was an oblique attack on Caesar is evident enough. Yet, unlike the proconsul, Vatinius was vulnerable. Admittedly he was Caesar's legate in 58 and therefore immune from prosecution under the same *lex Memmia* that protected his commander. However, Vatinius wanted to stand for the aedileship, which meant that he would soon be required to enter the city (thereby surrendering his immunity) in order to submit his *professio*—unless he chose not to stand at all, itself a victory for the *boni*.[138] Making a virtue of necessity, Vatinius entered Rome with a flourish, insisting that he preferred pleading his cause to hiding behind immunity. Clearly this was bravado, and he may have deemed it just possible that, confronted with his response, all efforts to convene a trial would evaporate. If so, he was mistaken. Preparations for his trial went ahead under the supervision of the praetor C. Memmius. At this point, Vatinius appealed to Clodius for his *auxilium*—in flagrant disregard of *mos maiorum* according to Cicero (though he could not have expected this inaccurate claim to make any great impression per se)[139]—perhaps on the (foggy) legalistic claim that Memmius's procedure for selecting the court's *quaesitor* violated the *lex Vatinia de alternis consiliis reicendis*.[140] In any event, some pretext was certainly advanced to justify the tribune's intervention, since, obviously, it was hardly illegal or exceptional to try Vatinius: the man had chosen to enter the city.

Thus Clodius was compelled at last to show his highest loyalties. Of course, Vatinius's appeal did not come unexpectedly: Clodius's willingness to respond had been secured in advance. But, in agreeing to support Vatinius, Clodius committed himself to a public demonstration of his alignment with the dynasts that was certain to alienate their enemies. That he was prepared to do so indicates the degree of political support that Clodius believed he had garnered from other places. Since there could be no middle ground in his gesture on Vatinius's part, the tribune saw to it that his intervention was impossible to dismiss (preparations demonstrated by the actual course of events). Clodius must have made it generally known that he would appear at Vatinius's trial. Then, on the actual day, in the presence of the praetor and of jurymen, Vatinius made his public and formal appeal for Clodius's *auxilium*. The tribune granted it. Resistance on Memmius's part either was offered or was by design perceived by Clodius to be offered, in reaction to which he summoned the *plebs* to support their tribune, no doubt invoking the tribune's right and duty to preserve a citizen's liberty from magisterial excess. It was then that Clodius's popular legislation paid its first dividends. Indeed, even Clodius may have been impressed by the readiness of the people to respond to his call: the court was completely disrupted, the praetor's benches were scattered, the urns were overturned—in short, the tribune's *auxilium* was violently enforced by the *plebs urbana*. Memmius made a note of it, a formal complaint for the official record, but Vatinius was free to return to his master (he finally stood for an aedileship of 56, but was defeated).[141] When Cicero recounted this episode in his *In Vatinium*, the outrage that he fully expected to tap hardly lay in lingering resentment over Vatinius's appeal to Clodius. Rather, it resided in the shocking quality of the tribune's response (which Cicero designates as *nefarium*). For the rescue of Vatinius was, to the best of our knowledge, Clodius's first exploitation of public violence in 58.[142]

The demonstration that disrupted Vatinius's trial was the first sign that Clodius's *lex de collegiis* and *lex frumentaria* had procured the tribune not only unprecedented *popularitas* but also a mechanism that could rally vocal and violent demonstrations whenever required. Indeed, it is no exaggeration to say that Clodius's political importance in the fifties was based primarily on his effective employment of popular violence, even after his opponents became determined to match him at his own game. But it goes too far, I think, to assume that Clodius's restoration of *collegia* was inspired by a calculated design to transform them into his private army (as Cicero and many modern scholars tend to depict Clodius's supporters).[143] For all his many political gifts, Clodius was not that perspicacious. Rather, it is more likely that Clodius's goal, both in legitimizing the outlawed *collegia* and in enlarging the scope of collegial organizations as well as in establishing free allotments of grain, was the broad and nonspecific one of winning *favor plebis*.[144] Past popular leaders had not relied extensively on the urban *plebs*, the object of Clodius's *popularis* legislation, nor had the *plebs* proved itself a conspicuously reliable support for violent politics, as the fates of the Gracchi and of Saturninus amply attest. Clodius's legislative benefactions were no doubt expected from the start to win popularity, and it is probably fair to credit him with discerning the potential gains to be earned by the politician who appealed to the *plebs'* hunger for dignity as well as bread.[145] But this perception on Clodius's part, realized effectually in his combined implementation of the two laws, is better conceived along the lines of what the French call an *idée mobilisateuse,* not a fully articulated master plan for winning political influence. Clodius's *beneficia,* joined with the elevation in local honor to be enjoyed by officers in *collegia,* whose recognition had been guaranteed by the tribune and whose functional importance was enhanced though their role in grain distributions, secured the deep gratitude of Rome's *collegiati,* which is to say the bulk of the *plebs urbana.* The depth of this gratitude was intensified by the social superiority of Clodius himself, who took care to oversee the enrollment of the *collegia* personally. And to be sure, Clodius's eminence and his ostensible personal commitment had been signaled all the more sharply by the past patrician's flamboyant *transitio,* a gesture that could hardly pass unnoticed by the common folk of the city.[146]

8

Who were the *Clodiani* who responded to the tribune's appeals for public support? The vocabulary of Cicero provides a rich selection of terminology: *operae Clodianae,*[147] *latrocinium Clodianum,*[148] *Clodiana multitudo,*[149] *seditio Clodiana,*[150] *exercitus Clodianus,*[151] to mention but a few. None of these designations, despite the acceptance of some into scholarly discourse as convenient shorthand expressions, was intended to provide an accurate or impartial description of Clodius's following. Cicero's depiction of the *exercitus Clodianus* is quite vivid: mustered and commanded by unsavory *duces,* heavily armed, Clodius's forces occupied the Aurelian tribunal and the temple of Castor as bases of operation. The composition of the *Clodiani* is, naturally, utterly disreputable: not merely criminals and slaves but *bankrupt* criminals and slaves, assassins and gladiators. Even when Cicero resorts to more mundane expressions— like *tabernarii, mercenarii,* or *conductii*—his emphasis is always on the low-life nature of the Clodian crowd, *omnis faex urbis* (*Pis.* 9).[152] Furthermore, according to Cicero's representations, Clodius drafted into his service the *veteres Catilinae milites,*[153] the *Catilinae copiae,*[154] the *coniuratorum reliquae.*[155] The orator's linguistic construction of his Clodian opposition has been extensively and admirably analyzed by Favory: Clodius and his supporters are systematically fashioned so as to constitute the negative aspect of a Manichaeistic political universe; the characteristics of the *Clodiani* are predicated on their being opposite to optimate virtues.[156] Not surprisingly, then, others among Cicero's enemies find themselves formulated similarly, as a comparison with Cicero's portrayal of Vatinius, A. Gabinius, Calpurnius Piso, and, especially, Mark Antony leaves undeniably evident. Cicero was effectively economic in his vilification: Catiline provides the paradigm of evil who gives literary shape to all the orator's central enemies.

All of which leaves to the historian the pedestrian task of sorting fact from fiction. We may begin with the idea, prevalent in modern scholarship, that Clodius's popular support was organized in a paramilitary fashion. This may well be true of the tribune's personal retainers: Clodius, like other aristocrats of his time, possessed a retinue part of whose purpose was to serve as a bodyguard. But this band cannot have constituted more than a small fraction of the *Clodiani*, else Clodius would hardly have represented a serious threat to anyone in 58. Most of the tribune's supporters were members of *collegia*—artisans and shopkeepers— as Cicero's contemptuous references to the laboring classes reveal.[157] In order to stage a demonstration, Clodius often issued a call to close up the shops—*tabernas claudi iubebas*, charged Cicero.[158] The *tabernarii* and *opifices* thereby summoned composed the backbone of Clodius's forces. Some of the *Clodiani* will have been laborers and underemployed poor, members of the *nova collegia*, though the very nature of their circumstances, which often left them available to muster when required, at the same time rendered them less reliable mainstays than the craftsmen and shopkeepers.[159] An unemployed man could not afford to pass up a day's wages however beholden he was to Clodius. This may help explain why in 56, in order to bolster Clodius's popular opposition to Pompey, Crassus provided the past patrician with money: there were times when the popular leader had to offer some of his supporters an immediate recompense to make their participation feasible. Although the *collegia* did organize themselves into *centuriae* and *decuriae*, they were not martial associations. *Collegiati* were ordinary urban citizens, hence untrained and unarmed. Their lack of training became evident in 57, when the hireling bands of Milo and Sestius proved superior fighters.[160] Still less were they heavily armed. It was illegal to carry weapons in the city of Rome, and even amid the disorder of the fifties a dropped dagger could engage the attention of a crowd.[161] Stones and other readily available projectiles, fire, clubs, and fists, these were the weapons with which the mob was regularly equipped. Which brings us to Clodius's seizure of the temple of Castor. This was a common site for *contiones*. Clodius did not transform the temple into a fortress or an arsenal: no doubt it was used as a rallying point for demonstrations because it was so familiar a point to Clodius's followers.[162] Cicero's military imagery, pervasive and persuasive, was intended to conjure fear of an army of have-nots waging war against the *boni*; in other words, it was meant to invoke the ghost of Catiline's rebellion.

Let us return once again (and finally) to the characterization of Clodius as Catiline's successor, an idea widely advertised by Cicero and often accepted (with varying degrees of conviction) by modern scholars.[163] The assimilation of Clodius to Catiline began, as we have seen, during the agitation preceding the Bona Dea trial. Given the *popularis* tactics of Clodius's supporters at that time—and given the schematic representation of *popularis* figures not merely in Cicero but in sources for the late republic generally—this is hardly surprising.[164] All of which urges care lest Cicero's early treatment of Clodius be promoted to the status of historical fact. That Clodius was not a participant in the Catilinarian conspiracy has been established. But did he, upon his personal transition to *popularis* politics, assume Catiline's mantle, did he inherit the revolutionary's following in any meaningful sense? This line of inquiry raises the question of the coherence of Catiline's actual organization, which, in view of his conspiracy's rapid failure as well as the spate of politically motivated accusations that supervened on defeat in the field, must remain difficult to answer with confidence.[165] But there seems little doubt that Catiline enjoyed the favor of the urban lower classes, at least until the announcement that his program included the complete elimination of debt (which alienated the shopkeepers and craftsman, it appears) and the rising fear that the Catilinarians intended destruction on the city itself. Catiline was apparently more popular in the Italian countryside. This, of course, was the opposite of Clodius's popular base, which was almost wholly urban and, one might add, wholly his own invention (however fortuitous).[166] One cannot ignore the fact that Clodius, like Catiline, had connections with Etruria—so did Caesar for that matter.[167] Yet the Claudians, like other families of their stature, were careful to cultivate *domi nobiles* throughout Italy. And it is worth observing that Cicero's complaints about Clodius's intrusive activities in Etruria come only after his death, which suggests that this was an endeavor occupying the latter years of the past patrician's life, years not especially remarkable for their *popularis* nature. Certain individuals who were conspicuous adherents of Catiline do reappear in the number of Clodius's friends and followers.[168] However, it is easy to exaggerate the significance of the freedman L. Sergius—*armiger Catilinae*—as it is that of the aristocratic friendships common to both men.[169] Catiline's circle was for a time quite wide, as Cicero admits, and its membership fluid enough for the orator to neutralize the charge of Catilinarian sympathies when it was directed at his client Caelius Rufus.[170]

In fact, when the collected evidence is examined, two common threads emerge connecting Clodius and Catiline: a willingness to exploit popular discontents and a willingness to turn to violent methods. But these traits were hardly the exclusive property of these two men. Still less do these qualities establish the much stronger claim advanced by Cicero. Clodius's political career followed a path dramatically different from Catiline's. The latter's was unimpeded if undistinguished until he met with rejection in his attempts to become consul. Clodius's career, on the other hand, hit the early obstacle of the Bona Dea scandal, but by 58 seemed well on track. However anxious the tribune was to form his own political base, he was hardly the desperate man Catiline appears to have become. Nor had Clodius the slightest intention of overthrowing the government. Quite the contrary. His later plans enjoined the co-opting of the consuls and the eradication of his opponents through legislation. Never mind that his actions were underscored by violence; they were not enforced by troops in the field. One may go so far as to assert that Clodius's success, both as a *popularis* and as an enemy of Cicero, which earned him the sobriquet *felix Catilina* (Cic. *Dom.* 72), owed itself not to his similarity with but to his differences from Catiline.[171] But Clodius's reputation, like Antony's, has suffered from Cicero's procrustean characterization. The frightening figure of Catiline was not solely Cicero's invention, to be sure, and an attachment to Catiline became a standard charge in the years after the infamous conspiracy. But few can have been more skillful at drawing damaging ethical portraits of their enemies in the likeness of the monstrous patrician revolutionary.[172] The matter can now be settled. Clodius was not the commander in chief of the *veteres Catilinae milites*.

The *Clodiani* did not comprise hired thugs and gladiators, nor did they aim at the violent overthrow of the established government. There was nothing novel or dangerous in popular demonstrations per se: the *plebs* expressed its will with cheers and jeers at the games and shows, at *contiones*, and at trials. The people sometimes became unruly; they even resorted to riot when they felt utterly stymied or were confronted with a frightening crisis, such as a food shortage. But this was a normal element of Roman politics.[173] As Yavetz aptly described matters: "democracy did not exist in Rome, but popular pressure did."[174] Nor was violence a facet of life alien to the Romans' existence. Devoid of a modern police force, Roman society regularly employed self-help as a means to securing property and maintaining local order.[175] For the privileged classes, the recognized principle of *vim vi repellere licet* translated itself into the acquisition of private guards. The necessity and respectability of personal violence were easily transformed into the utilization of violence to attain political goals—shocking when menacing to the *res publica*, admirable when vital to the state's preservation.[176] Political violence became endemic in the late republic, a familiar fact, though Clodius's exploitation of popular protests and demonstrations was a vital factor in the escalation of urban violence that characterized the fifties. Nevertheless, Clodian violence, as we shall observe, was normally accompanied by justifications that appealed to traditional Roman rights—like *provocatio*—or by the exigencies of food crises. The tribune was careful, for the most part, to satisfy the popular ideology of his constituents; in doing so he provided himself with a defense before his senatorial peers, some of whom will have been sympathetic to the rights of the *plebs*, at least on an abstract level, and all of whom understood the propriety of violence when legitimately employed and when not taken to extremes (the precise definition of that being impossible, of course). None of this was likely to be appreciated by Cicero, as a result of which Clodius's resort to violence is always displayed as the act of a criminal or madman.

Clodius's influence over the urban population, then, was based on appeals to popular ideology and on his personal claim on the people's gratitude. Still, important though *urbana gratia* undoubtedly was, the tribune's astonishing capacity to mobilize his backers also owes itself to the distribution of local prestige he had cultivated through the implementation of his legislation. In his denunciations of Clodius, Cicero mentions by name several of his supporters, mostly freedmen, who must have developed, at least in the course of events in 58 and later, a reputation as allies of Clodius, though allies of a very modest sort. Men such as Lentidius, Lollius, Plaguleius, and Sergius, cited by the orator as *duces tabernariorum*, are likely to have been leaders of *collegia*.[177] Though of dubious standing to a Cicero, they held an estimable station in their own wards among their own kind. Firmidius, who appears as a leader of *mercenarii*, must be of a similar mold.[178] He too will have been a leading member of a *collegium*. Of course, as we have seen, the distinguished Gellius was also a commander of *mercenarii*; his involvement in *collegia* will clearly have been of a different order, possibly as a patron. P. Pomponius, whose status is unknown, was another who possessed influence over the *plebs urbana*; he, likewise, was an intimate of Clodius. The obscure Fidulius was designated the first to vote for the *lex de exsilio Ciceronis*, a signal honor for a man of his rank: Clodius knew how to honor the humble.[179] These prosopographical traces hint at the extent of Clodius's personal role as a powerful benefactor to the people generally and as a superior friend to those holding positions of some significance in the world of the urban *plebs*. Consequently, his enjoyment of *favor populi* was never simply a matter of Clodius's own standing and of his own appeals to the crowd: his eager connections in the various *vici* could be, and had to be, relied upon.

Let us consider a hypothetical shopkeeper who has heard Clodius's call to close the stores and muster in the forum to demonstrate against, say, Cicero's violation of popular rights. Whatever the degree of his abstract allegiance to Clodius or to the principle he proposed to defend and whatever the depth of his personal feelings of gratitude toward the tribune, he must nonetheless consider the practicality of foregoing a day's profits (and its immediate consequences for himself and his family). He must also reckon with the possibility of suffering personal injury. Furthermore, the *tabernarius* might feel obliged to weigh his patron's requirements in the balance, especially if a freedman. Granted the ties of *clientela* were always strained under exceptional political or social circumstances, and Brunt and others have rightly questioned the extent of control exercised by noble patrons over the urban *plebs*, still, the part played by the patron cannot be mechanically dismissed.[180] Other factors also obtruded, perhaps tilting the balance decisively. Our shopkeeper would certainly take notice of how many of his neighbors, likely to be fellow *collegiati*, obeyed the tribune's summons; local societal expectations must have exerted considerable force in a culture that regarded conformity as a virtue.[181] And because Clodius and his associates had taken pains, through their personal involvement in the enrollment of the *collegia* and in their arrangements for the grain dole, to enhance the importance of the colleges' *magistri*, these neighborhood dignitaries had a personal stake in securing Clodius's position. Consequently, our hypothetical shopkeeper might be faced with the additional pressure of his *magister*, perhaps the most compelling consideration of all for some *tabernarii* (to the extent that the individual derived his own sense of honor and community from his membership in his college). Thus the ordinary plebeian confronted multiple and conflicting demands at any politically significant moment. Few will have reacted in the same way to every summons. But Clodius's *popularitas* was reinforced by his effectiveness at penetrating to the interests of simple Romans at a local level, which increased his capacity to appeal to the ordinary citizen through various channels, direct and indirect.

Perhaps we should not assume an intrinsic unwillingness on the part of our hypothetical shopkeeper to participate in a public demonstration. Such participation, as a member of a *collegium* (not as a random rioter), contributed to the individual's sense of political potency. And while it may be too much to assert that Clodius created a "collective identity" for the *plebs urbana*,[182] there seems no reason to doubt that the focused political activity of the *collegia* made possible an awareness of empowerment among ordinary Romans that exceeded their normal political experience. Thus Clodius's popular influence, founded on his dramatic *transitio ad plebem* and his ostentatiously *popularis* legislation, was constructed of the gratitude owed him (at various levels) for his past actions as well as a contemporary feeling of empowerment instilled by popular participation in behalf of ideologically suitable causes. Of course the *plebs* expected Clodius to defend their rights—he was tribune after all—but it would be ill advised to conclude that his control over his following depended largely on his ability to deliver a steady supply of *commoda populi*. He had done enough already to merit *urbana gratia*. No one among the common people could have expected the tribune's intimate relation with the *collegia* to last beyond his year in office; indeed, they must have been both astonished and delighted when the past patrician extended his *popularis* stance. This is why the *plebs* revered Clodius till the day he died—and beyond. His relationship to his urban following may be adequately understood without arguing that he was under pressure to produce new *beneficia*[183] or that he somehow stood *in loco patroni*.[184] After all, the importance of establishing friendships with the leaders of local associations was recognized by Q. Cicero, if, as seems likely, he was the author of the *Commentariolum Petitionis*: he admonishes Cicero to "take stock of the whole of the city, of all the *collegia*, the *pagi*, the *vicinitates*. If you make the leading men from these into your friends, you will easily hold the rest of the multitude through their agency" (*Comm. Pet.* 30). Clodius grasped that fact of life, events would soon demonstrate, far better than either Quintus or Marcus.

9

To return to the Vatinius episode, this event brought Clodius to what, from the perspective of his career heretofore, can only be viewed as a vertiginous height. At a word he had stymied Vatinius's enemies and scattered the praetor's court. Patently his situation was much changed from the commencement of his tribunate, when the expectations he had invested in his legislative program required him to seek the support or tolerance of every influential party. The power of his office and his pose of balance and potential tractability sufficed to neutralize Ninnius and Cicero and to win the passage of his four laws. These laws, however, transformed his political position: after winning enormous *favor populi* through the success of the Ludi Compitalicii and by dint of the creative and energetic implementation of his *popularis* legislation (once it had passed), Clodius emerged as a formidable political figure who was capable of enforcing his tribunician powers by means of organized popular violence. His defiance of Caesar's enemies revealed his confidence that he had become a force to be reckoned with. The success of this action made him a genuine factor in Roman politics and nobody's lackey. By February, then, the obstacle of the Bona Dea scandal, the *dolor* it provoked in Clodius and the suspicion it incited in others, had been cleared. And it was obvious to Clodius that his best opportunities for the remainder of his tribunate lay in pursuing an aggressively *popularis* course.

CHAPTER SIX

Demagogue

1

By the end of January, Clodius had emerged as a formidable figure in Roman politics, unexcelled in *popularitas* and unafraid to conjure its demonstration. Even the triumvirs were suitably impressed, and while most of Clodius's energies hitherto had been spent in facilitating the provisions of his own legislation, he had also given ample proof that he would champion the dynasts's interests as well.[1] That made it incumbent upon them to respect Clodius's prospects, which no doubt helps to explain Pompey's acquiescence when in February the tribune proposed a new bill, the *lex Clodia de insula Cypro*, annexing Cyprus and confiscating the property of its king, Ptolemy.[2] That this measure enabled Clodius to revenge himself on Ptolemy for his refusal to provide the appropriate succor when the young patrician had fallen into the clutches of pirates is patent enough and was surely one aspect of the law's attractiveness to its promulgator.[3] But vengeance was a collateral merit, not the law's main purpose. Although the resources of the treasury were adequate for the expenses necessitated by Clodius's *lex frumentaria*, senatorial anxiety over costs was nonetheless high. The annexation of Cyprus was intended to reassure the senate by securing new and continuing income to support a state expense that everyone recognized would go on forever.[4] In view of his violent intervention in Vatinius's behalf, Clodius could not risk any senatorial backlash cast in the form of protestations of fiscal responsibility. The tribune had a ready and recent precedent in the mission of P. Lentulus Marcellinus to Cyrene in 75 or 74, and the rhetoric of *commoda populi* will have rendered the measure irresistible.[5] Significantly, Clodius's bill did not stipulate to whom would fall the honor and the profit of annexing Ptolemy's kingdom, a cunning omission that must have suggested to several in the senate more than one possibility, even as it blunted, for the moment at least, the sharp *invidia* invariably aroused by special commands.

2

With this measure, Clodius placed the seal on his initial legislative program. It was time to enter the second, and for us more infamous, phase of his tribunate, the campaign against Cicero. Aggravated since the events of and subsequent to the Bona Dea trial, the enmity between the two men had become, for each of them, a defining attribute. Their peers and their public took for granted their mutual hostility, an expectation punctuated by the aftermath of Cicero's delivery of the *Pro Antonio* and the many-sided negotiations before and after Clodius's installation as tribune. But by February, all must have concluded, the possibility of a volatile conflict had been removed: Pompey had vouched, again and again, for Cicero's safety, and Clodius had given his pledge to the orator, and to key figures among the *optimates*, that he would forgo all attacks. Though in retrospect it may appear Clodius's destiny to have done so, in February 58 it could only have been considered an action as unlikely as it would be outrageous for the tribune to take up the cudgels against Cicero. This second and more hazardous phase of Clodius's tribunate required no less planning, though considerably more boldness, than the first.

In order to prevail against Cicero, whose resources, especially his influence among the equestrian order, were hardly to be despised, it was vital for Clodius to have the support or at least the consent of the consuls and of the triumvirs. Their backing would be crucial inasmuch as Clodius was certain to be confronted by *boni* furious at his unethical volte-face. Obviously, doing harm to Cicero required an enormous effort, which raises the question of Clodius's motivation. Was his hatred for Cicero so passionate that nothing could come between this dragon and his wrath? It would be unwise to discount the force of such personal animosities in Roman politics. Still, enmity does not seem a wholly satisfactory explanation for Clodius's unrelenting assaults. It must be observed that the tribune, having discovered the might of his *popularis* stance, could hardly have found a more appropriate icon at which to direct popular *invidia* than the man who had uncovered and crushed the Catilinarian conspiracy, whose own rhetoric cast himself as the very embodiment of *senatus auctoritas*. An enemy like Cicero justified Clodius's *popularis* tactics. And, because Cicero was an imposing figure in his own right, he was a more attractive target. Enmities as well as friendships defined the Roman politician. If Clodius could succeed in satisfying his hatred for the distinguished consular while enforcing the ideology subtending his role as tribune of the people, that success would guarantee his place among the leading politicians of the day. The gamble, even if against heavy odds, might be thought worth a little treachery.

The consuls had to be the tribune's first concern. For all the clout enjoyed by the dynasts, they were none of them magistrates in 58, which meant that they depended on agents holding offices, a fact all too well understood by Clodius since he was one. But the principal executives were Calpurnius Piso and Aulus Gabinius, and it was vital for Clodius to be confident of their disposition before he could act. Piso was an *adfinis* of the orator, after all, and Gabinius might feel obliged to enforce Pompey's guarantee of Cicero's security.[6] In such a circumstance, the assumptions we bring to the matter will largely dictate our interpretation of its final resolution. It is all too easy to view Piso and Gabinius (especially the latter) as simple ministers to the coalition's policy, in which case they tend to revert to the status of mere ciphers whose actions are deemed to be nothing more than clues to the hidden designs of the triumvirs. It would of course be ridiculous to doubt the consuls' loyalty to Caesar and Pompey, but that can hardly have extended to every particular. The consuls had minds of their own. Their ties to the dynasts meant that they would not see their friends' interests injured, but that, obviously, did not condemn the consuls to a supine disregard for their own interests. This provided Clodius his opening: it was certainly possible to complicate the consuls' network of obligations.[7]

As tribune, Clodius was in a position to promulgate bills assigning choice provinces and extraordinary commands to both consuls. It was an offer neither could refuse, nor could the dynasts expect them to do so. Indeed, the coalition must have felt obliged to promise its support for Clodius's measure. The price for the consuls was, as later events would show, made perfectly clear: they were not to interfere in Clodius's strikes against Cicero.[8] The prizes offered the consuls must actually have put pressure on the dynasts to concede Cicero to Clodius, a gesture that no doubt seemed the path of least resistance. What Crassus thought of it all remains typically vague.[9] Caesar certainly wanted a more manageable Cicero; consequently, he did nothing to stop Clodius even while he left open the possibility of Cicero's joining his staff, an appointment that would serve his purposes admirably.[10] It was Pompey, of all the triumvirs, who had the most to lose in terms of his reputation if at this point he turned his back on the orator, whose safety he had been promising for so long. But even he had become estranged from Cicero by the Vettius affair, and in this instance Gabinius's friendship was simply more valuable to the great man than was Cicero's.[11] Therefore Pompey too, not without genuine embarrassment, relented.[12] It was strictly business. Even Cicero, after his return from exile, admitted that the coalition had consented to his removal out of self-interest.[13]

Cicero was too well connected to be disposed of quite so easily, however, and Clodius had yet to contend with the *boni* whose trust he was poised to violate. Still, by building an alliance with the consuls and by securing the assent of the dynasts, Clodius had gained a considerable tactical advantage. And so, in February, the tribune promulgated two further bills: the *lex Clodia de provinciis consularibus*, which entrusted Piso with a five-year command in Macedonia and Gabinius with the same position in Cilicia, though his province was transferred, after mature consideration, to Syria; and the *lex Clodia de capite civis Romani*.[14] This second law reaffirmed every citizen's right of *provocatio* by interdicting from fire and water anyone who had put to death a Roman citizen without trial. *Provocatio* was a fundamental right, the very bulwark of freedom. Cicero himself describes it in an essay as "patrona civitatis ac vindex libertatis" (*De Orat.* 2.199) and Livy designates *provocatio* the "unicum praesidium libertatis" (3.55.4). Such sentiments tap a deep vein, and no undertaking by a tribune could be more suitable or more thoroughly Roman than the safeguarding of *provocatio*, which was tantamount to the preservation of *libertas*.[15] The cause, then, was a completely traditional one, but Clodius's law included two important innovations: the terms of the measure rendered culpable not only magistrates but also senators in their capacity as advisors to magistrates and the law allowed for retrospective application.[16]

The purpose of Clodius's law was as obvious to Cicero as it is to us, but its formulation was not merely window dressing. The orator's contest with Clodius had been configured from its inception around Cicero's symbolism as the consul who had vanquished the Catilinarians. Cicero embodied the conflict between the so-called *senatus consultum ultimum*, on the authority of which he had as consul executed the Catilinarians, and *provocatio*. By evoking *provocatio*, Clodius made it clear that the vocabulary of their hostility would not change. In fact, it was Clodius's intention to press—to the extreme—the implications of Cicero's public image.[17] No tribune could veto a measure that expanded the principle of *provocatio*, as Clodius's did, to include the senate's exercise of its *auctoritas*. Nor could the staunchest optimate deny that the premise of this expansion constituted a recognition of the legitimacy of the senate's actual role in governing Rome (and hence its responsibility for carrying out that role).

Clodius boasted that he would use his law *de capite civis Romani* to drive Cicero into exile and he further claimed that in this enterprise he had the endorsement of all the dynasts. The tribune even made so bold as to assert that the coalition would back him with Caesar's army.[18] Pompey simply shrugged his shoulders when faced with the proposition of this legislation, but Caesar, when asked, praised the merits of Clodius's law (how could he not?) even while he specified that he did not approve of retrospective legislation, which was at least a whiff of public sympathy for Cicero's circumstances.[19] Indeed, Caesar did not leave for his province until Cicero had departed into voluntary exile, thereby giving the orator every opportunity to seek his protection by joining his staff.[20] In constant *contiones*, however, Clodius clobbered the orator with threats of prosecution. The dynasts made no effort to rebut Clodius's asseverations, and Cicero was later to maintain that it was not their active participation but rather their *taciturnitas* that ruined him.[21] But the triumvirs were not alone in giving way to Clodius.

When Cicero learned of Clodius's law, he donned mourning and solicited the people's support. He got it, from his own sort of people at least.[22] *Equites* from the whole of Italy gathered in Rome and dressed in mourning as a public gesture of their solidarity with their hero. Municipalities and consortia of *publicani* passed resolutions in Cicero's behalf. More significantly, distinguished senators like Hortensius and the elder Curio (once Clodius's advocate) as well as M. Lucullus, L. Torquatus, and the praetor Lentulus Crus all championed Cicero's cause.[23] Acting on the proposal of the tribune Ninnius, the senate decreed that its membership should join the *equites* in wearing mourning in recognition of Cicero's plight. But despite pleas from *principes* and equestrians alike, the consuls took no action. Gabinius forbade a deputation of *equites* to address the senate and went so far as to hold a *contio* at which he denounced the higher orders for putting on mourning. To make his own position unmistakable, he reminded the *equites* that some of them had committed offenses against the principle of *provocatio* in the Catilinarian affair for which they too might one day be required to answer. One of Cicero's most zealous equestrian backers, L. Lemia, was relegated from the city on the ground that he was inciting the knights to riot. Thereafter both consuls, in a joint decree, required that the senate resume its normal attire. Hortensius and Curio were reprimanded. The consuls then called yet another *contio* in which they each of them denounced the execution without trial of Roman citizens, all of which was nothing less than a public demonstration in support of Clodius's bill.[24]

Nor was the tribune idle. Taking advantage of his popular following, he saw to it that Cicero was constantly molested on the streets. Hortensius, too, was attacked and allegedly nearly killed. Moreover, Clodius incited his *operae* to intimidate Cicero's equestrian partisans.[25] The violence that he had employed so effectively in Vatinius's behalf was rapidly becoming a reliable political resource. The senate, however, could not be expected to fold easily under the threat of popular violence or the intimidation of consular authority. The pangs of the previous year rendered a feeble response especially unattractive, and there was much at stake in safeguarding Cicero, not merely because he was so vital a symbol of senatorial authority but also, perhaps principally, because his situation portended future dangers for any and all the leading figures of the senate in view of the Clodian law's comprehensive retrospective application. Even the most obtuse among the *optimates* could not have failed to recognize that Clodius's betrayal of Cicero was likewise a betrayal of his optimate mediators—hence the very real possibility that the tribune would not limit his aggression to Cicero. At a public meeting, Clodius had brought Hortensius and Curio before the populace, which jeered them soundly enough for the senate to appreciate the intensity of the crowd's *invidia Ciceronis*, if not *invidia senatus*.[26] Consequently, it was important to the *boni* to protect Cicero—for their own sakes.

By a deft stroke, Clodius eliminated this motive for senatorial resistance. The tribune was able to alleviate the anxieties of the *optimates* by proposing to assign to Cato the responsibility of annexing Cyprus. The *lex Clodia de imperio Catonis* established Cato in an extraordinary command, *pro quaestore pro praetore*, so that he might supervise the annexation of Cyprus and restore certain exiles to Byzantium.[27] It was a signal honor for a man of Cato's rank, however vigorously Cicero endeavored to represent it otherwise. Clodius's law enhanced Cato's prestige and authority, and it presented him with an opportunity to reap a profit or to advertise his notorious rectitude. It is evident that Clodius had multiple motives in drafting this legislation. Cato's acceptance of this special honor would implicate him irretrievably in the *acta* of Clodius's tribunate, a condition that ensured a forceful spokesman for Clodius's legislative program should it be challenged after his resignation from office. Moreover, as Clodius recognized, matters were likely to run more smoothly for himself and for the triumvirs if Cato were occupied outside the city.[28] But the most immediate significance of the Clodian law was that, by offering public support of Cato, Clodius was able to split Cato and his circle from the resistance to the *lex de capite civis Romani*.[29] Cato, after all, was as logical a target as anyone for prosecution under the law's comprehensive terms. Yet Clodius, by proposing to set Cato in charge of the mission to Cyprus, made it perfectly plain that he had no intention of attacking anyone except Cicero. Thus Clodius, first by menacing, then by reassuring the *optimates*, succeeded in countering their feelings of betrayal. And this precipitated Cicero's sudden desertion by the *boni*.[30]

Suddenly Cicero was completely undone. Confronted by the certainty of prosecution under a law impossible to veto and under a charge that could hardly anticipate a friendly tribune's *auxilium*, the orator found himself without resource.[31] The consuls rebuffed him, the dynasts took no action, his public supporters could scarcely withstand the popular pressure brought against them, and, finally, Hortensius and Cato were advising capitulation. Cicero's refusal to take refuge with Caesar does him credit in an episode in which very few behaved honorably.[32] Some time in March, on the very day Clodius's law was ratified, Cicero left the city.[33] No sooner had he gone than rioters plundered his Palatine mansion.[34]

3

The suddenness of Cicero's collapse, though perfectly comprehensible from the isolated perspective of the orator, can only have been unforeseen by others, including Clodius.[35] And so the tribune's sudden triumph must have had an intoxicating effect, which helps to explain his rush to draft and promulgate a new measure, the *lex Clodia de exsilio Ciceronis*.[36] The haste with which the bill was composed, reflected in the modification of its text after promulgation and its curious, though unexceptionable, Latinity, as well as the turbulent circumstances of its passage and of its ultimate supersession, all underscore the urgency and passion of this measure.[37] Because the law is known only from Cicero's extended criticism of it in *De Domo*, its exact provisions—and the question of whether the legislation was in fact technically flawed—remain irrecoverable. Before turning to what can be said about the *lex Clodia*, then, it bears observing that irregularities seem not to have been noticed or pressed either at the time of the measure's introduction or of its subsequent ratification.

The law cited Cicero by name and recorded his misdeeds, the execution of the Catilinarians and the falsification of a *senatus consultum*. Cicero's voluntary exile was transformed into a legal and permanent banishment; he was forbidden under pain of death to come within 500 miles of Italy, and anyone who aided Cicero in violating this provision was likewise to be put to death. Furthermore, Clodius's measure confiscated Cicero's property, provided for its sale at auction (perhaps under Clodius's own supervision), and apparently assigned the tribune the responsibility of demolishing Cicero's *domus* on the Palatine. In addition, the law authorized the construction of a monument on the site. The measure also forbade Cicero's subsequent recall either by senatorial decree or by legislation.[38]

Much of this was highly traditional, despite the later complaints of Cicero, though little in our understanding of the law can safely be deemed unproblematic. To begin with, the main purpose of the law, obviously enough, was to make permanent and official Cicero's voluntary withdrawal from the city. In the past, defendants who fled the city were thereafter exiled by plebiscite, which is to say, through a tribunician enactment.[39] The crucial difference in Cicero's case lay in the fact that he had never formally been accused of anything, a reality that the law's catalog of misdeeds could in no way alter. This is why Cicero, in *De Domo*, can so effectively attack the law as a *privilegium* and as tantamount to proscription.[40] Whether this distinction, so forcefully pressed by the orator, was a matter of law or custom is obscure: Cicero cites no relevant statute, and this in a speech suffused with appeals to legal precedent. Nor can one be certain that traditional practice was ever clear on this point.

Cicero also claimed that Clodius's law was in violation of the *lex Caecilia et Didia* of 98, which forbade the drafting of a single law that dealt with unrelated subjects, and of the *lex Licinia*, which prohibited the author of a law from creating a *curatio* for himself.[41] The brief is formidable, but appeals to previous legislation (not always entirely legitimate)[42] characterize *De Domo*, and Cicero's objections might well have lacked substance. For instance, we have only Cicero's word for it that the *lex Clodia* specifically assigned to Clodius the confiscation, sale, and destruction of Cicero's property, a provision that would seem to contravene the *lex Licinia*. Yet Clodius's law need only have required that these actions take place; their performance, all would have understood, was naturally to become the responsibility of the law's promulgator.[43] Matters are complicated, however, by Clodius's apparent insistence in 57 that the *lex de exsilio Ciceronis* had actually granted him the appropriate authorization to construct and dedicate a shrine to Libertas, a claim that might be taken to imply that the law in fact mentioned him by name in stipulating the fate of Cicero's property.[44] If so, then Cicero's criticism carries conviction. The problem is that on this point Clodius's position was completely rejected by Cicero (and by the pontiffs who heard the *De Domo* in 57). Thus the relevance of the *lex Licinia* remains elusive.

Matters are less obscure when one turns to the Clodian law's observance of the *lex Caecilia et Didia*. The various measures affecting Cicero's property, especially the destruction of his house, and even the erection of some memorial on its site, must all from a Roman point of view have seemed relevant to Cicero's exile and therefore not unrelated items in an omnibus bill. The ideological essence of the accusation leveled by Clodius against Cicero was that, in his violation of *provocatio*, he was guilty of *regnum*. The tribune assailed the orator with recriminations of cruelty, tyrannical aspirations, and even pretenses to divinity.[45] For such an enemy of the people, the razing of his house was a spectacular but nonetheless traditional punishment: in the fifth century, the house of Sp. Cassius, who had plotted to seize royal power, was demolished; Sp. Maelius was slain by the "tyrannicide" Servilius Ahala and the Aequimaelium occupied the site of his wrecked manor; after M. Manlius Capitolinus was thrown from the Tarpeian rock in 384, the site of his ruined house was used to erect a temple to Juno Moneta.[46] Recent history, too, provided a pointed and significant precedent: the house of M. Fulvius Flaccus, the consul of 125 who became tribune in 122 only to perish with Gaius Gracchus in the subsequent year, was confiscated and destroyed by order of the senate; its location served as the site for Catulus's shrine, built *de manubiis Cimbricis*.[47] Exile, confiscation, destruction, and the erection of a public monument, then, were not individual and unrelated stipulations. Instead, they constituted, in the minds of most Romans, the sweeping and severe—and traditional—penalty appropriate for the elimination root and branch of the most dangerous enemies of the *res publica*.[48]

Clodius's law rendered Cicero an outlaw. Furthermore, it initiated a sequence of public actions that assimilated Cicero to the most infamous of the state's enemies. Cicero would later declare the law illegal, but only after it had been made irrelevant by the centuriate assembly's decision to recall him from exile. If Cicero's objections are difficult to substantiate, it is easier to appreciate his claim that Clodius's hatred for him was excessive and cruel (*Dom.* 60ff.). This was not, however, the immediate impression created by the enactment. The urban *plebs* had already pillaged Cicero's properties. When formal confiscations were undertaken, there seems to have been no shortage of willing buyers. Traces of this commerce mark the speeches of Cicero, enough at least for us to suspect Piso and Gabinius, Clodius's agent Scato, and, perhaps, others of the Claudii.[49]

4

That the destruction of Cicero's house signified his status as an outlaw is by now clear enough, but, in order to appreciate the full impact of Clodius's legislation and the intensity of the two men's later contest over the fate of this site, we must examine a little further the symbolic function of the *domus* in Roman society and we must consider the different, yet not unrelated, investments that Clodius and Cicero alike had made in the Palatine. The *domus* was not merely a residence for the Roman aristocrat. It defined the space and range of his immediate household, over whom he exercised *potestas* or *dominium*.[50] It was also the site of his family's cult, the *sacra* of his *gens*, so that Cicero could ask, with rhetorical passion but, other sources would indicate, without much rhetorical exaggeration, "What is more sacred, what is more strongly protected by every religious safeguard, than the *domus* of each and every Roman citizen?" (*Dom.* 109). Indeed, for imperial authors the very terms *domus* and *di penates* are interchangeable.[51] Most conspicuous of all, the *domus* provided a concrete display of a Roman's lineage, exposed in the *imagines* of the house's atrium that recorded his family's genealogy and accomplishments and in the trophies, often quite ostentatious, that became its fixtures.[52] The grand mansion was nothing less than the most visible and tangible symbol of a Roman's high birth and splendor. External display was a major component of this symbol. *Dignitas* demanded, and was enhanced by, ample *aedificatio* (though moderation, however fluid its definition, was felt to be a competing imperative as well).[53] Visibility was vital. Livius Drusus (tr. pl. 91), whose home would one day be Cicero's, reacted to his architect's assurances that his house, though it overlooked the forum, would be completely private and inaccessible to the inspection of others by saying "No, you should apply your skills to designing my house so that whatever I do will be visible to everybody" (Vell. Pat. 2.14.3). And in fact the Roman *domus* was a remarkably public structure, even in recesses that modern sensibilities would expect to be wholly personal and private.[54]

As a facility, the wholly public and the residential spheres of the *domus* were quite often blurred. Pompey's house in the Campus Martius was attached to his monumental theater complex, its temple to Venus Victrix and its porticoes.[55] There is reason to believe that Catulus's triumphal portico was an extension of his own *domus* on the Palatine.[56] And, in a later time, Augustus would find himself the neighbor of his patron god, Apollo. If the *domus* defined space so as to meld the public and private, it also combined the sacred and the profane—and not merely by housing the *di penates*. Perhaps because the Roman *domus* incorporated allusions to public spaces—Greek and Roman alike—it was inevitable that domestic architecture should evince aspects just as likely to be associated with sacred space.[57] The display of *spolia* and honorific statues at and in the entry areas of the *domus* parallels the look of temples constructed *ex manubiis*, as Wiseman has observed.[58] Less immediately obvious but equally important, domestic architecture of the late republic increasingly borrowed patterns of design from late Hellenistic sanctuaries: one may point to the relationship between the Horti Lucullani and the sanctuary of Fortuna Primagenia at Praeneste.[59] This last development has rightly been linked with the tendency of individual Roman politicians to appropriate particular cults for the sake of their personal advancement—a long-standing practice that accelerated rapidly with the civil wars of the late first century—as seen, for instance, early on in the attitude of Scipio Africanus (and his family) toward Jupiter Greatest and Best (Africanus's *imago* was housed in the temple by his descendants) and, more relevant to our purposes, the situation of Pompey's palace in the Campus Martius as well as Caesar's controversial addition of a *fastigium* to the *domus publica*.[60]

Thus the significance of the Roman *domus* emerges as something transcending the natural affection that a grandee of any culture might ordinarily be expected to feel for his property or the awe that a big house might inspire among the humbler sort in any society. The *domus*, in its combined representation of personal status and public image and in its affinities with sacred space, was at once a principal and living focus of an aristocrat's political activity and a vital symbol of his political power—hence the potency of the *domus* in the language of political imagery and in the actual discourse of politics. The example of Livius Drusus has already been cited. Cn. Octavius, who ennobled his family with the consulship in 165, may have owed a part of his electoral success to his splendid Palatine mansion, "plenam dignitatis domum," as Cicero described it.[61] On the other hand, the grandiose palace constructed on the Velia by P. Valerius Publicola (cos. suff. 509) so aroused popular suspicion that he was possessed of regal aspirations that it was demolished and Publicola removed himself to a home located at the base of the hill.[62] And Cicero himself, who went deeply into debt to purchase his beloved house,[63] was vulnerable to similar abuse, as when, in the aftermath of Clodius's acquittal in the Bona Dea trial, the angry patrician cast at Cicero with "quousque hunc regem feremus?"—a complaint buttressed by Clodius's critical and concise observation, "domum emuisti."[64]

Cicero's purchase warranted notice, be it envying or invidious, since it represented a move so spectacularly upward. By the late republic, the Palatine's northern slope was Rome's most fashionable neighborhood.[65] The lowermost portion of the Palatium was Lucus Vestae, that is, the Nova Via where stood the Atrium Vestae and Domus Regis, near Porta Mugonia. The principal streets distinguishing the upper region were the so-called Via Sacra, which Coarelli has now identified with the Vicus Fortunae Huiusce Diei, and the Clivus Palatinus.[66] Visible from the forum and possessing an easy view of the Capitol, the Palatine's political potential was appreciated and exploited as early as the second century B.C. Famous names occupied this district for centuries, even while other great men, some newly so, pressed to find a place for themselves in this elite neighborhood. Families such as the Aemilii Scauri, the Metelli, the Fulvii Flaccii, the Licinii Crassi, the Livii Drusi, to name but a few—and, of course, the Claudii—made their homes here. In all we know the names of nearly forty proprietors (of nearly thirty houses) from the mid-second century through the end of the late republic.[67] Although individual mansions varied in size and in luxury, to some extent because residents of the Palatine tended to join separate but adjacent houses into a single *domus* (and it must be borne in mind that the high cost and low availability of Palatine property encouraged building at several storeys), one can nonetheless approximate the size of the lot for the "typical" grand manor of this exclusive neighborhood: the finer late republican *domus* covered about 702 square meters (about 7,550 square feet).[68] Costs ran into the millions. Cicero, for instance, paid HS 3,500,000 for the house he bought in late 62.[69]

The Claudii Pulchri seem to have had a family residence of long standing on the Palatine, the possession of which had apparently devolved upon Clodius by the time of his election to the tribunate.[70] Clodius's *domus* was destined to become perhaps the largest property on the Palatine. This was by design, since it cannot be doubted that Clodius recognized the status to be gotten from acquisitions developed on a grand scale, especially in so elite and restricted a neighborhood.[71] The inventory of Clodius's property includes his original mansion, the apartments rented from him in 56 by Caelius Rufus (perhaps part of another *domus*, portions of which were leased to other aristocrats), and the properties acquired from Q. Seius Postumus in 58 and from M. Aemilius Scaurus (pr. 56) in 53, this last being itself a complex consisting of the past residences of the Octavii and the Licinii Crassi as well as the actual *domus Aemili*.[72]

Even if the latest archaeological data hold out the prospect of locating the site of Clodius's house with greater accuracy than past scholars could legitimately hope for, we must nonetheless admit that our ability to reconstruct the arrangement of Clodius's *domus* vis-à-vis his neighbors is still limited. We know well that he and Cicero owned adjacent properties. Clodius's other neighbors included Seius and the *porticus Catuli* (to which may have been attached the sumptuous home of the general who triumphed over the Cimbri; his son lived on the Palatine in any case). Nevertheless, their relative arrangement admits of several possibilities. We also know that Clodius's close neighbors included, in one constellation or other, Calpurnius Piso, Claudius Marcellus (cos. 50), M. Fadius Gallus (tr. pl. 75), Q. Cicero, and Clodius's own sister, Clodia, who lived with her husband, the consul of 60, in a house that shared a wall with the house of Catulus. In the same general vicinity one could likewise find the residences of Hortensius Hortalus, Annius Milo, and P. Sulla.[73]

Clearly, then, the neighborhood that Cicero joined with the purchase of his Palatine *domus* was nothing short of exclusive, and the setting of his house could scarcely be more prominent. This context is important: a visual awareness of the juxtaposition of Clodius's *domus* with Cicero's can only sharpen one's appreciation of the spectacle, viewable from the forum, of Clodius's urban followers laying riotous waste to the orator's mansion yet all the while respecting the sanctity of the tribune's residence next door.[74] The official confiscation and demolition that followed were also carried out in the shadow of Clodius's home and in full sight of the *plebs urbana*. The sheer pageantry, then, of Clodius's triumph over his enemy was striking advertisement to the undeniable political might of the tribune.

But the tribune's thirsty ambition was hardly slaked. If he had not done so already, he quickly acquired the property of Q. Seius Postumus, the Roman knight whose house adjoined Clodius's (and possibly either Cicero's or the *porticus Catuli*).[75] The knight was unwilling to sell, nor would he be intimidated by Clodius's threats to block out his sunlight through the construction of overshadowing additions to his own house. Charged with spunk in despite of Clodius, Seius, if Cicero is to be believed, vowed that the tribune would purchase his house only over his dead body, a condition soon realized, presumably by chance (though Cicero insisted that Seius had been borne off by poison). However it was that the stubborn soul of Seius was induced to shuffle off its mortal coil, Clodius purchased the property over heavy rival bidding at a strongly inflated price.[76] These properties, the houses of Cicero and Seius, along with the site of the *porticus Catuli*, were developed by the tribune into a public monument commemorating the victory of the cause of personal freedom, the *aedes Libertatis*.

We may postpone for the moment a thorough examination of the validity of Clodius's authority to construct and dedicate the *aedes Libertatis*. Presumably it stemmed from the *lex de exsilio*.[77] But uncertainty obtrudes, since Clodius's construction does not fall into the categories of republican building most familiar to us, such as manubial building; indeed, higher magistrates and triumphant generals, not tribunes, tend to dominate our accounts of the privileged activity of monumental construction.[78] Clodius was the first tribune we know of who dedicated an *aedes*.[79]

Whatever the exact formulation of the *lex de exsilio*, public sanctions beyond the law's ratification were necessary for Clodius to dedicate his shrine, even if the consecration of an *aedes* was a less complicated affair than the inauguration of a *templum* properly so called.[80] Clodius's shrine absorbed the portico of Catulus, the testimonial inscription of which Clodius stripped from the facade and replaced with his own epigraphic display. Cicero bewails the "destruction" of this portico in his *De Domo*, imploring the pontiffs to pity the reputations of the consul of 102 and his son, the consul of 78 who had once been *princeps senatus*. The *porticus Catuli* must at the very least have been *res publica* (certainly in 57, when the senate lifted the *religio* from Clodius's shrine, restoration of the portico was assigned to the consuls), which ought to mean that legislative or senatorial approval was required for its alteration.[81] Yet for all his tearful lamentations in *De Domo*, Cicero nowhere takes exception to Clodius's treatment of the *porticus Catuli* on the grounds of illegality or sacrilege (except insofar as he objects to the entire consecration of the shrine).[82] Nor, apparently, was there any obstruction of any kind in 58. It is well known, of course, that after his return from exile, Cicero insisted that Clodius had not observed the technicalities of the *lex Papiria de dedicationibus* in consecrating his shrine. Clodius disagreed, and an estimation of their respective arguments may for now be postponed.[83] But other particulars, not mentioned in Cicero's later criticisms, must have been seen to. For instance, at the dedication of the shrine there will have been posted the shrine's charter setting forth the sacred boundaries and special regulations (if any).[84]

Clodius consecrated the *aedes Libertatis* without consulting the college of pontiffs, a procedure whose irregularity Cicero was able to exploit in *De Domo*. Although conference with the college of pontiffs did not constitute a legal requirement for consecration, their approval and presence at the ritual was regular, as Cicero's acid remarks to Clodius make very clear (*Dom.* 132). In fact, however, the rites needed only a single pontiff's expertise, which in this instance was provided by the most junior pontifex, Q. Pinarius Natta, Clodius's brother-in-law.[85] Why Clodius snubbed the pontifical college is difficult to explain. Perhaps he feared that too many of the pontiffs would refuse to participate in the shrine's consecration and consequently he decided to avoid any public rebuff. Even so, this evasion of custom, especially in view of the controversial nature of his *lex de exsilio* as well as the novelty of a tribune's undertaking a public construction, must have provoked annoyance, and it ultimately proved quite damaging when the sanctity of the shrine was challenged before the college in 57. Consciously or not, Clodius was probing the limits of his recently acquired political might. The tribune's precipitous rush to settle Libertas on the Palatine was bound to eventuate in mistakes of process and of judgment. What is so arrantly unreasonable, and remains so hard to understand, is why Clodius should have hurried matters along in this way. He had won, after all. Which suggests that the tribune, if he was not actually overcome by the thrill of victory, foresaw the crystallization of opposition to his project if he did not finish it fast.

How, then, does Cicero describe the shrine to Liberty? It sat on the most visible, most beautiful location in the city.[86] The complex involved a paved *porticus cum conclavibus* whose frontal view was 300 feet long, an immense peristyle, and *cetera eius modi*, whatever that means (*Dom.* 115f.). There was a shrine (*aedes*) that presumably housed the goddess's cult statue, a piece imported by Clodius's eldest brother from Tanagra. Moreover, the complex also housed an honorific statue of Clodius erected by a certain Menulla of Anagnia in gratitude for the *lex Clodia de iniuriis publicis*, an otherwise unknown piece of legislation from which the dedicator had evidently benefited.[87] Finally, the edifice bore an inscription, which certainly contained the tribune's name, on its lengthy facade overlooking the forum. Cicero, striving to discredit Clodius's dedication of the site, makes much of the fact that this complex was integrated into (or at least appended to) Clodius's own home, a point that allows the orator to assert that Clodius was unmoved by religious or public concerns but merely hoped to enjoy the most spacious and prestigious *domus* in the city.

In view of the speed with which Clodius completed and dedicated the shrine, construction ex nihilo seems improbable. It is more reasonable to assume that Clodius did no more than renovate and expand what had been the portico of Catulus, integrating this facility with his own *domus*, which now absorbed the house of Seius. Certain additions will have been necessary to complete the design, but their exact nature remains unknown to us. The entire complex encroached upon the site of Cicero's house, but the shrine was not by any means a replacement for Cicero's *domus*.[88] It has been proposed that Clodius's shrine took the shape of a colonnaded *tholus* fronted by a rectangular portico.[89] The suggestion is intelligent, since this building type, derived from late Hellenistic sacred architecture, was contemporary both in Italian sacred and domestic designs, which means that such a structure would have been appropriate both to Clodius's purposes and to Cicero's criticisms.[90] Nevertheless, for all its attractiveness, this proposal can count only as speculation. There is absolutely no evidence to confirm or even to support it.[91]

That the *aedes Libertatis* had moment as a signal monument of Clodius's victory over Cicero is too apparent to call for further comment. And, in light of the symbolism of razing Cicero's *domus* in punishment of his "tyranny," the aptness of Freedom's shrine is also manifest. Yet Libertas was not exclusively the embodiment of the citizenry's political freedom. Liberty first found divine expression in Rome when Ti. Sempronius Gracchus (cos. 238) dedicated the temple of Jupiter Libertas on the Aventine, the proper purport of which was made clear by his son after he captured Beneventum in 214: he ordered painted in this temple a representation of himself freeing the slave volunteers who had assisted him in his victory.[92] This association of *libertas* with personal freedom (over against the position of the slave) is likewise reflected in the goddess's manifestation on republican coinage, where she generally appears in company with the *pileus*, the felt cap indicating free status.[93] But this conception of *libertas* cannot easily be separated from the political freedom of Roman citizens (to which idea the notion of personal freedom actually and obviously contributes). The Atrium Libertatis, a secular building in existence by 212, was employed in conducting the census, for storing records, and as a space for publishing legislation—as well as a site for manumitting slaves.[94] Furthermore, in republican coinage the goddess (with the attendant *pileus*) is found in conjunction with allusions to *leges tabellariae* and *leges de provocatione*.[95] Thus the traditional presence in Rome of the divinity Libertas underscores how Clodius's destruction of Cicero's house as well as his construction of the *aedes Libertatis* exploited the inherent duality of *libertas* as an idea incorporating, by the time of the late republic, both personal freedom and the political liberty of the Roman people.[96] Clodius, or so he hoped, was co-opting the cult of Freedom at Cicero's cost.

Clodius could also expect to derive from his building program at least some of the benefits that accrued from manubial construction.[97] The *triumphator* who chose to devote his booty to public building, frequently in the shape of a temple to the gods, earned a hefty return from his investment: a reputation for piety, the gratitude of equestrian contractors as well as that of common laborers in need of work, and—the most striking profit of all—a visible and enduring token of his glory. The dedicator of a public building could hope that, in addition to enjoying honor in his own lifetime, his family would preserve his monument's upkeep jealously. Thus his name would be perpetuated in a concrete form. Clodius's project, due to its scale, probably did not attract sensational attention either from contractors or from the unemployed. Still, Clodius's undertakings on behalf of the *plebs*, not only as its champion against Cicero and for *libertas* but also as a noble willing to lavish upon the city a new shrine speaking directly to the people's ideological concerns, could only enhance his already extraordinary popularity—all of which permitted Clodius to view himself, and to be viewed by others, as a real player in the game of civic display.

Nor should we overlook the prestige Clodius enjoyed on account of the substantial amplification of his *domus* represented by the *aedes*, which was now attached to it. The long portico would, among other uses, serve splendidly as a suitably grand and imposing environment in which to entertain the tribune's friends, clients, and fellow citizens. Indeed, if only owing to its increased size, Clodius's new *domus* complex enhanced his authority. But the force of the *domus Clodi* must have sprung mainly from its exceptional success in joining personal and political symbols even as it combined sacred and domestic space, an achievement at once compatible with the trends of the age yet innovative enough legitimately to be considered an influence on the building program of Pompey and especially on the domestic arrangements of Augustus.[98] Small wonder Cicero referred to the *aedes Libertatis* as the "monument of my pain," the "tropaea de me et de republica" (*Dom.* 100).

6

A brief retrospective is in order. The commencement of Clodius's tribunate saw him the dynasts' man, which is why it was so necessary for him to establish his own base within the senate and among the urban *plebs*. In order for him to accomplish this, however, Clodius had to secure the passage of his initial legislative program, a feat made difficult by Cicero's opposition. Consequently Clodius was constrained to negotiate with his enemy through the offices of the *boni*. But the concession was worth making: Clodius's laws, without alienating the senate, garnered their author unexcelled *popularitas*, the violent potential of which surfaced during the senate's attempt to try Vatinius. Thereafter Clodius cultivated his *popularis* profile by championing *provocatio*, a principle he enacted in congenial fashion by attacking Cicero. Clodius overcame Cicero's resources through a bold combination of treachery, brinksmanship, legislation, oratory, and popular violence, the last validated by traditional appeals to the rights of citizens in the teeth of magisterial excess. Cicero collapsed, and Clodius, flushed with victory, hastily declared him an outlaw, eradicated his Roman traces and erected the *aedes Libertatis*, a memorial to the cause of freedom—and to the enduring debt owed to Clodius by the urban populace.

But Cicero had fallen too suddenly. For it was in the *conflict* with Cicero that the tribune was able to exercise his might as a *popularis*. In triumph there were accolades, but no arena in which legitimately to demonstrate in action the extent of his newly acquired and redoubtable *potentia*. Clodius was, after all, merely a tribune, in spite of his ample clout and his enormous pretensions. Inactivity, then, was neither in Clodius's interests nor to his liking. It hardly constitutes a keen insight into Clodius's psychology to observe his passion for the whip hand or his penchant, only recently held in check, for overestimating his own circumstances. And in any case it would have been a sapient senator indeed who did not, in the rush of a tribunate so spectacularly successful so far, succumb to his own most flattering conception of his own capacities. All of which might help to explain Clodius's adoption of a new and extraordinary policy, in what may fairly be deemed the third phase of his tribunate, his undertaking of an unequal contest between himself and Rome's most powerful senator.

Yet even if we grant that it was not in Clodius's nature to rest satisfied, that is itself no explanation for his decision to make Pompey his next target. Prior hostilities between the two are inconspicuous; indeed, if anything Pompey can only be described as having been too cooperative in the early months of 58. Nor does it seem very likely that, at this juncture, Clodius considered Pompey a serious rival for popular affection.[99] It is important, of course, to make the observation that Clodius quite genuinely believed that in a struggle he could now prevail even against so formidable a figure as Pompey, but, once again, the motive for such a struggle in the first place must be accounted for.[100] It may simply have been the case that Clodius could see no better way to display his might than to turn it on Pompey. But more practical considerations may also have come into play. As we have seen, Clodius's victory over Cicero entailed the blunting and assuaging of senatorial sensibilities concerning the *fides* of the *boni* and concerning the scale of Clodius's assault on *senatus auctoritas.* Clodius never intended his *popularis* career to put him at war with the senate, nor will he have proved blind to the likelihood that his successful campaign against Cicero must leave him vulnerable to senatorial *invidia*. Still, whatever the suspicions and anxieties harbored against Clodius by the *boni*, they paled in comparison with the senate's resentment of Pompey's preeminence. A confrontation with Pompey, then, held the potential for attracting senatorial acceptance, if not its actual support, even while it shifted invidious attention to the exalted position of the great man.[101] Now Clodius could challenge Pompey only by resorting to his *popularis* arsenal, tactics he was keen to employ and whose use, remarkably enough, had to be viewed by the *boni* as being (for the moment at least) in their interests as well. The point, let us be clear, is not that Clodius would become any less *popularis* in posture in this phase of his tribunate, only that his posture, directed against Pompey, would become less offensive to the senatorial establishment. Of course, it was vital at the same time that Clodius limit his aggression to Pompey (as previously he had concentrated his energies specifically against Cicero). He could not by any means expect to stand up against the entire triumvirate. But he might well expect that Pompey's allies would, for a time and so long as their own immediate interests were unmolested, be content to see their senior partner tested. It was Clodius's intention, then, to make himself Pompey's principal rival in the city, an enterprise that would enable him to exploit his popular following even while he earned the senate's toleration.

This explanation of Clodius's motives makes the tribune's plan of attack on Pompey readily comprehensible: he struck at the general's eastern settlement. As is well known, the great man's victory over Mithridates had, by virtue of his unparalleled wealth and glorious achievement, brought him to a station that the leadership of the senate could only envy and fear. This is why the ratification of Pompey's eastern *acta* had provoked such stubborn opposition, in consequence of which the general was driven to unite with Crassus and Caesar. There were other ways to worry Pompey, but Clodius, by launching out against his eastern settlement, could assail the great man's prestige precisely by renewing the previous and unsuccessful optimate challenge to Pompey's preeminence. The implications of this coincidence could scarcely be lost on anyone.

7

Clodius set matters in motion by promulgating a bill *de rege Deiotaro et Brogitaro*.[102] In settling the affairs of Asia, Pompey had shown special favor to Deiotarus, the tetrarch of western Galatia. Pompey increased his territory and arranged for the senate to bestow on him the title *rex sociusque et amicus*. Pompey honored Deiotarus further by naming him high priest in the cult of Magna Mater at Pessinus, a principality dominated by that office. Deiotarus's elevation represented his reward for long loyalty to Rome. For Pompey, of course, this was the sort of benefaction that gave him license to style himself a maker of kings, a rare privilege that allowed for considerable pride and boasting.[103] The terms of Clodius's bill, however, removed Deiotarus from the high priesthood at Pessinus. In his stead Clodius appointed Brogitarus, Deiotarus's son-in-law and the ruler of the Trocmi in eastern Galatia. Brogitarus, too, by the stipulations of Clodius's law, was to be recognized as king, ally, and friend of Rome.

Clodius's support for Brogitarus, as Cicero would later insist, was the corrupt product of international graft.[104] That Clodius profited from his dealings with Brogitarus can scarcely be doubted. In fact, it would have been astonishing to his contemporaries had it been otherwise.[105] But Clodius's law was not primarily about increasing his own wealth or expanding the dimensions of his family's eastern *clientela*.[106] The tribune's purpose was to humiliate Pompey by abrogating the general's arrangements in Galatia. A large-scale cancellation of Pompey's eastern *acta* would have demanded a reaction from all the dynasts and would in any event have been tantamount to a reorganization of Roman foreign policy in the eastern Mediterranean, which the *boni*, whatever their attitude toward Pompey, would not by any means have permitted the tribune to undertake. But this specific abrogation sufficed to embarrass Pompey without raising senatorial or triumviral hackles. Thus the only legitimate recourse left to Pompey would have been to seek assistance from another tribune, an avenue Clodius closed by introducing an innovation into this law. The *appellatio* of a friendly king was traditionally conferred by senatorial decree, not by plebiscite. Clodius's law is in fact the sole exception.[107] This expansion of the competence of the *concilium plebis*, insignificant in itself, rendered the bill difficult to veto, especially since the innovation was bound to be trumpeted by Clodius in order to guarantee popular interest in the law and popular support should it prove necessary to resort to demonstrations or violence to secure its passage. Nor had Clodius cause to fret over senatorial disapproval over this small intrusion into senatorial prerogative. Though distasteful, it could be stomached since, in this instance, Pompey and not the senate was the real victim.

At about the same time as the *lex de rege Deiotaro et Brogitaro* was passed, Clodius made an even bolder, more flagrant assault on Pompey's authority. After the Mithridatic War, Pompey had restored Tigranes to to the throne of Armenia. The king's son, also named Tigranes, Pompey carried back to Rome as a political hostage. The prince was maintained in the house of Pompey's friend, L. Flavius, a praetor in 58.[108] According to Asconius, Flavius invited Clodius to supper one evening, in the course of which his guest asked to see Tigranes and requested the Armenian's presence at the banquet. Flavius complied, but astonishment supervened when the praetor saw his prisoner removed from his own house by an inviolable tribune. Pompey repeatedly sought Tigranes' return to Flavius, but to no avail. On the contrary, Clodius made arrangements for the prince to return to Armenia, a plan scuttled by a storm that drove Tigranes' ship to land at Antium, whereupon Clodius sent Cloelius to collect the Armenian and to return him to the city. Flavius, apprised of Tigranes' whereabouts, also set out for Antium. The two parties met on the Appian Way. A struggle ensued, in which the praetor's forces were bested by the scribe's. The clash was bloody, and among the slain was a publican, M. Papirius, an intimate of Pompey.[109] The ultimate fate of Tigranes is unknown, unsurprisingly since what mattered in this episode was Clodius's violent flouting of Pompey's *auctoritas*, for which the foreign prince was merely the token.

The disturbance on the Appian Way precipitated a complete rupture between Pompey and Clodius.[110] The equestrian Atticus, alarmed no doubt by the death of Papirius, anticipated a great political uproar over the incident, or so he told Cicero (*Att.* 3.8.3). Although Clodius's abduction of Tigranes was lubricated by his tribunician sanctity, he had held the prince in his custody and had endeavored to restore him to Armenia entirely on his own personal authority, with no recourse to plebiscite. Arrogance of this stripe was intolerable in itself, and Pompey's rage could only be aggravated by the senate's inaction after Clodius's initial interference with Tigranes and after the outrage of Cloelius's defiance of a praetor and the murder of Papirius. Indeed, the *boni* were actually encouraging Clodius in his effrontery.[111]

8

Pompey did not strike back directly, however. His loyal friend, the consul Gabinius, turned decisively against the tribune.[112] Alarmed by Clodius's violence, he collected his own gangs, but, even so amplified, the consul was now no match for the tribune. Clodius's *operae* fell on Gabinius in the streets of Rome. The consul's *fasces* were shattered in a symbolic rejection of Gabinius's authority, which marked the man out as an enemy of the urban *plebs*, a statement that was reinforced by Clodius's formal consecration of Gabinius's property to Ceres, the goddess of the *plebs*. The pageantry of the consecration allowed Clodius to make evident to all the extent of his popular following. It scarcely matters that this *consecratio bonorum* went unenforced and so had no practical effect on Gabinius's holdings. The real (and obvious) point of his gesture lay elsewhere.[113]

It had been especially shrewd of Pompey to allow Gabinius to react against Clodius on his behalf. For it was one thing, from a senatorial perspective, to see Pompey embarrassed, quite another to see the consul, whatever one's view of his personal merits, demeaned by the rabble whose objectionable actions were receiving public endorsement from a tribune. This constituted too severe a threat to public order, one consequence of which will have been that some in the senate began to think that Clodius was going too far, a shift in attitude that introduced complexities into Clodius's schemes against Pompey: the rift between Clodius and Pompey together with incipient ambivalence toward Clodius's tactics on the part of at least some senators made it possible for Cicero's genuine supporters to step up their efforts to reintroduce the issue of the orator's fate. The tribune Ninnius, in symbolic retaliation for Clodius's treatment of Gabinius, consecrated his colleague's property, a gesture that was made for Pompey's benefit and for the benefit of those in the senate who might be induced to welcome the return to Rome of Clodius's rival.[114]

On 1 June, Ninnius submitted to the senate a proposal, said to be backed by Pompey, to recall Cicero from exile.[115] The idea was attractive to many, which is hardly surprising since most senators had not been willing to see Cicero removed in the first place (although they, unlike the *optimates* or the dynasts, were impotent to resist Clodius and the consuls), nor did they view the orator's fate principally in terms of the strife between Clodius and Pompey. Indeed, not a few in the senate will have been perfectly happy to see Cicero restored yet at the same time will have remained hopeful that Clodius might do still further damage to Pompey's prestige. Inasmuch as the motion was doomed to failure anyway, since Clodius must be expected to veto it, nothing could be lost by casting a vote in favor of Cicero. The result was that Ninnius's proposition received the unanimous endorsement of a full senate, only to be derailed by the inevitable veto, which came not from Clodius but from Aelius Ligus. Nevertheless, the issue of Cicero's restoration had thereby been returned to the top of the political agenda. Subsequently, C. Piso,

Cicero's son-in-law, began to lobby his kinsman the consul; L. Domitius Ahenobarbus became a vocal proponent of the orator's recall, as did the elder Scribonius Curio, who in other respects was a friend to Clodius, while outside the senate equestrian support for Cicero began to resurface.[116] Eventually, the senate refused to address any matter until the consuls had brought a motion concerning Cicero, a move to which Clodius responded by posting in the Curia the relevant stipulation in the *lex de exsilio Ciceronis* banning any motion or mention of Cicero's recall.[117] Consequently, although there were intensive negotiations taking place on Cicero's behalf, in the senate there was silence.[118]

In all of this Pompey had remained very much in the background, tending to work through others, men like Terentius Varro and P. Plautius Hypsaeus.[119] But though Cicero doubted the great man's commitment, Pompey had every reason to welcome the resurgence of interest in Cicero. What Cicero of course failed to appreciate was that Pompey's purpose was not simply or primarily to secure the orator's homecoming: Pompey saw in Cicero's restoration the stick with which he intended to beat Clodius. Pompey's optimate rivals, so enthusiastic over Clodius's recent recklessness, could not honestly resist a push to restore Cicero, even with Pompey as the prime mover, a reality perceived by Atticus if not by his nervous friend.[120] For Pompey, it remained to cover his other flank. Clodius had, thus far, challenged Pompey without defying the coalition as a whole. Pompey hoped to make it impossible for Clodius to isolate him further. Consequently, he made a point of informing Cicero's adherents that he could not work on Cicero's behalf openly and vigorously until after he had secured the consent of his father-in-law. Pompey also made it clear that he anticipated no obstacles to getting that consent.[121] In this way, Pompey put oblique pressure on Caesar to take a stand that would put him at odds with Clodius or with Pompey, which leaves it a small wonder, then, that Caesar preferred to temporize. With characteristic shrewdness, Pompey was positioning himself to heed the call of the senate to rescue Cicero from Clodius's law.

9

Caesar's attitude now became crucial to the contest between Pompey and Clodius, and it is in this context that it makes the most sense to try to date the proposal, known only from a brief and oblique reference in Cicero's *De Provinciis Consularibus*, that Caesar reenact his *acta* of 59 in such a way that they would no longer be vitiated by their illegalities and especially by their religious violations.[122] We do not know by whom this suggestion was raised, nor do we know its details, all of which renders the matter difficult to interpret and any interpretation of it necessarily speculative. As it stands in Cicero's speech, the proposition seems rather pointless, given that Caesar was unlikely to admit that his *acta* required rectification of this or any sort. But if, as has been theorized, the actual suggestion was that all of Caesar's measures should be reenacted with the exception of Clodius's adoption, then the proposal had a real bite to it.[123] Under the circumstances of June 58, Caesar's acquiescence to such a proposal would clearly benefit Pompey, who would relish Caesar's public repudiation of the tribune and who would have in Caesar's action another tool to use against Clodius: if Caesar conceded the invalidity of his legislation, only to reenact the whole of it except for Clodius's adoption, then Clodius's entire tribunate would be technically invalid. Obviously that would not suffice to repeal the *leges Clodiae*, but it might so wound the patrician tribune that he would prove unable to remain a threat to Pompey thereafter. It is, however, unthinkable that Pompey could have made such a suggestion, though he was likely enough to favor its being floated, which means that the authors of this plan must have been Cicero's supporters in the senate, who no doubt hoped thereby to obviate the apparent finality of the *lex de exsilio Ciceronis*. If so, then they committed an enormous miscalculation, for this scheme presented Clodius with the opportunity to launch an attack on Caesar's *acta* that squashed their proposal altogether and positioned the tribune closer than ever to his optimate associates.

Clodius, who recognized more clearly than most that his tribunate was, by dint of his *popularitas*, inviolable, whatever the status of the *acta* of 59, renewed the optimate attack on the religious validity of Caesar's measures.[124] In the end, as even Clodius had to recognize, Caesar was certain to side with Pompey against him, which meant that he would need the continued favor of the *boni* if he hoped to maintain an advantage against Pompey in the contest over Cicero. Therefore Clodius, disregarding the strict logic that would tend to undermine his own position, joined with Bibulus and some of the augurs (by no means the entire college) at *contiones* summoned to confirm the religious improprieties of Caesar's legislation.[125] At the same time, the princes of the senate maintained that Clodius absolutely possessed the right to serve as tribune, which was the same sort of wink and nod that Clodius had extended to Cato in the aftermath of his *lex de capite civis Romani*.[126] The point of these exercises, for Clodius at least, was not to prevent the reenactment of Caesar's legislation (though nothing ever came of that proposal), nor was it likely to drive Caesar to put pressure on Pompey to give way to

Clodius, but rather these public displays were intended to reinforce in Rome the extent of Clodius's support among the *boni* and to prod the same *boni* to resist any effort to repeal or nullify the law exiling Cicero.

Irrespective of Caesar's attitude, it was clear that nothing substantive could be done for Cicero until 57, and so the elections were especially crucial for Clodius and for Pompey as well as for Cicero's supporters. The results were somewhat mixed. Of the tribunes-elect, none appeared to be hostile to Cicero, and two, Milo and Sestius, were determined friends.[127] The senior consul for 57 was to be P. Lentulus Spinther, who was deemed to be entirely in Pompey's pocket.[128] On the other hand, however, Clodius's eldest brother was to be praetor in the coming year, and the other consul was none other than Cicero's old enemy, and Clodius's kinsman, Metellus Nepos. Small wonder, then, that Cicero fretted over Clodius's continued influence even after he resigned his office.[129]

10

Cicero's anxieties were deepened by Clodius's resort to terrorism in the aftermath of the elections. On 11 August a slave of Clodius was observed dropping a dagger near a meeting of the senate. Brought before Gabinius, the slave confessed that he had been commanded by Clodius to assassinate Pompey.[130] It has been proposed that the slave's incompetence was calculated and that Clodius's plan was simply to frighten Pompey, who was without question constantly plagued by fears for his life.[131] Ruse or no, the episode was sufficient to drive Pompey to barricade himself in his house on the Carinae for the remainder of the year.[132] The great man had to have been struck by the complete absence of public sympathy for him after this incident. Nor was there any further investigation or censure of Clodius. Clodius did not stop with removing Pompey from public life. His gangs, led by the freedman Damio, stationed themselves around Pompey's house, continuously laying siege to the place.[133] The tribune went so far to threaten to seize the place and to build on the site another portico to match his monument on the Palatine, thereby associating Pompey with the orator's violation of *libertas* and helping to represent his public attack on Pompey as a *popularis* gesture.[134] This was a staggering turn of events. That Clodius should have succeeded to such a degree in humiliating and intimidating Pompey the Great could hardly have been expected by anyone. To all appearances, at least until December, the tribune was in complete control of the city. The *popularis* tribune was, for the moment, the champion of the urban *plebs* and of the princes of the senate.

Nevertheless, the industry devoted to restoring Cicero did not abate, and in fact Pompey's interest in its success became marked. But the great man was at a disadvantage, if he could not leave the confines of his mansion. A bill brought forward in October by eight of the tribunes of 58, which was no more than a futile gesture of continued support for Cicero's cause, attracted the frustrated orator's criticisms, as did the preparations of the tribunes-elect.[135] In November, Sestius set out to persuade Caesar to endorse or at least to tolerate Cicero's restoration.[136] Caesar was still pondering his best reaction to events in the city, and his response became all the more important as the likelihood of conflict in 57 heightened. For everyone had to know that Pompey would not remain in his house forever. The real question was whether Clodius would be able to persist in his opposition to Pompey once he was out of office.

CHAPTER SEVEN

Formidable Adversary

1

The tribunes of 57 entered office on 10 December 58, an event that had the effect of returning Clodius to the level of a *privatus* without, Cicero worried, diminishing his ability to hinder the orator's recall from exile. Although the elections of 58 had, by and large, gone Cicero's way, there seemed little doubt to him that Clodius would continue to exploit the violent capacities of his gangs or that he would find allies in the tribunician college.[1] As we have seen, however, powers greater and more various than those Cicero shows an awareness of were to determine his fate. Clodius's enemies, chief among them Pompey, were keen to see Cicero restored even in the teeth of Clodian resistance in order to tame the overweening past patrician, now former tribune and so no longer invulnerable. To these Cicero's numerous true supporters could appeal, and it is no accident that the first of the new tribunes to propose a bill to bring the orator home was C. Messius, Pompey's adherent. Moreover, Lentulus Spinther, the consul whose energetic championing of Cicero's cause would forge a genuine bond of friendship, was viewed by Atticus and by Cicero in November 58 as wholly under the influence of the dynast.[2] Yet Pompey and Cicero alike had enemies in the senate who, although perhaps concerned over the excesses of the latter months of Clodius's tribunate, nonetheless remained content to see Pompey restrained and shed few tears over Cicero's removal. These senators might naturally expect Clodius, his tribunate over, to lay aside the violence of the past year as he set his sights on higher magistracies and consequently to assume a less aggressively *popularis* posture in the senate.[3] Some were too notable to be allowed to keep their own counsel: Caesar, who had received Sestius's pleas coldly in November, would concede to Cicero's restoration only when, as Gelzer has put it, "he realized the inevitability of an event which he did not really desire." M. Crassus exerted himself (successfully, it would appear) to remain on estimable terms with both Cicero and Clodius. Clodius's kinsman and the other consul designate in December, Metellus Nepos, was lobbied diligently by Atticus in the hope of winning his acquiescence in Cicero's return; even Cicero attempted to assure his old enemy that a policy of *laissez-aller* was compatible with his familial obligations.[4] Clodius's temper goes unrecorded, of course, but in view of Cicero's anxiety, of the circumspection (if not, from Clodius's perspective, the cooperation) of Caesar and Crassus, of the presence of close relatives in the consulate and praetorship—as well as of his recent success in intimidating Pompey—the past tribune could hardly fail to feel secure in his victory over Cicero or indeed in his continued strong influence.[5]

C. Messius's bill was endorsed by seven other tribunes, the most en-thusiastic of whom was Q. Fabricius, who evidently drafted his own measure to recall Cicero.[6] Lentulus Spinther also lent his support to the measure at the time of its promulgation.[7] Opposed to the measure were Sex. Atilius Serranus Gavianus and Q. Numerius Rufus, though Cicero insists that at the start he enjoyed the support of all ten tribunes until these two were corrupted by his enemies.[8] Which ought to mean that before this time there was no conspicuous connection between Clodius and Serranus or Numerius, who need not be deemed the recipients of outright bribes but who were without doubt suborned by the prospects of Clodius's friendship. The bungling endeavors of his friends troubled the orator during December as much as Clodius's machinations: we learn from a scolding letter to Atticus that the knight and his associates had arranged it so that the allocation of consular provinces took place before the tribunes took office on the 10th, an arrangement that Cicero feared could well be taken as a slight upon the whole tribunician college (it being impossible for the tribunes to exercise a veto over the proceed-ings, should they wish).[9] Otherwise no further action was taken in De-cember, to Cicero's dismay though even he must have recognized that there was nothing to be done before the new consuls took office or the tribunes' bill came to a vote.[10]

Veniunt Kalendae Ianuariae: this day marked the return of Pompey to public life, a clear signal to Clodius that the struggle over Cicero's fate was about to be met. Lentulus Spinther, the presiding consul, convened the senate in the temple of Jupiter and spoke weightily in behalf of Cicero's restoration.[11] His colleague, while not denying his enmity with Cicero, yet made it plain that he would not block the will of the senate.[12]

As the day would prove, consular obstruction would be unnecessary, for Clodius had already secured his veto. L. Cotta (cos. 65), the eminent jurist, was the first to be asked his *sententia*: in his opinion the *lex Clodia de exsilio Ciceronis* was illegal; consequently a decree of the senate should suffice to recall the orator.[13] Pompey, however, while he commended Cotta's view, rejected it for a more pragmatic—and dramatic—course of action: the resolution of the senate should be bolstered by the passage of a law that would render Cicero's position secure beyond cavil.[14] Such, Cicero claimed, represented the manifest desire of the entire senate, when the tribune Serranus rose to request a recess of a single night in order to consider whether he should exercise his veto. After a brief and pointless hue and outcry, the senate capitulated, and the persistent Serranus succeeded in preventing the *patres* from resolving anything for the whole month.[15] As Cicero had feared, Clodius was proving scarcely less influential in 57, at least in the matter of preserving the force of his *lex de exsilio*, than he had been in the previous year.

The tribunician bill was slated to come to a vote on 23 January.[16] Q. Fabricius, its ardent champion, entered the forum before daybreak along with M. Cispius, a fellow tribune, and Q. Cicero in order to occupy the Rostra, doubtless with the intention of manipulating the vote.[17] But he had been anticipated by Clodius, who was already in position when Fabricius arrived. Clodius had borrowed from Appius the gladiators the latter had procured for the funeral games of a kinsman and these, assisted by the usual *operae Clodianae*, utterly routed Fabricius's supporters. The violence was extreme and deadly—Cicero asserts that the Tiber was clogged by corpses that day—and Cicero's brother, who was dragged from the Rostra, barely escaped with his life.[18] Even granted Cicero's exaggeration, this incident does seem to have been the bloodiest of Clodius's riots—largely because, for the first time, his forces were opposed by comparable numbers and comparable determination.[19] T. Annius Milo, the gruff tribune destined to become Clodius's own bête noire, responded to the riot energetically by arresting many of the Clodian gladiators, whom he interrogated before the senate and subsequently placed in chains. But Serranus ordered them freed, and nothing came of the gladiators' confessions. Milo, however, thereafter became an object of Clodian violence.[20]

Why should Clodius have had recourse to a riot on 23 January? His tribunician allies ought to have been able to prevent the ratification of Messius's *rogatio* through constitutional methods, either through *obnuntiatio* or an outright veto.[21] Yet Fabricius's plans were such as to make constitutional obstruction impossible. Unable to deploy his tribunes,

Clodius may have found no choice but to revert to the techniques of terrorism. Which is not to suggest that Clodius found such methods uncongenial, and, to be sure, Clodius's actions must certainly have been cast as protective of the popular will.[22] After all, Fabricius could be portrayed as the original aggressor—and perhaps Cicero's champions had actually made it impossible for a Clodian tribune to obstruct the proceedings constitutionally. Though we hear little of it, the case for *provocatio* and the vilification of Cicero as the enemy of popular liberty must have constituted the bulk of the propaganda by means of which Clodius motivated his following (along with, one must add, his claims to gratitude). Unfortunately for him, however, the bloody success of 23 January brought a backlash. For this riot, though it plunged Cicero into despair, proved galvanizing for Clodius's enemies, and, for many of Clodius's erstwhile supporters in the senate, it removed any basis for further neutrality. Clodian violence had again proven unbeatable, but the attendant destruction and instability constituted too great a price to pay for Pompey's continued embarrassment.[23]

Milo's efforts to investigate the causes of the rioting on 23 January were repaid in the coin of Clodian abuse. Milo was molested on the streets and his home was attacked by gangs.[24] Unintimidated, Milo indicted Clodius under the *lex Plautia de vi*, a suitable charge and one likely to have prevailed in court had not Clodius's supporters among the magistrates intervened. As Cicero complained, a consul (Nepos), a praetor (Appius), and a tribune (either Serranus or Numerius) published decrees making it impossible to try Clodius, "nova novi generis edicta" (*Sest.* 89). This suppression of the courts succeeded owing to the invincible combination of the highest magistracies and a representative of the *plebs*, cooperation reminiscent of the arrangements of 58 and unquestionably legal (else Cicero would surely have pointed it out). This was the first of the two times that Nepos rescued his *frater* from criminal prosecution in 57.[25] Finding no justice in the courts, Milo began to organize his own defenses.[26]

Clodius's next act of terrorism remains unexplained. At a meeting of the *comitia tributa*, the tribune P. Sestius attempted to approach Nepos, who was conducting the assembly in front of the temple of Castor, in order to stop the proceedings through *obnuntiatio*.[27] Unfortunately we know nothing of the purposes either of the *comitia* or of the obstructing tribune.[28] Perhaps Sestius meant to enforce the governmental inactivity that had been senatorial policy since the movement to recall Cicero had begun in 58 and continued into 57, at least under the leadership of Spinther.[29] That Nepos had convened the tribal assembly, however, suggests that he had other intentions, at least during his watch. While Clodius's kinsman would not actively prevent Cicero's restoration, neither did he wish it to become the sole issue of his consulship, and there must have been considerable pressure from several quarters pushing for government to proceed. Clodius, who must have been pleased to see the republic move on to other matters, added his own muscle (invited or not) to Nepos's *auctoritas*. For *Clodiani* led by Lentidius and Titius descended on the tribune, whose *sacrosanctitas* was ruthlessly and painfully ignored.[30] The fighting resisted even the consul's exertions to restore order, as a result of which the *fasces* were shattered. Sestius was sorely wounded; indeed, he escaped death only because he was believed by those on the spot to have perished in the assault (so Cicero in the *Pro Sestio*) or, perhaps more likely, because he was rescued by the aedile L. Calpurnius Bestia (so Cicero in his *Pro Bestia*, as reported in Q.F. 2.3.6).[31] The *Clodiani*, conscious of their culpability in murdering (so they believed) a tribune, attempted to murder Q. Numerius in the hope of laying the blame on Cicero's supporters—or, again, so Cicero claimed. Numerius, however, contrived to escape the bloodthirsty *Clodiani* by donning a humiliating disguise. This is fantasy, but the violence done Sestius may well have sparked demonstrations and denunciations.[32] Sestius, taking his lesson from Milo, eschewed vain indictments and collected his own combative retinue.[33]

The establishment of massive private guards by Milo and Sestius constitutes a turning point for Clodius's politics. Equipped with armed slaves, freedmen, clients—and gladiators—the tribunes could match Clodius in brazen boldness and excel him in resources. Senators exasperated by Clodius or favorable to Cicero offered money to their cause, and Pompey, seeing his chance to exploit the tribunes' daring, imported roughs from his estates to swell their ranks further.[34] Clodian violence, as we have seen, relied mainly on *tabernarii* (and other citizens of the lower classes) and not on professional thugs. Milo and Sestius had recruits of a different stripe, who, better equipped and more efficiently deployed than Clodius's popular following, soon put an end to Clodius's monopoly on street violence.[35] Indeed, the former tribune was now at a distinct disadvantage, though he and his supporters remained unflinching, with the result that gang violence dominated Rome through the spring—and beyond.[36] This turn of events admittedly had the effect of postponing any action on Cicero, but hardly of eliminating the issue. At the same time, the constant violence diminished Clodius's support among men of substance and even among humbler citizens with an interest in stability.

Cicero's recall had by now assumed a significance transcending the quarrel between Clodius and the orator, or even between Clodius and the great dynast. Caesar, seeing no benefit in supporting Clodius when so many opposed him, yielded to necessity and to his son-in-law. At once Pompey began to mobilize the *domi nobiles* throughout Italy. By virtue of his office as *duovir* in Capua, he induced that city to pass a decree denouncing the *lex de exsilio Ciceronis* as a *privilegium* and calling for Cicero's restoration.[37] He toured Italy winning similar resolutions from various colonies and municipalities.[38] Nor had the politics of Rome been limited to street fighting. Spinther continued vigorously to represent Cicero's interests in the senate, in response to which Appius held rallies hoping to demonstrate to the *patres* the popular opposition to Cicero's homecoming.[39] Yet when they contemplated the clashes between the forces of Clodius and those of the tribunes as well as Pompey's inexpugnable resolve to return Cicero to Rome, few senators, even Clodius's associates, had the stomach to endure the continuation of this contest. In addition to the other pressures being brought to bear on the senate's judgment, the demands of responsible government acted to erode Clodius's position.[40] It might have been different had Clodius been content with Cicero's voluntary exile or had he actually indicted the orator in court. But the *lex de exsilio Ciceronis* was ever more appearing too much the exercise of personal enmity, and Clodius's vendetta against Cicero, once tolerable, even welcome in certain quarters, was moving beyond the pale of acceptable hatred. Cicero would later complain of Clodius's *crudelitas* and, by Roman standards, not unreasonably.[41] Consequently, early in May, on the motion of Lentulus Spinther, the senate decreed that all citizens who treasured the safety of the republic should assemble in Rome to support Cicero's recall; furthermore, the senate offered its gratitude to all those who had assisted Cicero during his exile and encouraged provincial magistrates to continue to favor him.[42] This time there was no tribunician veto. Clodius, checked in the streets, had lost the senate.

This defeat was underscored by events in the theater on the same day. The senate had met to pass its resolution during the Ludi Florales (1–3 May), a festival that ordinarily encouraged substantial citizens to gather in Rome and all the more so in this year owing to Pompey's industry. Following the meeting, the senate's decisions regarding Cicero were announced in the theater to great acclaim.[43] The senators, the orator gleefully reports in the *Pro Sestio*, were greeted with cheers, and the entrance of Spinther, who was the sponsor of the games, brought the house down. But when Clodius came in, the Roman people barely restrained themselves from lynching the man, electing instead to satisfy themselves with jeers and obscene gestures. A claque, taking up a menacing line from the comedy being performed at the time, finally drove Clodius, who was more accustomed to directing than receiving popular abuse, from the theater (*Sest.* 118). At a later performance of Accian tragedy, the actor Claudius Aesopus repeatedly roused his audience in support of the exiled Cicero; "Tullius, qui libertatem civibus stabiliverat," became a virtual slogan (*Sest.* 123). Further testimony to Clodius's unpopularity came only days later when, at the splendid funeral games given by the aedile Q. Metellus Scipio in honor of his adoptive father, Sestius was roundly applauded whereas Appius Claudius was so harshly hissed whenever he entered to view the gladiators that he took to following a discreet path to his seat which his enemies dubbed "the Appian Way."[44] Clodius, wholly unaccustomed to such receptions at public entertainments, could not fail to appreciate the weight of public opinion against him; such demonstrations had to sting, however much he might recognize the exceptional nature of the crowds at the Floralia of this year and at Scipio's gladiatorial shows.[45]

Clodius's main constituency remained loyal, but other categories of the general public, especially those with a greater stake in stability than in the abstract principle of *provocatio*, had soured.[46] The publicans passed resolutions demanding Cicero's return, as did the powerful order of the *scribae*. Other associations, even the *collegia* according to Cicero's claims, followed their lead.[47] By July only the *plebs urbana* remained devoted to Clodius—and he meant to put them to use even until his final opportunity to block Cicero's recall, a strategy that can only be described as desperate and hardly redounds to the political *sapientia* of the former tribune.[48] Nepos and Appius, as events were shortly to prove, were too astute for such outré stubbornness.[49]

By July Pompey was ready to deliver the coup de grâce. Rome was filled with supportive citizens assembled from throughout Italy for the Ludi Apollinares (5–13 July), in the midst of which the great man planned to introduce a motion to the senate that would guarantee the orator's recall.[50] Clodius, however, was able to make a final attempt to distract the senate from Cicero's restoration by staging food riots at the theater shows of the *ludi* and at the house of the urban praetor, L. Caecilius Rufus— though it remains unclear whether Clodius directed the demonstrations or simply took advantage of popular unrest to press for his own agenda.[51]

From the summer of 58 through 56 Rome experienced grain shortages and erratic price fluctuations. The crises were real though their causes were uncertain, as a consequence of which recriminations multiplied as the problem proved intractable.[52] Natural causes were at least partly to blame but not useful as political ammunition. Cicero would hold Clodius's grain law responsible, predictably enough, whereas the past tribune alleged that Pompey and his friends—including Spinther and Cicero—had colluded with suppliers to contrive an artificial shortage in order to manipulate the people by controlling prices.[53] Suspicions of speculation, untethered to any political cause, ran rife, and at least one *eques*, P. Sittius, was condemned in court in large measure because he was believed to be involved in price gouging.[54]

Clodius's law hardly seems a likely culprit or even an accessory: only the state, not the grain merchants, bore the cost of *publicum frumentum* and, as we have seen, the tribune's interference in the city's procurement practices was if anything minimal—despite Cicero's allegations to the contrary.[55] Admittedly, free rations in place of subsidized ones may have proved a less stabilizing influence on the marketplace inasmuch as a notional fair price will have been removed from public view even as many ordinary Romans found themselves with more money for purchasing supplies (thereby inviting rises in price), but this can hardly have been more than a minor factor. Nor can Pompey be held solely responsible. If he had any control over grain dealers in the early crises, it unmistakably escaped him after he assumed his *cura annonae*, which was by no means an immediate or conspicuous success.[56] The exceptionally large number of visitors to Rome in 57 played a highly visible but probably inconsequential (and, in any event, temporary) role in the shortages. Which leaves poor harvests and speculation (by businessmen instead of conspiratorial politicians) the most probable suspects.

The *plebs urbana*, hungry or uncertain of future supplies, was not inclined to protracted analysis. Even a mild shortage could prompt strong reactions as the fear of famine alone, a powerful force that needed no assistance from political leaders, roused the people to demonstrations.[57] In the antagonistic atmosphere of 57, as the urban poor were pitted against the municipal citizenry, popular resentment was all the more easily inflamed by *inopia* and unaffordable food. As a result, an *infima coacta multitudo*, as Asconius describes it, set upon the audience at the shows, theatergoers who may be presumed in this instance to have been municipal or apparently less in distress than the very poor, thereby causing a tumult. At about the same time, Clodius's gangs assaulted the house of the *praetor urbanus*, which has suggested to many that he was also responsible for the riot at the theater.[58] Perhaps. However, there can be little doubt that Clodius seized the moment to direct popular hostility over the food crisis toward Caecilius, a friend of Cicero but more importantly the highest magistrate responsible for overseeing Rome's grain supply.[59]

A word should be said about Clodius's role in providing *publicum frumentum* after he left the tribunate. Presumably, he had none.[60] The normal duties of Rome's magistrates remained unchanged and, if we are correct in concluding that the free rations were dispensed by *vici* with the assistance of the *collegia*, that procedure did not require Clodius's continued supervision. In short, while Clodius enjoyed the people's gratitude for his *lex frumentaria*, he had laid down his administrative responsibilities (which were ad hoc from the start) along with his office. Nothing suggests that the *plebs* blamed Clodius for the food crises of this period. Quite the contrary. The people seemed very willing to follow his lead in demanding governmental action to resolve matters.[61] The senate's ultimate solution, however, was not to be to Clodius's liking.

But let us return to the demonstrations of early July. The disruption of the games and the attacks on Caecilius did nothing to deter the senate from its purpose. Grain prices did drop, at least temporarily, in response to the riot, a success the *plebs* may have credited to Clodius but which did nothing whatsoever for his position in the senate.[62] When the senate met a few days later in the temple of Jupiter to debate Cicero's restoration, Clodius was completely isolated. Even Nepos deserted Clodius to speak in support of Pompey's resolution hailing Cicero as Rome's savior and directing that legislation be promulgated for his recall. Of 417 senators in attendance, only Clodius voted against the measure.[63] As Robin Seager has aptly remarked, "whatever else he was, Clodius was no coward."[64] Quite so. But he had been a fool.

Even in the face of such massive opposition, forged by his own excesses, Clodius refused to go gently into the back benches. He kept the passive loyalty of the two tribunes, Serranus and Numerius, who declined to endorse the promulgated legislation. And, of course, Appius continued to side with his brother.[65] But every other magistrate signed the bill. Spinther, on the day following the senate's decree, held a *contio* in which he, Pompey, and the whole of the *consulares* and *praetorii* spoke out for Cicero's restoration.[66] Clodius prolonged his resistance, but insofar as the senate was concerned, his was a voice in the wilderness.[67] On the same day the senate convened to forbid the obstruction of Cicero's recall by any means, constitutional or otherwise, and declared that anyone blocking the legislation proposed in the orator's behalf would be declared a public enemy.[68]

The senate's warning did nothing to intimidate Clodius, however. On 4 August, the date for the centuriate assembly's consideration of the senate's bill, Clodius disrupted a preliminary *contio* held in the forum: Q. Cicero, escorted by Pompey, mounted the Rostra to speak on his brother's behalf. The *Clodiani* were unleashed, violence erupted, but

Pompey's adherents managed to eject Clodius from the forum.[69] This final, pointless delay merely underlined Pompey's triumph. The great man's strategy of overwhelming Clodius's urban supporters in the streets and the assembly by mobilizing the municipalities—as Cicero would later put it, "non tabernis sed municipiis clausis" (*Dom.* 90)—had proved a stunning success and had clearly exceeded Clodius's calculations.

2

Cicero's homecoming parade through Italy and his triumphal entry into Rome, staged to coincide with the start of the Ludi Romani (4 September), are familiar events, celebrated more than once by the vindicated orator.[70] But the thrill of victory was exceedingly short-lived. September had already seen food prices rise severely and once again the fear of famine gripped the urban *plebs*. The precise chronology of the events of early September is not easy to retrieve, despite what by classicists' standards is a plethora of data, but it appears that the senate was already debating what to do about the grain supply when popular discontent erupted on 6 September into demonstrations at the theater followed by rioting in the forum. The senate was besieged as it met in the temple of Concord.[71]

Cicero ascribed the turmoil to Clodian initiative—the *popularis* is condemned by the orator as the "seditionis quidem et instimulator et concitator"—but also to genuine popular outrage.[72] Once again, it would seem, Clodius was endeavoring to channel the discontent of the *plebs* against his own enemies: during the night preceding the riot, Clodius's adherents, by resorting to a nocturnal *flagitatio* (a traditional form of public defamation) incited the masses to blame Cicero for the grain crisis.[73] When the mob arrived at the forum the following day, Clodius was present with his stalwarts, Sergius and Lollius, whose following certainly included *tabernarii* as well as more desperate sections of the populace.[74] The senate was disrupted, nor were the consuls able to quell the turbulence: indeed, the presiding consul, Metellus Nepos, was injured by stones thrown by the rioters, proof that the disturbance had passed beyond Clodius's control. Random violence against the senate was not in Clodius's interest at this point nor did it constitute part of his intention: the *Clodiani* clamored against Cicero. The orator, forewarned of Clodius's agitation, remained at home.[75]

Matters were quite different the next day. The *Clodiani* were, if not actually driven from the forum as Cicero alleges, then certainly suppressed by superior forces put into action by Pompey. The situation was unquestionably a tense one, since the *consulares*, fearing violence, stayed away from the senate—except for the staunch Pompeians, Massala and Afranius, and except for Cicero. This time the *multitudo* cried out for Pompey to save them, as indeed did some of the *boni* (so Cicero insists). An appeal was made to the restored savior of the republic to move the appropriate proposal in the senate: he did. Pompey, Cicero confided to Atticus, lusted after the assignment. The orator could not have acted otherwise.[76]

In the senate, Cicero proposed a decree that Pompey should be asked to solve the grain crisis. The senate passed Cicero's resolution, which was proclaimed immediately to popular applause. Cicero then addressed the people at the invitation of all the magistrates—except for one praetor and two tribunes. The following day a crowded senate met to consider Pompey's particular requirements for his *cura annonae*: he was denied nothing. The consuls drafted a bill providing him with fifteen legates (of whom Cicero was the first named) and, for a period of five years, "omnis potestas rei frumentariae toto orbe terrarum" (*Att.* 1.4.7). The tribune Messius offered an alternative measure according to which Pompey would receive control over the treasury, a fleet, an army, and *imperium maius* in the provinces. This bill provoked such instant and intense fury that Pompey's public preference for the consuls' *rogatio* appeared positively modest by comparison, which was no doubt the essential purpose of Messius's proposal. Pompey's *cura annonae* was passed, a significant event in Rome's history, and that stalwart servant of the state took up his new responsibility with his regular industry and efficiency, though success, as we have noted, would prove elusive.

All of which helps to clarify Clodius's conduct. The need to respond to the grain crisis had been recognized in the senate and the possibility of Pompey's appointment to a special command had already been mooted before the crowd beseeched Cicero to recommend the great man in the senate.[77] In other words, Clodius was not the only senator interested in exploiting the hunger of the *plebs*: Pompey's conniving after the *cura annonae* (designed both to boost his own prestige in obvious ways but equally to overshadow Clodius's tribunician accomplishments) had to be known to Clodius. Indeed, Clodius insisted that Pompey was engineering the shortage in order to extort his appointment.[78] No doubt he would have liked to block Pompey's scheme altogether, but, failing that, he could certainly deploy his popular following so as to embarrass Cicero, whose unpopularity with the urban *plebs* was undiminished.[79] Cicero had hoped to avoid controversy until he had completely recovered his prestige and—to be blunt—his property. Clodius's *aedes Libertatis* still

FORMIDABLE ADVERSARY

loomed over the city, while Cicero resided in a house on the Carinae. Many in the senate would regard Pompey's *cura*, a distinguished appointment eminently reasonable in itself (as events would ultimately prove), as objectionable nonetheless—jealousy being a law of oligarchy every bit as reliable as the principles of physics—yet the orator, however much he might prefer to keep his peace until he could settle his private affairs, could hardly deny the demands of the gratitude he owed to Pompey.[80] By focusing public attention on Cicero, Clodius not only underscored the orator's unpopularity, he spotlighted Cicero's awkward posture suspended betwixt Pompey and the *optimates*. The violence of Pompey's forces—Clodius later claimed (and Cicero could not categorically deny) that even the senate was intimidated on 7 September—only worsened Cicero's position, especially since Clodius could seize the moment to associate Cicero with Pompey's putative *argumentum baculinum* by assailing him as *hostis Capitolinus* and with other such insults.[81] Clodius was able to claim to great effect that Cicero had betrayed the *optimates* in handing over so much power to a single man.[82] The struggle for Cicero's house was in the offing, and Clodius meant to extract every advantage from the burgeoning *invidia Ciceronis*, which was perceptible even to the orator himself.[83] A sensible tack, for the former tribune, as we have seen, had image problems of his own.

3

Cicero's recall, while it most certainly did not represent Clodius's political annihilation, had nonetheless demonstrated beyond doubt Pompey's recovery of his old preeminence in Rome, a lesson reinforced by the great man's appointment as guardian of the city's grain supply. Indeed, one might do well to speak not of Cicero's but of Pompey's restoration in September 57. Clodius's violent reprisals had certainly not improved his standing in the senate. Quite the contrary. And while Pompey's refurbished prestige as well as Cicero's honored homecoming could be expected to attract their share of *invidia*, it remained to be seen if these developments had diluted the senate's anti-Clodian mood. In this uncertain climate, the pontiffs were asked to render an opinion on the consecration of Cicero's *domus*.

The repossession of his goods was, naturally enough, a high priority for Cicero even during the dark days of exile. Already in 58 he had criticized the efforts of Clodius's tribunician colleagues to restore him because they had neglected to deal with the question of his property: "nothing is restored except my citizenship and my rank" (*Att.* 3.23.2). His apprehensions persisted into the next year: "What of my property?" he asked Atticus in August 57, "What of my *domus*? Can it be restored? And if it cannot be restored, how shall I myself?" (*Att.* 3.15.6). Clearly the cancellation of exile did not per se recover for Cicero his lost properties. But by the time of his return, the problem had been dealt with, if not to Cicero's full satisfaction (*Att.* 4.1.3). One issue remained unresolved, by far the most important for Cicero, and that was the repossession of his Palatine *domus*, which was possible only if the religious impediment imposed by the consecration of the *aedes Libertatis* could be removed.

This brings us to a vexed passage in a crucial letter of Cicero to Atticus, written around 10 September 57, in which the author has just recounted the results of a senate meeting (the subject of which was Pompey's *curatio*) at which the orator felt obliged to sit quietly in deference to the pontiffs' imminent hearing on the issue of his *domus*. The text of W. S. Watt is the safest on which to base discussion (*Att.* 4.1.7):[84]

> nos tacemus, et eo magis quod de domo nostra nihil adhuc pontifices responderunt. Qui si sustulerint religionem, aream praeclaram habebimus, superficiem consules ex senatus consulto aestimabunt; sin aliter, demolientur * * * suo nomine locabunt, rem totam aestimabunt. Ita sunt res nostrae, "ut ín secundis flúxae, ut in adversís bonae." In re familiari valde sumus, ut scis, perturbati.

> I remain silent, all the more because the pontiffs have not yet issued a response concerning my house. If they lift the sanction, I will have a splendid site; the consuls, in accordance with the senate's decree, will estimate the value of the building. If not, they will demolish * * * they will let a contract in their own name, they will make an estimate for the whole. That is how my affairs stand, "unsettled in prosperity, in adversity, fine." Indeed, my personal finances are, as you know, a mess.

It has been suggested that this letter informs us that, regardless of the pontiffs' decision, Clodius's shrine, "a conspicuous reminder of the senate's defeat," was destined for destruction, the real question being whether the site would contain another shrine (dissociated from the tribune) or if that portion which had once belonged to Cicero would regain private status and so be reversionary.[85] Now there can be no doubting that the *aedes Libertatis*, a very concrete symbol of *provocatio*, could be construed as a challenge to *senatus auctoritas*. Nor can it be denied that Clodius's senatorial standing was extremely low in September 57. But as Cicero himself remarked with some dismay in this very letter (*Att.* 4.1.8), the gilt was off the lily so far as his homecoming was concerned, in some quarters at least, and the exceptionable proposal of Messius in Pompey's behalf might have suggested to some that it was too soon to discard Clodius altogether as a foil to Pompey (or to Cicero for that matter).[86] Certainly Cicero was concerned, hence "nos tacemus." It seems more likely, as Shackleton Bailey (at least originally) saw matters, that while Cicero was in real doubt as to the fate of the *aedes Libertatis*, in this passage he was informing Atticus that even if the consecration should be upheld, the senate would compensate him for his site and for his *domus*. All of which had left his personal finances confused and consequently in need of Atticus's expertise.[87] The salient point for our purposes is that the issue to be settled by the senate, on the pontiffs' advice of course, was whether the *aedes Libertatis* would remain on the Palatine or be replaced by Cicero's restored house. Clodius's shrine was not doomed from the start.

At the same time, one notes in this letter none of Cicero's usual hand-wringing over the question. Momentum was clearly with him if in his appearance before the pontiffs he could capitalize on Clodius's current unpopularity in the senate and if he could isolate vitiating objections that might legitimately undo Clodius's consecration. The pontiffs had to decide upon a matter that was genuinely debatable and, as the conduct of Clodius and Appius would later show, far from straightforward. If the prejudices of the pontifical college or of the senate seem perhaps unduly emphasized here, it is only because it is too easy to overlook the actual complexity of the pontiffs' situation. In the aftermath of Cicero's departure from Rome, no objection had been raised against Clodius's building project (else Cicero would certainly have made mention of it in his oration) by any competent magistrate or by any religious authority. Yet impediments to religious dedications or to public building in general are hardly uncommon in the record of the Roman republic. Granted that Clodius's political might in 58 constitutes the most immediate explanation for such public compliance, the establishment of his shrine was not easily reversed. And we can be sure that such considerations were raised by Clodius in his own oration before the pontiffs. Although Cicero was ultimately the victor, Clodius and Appius were able at least to try to portray the pontiffs' verdict as favorable to Clodius—and even in the senate, which was quick to take Cicero's side in response to the college's decision, the consuls were curious as to how the priests could have reached their conclusion. In other words, while many in the senate inclined to view the fate of Cicero's *domus* in terms of how best to curtail Clodius, so that it was by no means a question purely of *religio*, this attitude hardly freed the pontiffs to ignore pontifical law and tradition as they chose.[88]

On the motion of M. Bibulus, possibly as early as the passage of Cicero's recall, the senate had referred to the pontiffs the problem of Cicero's *domus*.[89] While the ultimate and official decision would reside with the senate, normal practice rendered the pontifical verdict the crucial one.[90] Cicero, as we have seen, felt obliged to be especially circumspect in anticipation of the pontiffs' response. This tribunal convened on 29 September, at which time Clodius and Cicero—as well as at least one other pleader—spoke.[91] They addressed a distinguished body. Indeed, Cicero catalogs the attending college at *Har. Resp.* 12 (he omits Clodius's brother-in-law, L. Pinarius Natta, though that hardly requires the conclusion that he was absent from the proceedings), which included seven consulars (and two future consuls) as well as numerous other notables of patrician and plebeian extraction alike.[92] Some were unquestionably enemies of Clodius: the consul, Lentulus Spinther; M. Valerius Messalla Niger, an opponent from the Bona Dea affair; C. Fannius, one of Clodius's accusers at the Bona Dea trial (which explains Cicero's recurrence to the scandal throughout his speech). But others might be expected to be friendly, certainly L. Claudius (though little is known of the man),[93] M. Crassus (if he is the triumvir), and most definitely C. Scribonius Curio (despite his own opposition to Cicero's exile) and Pinarius. Thus Cicero, in belittling the tribune's reliance on young Pinarius, could make the point that Clodius had enjoyed the advantage of *familiarissimi* in the pontifical college.[94] Arguments were heard before a massive throng, not *hoi polloi*, however, but a crowd of wealthy, sophisticated citizens, "maxima frequentia amplissimorum ac sapientissimorum civium astante" (*Har. Resp.* 12), including Pompey the Great, all of which yielded circumstances that made it possible for Cicero to play to the social prejudices of the elite classes.[95]

The contents of Clodius's oration we can only infer from Cicero's most obvious ripostes. Alarmed at Pompey's successful resurgence, Clodius endeavored to portray the great man—and Cicero, his henchman—as menaces to senatorial preeminence, thereby (so he hoped) regaining his old appeal as a counterweight to Pompey's authority. Clodius bemoaned the shortage of grain, which, he maintained, had been engineered by Cicero and Pompey so as to secure the latter's extraordinary, and exceptionable, appointment. Every pontiff, he insisted, ought to be offended by Pompey's *curatio* and by Cicero's oratory, which had secured the great man's *imperium*.[96] We can speculate further with some confidence. That Cicero was insufferable was something of a topos in the late republic, one usually allied with the imputation that he strove for unacceptable political supremacy.[97] In later speeches (as we learn from *Har. Resp.* 17) Clodius would say that Cicero had been recalled from exile only through violence and factional machinations; such imputations would not have been inappropriate in an attack on Cicero's ostentatious proposals on Pompey's behalf. *Amicitia* thereby becomes *factio*, and Clodius could depict the exiled consular not as the *defensor Capitoli* he incessantly insisted he was, but as *hostis Capitolinus.*[98] The implicit argument is plain enough: advancing Cicero's interests at Clodius's expense would further entrench Pompey's superiority—at the senate's expense. But this rhetorical strategy, however promising, could hardly be certain to persuade in September of 57. Recent events had probably underscored too sharply Clodius's own excesses, even if the senate did actually harbor suspicions of Pompey and jealousy of Cicero. Still, Cicero's lengthy and labored response (*Dom.* 3–31), thoroughly optimate in sentiment, reveals how vital it was to his oration's success that he receive a sympathetic hearing from the pontiffs in order to overcome the other, more formidable prong of Clodius's sally: religious scruple.

"Dedicatio magnam, inquit [Clodius], habet religionem" (*Dom.* 127). This was evidently, and quite naturally, the principal thrust of Clodius's oration. Clodius claimed that, under the supervision of Pinarius, the *aedes Libertatis* had been consecrated in proper accordance with Roman ritual.[99] "Aedis sacra a magistratu pontifice praeeunte dicendo dedicatur" (Varro *L.L.* 6.61). On this point alone the entire issue might be thought to depend in view of the centrality of punctilious ritual performance in Roman religion and in Roman feelings of religiosity, aspects of Roman culture that have been widely discussed of late.[100] Furthermore, for all their confidence in divine favor, Romans frequently displayed anxiety over the efficacy of their ritual practices in securing divine cooperation.[101] Clodius, backed by his notoriously pious brother, made heavy weather of his own commitment to civic religion (Clodius was a *quindecimvir sacris faciundis*) and, like Ap. Claudius in his censorship, adopted a posture of old-fashioned rectitude.[102] The righteous brothers may have gone so far as to instruct the pontiffs as to their priestly duties in such a matter, a presumption that would explain Cicero's exaggerated deference in this case as well as Cicero's request that the college outline for Clodius the proper boundaries of religiosity.[103] The extremes to which Cicero is compelled in his refutation suffice to demonstrate the force of Clodius's argument and the apparent soundness of his claims. Indeed, if we actually possessed Clodius's oration, we might share more fully in Cicero's admiration for the *De Domo*.

But the issue was by no means straightforward, nor was the attitude of the college toward the disputants' claims a positively known quantity. Clodius's recent enormities lent urgency to Cicero's denunciations of the ex-tribune as an immoral menace to private property and to the stability of the state.[104] And it was unquestionably Cicero's hope that the pontiffs would at some level recognize the restoration of his Palatine *domus* as the only appropriate sequel to the centuriate assembly's de facto abrogation of the *lex Clodia* that confiscated his house when it banished him. Yet, at the same time, the orator had every reason to fear that the priestly college, whatever its private sentiments, would in the end prove too scrupulous, even superstitious, to find in his favor. Hence the need for technicalities. The complicated sophistry, both legal and theological, by means of which Cicero convinced the pontiffs to nullify Clodius's consecration, need not delay us.[105] Suffice it to say that his combination of antiquarian legalism and quasi-philosophical moralism went a long way toward providing what was at least an apparently legitimate basis for rejecting Clodius's all-too-traditional claims. It was not that Clodius's law banishing Cicero was defective or illegal in itself. Rather, because the law had been so hastily composed, and with no consideration of the possibility that all its provisions and consequences might one day require a detailed defense, Cicero was able to isolate a specific omission that satisfied the religiosity as well as the mood of the pontiffs. The priests reported to the senate that, if the Roman people had not explicitly authorized Clodius to dedicate the *aedes Libertatis*—which exact stipulation was evidently not to be found in the *lex de exsilio Ciceronis*—then the shrine could be removed from its site *sine religione*.[106]

Clodius reacted to the pontiffs' decision with his usual vigorous obstinacy. At a *contio* called by his brother, he claimed that the pontifical decree was in fact in his own favor and furthermore that Cicero was trying to regain his property by force. The *plebs*, he urged, ought to defend its Libertas.[107] But the gesture pointed to nothing in the end, and when the senate convened on 1 October, the consul designate, Cn. Lentulus Marcellinus, who was first to be asked his opinion, came out strongly in Cicero's behalf, eventually proposing that a decree be passed providing for the restoration of Cicero's properties and the reconstruction of the portico of Catulus. Clodius attempted a filibuster, three hours into which, however, he was hooted down. As Marcellinus's motion came to a vote, it became clear that there would be only a single dissent, at which moment Serranus interposed his veto. The senate's stern opposition to his intercession so frightened the tribune that he requested (yet again) a night's recess to ponder the matter, an action too redolent of January's delaying tactics to find any favor with the senators. Only Cicero's own intervention won Serranus his face-saving postponement. The following day Marcellinus's proposal passed in the senate, thereby completing Clodius's defeat.[108]

4

He responded with what Cicero describes as unbridled fury. On 3 November armed men disrupted the rebuilding of Cicero's *domus* as well as the *porticus Catuli*. They then set themselves to attacking the house of Cicero's brother. On the eleventh, Clodius and his gangs actually ambushed the orator on the Via Sacra. Cicero retreated into the house of Tettius Damio, and his companions held off the Clodian onslaught. The next day, Clodius launched a daylight raid against Milo's house in the Cermalus. He met with fierce resistance, however, in the shape of Q. Flaccus (an adherent of Milo), whose forces killed many of the *Clodiani* (so Cicero) and hotly desired to kill Clodius himself. He, alleges Cicero, had fled the scene to hide in the basements of P. Sulla.[109]

The violence with which Clodius prosecuted his grudge against Cicero and Milo offended many. Two of his better-connected associates, Decimus and Gellius, became estranged.[110] Yet Clodius, however unwilling to pursue a subtler tack against his enemies, continued to rely on *popularis* propaganda to justify his actions. Cicero describes the ex-tribune in the following hostile terms: "he campaigns in every district, he openly holds out the expectation of freedom to the slaves" (*Att.* 4.3.2). Now Cicero's proclivity for describing the *plebs* in servile terms whenever it failed to toe the proper line has been remarked upon. Clodius, of course, had no intention of freeing the city's slaves—at this time or at any other in his career. Rather, the former tribune was mustering the support of the *collegia* with appeals to the popular ideology of *libertas*—the protection of which could be represented (as we have seen) as requiring assaults on Cicero's house or even on his person, not that such actions were necessarily unwelcome to those whom Cicero regularly described as scum.

Such posturing aside, escalating the level of violence had not helped Clodius to intimidate Milo or Sestius—or anyone else for that matter—and his impotence made his actions appear unduly obstinate and so offensive rather than menacing. None of which should lead us to overlook the magnitude of effort that had been required in order to defeat Clodius in the matter of Cicero's homecoming and restoration. Yet Pompey could hardly sustain his coalition indefinitely. Clodius's *popularitas* remained intact and although many leaders in the senate had turned their back on him at this most recent juncture, his connections were hardly severed. What Clodius required was a political stratagem that, from the senate's perspective, transcended personal animosity. For in the fall of 57 it was clear that, whatever the faults or crimes of his enemies, the senate was for the moment inclined to blame Clodius for his excessive reliance on the violence of the mob. It was incumbent upon Clodius to revive his support, a far from hopeless assignment. The urban *plebs*, after all, was not Clodius's sole support even in this time of relative isolation.[111] While many younger men of the elite classes recoiled from Clodian violence, the past patrician found a friend in the wealthy P. Sulla—the man's house was being used by Clodius *pro castris*—and as Cicero complained to Atticus, when on 14 November Clodius's combats constituted the central topic of senatorial debate, not only did Metellus and Appius come to Clodius's rescue but so, apparently, did Hortensius (or one of that crowd—Cicero's expression to Atticus is "etiam hercule familiari tuo").[112] Whence, in the face of such reprehensible behavior, this optimate support?

Cicero, in a characteristic analysis, blamed the envy that the *optimates* felt against himself and his preeminent friend.[113] This was indisputably an important factor, but not the only one (or, put another way, not a factor sufficiently illuminating without further explanation). The senate, after all, had only just set the finishing touches on Clodius's overwhelming loss to the orator and the general. But the Moving Finger of political rivalry, having writ, moves on. In the East lay not a new but rather another object of competition and discord about which new alignments might be arranged—and Clodius's situation improved, in large measure, it must be said, owing to the bounty of Fortuna, or rather, of Tyche. The Egyptian question, which had for some time been a matter of substantial importance to Pompey, was coming into the foreground of the senate's attentions.

5

Ptolemy XII "Auletes," *Theos Philopator Philadelphos Neos Dionysos*, had been placed precariously on the throne of Egypt in 80 by Mithridates VI of Pontus. Auletes, dissolute and much maligned by ancients and moderns alike, owns an honest claim to being one of history's great survivors, reigning (on and off) for almost thirty years until his death in 51—but never without uneasiness. Immediately upon his accession the king began to forage for recognition in the Roman senate, as well he might in view of the testament of Ptolemy X Alexander, who in 87 had willed his kingdom to the Romans and promptly fallen in battle. This legacy had not yet been claimed, though the idea had certainly been floated by some, and the matter remained a concern both in Rome and especially in Alexandria. Finally, during Caesar's consulship, owing to heavy bribery (of which Caesar and Pompey were the chief beneficiaries), Auletes was recognized by the senate as the legitimate king of Egypt and as *socius et amicus populi Romani*. Yet in 57 the New Dionysus was driven from his realm. He sought refuge—and restoration—from his Roman friends.[114]

The king enjoyed an indisputable claim on Roman *fides*. Moreover—and, from a jaded perspective, more important—the overextended monarch owed such huge sums to Pompey and to Roman capitalists like Rabirius Postumus that his return to power, which represented his only prospect for making good on his debts, clearly constituted an economic incentive of the highest magnitude: too much money was at stake for the senate not to respect the monarch's legitimate rights.[115] Pompey received the king and his entourage into his Alban villa, where he also assisted in arranging the exiled sovereign's finances. Auletes found that there were businessmen enough who were keen to invest in his future and, furthermore, that there were more than enough senators with their hands out to accept all the largesse that royal generosity might proffer. These sordid arrangements guaranteed the king a friendly reception when Pompey formally recommended him to the senate, perhaps as early as mid-May and certainly before Cicero's actual return to the city.[116]

The government in Alexandria dispatched an embassy of 100 delegates, including Dio the Academic philosopher, to speak in rebuttal of Auletes' claims. The Flute Player plotted the murder of some of these ambassadors, the intimidation or corruption of the rest.[117] The resulting scandal seems to have done remarkably little harm to the monarch's position in Rome. The wealth of Egypt and the cachet of a royal client—as well as the military glory likely to derive from the mission to reinstall Auletes—proved an irresistible combination. It was rumored that Spinther had at once set his sights on the command (hence his support for Pompey's *cura annonae*, a task whose demands and prestige ought to have satisfied Pompey even while excluding him from consideration for additional assignments).[118] The consul in fact enjoyed Pompey's public support, nor could Cicero fail to endorse his friend. In September, it appears, the senate decreed that the governor of Cilicia and Cyprus, who was to be Spinther himself, was the man to restore the Egyptian king to his throne. By November Spinther had departed Rome to take up his province.[119]

Matters were complicated, however, when Auletes and his Roman financiers wished the restoration to be placed in Pompey's hands, either due to covert pressure from the great man or because they genuinely (and reasonably) believed him the best man for the job.[120] No explicit controversy over the Egyptian command emerges in the senate until December, but once the king and his equestrian supporters had made their preference clear, maneuvering for and against Spinther or Pompey was inevitable. Obviously, few in the senate would look favorably upon yet another Pompeian distinction. Yet at the same time it was difficult to ignore or offend Pompey's supporters, not so much Auletes as the capitalists whose investments were at stake.[121] Hence Clodius's violent attacks on Cicero and Milo—Pompey's men in the eyes of many—and his open hostility toward the great man himself began to appear less objectionable than only a few months ago. Clodius as counterweight to Pompey was a familiar role to all concerned, and it allowed the past tribune to maintain crucial senatorial support at a time when his tactics were threatening to isolate him completely. By November Clodius was in a position to exploit the Auletes issue so as to render his own participation in public life more palatable to leading senators than Cicero for one should have cared to see.

6

So we may return to the meeting of the senate that took place on 14 November, whose main topic of debate was Clodian violence. The issue had special moment because Clodius was by then a candidate for the aedileship, elections having been announced in October.[122] If elected—and that was hardly to be doubted—Clodius would be immune to prosecution; consequently, his enemies sought a speedy trial *de vi*. That was the proposal of no less a figure than the consul designate, Lentulus Marcellinus, long an enemy of Clodius.[123] However, as we have seen, Clodius's supporters talked out the session. Hence rage and tears. Sestius exploded with fury. Clodius, who had not been present at the senate that day, threatened the city with more violence if elections were not held. Milo published Marcellinus's *sententia*, indicted Clodius *de vi* (if he had not actually done so already), and announced by edict that he would observe the heavens on all comitial days. Clodius, Appius, and Nepos each responded with an angry public speech. Only Milo's *obnuntiatio*, Nepos made clear, would prevent the elections taking place.[124]

On 19 November Milo prevented the *comitia* by *obnuntiatio*. Clodius had been prepared to eject Milo from the Campus Martius, but the tribune's superior violence prevailed—*summa cum gloria* in Cicero's words.

The following day witnessed Nepos's unsuccessful attempt to avoid Milo's *obnuntiatio* by guile: the consul had arranged to meet the tribune in the forum (so as to spare each of them the trip to the Campus Martius) but instead tried to make his way to the Field of Mars undetected and unobstructed by the proclamation of ill omens; Milo caught him, however, and Nepos retired not only stymied but also rather humiliated. Clodius complained that Cicero was the mastermind holding up the elections, hindrance that was no doubt represented as opposition to the people's exercise of its right. For his part Milo threatened to murder the past patrician if he attempted to override the tribune's *obnuntiatio* by means of violence, a threat that Cicero believed to be thoroughly sincere. On 22 November the orator was confident that Clodius had been beaten and would stand trial.[125]

But Clodius's cause enjoyed a welcome though indirect and unintended boost when L. Caninius Gallus, upon entering his tribunate (or very soon thereafter) promulgated a bill that would take Ptolemy's restoration out of Spinther's hands and entrust it to Pompey. The obtruded audacity of Pompey's ambition restored to Clodius much of his former appeal to the princes of the senate. Thus Clodius, although far from being the darling of the *optimates*, could at least have reason to expect a greater degree of tolerance from the senate for his recent conduct. And he had already won over allies in the new tribunician college, chief of whom was C. Cato.[126]

Such support would be needed. When the senate was convened in early December, one of the new tribunes, L. Racilius, in an urbane yet combative speech, raised again the issue of Clodius's impending trial.[127] The matter had now reached a technical impasse. The quaestors of 57 had left office on 4 December, but their successors had not yet been elected owing to Milo's frustrating the aedilician *comitia* (which were required to precede the quaestorian elections). The problem—for Clodius's enemies—lay in the fact that the quaestors held the responsibility for assigning jurors in cases *de vi*.[128] No quaestors, no jury, no trial. Marcellinus hoped to surmount this obstacle by proposing that the senate authorize the *praetor urbanus* to select the jury by sortition. He furthermore proposed that elections proceed only after the jury had been constituted and that anyone who sought to impede Clodius's trial be considered to be acting *contra rem publicam*. C. Cato and another tribune opposed the idea—to the senate's consternation in Cicero's account to his brother. The other consul designate, L. Marcius Philippus, sided with Marcellinus, as did Cicero when called upon. Indeed, the orator spoke at length "de furore latrocinioque P. Clodi." He was followed by L. Antistius Vetus (tr. pl. 56), who spoke with eloquence in Marcellinus's favor. When it came time for Clodius's opinion, he directed his wrath at Racilius, who had, it would appear, been most effective of all in getting Clodius's goat. He meant to talk out the session, which proved unnecessary when his bands engaged Milo's outside the senate in so great a clamor that the body dissolved in fear, haste, and mutual recriminations. Cicero expected no new action in the senate until January.[129]

Cicero, in his description of this meeting, emphasized the senate's distinct support for Marcellinus's proposal. Yet Nepos, who had been absent from this meeting, forbade the praetor's constituting a jury before the election of new quaestors. The matter was dropped by the senate or, if raised again, blocked once more. Nepos later claimed that this was the second time he saved his *frater*.[130] However, while the consul's authority was clearly significant to Clodius's salvation, it was also clearly the senate's will that the elections proceed.[131] And by 17 January 56 Cicero was apprehensively reckoning with the prospect of Clodius's *furiosa aedilitas*.[132] As the orator would later admit, the same aristocrats who had secured his restoration had also preserved his archenemy from prosecution. This state of affairs was disillusioning if not shocking to Cicero, yet it made perfect sense in the political environment of senatorial competition. During the course of 57 the balance not of power but of prestige had shifted: at the year's commencement Pompey and Cicero had to be restored in order to curb a reckless and formidable ex-tribune; by December it was Pompey who loomed most terrible, hence the necessity of Clodius's rehabilitation.[133]

7

Clodius was elected aedile for 56 on 20 January of that year. He was returned at the top of the polls, incontestable proof of his continued popularity and also evidence of his senatorial acceptability.[134] The office was an eminently suitable one for Clodius: aediles enjoyed ample opportunity to attend to the needs of ordinary Romans, especially shopkeepers, and consequently presented a legitimate path to enhanced popularity.[135] Great expectations attended the new aedile: Cicero grumbled on the eve of Clodius's election that the eminent architect Vettius Cyrus was avoiding contractual engagements in anticipation of Clodius's year in office.[136] In view of the *aedes Libertatis* of Clodius's tribunate as well as the man's proclivity for *aedificatio*—not to mention Clodius's *popularis* career of the previous two years—the architect and the orator no doubt predicted a massive program of public building. If so, they were to all appearances disappointed. Clodius's aedileship was an eventful one, but not a hint (apart from this mention of Cyrus's anticipation) of the aedile's building activities is preserved to us.

Financial impediments may have been partly responsible. It cannot have been cheap to show his steadfast friendship, even through tokens and by means of his indirect network of support, to the multitudes who supported him throughout 57 by closing their shops for demonstrations. Nor in that year had Clodius enjoyed the sort of financial backing Milo had received from optimate senators. The destruction of the shrine of Liberty constituted a serious (and uncompensated) loss. And Clodius had by the time of his election only just concluded a prolonged and therefore more than normally expensive candidacy. Given that, as aedile, Clodius would be expected to sponsor games and public works of a relatively inconspicuous, utilitarian nature, it may have been the case that he lacked the ready cash for anything grandiose (especially if he intended to carry on his campaign against Pompey). Financial considerations of this sort would not spring immediately to mind were it not for two statements in Cicero's correspondence that suggest Clodius was in need of money in 56 and perhaps even later. At *Q.F.* 2.3.4. Cicero informed his brother that Pompey had learned that Clodius was being supplied with funds ("Clodio pecuniam suppeditari") and, much later (in 55), he reported at *Q.F.* 2.8(7).2 that Clodius was very keen to receive a *legatio libera* in order to visit his clients in the East—"plena res nummorum," Cicero calls it. None of which means that Clodius was especially disadvantaged in 56 even by senatorial standards. But money appears to have been a concern, as a consequence of which the aedile may not have been in a position to launch a program of public munificence along the lines envisioned by Cyrus and by Cicero.

8

The bill promulgated by Caninius Gallus, by the terms of which Spinther's responsibility for restoring Auletes would be transferred to Pompey, excited such a fury of resentment that the Egyptian question came to dominate senatorial politics through the early months of 56, to the advantage of Clodius as we have seen. The king himself endorsed Caninius's bill through a letter read to the public by the tribune A. Plautius. Pompey, however, in a vain effort to dissipate senatorial *invidia*, continued to support Spinther's position ostentatiously, while the great man's detractors, seizing upon the unresolved difficulties of the grain supply, argued that Pompey had far too much on his plate to permit himself to be distracted by the needs of Egypt's king. Even the gods had an opinion: early in January a statue of Jupiter on the Alban Mount was struck by lightening, clearly an omen, though alas unilluminating (as omens are wont to be) without skilled interpretation.[137]

For that the senate turned to the college of the *quindecimviri sacris faciundis*, the elite priests who oversaw the operations of the *haruspices* (when they were consulted by the state) and who preserved, consulted, and interpreted the *libri Sibyllini*.[138] Since the portent was a thunderbolt, for the decipherment of which the *disciplina Etrusca* was superbly proficient,[139] it is perhaps odd that the Sibylline books were investigated instead of the *haruspices* summoned, a curiosity rendered suspicious by the quindecimvirs' discovery of an oracle warning against either rejecting or embracing too closely the king of Egypt, should he require assistance, and forbidding the monarch's restoration "with a crowd," a phrase not unnaturally understood to mean "with an army." Little is known of the composition of the quindecimvirate at this time, but Clodius was a member. And one eminent scholar has speculated that M. Crassus too was a *quindecimvir*, though, as so often in matters pertaining to Crassus, proof eludes.[140] The college's response radically altered the Egyptian question without diminishing its controversy. The presentation of the oracle to the senate was preempted by Clodius's friend, C. Cato, who was already on record as hostile to Spinther's position.[141] He summoned the college before the people in order to compel them to reveal the Sibyl's words. After a brief and perhaps sincere show of resistance, they acquiesced in the tribune's demand.

Cicero privately denounced the oracle as a forgery, disparaging it as a "calumniam religionis" (*Fam.* 1.1.1).[142] In fact, however, there exists every possibility that, owing to the recent collection of Sibylline oracles (many of Hellenistic and eastern provenience) to form the reconstituted *libri Sibyllini*, the references to the king of Egypt were quite genuine.[143] Nor do we know enough about the methods by which the Sibylline books were consulted to declare with certainty that it was inappropriate for the college to seek out a passage of topical relevance.[144] Granted that Cicero's apprehensions fail to constitute proof of fraud, nor need his views be considered representative of current opinion, still the involvement of Clodius with his ally C. Cato (and, possibly, Crassus) lends support to the conclusion that religious manipulation was being employed to blight the prospects of Pompey and Spinther alike. This is not to lay the credit or opprobrium on Clodius's head alone: the college acted as a body, after all, and it was C. Cato who sensationalized the college's response. Nor did Cicero blame Spinther's misfortunes on Clodius. In fact, the Sibyl's oracle was received enthusiastically by Marcellinus as well as the majority of the senate, which voted to accept the oracle's prohibition, thereby excluding the prospect of military glory in the restoration of Auletes.[145] None of which lessened the energies of Pompey's adherents or of Spinther's—or of their opponents for that matter. The appointment still carried with it ample prestige, nor was it rendered impracticable by the prohibition on an army's employ (certainly there is not the slightest hint that the senate perceived the mission to be impossible as a result of the oracle's ban).[146] Alternative proposals proliferated, while Cicero feared that Caninius's *rogatio* would be passed *per vim*.[147] The touch of the gods had done nothing to defuse the issue.

The crusty Servilius Isauricus (cos. 79) proposed forgetting about Ptolemy altogether, a suggestion whose admirable simplicity attracted no one. Cicero, Hortensius, and M. Lucullus—and Pompey, of course—persisted in their support for Spinther. Rutilius Lupus came out for Pompey, as did Pompey's intimate associates, including Volcacius Tullus (cos. 66) and the loyal Afranius (cos. 60), whose endorsement of Rutilius's motion was taken as indicative of the great man's true feelings. Still others in the senate—notably the consuls and the rest of the *consulares*—looked favorably on Bibulus's proposal that a delegation of three *privati* handle the Egyptian affair. Crassus had floated a similar scheme, whereby the king would be restored by three legates any of whom might hold *imperium*. Although Crassus dropped his plan, probably because it had even less chance of passage than Bibulus's, it is notable that on this issue Crassus emerged from the shadows to stake out a position that, while not openly hostile to Pompey's interests, could hardly be said to strengthen the bond between them. After all, Crassus, by proposing to dilute the prestige of restoring Auletes, supported neither Pompey's public nor his private desire. The various propositions were debated in the senate on separate meetings held on 13, 14, and 15 January. Bibulus's motion went down in defeat, while parliamentary maneuvering kept the others even from coming to a vote. The issue had to be postponed until February.[148]

9

The question of Pompey's role in the restoration of the king would be decided not in senatorial debate, however, but in popular demonstrations. On 2 February Clodius commenced his prosecution of Milo.[149] By virtue of his office, Clodius brought Milo to trial before the people for his violent utilization of gladiators to disrupt the state during his tribunate.[150] An aedilician *iudicium populi* held out the prospect of grand political drama, whose consequences Clodius, confident in his forensic capacities, could hope to be shaming if not downright tragic for Milo and his allies, principally Pompey and Cicero. Clodius was able to bring his case without hindrance from the senatorial elite, who were pleased enough to see Pompey and his friends discomfited (though some in the senate had not long before lent their support to Milo, as we have seen). Nor could the presence of Vatinius as witness for the prosecution pass unnoticed: his obligations to Clodius were indisputable, but no less his friendship with Caesar.[151] Indeed, when Cicero one month later delivered his *In Vatinium* he felt compelled to make explicit that his attack on Vatinius was not an attack on the proconsul of Gaul.[152] The aedile, in his renewed struggle with Pompey, meant to advertise (as he had during his tribunate) his ties with Caesar. Milo's defense was to be argued by Cicero, M. Marcellus, and Pompey, who, though only designated an *advocatus* in this process, in the end played the major part on Milo's side in this trial.[153]

The first day ended well, in Cicero's opinion. But on 7 February, when next the court convened, violence resulted.[154] When Pompey rose to speak on Milo's behalf, the *operae Clodianae* raised a loud ruckus, in despite of which the great man tenaciously completed his oration. Then Clodius spoke, but, in the face of an even greater uproar on the part of Milo's supporters, the aedile, if we can believe Cicero, lost his head. Clodius's opponents berated him with every resource of Roman malediction, including the chanting of obscene verses on the topic of his incestuous relationship with Clodia. Outraged, Clodius departed from his speech to lead his followers in a chorus against Pompey.[155] More than one version of their refrain has come down to us, owing possibly to the selectivity of our particular sources and definitely to the fact, mentioned explicitly in Dio, that during this period Clodius frequently assailed Pompey's looks, character, and conduct by means of responsive jeering from his *operae*.[156] The aedile's claques were well rehearsed: at a tug of Clodius's toga they would answer "Pompey!" to whatever inquiry was put them.[157] On this day the most stinging barbs were recorded by Cicero: "Who is destroying the *plebs* by starvation?" "Pompey!" "Who burns to go to Alexandria?" "Pompey!" "Whom do the people desire to go to Alexandria?" "Crassus!"

Crassus was present at Milo's trial, though clearly hostile and not as a supporter.[158] The people's choice on this day can hardly have been spontaneous, in view of Clodius's obviously careful coaching, nor would the aedile have put the spotlight on the triumvir without his consent: what little we know of Crassus makes it plain that, while he might be over-looked, he was too dangerous to offend.[159] In fact, as Cicero was soon to learn, Crassus was financing Clodius's anti-Pompeian demonstrations. For their finale, the *Clodiani*, as if on cue (so Cicero noted), spat on Milo's supporters, an unmistakable act of contempt. At this provocation, the forces of the defense sprang at their enemies. Clodius's gangs fled, while he himself was rudely ejected from the Rostra.[160]

The senate was immediately summoned to the Curia. Pompey went home, as did Cicero, who wanted to avoid offending the *boni* by defend-ing Pompey (the alternative, silence, he admitted to finding equally dis-tasteful). For the great man was being denounced by Bibulus, Scribonius Curio (who was of course Clodius's friend), M. Favonius, and Servilius Isauricus, the son of the consul of 79 and married to M. Cato's niece. Milo's trial, so unceremoniously adjourned, was scheduled to reconvene 17 February.[161]

On the day following the violence, that is, on 8 February, the senate met outside the *pomerium* so that Pompey could attend and give an account of himself. Plainly Milo's supporters, not Clodius's, were blamed for the disorder, and it is equally clear that Pompey was held responsible for the excesses of the defense. On the ninth Pompey again addressed the senate, but to no avail. The conscript fathers passed a decree declaring that the events of 7 February had been *contra rem publicam*, which was tantamount to a vote of censure against Pompey.[162] This was a reversal that Cicero was able to bear with some fortitude, not least because C. Cato, who delivered a searing diatribe against Pompey, included in his harsh remarks a lengthy and laudatory reference to Cicero (whom Pom-pey had betrayed, C. Cato hypocritically asserted, at the time of his exile).[163] In this way Pompey was singled out as the sole object of the senate's opprobrium. Pompey exploded with fury at C. Cato's invective, making it plain that he blamed Crassus for everything; furthermore, he vowed to protect himself from harm, not the great man's first public admission of feeling a tinge of anxiety over assassination.[164]

Afterward, Pompey confided to Cicero that he believed that there actu-ally were plots against his life. He knew that Crassus was encouraging Clodius and C. Cato and that these two enjoyed the additional assent of the *optimates*. He recognized that the senate was thoroughly alienated from him. Pompey, dejected and concerned about his position in Rome, abandoned his designs on the mission to Alexandria.[165] Caninius's bill was soon forgotten.[166] But just prior to the tumultuous judicial assembly of 7 February, C. Cato had promulgated a bill to abrogate Spinther's *imperium*.[167] There can have been little hope of success for the measure despite the burgeoning unpopularity that attended Spinther's absence from Rome. Still, inasmuch as Pompey felt that he would require every friend now, he permitted Cicero to convey to Spinther his assurances that he would support the proconsul loyally.[168] He also began to summon his clients from Picenum and Cisalpine Gaul both for his personal protection—Clodius likewise was strengthening his gangs (sensible enough in response to the rout he suffered at Milo's trial)—and in expectation of a violent struggle to block C. Cato's *rogatio*. Moreover, the industrious tribune had promulgated another bill "de Milone," the nature of which is unknown but which was without doubt of Clodian inspiration.[169] In the event, the consul Marcellinus resorted to religious delays to prevent C. Cato's legislation from coming to a vote.[170] Nonetheless, the message of the bill that would have affected Spinther was unmistakable: the proconsul of Cilicia should forget about Egypt. Even in July 56, when Spinther's original authorization to restore Auletes remained the senate's official policy, Cicero and Pompey advised him to reckon his chances of success carefully before embarking upon an Egyptian expedition.[171] Wary of his opposition in Rome and informed of the consequences should he fail in Alexandria, the prudent Spinther chose inactivity instead.

As for Milo, his trial reconvened on 17 February and a hearing was also scheduled for 7 May.[172] By then, however, the conference at Luca had transformed Clodius and Pompey into allies and *adfines*.[173] This prosecution of Milo, so embarrassing for Pompey, was then dropped—though by no means did Clodius surrender his enmity toward Milo.

Dio believed that Clodius prosecuted Milo not in order to win a conviction but rather to humiliate Milo's supporters, a perfect specimen of *post hoc ergo propter hoc* logic.[174] Yet it remains true that Clodius's prosecution utterly demolished Pompey's Egyptian ambitions, and that the censure of the senate proved devastating.[175] Cicero had been less grievously harmed, yet he had been shown unequal to the task of securing his own savior's reward, a state of affairs that brought the orator considerable *dolor*.[176] Clodius, on the other hand, found himself maintaining his ties to Caesar and working in close cooperation with Crassus—all the while basking in the approval of the senatorial elite, a stark contrast to his circumstances only short months previously. Milo had escaped, true, but the cloud of accusation could be said to hang over him. And in any event, Clodius had played more than a spectator's part in the reversals suffered by his most prominent enemies, all of which, if not victory, was yet revenge.

While Pompey sulked and Milo pondered his fate, the business of state-craft proceeded. On 10 February the senate passed a decree disbanding *sodalitates*, upper-class associations often united behind a single figure in order to exercise influence at elections and at trials. The senate also outlawed *decuriati*, which ought to mean no more than associations organized into *decuriae*, a vague and widely ranging category; after all, even juries were arranged in *decuriae*—and there can be no question of the senate's banishing them—which must mean that Cicero, who provides us the only account of this *senatus consultum*, expected his brother (who is the addressee of the letter reporting it) to take his meaning without careful elaboration. The senate's decree went on to recommend that legislation be introduced to the assemblies to the same effect as the terms of the decree.[177] Cicero mentions this *senatus consultum* to his brother with little detail or obvious interest. Yet the requirements of the decree anticipated the major reforms of Crassus's *lex Licinia de sodaliciis*, passed in 55.[178] Like Crassus's law, the *senatus consultum* of 56 was aimed at eliminating corrupt electioneering practices. It did not impinge upon the terms of the *lex Clodia de collegiis*, nor can the decree have had any directly adverse effect on Clodius whatsoever: *sodalitates* were not *collegia*, and although *collegia* were arranged internally by *decuriae*, there is no necessary reason to conclude that in the senate's resolution *decuriati* refers to colleges.[179] One is loath to work to death the argument from silence, but in a letter otherwise obsessed with Clodius's sordid political practices—and their efficacy—it is inconceivable that Cicero could have mentioned so matter-of-factly a senatorial decree that damaged Clodius in any way whatsoever. The *senatus consultum* of 10 February was a positive effort at campaign reform (not every senator or even every successful one was a scoundrel); it was unrelated to Clodius's activities at Milo's trial or to his previous use of *collegia* for public demonstrations.[180]

11

On the same day as the senate's decree, P. Sestius was indicted on two counts: violation of the *lex Tullia de ambitu*, a charge leveled by the otherwise unknown Cn. Nerius, and of the *lex Plautia de vi*, this accusation being brought by a certain M. Tullius.[181] The prosecution *de ambitu* fizzled, but Sestius soon came to trial *de vi*. Although M. Tullius brought the original indictment, the principal prosecutor was evidently P. Albinovanus, whom Tullius may have assisted along with T. Claudius.[182] The prosecuting attorneys were undistinguished, but they brought before the court, as witnesses against Sestius, L. Aemilius Paullus, who may have been aedile in 56 and was destined to be consul in 50,[183] Clodius's friend the equestrian Gellius Publicola (their estrangement may be presumed to have ended, though of course Gellius may have had his own reasons for testifying against Sestius), and—infamously—P. Vatinius, *adsecula Caesaris*. Standing behind the prosecution, or so Cicero insisted and it is widely believed, was Clodius.[184]

Sestius's cause brought an impressive collection of advocates: Cicero, of course, as well as Hortensius, the brilliant and youthful Licinius Calvus, and M. Crassus—all in all a vastly superior defense to Milo's (whose trial, it should not be forgotten, was technically still in progress). In addition, Sestius may have spoken in his own behalf, and Pompey delivered a *laudatio*. The presence of Crassus alongside Cicero and Pompey—in support of Clodius's enemy—has raised eyebrows and prompted speculation.[185] But it must be remembered that Crassus was at once a tireless and indiscriminate advocate and a very nimble politician. He no doubt recognized that Sestius enjoyed wide support from the princes of the senate—unlike Milo—as Hortensius's participation made clear.[186] Furthermore, the urge to view trials as solely political and as politically defining must be resisted.[187] Sestius's trial, the content of Cicero's oration notwithstanding, was not primarily a referendum on Cicero or Clodius.[188] It was the morose ex-tribune, the defendant, whose future was at stake.

There is actually reason to query the extent to which Clodius was involved in Sestius's trial. Obviously Clodius would have been delighted to see Sestius condemned, nor is there any questioning his connection to two of the prosecution's star witnesses. But this is not really the point: what is commonly asserted is that Clodius engineered the prosecution, if discreetly, and that Sestius's unanimous acquittal on 11 March represented a severe political defeat for the past patrician.[189] On closer scrutiny, however, problems emerge from this reconstruction. It seems odd that the prosecution went to great lengths to praise Milo—Clodius's bitterest enemy after Cicero—in the hope of blackening Sestius's character by contrast.[190] Clodius had little to gain in his ongoing case against Milo from encouraging his putative lackeys to glorify Milo's tribunate. Indeed, the artless ploy makes so little sense and is so obtrudedly clumsy that it lends support to Vatinius's claim that the prosecution was in collusion with the defense. In fact, Vatinius insisted that he had preferred to see Sestius tried *de ambitu* and that it was only after he had begun to cooperate with Albinovanus that he came to recognize the *praevari-catio*.[191] Now there is no compelling reason to disbelieve Vatinius, which means that Clodius's efforts to condemn Sestius may have been frustrated from the start, perhaps when the effort to try Sestius *de ambitu* faltered. In any case, while Cicero's performance at the *quaestio* provided an opportunity to expound his political principles, in his private correspondence the orator viewed the significance of Sestius's trial in terms of the disgrace he had heaped on Vatinius.[192] No word of Clodius, who, however vigorous his encouragement to Vatinius or Gellius, probably should not be judged the mastermind behind the prosecution of Sestius.

Insofar as Sestius's trial had larger political ramifications, these may lie in the attack on Caesar contained in Cicero's invective against Vatinius. Attempts to rescue Cicero's speech from the charge of being critical of Caesar have not succeeded.[193] What is less certain is why the orator chose Sestius's trial as the forum for his reflections on the proconsul in Gaul. It seems difficult to believe that he was deceived by the erstwhile *concordia* of Sestius's defenders and consequently emboldened to exploit the budding senatorial hostility to Caesar. A larger tendency in senatorial politics was at work. Caesar's victories had brought him a *supplicatio* of unprecedented magnitude in 57 and had inspired tremendous popularity among the people, not unnaturally. And Caesar had as always been energetic in cultivating his political associates in the city, insofar as he had been able under the circumstances.[194] Friendship with Caesar, though it had not delivered Vatinius success in the aedilician elections for 56, was yet a valuable commodity.[195] And in March the consul Marcellinus was busy preventing the passage of *de Caesare monstra*, whatever they were, presumably extravagant honors or a prorogation of Caesar's command.[196]

Not unexpectedly, there was opposition, which was amplified by the nature of Caesar's recent successes and which must have left Cicero's harsh language a matter of mild concern by comparison. L. Antistius, a tribune, went so far as to attempt to bring the proconsul to trial, an effort that failed when Caesar appealed to the other tribunes, who supported his claim to immunity from prosecution on the ground that he was *rei publicae causa absens*.[197] But even that refuge came under assault. L. Domitius Ahenobarbus planned to stand for the consulship of 55; he was decidedly vocal in his intention to remove Caesar from his command and to return him to Rome for trial.[198] Clodius, though he was never slow to flaunt his friendship with Caesar, took no part either in these attacks or in the proconsul's defense.[199] However, his brother Gaius was under Caesar's command, and his eldest brother visited the proconsul at

Ravenna for protracted consultation.[200] The rising anti-Caesar sentiment in the senate constitutes an important backdrop to the aedile's struggle against Pompey and Cicero in early 56.

12

The early months of 56 continued to teem with litigation involving Cicero. One of his tribunician supporters in 57, M. Cispius, was prosecuted *de ambitu*.[201] Cicero defended the man, but unsuccessfully, and at the trial of Cn. Plancius in 54 the orator was ridiculed for the quality of his performance in Cispius's behalf. It is likely enough that, in making his defense, Cicero introduced Cispius's efforts to recall the orator from exile. That, however, hardly justifies the further inference that Cispius was prosecuted by Clodius or one of his associates.[202] Cispius had enemies of his own—he and Cicero had been on poor terms before 57—so there is little to recommend the addition of poor Cispius to the list of Clodius's enemies and victims.[203]

More pertinent to Clodius's concerns was the trial of his intimate friend Sex. Cloelius, presumably *de vi*, in March.[204] Milo either participated in the prosecution himself or directed it. Either way, it was bungled and Cloelius won acquittal—by three votes—thanks to the support he received from half the *equites* and most of the senators. Cicero blamed the senate's hostility to Pompey for the jury's vote, a conclusion we may accept as partly valid. But one should not overlook the senate's tendency to avoid offending the scribal order, which was doubtless a factor in Cloelius's acquittal.[205] Still less should the potency of Claudian advocacy, marshaled in full for this trial, be discounted merely because Cicero chose not to acknowledge it. The loss, attributed to Milo's *imprudentia* and *Pompei offensio*, clearly stung, hence Cicero's remark to his brother that his disappointment in the matter was diluted by the daily convictions of his enemies.[206] Not a very substantial remark, one should think, and Cicero made no effort to expand on it. Which leaves little reason to imagine that when Cicero referred vaguely to his *inimici* he had in mind "lesser hirelings of P. Clodius."[207]

The involvement of the *gens Clodia* in the trial of M. Caelius Rufus is indisputable.[208] In this fabulous trial, so alluring as a possible glimpse into the glamorous if seamy world familiar from Catullan verse, young Caelius, the protégé of Crassus and student of Ciceronian rhetoric, was accused *de vi* largely on the basis of his alleged role in the harassment of the Alexandrian deputation sent to oppose Ptolemy Auletes' restoration to the throne and especially for his (again alleged) participation in the conspiracy to murder the philosopher Dio. Caelius had himself won early forensic notoriety by securing the conviction of C. Antonius, the vanquisher of Catiline's army, in the teeth of a defense by Cicero. Caelius had been quaestor, probably in 58, and was a prominent, and promising, young man. Indeed, his resources in charm and in political acuity were vast.[209] Crassus's tutoring taught him the advantage of flexibility, and he was very likely a supporter of Clodius during the past patrician's tribunate.[210] He was certainly leasing a luxurious apartment on the Palatine from Clodius, and he was extremely fond of his sister, as was well known, at least for a time.[211] Caelius's participation in the intimidation of the Alexandrians, in view of his unscrupulous ambitions, lies well within the boundaries of possibility. The sordid business attracted influential men and large sums of money, thereby creating prospects for lucre and friendships for anyone bold enough to seize them. As his father already owned extensive properties in the province of Africa, Caelius's own family may have considered an investment in the monarch's return to power a convenient venture.[212] Whether Caelius had by late 57 allied himself to Pompey and whether that caused the rupture with Clodia and her brother must be deemed extremely uncertain.[213] Still, Pompey was the natural man to support for the Egyptian commission—and by late 57 the great man had recovered a good deal of his old clout (at heavy cost to Clodius). Nevertheless, personal animosities may explain the hostility of the Clodians at Caelius's trial as much as they do that of the other prosecutors.[214]

Caelius was accused by L. Sempronius Atratinus, a youth of seventeen years, whose father, L. Calpurnius Bestia, Caelius had supported for the praetorship in 57 only to turn and prosecute the man *de ambitu* in January 56 (unsuccessfully—Cicero defended). Undeterred, Caelius had lodged another indictment.[215] Hence the laudable nature of Atratinus's motive—*paternae inimicitiae*—the force of which induced Cicero to address the callow youth in magisterial rather than menacing tones.[216] Atratinus was assisted by a certain P. Clodius—not the aedile of 56 of course but rather his client—and L. Herennius Balbus. Herennius was a friend of Bestia, thus a suitable participant, but he also had connections with Clodius's circle.[217] Nor can one overlook the spectacular witness for the prosecution, no other than Clodia Metelli herself.

The prosecution did not merely emphasize Caelius's alleged crimes, but also conducted the usual smear campaign against the accused, whose dissolute past both in politics—he had undeniably been an associate of

Catiline after all—as well as amid the *demimonde* offered ample and easy targets.[218] Nor had Caelius, a renegade *novus homo*, the heritage or the extensive senatorial connections to be certain of the jury's sympathetic discrimination. Fortunately, however, the defendant enjoyed faithful mentors: his own oratorical skills were richly complemented by the advocacy of Crassus and Cicero (each of whose motives, one must say, appear more personal than political in inspiration).

Excellent accounts of Caelius's trial and intelligent analyses of Cicero's brilliant oration are plentiful enough, which justifies the absence of a full rehearsal here.[219] Too many of the facts of the case have been occluded anyway by the sand cast in posterity's eyes by the author of the *Pro Caelio*. Caelius came to trial 3–4 April, the start of the Ludi Megalenses. Taking his cue from Rome's festive atmosphere, the orator produced a show of his own, replete with the motifs of Roman comedy and featuring cameo appearances from Appius Claudius Caecus, in the part of the *durus pater*, and Clodia's *frater urbanissimus*, as the pimp.[220] The effect of Cicero's entertaining performance resists simple formulation, yet one dimension is unmistakably prominent: by depicting the prosecution of Caelius as the silly saga of an angry, scorned lover—an immoral older woman—Cicero decisively trivialized the real charges against his client. Consequently, the search for political motives and factors in the trial is condemned to a degree of speculation daunting even by the standards of classical scholarship.

The trial has been interpreted as another of the strikes against Pompey's assumption of the assignment to restore the king.[221] However, inasmuch as Pompey had removed himself from the competition after the senate's censure in February, this hypothesis must be rejected.[222] Indeed, Pompey's presence goes remarkably undetectable in the testimonia to Caelius's trial.[223] It seems more likely that Caelius was nobody's proxy: his own enemies sought to ruin him. If Caelius was in fact cooperating with Pompey in late 57, then it may be supposed that Clodius's support for Atratinus resulted from political considerations in addition to whatever personal pique he felt on his sister's behalf. Of course, Clodia Metelli had the resources and determination to support Atratinus on her own, though it is hard to imagine that she would engage in such a contest without her brother's consent.[224] Unfortunately, little more can be said. The *gens Clodia*, though sorely bruised, was not utterly crushed by the mace of Cicero's oratory.[225] Nor did Clodia Metelli vanish from sight as a consequence of this trial.[226] However hot his hatred for Cicero and Caelius burned, Clodius's energies were directed elsewhere during the Megalesia.

13

Cicero's letters of March and April 56 tend to concentrate on forensic matters: he was busily engaged in courtroom affairs in the hope of revivifying his influence and prestige. The meaner world of the streets goes unobserved. Yet Cicero himself is our source for the fact that in February 56 both Clodius and Pompey were reinforcing their violent resources.[227] Clodius relentlessly attacked Pompey's weak performance as the curator of Rome's grain supply—and it seems a reasonable surmise that demonstrations and scuffles took place between the adherents of the aedile and those of his enemy. At one such confrontation, probably in late February or early March, the temple of the Nymphs was burned.[228] This temple, the site of Pompey's administration of grain distributions in the city (a process that the great man was revising so as to correct the lassitude of Clodius's distributions), was a natural location for a food riot, especially one designed to embarrass Pompey.[229] The *Clodiani* in this perturbation were led by Sex. Cloelius, though it is by no means necessary to accept Cicero's allegation that Cloelius (and Clodius) *intended* to destroy the temple in order to foil Pompey's efforts. No doubt that construction was placed upon the event when it was recalled (as it must have been) at Cloelius's trial *de vi*. But such hostile rhetoric (of a sort which did not persuade the jury at Cloelius's trial) hardly constitutes compelling evidence.[230] The most important implications of the destruction of the temple of the Nymphs are that Clodius and Pompey were colliding violently during this period and that the aedile was exploiting once again the *plebs'* discontent over the food supply to stir up popular animosity against Pompey.

The riot at the Megalensian Games, games conducted by Clodius in his capacity as aedile, must be understood in this context.[231] According to Cicero, in his retrospective account in the speech *De Haruspicum Responso*, Clodius ruined his own dramatic productions at the Megalesia by gathering slaves from all the neighborhoods of the city and, at a given sign, allowing them to storm the theater. The consul, the senators, the *equites*, indeed all the *boni*, withdrew in protest, while the remaining spectators were forced out. The result was that the games were performed for the slaves exclusively. Now no one doubts that Cicero has distorted the facts of this event, hence the numerous hypothetical substitutes for the orator's version of things that have been contrived. Certain canards are easily discerned: Cicero regularly exaggerates the servile percentage of Clodius's following, and in view of the expense of aedilician games and their importance for cutting the *bella figura* deemed helpful for subsequent electoral success, the idea that Clodius intentionally alienated the upper classes and the citizen population of the city must be considered absurd.[232] Cicero's undue emphasis on class hatred has led some scholars to see in Clodius's actions a challenge to the "elitist" nature of the Megalensian games, others to view the demonstration as another episode in Clodius's expansive patronage of the urban *plebs* at the expense of the upper classes and the rural *plebs*.[233] Far more likely is the conclusion that the Megalensian Games provided an occasion for yet another food riot—perhaps in reality spontaneous and unforeseen—perturbation unsurprisingly attributed to Clodius's instigation.[234] That the grain supply was the cause of the disruption finds support in the fact that the senate, on 5 April, voted to allocate 400,000 sesterces to Pompey to help to fund his *cura annonae* adequately.[235] Because Cicero does not mention the disturbance at the Megalesia in his correspondence, there is a tendency to assume that the riot must have taken place after his departure from Rome on 8 April.[236] But given the orator's lack of interest in popular violence in his correspondence at this time, his silence in this instance is probably insignificant, especially since, as we shall see presently, Cicero had larger issues on his mind on 5 April and subsequently. This increases the probability that the senate's action of 5 April—at a time when the body was by no means partial to Pompey, as we have seen—was in reaction to popular discontent, exploited by Clodius, which had already brought the destruction of the temple of the Nymphs and had culminated in violence at the games.

14

Other matters preoccupied Cicero. Even as he left Rome on 8 April Cicero was reckoning with the next stage of Milo's trial.[237] Of greater moment was his proposal, made at the meeting of the senate on the fifth, that the disposition of the Campanian land allocations be reviewed by the senate. One of the more controversial elements of Caesar's legislation in 59 had been the distribution of land in Campania to men (presumably poor men) with three or more children. A suggestion to reconsider, and possibly to repeal, Caesar's law had been floated already by Rutilius Lupus early upon his assumption of the tribunate. But the issue had lain dormant since. Sound arguments, in addition to political intrigue, can explain the senate's willingness to reconsider the law, among them the belief that the state's coffers were low and the hope on the part of some that any revision of the law would be a blow to Caesar's position. The senate agreed to debate the matter on 15 May.[238] The debate would never transpire, however. The conference of Luca supervened first. The renewal of the dynasts' friendship brought Pompey's pressure to bear on Cicero to quash the Campanian land debate.[239] But there was a much more significant consequence to the conference: the political realignment of the Claudii Pulchri, who buried the hatchet with Pompey. Clodius, hitherto Pompey's bitter and formidable enemy, was henceforth to be both friend and kinsman to the great man.[240] All to Cicero's disapprobation—and disillusionment—of course.[241]

CHAPTER EIGHT

The Appian Way

1

Striving to keep in repair their disintegrating friendship, the dynasts convened at Ravenna (Caesar and Crassus) and at Luca (Caesar and Pompey—and perhaps Crassus). The manifold motives and goals that provoked them have been examined often enough, but what has perhaps been too little stressed, owing to the inevitable emphasis placed on the big three, is the involvement of other powerful senators, each with his own agenda, in the deliberations at Luca. The accounts of later sources, wherein no fewer than 200 senators (accompanied by 120 lictors) attended the proceedings, will best be regarded with skepticism. Yet there can be no denying the obvious implication of such a tradition, namely that the conference at Luca was by no means a covert or exclusive affair. However fantastical the veritable forest of *fasces* imagined by later writers, two influential senatorials were indubitably present: Metellus Nepos and Appius Claudius Pulcher.[1] Indeed, Appius had been with Caesar for some time, a visit of key importance for the subsequent career of his youngest brother.

The dynasts stood in need of friends, nor were the Metelli or the Claudii Pulchri families to be despised at any time, as Pompey for one was all too aware.[2] For reasons that no longer require rehearsal, Appius brought much that was attractive to any bargaining table. Gaius's praetorship could prove useful as the year unfolded, since the dynasts would require every scrap of executive support in the teeth of Marcellinus's inevitable and formidable hostility. Yet it was Clodius who represented the chief prize of a new alliance: he enjoyed the devotion of a loyal and energetic tribune (C. Cato) and, more to the point, he could deliver to the assemblies the stout and violent endorsements that would be necessary if Crassus and Pompey hoped to overcome senatorial opposition to their candidacies for the consulship. Under such circumstances, Milo was hardly a reliable man. At one stroke, then, the dynasts could not merely eliminate the redoubtable threat that Clodius continued to pose to Pompey but actually enlist the vigorous talents of Clodius and his elder brothers.

Our attention must focus on the role of Appius. At this juncture it was he who represented the position of his entire family, though one can scarcely doubt that his own aspirations for the consulship weighed heaviest in his personal deliberations. For the two elder Claudii, Rome's highest and most contentiously pursued magistracy remained the sole object in the *cursus* of each. Neither could tolerate a Clodius who failed to cooperate in the preparations for their campaigns—all the more so in view of their past support for their young brother's career.[3] For his part, Clodius must have recognized the special demands imposed on one who sought a curule magistracy, be it the praetorship or the consulship.[4] Raw popularity (which he was unlikely to lose whatever his relationship with Pompey) was no substitute for the backing of his own clan and its powerful associates—and he must have assumed that he was likely to reap far more in the electoral *comitia* from the friendship of the dynasts than from their enmity.[5] Clodius's loyalty to Appius cannot have been a question in the latter's mind when he sought Caesar's counsel before removing himself to his province in Sardinia.[6] Once again Clodius proved himself, for all the remarkable and provocative qualities of his political conduct, no maverick. Pompey's son was married to Appius's daughter. Clodius obeyed his brother by observing enthusiastically the courtesies and fealties required by this new *adfinitas*. In a public speech—his own palinode—Clodius sought Pompey's friendship.[7]

2

Nothing in Clodius's new relationship with Pompey obliged him to desist from his hatred for Cicero.[8] Nor, apparently, did this new Claudian affinity for the great man noticeably harm Clodius's resurgent standing among the nobility, a point of extreme displeasure to Cicero, for whom the unrelenting resentment of the *optimates* eventually served as an excuse for his capitulation to the dynasts.[9] Yet he continued to be harassed by the hostile aedile. Even as Clodius was celebrating his reconciliation with Pompey, he was thundering jeremiads decrying the ruin for Rome threatened by Cicero's sacrilege and misconduct, by which Clodius referred to the destruction of the shrine of Libertas.

For varied prodigies had manifested themselves during the spring and summer, all intimating (as prodigies tend to do) the displeasure of the gods. According to Dio, the list included the inexplicable reorientation of a (small) temple to Juno on the Alban Mount, a wolf's entering the city, an earthquake, the death of several citizens by lightning, and the sound of unnatural rumblings in the *ager Latiniensis* (just northeast of Rome).[10] This last event stimulated the senate into consulting the *haruspices*, whose response, which was reported to the senate, can be recovered from its scattered traces in Cicero's *De Haruspicum Responso*:[11]

> quod in Agro Latiniensi auditus est strepitus cum fremitu, postiliones esse Iovi Saturno Neptuno Telluri dis caelestibus (20); ludos minus diligenter factos pollutosque (21), loca sacra et religiosa profana haberi (9), oratores contra ius fasque interfectos (34), fidem iusque iurandum neglectum (36), sacrificia vetusta occultaque minus diligenter facta pollutaque (37); ‹videndum esse› ne per optimatium discordiam dissensionemque patribus principibusque caedes periculaque creentur auxilioque divinitus deficiantur, qua re ad unius imperium res redeat exercitusque † apulsus deminutioque accedat † (40), ne occultis consiliis res publica laedatur (55), ne deterioribus repulsisque honos augeatur (56), ne rei publicae status commutetur (60).

> Whereas in the Ager Latiniensis a loud noise and a clashing has been heard, whereas expiations are due to Jupiter, Saturn, Neptune, Tellus, and the heavenly gods, whereas games have been incorrectly performed and profaned, whereas sacred and hallowed places have been profaned, whereas orators have been slain in violation of the laws of men and of gods, whereas good faith and oaths have been neglected, whereas ancient and secret sacrifices have been incorrectly performed and profaned, beware lest, through discord and dissension among the best men, slaughter and danger be created for the senate and its leaders and they be without the aid of the gods, as a result of which the state may pass into the power of one man and . . . , beware lest the state be harmed by secret schemes, beware lest honor be increased for the worse sort and those who have been rejected, beware lest the condition of the state be changed.

This is the best-known *responsum* from the time of the republic.[12] We remained uninformed of the protocols and techniques by which the *disciplina Etrusca* translated particular omens into divine advice, so the door is always open to speculation about hidden political agenda. The pro-

nouncements of the *haruspices*, it seems, tended conservatively to encourage stability (unsurprisingly enough), nor does this response, with
its cautions against discord among the elite and its warning against the
danger of one-man rule, fail to conform to that general habit.[13] But,
faced with such signs, the primary responsibility of divination, it should
be stressed, was not the interpretation of the gods' will but the isolation
of definite actions that would avert any supernatural hostility by restoring the *pax deorum*.[14] Thus attention is naturally concentrated on those
clauses which delineate which gods require sacrifice (under which category might be subsumed the gods' criticism of the games' observance)
and those which declare that sacred places have been profaned. Unsuccessful or overlooked rituals were easily made good by the Romans. The
discovery of profaned sites, however, and their restoration might prove
more exacting. It was upon this latter concern that Clodius seized.

Clodius insisted that the gods, through the visitation of their scowling
signs, were demonstrating their outrage over Cicero's restored Palatine
domus, thereby vindicating the ex-tribune's past defense of the shrine to
Libertas. Clodius's point was apparently well taken, since the senate decreed that there should be a debate and a resolution "de locis sacris
religiosis" (*Har. Resp.* 11; cf. 14).[15]

One cannot completely discard the possibility that Clodius honestly
believed that an opportunity to restore Libertas to the Palatine hill had
presented itself. But his chances for success must have seemed slender at
best. After all, as Cicero was to underscore at length, the senate had, after
a full pontifical investigation of the matter, decreed that no religious
impediment prohibited the restoration of the orator's house. That the
pontiffs and the senate should stomach the reversal of their determina-
tions was improbable to say the least. Still, the issue of Cicero's *domus*
provided his enemy with a focus on which to center alike popular and
noble hostilities toward the orator and a chance to rehearse yet again the
indignities Cicero had suffered at Clodius's hand. Portraying Cicero's
political position as precarious and of dubious integrity constituted an
attack on his dignity and could not fail to affect his public standing. The
clash was over honor. Though the whole affair tends to take on the
appearance of a side show in view of the political perturbations striking
Rome in the aftermath of Luca, its contemporary importance can be
gauged by the intensity of the *De Haruspicum Responso* as well as by the
orator's effort to see his (successful) speech published.

Before the senate was able to convene its debate on the *responsum*,
Clodius took the issue to the people. At a *contio*, held in Cicero's absence
but whose proceedings were taken down and delivered to him, Clodius

read to the throng the *haruspices*'s response and incited the crowd to attempt once more to demolish the orator's house.[16] Because he was a member of the college of *quindecimviri sacris faciundis*, whose duties included the supervision of the *haruspices*, Clodius was able to speak with ample authority as he again adopted the posture of the *homo religiosus*.[17] At this same *contio*, Clodius once more emphasized his recently recovered friendship with Pompey, a maneuver the purpose of which was to render Cicero's position more isolated and hence more vulnerable. And—possibly—Clodius went on to demand a suspension of public business until the *pax deorum* was mended.[18] The aedile, loosened from his unequal struggle with Pompey and for the moment distracted from Milo, continued to indulge unabated his animosity toward Cicero even as he advertised before the city his own fealty toward liberty and his piety toward the gods.

In May Cicero had returned to Rome. He had previously learned, from Pompey's agent L. Vibullius Rufus as well as from his brother, of the new arrangements at Luca (though that perhaps only sketchily) and certainly of Pompey's urgent wish that the matter of the Campanian land not be discussed without his being present.[19] It was an unsettling revelation. At the same time, he was, as we have seen, feeling considerable pressure from Clodius. The two men clashed early in the month.

A day had been designated by the senate for the discussion of Syrian tax contracts.[20] Gabinius had evidently angered the *publicani* by showing too much consideration to the provincials (or for his own profits).[21] The arguments both of the tax farmers and of the Syrians were heard by the senate. The provincials and their representative, P. Tullio, were roundly criticized by Cicero, who resumed his normal role as the publicans' champion. Furthermore, Cicero seized the moment to lambaste, with some amplitude it would seem, the hated Gabinius. Clodius, who of course owned investments in Syria, which may have implicated him in the concerns of the provincials, and who had had in his youth some experience of Syrian politics, took a stand hostile to the interests of the *publicani*.[22] Although Clodius and Gabinius had become estranged during the former's tribunate, their enmity had apparently dissolved in the warmth of Clodius's new association with Pompey, a circumstance that sharpened further the conflict between Cicero and his enemy. Clodius interrogated Cicero severely, and a shouting match ensued, with the result that both sides threatened prosecutions and Clodius made a great show of walking out in high dudgeon, offended by Cicero's outrageous conduct. The always severe P. Servilius sided with Cicero. But it was plain that the past patrician had not been alone in taking umbrage at Cicero's behavior, as even the orator had to admit. After all, taking a position against the depredations of the *publicani* was an action susceptible of assuming a noble luster, as Cato's past performances had shown.[23] In addition, Cicero's personal animosities were simply too obvious that day, and his deportment must have failed to conform even with the generous latitude ordinarily accorded to angry senators. The bitter confrontation was clearly still weighing on Cicero's mind when the senate met on the following day.

Which brings us to the *De Haruspicum Responso* itself, about which little need be said. Cicero's purpose was to refute Clodius's earlier attacks, a goal arrived at by smearing Clodius's entire career hitherto. Amid his heavy invective, Cicero proposed his own interpretation of the *responsum*, wherein virtually every offense and every danger enumerated by the *haruspices* derived ultimately from Clodius himself. Cicero's dazzling eloquence, at once vicious yet (unlike the previous day) possessed of a certain dignity, succeeded in demolishing Clodius's continued objections to Cicero's house. But he by no means eliminated the envy that had attached itself to his now sensational *domus*. And the orator had soon to confront other difficulties, most notably the exorbitant demands of his creditors in gratitude, Pompey and Caesar.[24]

3

Here Clodius vanishes briefly from the record, while the implications of Luca come to involve Cicero more intimately. On 15 May, to the orator's satisfaction, Gabinius was denied a *supplicatio* for his military successes against rebellious Jews in Syria.[25] Still, that could hardly compensate for the abandonment of the debate on the Campanian land, which had, at Cicero's request one recalls, been scheduled for that same day. Cicero began to feel the full burden of the debt he owed to Pompey—and to his own brother, Quintus. He sang his palinode (whatever the actual shape it took), a recantation the no longer idealistic statesman could only describe as ignominious.[26] And he exerted himself on Caesar's behalf. At Cicero's motion the proconsul was finally honored by the senate with a *supplicatio*, was granted ten additional legates, and was allocated funds with which to pay his legions. In addition, Cicero's eloquence preserved undiminished Caesar's Gallic province, though it failed to recall either Piso or Gabinius from their proconsular commands.[27] So the summer advanced, with Cicero feeling ever more dissatisfied with the state of things generally and with his own political prospects in particular.[28]

The orator's hatred for Clodius left at least one avenue open for independent action. Or so he believed. Cicero, in company with Milo and certain of the tribunes (perhaps L. Racilius or Antistius Vetus), ascended the Capitoline and removed from public display the tablet on which was inscribed the *lex Clodia de exsilio Ciceronis*.[29] Though plainly provocative, Cicero's gesture was neither inscrutable nor unreasonable. After all, by voting to recall the exiled orator the centuriate assembly had in essence abrogated the Clodian measure, the presence of which among Clodius's legislative program served primarily to advertise Cicero's past humiliation, ever a sore point and all the more so in view of the recurrence of the controversy over Cicero's house. Posted documents were possessed of signal authority in Rome, whatever their official status as simple records.[30] Defended by tribunician *potestas* and Milo's *vis*, Cicero banished the offending tablet, a symbolic act performed in protection of his blemished honor. He could hardly doubt but that the tablet would be recovered and restored by the praetor, Gaius Claudius, but nor need he fear censure for his pageant.[31]

The sequel, however, revealed the purblind quality of Cicero's hatred. For the orator elected to take advantage of Clodius's absence from the city to make yet another assault on Clodius's tribunician monument.[32] This time Cicero, with a large band and with recourse to violence, seized not only the hateful *privilegium* but all of Clodius's tablets.[33] He either hid them within his own house or he destroyed them. This action translated Cicero's gesture from an understandable expression of his own sense of dignity into an attack on the very legitimacy of Clodius's entire tribunate, a matter that in the minds of most had long been settled. Nor, given the heavy contemporary concern with concord manifested (for instance) in the haruspical response only recently examined in the senate, could so brazen a demonstration fail to attract critics. Upon his return to Rome, Clodius castigated Cicero's behavior in a session of the senate called to consider this very matter. In his reply, Cicero once more rejected the validity of Clodius's transition to plebeian status, thereby denying the legitimacy of all his tribunician legislation and, necessarily, of all acts pertaining thereunto.[34] This brought a sharp rebuke from M. Cato, recently returned—to exuberant senatorial acclaim—from Cyprus. Cato interrupted Cicero's virulent charges to insist upon a distinction between Clodius's conduct while tribune (to much of which Cato, too, took exception) and the actual legality of Clodius's tenure of office.[35] To abrogate Clodius's legislation, Cato observed unabashedly, would be to reduce to nothing his own brilliant performance in Cyprus, the success of which at that time constituted the focus of the senate's galvanizing rally against the arrangements made at Luca.[36] By a remarkable twist, then, Clodius's legislation had become a crucial element in the optimate cause, thereby rendering the past patrician's tribunate an inviolable issue. Cicero had severely miscalculated, and he continued to misunderstand the attitude of the senate's best men. The whole affair, then, helped to solidify Clodius's appeal to some of the *optimates* and was, in the end, a victory for Clodius over his increasingly frustrated enemy. Perhaps it was then that Clodius affixed to the walls of his Palatine mansion tablets that advertised his past legislation as well as Cicero's crimes against the *res publica*.[37] Cicero, understandably, continued to nurse fears for his safety.[38]

4

It was to Cicero's exasperation that Clodius never really fell out with the *boni* even after the realignment at Luca. By that time, however, it was clear that the past patrician was not likely, in the short term at any rate, to constitute a menace of Pompeian or, a matter of increasing concern, of Caesarian dimensions, and the possibility always remained, if recent events were any guide, that he might in the end be turned against the coalition. At the moment, his *amicitia* with Pompey could hardly be seen as anything short of familial *pietas*, in its own way a public proof of Clodius's conventionality. None of this, however, prevented Clodius from competing with the *boni* for his share of glory, even if it came at the expense of the senate's darling, Cato. Among the goods that Cato carried to Rome from Cyprus was a number of slaves, confiscated from the king and therefore public slaves of Rome. Such slaves were naturally to be called *Cyprii*, but Clodius, anxious to receive his share of the credit for Cato's successful mission, proposed that they should additionally be named *Clodiani*, in his own honor. This suggestion was strenuously opposed by Cato himself and by his allies in the senate, unsurprisingly in view of Cato's importance as a counterweight to the coalition. In order to make that very point clear, the proposition was raised that these slaves should be called *Porciani*, another distinction rejected by Cato's calculated modesty. In the end, the slaves received no special designation, but all this fuss over so minor a matter made it an issue in its own right.[39] The refusal by Cato and by the senate to deflect even a single ray of the Cyprian annexation's luster onto Clodius proved a mistake: the aedile attacked Cato's administration of the island and demanded a review of his accounts, which was an impossibility because all of Cato's documentation had been lost at sea. As he impugned Cato's celebrated integrity, Clodius was able to advertise his own claim that he had the firm approval of Caesar, who was of course delighted at Cato's discomfiture.[40] The whole affair never came to a prosecution—that was hardly the point—but it sufficed to sully what was meant to be an easy optimate triumph. One lesson had to be clear: there was little to be gained and still much to be lost from alienating Clodius unnecessarily.

5

Greater matters were pressing. The key decision made at Luca was that Crassus and Pompey should be elected consuls for 55, thereby securing executive positions in which they could insure the continuation of their faction by creating special provincial commands for Pompey and Crassus and by protecting Caesar's tenure in Gaul. This was easier said than done, however, as the triumvirs could be certain of heavy senatorial opposition to their plans and of the hostility of the consuls, most certainly that of Cn. Lentulus Marcellinus, who adamantly refused to accept their candidacy.[41] In order to overcome this obstacle, Pompey and Crassus prevailed upon the tribune, C. Cato, Clodius's close friend and now a supporter of the coalition, to prevent the consular elections from taking place for the remainder of the year. In this way, the elections, postponed until 55, would be handled by an *interrex*, who would find himself, so the dynasts had determined, with only two possible candidates to recommend.[42] C. Cato's tenacity matched that of his optimate namesake. In reaction, the senate donned mourning and, under Marcellinus's leadership, roused the people, with considerable success, to oppose the dynasts' tactics. C. Cato, however, was not intimidated, and his resistance received public support from Clodius, who refused to follow the senate in changing his attire and, furthermore, harangued the people in public speeches. Clodius insulted the consul and inveighed against the senate. In the end there was violence in which Clodius was blocked from entering the senate and very nearly lynched by a band of equestrians: only the forceful intervention of his urban supporters, who threatened to destroy the Curia, rescued him from harm.[43] The extraordinary violence required to sustain C. Cato's thwarting of normal consular elections constitutes a fair indication of the extreme and critical circumstances in which the dynasts found themselves in late 56. But already the realignment at Luca was paying its dividends: Clodian boldness—and violence—in tandem with C. Cato's unyielding obstruction were vital to the postponement of the elections until 55.[44]

Even in that year, however, violent opposition to the coalition's schemes persisted. Domitius Ahenobarbus, backed by M. Cato, had refused to withdraw from the consular elections. In order to strengthen the position of his friends at Rome, Caesar sent soldiers to the city, under the leadership of P. Crassus, the triumvir's son, so that they might participate in the elections. Cato and Domitius Ahenobarbus tried to seize the Campus Martius on the night preceding the elections; in the event, they were anticipated by Pompey and Crassus. The fighting that supervened left Cato seriously wounded and the optimate forces driven to retreat. Thereafter intimidation promoted Crassus and Pompey to their consulships.[45] Clodius's presence in this violence is not attested, but it must be considered a possibility. Indeed, inasmuch as Pompey's opponents resorted to *libertas* as a rallying cry, Clodius's presence would have served as a significant counterweight against the effect of that sort of propaganda.[46] And since our sources for this episode are either very concise or configured around the specific subject of a Plutarchan biography, Clodius's omission might fairly be deemed natural. The same can be said for the violence attending the aedilician elections in 55, at which the rioting was so severe that several were killed and Pompey returned to his home in blood-stained clothes, or the furious events surrounding the passage of the legislation of the tribune C. Trebonius, who finally secured the dynasts their desired provincial commands.[47] Nevertheless, it was one thing to risk the senate's wrath in support of tribunician rights, which was the obvious public posture adopted by Clodius in his cooperation with C. Cato, especially when Clodius's *popularis* stance could be, and certainly was, understood by everyone as a predictable expression of *amicitia* with C. Cato and of *adfinitas* with Pompey. It was quite another to commit mayhem at the elections themselves, especially when it was possible to leave the worst of it to the dynasts themselves, who by then were in a position to deal with their competitors with other violent resources. In short, we simply are not able to know to what extent, if any, Clodius participated in the violence of 55. And at the same time, even on the most minimal estimation of his participation in Pompey's and Crassus' success, Clodius's actions had been such as to earn him, and his brothers, the coalition's gratitude.[48]

The past patrician was not slow to seek his quid pro quo. In a letter to his brother, composed in February, Cicero recounts discussions he has had with Pompey and Crassus concerning a project of interest to Quintus but otherwise unknown to us.[49] In his conversation with Crassus, Cicero tells his brother, it was made clear that the consuls were under pressure from Clodius to secure their friend a *legatio libera*, a state-sponsored junket, presumably to the East (Cicero speculated that it was to Byzantium or to King Brogitarus, but in actuality he did not know). Crassus made it plain that, if Cicero offered no impediment to Clodius's *legatio*, then the orator should be able to have his way in his own project. Cicero left it in the consuls' hands. Crassus was prudent to take up the issue with Cicero in advance: in theory the *legatio libera* was a senatorial mission on behalf of the state or in pursuit of some worthy undertaking (such as the fulfillment of a religious vow) but in practice had become a self-serving expedition that cost a senator nothing even while it enabled him to wield the full majesty of the senate as he set forth to manage his personal investments abroad.[50] Such legations were not infrequently granted by the senate; nevertheless, they were an aspect of senatorial practice so visibly sordid that they were easy to denounce and, in fact, Cicero had tried to curb the practice as consul and he would one day make plain his opposition to it in his philosophical writings.[51] It was predictable that Cicero's personal principles were likely to combine with his hatred of Clodius to stage an embarrassing scene in the senate, one that the consuls sensibly preferred to avoid. It was all clear enough to Cicero, who also wanted to elude senatorial impediments, which is why he was willing to acquiesce.

Cicero had no idea where it was Clodius longed to travel, but he did know that large sums of money were involved. The orator's guess that his enemy might yet expect to collect money from the Byzantine exiles whose restoration he had provided for during his tribunate or from Brogitarus, whose circumstances Clodius had, again while tribune, improved, was perfectly reasonable. And Clodius had other eastern investments, a fact that has by now been remarked on more than once. This is a convenient place, however, to make the point that Clodius's activities were not always exclusively political: Clodius was a rich man keen to become richer. His acquisitiveness for land in Italy was enormous: Cicero claimed, after Clodius's death, that his enemy had hoped to own everything between the Alps and the Janiculum. Clodius had ample possessions in Etruria, to be sure. In the city itself, his holdings on the Palatine were conspicuous and, politics aside, open to censure.[52] So it is in itself unsurprising that Clodius might seek to profit from his services to Pompey and Crassus. To return to politics, however, the demands of Clodius's *cursus* meant that he would soon require large sums of cash, since his next office was the praetorship, and even a relatively honest campaign was likely to be expensive. Furthermore, Appius was poised to stand for the consulship of 54. He, too, even with the support of the sitting consuls, would need cash, and Clodius had an obligation to support his brother's canvass. It is sometimes asserted that Clodius did not receive or did not take up his *legatio libera*, but there is no reason for such a conclusion.[53] Quite the contrary, for in fact very little is heard of

Clodius in 55. A sequence of three letters from Cicero, who was writing to Atticus in April from Cumae and Naples, asks after the security of his house, but this will hardly suffice to prove that Clodius was in Rome and running riot.[54] When out of the city, Cicero had every reason to be anxious about his *domus*: the urban *plebs* did not require Clodius's actual presence in order to vandalize the orator's house (Clodius had at his disposal, after all, an adequate supply of lieutenants). In any case, none of these letters mentions Clodius or any specific menace: each is a very concise request, none is very pressing: for example, "please keep an eye on my house, insofar as you can" (*Att.* 4.6.4). Clodius himself does not again surface in the correspondence until late June, when the orator, now writing from one of his country estates nearer to Rome, inquires after Appius and *illa populi Appuleia*, an insulting reference to Clodius but a reference that indicates no more than that Cicero expected Clodius to be in Rome for the run up to the elections.[55] The query does not even prove that Clodius was actually in Rome then. In fact, the evidence of Cicero's correspondence, such as it is, is entirely consistent with the proposition that Clodius got his *legatio libera*, took advantage of it, and was expected to return to Rome in time to campaign for Appius. There is no further mention of Clodius in 55.

6

Not every item of legislation proposed and passed in 55 was so out-rageous or self-serving that it invited strong opposition. In response to the still-rising concerns over corrupt electioneering practices, practices and attendant concerns that had not been put to rest by the *senatus consultum* of 10 February 56 aimed at that very point, Crassus put through a law, the *lex Licinia de sodaliciis*, which punished candidates who made use of *sodalitates* in order to influence elections improperly.[56] It was a sound reform about which we know very little, despite the fact that we possess Cicero's *Pro Plancio*, delivered at a trial, conducted in 54, con-cerned with Cn. Plancius's alleged violation of the *lex Licinia* in the aedilician elections for 54.[57] This law is of interest here because, it has been claimed, the measure was designed to reduce or even to eliminate the activities of *collegia* faithful to Clodius.[58] The same suggestion has been advanced regarding the *senatus consultum* of 56, a view that has already been discussed and rejected.[59] Similarly, there is no compelling reason to conclude, simply because the *lex Licinia* apparently employed references to organization by *decuriae*—always, if the *Pro Plancio*, our only witness, is to be believed, in strict conjunction with provisions against corrupt electioneering—that the law in any way dealt with *collegia*.[60] Words like *decuriae* or *decuriati* lack the specificity required to sustain so powerful a claim with evidence so flimsy. The *lex Licinia*, like the *senatus consultum* whose wishes it elevated into law, was concerned with excessive bribery in the elections, objectionable actions sometimes carried out by *sodalitates*, a problem so widely recognized that there could be no opposition to any attempt at reform. It is beside the point that *collegia* played a part in the pageantry important to a candidate's electoral success: the *lex Licinia* did not prohibit traditional and legitimate campaigning practices but rather the use of bribery to win office, and *collegia* did not play that role in Roman elections.[61] It is hardly necessary to add how remarkable it would be, if those who have wanted to connect the *lex Licinia* to Clodius were correct, that so dramatic a volte-face on the part of Crassus, and on the part of his colleague (who did not oppose the measure), went unnoticed in all of our sources, including the *Pro Plancio*, in which speech Clodian wickedness receives its due treatment—especially since the law, understood as an attack on Clodius, would mark a precipitous and wholly unexpected (and unexplainable) collapse in the former tribune's political position in 55.[62] But such was not the case. The year 55 was heavy with sentiment for reform, much of it hypocritical or, at the very least, ironic. Nevertheless, there was no reason for Crassus or Pompey to seek to eliminate Clodius's *popularitas*, even if it could have been accomplished in so oblique a manner, and they did not. It was electioneering that Crassus, like many in the senate, wanted to remedy.

7

In 54 Clodius was once more very much a presence in urban politics, not least in the courts. The first issue that must be addressed, however, is whether in this year Clodius was making himself a candidate for the praetorship. In his *Pro Milone*, Cicero insinuates that Clodius was at first a candidate for the praetorship of 53, but later, when, owing to the extreme postponement of elections (the praetors of 53 were not elected until late in 53), it was clear that election to the praetorship would afford him too narrow an opportunity for wickedness, he abandoned his campaign. Apparently the orator had attacked Clodius along similar lines during the campaigns of 53.[63] Cicero's version of events is sometimes accepted as it stands.[64] However, Badian is surely correct to regard the whole matter as a clever slur and, for the historian, a red herring.[65] Admittedly praetors elected in 53 for 53 could not hold their office for a full year. But, as Badian observes, a gain of a year in the *cursus honorum* and the attainment of praetorian standing were advantages that more than compensated for the loss of a few months of actual tenure. Cicero's assertion need not have been complete nonsense: the special circumstances of 53 may have meant that Clodius had in fact come of age in time to submit his *professio* for the much delayed praetorian elections, though a sudden and unnatural candidacy of that sort may have proved controversial in the event and in any case would not have offered him any real gain in the *cursus* (while depriving him of time in office). On balance, then, it seems best to accept Badian's explanation of Cicero's allegation, which means that in 54 Clodius was beginning to position himself for the praetorian elections to be held in 53 for the year 52. Such advanced planning, as Cicero's preparations for his consular campaign make absolutely plain, was perfectly normal.[66]

It was an opportune time for Clodius to accumulate *gratia*, inasmuch as his brother was one of the consuls for this year. Unfortunately, we are not in a position to know to what extent and in what style Clodius flaunted Appius's station; the boldness with which Clodius tended over his career to invoke other powerful allies, notably Pompey and especially Caesar, leads one to suppose that he will not have been too shy to exploit his brother's position. Nevertheless, it is in the courts that one spots Clodius most often in 54, not least because that year was an active one for Cicero—hence our welcome glimpses into what, even when one takes into consideration the sheer accident of Ciceronian *testimonia*, seems to have been a year of frenzied forensic activity. Much of the bustle must be credited to Clodius's tribunate: the censors elected in 55, Valerius Messalla and Servilius Isauricus, were still in office in July, hopeless of completing the *lustrum* owing to the countless hearings mandated by the *lex Clodia de censoria notione*.[67] That there were many trials can only mean that there were many senators marked for expulsion from the *album senatorum*, and the frustration of the census will not have been an unwelcome event to those who enjoyed the fresh right to defend themselves from the censorial stigma. Although Clodius's legislation had not solved the problems of the census, as the events of this year would demonstrate to the disinterested, it was bringing its promulgator timely dividends from the *pedarii* he had long ago hoped to cultivate. But there were other and traditional routes to gratitude, not least of which was actually pleading in court. Clodius left to posterity a reputation for forensic excellence that even Ciceronian hostility could not eclipse.[68] And in 54, as we shall see, Clodius was active and influential in the courts.

In February, Appius's friend, Servius Pola, brought Caelius Rufus to trial. Cicero was not directly involved, and Caelius apparently escaped harm, but it was clear to the orator that his friend was under heavy assault by the *gens Clodia*, a formulation that ought to suggest that Clodius—and Clodia—were still nursing their personal grudge against Caelius.[69] As in the trial of 56, it was left to surrogates to deal with the actual prosecution. It may have been the case that by 54 Caelius no longer required the advocacy of his mentor, and it is hard to escape the conclusion that it was a petty affair (for all save Caelius), but it is equally likely that Cicero was anxious not to leap into a contest with his old enemy: more than once in 54, Cicero confesses to Atticus and to his brother Quintus, that he is avoiding certain confrontations in court for fear of offending Clodius.[70] Though he tried to persuade himself that he was safe, it was concern over Clodius that led Cicero to reduce the number of his enemies: by July he had reconciled with C. Cato, Clodius's friend, and before the year was out he succeeded in cultivating the friendship of Appius Claudius.[71] Each of these instances serves to remind one of the political benefits that can accrue to aggression. Cicero and Hortensius may have felt compelled to avoid prosecutions in order to construct their public images, but that should not obscure the fact that prosecutions in the furtherance of traditional hostilities, such as the contest between the Claudii and Caelius, or prosecutions that permitted one to champion traditional causes, could enhance a politician's image at any stage of his career and could certainly remind others of the perils concomitant with confronting one not afraid (and not unable) to win convictions in the courts.

We come now to three trials of which we know very little, although each had a claim on Clodius's sympathies.[72] Sometime before July, C. Cato was prosecuted under the *lex Licinia Iunia* of 62 (legislation that required copies of all proposed legislation to be deposited in the *aerarium*), no doubt in retaliation for his part in obstructing the consular elections in 56.[73] That one of his prosecutors was the young Asinius Pollio (cos. 40) is certain. Another pleader in the case was Licinius Calvus, whose role, while it cannot be determined with complete confidence, seems most likely to have been that of a fellow prosecutor with Pollio.[74] The trial was marred by violence, and Pollio nearly came to harm, but all such perturbation was efficiently put down by the courage and resolution of Calvus. Thereafter, according to our only account of the incident, Pollio suffered no offense of any sort from Cato or from his advocates.[75] In the event, such tactics proved unnecessary, since Cato was acquitted. The political dimensions of this trial are obvious. The relevant question for our purposes is whether Clodius was one of Cato's advocates, either as a pleader or as an advisor. The case was patently pertinent to Clodius, inasmuch as he had worked so closely with Cato in 56. On the evidence it seems a fair surmise that Clodius was somehow involved in the defense—of course, he need not have been a formal participant to lend his public support to Cato—and that the exiguous nature of our sources is responsible for the omission.

We are better informed of Cato's second trial in 54, this time under the charge of violating the *lex Fufia*.[76] In this trial, once again, Cato's actions as tribune came under attack. And once again, it seems, Asinius Pollio was the prosecutor. For this trial there is no uncertainty over the identity of Cato's *patronus*: he was M. Aemilius Scaurus (pr. 56), recently returned to Rome from his province. Clodius had much less opportunity to play a central role in this trial, as he was otherwise engaged with a prosecution, and there was, if Cicero's imputation of *praevaricatio* is to be believed, less urgency for him to do so.[77] Regardless of such machinations, Clodius may well have made an appearance as a witness for the defense. Again, to Cicero's disgust, Cato was acquitted.

Finally, we may turn to the trial of M. Nonius Sufenas, which reached its verdict on the same day on which Cato's second trial was concluded.[78] That of course means that Sufenas had to have been tried in a different court, on a different charge, from that of Cato, very probably under a charge of electioneering. In reality, of course, Sufenas had incurred displeasure on account of his cooperation with C. Cato in 56, so once again there is a connection to Clodius, though, in this instance, a more tenuous one. How actively Clodius supported or encouraged Sufenas's defense must lie outside the boundaries, perhaps already trespassed, of tolerable speculation.

At last we may crawl toward the light of an explicit testimonium, though one vexed by textual controversy. If we accept the apparent reading of *Att.* 4.15.4, Clodius was the prosecutor at the trial of a certain Procilius:

Publius sane diserto epilogo criminans mentis iudicum moverat. Hortalus in ea causa fuit cuius modi solet. Nos verbum nullum; verita est enim pusilla, quae nunc laborat, ne animum Publi offenderem.[79]

Publius, in making the case for the prosecution, moved the jury with a truly eloquent peroration. Hortalus, in this case, was in his usual form. Not a word from me: my little girl, who is now in some distress, was afraid that I might offend Publius.

Procilius was condemned, by a vote of 28 to 22, on the charge of murder. Just who this Procilius was remains quite uncertain. There is absolutely no evidence that Procilius was, like Cato and Sufenas, a tribune of 56, so it would be unreasonable to imagine that Procilius was involved in the violent obstructions of that year. Nor would it be fair to think that Cicero considered Procilius a creature of the same ilk as Cato or Sufenas: he apparently feared for Procilius's conviction at *Att.* 4.16.5 (though he may simply have been worried that Clodius would score a forensic success), and the fact that Procilius was defended by no less a figure than Hortensius Hortalus must go a long way to suggest that, whatever else he was, Procilius was a presentable *bonus*. Beyond that, however, nothing more can be said. In other words, if this trial involved political issues, they remain stubbornly elusive. Consequently, there is little incentive to accept Shackleton Bailey's emendation of this passage; he wishes to read *lacrimans* for *criminans*, a conjecture that is based largely on (untenable) political arguments and not at all on philological ones.[80] Were the emendation to be accepted, Clodius would be shifted to the other side of the case and become partner with Hortensius in the unsuccessful defense, a not impossible configuration, of course, but one for which there is no necessity. Indeed, if there were wider political issues involved in Procilius's trial, they are irretrievable, and the fact is that Cicero's letter tends to suggest that he saw nothing whatsoever of a political nature in Procilius's trial (in contradistinction from the trials of C. Cato and Sufenas, on which he reports in the same letter). What we are left with, then, is Cicero's grudging report to Atticus of a Clodian victory over Hortensius, a victory that was, irritatingly enough, based on genuine oratorical excellence, all of which must have been quite enough to pain Cicero, especially at a time when so much of his public esteem was concentrated on his status at the bar. The orator, very much wary of Clodius, could neither complain of his enemy's success nor offer public comfort to the defeated Hortensius. Nor, one should add, could he complain publicly of Cato's or Sufenas's acquittal. His daughter's frailty provided a convenient excuse. For Clodius, on the other hand, it was a day of real triumph. His political associates escaped conviction, he himself could savor an oratorical triumph, and as prosecutor he had succeeded in making a convincing case for his passion for traditional family values.[81]

At some point, we cannot say for certain when, Clodius defended one of the Lentuli who had prosecuted him during the Bona Dea affair. Our sole evidence is an *exemplum* recorded by Valerius Maximus in which Clodius is said to have imitated Cicero by being reconciled to his enemies.[82] Valerius cites Cicero's reconciliation with Gabinius and Vatinius, each of whom he defended in 54. Now that is hardly strong evidence that Clodius's defense of Lentulus also occurred in that year, but the time was right for Clodius the candidate to collect all the goodwill that he could. In his defense, so Valerius makes clear, Clodius conspicuously invoked the temple of the goddess Vesta, a detail that makes it clear that Clodius was not only reconciling himself to old enemies but making a bold claim for his religiosity. However distasteful Clodius remained to Cicero, he was forging *amicitiae* with former foes and posing as a sound and reliable figure: just the sort to make an excellent praetor.

8

The narrower interests of Clodius's precampaign positioning must now yield to the electoral contests actually taking place in 54, in which Clodius could hardly avoid involvement. The consular elections for 53, which had looked to be close from the start, accelerated into one of the most corrupt races that the Romans had ever seen.[83] There were at least four, and for a time there was the possibility of there being five, candidates: Cn. Domitius Calvinus and C. Memmius, each of whom was plebeian, were standing for the office, while M. Aemilius Scaurus and M. Valerius Messalla, both patricians, competed against the others and against one another for the sole potential patrician consulship; matters were complicated by the strong possibility that C. Claudius Pulcher would return from his governorship in Asia, thereby adding another patrician to the mix.[84] The competition was intense, the bribery outrageous, with the result that elections were postponed until September. Tensions were running high, however, and already in June there arose rumors of a dictatorship.[85] In the midst of such rivalries, few loyalties could be counted as certain. C. Memmius was the coalition's man, but events would later show that he was unwilling to rely on support only from that quarter. Scaurus, too, was Pompey's choice, or so it was said, but his governorship in Sardinia had been a disaster and the extent of the dynast's support for Scaurus—*utrum fronte an mente*—was unclear, at least to Cicero.[86]

For Appius and, presumably, for Clodius, the highest priority was to protect the interests of Gaius. Consequently, Appius cooperated with the Sardinians in encouraging *repetundae* proceedings against Scaurus, whom he thought to be the more formidable of his brother's patrician rivals.[87] For the Claudii Pulchri to support their brother's interests was unobjectionable, as Cicero himself was at pains to observe in his defense of Scaurus; whatever the family's attachment to Pompey, *pietas*—or in this instance, *Appietas*—transcended *adfinitas* and *amicitia*.[88] When it became clear, however, that Gaius would remain in Asia, Appius had by then made such excessive commitments to the Sardinians that he could hardly repudiate Scaurus's prosecution.[89] Instead, he scrambled for personal advantage by entering into an electoral coalition between himself and his consular colleague, Domitius Ahenobarbus, on the one hand and with the candidates Memmius and Calvinus on the other.[90] This was a deal that cut across all previous loyalties, as Memmius was the darling of the dynasts and Calvinus their opponent. The whole matter was made more thoroughly sordid by the nature of the payoff: Memmius and Calvinus promised, if elected, to fabricate a *lex curiata* and a senatorial decree giving the two consuls choice proconsular commands (or, failing that, to pay Appius and Domitius an enormous sum of money). The four even put their agreement in writing. The arrangement, though ostensibly secret, was out by July and the news sent interest rates soaring as the excluded candidates mounted massive bribery campaigns in retaliation.

In the midst of this came Vatinius's trial for his alleged violation of the *lex Licinia de sodaliciis*.[91] He was an obvious target of the coalition's noble opposition, given his tribunician career and, what was perhaps less forgivable, his success in the praetorian elections of 55, when the machinations of Crassus and Pompey spoiled M. Cato's candidacy for the same magistracy.[92] Pompey and Caesar brought heavy pressure to bear on Cicero, who was, in the end, compelled to defend a man whom he had consistently opposed (not least during the elections of 55) and whom he sincerely detested.[93] The whole affair was an extremely debasing one for Cicero. If we can believe what Cicero wrote to Lentulus Spinther in a famous letter, composed at the end of the year, in which the senior consular attempted to defend his career since the arrangements at Luca, his defense of Vatinius included an attack on the *nobiles* for their too enthusiastic support of Clodius Pulcher.[94] If so, this was a public expression of some importance, since it signals, not merely Clodius's continuing respectability but his success in preserving his own reputation even while his brother was known to be implicated in a most reprehensible scheme.

Meanwhile Scaurus's trial continued. The long and illustrious list of orators and character witnesses who participated in the defense testifies both to Scaurus's expansive network of personal connections and, more importantly, to the significance this trial had attracted in the squalid atmosphere of the consular elections.[95] As scholars have long recognized, the trial was exceptional, not least because it saw Clodius and Cicero pleading in behalf of the same client. The motives that led so many to rally around Scaurus, and to do so at this single moment (since, follow-

THE APPIAN WAY

ing his acquittal, few rallied around his candidacy for the consulship), will have been manifold, but one certain factor had to be sheer disgust produced by the growing awareness of Appius's disreputable pact with Scaurus's rivals and its baleful consequences for the conduct of the elections. Consequently, it will have been important to the Claudii Pulchri to have a foot in both camps, hence Clodius's role as an advocate. In this context, however, Clodius, soon to be a proper candidate himself, must have sensed the need to establish some distance between himself and his brother's recent deportment. How he did this one cannot say with confidence, but we may draw a hint from Cicero. Though they spoke on the same side, the orator could not resist a few jabs at his enemy, who had spoken before him.[96] In his own account of Appius's motives in instigating Scaurus's trial, Cicero indicates that Clodius had spoken at great length on the subject of Appius and had done so in a less friendly manner than that of the orator.[97]

Ironically enough, then, it was Clodius and not Appius who in 54 had to be troubled by the maverick tendencies of his brother.[98] Appius's reputation was scarcely improved when, later in September, Memmius, at Pompey's urging, made a formal disclosure of the electoral pact to the senate, a move that perhaps did not damage Memmius's prospects so greatly as is often supposed (given that the arrangement was already an open secret). In any event, Appius, far from showing embarrassment, remained imperturbable.[99] A bill was then floated to establish a special court to deal with the matter, but it came to nothing, and it was decided that the elections should proceed. That proved impossible, however. All four candidates—none withdrew from the race—were indicted *de ambitu*, and various obstructions prevented the elections from taking place for the remainder of the year.[100] Again there were rumors of a dictatorship.[101]

But let us return to the events of September. Late in this month Gabinius returned to Rome from his province. In view of his past struggles with the *publicani* and with Crassus—and especially in view of his Egyptian expedition—Gabinius knew that his reception would be stormy and that indictments were inevitable.[102] Indeed, his entire fate hung on the strength of Pompey's *auctoritas*. When Gabinius entered the senate, on 7 October, he was assailed by angry senators, chief of whom was Cicero, and by representatives of the *publicani* (invited for the very purpose). Of even greater moment, he was attacked by Appius, who denounced him for *maiestas*.[103] What cannot be overlooked is that, despite the universal hostility toward the man, Cicero was utterly shocked when Appius assailed Gabinius in the senate. In other words, nothing in Appius's bungling attempt to manipulate the consular elections had provoked an open breach between Pompey and Appius and, it is safe to conclude, Cicero had rather expected Appius to come to Gabinius's aid. That he did not do so should be attributed to recent events: the outrage of the infamous electoral pact made it imperative that Appius, however poised his public demeanor, make a display of standing firm in the ranks of the respectable insofar as Gabinius was concerned. Perhaps he need have not worried greatly about Pompey's reaction to this: the great man, in his attempt to rescue Gabinius, found himself deserted at his utmost need.[104] His brother-in-law, P. Sulla, brought in a charge *de ambitu*, and his nephew, C. Memmius, a tribune of the *plebs*, roasted Gabinius in a searing public oration.[105] Hostile speeches in the senate were one thing; it was quite another to speak against Gabinius in court, as Cicero did during Gabinius's trial for *maiestas*, which was concluded in late October.[106] There were some, Cicero reported to his brother, who felt that he himself ought to have been the one to prosecute. But, as Cicero explained to Quintus, to prosecute Gabinius would have been to initiate a struggle with Pompey, who would have viewed the matter as an affront to his *dignitas*—and who would certainly have unleashed Clodius against the orator.[107] The past patrician's violent capacities had not vanished in 54, even if they had not for some time proved necessary. They were enough, in the event, to keep Cicero in check.

9

The failure to conduct elections in 54 did not prevent candidates hopeful of a magistracy in 52 from commencing their campaigns for public favor. Clodius, of course, was to stand for the praetorship of 52. However, it is not Clodius the candidate but Clodius the hatchet man who dominates the attention of our sources. In fact, the past patrician's elevation to the praetorship hardly seems in doubt—even Cicero concedes its inevitability—and this is unsurprising in view of his heritage, his popularity with the *plebs* and with the senate alike, and his association with the dynasts.[108] It is this last item that goes the farthest to characterize Clodius's actions during the turbulence of 53, since Clodius roused himself to violence once again in order to support consular candidates who were to Pompey's liking, and to his own. Seeking the consulship of 52 were Milo, P. Plautius Hypsaeus, and Q. Caecilius Metellus Pius Scipio Nasica. That Clodius would oppose Milo's candidacy was obvious. In the event, it was an action congenial to Pompey as well. He had made it clear, before 54 was out, that he would work against Milo in the elections.[109] To some degree, Pompey was bound to accommodate Clodius in this matter; furthermore, it was very much in the great man's interest that Plautius Hypsaeus succeed at the polls. Plautius had been Pompey's quaestor during the eastern wars and his loyal supporter ever since, and he was the principal object of Pompey's electoral industry.[110] Milo's other rival, Metellus Scipio, was a mediocrity of questionable moral fiber, but his *summa nobilitas* was an important asset; at the very least he could be expected to prove an unproblematic ornament to the consular *fasti*.[111] Clodius threw himself behind the candidacies of Plautius and Metellus Scipio—and against Milo's.[112]

Milo, however, was a formidable candidate. He enjoyed the support of the *boni*—especially M. Cato—and many among the youth. Cicero was utterly devoted to his cause. And he was widely appreciated by the masses, and not only by the masses, on account of the magnificent entertainments he provided.[113] Indeed, there will have been Romans in every class who intended to vote for Milo in the consular elections and for Clodius in the praetorian ones. In 53, once again, there was rampant bribery. Clodius himself sedulously cultivated the various tribes in support of Plautius and Metellus Scipio.[114] And, once again, there was violence.[115] Clodius and Milo reprised their past struggles, with equal ruthlessness. Clodius was not content to struggle in the streets. In a meeting of the senate, Clodius took Milo to task for the enormity of his debts.[116] The issue was an important one, since Milo had vastly overextended himself, a strain that, given sufficient publicity, could only harm him politically.[117] Clodius was able to posture as a proper *bonus*, a champion of solvency hostile to deeply indebted *egentes* who sought to remedy their financial problems by exploiting the *res publica*. That, of course, is merely a speculative version (however plausible) since Clodius's actual speech does not survive. We do know, however, that much of Clodius's diatribe consisted of contumely aimed at Cicero, to which the orator responded with a lengthy laceration of his enemy's career and character.[118] How these speeches affected the senate must remain unknown, but Clodius had struck a nerve: even Cicero nursed concerns over Milo's extravagance.[119] In the end, however, invective gave way to tumult: even the freshly elected consuls could not control the unbridled violence of Clodius and Milo.[120] At one point the supporters of Plautius, led by Clodius, fell upon Milo and his entourage as they were in the Via Sacra; Milo was put to flight. During one attempt at conducting the elections, Clodius tried to rush into the voting area; he was repulsed, with violence, by Milo.[121] Consequently, elections became impossible. In this brutish atmosphere, the young Mark Antony went so far as to offer to assassinate

Clodius, or so Cicero later claimed.[122] Elections were, once more, postponed until the next year, and even then the tribune T. Munatius Plancus, backed by Pompey, blocked efforts to appoint an *interrex*, a move that indicates that Milo's prospects continued strong.[123]

Clodius, meanwhile, fortified his own chances for election. We must return to Clodius the candidate. During his campaign, early enough for Cicero to make animadversion in his *De aere alieno Milonis*, Clodius had let it be known that, as praetor, he intended to revive the law, thoroughly *popularis*, whereby freedmen, or at least those freedmen resident outside the city, were to be registered in the appropriate rural tribes.[124] This was remarkable in several respects. In the first place, it was not normal practice for candidates in Rome to make promises of the "if I am elected" variety. Second, although it was possible and unexceptionable, it was hardly normal practice in Clodius's day for praetors to bring forward legislative proposals. So far, so Clodian, one might say, in that Clodius, confident of his success, could risk being attacked for his magisterial agenda and, further, in that he was perfectly willing to stretch the capacities of an office to their uttermost. One might also judge the proposal itself typically Clodian insofar as it invoked a standard *popularis* theme, an estimation immune from fundamental challenge, though perhaps more than that should be said. The status of freedmen within the electorate of Rome was periodically controversial, sometimes owing to purely political machinations, of course, but mainly because the aristocracy was torn between its insurmountable class bias, which remained hostile to the social advancement of ex-slaves as a group, and the patent injustice of assigning all freedmen, who were after all *cives Romani*, exclusively to the four urban tribes regardless of their place of domicile.

In past years, various politicians of *popularis* bent had tried to remedy this state of affairs by proposing a redistribution of freedmen: P. Sulpicius had passed such a law, later annulled by Sulla, then revived under Cinna only to be abolished by the dictator; in 66, C. Manilius brought the same measure before the people, but it, too, was invalidated, this time by the senate.[125] Consequently, Clodius could claim no originality when he floated the idea. Nor could anyone miss its *popularis* quality. But Clodius enjoyed a special claim on the issue that complicates its significance: the great Appius Claudius Caecus, when censor, had attempted unsuccessfully to adlect the sons of *libertini* into the senate; when that failed, he resorted to a redistribution (of some sort) of freedmen voters; furthermore, in 169, the censor C. Claudius Pulcher prevented his colleague, Ti. Sempronius Gracchus, from disfranchising freedmen entirely.[126] In other words, the protection and enhancement of freedmen's electoral rights could be represented as a traditional Claudian calling. A political campaign was an appropriate time for Clodius to advertise his ancestry. Nor, it was suggested previously, had Clodius failed in the past to imitate Caecus.[127] It was probably no accident that Clodius's plans became so well known to his contemporaries. After Clodius's death, during the riots that led to the cremation of his corpse in the Curia, Sex. Cloelius brandished before the people a *librarium* containing Clodius's legislative program.[128] Cicero makes much of this incident, which leads one to suspect that this *librarium* had been a prop of Clodius's campaign for the praetorship. The rights of freedmen were clearly meant to be something of a theme in Clodius's tenure of office, and it would be rash to doubt that his vigorous *popularis* pose was helpful to Clodius in rallying the crowds in opposition to Milo and his supporters. Still, Clodius's continued good standing within the senate and his certain prospects for electoral success in the coming *comitia* make it plain that Clodius's program was not by any means perceived to be subversive, dangerous, or objectionable by those who were not already his enemies.

This point must be developed somewhat further. The political gain to be gotten from the passage of this law, if Clodius had lived to promulgate it, can easily be overestimated. There can hardly be a question of Clodius's enhancing his already unprecedented popularity with the urban populace. Admittedly, the redistribution might have benefited Clodius in the centuriate assembly by its removal of some wealthy freedmen to the rural tribes within the first class (on the likely assumption that they appreciated the transfer), but it is unclear how significant an advantage would actually eventuate from that.[129] In any event, this legislation, though *popularis*, was hardly the lightning strike of Clodius's *lex frumentaria* or his *lex de collegiis*. Although it was not the sort of legislation to win enthusiastic support in the senate or to forge for himself another political weapon, nevertheless Clodius clearly felt that, as praetor, it was a bill worth proposing. We are scarcely in a position to know just how deep was Clodius's sense of family tradition and whether it was the example of Caecus or the censor of 169 that inspired him. But it is perhaps worth considering an idea advanced in the first chapter of this book, that some Romans, whatever their opportunistic instincts, whatever their willingness to resort to any tactic to win advancement, could nonetheless genuinely respect the *iura populi* at the same time and could do so in deference to the past.[130] For Clodius, it is not unreasonable to suggest, the redistribution of freedmen did indeed have more to do with Claudian traditions and with actual principle than with mere politicism, which is not the same thing as saying that Clodius was uninterested in whatever practical benefits might ultimately accrue from his enactments. The *popularis* tribune was soon to become a *popularis* praetor, but by now Clodius had shown how the *via popularis* could safely, even triumphantly, be trod.

Another possible Clodian proposal concerning freedmen must be addressed. In his *Pro Milone*, Cicero alleged that part of Clodius's praetorian legislative program included a new law that would have made the Romans' slaves into Clodius's freedmen (*Mil.* 89: "lege nova, quae est inventa apud eum cum reliquis legibus Clodianis, servos nostros libertos suos effecisset"). It is difficult to determine what should be made of this. It is always possible that this is simply an instance of misleading or baseless Ciceronian slander: after all, Clodius's plan to redistribute freedmen voters was certainly well known by the time of Milo's trial, and elsewhere in *Pro Milone* Cicero makes exaggerated assertions about Clodius's plans for Rome's servile population (e.g., *Mil.* 87). But this claim seems too vehemently specific to be the usual fear-mongering resorted to in order to raise an audience's indignation, and Quintilian (9.2.54) adds that this law was one in whose originality Clodius took special pride (though one may wonder how Quintilian knew that), all of which speaks against Cicero's reference here being to the *rogatio de libertinorum suffragiis*, which was by no means new or original.

T. Loposzko has made the intriguing suggestion that Clodius had intended to propose a law that would deal with the problem of informally manumitted slaves.[131] Such freedmen possessed their liberty only at the discretion of their masters, for they were in point of law still *servi*. Under the empire this condition was remedied by the *lex Junia* (of uncertain date) which made informally manumitted slaves into *de jure* freedmen and Latins.[132] It is Loposzko's attractive proposition that Clodius's law was designed to do something to secure the liberty of freedmen of this type. If so, it would have been a timely reform, and one appropriate to the responsibilities of a praetor, since, during the republic, the only safeguard to their freedom that was available to informally manumitted freedmen was the intervention of the praetor.[133] What was regulated in *ad hominem* fashion by the praetor, then, was to become regularized in such a way that the informally manumitted would no longer technically be slaves. If this was in fact so, then Cicero's depiction of Clodius's law, though tendentious, was not entirely inaccurate, since the promulgator of such a law could expect the gratitude of those who benefited by it, though it is unthinkable that freedmen so created would become, in any real sense, Clodius's *libertini*. Of course, the evidence is insufficient for a firm conclusion. But, if Loposzko is correct, then once again we have to do with a piece of legislation which, though a needed reform, was unlikely to win abundant approval from the elite or to affect his standing with the urban populace in any significant way. It would, however, promote Clodius's reputation as a champion of *libertas*.

10

The year 52 began with warnings and portents and evils imminent: an owl was captured in the city; a statue sweated for three days; a flash appeared in the sky; there were many thunderbolts; clods of earth, stones, shards—and even blood—were seen flying through the air. Such signs, and the rumor of such things, quite naturally increased the trepidation of a city whose government had, once again, failed to perpetuate itself without resort to emergency methods.[134] But the occurrence that did the most to unleash the festering anxieties and rage of the Romans was not heaven sent: it was the murder of Clodius. The importance of this episode resulted in its assuming more than one version, unsurprisingly in view of the varying personal political sentiments that underlay its every telling. When Milo came to trial, the prosecution made the claim that Milo had contrived a journey to Lanuvium so that he might confront and waylay Clodius on the road. Speaking for the defense, Cicero put forward the counterclaim that it was Clodius who had plotted to ambush Milo. Cicero's brilliant *narratio* in *Pro Milone* is an unrivaled specimen of the orator's genius in that department and consequently difficult to resist. Fortunately, it can be corrected by the more sober, and carefully researched, account to be found in Asconius.[135]

On 17 January, Clodius left Rome in order to address the decurions of Aricia, a municipality south of Rome on the Appian Way.[136] Presumably the visit was related to his campaign for the praetorship. Clodius was traveling lightly, a point stressed by Cicero in his defense of Milo: he did not carry with him his usual cortege of Greeks or his wife, who was his habitual companion. Instead, he journeyed on horseback, accompanied by two friends, the equestrian C. Causinius Schola, the man who had provided Clodius his alibi during the Bona Dea trial, and a certain P. Pomponius, a man who was, according to Asconius, a well-known figure among the urban *plebs*; in addition, he was conducted by approximately thirty armed slaves, a fairly typical bodyguard for such an expedition.[137] On the following day, the 18th, Clodius was returning to the city, again by the Appian Way. He stopped at his Alban villa, near Bovillae. Later in the day he visited Pompey's Alban villa, at Alsium. Meanwhile, Milo had left Rome on the 18th: that morning he had been abused by Pompeius Rufus and Sallust at a *contio* the two had summoned, after which he attended a meeting of the senate; thereafter, he began his journey to Lanuvium, his hometown, where he was the chief magistrate for that year and where he was obliged to install a local priest, the flamen of Juno Sospes. Milo traveled in a wagon with his wife, Fausta, and with a friend named M. Saufeius and another whose name was either Fufius or Fusius; he was accompanied by an entourage of slaves, some of whom were gladiators, including two famous ones, Eudamus and Birria, who brought up the rear of Milo's escort.[138] In the late afternoon, near Bovillae and more specifically, so we are told, near a shrine of the Bona Dea, Milo's party passed that of Clodius.[139] Words were exchanged on both sides, culminating in a brawl of sorts between the gladiators and the slaves at the rear of Clodius's train. Clodius looked back menacingly, at which moment Birria hurled a lance, which wounded Clodius in his shoulder. At that, a full-scale fracas broke out, during which Clodius was taken to an inn in Bovillae. Milo's forces overpowered Clodius's, at which time Milo made the calculation that a stricken and vengeful Clodius was infinitely more dangerous than a dead one, whereupon he ordered Clodius to be ejected from the inn.[140] M. Saufeius saw to it that Clodius was finished off.[141] His body was left on the road. Back in Rome, it would become a refrain of Clodius's champions and of Milo's enemies that their hero had been slain on the Appian Way, amid the monuments of his own ancestors.[142]

A passing senator, Sex. Teidius, returned Clodius's body to Rome, where popular grief and rage culminated in riot. The passions of the crowd were further incited by Fulvia, by Sex. Cloelius, and by the tribunes T. Munatius Plancus and Q. Pompeius Rufus. In the end, Clodius's body was carried to the forum, where it was cremated in a blaze that consumed the Curia. Mobs attacked the house of Milo and the house of M. Aemilius Lepidus, who was *interrex*. Such flaming violence, however, evaporated enough of the outrage over Clodius's death that Milo deemed it safe to return to the city. Finally, the senate was forced to pass the ultimate decree, which, there being no consuls, appealed to the *interrex*, to the tribunes, and, most significantly, to Pompey.[1] Order was restored, and soon Pompey was made the sole consul of Rome, an event of momentous consequences for his relationship with the *optimates* and with Caesar.[2] The senate resolved that Clodius's murder and the urban violence that attended it were *contra rem publicam*. The new consul promptly promulgated a law *de vi* that explicitly cited Clodius's murder and the rioting that led to the Curia's destruction: the law instituted special proceedings that would bring to justice all who had acted against the republic.[3] Clodius's nephews brought Milo to trial, and he was condemned.[4] But Cicero, who had failed in Milo's defense, prosecuted Plancus and Pompeius Rufus as soon as both men had left office, and he secured the condemnation of each.[5] So, too, was Sex. Cloelius sent into exile, though he would one day be recalled, in 44, by the consul Mark Anthony as a favor to Clodius's young son.[6] This young man, P. Claudius Pulcher, is said by Valerius Maximus to have been utterly depraved and to have suffered an embarrassing death. Nevertheless, he prospered well enough in the meantime, joining the college of augurs and winning elevation to a praetorship.[7] No doubt it was his death and not his morals that kept him from the consulship. Whether the augur was father to the P. Claudius Pulcher who was consul in A.D. 21 or 22 or to the Appius Claudius who was condemned as one of Julia's lovers must remain uncertain; the second possibility, which would be so deliciously poetic, requires special resistance.[8] Clodius also left a daughter, who was briefly the wife of Octavian; thereafter she disappears from view.[9]

The memory of Clodius's success with the people survived him, at least for a time. That dashing and degenerate patrician, P. Cornelius Dolabella, who had entered public life in 50 by prosecuting Appius Claudius even while he was sweeping Cicero's Tullia off her feet, imitated Clodius by becoming a plebeian through adoption (by a P. Lentulus) in order to stand for the tribunate, an office he held in 47.[10] Although Cicero did not regard Dolabella as a satisfactory son-in-law, it was on Dolabella that his hopes for security rested in that year: Cicero, having returned to Italy from the republican camp, feared his enemies among the Caesarians, so much so that, though he had decided that it would be best for Tullia to divorce her husband and though he was himself quite strapped for funds, he nevertheless continued to make payments on Tullia's dowry.[11] Still, Dolabella's politics were as disturbing as his carousing and womanizing. The tribune had proposed a bill to abolish debts, a sore problem in 48 and 47 that had not been alleviated by Caesar's own legislation on that score, and the resulting perturbations eventually led to the intervention of Antony, who was master of the horse.[12] Another Dolabellan proposal, which deeply wounded Cicero, was to erect an honorific statue to Clodius Pulcher. "That my own son-in-law should propose this," exploded Cicero in a letter to Atticus (*Att.* 11.23.3), "or debt cancellation!" But in 47, the orator was hardly in a position to do more than to complain privately. Dolabella's political instincts, attuned as they were to the requirements of the moment, were such that his alliances shifted rapidly. His keenness to model his urban image on that of Clodius makes it plain that there was still political capital to be drawn from that past patrician's *favor plebis*.

But it is time to have done with narration and to turn to the final issue: did Clodius matter? In many ways, the very question signals an appeal to the prepossessions that one entertains about history. If, for instance, one is mostly concerned with that impersonal groundswell on which the more obvious men and events of our period were borne, to borrow an expression from Hobsbawm, then the question is hardly worth bothering about at all. The structures of urban life and of urban politics probably meant that, sooner or latter, someone would promulgate a *lex frumentaria* that established a grain dole. But it was perhaps not inevitable that one politician in Rome would eventually recognize the full potential of the *via popularis* for establishing a position of sustained power and influence within the city itself, for forging a career that, while remarkable and at times even dangerous, did not lead either to complete political isolation or to a state of affairs in which senatorial forces could inflict on it a legitimate deathblow. Clodius's success in doing just that was, for the most part, the product of a series of accidents, though it was aided by an arrogant pertinacity and at the same time by a degree of political acumen and political carefulness, this last item being a quality that developed, in its own way, as time went on. In no small measure, Clodius was able to locate himself within the boundaries of political reasonableness by the tendency of some his opponents to resort to enormities that equaled or surpassed his own (or at least were perceived by many to do so) and by the presence in Roman politics of figures regarded by the senatorial majority as ultimately more threatening than Clodius himself. His obsession with his own ends and with his own *dignitas*, all would presumably agree, was so much an aspect of his times that it hardly represented a quality that confounded any of his peers.[13] Clodius the *popularis*, then, was not so maverick a senator that his colleagues were unable to deal with him. That Clodius was no mere "instrument" was securely established long ago. What I hope has emerged from the preceding pages is a clearer understanding of the extent to which Clodius—like everyone else in the senate—was obliged to cooperate with others, to find in the configuration of power that centered around a political issue a place that would advance his own interests without incurring more enmity or envy than he could cope with. Clodius did not always negotiate these matters successfully, as the events of early 57 show. But he became increasingly adept at the game, as indeed he had to become.

Clodius's political disappointments, like his achievements, are not always to be explained in terms of the opposition between *optimates* and *populares*. Even the exile of Cicero, which was made possible by the influence resulting from the tribune's *popularis* legislation and was shaped by the rhetoric of *provocatio* and *libertas*, required the sordid cooperation of Cato and his circle. Nor was Cicero's restoration inspired solely by loyalty to the cause of *senatus auctoritas*. This is not to say that senatorial prestige and popular rights were not important factors in all of this—far from it—but rather than they were not the only or even the most important ones. And for the rest of Clodius's career, the flamboyant *popularis* remained all too acceptable to the *optimates*, as Cicero complained, and he all too readily cooperated with them to discomfit Pompey. All of which exemplifies Meier's emphasis on the ad hoc quality of so many (if not most) political contests in Rome: principles were important, but there were many principles, not the least of which was the hostility that oligarchies naturally direct against any paramount leader. Hence, although some associations remained steadfast, most did not, and care must be exercised to avoid neglecting the shifting concerns of Roman politicians (which is not quite the same thing as viewing the Roman senate with total cynicism).

In the end, Clodius's career displayed all the strengths, and all the weakness, that lay in the mobilization of the urban *plebs* for political gain. Though there is no denying the advantage of crowds and popular pressure, the urban *plebs* was not sufficiently important on its own to raise one to the highest magistracies, which is why, in the latter years of Clodius's life, he began to appear ever more the typical senator, pleading in the courts and accumulating the wealth and connections needed to succeed at the polls. The distinctive narrowness of Clodius's entire career, however, stands revealed when one wonders what, had he survived, he might have done for either side during the civil war, when the Romans had to come to terms with the deployment of violence on a grand and serious scale.

Clodius's one abiding contribution to the structure of Roman society was the grain dole. Nevertheless, the practice persisted without its remaining any sort of memorial to its creator. Simply put, then, it is fair to say that Clodius did not leave a lasting *personal* impression on Rome. Dolabella's impersonations demonstrate his abiding popularity, but little more than that survived or could be expected to survive. When young Caesar married young Claudia, it was the importance of Fulvia and of Antony and not of Clodius that actuated the entanglement. Nor did the future Princeps require the example of Clodius to perceive the value of *tribunicia potestas* or of the curatorship of the grain supply, even if it is true that Clodius's career had raised the stakes of such matters.[14] And the complications of Augustus's building program, whatever it owed to its predecessors—and Clodius's Palatine shrine to Libertas was an important precedent—constitute in themselves a transformation of public building so thorough that, in the end, aristocratic competition along those lines was consumed and eliminated.[15] Admittedly, Augustus's cultivation of the cult of the Lares Compitales, which fostered the dignity of freedmen, may perhaps owe something to Clodius's perception of the value of *collegia* and to his late interest in the circumstances of freedmen.[16] Still, Clodius's *popularis* tactics, which invoked long-standing values and concepts for ephemeral and limited purposes, were not designed to change the nature of things, only to focus attention on particular issues (none of them novel) and to advance Clodius's career. In fact, it may safely be said that the past patrician was on the wrong side of his epoch's history: there is no reason to suppose that, had he escaped Milo,

Clodius would have joined the Caesarian cause in the civil war; more importantly, Clodius—like the vast majority of his class (with the notable exception of Octavian)—failed to appreciate the far more consequential class tensions that reverberated throughout the municipal elite up and down the peninsula, compared with which the discontents of the urban poor were, alas, merely a local racket. That story, of course, has been told elsewhere, and Clodius has no real part in it.[17]

Nevertheless, Clodius's transformation of *favor plebis*, which under his direction came to manifest itself in organized demonstrations and in violence, altered the political profile of the urban populace. Owing to its long association with Clodius, the *plebs urbana* developed a sense, however inchoate, of political identity and of political entitlement. Subsequent leaders were obliged to seek popular support with grand and continual gestures if they hoped to dominate the city—not because they had as a conscious purpose the specific imitation of Clodius (as Dolabella did), but because the heightened awareness and volatility of the people required the perpetuation of some aspects of his style. Hence the celebrated aedileship of the distinguished consular M. Agrippa in 33, a move which recognized popular concerns and yet avoided the tribunate, and hence Augustus's assumption of tribunician powers (as well as his attention to other matters important to the well-being of the *plebs*).[18] This was certainly an effect of Clodius's career that outlasted his personal reputation.

But, to return to the question, even if Clodius did not greatly matter to the transactions or structures of the Triumviral period or to the Principate that succeeded it, he certainly did matter to his own times, and it is perhaps best not always to regard the late republic as if it were merely a prelude to the empire. It was Clodius's corpse and no other whose cremation destroyed the Curia and set the stage for Pompey's sole consulship. The death of Milo along the Appian Way could have caused no similar perturbation, and Milo was by no means an inconsequential figure. In any event, it is vital to bear in mind, the 60s and 50s were not merely run-ups to the civil war: a day or a year does not derive its sole importance only from its place in the cosmic chain of events, but rather, and one might even say mostly, it has importance for its own sake. It is quite simply impossible to imagine Roman politics in the 50s without Clodius and without his particular combination of demagoguery and statesmanship. Change the fifties, historians of a certain stripe might insist, and one changes everything, but there is no desire here to enter into a philosophical discussion either of Roman history or of history (full stop). The purpose of this book has been to concentrate on matters far narrower in scope: on the events, or rather, on some of the events of the 60s and 50s, all of them connected with the life and career of Clodius Pulcher. In view of this accounting of things, it is enough, I hope, to say that, for all his complications and for all his failures, Clodius mattered— briefly, but intensely.

1. Clodius or Claudius?

"P. Clodius, whom some call Claudius" (Dio 36.14.4). And therein, of course, lies a difficulty, since the exact significance of this variation, or whether the variation possesses any significance whatsoever, is unclear. The most commonly asserted view is that Publius's use of the form Clodius represented one aspect of his *popularis* posture: a recent and typical specimen of this point of view is C. Habicht, who remarks without further comment of our subject that "Clodius was a patrician, a Claudius, who had changed his name to the proletariat Clodius in order to win favor with the crowd" (*Cicero the Politician*, 46). In fact, the present condition of our evidence is unlikely to substantiate any hypothesis seeking to explain Publius's preference for Clodius instead of Claudius. The political explanation, however, is almost certainly wrong.

The two forms of Publius's *gentilicium* may be referred to as the o-form and the au-form. The variation of *o* for *au* was a characteristic of Umbrian, which by Publius's day was either rustic, vulgar, or archaic (Lindsay, *The Latin Language*, 41; Leumann, *Lateinische Laut- und Formen-Lehre*, 79f.). Publius's use of the o-form is characteristic from the onset of his public career, but one cannot say with certainty that he was the first member of his *gens* so to style himself. A Greek inscription has been thought to indicate that Publius's uncle, the consul of 92, used the o-form (Gasperini, "Due nuovi apporti epigrafici," 53), but the unreliability of Greek transliterations of Latin names renders this evidence problematic (Startevant, *The Pronunciation of Greek and Latin*, 58ff.). The same can be said for the epigraphic and literary evidence that Publius's eldest brother likewise employed the o-form (*IG* 3:566; Plut. *Luc.* 21). We are on surer ground with Publius's other brother, however: Gaius is twice called Clodius by Cicero, and in neither instance is an allusion to Publius possible (Cic. *Att.* 3.17.2, 4.15.2). Publius's sisters were apparently called Clodiae (passages collected in Drumann and Groebe, *Geschichte Roms*, 2:313ff.). All of which raises the question of Publius's actual distinctiveness in preferring the o-form to the au-form.

The distinction between the two forms has nothing whatsoever to do with patrician or plebeian status, as the existence of the plebeian Claudii Marcelli suffices to demonstrate. Nor is there much to commend the view that Publius's resort to the vulgar pronunciation of his name was intended to win popular favor. It should be clear from the first chapter of this book that *popularitas* was not won by politicians who eliminated the social distance between themselves and the *plebs urbana*. Quite the contrary: the mob valued nobility, and the superiority of their benefactors tended to enhance *favor plebis*. *Popularis* politics was not about egalitarianism. This is no doubt the reason that, for all the rich abundance of anti-Clodian invective in the extant writings of Cicero, there is not so much as a hint that Publius's use of the o-form is exceptionable for political reasons. Indeed, the only text in which Cicero makes a conscious effort to employ one form of the *gentilicium* instead of the other comes in a letter written to Metellus Celer in which reference to the arrogant noble's wife takes the au-form (Cic. *Fam.* 5.2.6; elsewhere in Cicero she is regularly Clodia). But this simply indicates that the two forms belonged to different registers of speech, hardly that the o-form had political implications.

The pronunciation of *o* for original *au* was, by the first century of our era, so common that au-forms could be treated as pedantic (e.g., Suet. *Vesp.* 22). The situation was not quite the same in Publius's day, but o-forms of certain nouns were used colloquially by Cicero (e.g., *Att.* 5.2.6; *Fam.* 12.12.2; *Q.F.* 2.13.4). It may well be that the use of Clodius and Clodia by Publius and his sisters (if not also by Gaius) was one manifestation of contemporary fashion among their stylish circle. The trendy language of the sophisticated set, if Catullus's poetry is any guide, included colloquialisms in grammar and homely, provincial diction (e.g., *basium* in Cat. 5.6; *ploxenum* in Cat. 97.6). Evidently such expressions, daring vernacular intrusions into the *sermo urbanus*, came into vogue in the fifties. In view of the fact that not a scrap of evidence exists for a political interpretation of Publius's use of the o-form of his *gentilicium*, it can hardly be unreasonable to look elsewhere for his motive in making what was certainly a choice. Faddism then emerges as a very likely motive indeed. And if so, then it is perhaps an error (caused by the bias of our sources, which regularly prefer the political and the masculine) to assume that Publius was the key figure in his family's recourse to the o-form: Clodia Metelli, who was the embodiment of chic, did not (despite Cicero's treatment of her in *Pro Caelio*) need her younger brother's advice when matters came to fashion. Perhaps it was the style of his elder sister that led young Publius to prefer Clodius to Claudius.

In any case, the trend was short lived. Publius's children each resorted to the au-form. This is undeniably the case for Publius's son, whose official preference is preserved in *ILS* 882 (for Claudia, see Vell. 2.65.2; Suet. *Aug.* 62.1; Dio 46.56.3, 48.5.3). Mark Antony called the young man Claudius, whereas Cicero, in a highly formal letter to Antony, took pains to designate Publius's son as Clodius in order to underscore his (feigned) willingness to accommodate the consul and to prove that he did not extend to the son his hatred for the father (Cic. *Att.* 14.13B.4).

Bibliography: The best treatment of this issue is Hillard, "The Claudii Pulchri," 425ff. Other discussions, in addition to the works cited above, include: Drumann and Groebe, *Geschichte Roms*, 2:172f.; *OLD* s.v. Clodius.

2. The Identity of Clodius's Mother

Having disposed of the previous suggestion that the wife of the consul of 79 was a Caecilia, Wiseman ("Celer and Nepos," 182) proposed a daughter of Q. Servilius Caepio (cos. 106), a hypothesis accepted by Shackleton Bailey ("Brothers or Cousins?" 149) and Hallett (*Fathers and Daughters in Roman Society*, table III), but now doubted by Wiseman himself (*Catullus and His World*, 19), though on rather dubious grounds that do not settle the matter. Wiseman's original identification rests on two points: (1) Nepos's mother was notoriously promiscuous (Plut. *Cic.* 26.2), as were Servilius's daughters (Strabo 4.188); (2) the Serviliae were the sisters of M. Cato's stepfather (Plut. *Cato Min.* 1), and Cato was related to Mucia, who was *soror* to the Metelli. Thus Wiseman concluded that a Servilia is a likely candidate for the wife of the consul of 79. Wiseman's first point is objectionable not only because it is too coincidental to mean very much, but also because it requires that we share Plutarch's naive construction of Cicero's insult. When confronted with Nepos's ridicule of his own origins, Cicero retaliated with an outrageous slander, effective if only for its shock value. The actual reputation of Nepos's mother was irrelevant to its sting. As to the second point, it hardly requires that we look to a Servilia: the web of aristocratic relationships in the first century is so complex (see Brunt, *Fall of the Roman Republic*, 451ff.) that much more specific data are necessary before an educated guess is truly possible. Clodius's mother, therefore, must remain *ignota*.

3. Other Clodian Legislation

Lex Clodia de iniuriis publicis. This law is known only from Cicero's passing remark at *Dom.* 81, a testimonium the very exiguousness of which has tended to encourage speculation. Nisbet (*M. Tulli Ciceronis De Domo Sua*, 143) proposed that the law might have given Menulla a special exemption from Sulla's law *de iniuriis*. Wiseman (*New Men*, 141) has suggested that the law, whatever its exact nature, was intended to win Clodian support in the Poblilian tribe, which was centered in Anagnia. Rawson (*Roman Culture and Society*, 236), who mentions Wiseman's idea, remained unconvinced, or at least took seriously Cicero's report that Menulla, the special beneficiary of Clodius's law, was unpopular with the *municipes Anagnini*. The fact is that nothing of the actual nature or purpose of this law can be retrieved.

   Lex Clodia de scribis quaestoriis. The law is mentioned only by Suetonius (*Dom.* 9.3): "scribas quaestorios negotiantes ex consuetudine, sed contra Clodiam legem, venia in praetertitum donavit." The general nature, though of course not the precise details, of this law is easily inferred. Gruen (*Last Generation*, 255) has aptly compared Clodius's law to the efforts made by Cato (Plut. *Cat. Min.* 17.3) to curb the abuses of quaestorian scribes. Clodius's law, though ineffectual in the event (or so it would seem on the basis on Suetonius's remark), is worth noticing if only because it helps to break the impression that all Clodian legislation was somehow *popularis* in principle or chiefly self-serving in purpose. None in the senate (or among those who had to conduct business with quaestorian scribes) will have failed to appreciate the value of this law. And, in view of the influence of the scribal order (Badian, "The *scribae* of the Roman Republic"), the proposal of such a law required a certain degree of political nerve.

Abbreviations

References to certain ancient sources perhaps require comment. As is common practice, references to Asconius are to the page numbers of the edition of A. C. Clark, *Q. Asconii Pediani orationum Ciceronis quinque enarratio* (Oxford, 1907). Similarly, references to the Bobbio Scholiast (and to other Ciceronian scholia) are to the page numbers of the edition by T. Stangl, *Ciceronis orationum scholiastae* (Hildesheim, 1964). References to Cicero's fragmentary orations are to the edition and commentary by J. Crawford, *M. Tullius Cicero: The Fragmentary Speeches*, 2nd ed. (Atlanta, 1994). The fragments of Sallust's *Historiae* are cited by reference to the edition of B. Maurenbrecher, *C. Sallusti Crispi Historiae reliquae*, 2 vols. (Stuttgart, 1893), as well as to the recent translation and commentary by P. McGushin, *Sallust: The Histories*, 2 vols. (Oxford, 1992, 1994). Finally, for the sake of convenience, Cassius Dio and Plutarch are cited with reference to their Loeb editions.

CIL	*Corpus Inscriptionum Latinarum*. Berlin, 1831–.
F. Gr. H.	F. Jacoby. *Fragmente der griechischen Historiker*. Berlin, 1923–58.
IG	*Inscriptiones Graecae*. Berlin, 1873–.
ILS	H. Dessau. *Inscriptiones Latinae Selectae*. 3 vols. Berlin, 1892–1916.
LSJ	H. G. Liddell, R. Scott, and H. S. Jones. *A Greek-English Lexicon*. 9th ed. Oxford, 1940. *Supplement*. Oxford, 1968.
MRR	T. R. S. Broughton. *The Magistrates of the Roman Republic*. Vols. 1–2. New York, 1951–52. Supplement. New York, 1960. Vol. 3. Atlanta, 1986.
OLD	P. G. W. Glare. *Oxford Latin Dictionary*. Oxford, 1982.
PIR	E. Groag and A. Stein. *Prosopographia Imperii Romani*. 2nd ed. Berlin, 1965–.
RE	G. Wissowa, W. Kroll, K. Mittelhaus, and K. Ziegler. *Paulys Realencyclopädie der classischen Altertumswissenschaft*. Stuttgart, 1893–1980.
Rhet. Lat. Min.	K. Halm. *Rhetores Latini Minores*. Frankfurt am Main, 1863.
TLL	*Thesaurus Linguae Latinae*. Leipzig and Munich, 1900–.

Chapter 1

1. *B.Iug.* 41; cf. *Cat.* 37f.; *Hist.* 1.12 (M) = 1.12 (McGushin).

2. Ungern-Sternberg, "The End of the Conflict of the Orders," 376. Discussions of this fundamental conundrum posed by the Roman constitution are legion; see the authorities cited below.

3. The bibliography is daunting. Fundamental are Taylor, *Party Politics*, esp. 11–24; Wirszubski, *Libertas as a Political Idea*; Strasburger, *RE* 18.1:773–98; Hellegouarc'h, *Le vocabulaire latin*, 518–65; Meier, *RE Suppl.* 10:549ff.; Meier, *Res Publica Amissa*, 144ff.; Martin, *Die Popularen*; Seager, "Cicero and the Word *Popularis*," 328ff.; Seager, "'Populares' in Livy," 377ff. Recent discussions include Perrelli, *Il movimento popolare*; Vanderbroeck, *Popular Leadership*; Burckhardt, *Politische Strategien der Optimaten*; Brunt, *Fall of the Roman Republic*, esp. 32–68; Mackie, "*Popularis* Ideology," 49ff.

4. Seager, "Cicero and the Word *Popularis*," 328 n. 1 (this is missed by Vanderbroeck, *Popular Leadership*, 26).

5. Vanderbroeck, *Popular Leadership*, 178–85; the same may be said of Sallust and Appian, though their divergences (from Cicero) in expression must be respected. The "true" or "good" *popularis* in Cicero's writings: Seager, "Cicero and the Word *Popularis*," 333–38; Achard, *Pratique rhétorique et idéologie politique*, 193ff.

6. Martin, *Die Popularen*, 7f., discusses the emergence of *popularis* as a political term. But cf. Seager, "'Populares' in Livy," 380f.

7. Cf. *Sest.* 99 and *Brut.* 273 (*furor*). Other Ciceronian explanations for a *popularis* career can be found, though they seem secondary: *metus poenae*; *implicatio rei familiaris* (*Sest.* 99). For political obstruction as an explanation, see below. Cicero's attitude is hardly unique: Plutarch must explain that the democratic tendencies of Pericles and the Gracchi existed *despite* their nobility of character and their education; see Pelling, "Childhood and Personality," 233.

8. On *fides* here, however, cf. Wiseman, Review of Brunt, 107.

9. Seager, "Cicero and the Word *Popularis*," 329; Brunt, *Fall of the Roman Republic*, 52ff.

10. Meier, *RE Suppl.* 10:599ff.; Martin, *Die Popularen*, 210ff. Nonetheless, it should not be forgotten that it is, for the most part, the description of a politician or his legislation as *popularis* (or a related term; cf. Hellegouarc'h, *Le vocabulaire latin*, 525ff.), mostly by Cicero but also by other ancient sources, that determines the identification of *populares*. Extrapolation is rare.

11. The exception was Gellius Poplicola, Clodius's intimate (*Sest.* 110). For a list of nontribunician *populares*, see Meier, *RE Suppl.* 10:579ff.

12. Meier, *RE Suppl.* 10:555; Meier, *Res Public Amissa*, 116ff.

13. Examples are cataloged by Meier, *RE Suppl.* 10:599ff. In the seventies (especially), issues important to specific groups were represented as *popularis*: see Martin, *Die Popularen*, 7ff.

14. Gruen, Review of Burckhardt, 179ff.

15. Meier, *Res Publica Amissa*, 95f.; Evans, "Plebs rustica," 134ff.; Rathbone, "The Slave Mode of Production," 160ff.; de Neeve, *Peasants in Peril*; Wickham, "Marx, Sherlock Holmes, and Late Roman Commerce," 183ff.; Brunt, *Fall of the Roman Republic*, 254ff.

16. Brunt, "The Roman Mob," 3ff.; Scobie, "Slums, Sanitation, and Mortality," 399ff.; Duncan-Jones, *Structure and Scale*, 77ff.

17. Frier, *The Rise of the Roman Jurists*, esp. 256ff.; more generally, see Brunt, *Fall of the Roman Republic*, 93ff.

18. De Blois, *The Roman Army and Politics*. But see the cogent criticism of Lazenby, Review of De Blois, 150f., and the evidence, tending against De Blois's conclusions, assembled in Brunt, *Fall of the Roman Republic*, 253ff.

19. A recent, comprehensive discussion is provided by Brunt, *Fall of the Roman Republic*, 1–92.

20. Long recognized and often repeated: cf. Strasburger, *RE* 18.1:797; Meier, *RE Suppl.* 10:557; Martin, *Die Popularen*, 223.

21. Strasburger, *RE* 18.1:797; Meier, *RE Suppl.* 10:563, 566f.; Meier, *Res Publica Amissa*, 95ff.

22. Gruen, *Last Generation*, 211ff.; Thommen, *Das Volkstribunat*, 126ff.

23. Meier, *RE Suppl.* 10:580ff.

24. Meier, *RE Suppl.* 10:567, a point properly stressed by Benner, *Die Politik des P. Clodius*, 34f., 104f.

25. Bleicken, *Das Volkstribunat*; Thommen, *Das Volkstribunat*. The role of the tribune was nonetheless important for defining the *popularis* stance, a point to be discussed subsequently, and it must be appreciated how poorly informed we are regarding the tribunate during the early and middle republic; see Badian, "*Tribuni Plebis* and *Res Publica*," 187ff.

26. On wayward *populares* returning to the fold, see Cic. *Prov. Cons.* 38. The temporary nature of political stances is further discussed below.

27. Meier, *RE Suppl.* 10:555; Martin, *Die Popularen*, 2.

28. Meier, *Res Publica Amissa*, XXXII–XLIII, 163–90.

29. Not parties: Brunt, *Fall of the Roman Republic*, 35ff. (the observation can be traced back to the nineteenth century; see Meier, *RE Suppl.* 10:563). No necessary affinity: Meier, *RE Suppl.* 10:558f., contra Martin, *Die Popularen*, 70.

30. Cato's grain law: Rickman, *The Corn Supply of Ancient Rome*, 169; Thommen, *Das Volkstribunat*, 58ff.

31. Burckhardt, *Politische Strategien*, 241ff., discusses *die optimatische Getreideversorgungspolitik*; pp. 253–54 deal specifically with Cato's law. The circumstances of Cato's special command: Tatum, "Cicero's Opposition," 193 (with further references) and see chapter 6, sections 1 and 2.

32. Cic. *Mil.* 16: "senatus propugnator atque illis quidem temporibus paene patronus."

33. Even when Drusus is criticized for his demagoguery—in Appian (*B. Civ.* 1.21–22), Tacitus (*Ann.* 3.27), and Plutarch (*C. Gracch.* 9.1)—it is made explicit that he acted in the service of the senate. Sources for Drusus's tribunate: *MRR* 2:21f. Of course, Ti. Gracchus had enjoyed similarly powerful support in the senate in the persons of Ap. Claudius Pulcher (cos. 143), P. Licinius Crassus (cos. 131), and P. Mucius Scaevola (cos. 133).

34. See Burckhardt, *Politische Strategien*, 256ff.

35. In the writings both of Cicero and of Sallust, it is ordinarily persons, not political methodologies, that are attacked. Cf. Weische, *Studien zur politischen Sprache*, 55ff.; Vanderbroeck, *Popular Leadership*, 190ff.

36. Claims: Cic. *Leg. Agr.* 2.10; *Rab. Perd.* 11ff.; *Cat.* 4.9. Usurpations: Cic. *Leg. Agr.* 2.6. Cf. Seager, "Cicero and the Word *Popularis*," 333ff.

37. Yavetz, *Plebs and Princeps*, 49ff., discusses this point, adducing examples of politicians who were unsuccessful at securing *popularitas*.

38. Categorically denied by Martin, *Die Popularen*, 216ff., and Vanderbroeck, *Popular Leadership*, 32.

39. Earl, *The Moral and Political Tradition of Rome*, 11ff.; Meier, *Res Publica Amissa*, 162ff.; Brunt, *Fall of the Roman Republic*, 351ff.

40. E.g., Cic. *Att.* 4.5.1, 4.6.2; *Fam.* 1.9.

41. Cic. *Att.* 8.1, 8.3, 8.9, 8.14, 8.15, 9.1, 9.4; *Fam.* 7.3.2. It is worth noting that Cicero did not change his opinion even in the aftermath of Caesar's victory: *Marc.* 16; *Off.* 2.45. One might compare Metellus Numidicus, who preferred exile to an appeal to the ὄχλος (App. *B. Civ.* 1.31).

42. Cic. *Fam.* 8.14.3.

43. Cf. the explicit appeal to the demands of *dignitas* on the part of Catiline (Sall. *Cat.* 35.3) and Caesar (*B. Civ.* 1.7.7) or of expediency on the part of Cicero (*Att.* 2.1.8, explaining his defense of equestrian interests in the senate).

44. Discussed in detail by Brunt, *Fall of the Roman Republic*, 54ff.

45. Ungern-Sternberg, "The End of the Conflict of the Orders," 355ff. A recent treatment of the Conflict, espousing a different point of view, is Cornell, *The Beginnings of Rome*, 242ff.

46. On *invidia senatus*, which existed alongside the public's general admiration of its leadership, see Meier, *RE* 10:612; Meier, *Res Publica Amissa*, 109; Seager, "Cicero and the Word *Popularis*," 329 (each with references to sources). *Populares* who became overweening could also feel the brunt of public disapproval, as Caesar and Pompey learned in the latter part of 59; cf., e.g., Cic. *Att.* 2.20.4: "populare nunc nihil tam est quam odium popularium."

47. Veyne, *Le pain et le cirque.*

48. This problem receives thorough treatment in various essays by Raaflaub, Cornell, Ungern-Sternberg, and Develin in Raaflaub, *Social Struggles in Archaic Rome*, where an excellent bibliography may also be found, to which one may add Cornell, *The Beginnings of Rome.*

49. Bleicken, *Lex Publica*, 288ff.

50. App. *B. Civ.* 1.114–18; Vell. 26.4–7; Plut. *C. Gracch.* 15–16. On the justificatory appeal to *mos maiorum* on the part of *populares*, see Brunt, *Fall of the Roman Republic*, 330f., 521.

51. Millar, "The Political Character"; Millar, "Politics, Persuasion and the People"; Millar, "Political Power in Mid-Republican Rome."

52. Cf. the criticisms of Burckhardt, "The Political Elite." The people's lack of initiative in government: Bleicken, *Lex Publica*, 244–58. On this controversy, see Jehne, *Demokratie in Rom?*

53. *Res publica* means *res populi*: Cic. *Rep.* 1.39. The role of the *populus* in government: Polybius 6.13ff.; see Brunt, *Fall of the Roman Republic*, 14ff.; Cic. *Rep.* 2.57, 3.23.

54. Brunt, *Fall of the Roman Republic*, 32ff., 346ff.

55. Gell. 13.12; Plut. *Quaest. Rom.* 81.

56. Millar, "Political Power in Mid-Republican Rome," 145.

57. The early supporters in the senate of Ti. Gracchus's reforms, who fell away when the tribune's conduct turned to extremes, are likely instantiations.

58. Cicero's exasperation: *Att.* 2.1.8; cf. *Mur.* 3ff. On Cato's reputation generally, see Fehrle, *Cato Uticensis*, 22ff., 279ff.

59. App. *B. Civ.* 2.1; Sall. *Cat.* 49.3.

60. Caesar deprived the people of voting rights (see Taylor, *The Roman Voting Assemblies*, 113, for discussion), dissolved *collegia* (Suet. *Iul.* 42), and reduced the number of dole recipients (Suet. *Iul.* 42). This is not to say that Caesar did not introduce some measures that benefited the *plebs* (Yavetz, *Plebs and Princeps*, 45ff.),

but the elevation or even the maintenance of *libertas populi* was clearly not a priority of Caesar's dictatorship.

61. Caes. *B. Civ.* 1.4. On Roman invective, see Nisbet, *M. Tulli Ciceronis in L. Calpurnium Pisonem Oratio*, 192ff.; Koster, *Die Invektive*; Corbeill, *Controlling Laughter*.

62. E.g., *Mil.* 99; *Brut.* 273. Cf. Vanderbroeck, *Popular Leadership*, 178ff.

63. Badian, "Tiberius Gracchus," 692; Morgan and Walsh, "Tiberius Gracchus," 200ff.

64. Augurs: Asc. 21.4 (C). Pontiffs: Suet. *Nero* 2.1. The date of Domitius's tribunate is itself controversial. For a rehearsal of the difficulties and arguments, see Marshall, *A Historical Commentary on Asconius*, 277f.; *MRR* 3:82f.

65. Sources in *MRR* 2:559. Such legislation is explicitly adjudged *popularis* by Cicero *De Amicitia* 96.

66. Caes. *B. Civ.* 3.83.1.

67. Syrus, fr. 95 [Loeb]: "beneficia donari aut mali aut stulti putant."

68. Millar, "The Political Character"; Millar, "Politics, Persuasion and the People"; Cic. *Brut.* 290.

69. Cic. *Att.* 4.15.6. Of course, Cicero was keenly interested in the reactions of audiences at spectacles: e.g., Cic. *Sest.* 115–25; *Att.* 1.16.11, 2.19.3.

70. Plut. *Pomp.* 68.

71. Gell. 11.10.

72. That the Roman people venerated aristocracy, whatever social tensions obtained, hardly requires proof; see Meier, *Res Public Amissa*, 112. In the case of *populares* it must be remembered that the social superiority of a benefactor enhanced the perceived value of his *beneficia* and consequently the depth of gratitude they inspired; see Saller, *Personal Patronage*, 38.

73. On the political value of certain acts of solidarity with the commons see Vanderbroeck, *Popular Leadership*, 118f. (with examples); cf. Cic. *Mur.* 76: "odit populus Romanus privatam luxuriam, publicam magnificentiam diligit."

74. The subject overall in *Comm. Pet.* 41–53 is *quae in populari ratione versatur*, a category broken down into *nomenclatio, blanditia, adsiduitas, benignitas, rumor*, and *pompa*. The *Comm. Pet.* is discussed in further detail below.

75. Honorable retirement: Cic. *De Orat.* 1.1–4. Piscinarii: Cic. *Att.* 1.19.6, 1.20.3.

76. It must be borne in mind that, because of its lack of political initiative, the *plebs* needed to support what leaders it could. That is, although not every would-be *popularis* was successful, the *plebs* could not be too recalcitrant; see Meier, *Res Publica Amissa*, 110f. Of course, this tension does not take into consideration the fragmentary nature of the *plebs*, a point to be treated subsequently.

77. Introductions to stratification: Hamilton and Hirszowicz, *Class and Inequality*; Jackson, *Social Stratification*; Tumin, *Social Stratification*. Each provides further bibliography.

78. Consult the intelligent and concise discussion of Harris, "On the Applicability of the Concept of Class."

79. See the examples collected by MacMullen, *Roman Social Relations*, 138ff.

80. Astin, "Regimen Morum."

81. Nicolet, *L'ordre équestre*, 162ff.; Badian, *Publicans and Sinners*, 82ff.; Brunt, *Fall of the Roman Republic*, 144ff.

82. *Tribunii aerarii*: Badian, *Publicans and Sinners*, 84; Brunt, *Fall of the Roman Republic*, 210f., 515f. *Apparitores*: Purcell, "The Apparitores." But see Badian, "The *scribae* of the Roman Republic," on the power of the scribes and the respect (or fear) it could inspire even among senators.

83. Weber, *Wirtschaft und Gesellschaft*, 631ff.; cf. Hamilton and Hirszowicz, *Class and Inequality*, 12ff.

84. App. *B. Civ.* 1.39ff. Cf. Arist. *Pol.* 4.11.1295b1–3. The imperial division into *honestiores* and *humiliores* indicates that this fundamental configuration, so self-evident one should think, was by no means confined to the theoretical realm; see Garnsey, *Social Status and Legal Privilege*.

85. For a critique of analysis predicated on *ordines* (and bibliography) see Harris, "On the Applicability of the Concept of Class."

86. The sources indicate potential tensions between the urban and rural *plebs* (e.g., Cic. *Leg. Agr.* 2.79; App. *B. Civ.* 1.28ff.), and MacMullen, *Roman Social Relations*, 28ff., substantiates the antipathy, but the interpenetration of the two groups cannot be overlooked: *non occupati* amid the *plebs urbana* were available for local agricultural labor; many of the urban poor were themselves dispossessed peasants (Meier, *Res Publica Amissa*, 100); and the veterans often fell between stools (Meier, *Res Publica Amissa*, 104).

87. MacMullen, *Roman Social Relations*, 138ff., collects samples.

88. Treggiari, "Urban Labour in Rome," with further references. The most thorough study is Huttunen, *The Social Strata in the Imperial City of Rome*, who examines the epitaphs in *CIL* VI.

89. Treggiari, "Urban Labour in Rome," 52ff. Cf. Treggiari, *Roman Freedmen*, 98ff.

90. Sall. *Cat.* 37.1–8, but cf. Balsdon, "Panem et circenses."

91. See, e.g., Meier, *Res Publica Amissa*, 114f.; Sternberg, "Zur sozialen Struktur der plebs urbana"; Benner, *Die Politik des P. Clodius*, 74ff.; Vanderbroeck, *Popular Leadership*, 81ff. These samples represent varying opinions.

92. Treggiari, *Roman Freedmen*, 99.

93. Ibid., 95ff. (though in certain trades freedmen apparently "excluded" freeborn, as Treggiari argues); a more nuanced (and qualified) picture appears in Treggiari's later contribution, "Urban Labour in Rome." And it must be recognized that *libertini*, whose offspring very likely continued as craftsmen if not necessarily in the same trade, did not beget *libertini* but *ingenui*. See Kühnert, *Die Plebs Urbana*.

94. Treggiari, *Roman Freedmen*, 99f.

95. Garnsey, "Independent Freedmen."

96. Craftsmen contemptible: e.g., Cic. *Flacc.* 18. On the distinctions to be drawn among the various "sordid" occupations, see Treggiari, "Urban Labour in Rome." See the useful collection of material by De Robertis, *Lavoro e lavoratori*.

97. Sall. *Cat.* 37.3; Cic. *Off.* 2.24.85.

98. MacMullen, *Roman Social Relations*, 120.

99. *Comm. Pet.* 3, 6, 18–19, 24, 29, 30. These groups are discussed in greater detail below. The attribution of the *Comm. Pet.* to Quintus Cicero, though likely enough, is irrelevant to the uses to which that text will be put in this chapter. That the document reflects late republican practice, on the other hand, is taken for granted. Cf. David et al., "Le 'Commentariolum Petitionis,'" and Nardo, *Il Commentariolum Petitionis*.

100. See *Comm. Pet.* 24, 30.

101. *Comm. Pet.* 3. There is the problem that a Roman may have belonged to several

groups that might ultimately find themselves in competition, but we are here concerned with groups and the group will in the end be defined by those who, when faced with a choice, elect to identify with that particular association rather than another. Self-identity and organization were no doubt facilitated by the frequent coincidence of *collegium*, occupation, and neighborhood; cf. MacMullen, *Roman Social Relations*, 129ff.

102. Extensive and authoritative treatment can be found in Taylor, *The Voting Districts*; Staveley, *Greek and Roman Voting*, 121ff.; Nicolet, *World of the Citizen*, 207ff.

103. Inequities: Taylor, *The Voting Districts*, 116ff. Freedmen: ibid., 132ff. Legislative assemblies, as Vanderbroeck, *Popular Leadership*, 70, points out, differed in character from elective ones: in the former the urban *plebs* could play a much more prominent role.

104. Cameron, *Circus Factions*, 157ff.; Nicolet, *World of the Citizen*, 361ff.; Frézouls, "La construction du *theatrum lapidum*"; Vanderbroeck, *Popular Leadership*, 77ff. (arguing that audiences at spectacles were "optimate" in sympathy, largely due to the aristocracy's partial distribution of tickets); cf. Tatum, "Another Look" (refuting Vanderbroeck).

105. E.g., Cic. *Att.* 2.19.3 and Cicero's challenge to Calpurnius Piso: "da te populo, committe ludis. sibilum metuis?" (*Pis.* 65).

106. See Badian, *Foreign Clientela*, 1ff.; Saller, *Personal Patronage*; Brunt, *Fall of the Roman Republic*, 382ff.; and the essays contained in Wallace-Hadrill, *Patronage in Ancient Society*, all with extensive references.

107. Dion. Hal., *Ant. Rom.* 2.9.3. See Drummond, "Early Roman *Clientes*."

108. Brunt, *Fall of the Roman Republic*, 406ff.; Garnsey and Woolf, "Patronage of the Rural Poor."

109. Wallace-Hadrill, "Patronage in Roman Society," 72f.

110. In the opinion of Proculus, *Dig.* 49.15.7.

111. Brunt, *Fall of the Roman Republic*, 420, seems to me to draw the wrong conclusions on this point. The prestige wrought from client collecting is elsewhere recognized by Brunt: see ibid., 393 (on foreign *clientela*).

112. Clients' votes: ibid., 424ff. Clients and violence: ibid., 431ff., though I think Brunt underestimates the uses to which willing clients might be put as bodyguards. The standard work is Nowak, *Der Einsatz privater Garden*.

113. See Brunt, *Fall of the Roman Republic*, 382ff., who of course surveys these views only to dispel them.

114. This view can be traced back to antiquity, e.g., Dion. Hal. *Ant. Rom.* 2.11.3. Cf. Brunt, *Fall of the Roman Republic*, 415ff. This certainly represents the view of Benner, *Die Politik des P. Clodius*, 20ff. (with further references), a chapter entitled "Die Denaturierung des Bindungswesens." Similarly, Vanderbroeck, *Popular Leadership*, 81ff., detects the emergence of a "public clientele" (identified by him as the *tabernarii*) resulting from the loosened vertical social obligations of the late republic.

115. Brunt, *Fall of the Roman Republic*, 398ff.; Saller, "Patronage and Friendship." That this practice on the part of lower sorts was felt by the aristocracy to be objectionable is made quite clear at *Comm. Pet.* 35, where nonetheless Cicero is urged to look the other way.

116. Brunt, *Fall of the Roman Republic*, 399f., who points out that patriotic motives might also play a factor in the selection and desertion of patrons at critical junctures.

117. Discussion and sources in Stockton, *The Gracchi*, 74ff.

118. Testimonia for the importance of *clientela* in Roman politics are collected by Brunt, *Fall of the Roman Republic*, 416 n. 87, 435 n. 139. Vanderbroeck, *Popular Leadership*, 74ff., argues that ties of patronage actually became stronger for the *plebs rustica* during the late republic.

119. Staveley, *Greek and Roman Voting*, 143ff.; Nicolet, *World of the Citizen*, 297ff. For a more technical discussion of *professio*, see Earl, "Appian *B.C.* 1, 14 and 'Professio,'" 325ff.; Linderski, *Roman Questions*, 88.

120. Earl, "Appian *B.C.* 1, 14 and 'Professio,'" discusses the distinction between informal and formal professions of candidacy.

121. David et al., "Le 'Commentariolum Petitionis,'" 275ff.; Lintott, "Electoral Bribery," 9.

122. It remains unclear whether the coordination of tribes and centuries extended through all classes. For arguments and further references, see Staveley, *Greek and Roman Voting*, 125f., 256f.

123. Tribal organization: Taylor, *Party Politics*, 63ff.; Taylor, *The Voting Districts*, 14f. Status of *curatores* and *divisores*: Nicolet, *L'ordre équestre*, 603f.

124. See the valuable collection of essays in Cébeillac-Gervasoni, *Les "Bourgeoisies" municipales italiennes*, for further discussion of *domi nobiles* and prosperous municipal figures.

125. It is worth noting the extent to which the influence even of the wealthy *publicani* was derived from their organization; see Brunt, *Fall of the Roman Republican*, 165, 172. A very few *collegia*, it should be noted, evidently included men of considerable substance, wealthy enough to qualify as equestrians, but even these men were apparently not very well known; see Treggiari, *Roman Freedmen*, 196f.

126. Important (and recent) bibliography on *collegia* includes Mommsen, *De collegiis*; Liebenam, *Zur Geschichte und Organisation des römischen Vereinswesens*; Waltzing, *Étude historique sur les corporations professionnelles* (fundamental); Accame, "La legislazione romana intorno ai collegi"; Lintott, *Violence*, 78ff.; Treggiari, *Roman Freedmen*, 168ff.; MacMullen, *Roman Social Relations*, 72ff.; Schulz-Falkenthal, "Zur politischen Aktivität der römischen Handwerkerkollegien"; Flambard, "Clodius, les collèges, la plèbe et les esclaves"; Flambard, "Collegia Compitalicia"; Ausbüttel, *Untersuchungen zu den Vereinen*; Royden, *The Magistrates of the Roman Professional Collegia*; Linderski, *Roman Questions*, 165ff., 645ff.

127. Schultz-Falkenthal, "Zur politischen Aktivität der römischen Handwerkerkollegien," 88; Flambard, "Collegia Compitalicia," 154f.; Nippel, *Aufruhr und Polizei*, 111f.; Vanderbroeck, *Popular Leadership*, 112ff.

128. Flambard, "Les collèges et les élites locales."

129. Flambard, "Collegia Compitalicia," 151, 155ff. See also Ling, "A Stranger in Town."

130. Flambard, "Les collèges et les élites locales."

131. *Collegia*: Ausbüttel, *Untersuchungen zu den Vereinen*, 36f. *Vici*: Flambard, "Collegia Compitalicia," 147. Owing to the paucity of our data, this distinction may be delusory.

132. Honor was a paramount concern of *collegia*: Liebenam, *Zur Geschichte und Organisation des römischen Vereinswesens*, 260; McMullen, *Roman Social Relations*, 76; Flambard, "Collegia Compitalicia," 165f.; Nippel, *Aufruhr und Polizei*, 111f. The role of funeral provision may be exaggerated by modern scholarship: Ausbüttel, *Untersuchungen zu den Vereinen*, 34, but cf. Lintott, Review of Ausbüttel.

133. Flambard, "Collegia Compitalicia," 154.

134. Ibid., 155ff.

135. *Collegia* required financial contributions and so were not ordinarily for those who were absolutely destitute: Ausbüttel, *Untersuchungen zu den Vereinen*, 43f. *Collegia* reflected timocratic biases: Flambard, "Collegia Compitalicia," 154, 165f. Relative positions of *ingenui, libertini*, and *servi*: Welwei, "Das Sklavenproblem," 66; Flambard, "Collegia Compitalicia," 157f. (citing epigraphical evidence). Women in *collegia*: Ausbüttel, *Untersuchungen zu den Vereinen*, 42.

136. Lintott, *Violence*, 82; Royden, *The Magistrates of the Roman Professional Collegia*, 13f. It need not follow from their quasi-military organization that *collegia* had a military purpose, a point to be borne in mind when considering Clodius's enrollment of *collegia* in 58. It was simply the case that for Romans the military's structure provided the most conspicuous, most glorious, and most efficient model: see Garnsey and Rathbone, "The Background to the Grain Law of Gaius Gracchus," 24.

137. Ausbüttel, *Untersuchungen zu den Vereinen*, 85ff., surveys the political roles of *collegia*.

138. Ibid., 86.

139. The phenomenon is well attested for imperial *collegia*: Clemente, "Il patronato nei collegia."

140. Aristocratic disparagement of *divisores*: *Att.* 1.16.2, 1.18.4 (actually an insult directed at C. Herennius [tr. pl. 60]); *Verr.* 3.161; *Planc.* 48; *De Orat.* 2.257. Of course, by Cicero's day the term was tainted by corruption. A more neutral sense may be detected in *Verr.* 1.22f.

141. On electoral corruption, see Gruen, *Last Generation*, 212ff., 271ff.; Nicolet, *World of the Citizen*, 297ff.; Lintott, "Electoral Bribery"; Yakobson, "*Petitio et Largitio*." Best of all see Linderski, *Roman Questions*, 107ff., 638f. The power that corrupt *divisores* were capable of mustering is evidenced by Asc. 75(C).

142. *Comm. Pet.* 34–38.

143. As does Vanderbroeck, *Popular Leadership*, 82ff.

144. Saller, "Patronage and Friendship," 57f.

145. *Equites* in *deductiones*: e.g., Cic. *Mur.* 70.

146. Noble youths: *Comm. Pet.* 6. Satisfying an obligation: *Comm. Pet.* 37–38.

147. MacMullen, "How Many Romans Voted?" Cf. the approach of Nicolet, *World of the Citizen*, 289ff.

148. By now it should be clear that there were reasons to participate in the election process other than simply selecting magistrates. Furthermore, elections can play a role in reaffirming societal structures and norms; cf. O'Gorman, "Campaign Rituals and Ceremonies."

149. Vanderbroeck, *Popular Leadership*, 126–27, collects numerous examples of *tabernarii* closing their shops.

150. The importance of veterans in politics should not be overestimated, however; see Meier, *Res Public Amissa*, 100ff.

151. Ibid., 114f. The expression is accepted by Benner, *Die Politik des P. Clodius*, 71ff. (for whom it is the urban poor and unemployed), and Vanderbroeck, *Popular Leadership*, 86ff. (for whom, following Meier, it is the *tabernarii*).

152. Nicolet, *World of the Citizen*, 237.

153. Vanderbroeck, *Popular Leadership*, 165ff., discusses some of the impediments to the politicizing of the *plebs*.

154. Rudé, *Ideology and Popular Protest*, 27ff.

155. See Martin, *Die Popularen*, 7ff. This category includes legislation in behalf of special interests, such as legislation promulgated in the interests of the equestrian class, extraordinary military commands, and technical political measures, on which see Vanderbroeck, *Popular Leadership*, 100ff.

Chapter 2

1. The early history of the Claudii was confused already in antiquity and has become increasingly controversial; see Levick, *Tiberius the Politician*, 11ff.; Wiseman, *Clio's Cosmetics*, 57ff. (and literature there cited)—but cf. Cornell, Review of Wiseman; Vasaly, "Personality and Power." The Sabine origins of the Claudii have been questioned by Hollemann, "The First Claudian at Rome," but the discussion by Keaney, "Three Sabine Nomina," leaves little doubt that the tradition is accurate in this respect.

2. Suet. *Tib.* 2. Caecus actually had four sons and five daughters (Cic. *Sen.* 37); the patrician Claudii Centhones also derived from a son of Caecus. Syme quotation: *The Roman Revolution*, 19. No eclipse: Cic. *Cael.* 33–34.

3. Wiseman, *Catullus and His World*, 15ff., discusses the family's prominence. A valuable study of the family's politics during the late republic is Hillard, "The Claudii Pulchri."

4. *Cael.* 33, 68.

5. Sources for Appius (cos. 143): *MRR* 1:471–72, 486; relationship to Ti. Gracchus: Stockton, *The Gracchi*, 29f.; sources for Gaius: *MRR* 2:17, 3:57–58; sources for Appius (cos. 79): *MRR* 2:33, 48, 82, 86, 89, 94, 3:56. The identity of Clodius's tribe is not uncontroversial: see Taylor, *The Voting Districts*, 145ff.

6. Birth date: Hillard, "The Sisters of Clodius Again," 508. See also Badian, *Studies*, 140ff., esp. 150, for the evidence of Clodius's eligibility to submit his *professio* for the praetorian elections for 52. Roman youth orphaned by their fathers: Saller, *Patriarchy, Property and Death*, 12ff., 181ff.

7. E.g., when his infamous electioneering pact with Domitius Ahenobarbus (cos. 54), C. Memmius (pr. 58), and Domitius Calvinus (cos. 53) surfaced in 54 (*Att.* 4.17.2). Appius's notorious arrogance: Cic. *Fam.* 3.7.5, 5.10.2, 8.12.3 (Caelius).

8. Sources for consulship and censorship: *MRR* 2:221, 247–48; cf. Constans, *Un correspondant de Cicéron*.

9. Sources: *MRR* 2:208, 218, 224, 3:58. Gaius's condemnation: Caelius *apud* Cic. *Fam.* 8.8.2–3. Gaius's culture: Cic. *Att.* 4.15.2.

10. Recent studies include Skinner, "Clodia Metelli," and Wiseman, *Catullus and His World*, 15ff. Both provide ample bibliography. Despite the reservations of Wiseman, *Catullan Questions*, 50ff. (often repeated in his subsequent publications), and Hillard, "*In triclinio Coam,*" most scholars continue to accept the traditional identification of Catullus's Lesbia with Clodia Metelli: cf. Deroux, "L'identité de Lesbie."

11. Marriage in 79: Wiseman, *Catullus and His World*, 24. *Univira*: Skinner, "Clodia Metelli," 285, an assertion not susceptible of proof, but likely enough; contra: Wiseman, *Catullan Questions*, 57ff. The moral superiority of the *univira*: Treggiari, *Roman Marriage*, 229ff.

12. Marriage to Lucullus: Varro, *R.R.* 3.16.2; Plut. *Luc.* 21.1; Dio 36.14.4, 38.1. Marriage to Marcius Rex: Plut. *Cic.* 29.4; Dio 36.17.2. The relative ages of the sisters are

discussed by Hillard, "The Sisters of Clodius Again," 505ff.; the proper significance of the cognomen *Tertia* remains elusive.

13. Syme, *The Augustan Aristocracy*, table I (p. 509), table VII (p. 519). *Fratres*: Cic. *Att.* 4.3.4; *Fam.* 5.3.1; *Dom.* 7, 87; *Har. Resp.* 45; *Cael.* 60; cf. Dio 37.51.2. Earlier reconstructions are discussed in Wiseman, "Celer and Nepos." Shackleton Bailey's reconstruction: "Brothers or Cousins?"

14. Wiseman, *Catullus and His World*, 20.

15. Hillard, Taverne, and Zawawi, "Q. Caecilius Metellus (Claudianus)?"

16. Saller, *Patriarchy, Property and Death*, 74ff.

17. Varro, *R.R.* 3.16.1–2; Syme, *The Augustan Aristocracy*, 17.

18. Tatum, "The Poverty of the Claudii Pulchri."

19. Syme, *The Roman Revolution*, 10ff.; Wiseman, *New Men*; Gruen, *Last Generation*, 47ff.; Dondin-Payne, "*Homo Novus*"; Brunt, "Nobilitas and Novitas"; Shackleton Bailey, "*Nobiles* and *novi* Reconsidered"; Vanderbroeck, "Homo Novus Again."

20. Hopkins, *Death and Renewal*, 31ff.

21. Millar, "The Political Character," 11. Millar's comparison of the results of elections with co-optation is meant to apply to the period relevant to his article.

22. Hellegouarc'h, *Le vocabulaire latin*, 369ff., with ample documentation; Earl, *The Moral and Political Tradition of Rome*, 11ff.; Harris, *War and Imperialism*, 17ff.

23. Hellegouarc'h, *Le vocabulaire latin*, 369, 375ff.

24. For the relationship between *dignitas* and *gloria*, see Hellegouarc'h, *Le vocabulaire latin*, 400; cf. 366ff. (on *laus*).

25. Elections: Hopkins, *Death and Renewal*, 113ff.; *contentio dignitatis*: Cic. *Mur.* 14; *Planc.* 8; *Off.* 1.38; the term is common in municipal politics, cf. Hellegouarc'h, *Le vocabulaire latin*, 398 n. 5.

26. Cic. *Cat.* 4.21; *Phil.* 2.20, 8.30.

27. Devotion to *res publica*: Brunt, *Fall of the Roman Republic*, 40ff., 49f.; *invidia*: Odelstierna, *Invidia*; Pöschl, "Invidia nelle orazione di Cicerone"; Wlosok, "Nihil nisi ruborem"; Veyne, "La folklore à Rome."

28. Competition for office ideally should not spoil a friendship: Brunt, *Fall of the Roman Republic*, 369ff.

29. Cic. *Planc.* 15. Cicero's famous allusion to Domitius Ahenobarbus as a man who "tot annis quot habet designatus consul fuerit" (*Att.* 4.8A.2) is, in its context, too tendentious to be taken *au pied de la lettre.*

30. *ILS* 6: "facta patris petei. Maiorum optenui laudem, ut sibei me esse creatum laetentur"; cf. also *ILS* 4, 7; Plautus, *Trin.* 642ff.; Cic. *Off.* 1.116; *Verr.* 79; Livy 1.22.2. Cf. Rawson, *Roman Culture and Society*, 88; Tatum, "The Epitaph of Publius Scipio," 253f.

31. Caes. *B. Civ.* 1.4.

32. See Caes. *B. Gall.* 7.80, where *laudis cupiditatis* is made parallel with *timor ignominiae.*

33. Often discussed. See Levick, "Morals"; Brunt, *Fall of the Roman Republic*, 424ff.

34. Wiseman, *Catullus and His World*, 20.

35. Cic. *Fam.* 3.7.5.

36. Patrician privileges at elections to higher magistracies: Badian, *Studies*, 140ff.

37. This, of course, is not to say that *nobiles* did not enjoy special advantages that paved their way toward the top, but rather that these advantages probably were more obvious and mattered more to those lacking them than to the *nobilitas* itself. Benner,

Die Politik des P. Clodius, 18, accurately situates Clodius's ambition in terms of his family's heritage.

38. Publication of senatorial proceedings: Suet. *Iul.* 20. Clodius's records: Cic. *Mil.* 89; see Moreau, "La lex Clodia sur le bannissement de Cicéron," 467 n. 4. Yet it must be borne in mind that Clodius left no writings known to us, despite the suggestion of Hejnic, "Clodius auctor." The problems posed by derivative accounts of the late republic are examined by Brunt, *Fall of the Roman Republic*, 213.

39. Marshall, *A Historical Commentary on Asconius*, 39ff., on the sources and reliability of Asconius's commentaries.

40. Plutarch: Pelling, "Plutarch's Method of Work"; Pelling, "Plutarch's Adaptation of His Source Material." The wide diversity of Plutarch's sources for his late republican biographies is stressed by Hillard, "Plutarch's Late Republican Lives." Dio: Reinhold, *From Republic to Principate*, 1ff. Dio's sources: Millar, *A Study of Cassius Dio*, 34ff. On Dio's methods, see Moscovich, "Historical Compression," 137ff., and Reinhold, *From Republic to Principate*, 6ff. (with literature there cited).

41. Sen. *Ep.* 97.10; Gellius 2.7.18–20.

42. See Havas, "Schemata und Wahrheit," 216ff. Pelling, "Plutarch's Adaptation of His Source Material," 132f., shows how Plutarch tends to use Clodius as a literary foil in his portrayal of the central characters of his Roman *Lives*. Image of the demagogue: Vanderbroeck, *Popular Leadership*, 175. The ancient view of characterization is intelligently discussed by Gill, "The Character-Personality Distinction."

43. E.g., Meier, *Res Publica Amissa*, 114f.; Meier, *Caesar*, 267, 325. Such views are rightly dismissed by Benner, *Die Politik des P. Clodius*, 116.

44. Cic. *Dom.* 116; *Har. Resp.* 26. Clodius's penchant for excessive conduct: Sall. *Hist.* 5.12 (M) = 5.10 (McGushin); Vell. 2.45.1; Plut. *Luc.* 34.1; *Pomp.* 48.6; Cic. 28.1; Dio 36.14.4. Wiseman, *Clio's Cosmetics*, 123ff., argues that the proverbial *superbia Claudiana* detectable in our sources "can be accounted for by the behaviour of the patrician Claudii of the 50s B.C." (p. 125), though one should compare the comments of Cornell, Review of Wiseman.

45. Cic. *Dom.* 60ff.

46. Vell. 2.45.1; Plut. *Caes.* 9.1; Tac. *Ann.* 11.7. Cic. *Att.* 4.15.4 relates that Clodius's peroration at the trial of L. Procilius (tr. pl. 56) was *sane disertus*. On the partisan nature of the *Brutus*, see Tatum, "Cicero, the Elder Curio, and the Titinia Case."

47. Cic. *Dom.* 7, 21. Val. Max. 4.2.5 illustrates Clodius's capacity for making grand visual gestures when speaking.

48. See Rawson, *Roman Culture and Society*, 115ff. (see pp. 119ff. for discussion of Clodius himself). Clodius's Greek companions: Cic. *Mil.* 28, 55; Appius also had a Greek retinue: Cic. *Q.F.* 2.11.4.

49. *Barbatuli iuvenes*: Cic. *Att.* 1.14.5, 1.16.11. Calvus: Plut. *Pomp.* 48.7; Calvus *apud* Sen. *Contr.* 7.4.7 and *Scholia ad Luc.* 7.726 (fr. 18 Morel); cf. Wiseman, *Catullus and His World*, 37.

50. Cat. 79; see Tatum, "Catullus 79."

51. Cic. *Cael.* 36.

52. Cic. *Att.* 2.3.2; *Mil.* 48.

53. Fantasies about the rites of the *Bona Dea*: Juv. 6.314ff. (cf. 2.83ff.); see Richlin, *The Garden of Priapus*, 78 n. 6.

54. Cicero and Tullia: [Sall.] *Inv. in Cic.* 2; Dio 46.18. Clodius and incest: Tatum, "Catullus 79," 34f.

55. Val. Max. 4.2.5; Schol. Bob. 89 (St). See the discussion of this episode (and the purposes to which Valerius puts it) in Mueller, "Exempla Tuenda," 222ff.

56. Cic. *Dom.* 105, 127; *Har. Resp.* 9; Schol. Bob. (St) 88; Quint. 8.6.56; see Lenaghan, *A Commentary on Cicero's Oration De Haruspicum Responso*, 77.

57. Caelius: Fortunatianus, *Rhet. Lat. Min.* 124 (H). Aelius Lamia: Cic. *De Orat.* 262.

58. Cicero's puns on Pulcher: examples include *Att.* 1.16.10, 2.1.4, 2.18.3, 2.22.1. Cf. Catullus 79. The Roman sense of humor: Corbeill, *Controlling Laughter*, 14ff. Cicero's fondness for mocking physical deformities: Plut. *Cic.* 26. I am not persuaded that the cognomen *Pulcher* originally suggested effeminacy, as Corbeill, *Controlling Laughter*, 37, 80, proposes.

59. Cic. *Cael.* 36.

60. Pelling, "Childhood and Personality" (material describing an individual's childhood tends to appear in encomia, invective, and biographical novels; see 217f.). At the same time, it must be noticed that Greek writers were quick to consider the importance of εὐγένεια in delineating character: Halliwell, "Traditional Greek Conceptions of Character."

61. Lucullus and the Third Mithridatic War: Liebmann-Frankfort, *La frontière orientale*, 219ff.; Sherwin-White, *Roman Foreign Policy*, 159ff.; Keaveney, *Lucullus*, 75ff.

62. Plut. *Luc.* 21, 23.2; Memnon, *F. Gr. H.* 3B:360.

63. Harris, *War and Imperialism*, 11ff. Even if there was no legal requirement for ten years of military service (and clearly there was none by the time of the late republic), there remained the clear expectation of some military experience. Furthermore, the traditional place of military service in the aristocratic ideology can only have enhanced its attraction: hence even Cicero complied with prevailing expectations (however minimally); see ibid., 12. A different view (even of the middle republic) can be found in Rosenstein, *Imperatores Victi*, 174 (but cf. 108ff.).

64. As suggested by Carcopino, *Jules César*, 70.

65. Clodius as Catiline's prosecutor in 73: *MRR* 2:107f., 114, 142 n. 10; Twyman, "The Metelli," 857; Gruen *Last Generation*, 41; Epstein, "Cicero's Testimony," 232f. But see Shackleton Bailey, *Cicero's Letters to Atticus*, 1:319; Moreau, *Clodiana Religio*, 234ff. Alexander, *Trials in the Late Roman Republic*, 83, registers Clodius's participation as uncertain.

66. Sources and scholarship assembled in Tatum, "Lucullus and Clodius at Nisibis."

67. For a fuller discussion of these points see ibid., 572ff. Other sources for the *Lucullus* are discussed by Hillard, "Plutarch's Late-Republican Lives," 37ff.

68. Eutropius 6.9, properly and fully explicated by Sherwin-White, *Roman Foreign Policy*, 183.

69. Adiabene had been annexed by Tigranes only in the eighties. The (false) tradition that Lucullus planned an invasion of Parthia (Plut. *Luc.* 30.2–4; Eutropius 6.9) is discussed by Sherwin-White, *Roman Foreign Policy*, 180ff.

70. Tatum, "Lucullus and Clodius at Nisibis," 574f. Cf. Bosworth, "History and Artifice," 63ff.

71. The historicity of the mutiny has been doubted (without foundation) by Mulroy, "The Early Career of P. Clodius Pulcher," 161ff. Responses to Mulroy: Tatum, "Lucullus and Clodius at Nisibis," 577f.; Keaveney, *Lucullus*, 239. Speeches in Sallust: Tatum, "Lucullus and Clodius at Nisibis," 575, 578 (and literature there cited). The

anti-Pompeian aspect of Clodius's speech: Clodius denigrates the accomplishments of Pompey's troops much in the same manner as does Lucullus in his interview with Pompey in Galatia; cf. Plut. *Pomp.* 31; Dio 36.46.1.

72. Moreau, *Clodiana Religio*, 180f.; Williams, "The Appointment of Glabrio." A similar position is taken by Benner, *Die Politik des P. Clodius*, 38 n. 1.

73. Removal of Asia: Dio 36.2.2. Quinctius: Sall. *Hist.* 4.71 (M) = 4.68 (McGushin); Plut. *Luc.* 33.4–5.

74. A state of affairs that partially explains Lucullus's strategic decisions; see Sherwin-White, *Roman Foreign Policy*, 178f.

75. Cilicia: Dio 36.2.2. Sources for the proconsulship of Marcius Rex: *MRR* 2:146. Release from service: Plut. *Luc.* 33.5, 34.1; Dio 36.14.3. Fabius's defeat: Sherwin-White, *Roman Foreign Policy*, 184 n. 95.

76. Dio 36.14.4; Sall. *Hist.* 5.12 (M) = 5.10 (McGushin); for discussion, see Mc Gushin, *Sallust: The Histories*, 211f.

77. The mutiny is narrated at *Luc.* 33–34. At *Luc.* 34.1 Clodius is characterized as follows: Πόπλιος Κλώδιος, ἀνὴρ ὑβριστὴς καὶ μεστὸς ὀλιγωρίας ἁπάσης καὶ θρασύτητος. On Plutarch's use of these terms, see Büchler-Isler, *Norm und Individualität*, 54f.

78. The unsavory connotations of φιλοστρατιώτης: cf. Xen. *Anab.* 7.6.4. Clodius as a foil in Plutarchan biographies: Pelling, "Plutarch's Adaptation of His Source Material," 132f. It is no doubt true that the mutiny at Nisibis gave Clodius "experience in the mobilization of large crowds," as observed by Vanderbroeck, *Popular Leadership*, 30, but only in a trivial sense.

79. Anger and revenge in Roman society: Wlosok, "Nihil nisi ruborem," 156ff.; Epstein, *Personal Enmity in Roman Politics*, 30ff.

80. Challenge to defenders of the Sullan constitution: Benner, *Die Politik des P. Clodius*, 38.

81. The potential legal ramifications of Clodius's mutiny are discussed in detail by Moreau, *Clodiana Religio*, 178ff. Roman mutinies often unpunished: Messer, "Mutiny in the Roman Army"; Watson, *The Roman Soldier*, 118.

82. Rex's jibe: Dio 36.15.1, 17.1. Rex's marriage tie to the Claudii Pulchri: Plut. *Cic.* 29.4; Dio 36.17.2.

83. Sources for *lex Gabinia*: *MRR* 2:144f. Cicero on the mutiny: *Har. Resp.* 42. Lucullus was finally superseded (by Pompey) in 66 on the terms of the *lex Manilia* (cf. *MRR* 2:153).

84. Dio 36.17.2 Κλώδιον ἀποστάντα ἀπὸ τοῦ Λουκούλλου δέει τῶν ἐν τῇ Νισίβι γενομένων suggests desertion, though this may well be based on hostile sources, as Hillard, "The Claudii Pulchri," 213, maintains. Clodius as deserter: Reinach, *Mithridate Eupator*, 369; *MRR* 2:148; Moreau, *Clodiana Religio*, 178ff. By summer 67 Marcius Rex had arrived in the East, though he may have been on the scene earlier: whether Marcius was delayed in Rome depends on the correct interpretation of Suet. *Iul.* 8; see Downey, "The Occupation of Syria," 152 (delayed), and *MRR* 2:646 (not delayed).

85. E.g., Magie, *Roman Rule in Asia Minor*, 296ff., 1179 (with further references).

86. Sherwin-White, *Roman Foreign Policy*, 185, criticizes Marcius for not involving himself in the war with Mithridates, but that was not his assignment.

87. The military significance of Cilicia: Syme, *Roman Papers*, 124ff. Cilicia and piracy: Magie *Roman Rule in Asia Minor*, 283f.; Badian, *Studies*, 162; Benabou, "Rome

et la police des mers"; Marasco, "Roma e la pirateria cilicia." With Cilicia as his province, Sulla had been employed in Cappadocia; Lucullus appropriated the Cilician command with a mind to secure the leadership of the war against Mithridates.

88. Honored in Argos: *ILS* 867, 868, with the interpretation of Münzer, *RE* 14:1585; Magie, *Roman Rule in Asia Minor*, 1178f., expresses doubts. Deserved triumph: Sall. *Cat.* 30.2; Sallust blames the delay in Marcius's triumph on the *calumnia paucorum*. We do not know whether Marcius triumphed.

89. Sall. *Cat.* 34.

90. Cic. *Att.* 1.16.10. On the importance of wills as indicators of genuine affection, see Champlin, *Final Judgments*.

91. Omerod, *Piracy in the Ancient World*; Magie, *Roman Rule in Asia Minor*, 281ff., 1159f. (with further references); Sherwin-White, *Roman Foreign Policy*, 186f.

92. Flourishing of piracy: Omerod, *Piracy in the Ancient World*, 199ff. Pirate fleets: ibid., 210; App. *Mith.* 63. Cilicia: Omerod, *Piracy in the Ancient World*, 192.

93. Dio 36.17.2–3. That Clodius's appointment was a prefecture is the very plausible suggestion of Broughton (*MRR* 2:148), though there is no evidence. Sherwin-White, *Roman Foreign Policy*, 211, considers Clodius's sea command and his encounter with the pirates as an episode in his mission to Antioch, not as a distinct assignment, though dealing with piracy clearly held a higher priority in Marcius's brief than did Syrian intrigue.

94. Prestige and responsibility: Suolahti, *The Junior Officers*, 198ff., 204f. Danger: Cic. *Brut.* 168 (M. Gratidius, M. Antonius's prefect in 102, was killed in Cilicia).

95. Cic. *Har. Resp.* 42; App. *B. Civ.* 2.23; Dio 38.30.5.

96. Plut. *Caes.* 2.1: young Caesar, also abducted by pirates, was irritated when his captors demanded only twenty talents in ransom. Rawson, *Roman Culture and Society*, 234, speculates that Ptolemy may have been a client of the Claudii Pulchri, but the situation is probably better understood in terms of the regal generosity that important Romans could expect from kings, on which see Braund, *Rome and the Friendly King*, 79ff.

97. Cic. *Har. Resp.* 42.

98. Vell. 2.32.4; Plut. *Pomp.* 28; Liv. *Per.* 99; Flor. 1.41.14; see Seager, *Pompey*, 37f.

99. This seems to me the best interpretation of Dio 38.15.6: ὁ Κλώδιος, ἅτε καὶ ἐν γένει ποτὲ αὐτῦ̈ γενόμενος καὶ συστρατεύσας ἐπὶ πολὺν χρόνον. The relationship in question refers to Pompey's marriage to Mucia, Clodius's half sister; this marriage was dissolved in 62. Lacour-Gayet, *De P. Clodio Pulchro*, 12, and "P. Clodius Pulcher," 5, infers from this passage that Clodius served with Pompey after his intrigues in Antioch. This is not impossible. But there can be no question of Clodius serving under Pompey *after* Marcius had been replaced by him. Since Clodius and Marcius were still friends in 61 (or so Clodius at least believed)—at the time of the latter's death—it cannot be the case that Clodius forsook his brother-in-law for the man who superseded him *ante tempus*. Wiseman (*apud* Hillard, "P. Clodius Pulcher," 40 n. 37) refers the passage to Pompey's Spanish campaign: when Pompey requested new troops in 74, Clodius joined him, thereby escaping the wrath of Cato (Plut. *Cat. Min.* 19.3). But this passage has no bearing on the seventies, as we have seen. The most likely time for Clodius and Pompey to have campaigned together is during the Pirate War following Clodius's release. Dio's ἐπὶ πολὺν χρόνον is either imprecise or false; he is, it should be noted, reporting Cicero's thoughts, and so some fuzziness should be allowed for. The joint service of Pompey and Clodius, however, cannot be ignored.

That Clodius served with Pompey while still Marcius's officer is no problem. The *lex Gabinia* required governors to cooperate with Pompey (Vell. 2.31.2; Plut. *Pomp.* 25.3–6, 26.2–3; App. *Mith.* 94; Dio 36.23.4), although Piso in Gallia Narbonensis and Metellus on Crete resisted. Marcius's assistance was presumed (none of Pompey's legates was sent to Cilicia, though Metellus Nepos cruised the coast of Asia Minor; see Omerod, *Piracy in the Ancient World*, 238), especially since Cilicia was the anticipated site of the final conflict. Marcius had no legitimate reason to object to Clodius's service, and it is not likely that he foresaw his own imminent succession at this time.

100. Downey, *A History of Antioch*, 140. A concise narrative of the demise of Seleucid Syria can be found in Green, *Alexander to Actium*, 549ff. and esp. 658f.

101. Just. 40.1–4 portrays Tigranes as the popular choice; App. *Syr.* 48 and Strab. 11.14.15 give an account of conquest. See Bellinger, "The End of the Seleucids," 80f. The intrigues of Ap. Claudius Pulcher while acting in Antioch as Lucullus's ambassador to Tigranes indicate that the Armenian peace had been imposed on the factious Syrians; Plut. *Luc.* 21.1–2. Earthquake: Just. 40.21.

102. Plut. *Luc.* 21–22; App. *Mith.* 82; Memnon *F. Gr. H.* 38; see Sherwin-White, *Roman Foreign Policy*, 174.

103. App. *Syr.* 49; Just. 40.2.2; Downey, *A History of Antioch*, 139.

104. Cic. *Verr.* 4.27–30.

105. App. *Syr.* 49.

106. Diod. 40.1a–1b; Euseb. *Chron.* 261 (Schoene); Jerome *Chron.* p. 150 (Helm); Bellinger, "The End of the Seleucids," 83.

107. On Aziz and Sampsigeramus, see Sullivan, *Near Eastern Royalty and Rome*, 63f.

108. Sherwin-White, *Roman Foreign Policy*, 211, correctly maintains that Marcius acted independently.

109. Though it would be necessary for the *appellatio* to be approved by the senate; Braund, *Rome and the Friendly King*, 24.

110. Eckstein, *Senate and General.*

111. Badian, *Foreign Clientela*, 162f.; Braund, *Rome and the Friendly King*, 26, 58ff.

112. The Italian business community in Antioch: Rostovtzeff, *The Social and Economic History of the Hellenistic World*, 981.

113. Badian, *Foreign Clientela*, 158, 163, 272.

114. Keil and Wilhelm, *Monumenta Asiae Minoris Antiqua*, 64ff., no. 62. On the use of the epithet, see Braund, *Rome and the Friendly King*, 107.

115. On the political role of euergetism in the Hellenistic world, see Veyne, *Le pain et le cirque*, 264ff.; Braund, *Rome and the Friendly King*, 75ff. The sole source for Marcius's trip to Antioch is the *Chronicle* of John Malalas (p. 225.4–11 [ed. Bonn]), a garbled and variously interpreted passage. For discussion, see Downey, "Q. Marcius Rex," though Downey assumes throughout that Marcius acts essentially as the agent of senatorial policy.

116. Dio 36.17.3. This vague account, whose point is to highlight Clodius's failure, depicts him as acting alone and on his own authority. More likely he was in Marcius's service. Coracesium was captured in April 67, a convenient time for Clodius to return to his place on Marcius's staff (as he would no longer be needed by Pompey).

117. No chronological clues enable us to determine with absolute certainty whether Clodius went to Antioch before or after Marcius's visit. But, if it is correct to conclude that Clodius served with Pompey in the war against the pirates, then it is probable

that Clodius's visit followed Marcius's. Since Clodius's mission to Antioch failed, there would not have been enough time for Marcius to salvage Philip's position in Antioch—to the point that a major building project would be feasible and desirable—before his supersession by Pompey in spring 66. On the other hand, the conclusion of the Pirate War and Pompey's vigorous presence in Cilicia might encourage Philip's enemies to seek a second Roman opinion: Pompey's rather than Marcius's. Sampsi-geramus, whose prisoner had senatorial approval already, would have a fair case—especially if he could plead it from the palace in Antioch.

118. Claudian links to Syria: Rawson, *Roman Culture and Society*, 116ff. Ap. Clau-dius: Plut. *Luc.* 19.1, 21–23.2; Memnon *F. Gr. H.* 38:360.

119. The two families continued to cooperate into the next generation: *ILS* 4041.

120. Rosenstein, *Imperatores Victi* (see 172 for the quotation). Cf. Tatum, "Military Defeat and Electoral Success," and Tatum, "Military Defeat and Electoral Success—Two Corrections."

121. Youthful prosecutions: Cic. *Acad.* 2.1; Plut. *Luc.* 1.2; Quint. 12.7.3. The varied motives for prosecutions and the risk of incurring enmity: Gruen, *Last Generation*, 260ff.; Epstein, *Personal Enmity in Roman Politics*, 90ff.; David, *Le patronat judiciaire*, 497ff. Potential rewards (most of which were inaccessible to Clodius, since he was not yet a senator): Taylor, *Party Politics*, 112ff.; Alexander, "*Praemia* in the *Quaestiones.*"

122. *Inimicitiae* were more pervasive and respectable than Brunt, *Fall of the Roman Republic*, 370f., allows, though Brunt is correct to observe that Romans believed that there were limits to be set on the exercise of one's hostility and in all cases the requirements of the *res publica* must supersede any personal grudge, however bitter. The acceptability of noble enmities: Cic. *Scaur.* 32–33. See Syme, *The Roman Revolution*, 12; Epstein, *Personal Enmity in Roman Politics*, 12ff.

123. Cic. *Har. Resp.* 42: "cum propinquis suis decidit ne reus faceret, a Catilina pecuniam accepit ut turpissime praevaricaretur."

124. Lenaghan, *A Commentary on Cicero's Oration De Haruspicum Responso*, 163.

125. Cicero elsewhere in the *Har. Resp.* stresses this unnatural quality of Clodius's career, for instance, at *Har. Resp.* 45 (see Tatum, "The Marriage of Pompey's Son," 128f.).

126. Sources for Catiline's praetorship and governorship are collected in *MRR* 2:138, 147, 158. Catiline's unsuccessful *professio*: Sall. *Cat.* 18.2–3; Asc. 89 (C); Dio 36.43.3–4. Discussion: Marshall, "Catilina," and Marshall, *A Historical Commentary on Asconius*, 302ff. (each with further literature).

127. Political considerations behind Volcacius's behavior are examined by Vretska, *C. Sallustius Crispus*, 294, and Marshall, *A Historical Commentary on Asconius*, 303f., each with additional references.

128. Asc. 89 (C).

129. Cic. *Har. Resp.* 42; *Pis.* 23.

130. This view may be found in (e.g.) Tyrrell, *The Correspondence of M. Tullius Cicero*, 1:152; Drumann-Groebe, *Geschichte Roms*, 175; Lintott, "P. Clodius Pulcher," 158. Moreau, *Clodiana Religio*, 198f., is uncertain, while Alexander, *Trials in the Late Roman Republic*, 106f., reports this view without expressing a judgment of his own.

131. Asc. 87 (C): "Ita quidem iudicio absolutus est Catilina ut Clodius infamis fuerit praevaricatus esse: nam et reiectio iudicum ad arbitrium rei videbatur esse facta." Presumably Clodius believed that *any* jury would convict Catiline; compare Horten-sius's similar miscalculation in the Bona Dea affair (Cic. *Att.* 1.16.2).

132. Asc. 85 (C).

133. *Comm. Pet.* 10.

134. Shackleton Bailey, *Cicero's Letters to Atticus*, 1:296; Phillips, "Cicero, Ad Atticum I 2"; Gruen, "Some Criminal Trials," 59ff. (see also *Last Generation*, 271).

135. Sources for the trial: Cic. *Att.* 1.1.1, 1.2.1; *Cat.* 1.18; *Sull.* 81; *Cael.* 10, 14; *Har. Resp.* 42; *Pis.* 23; *Comm. Pet.* 10; Asc. 9, 85, 89, 92 (C).

136. The ballots of the orders were not tabulated separately at trials before 59 (Dio 38.8.1), so the question of Asconius's reliability, especially in view of the uncertainty hanging over many details from this trial, is particularly acute here; see Marshall, *A Historical Commentary on Asconius*, 305, for the problems associated with Asc. 89 (C) on this point.

137. Sources in *MRR* 2:119, 134.

138. Plut. *Luc.* 19.

139. Hillard, "Plutarch's Late-Republican Lives," 43ff. Coarelli, "Alessandro, i Licinii e Lanuvio," examines the decorative remains of the temple of Juno Sospita at Lanuvium, which Murena apparently refurbished in such a way as to commemorate his achievements in the Mithridatic War: in his interpretation of these remains, Coarelli postulates continued close cooperation between Murena and Lucullus; in view of Hillard's discussion, however, this seems untenable.

140. Plut. *Luc.* 33.2; this criticism, as we have seen, derives from Sallust.

141. Murena was *pr. urbanus* in 65: *MRR* 2:158; his proconsulship in Gaul is, of course, much discussed by Cicero in the *Pro Murena*; see *Mur.* 42, 53, 68f., 89.

142. Cic. *Har. Resp.* 42. Broughton (*MRR* 2:156 n. 6) suggests that Clodius held a military tribunate in 64, but for no good reason.

143. Clodius a forger: Cic. *Sest.* 39; Plut. *Cic.* 29.3. These passages do nothing to strengthen Cicero's asseveration in the *Har. Resp.*, *pace* Moreau, *Clodiana Religio*, 188ff. Avarice and theft were standard topics of invective: Süss, *Ethos*, 247ff.; Nisbet, *M. Tulli Ciceronis in L. Calpurnium Pisonem Oratio*, 195; see Cic. *Off.* 3.73 for a typical table of misconduct that includes the crime of forging wills. The significance of wills: Champlin, *Final Judgments*.

144. Neatly illustrated by the assumptions operative in Catullus 10 and 28.

145. Cic. *Mur.* 42, 69.

146. The consular elections for 62 are discussed (with ample references) in Gelzer, *Cicero*, 80ff., and Stockton, *Cicero*, 105ff. Murena's father: Münzer, *RE* 13:444ff. Lucullus's troops: Cic. *Mur.* 37ff., 53, 69. Electoral corruption in 63: sources collected in *MRR* 2:172f.

147. *Comm. Pet.* 6, 33; Cic. *Fam.* 2.6.3; Sall. *Cat.* 14.

148. Linderski, *Roman Questions*, 107ff.; Lintott, "Electoral Bribery"; Yakobson, "Petitio et Largitio."

149. On the basis of Schol. Bob. 87 (St), who remarks of Clodius "plerisque in locis interversas ab eodem Clodio criminatus est pecunias candidatorum," Moreau, "Cicéron," 227f., infers that Murena and Iunius Silanus had formed a *coitio* and that Clodius acted as *sequester* to both. However, the scholiast's comment actually refers to the consular elections in 61, which makes it rather difficult to extract so specific a conclusion regarding the elections of 63 from the plural *candidatorum* (which itself follows *plerisque* etc. naturally enough and suits the scholiast's general and vague tenor here).

150. Moreau, *Clodiana Religio*, 50; Benner, *Die Politik des P. Clodius*, 68.

151. Aigner, "Gab es im republikanischer Rom Wahlbestechungen für Proletarier?"

152. Plutocratic nature of centuriate assembly: Staveley, *Greek and Roman Voting*, 123ff. The significance of elections as civic ritual: O'Gorman, "Campaign Rituals and Ceremonies." Cultivation of lower classes: Aigner, "Gab es im republikanischer Rom Wahlbestechungen für Proletarier?," 236f.; Yakobson, "*Petitio et Largitio*." The logistics of electoral bribery were rendered less formidable by the low number of active voters; see MacMullen, "How Many Romans Voted?"

153. Sources for this trial: Alexander, *Trials in the Late Roman Republic*, 111f.

154. Silanus was married to Servilia, Cato's stepsister: Plut. *Cat. Min.* 21.2.

155. Pliny *Ep.* 1.20.7. Moreau, "Cicéron." It follows that Moreau sets the publication of the *Pro Murena* after 61, that is, after Cicero and Clodius had become enemies.

156. Plut. *Cic.* 29.1.

157. Cic. *Att.* 1.16.3. Cf. Schol. Bob. 87 (St).

158. Cic. *Har. Resp.* 42.

159. No one believes that Clodius actually murdered *divisores*, but the allegation that Clodius cheated them is commonly accepted: see Moreau, *Clodiana Religio*, 188; Benner, *Die Politik des P. Clodius*, 68.

160. Asc. 50 (C). Asconius may have mistaken the intention of Cicero's phrase, as Marshall, *A Historical Commentary on Asconius*, 202, suggests, but his statement that Cicero often painted Clodius a *socius coniurationis Catilinae* remains credible.

161. Lintott, "P. Clodius Pulcher," 158f., accepts the rumor reported by Asconius.

162. Murena was not merely Catiline's opponent in the consular elections: at the debate concerning the fate of the arrested conspirators in December 63, Murena cast a firm vote for the death penalty (Cic. *Dom.* 134; *Att.* 12.21.1) and Murena's brother and legate, C. Licinius Murena, seized the Catilinarian envoys he found in Gaul (Sall. *Cat.* 42.3).

163. Sall. *Cat.* 30.3, 33–34.1.

164. Cicero's bodyguard of young nobles: Cic. *Att.* 2.19.4, 2.1.7; *Red. Sen.* 32; *Phil.* 2.16; Plut. *Caes.* 8.3–4.

165. Cic. *Mur.* 73.

166. Taylor, "Caesar's Colleagues," 396f., followed by Babcock, "The Early Career of Fulvia," 6f. Moreau, *Clodiana Religio*, 183f. Cic. *Phil.* 2.48 indicates that Clodius and Fulvia were certainly married by 58.

167. Natta in 58: Cic. *Dom.* 139. Sempronia and Fulvia in 52: Asc. 40 (C).

168. Ages for marriage, for both men and women: Treggiari, *Roman Marriage*, 398ff. (and literature cited there).

169. Claudia was married to Octavian in 43, when she was "vixdum nubilem" (Suet. *Aug.* 62.1; cf. Vell. 2.65.2; Plut. *Ant.* 20; Dio 46.56.3, 48.5.3). In 43 Claudia was probably no more than thirteen.

170. See *PIR* 2.240. Claudius's praetorship is attested by *CIL* 6.1282 = *ILS* 882.

171. *Parvulus*: Asc. 30 (C). *Puer*: Cic. *Att.* 14.13A.2, 14.13B.4.

172. According to Gellius (10.28.1), one may be a *puer* until age seventeen, while Isidore (*Etymol.* 11.2.4) sets the limits from seven to fourteen. But these definitions are hardly prescriptive since the donning of the *toga virilis* was a movable feast.

173. Fulvia's wealth: Babcock, "The Early Career of Fulvia," 3f.

174. Bambalio was still alive when Antony was Fulvia's husband: Dio 45.47.4, 46.7.1, 46.28.1.

Chapter 3

1. A convenient narrative is provided by Stockton, *Cicero*, 99ff. See also Fehrle, *Cato Uticensis*, 87ff., and Drummond, *Law, Politics and Power*. Recent discussion (with further literature) of the *senatus consultum ultimum*: Burckhardt, *Politische Strategien der Optimaten*, 86ff.; Nippel, *Public Order in Ancient Rome*, 59ff.

2. For sources on the tribunate of Nepos: *MRR* 2:174. The basic discussion is Meier, "Pompeius' Rückkehr." See also Afzelius, "Die politische Deutung des jüngeren Catos," 143ff.; Sumner, "The Last Journey of L. Sergius Catilina"; Stockton, *Cicero*, 135ff.; Seager, *Pompey*, 68ff.

3. Nepos's independence: Meier, "Pompeius' Rückkehr," 105. Greenhalgh, *Pompey*, 184, argues that the bill to recall Pompey would *not* have pleased the general, but this is unconvincing.

4. Meier, "Pompeius' Rückkehr," 119. Cf. Sall. *Cat.* 57.1; Plut. *Cic.* 16.6, 22.4; App. *B. Civ.* 2.7.23; Dio 37.39.2, 37.40.1.

5. Sall. *Cat.* 27.1, 30.3–5, 42.1; Cic. *Cat.* 4.6; Plut. *Cic.* 10.5, 14.2; App. *B. Civ.* 2.2.7; Dio 37.30.2, 37.33.4; Oros. 6.6.7.

6. Sources for Caesar's activity in 62: *MRR* 2:173. Discussion: Gelzer, *Caesar*, 56ff.

7. Sumner, "The Last Journey of L. Sergius Catilina," provides a detailed discussion of Catiline's military situation.

8. Plut. *Cic.* 23; *Cat. Min.* 27–28; Dio 37.43.1–2. *Senatus consultum ultimum*: Dio 37.43.3, but see also Cic. *Fam.* 5.2.9; Suet. *Iul.* 16.1; Dio 37.44.2. Plut. *Cat. Min.* 29 is incorrect in its claim that Nepos was not suspended from office.

9. Nepos's flight: Plut. *Cat. Min.* 29.1–4; Dio 37.43.4. Caesar's conduct: Suet. *Iul.* 16.1–2; Dio 37.44.2.

10. Lucullus: *MRR* 2:169. Creticus: *MRR* 2:176. On the general anxiety and the marshaling of Pompey's *inimici*, see Gruen, *Last Generation*, 84f.

11. Plut. *Pomp.* 43.1. Most scholars agree Crassus's flight was not truly motivated by fear; after all, he traveled eastward (Cic. *Flacc.* 32). See Marshall, *Crassus*, 93f.; Ward, *Marcus Crassus*, 193ff. In general on the fears of the time, see Vell. 2.40.3 and Plut. *Pomp.* 43.

12. Cic. *Fam.* 5.7.1.

13. Cic. *Att.* 1.12.3; Plut. *Pomp.* 42.7. The resentment of the Metelli: Dio 37.49.3. The divorce hardly seems an implicit criticism of Caesar (as Shackleton Bailey, *Cicero's Letters to Atticus*, 1:299, suggests). Nor was it a clumsy move to attach himself to Cato. Pompey meant to dissociate himself from Nepos. If Celer took his brother's part (as he did), so be it; Nepos was simply too great a liability.

14. Vell. 2.40.3; Plut. *Pomp.* 43; Dio 37.20.6.

15. Plut. *Cat. Min.* 30.2–5, 45.2; *Pomp.* 44.2–4. Cf. Fehrle, *Cato Uticensis*, 105.

16. Asc. 52f. (C); Schol. Bob. 86, 89 (St). The events of the Bona Dea scandal suggest that Clodius was popular with the people even at this stage of his career (owing no doubt to his family's nobility), and one may be certain that his success at the quaestorian elections was a strong one.

17. Brouwer, *Bona Dea*, 358ff., for a description of the December rites; Scullard, *The Festivals and Ceremonies*, 199ff. The festival was celebrated on 3 December in 63 (Plut. *Cic.* 19). Since Clodius was quaestor-elect at the time of the incident (Asc. 52–53 [C]) and inasmuch as quaestors enter office on 5 December, the sacrifice must have taken place no later than the night of the fourth. Even that is unlikely, in view of

Clodius's alibi. The very exclusive nature of the festival is noted by Wiseman, *Cinna the Poet*, 130, and Scullard, *The Festivals and Ceremonies*, 200. Exclusive rites are by no means unique in Roman religion: at the Veneralia (1 April), women of rank worshiped in a manner and at a place different from humbler women (Scullard, *The Festivals and Ceremonies*, 96). The Bona Dea's rites were more exclusive yet, being limited to the *nobilissimae feminae* (Cic. *Mil.* 72) and by the size of a single *domus*.

18. Sources for the Bona Dea scandal (excluding incidental references by Cicero): Cic. *Att.* 1.12, 1.13, 1.14, 1.16, 2.1.5; *Fam.* 1.9.15; *Har. Resp.*; *Prov. Cons.* 24; *Mil.*; *Parad. Stoic.* 32; Asc. 45, 49, 52–53 (C); Schol. Bob. 85–91 (St); Livy *Per.* 103; Sen. *Ep. Mor.* 97; Val. Max. 8.5.5, 9.1.7; Suet. *Iul.* 74; Juv. 6.314–45; Plut. *Caes.* 9–10; *Cic.* 28–29; App. *Sic.* 7; *B. Civ.* 2.14; Dio 37.45–46.

19. Balsdon, "Fabula Clodiana," 71f.

20. Ibid., 65f. See also Tatum, "Cicero and the *Bona Dea* Trial," 202f.

21. Cic. *Att.* 1.12.3. Despite Plut. *Cic.* 29.1, Clodius and Cicero were probably *not* friends before the time of the Bona Dea scandal: Epstein, "Cicero's Testimony."

22. Among the examples of Ciceronian distortion are Cic. *Parod. Stoic.* 4.32 and *Har. Resp.* 8, despite Moreau's willingness (*Clodiana Religio*, 194f.) to accept them as sound evidence.

23. Suet. *Iul.* 74.4; Schol. Bob. 89 (St).

24. Typical are Stockton, *Cicero*, 159; Rundell, "Cicero and Clodius," 303; Gruen, *Last Generation*, 273; Seager, *Pompey*, 74. But cf. Tatum, "Cicero and the *Bona Dea* Trial," 207f.

25. *Att.* 1.12.3: "P. Clodius Appi f. credo te audisse cum veste muliebri deprehensum domi C. Caesaris cum sacrificium pro populo fieret, eumque per manus servulae servatum et eductum; rem esse insigni infamia. quod te moleste ferre certo scio." This letter, written 1 January 61, makes no mention of any action on the senate's part concerning the scandal. Though the meeting on the Kalends, devoted to religious matters, was an appropriate time to raise the Bona Dea issue (earlier than that seems out of the question; see Moreau, *Clodiana Religio*, 61 n. 149), the earliest report of its being discussed in the senate is *Att.* 1.13.3, which was composed 25 January, some time after the event to be sure. Still, there was a delay, which seems to me sufficient to contradict Moreau's assertion (*Clodiana Religio*, 58) that everyone will have expected the senate to pursue the scandal.

26. See Tatum, "Cicero and the *Bona Dea* Trial," 207f., for discussion and doxography.

27. *Pace* Moreau, *Clodiana Religio*, 262, but cf. Cic. *N.D.* 1.123 and Diog. Laert. 10.120 for evidence that even Epicureans respected public conventions where religion was concerned. And, in any case, what we possess is a specimen not of Atticus's actual opinion but rather of Cicero's estimation of his friend's opinion.

28. Moreau, *Clodiana Religio*, 52 (with further discussion).

29. Cic. *Har. Resp.* 8, 37, 57. See further Cripiano, *Fas et Nefas*, 44f.

30. Cic. *Att.* 1.12.3, 1.13.3; *Har. Resp.* 37; Schol. Bob. 89 (St); Sen. *Ep. M.* 97.2; Suet. *Iul.* 6.3; Dio 37.35.4.

31. On this point see especially Price, *Rituals and Power*, 7ff. Any selection of the recent and excellent work on Roman religion must include Liebeschuetz, *Continuity and Change*; Wardman, *Religion and Statecraft*; Linderski, "The Augural Law"; Beard, "Religion," each with ample bibliography.

32. Linderski, *Roman Questions*, 458ff., 667f.; Momigliano, "The Theological

Efforts"; Beard, "Cicero and Divination"; Schofield, "Cicero for and against Divination"; Morgan, "Politics, Religion and the Games"; Tatum, "Ritual and Personal Morality."

33. Manfredini, "*Qui commutant cum feminis vestrem*"; Dallo, *Ubi Venus Mutatur*, 18ff.; cf. Sen. *Contr.* 5.6.1.

34. Veyne, "La folklore à Rome." One should also bear in mind the Romans' moralistic disapproval of *curiositas*.

35. Moreau, *Clodiana Religio*, 51ff., 81ff., reviews the nature of Clodius's sacrilege and the limited legal avenues for punishing him.

36. Moreau, *Clodiana Religio*, 26ff.

37. Suet. *Iul.* 74; App. *B. Civ.* 2.14; Dio 37.46.

38. The mention at Cic. *Att.* 1.16.1 of *libidenem iuventis* need not be an allusion to adultery. The passages that name adultery—or more commonly *stuprum* (which is not the same thing)—are all late and all dependent (it seems) on Cicero's invective after the trial. The passages are collected by Moreau, *Clodiana Religio*, 24 n. 30.

39. Moreau, *Clodiana Religio*, 26. See ibid., 13 n. 8, for the difficulties in determining the name of Pompeia's slave.

40. Plut. *Caes.* 10; *Cic.* 29. In Plutarch's account, Clodius is driven out by the women, while in Cicero's he escapes with the slave's help (*Att.* 1.12.3; *Har. Resp.* 44). Moreau, *Clodiana Religio*, 15 n. 11, suggests that Cicero's version may be the less trustworthy inasmuch as he hoped to emphasize "l'humiliation de Clodius, réduit à devoir son salut à un *beneficium* d'une ou plusieurs esclaves." Pompeia's slave under torture: Schol. Bob. 90–91 (St).

41. Plut. *Cic.* 28.3 suffers from historical error and textual difficulty. Caesar did not prosecute Clodius; see Pelling, "Plutarch's Method of Work," 90; Moreau, *Clodiana Religio*, 42f., 385.

42. *Pace* Moreau, *Clodiana Religio*, 24.

43. Cic. *Att.* 1.13.3, correctly understood by Balsdon, "Fabula Clodiana," 67, wrongly by Moreau, *Clodiana Religio*, 38.

44. Caesar's election: *MRR* 2:171. The precariousness of Caesar's political position in 62: Dio 37.44. Caesar keen to depart Rome: Suet. *Iul.* 18.

45. E.g., Gruen, "P. Clodius," 121f.; Moreau, *Clodiana Religio*, 44ff.

46. Schol. Bob. 85 (St); Dio 37.45.2; Plut. *Cic.* 29.5; *Caes.* 10.5; App. *B. Civ.* 2.14.

47. Rundell, "Cicero and Clodius," 303 n. 10.

48. Moreau, *Clodiana Religio*, 47ff. Moreau erroneously believes Clodius's gang network was in place by 61 and generally overestimates his influence over the *plebs*. Cf. Linderski, *Roman Questions*, 112; Lintott, "P. Clodius Pulcher," 160; Rundell, "Cicero and Clodius," 303.

49. Wiseman, *Catullus and His World*, 20f.

50. Scullard, *The Festivals and Ceremonies*, 116f.; Brouwer, *Bona Dea*, 370ff.

51. Pupius Piso: Cic. *Att.* 1.13.3 ("Piso amicitia P. Clodi ductus"); Plut. *De garrulitate* 18. Pupius Piso had received Pompey's special support in his bid for the consulship (Plut. *Pomp.* 44; *Cat. Min.* 30; Dio 37.44.3), but it does not follow from that that Pompey was also Clodius's *amicus*. On Piso, see Moreau, *Clodiana Religio*, 104ff. (and literature there cited), and *MRR* 3:177. The elder Curio: Moreau, *Clodiana Religio*, 158ff. (with bibliography); his defense of Clodius: Cic. *Att.* 1.14.5; Schol. Bob. 85 (St). His relationship with Clodius is correctly inferred by Meier, *Res Publica Amissa*, 20.

52. Cic. *Fam.* 5.2. See Hillard, "P. Clodius Pulcher."

53. Their attachment to Clodius is revealed in their energetic support during the trial: Cic. *Att.* 1.12, 1.16. Meier, *Res Publica Amissa*, 20, suggests a traditional obligation to Clodius on the part of Curio and his family.

54. Cic. *Att.* 1.13.3. *Operae* refers to hired supporters and dependents: Martin, *Die Popularen*, 36ff.; Treggiari, *Roman Freedmen*, 75ff. Clodius's support in 61: Lintott, "P. Clodius Pulcher," 160; Rundell, "Cicero and Clodius," 303.

55. On this point and on the subject of Clodius's youthful supporters during the Bona Dea trial, see (with caution) Dettenhofer, *Perdita Iuventus*, 34ff.

56. Curio and Antony: Cic. *Phil.* 2.44–46. Antony Clodius's intimate: *Phil.* 2.48. Antony's threat against Clodius: *Mil.* 40; *Phil.* 2.21, 49.

57. Discussion in Wiseman, *Cinna the Poet*, 119ff. See also Benner, *Die Politik des P. Clodius*, 160f.

58. Wiseman, *Cinna the Poet*, 151ff., but see Benner, *Die Politik des P. Clodius*, 159f., for a brief examination of other opinions concerning the proper identification of Clodius's friend.

59. Herennius: Cic. *Att.* 1.18.4, 1.19.5; see Gruen, *Last Generation*, 185, on his probable senatorial origins. Fonteius: Cic. *Dom.* 35ff.; see Rawson, *Roman Culture and Society*, 235 n. 60.

60. The Porcius of Cat. 47 is sometimes identified as the tribune of 56, but without good reason; see Fordyce, *Catullus: A Commentary*, 211.

61. Sen. *Contr.* 7.4.7; cf. Plut. *Pomp.* 48.7.

62. Cic. *Cael.* 10–17; see Frank, "Cicero and the Poetae Novi."

63. So Rice Holmes, *The Roman Republic*, 1:297, followed by many scholars since.

64. Taylor and Broughton, "The Order of the Two Consuls' Names"; Linderski, *Roman Questions*, 71ff. Of course, the right to make a *relatio* in the senate was not strictly limited to the consul holding the *fasces*: Drummond, "Some Observations."

65. Cic *Att.* 1.13.3. This seems to me to contradict Moreau's assertion that everyone expected the senate to take up the Bona Dea scandal; cf. Moreau, *Clodiana Religio*, 58.

66. The nature of Clodius's infraction was unprecedented: Cic. *Har. Resp.* 12, 37.

67. Censors were elected in 61: Dio 37.46.4; Cic. *Att.* 1.18.8, 2.1.11. Their identities are unknown. That the senior Curio was one of these censors is the theory of Borghesi, *Oeuvres*, 40ff., followed by Willems, *Le sénat*, 1:430, MRR 2:179, and Suolahti, *The Roman Censors*, 650ff. Cram, "The Roman Censors," 101, opposes this view. Moreau, *Clodiana Religio*, 162ff., argues further for the identification, making the additional suggestion that Clodius began to cultivate Curio straightaway in order to fend off a censorial *nota* as well as to secure a prestigious counsel.

68. Cic. *Att.* 1.13.3. For sources on Cornificius: MRR 2:132, 152. He was not a *novus*, see Wiseman, *New Men*, 227.

69. Cic. *Att.* 12.17.

70. Cic. *Verr.* 1.30. Asc. 82 (C). Correspondence with Cornificius *filius*: Cic. *Fam.* 12.7, 12.8.2.

71. Cic. *Att.* 1.13.3. Whether Cornificius conceived of himself as the senate's moral vanguard is a difficult question. He drops out of the picture once the issue begins to matter, yielding place to the consulars, to Cato, and to the Cornelii Lentuli. Moreau, *Clodiana Religio*, 60 n. 145, is correct to reject Gruen's idea that Cornificius acted in Caesar's behalf (cf. Gruen, *Last Generation*, 275 n. 51). For the procedure of referring to the pontiffs, see O'Brien Moore, *RE Suppl.* 6:714. Moreau, *Clodiana Religio*, 64f., discusses their consultation with the Vestals.

72. Moreau, *Clodiana Religio*, 66ff., attempts to determine the membership of the pontifical college in 61, then to recover the political motives of the individual pontiffs. Unfortunately, his methodology for deducing each priest's attitude toward Clodius fails: for Moreau, Clodius is a *popularis*; therefore, if a pontiff can be shown to be even remotely associated with the *optimates* at any point in his career, he will have been opposed to Clodius in 61. Such reasoning, and the prepossessions governing it, must be rejected. Yet there were in 61 at least two hostile pontiffs sitting in the college: Catulus (who surely hoped to embarrass his enemy Caesar) and L. Cornelius Lentulus Niger, the *flamen Martialis* and one of Clodius's prosecutors during the actual trial (the grudge held against Clodius by the Cornelii Lentuli is discussed by Epstein, *Personal Enmity in Roman Politics*, 108).

73. For the procedure see Willems, *Le sénat*, 2:299ff., and O'Brien Moore, *RE Suppl.* 6:714. Senatorial authority: Linderski, *Roman Questions*, 505f.; Linderski, "The Augural Law," 2161f.; Beard, "Priesthood in the Roman Republic." The pronouncements of the sacred colleges were not invariably accepted by the senate in its deliberations: see Morgan, "The Introduction of the Aqua Marcia," 48ff.

74. Moreau, *Clodiana Religio*, 80, following Dio 37.46.1.

75. Livy 31.12.

76. Cic. *Att.* 1.13.3. The details of the *rogatio Pupia Valeria* are provided by Moreau, *Clodiana Religio*, 92ff. Lacey, "Cicero and Clodius," 86, wrongly construes Pupius Piso's opposition as evidence that the *rogatio* was actually drafted by the consuls of 62 or by Valerius Messalla: but Cicero makes plain the contradictory and awkward nature of Pupius Piso's position. Moreau, *Clodiana Religio*, 100ff., proposes two motives for Pupius Piso's conduct: (1) he wished to keep the initiative from passing to Messalla (who would hold the *fasces* in February) and thus maintain some control over the situation, and (2) by proposing the bill at his own *contio* he could guarantee his chance to speak against it. One might add, from a somewhat different perspective, that Pupius Piso was put to the necessity of promulgating the bill by senatorial pressure: too stubborn a resistance could only exacerbate Clodius's problem. Since he felt unable to stop a bill from being promulgated, he might as well try to take advantage of his position.

77. Lycurgus: Cic. *Att.* 1.13.3. Areopagus: Cic. *Att.* 1.14.5. Cf. also *Att.* 1.18.2. Morality in Roman religion (neither to be exaggerated nor to be ignored): Liebeschuetz, *Continuity and Change*; Tatum, "Ritual and Personal Morality."

78. Two examples: Gallini, "Politica religiosa di Clodio," views Clodius's action as a protest against the exclusion of the lower orders from the worship of the Bona Dea in December. Benner, *Die Politik des P. Clodius*, 39f., suggests that Clodius invaded the Bona Dea's rites in the hope of being apprehended, a gesture that would help him to distance himself from the Sullan establishment.

79. Balsdon, "Fabula Clodiana," 68f. Cf. Dio 37.46.2.

80. Epstein, *Personal Enmity in Roman Politics*, 12ff.

81. Lucullus's divorce: Cic. *Mil.* 73; Plut. *Luc.* 38.1; *Cic.* 29; *Caes.* 10. Presumably she had borne Lucullus children already; see Ooteghem, *Lucius Licinius Lucullus*, 168 n. 3. Lucullus's triumph: *MRR* 2:169.

82. Keaveney, *Lucullus*, 138ff.

83. The close friendship of Lucullus, Catulus, and Hortensius: Gruen, *Last Generation*, 51ff. The hostility of the Cornelii Lentuli: Dio 39.6.2.

84. Valerius Messalla was an opportunist whose motives are difficult to discern; see

Moreau, *Clodiana Religio*, 103f., for a summary of his career with further references. C. Piso and Clodius: Epstein, *Personal Enmity in Roman Politics*, 109. Cicero influenced by Lucullus and his circle: Stockton, *Cicero*, 161.

85. Cic. *Att.* 1.13.3. See Fehrle, *Cato Uticensis*, 106ff.

86. Clodius's gestures in the senate: "boni viri precibus Clodi removentur a causa" (Cic. *Att.* 1.13.3).

87. Cic. *Att.* 1.13.3; Schol. Bob. 89 (St). See Moreau, *Clodiana Religio*, 83ff., 92ff. (on the details of the *rogatio Pupia Valeria*).

88. Isid. *Orig.* 5.26.24. See Mommsen, *Römisches Strafrecht*, 407; Cornell, "Some Observations on the *crimen incesti*"; Sheid, "Le délit religieux."

89. Such accusations, as Moreau, *Clodiana Religio*, 168, correctly observes, formed part of the prosecution's attempt to blacken Clodius's character in order to convince the jury of his guilt, a standard rhetorical procedure.

90. See the excellent discussion by Cornell, "Some Observations on the *crimen incesti*."

91. Mommsen, *Römisches Strafrecht*, 18ff.

92. On the *lex Peducaea* see Rotondi, *Leges Publicae*, 321, for sources. Discussion: Gruen, "M. Antonius"; Weinrib, "The Prosecution of Roman Magistrates," 44f.; Rawson, *Roman Culture and Society*, 163f. Rawson's suggestion that the *lex Peducaea* created a standing *quaestio* is most unlikely; her reference to Plut. *Crass.* 1 proves nothing (see Moreau, *Clodiana Religio*, 91 n. 240) and Clodius's predicament in 61 demonstrates the absence of any general precedent for problematic *incestum* trials.

93. Moreau, *Clodiana Religio*, 95.

94. *Libera interpretatio*: Cic. *Caec.* 51f.; *Inv.* 1.17, 2.127f.; *Top.* 25; Asc. 62 (C). Quint. 7.8.7 provide examples.

95. See Cornell, "Some Observations on the *crimen incesti*"; Sheid, "Le délit religieux"; Moreau, *Clodiana Religio*, 84ff., who provide further bibliography.

96. Moreau, *Clodiana Religio*, 96, with full documentation.

97. Quaestors were evidently not immune from prosecution *de incestu*, as the case of M. Antonius in 113 demonstrates: see Gruen, "M. Antonius," 61; Weinrib, "The Prosecution of Roman Magistrates," 36, 44f. Nor was Clodius immune when quaestor designate, a point Weinrib (p. 51) argues convincingly. Shackleton Bailey, "The Prosecution of Roman Magistrates-Elect," asserts the contrary, supposing that Paulus's list of unsuitable *defensores* (*Dig* 3.3.54) is also a list of unsuitable defendants, since "defendere est eandem vicem quam reus subire." That is, those in Paulus's list could not be *defensores because* they could not be *rei*. This does not follow. Clearly "qui rei publicae causa *afuturus* est" can be prosecuted, though he is found on Paulus's list. And, according to Shackleton Bailey's principle, magistrates holding *imperium* should a fortiori be in Paulus's list of ineligible *defensores*, since they are positively ineligible defendants.

If Weinrib is correct to argue that each *quaestio* will have established exemptions, and that magistrates without *imperium* were liable unless exempted, then the *rogatio* setting up an extraordinary *quaestio* to try Clodius need not have included a clause denying him immunity (as Moreau, *Clodiana Religio*, 127f., suggests).

98. See Gruen, "M. Antonius," 61, for discussion of the *lex Memmia*; sources in Rotondi, *Leges Publicae*, 321.

99. Cic. *Att.* 1.14.5. It had the effect of preventing Clodius from skipping town, as Balsdon, "Fabula Clodiana," 68, rightly observed.

The *crimen maiestatis* was probably not a real possibility, since it seems only magistrates and senators (and Clodius was not a senator when he committed his offense) could commit *maiestas*; see Bauman, *The Crimen Maiestatis*, 87ff. Moreover, *maiestas* would have been more difficult to prove: first it would have been necessary to establish that Clodius had violated the Bona Dea's rites, then that by such action he had diminished the people's *maiestas*. Though the gods possessed *maiestas*, the *crimen maiestatis* referred only to *maiestas populi Romani* (so Bauman, *The Crimen Maiestatis*, 13). It is perhaps worth observing that when Plutarch (*Caes.* 10.5) and Appian (*B. Civ.* 2.14) report that Clodius was accused of ἀσέβεια, the idea thereby conveyed is (probably) that he was tried for a religious offense, not *maiestas*, though ἀσέβεια is admittedly the standard Greek translation for *maiestas* (see Bauman, *The Crimen Maiestatis*, 1). Moreau, *Clodiana Religio*, 88f., is clearly correct to reject the suggestion of Latte, *Römische Religionsgeschichte*, 230, and Sheid, "Le délit religieux," 131, 133, that Clodius's friends arranged for his prosecution *de incestu* so that he could avoid a more serious charge.

100. Cic. *Att.* 1.14.1, 1.16.2.

101. The danger of a packed jury: Balsdon, "Fabula Clodiana," 69. On this point, see Moreau, *Clodiana Religio*, 97f. Todd, "*Lady Chatterly's Lover* and the Attic Orators," offers a useful discussion of ancient and modern concerns over the composition of juries and of the perceived importance to all parties of a jury's precise composition.

102. *Album iudicum*: Greenidge, *The Legal Procedure of Cicero's Time*, 445. *Reiectio*: since it was preserved in the *lex Fufia*, it must have been part of the *rogatio Pupia Valeria*; see Cic. *Att.* 1.16.3. *Lex Aurelia*: Rotondi, *Leges Publicae*, 369.

103. Mommsen, *Römisches Strafrecht*, 221.

104. *Pace* Moreau, *Clodiana Religio*, 142.

105. On the controversial nature of legislation affecting juries, see Brunt, *Fall of the Roman Republic*, 194ff. (with further literature). The point at issue in the Bona Dea affair was not whether the praetor's selection of the jurors was actually a senatorial infringement, but whether Fufius could represent it as such; see Lacey, "Cicero and Clodius," 88f.

106. Cic. *Att.* 1.14.1.

107. The *lex Gabinia* was vehemently resisted by C. Piso (Plut. *Pomp.* 25), Hortensius (Cic. *Leg. Man.* 52), and Catulus (Cic. *Leg. Man.* 59; Sall. *Hist.* 5.24 [M] = 5.20 [McGushin]; Vell. 2.32.1; Dio 36.30.4ff.). Catulus and Hortensius also opposed the *lex Manilia* (Cic. *Leg. Man.* 51f.).

108. Ooteghem, *Lucius Licinius Lucullus*, 159ff., with citations. Keaveney, *Lucullus*, 37f., is only the latest to trace their enmity to the terms of Sulla's will, an idea that has been challenged by Hillman, "The Alleged *Inimicitiae*." On the use of wills to convey a final and lasting insult, see Champlin, *Final Judgments*, 13ff. (too late for consideration by Hillman).

109. Sall. *Hist.* 4.45f. (M) = 4.40f. (McGushin). See also Sall. *Hist.* 4.42 (M) = 4.37 (McGushin); Plut. *Pomp.* 22.

110. Cic. *Att.* 1.14.1. It is Cicero who adds the comment that this would be the procedure in the Clodius case.

111. Cic. *Att.* 1.14.1. On the derogatory use of *levitas* to describe *popularis* politicians, see Hellegouarc'h, *Le vocabulaire latin*, 518, 558, and Yavetz, *Plebs and Princeps*, 51ff., 99ff.

112. Cic. *Att.* 1.14.2. Given the Nepos debacle and his own ongoing efforts to ingratiate himself with the established oligarchy and the senate as a whole, Pompey could not afford to side with a *popularis* tribune.

113. Cic. *Att.* 1.14.2.

114. Cic. *Att.* 1.14.4. The thematic continuity of Pompey's speeches and those of Crassus and Cicero are sufficient to show that when Pompey remarked to Cicero that he hoped he had said enough "de istis rebus" (*Att.* 1.14.2) the phrase meant "on your characteristic themes." Modern scholars incline to take the phrase as a reference to the Bona Dea scandal: Shackleton Bailey, *Cicero's Letters to Atticus*, 1:307; Lacey, "Cicero and Clodius," 87; Seager, *Pompey*, 75 n. 3; Moreau, *Clodiana Religio*, 111. By now it should be clear that this is not the obvious implication of Cicero's letter, which goes to great lengths to make the point that Pompey did *not* give a straight answer to the question put to him. Nor need Pompey's remark be taken as rude; *istis* here means "such things as you characteristically talk about"—a neutral, not derogatory, sense (see *OLD* 971)—a usage conveniently paralleled by Cic. *Att.* 1.16.13 (*istos consulatus*). Tyrrell, *The Correspondence of M. Tullius Cicero*, 1:199, gets it right.

115. This is discussed in more detail in Tatum, "Cicero and the *Bona Dea* Trial," 205ff. See also Nippel, *Aufruhr und Polizei*, 108f.

116. Sergius was apparently a freedman of Catiline. See Benner, *Die Politik des P. Clodius*, 163, and Lewis, "Inscriptions of Amiternum," 35ff.

117. The continuity of Cicero's invective against Catiline, Clodius, and Antony is clear: cf. (e.g.) Cic. *Cat.* 2.22; *Mur.* 49 (Catiline) with *Att.* 4.3.3; *Dom.* 24, 45, 48, 53, 64, 89; *Sest.* 2, 53, 76, 81, 89; *Vat.* 40; *Mil.* 36 (Clodius) with *Phil.* 5.18, 12.17, 27 (Antony). This continuity is discussed in detail by May, "Cicero and the Beasts." See also Gonfroy, "Homosexualité et idéologie esclavagiste" (on certain aspects of the continuity of Cicero's invective throughout his career), and, more to the present point, Rink, "Diskussionsbemerkungen," and Havas, "Schemata und Wahrheit." Some scholars, it should be pointed out, continue to accept Cicero at his word: for instance, Lewis, "Inscriptions of Amiternum." The schematic quality of anti-*popularis* rhetoric is also examined by Brunt, *The Fall of the Roman Republic*, 53ff.

118. Cic. *Att.* 1.14.5.

119. Moreau, *Clodiana Religio*, 112ff., with further references.

120. Cic. *Att.* 1.14.5. Cato, *privatus* in 61, had no right to address the people unbidden; see Bauman, *The Crimen Maiestatis*, 46f., 87, 90. M. Favonius (pr. 49): Gruen, *Last Generation*, 56ff., 275.

121. The senate meeting is recounted at Cic. *Att.* 1.14.5.

122. For the career of Curio *pater*, see the recent summary in Moreau, *Clodiana Religio*, 157ff., with important bibliography. See also Tatum, "Cicero, the Elder Curio, and the Titinia Case." Although he supported the *lex Manilia* (Cic. *Leg. Man.* 68) and saved Caesar after the judgment of the conspirators (Plut. *Caes.* 8.3), neither is evidence of an antagonistic attitude toward the senate. The *lex Manilia* was a sure thing, and saving Caesar was both decent and prudent, as even Cicero realized. But it is worth noting that Curio may have been an enemy to Lucullus; see Gruen, "Pompey," 76; Moreau, *Clodiana Religio*, 160; a different view is to be found in Keaveney, *Lucullus*, 47, 56.

123. Cic. *Att.* 1.14.5. As Shackleton Bailey, *Cicero's Letters to Atticus*, 1:312, correctly observes of *decernebat*: "The tense seems to have been influenced by the preceding epistolary imperfects, for 'is decreeing' in the context can scarcely mean anything but

'has decreed.'" The effects of this resolution were (1) to hold up the allotment of *provinciae*, thereby keeping Caesar and especially Clodius in Rome (and preventing Clodius from invoking the *lex Memmia*) and (2) to postpone the reception of foreign *legationes* (see Balsdon, "Fabula Clodiana," 68). This action made Clodius's case *the* central issue of Roman politics.

124. Cic. *Att.* 1.14.5; see Tatum, "Cicero, *ad Att.* 1.14.5."

125. Cic. *Att.* 1.14.5, 1.16.1.

126. Lacey, "Cicero and Clodius," 88, though I do not think it necessary that Cicero's reference to "odia et inimicitias rei publicae causa" in *Att.* 1.15.1 refers specifically to the events of the Bona Dea trial; Rundell, "Cicero and Clodius," 304f.

127. Cic. *Att.* 1.14.5. Cf. Cic. *Cat.* 1.10, 1.27, 3.4. Clodius later parodied Cicero in their famous exchange in the senate (*Att.* 1.16.10: "quousque, inquit, hunc regem feremus?"). Caesar and others: Suet. *Iul.* 74.2, on which passage see McDermott, "Suetonius, *Iul.*, 74, 2"; Cic. *Fam.* 5.5.2; *Acad.* 2.62; [Sall.] *In Cic.* 3. Caesar did not make his joke at Clodius's actual trial, however; by May he had left for his province: Gelzer, *Caesar*, 60 n. 3. Compare the effectiveness of Laterensis's use of *quousque* in needling Cicero during the trial of Cn. Plancius in 54 (Cic. *Planc.* 75).

128. Cic *Att.* 1.16.1. Balsdon, "Fabula Clodiana," 71, suggested that the invective of these speeches turned Clodius into Cicero's enemy. It seems to me difficult to discern in our meager evidence so precise a turning point; surely Clodius's attacks (after Nepos's attacks at the end of Cicero's consulship) expected a forceful reaction. For other propositions as to *the* cause of Clodius's enmity, see Stockton, *Cicero*, 160f.; Rundell, "Cicero and Clodius," 304f.; Moreau, *Clodiana Religio*, 254ff.

129. Cic. *Att.* 1.16.2, a fear Cicero did not take seriously.

130. Not only promagistrates but foreign legations were anxious to see matters proceed. Businessmen had a stake as well, since their dispositions in the provinces relied to a high degree on the governor in power. Cicero himself (*Att.* 1.16.2) ascribes Hortensius's behavior to *odium*. After the trial, others joined Cicero in criticizing Hortensius's tactics (*Att.* 1.16.3).

131. Cic. *Att.* 1.16.4: "triumphabat Hortensius se vidisse tantum, nemo erat qui illum reum ac non miliens condemnatum arbitraretur."

132. Lacey, "Cicero and Clodius," 89.

133. Balsdon, "Fabula Clodiana," 70; Cic. *Att.* 1.16.2; Asc. 44f. (C).

134. Moreau, *Clodiana Religio*, 125ff. For sources on the *lex Fufia*, see Rotondi, *Leges Publicae*, 385.

135. On Curio's underrated capacities as an orator, see Tatum, "Cicero, the Elder Curio, and the Titinia Case."

136. Curio: Schol. Bob. 85–89 (St). Clodius's *patroni*: Cic. *Att.* 1.16.5 ("patroni omnes conciderunt"); *Har. Resp.* 38. Clodius's *advocati*: Cic. *Att.* 1.16.4. On *advocati* generally, see Greenidge, *The Legal Procedure of Cicero's Time*, 474f.

137. Cic. *Har. Resp.* 37; Schol. Bob. 85, 89 (St); Val. Max. 4.2.5. Plutarch (*Caes.* 10.5), confusing Fufius's role in creating the *quaestio*, mistakenly believes that Fufius was a prosecutor of Clodius; cf. Moreau, *Clodiana Religio*, 133 n. 185. On the other hand, Moreau's view that Lentulus Crus's prosecution of Clodius was in reality an attack on Caesar, a view based on Lentulus Crus's opposition to Caesar in 49 (Caes. *B. Gall.* 8.50.4; *B. Civ.* 1.2), is hardly tenable; see Moreau, *Clodiana Religio*, 135f.

138. Dio 39.6.2. See Gruen, *Last Generation*, 273ff.; Moreau, *Clodiana Religio*, 135.

One of Clodius's prosecutors, a Cornelius Lentulus, was later defended by him in a trial *de ambitu* (Val. Max. 4.2.5); see chapter 2, section 3.

139. The prosecutor was ordinarily assisted by one or two *subscriptores*; see Greenidge, *The Legal Procedure of Cicero's Time*, 475f. However, three *subscriptores* are recorded for Clodius's trial: the two Cornelii Lentuli mentioned in the text (Schol. Bob. 89 [St]; Val. Max. 4.2.5) and C. Fannius (Cic. *Att.* 2.24.3). Moreau, *Clodiana Religio*, 133ff., is surely correct to accept the evidence of Cicero's letter, which cannot be mistaken on this point.

140. Dio 39.6.2.

141. Cic. *Att.* 2.24.3.

142. Cic. *Att.* 1.16.3.

143. Cic. *Att.* 1.16.4. Moreau, *Clodiana Religio*, 144, notes Cicero's contradictory attitude.

144. Schol. Bob. 90 (St).

145. Aurelia and Julia: Schol. Bob. 89 (St); Suet. *Iul.* 74.4. Cato: Sen. *Ep. M.* 97.3. Lucullus: Cic. *Mil.* 73; Dio 37.46.2 (by implication). Cicero: Cic. *Att.* 1.16.2, 2.1.5; *Dom.* 80; Schol. Bob. 85 (St); Quint. 4.2.88.

146. Seneca is the only source naming Cato as a witness. His contribution is difficult to fathom and Seneca may be in error, but that has yet to be proved; see Moreau, *Clodiana Religio*, 200.

147. Val. Max. 8.5.5 cannot be correct when he says "illo [i.e., Clodius] sacrilegium flagitium *uno argumento* absentiae tuente." Moreau, *Clodiana Religio*, 201ff., reviews the possible identifications of Interamna.

148. Cic. *Mil.* 46; Asc. 49 (C); Schol. Bob. 85 (St); Quint. 4.2.88. See Nicolet, *L'ordre équestre*, 2:834. Causinius Schola was with Clodius when he was killed: Cic. *Mil.* 46; Asc. 31 (C).

149. Balsdon, "Fabula Clodiana," 71. Aurelia and Julia, for example, contradicted Clodius's testimony when they testified to *his* presence—not merely *a man's* presence—at the sacrifice; see Moreau, *Clodiana Religio*, 197, against Ciaceri, *Cicerone e i suoi tempi*, 2:25.

150. Cic. *Att.* 1.16.2: "neque dixi quicquam pro testimonio nisi quod erat ita notum ut non possem praeterire."

151. Cic. *Att.* 1.16.4–5.

152. Moreau, *Clodiana Religio*, 203, notes how seriously the prosecution took Cicero's testimony, but takes the reason to be that his evidence would wreck Clodius's alibi. More likely they feared Cicero's authority and his powerful eloquence; see Tatum, "Cicero and the *Bona Dea* Trial," 205ff.

153. Cic. *Att.* 1.16.5. Plut. *Cic.* 29.6, reporting that some jurors handed in unintelligible tablets, must be rejected; see Greenidge, *The Legal Procedure of Cicero's Time*, 389; Balsdon, "Fabula Clodiana," 72 n. 46; Moreau, *Clodiana Religio*, 223.

154. Cic. *Att.* 1.16.5; *Har. Resp.* 36ff.; Dio 37.46.3; Plut. *Cic.* 29.5f.; Val. Max. 9.1.7; Schol. Bob. 86, 90, 91, 173 (St).

155. The bitter observation of Q. Calidius, that a bribe of HS 300,000 was necessary to secure the conviction of a *praetorius* (Cic. *Verr.* 1.38), implies that bribery on the side of the defense was the norm. Examples of bribery from the late republic include, in addition to the sensational case of Verres: Terentius Varro (Cic. *Verr.* 1.40; *Clu.* 130); Oppianicus (Cic. *Clu.* 62–116; *Verr.* 1.29, 39, 2.79; *Caec.* 28; *Brut.* 241); P. Lentulus

Sura (Cic. *Att.* 1.16.9; Plut. *Cic.* 17.2–3), and examples could be further multiplied. Clodius's older brother, Gaius, attempted unsuccessfully to bribe the jury trying him for extortion, as his son tastelessly and casually remarked (Cic. *Fam.* 8.8.2–3, 11.22.1). The *lex Pompeia* of 52 had as one of its goals the minimizing of opportunities for corrupting jurors; see Gruen, *Last Generation*, 237f.

156. Catulus: Cic. *Att.* 1.16.5. Cicero's jibes: Cic. *Att.* 1.16.10.

157. Cicero's accusations of dishonesty plainly focus on the lower orders in the jury: e.g., Cic. *Att.* 1.16.3; Schol. Bob. 90–91 (St). Cato's jury bill: Cic. *Att.* 1.17.8, 1.18.3, 2.1.8. The precise nature of the bill is debated; see Moreau, *Clodiana Religio*, 239f., 246, for a recent discussion. Moreau (pp. 241, 248ff.) links Cato's jury bill to his opposition to the publicans' request to renegotiate their tax contracts in 61/60. This seems unnecessary: even Cicero, who publicly supported the publicans, considered their request objectionable.

158. Gruen, *Last Generation*, 275; Seager, *Pompey*, 76. An excellent bibliography on the topic is provided by Moreau, *Clodiana Religio*, 210 n. 642. Important discussions include Frank, "Cicero and the Poetae Novi"; Hathorn, "The Political Implications of the Trial of P. Clodius," 49ff.; Hathorn, "Calvum ex Nanneianis"; Trencsény-Waldopfel, "Calvus ex Nanneianis"; Wiseman, *Cinna the Poet*, 147ff.; Loposzko, "Die Bestechung der Richter," 298ff.; Moreau, *Clodiana Religio*, 209ff. Moreau joins the majority of scholars in accepting the identification with Crassus. The identification with Calvus is argued by Frank, Hathorn, Wiseman, and Loposzko.

159. E.g., Marshall, *Crassus*, 113ff.; Ward, *Marcus Crassus*, 227ff.

160. Schol. Bob. 86, 91 (St). For comparison, see Cic. *Clu.* 68f.; *Verr.* 1.38. On Cicero's figures, see McDermott, "The Verrine Jury," 65.

161. Schol. Bob. 90 (St). In the senate: Cic. *Att.* 1.16.3.

162. Schol. Bob. 86 (St).

163. Schol. Bob. 87 (St). Clodius's "poverty" is stressed in Cicero's *In Clod. et Cur.*; see Schol. Bob. 87f. (St).

164. Schol. Bob. 91 (St).

165. Hathorn, "The Political Implications of the Trial of P. Clodius," 49; Wiseman, *Cinna the Poet*, 147f.

166. Frank, "Cicero and the Poetae Novi."

167. Proponents of the identification with Calvus include Frank, "Cicero and the Poetae Novi"; Hathorn, "The Political Implications of the Trial of P. Clodius," 49ff.; Hathorn, "Calvum ex Nanneianis"; Wiseman, *Cinna the Poet*, 147ff.; Loposzko, "Die Bestechung der Richter," 298ff.; Dettenhofer, *Perdita Iuventus*, 38.

168. Wiseman, *Cinna the Poet*, 147ff. The coarseness of *calvus*: ibid., 148 n. 9. *Calvus* in mime: Cicu, "Moechus Calvus."

169. Ward, *Marcus Crassus*, 206.

170. Cic. *Har. Resp.* 45.

171. The former view is the more common; see, e.g., Lenaghan, *A Commentary on Cicero's Oration De Haruspicum Responso*, 169; Moreau, *Clodiana Religio*, 205. The view adopted here is that of Hillard, "P. Clodius Pulcher," 41, though for reasons somewhat different from those which Hillard advances.

172. Gagé, *Matronalia*, 141; Ovid, *Fasti* 5.155f.

173. Moreau, *Clodiana Religio*, 24f.

174. Juv. 6.314–45; cf. 2.83ff. See Richlin, *The Garden of Priapus*, esp. 78 n. 6.

Chapter 4

1. Lacey, "Cicero and Clodius," 85ff. Gruen, *Last Generation*, 275, less plausibly takes the contrary view. T. N. Mitchell, *Cicero*, 118f., also overestimates Clodius's position at this time (and in fact through 59).

2. Cato's bill: Cic. *Att.* 1.17.8, 2.1.8. Owing to heavy equestrian opposition, the bill ultimately failed. Piso deprived of Syria: Cic. *Att.* 1.16.8. This is the natural inference to be drawn from Cicero's expression "desponsam . . . Syriam"; see Balsdon, "Roman History, 65–50 B.C.: Five Problems," 140. Clodius deprived of Syria: Cic. *In Clod. et Cur.* fr. 8 (Crawford); cf. Schol. Bob. 86–87 (St). That Piso intended to choose Clodius as his quaestor (not every quaestor was assigned his duties by the lottery) is the reasonable proposal of Moreau, *Clodiana Religio*, 230f. Clodius's debts: Cic. *In Clod. et Cur.* fr. 6 (Crawford); cf. Schol. Bob. 86 (St).

3. J. W. Crawford, *M. Tullius Cicero: The Fragmentary Speeches*, 229ff., but see McDermott, "Curio Pater and Cicero," 407ff.; Tatum, "Cicero, the Elder Curio, and the Titinia Case," 370 n. 17 (not adequately addressed in J. W. Crawford, *M. Tullius Cicero: The Fragmentary Speeches*, 230 n. 9).

4. Geffcken, *Comedy in the Pro Caelio*, 64.

5. This performance is regularly deemed to be the basis of the *In Clodium et Curionem*, perhaps rightly. See J. W. Crawford, *M. Tullius Cicero: The Fragmentary Speeches*, 229f. (with further literature).

6. Cic. *Att.* 1.16.9–10. The assimilation of Clodius to Catiline: see chapter 3, section 4.

7. Cic. *Har. Resp.* 43.

8. Badian, "Tiberius Gracchus," 692.

9. *Contiones*: Cic. *In Clod. et Cur.* frr. 2, 3 (Crawford). Clodius's attack on the Vestals: Plut. *Cat. Min.* 19.5–6, properly interpreted in Moreau, *Clodiana Religio*, 233–39, 253; see also Tatum, "Cicero and the *Bona Dea* Trial," 203f.

10. Cic. *In Clod. et Cur.* fr. 11 (Crawford); cf. Schol. Bob. 87 (St).

11. Cic. *Att.* 1.16.13.

12. Cic. *Att.* 1.16.12; Plut. *Pomp.* 44; *Cat. Min.* 30.

13. *Dolor* and tractability: Morgan and Walsh, "Tiberius Gracchus," 204.

14. Cic. *In Clod. et Cur.* 15 (Crawford); Schol. Bob. 87 (St).

15. Balbus: *MRR* 2:133, 155, 181; *MRR* 3:218. Quaestors in Sicily: Ps.-Asc. 187 (St).

16. Admitted by the orator at *Planc.* 64–65.

17. Cic. *Att.* 2.1.5.

18. See Badian, "The Silence of Norbanus," 156ff., for the expectations, traditional and legal, affecting provincial quaestors.

19. Cic. *Att.* 2.1.5.

20. Mommsen, *Römische Forschungen*, 126ff.; Lange, *Über die Transitio ad Plebem*; Holzapfel, *De transitione ad plebem*; Botsford, *The Roman Assemblies*, 162f. More recent treatments are Kübler, *RE* 6.2:2154ff.; Ranouil, *Recherches sur le patriciat*, 160ff.; Slagter, "Transitio ad Plebem"; Cornell, *The Beginnings of Rome*, 253ff.

21. *Transitio* was a process distinct from adoption, though admittedly confusion can arise from the inconsistency of Roman terminology concerning the case of Clodius. Clodius, as we shall see, became a plebeian by *adrogatio* (by which action a Claudius Pulcher did not actually become a plebeian but rather a Claudius Pulcher

became a Fonteius and consequently a plebeian); on this point there is absolutely no uncertainty (Cic. *Dom.* 34ff.; *Har. Resp.* 48, 57; *Sest.* 15f.; *Prov. Cons.* 45; *Att.* 7.7.6, 8.3.3). Nevertheless, Cicero sometimes makes casual reference to Clodius's adrogation as a *transitio* (*Har. Resp.* 44; *Prov. Cons.* 42; *Att.* 2.7.2, 2.9.2, 2.22.2), a habit of expression followed in later sources: Vell. 2.45.1; Liv. *Per.* 103; Suet. *Iul.* 20.4 (cf. *Tib.* 2.4); Plut. *Caes.* 33.3; *Cat. Min.* 34.1. See the discussion in Slagter, "Transitio ad Plebem," 8f.

22. Cic. *Brut.* 62; *Fam.* 15.20.1; Plin. *N.H.* 35.8; see Wiseman, *Roman Studies,* 207ff.

23. M. H. Crawford, *Roman Republican Coinage,* 1:441 (with further discussion and references); see also *MRR* 3:9.

24. Liv. 8.40; cf. 4.16.3–4. See Ridley, "*Falsi triumphi, plures consulatus,*" 372ff.

25. For example, Beloch, *Römische Geschichte,* 10f.; Palmer, *The Archaic Community of the Romans,* 290; Cornell, *The Beginnings of Rome,* 242ff.

26. The scholarship is at once immense and formidable: cf. the valuable summary by Ridley, "Fastenkritik."

27. Fundamental is De Sanctis, *Storia dei Romani,* 1:224ff. The scholarly tradition is collected in Ranouil, *Recherches sur le patriciat,* and Richard, *Les origines de la plèbe romaine.* See also Staveley, "The Nature and Aims of the Patriciate"; Richard, "Patricians and Plebeians: The Origin of a Social Dichotomy." With caution, see R. E. Mitchell, *Patricians and Plebeians;* Cornell, *The Beginnings of Rome,* 242ff.

28. Badian, "The Clever and the Wise," 8ff.

29. Ranouil, *Recherches sur le patriciat;* Shatzman, "Patricians and Plebeians." The argument of Cornell, *The Beginnings of Rome,* 253f., constitutes a *petitio principi.*

30. Servius Tullius: Cic. *Tusc. Disp.* 1.38: "meo regnante gentili." Tullus Attius: Plut. *Cic.* 1.2. Octavii: Suet. *Aug.* 2.1.

31. Liv. 4.12–16; the critique comes at 4.16.3–4. See Ogilvie, *A Commentary on Livy,* 550ff., for discussion and details.

32. Plin. *N.H.* 18.15. The *titulus* is cited by Livy at 4.16.4 ("falsum imaginis titulum").

33. Mommsen, *Römische Forschungen,* 124.

34. Clodius and Dolabella, however, became plebeian by adoption, the latter being adopted by a plebeian Lentulus: Dio 42.29.1; Shackleton Bailey, *Two Studies,* 29ff.

35. Papirii Masones: The late republican or early Augustan C. Papirius Maso whose career is preserved on *CIL* 6.1480 was plebeian; the Papirii were a minor patrician *gens,* but the Papirii Carbones and Turdi were plebeian. Sempronii Atratini: After the fifth century the patrician Sempronii Atratini tend to vanish, whereas the plebeian Sempronii attained the consulship in 304 and remained estimable thereafter. The Atratini reappear in the late republic, however. C. Sempronius Atratinus, the youthful prosecutor of Caelius Rufus and cos. suff. in 34, was the son of L. Calpurnius Bestia (aed. by 57) and adopted by a L. Sempronius Atratinus; see *ILS* 9461 and Münzer *RE* 2A.2:1366ff. (the relationship is inadvertently reversed in *MRR* 3:188). Whether the cognomen was legitimate or a pretension remains unclear; if the former, there is of course no evidence of *transitio.*

36. Sources and discussion in Badian, "The House of the Servilii Gemini," 50f.; Slagter, "Transitio ad Plebem," 168ff.

37. See, in addition to the passages in Livy already cited, Zon. 7.15.

38. Cornell, *The Beginnings of Rome,* 246.

39. Münzer, *RE* 4A.1:850f.

40. The jurist: Münzer, *RE* 4A.1:851ff. The orator: Syme, *The Augustan Aristocracy*, 205f.; *MRR* 3:203. The quaestor and proconsul: Sumner, "The Lex Annalis," 249f.

41. Val. Max. 6.5.7. Valerius hardly represents the most solid evidence for such a point as this: Maslakov, "Valerius Maximus."

42. *MRR* 3:202f.

43. Mattingly, "The Consilium of Cn. Pompeius Strabo in 89 B.C."; Gruen, *Last Generation*, 199; Shackleton Bailey, *Two Studies*, 131f.; Harvey, Review of Shackleton Bailey, 119; *MRR* 3:262.

44. Slagter, "Transitio ad Plebem," 33ff.

45. Schol. Bob. 87 (St).

46. Cic. *In Clod. et Cur.*, frr. 2, 3 (Crawford); Plut. *Cat. Min.* 19.5–6 (see discussion above in section 1 above).

47. J. W. Crawford, *M. Tullius Cicero: The Fragmentary Speeches*, 251.

48. Consider Cicero's (perhaps mild) surprise when, in June 60, he realized that Clodius genuinely intended to become a tribune (*Att.* 2.1.5: "ille autem non simulat, sed plane tribunus pl. fieri cupit").

49. Cic. *Att.* 1.18.4, 1.19.5.

50. Cic. *Att.* 1.19.5.

51. Shackleton Bailey, *Cicero's Letters to Atticus*, 1:332.

52. Cic. *Att.* 1.19.5 is dated to 15 March 60.

53. Cic. *Att.* 2.1.5.

54. At Cic. *Har. Resp.* 41, 43, Cicero compares Clodius unfavorably to Sulpicius Rufus, but without a word about *transitio*.

55. Dio 37.51.1, however, attributes Clodius's desire to his hatred of the leaders (τοὺς δυνατούς) of the senate. Clodius and vengeance: Martin, *Die Popularen*, 81ff.; Gruen, "P. Clodius," 124f.; Lintott, "P. Clodius Pulcher," 167; cf. Moreau, *Clodiana Religio*, 255ff., and Benner, *Die Politik des P. Clodius*, 54ff., for more complicated views of Clodius's motives for seeking the tribunate (each accepting nevertheless that Clodius was motivated by the desire for vengeance).

56. *Att.* 2.1.5.

57. Well discussed in Slagter, "Transitio ad Plebem," 26ff.

58. Ibid., 51ff.

59. Badian, "Tiberius Gracchus," 692; Morgan and Walsh, "Tiberius Gracchus," 204.

60. *Har. Resp.* 43. Sulpicius Rufus is also mentioned there, but his reckless tribunate is not ascribed to *dolor*.

61. The varied possibilities of the tribunate: Bleicken, *Das Volkstribunat*; Gruen, *Last Generation*, 23ff.; Thommen, *Das Volkstribunat*.

62. After Celer's death, Cicero claimed that the noble had threatened to slay Clodius with his own hand if he persisted in trying to transfer to the *plebs*: Cic. *Cael.* 60.

63. Metellus opposed the measures sought by Pompey and pushed by the tribune L. Flavius; see *MRR* 2:183f. for sources. Celer's younger brother, Nepos, who held the praetorship in 60, was making himself unpopular with the senate: Dio 37.51.3–4.

64. Dio 37.51.1–2.

65. Mommsen, *Römische Forschungen*, 125ff.; Lange, *Über die Transitio ad Plebem*, 19ff.

66. Liv. 3.65.1, 4.16.3, 5.10.11. See Ogilvie, *A Commentary on Livy*, 513ff.

67. *Lex Trebonia*: Liv. 3.65.4; Rotondi, *Leges Publicae*, 206f.

68. Slagter, "Transitio ad Plebem," 67, accepts Dio's account as it stands.

69. Cf. the language at Zon. 7.15, also describing *transitio ad plebem*: εἰ δέ τις (a patrician) τὸ τοῦ γένους ἀξωμόσατο καὶ πρὸς τὴν τοῦ πλήθους νόμισιν, ἀσμένως αὐτὸν προσεδέχοντο.

70. So Mommsen, *Die römische Chronologie*, 241.

71. Cic. *Mur.* 27 suffices to show that Sulpicius was by then a recognized expert on the subject. Sulpicius's treatise may well have been a source (and a spur) for Clodius.

72. It seems unlikely that Pompey forcefully opposed Clodius's intentions at this time, despite the claim of Cicero at *Har. Resp.* 45. Had he done so, Cicero would surely have made some notice of it to Atticus in *Att.* 2.1, in which letter the orator is at pains to underscore his intimacy with the great man.

73. Seager, *Pompey*, 72ff., provides a succinct yet thorough account.

74. Sources in *MRR* 2:184.

75. Cic. *Att.* 2.1.6.

76. Plut. *Pomp.* 46.4–47.1; *Cat. Min.* 31.2.

77. Clodius as a foil in Plutarch's *Lives*: Pelling, "Plutarch's Adaptation of His Source Material," 132f.

78. Caesar's canvass, the formation of the triumvirate, and the events of Caesar's consulship are too familiar to require review here; see Gelzer, *Caesar*, 71ff.; Seager, *Pompey*, 83ff.

79. App. *B. Civ.* 2.14 and Dio 38.12.1 suggest that Clodius took seriously his indebtedness to Caesar.

80. Cic. *Att.* 2.3.3.

81. Sources and discussion in Gelzer, *Caesar*, 71ff. Caesar's use of force: Lintott, *Violence*, 213.

82. Gruen, "The Trial of C. Antonius"; Rundell, "Cicero and Clodius."

83. Sources for Antonius's trial are assembled in Alexander, *Trials in the Late Roman Republic*, 119f.

84. That Cicero's speech offended Caesar is amply attested by the orator himself: *Dom.* 41; *Sest.* 116; *Prov. Cons.* 42; cf. Suet. *Iul.* 20.4; App. *B. Civ.* 2.14; Dio 38.10.1.

85. Sources for Clodius's adoption: Cic. *Dom.* 34–42; *Sest.* 15–16; *Prov. Cons.* 45–46; App. *B. Civ.* 2.14; Plut. *Caes.* 14.9; Dio 38.12.1–2, 39.11.2, 39.21.4. *Obiter dicta* include: Cic. *Att.* 2.7.2, 2.12.1, 8.3.3; *Dom.* 77; *Leg.* 3.9.21; Vell. 2.45.1; Suet. *Tib.* 2.

86. *Adrogatio*: Gell. 5.19; Gaius, *Inst.* 1.97–107; see Crook, *Law and Life of Rome*, 111f.; Watson, *The Law of Persons*, 83ff. *Comitia curiata*: Taylor, *Roman Voting Assemblies*, 3ff., and Nicolet, *World of the Citizen*, 219 (with further references).

87. It seems likely that even when meeting for the purpose of passing a *lex curiata* for adrogation the curiate assembly was convened by a competent magistrate; see Bleicken, "Oberpontifex und Pontifikalkollegium."

88. *Dom.* 37. Nothing is known of young Fonteius. Rawson, *Roman Culture and Society*, 235 n. 60, links him to the Fonteii from Tusculum. He is often identified with the moneyer of 55 (P. Fonteius P. f. Capito), but this is doubted by M. H. Crawford, *Roman Republican Coinage*, 1:453. The irrepressible Cicero hints at immoral relations between Fonteius and Clodius (*Dom.* 35–36).

89. *Dom.* 34–42; cf. Dio 39.11.2, 39.21.4.

90. *Dom.* 37.

91. *Dom.* 35–41. I have preserved the order of the objections in Cicero's speech.

92. Cic. *Att.* 2.4–17 were written from various estates.

93. Cic. *Dom.* 34, 42; *Prov. Cons.* 45. Cic. *Att.* 2.9.1 is a reference, not to Clodius's adoption, but to Vatinius's legislation (cf. *Sest.* 135). When Cicero learns of Caesar's (vain) effort later in 59 to repudiate Clodius's adoption, he responds by writing: "hoc vero regnum est et ferri nullo pacto potest. emittat ad me Publius qui obsignent; iurabo Gnaeum nostrum, collegum Balbi Ati, mihi narrasse ⟨se⟩ in auspicio fuisse" (*Att.* 2.12.1). Of course, by then Clodius was posing as Caesar's enemy.

94. Gell. 5.19; Gaius, *Inst.* 1.97–107; Just. *Inst.* 1.11.4 (the practice illegal). Given that one was forbidden to hold plebeian office if one's father had held curule office and was still living, Clodius's choice of a man younger than himself may have been at least partly intended to dispose of that problem. Vernacchia, "L'adopzione di Clodio," 208, postulates that Clodius's adoption by a younger man was the first such and set in motion the subsequent legal debate.

95. Gell. 5.19.6–7. *Sacrorum detestatio* and *adrogatio*: Kübler, *RE* 1.2:1682ff.; Watson, *Rome of the XII Tables*, 40f.

96. Slagter, "Transitio ad Plebem," 121ff.

97. Though it was perfectly natural and even expected that an augur be present at a meeting of the curiate assembly.

98. Cic. *Att.* 2.12.1–2.

99. Shackleton Bailey, *Two Studies*, 84f.

100. Clodius's children: Wiseman, *Roman Studies*, 42ff. Shackleton Bailey's suggestion (*Two Studies*, 109) that Clodius's son "may have been born before the adoption" will not explain his nomenclature, since *adrogatio* transferred all a man's property and descendants into the *potestas* of his adoptive father; see Crook, *Law and Life of Rome*, 112; Watson, *The Law of Persons*, 86 (of course, it would not have been impossible for Clodius to emancipate his young children before his *adrogatio*, but this seems farfetched).

101. Shackleton Bailey, *Two Studies*, 65ff.

102. Ibid., 118 (Brutus); 113f. (Spinther); 90 (Dolabella and his son). The other cases are T. Pomponius Atticus, L. Cornelius Balbus, C. Rabirius Postumus, Q. Servilius Caepio Brutus, and Ti. Claudius Nero.

103. Gell. 7.22; Festus 466L.

104. Rotondi, *Leges Publicae*, 335; see the discussion in Hardy, "Three Questions," 262, and Lintott, *Violence*, 140f. *Trinum nundinum*: Lange, *Römische Alterthümer*, 2:469ff.; Lintott, "Trinundinum."

105. Drusus's legislation: *MRR* 2:21f.

106. *Per vim*: Liv. *Per.* 71; Florus 2.5.9. *Contra auspicia*: Asc. 69 (C). *Per saturam*: Hardy, "Three Questions," 262.

107. Tatum, "The *Lex Papiria de Dedicationibus*."

108. Crassus's role is extremely difficult to fathom. He may have been consulted about Clodius's adoption, as suggested by Ward, *Marcus Crassus*, 219f., but, whatever his actual role, Crassus would hardly have resisted any threat to Cicero. Once Clodius was menacing the orator, Crassus seems to have urged (or at least seems to have been believed by Cicero to have urged) Pompey to give way to Clodius's designs; see Cic. *Att.* 2.22.5, with the interpretation offered by Shackleton Bailey, *Cicero's Letters to Atticus*, 1:397. Ward, *Marcus Crassus*, 243f., however, maintains that Crassus's hostility toward Cicero was merely Clodian propaganda.

109. Cic. *Att.* 2.4–17. Mitchell, *Cicero*, 117ff., argues at length against the significance of Antonius's trial and its connection with Clodius's adrogation, unconvincingly in my view. Mitchell tends to believe that we know more about *adrogatio* than we in fact do, and his assertion that, as a move to control Cicero, Clodius's adoption "was largely, if not completely, negatived by the fact that Pompey gave Cicero immediate and repeated assurances that the adoption was not aimed against him and that he had, in fact, before consenting to it, exacted a pledge from Clodius that he would not use his tribunate to harm Cicero" (p. 118), entirely misses the point.

110. Cic. *Att.* 2.9.1, 2.12.2, 2.14.1, 2.15.2, 2.22.5.

111. Clodius's support: App. *B. Civ.* 2.14. This dating reflects the likeliest implication of Pompey's remark recorded at Cic. *Att.* 2.16.2; see Meier, "Zur Chronologie und Politik," 80ff. But, as Shackleton Bailey, *Cicero's Letters to Atticus*, 1:408, and Seager, *Pompey*, 191f., point out, it is just possible to conclude that Pompey (and Cicero) were relying on informed expectations and gossip for context instead of an actual *rogatio*. If the bill was promulgated later, Clodius's support will then be best placed in May, when he was seeking a *rapprochement* with Caesar, following their brief disaffection (see below).

112. Caesar's land law: *MRR* 2:187f. The agrarian commission: *MRR* 2:191f. Clodius's expectations: Cic. *Att.* 2.7.3.

113. Sources: *MRR* 2:188. Clodius's expectations: Cic. *Att.* 2.7.3. Cicero, too, coveted the assignment: *Att.* 2.4.2, 2.5.1.

114. Cic. *Att.* 2.7.3. Cicero was prepared to envy the embassy to Tigranes before he knew that Clodius was opposed to it: cf. *Att.* 2.4.2 (that much is recoverable despite the textual difficulties, on which see Shackleton Bailey, *Cicero's Letters to Atticus*, 1:359).

115. Cic. *Att.* 2.7.3.

116. Cic. *Att.* 2.22.2 (cf. 2.20.2).

117. Cic. *Att.* 2.12.2. Clodius's attitude is described in *Att.* 2.22.1 (written somewhat later): "cum videt, quo sit in odio status hic rerum, in eos, qui haec egerunt, impetum facturus videtur." Yet Clodius remained conscious of the coalition's superior power; see Rundell, "Cicero and Clodius," 309.

118. Cic. *Att.* 2.12.1.

119. Cic. *Att.* 2.15.2.

120. Stockton, *Cicero*, 179.

121. Cic. *Att.* 2.8.1, 2.12.2, 2.19.3. For a recent treatment of Curio during this period, see Dettenhofer, *Perdita Iuventus*, 38ff.

122. Cic. *Att.* 2.12.2. On the prominent opposition to the triumvirate, see Mitchell, *Cicero*, 106ff.

123. The view of Seager, "Clodius, Pompeius and the Exile of Cicero," 522f., and Ward, *Marcus Crassus*, 234.

124. Cic. *Att.* 2.16.2.

125. Speaking order in the senate: Suet. *Iul.* 21; Gell. 4.10.5. Marriage tie: Cic. *Att.* 2.17.1, 8.3.3; Vell. 2.44.3; Suet. *Iul.* 21; Plut. *Pomp.* 47; *Caes.* 19; *Cat. Min.* 31; Dio 38.9.1. Perhaps it is at this time that Caesar made Pompey his heir: Suet. *Iul.* 83.1; see Seager, *Pompey*, 96.

126. See, for instance, the reference to Clodius's *pudor* at Cic. *Att.* 2.18.3.

127. Cic. *Att.* 2.18.1.

128. Cic. *Att.* 2.18.2. On Caesar's law and the controversy it provoked, see T. N. Mitchell, *Cicero*, 102, 105–7.

129. Linderski, *Roman Questions*, 87ff.

130. Cic. *Att.* 2.19.4, 2.20.2, 2.23.3.

131. Cic. *Att.* 2.21.4.

132. Cic. *Att.* 2.22.2.

133. Cic. *Att.* 2.22.1.

134. Cic. *Att.* 2.9.1.

135. Clodius was elected by 22 October; see Cic. *Q.F.* 1.12.16. Although consular elections were postponed in 59 (Cic. *Att.* 2.15.2), there is no indication that that was the case for tribunician elections as well; so, rightly, Seager, *Pompey*, 99.

136. Sources: Cic. *Att.* 2.24; *Flacc.* 96; *Sest.* 132; *Vat.* 24–26; Schol Bob. 139 (St); Suet. *Iul.* 17, 20.5; Plut. *Luc.* 42.7–8; App. *B. Civ.* 2.12; Dio 37.41.2–4, 38.9.2–4. McDermott, "*Vettius ille, ille noster index*," summarizes previous scholarship. Important and recent treatments include Taylor, "The Date and Meaning of the Vettius Affair"; Ward, *Marcus Crassus*, 236ff.; Seager, "Clodius, Pompeius and the Exile of Cicero"; Greenhalgh, *Pompey*, 224ff.; T. N. Mitchell, *Cicero*, 111f.

137. Pompey is Ward's candidate: *Marcus Crassus*, 238ff. Greenhalgh, *Pompey*, 224ff., suggests that Vettius acted on his own.

138. Seager, "Clodius, Pompeius and the Exile of Cicero," and *Pompey*, 99ff.

139. Seager, *Pompey*, 101f.

140. Cic. *Pis.* 3; Plut. *Pomp.* 48; *Cat. Min.* 33; App. *B. Civ.* 2.51.

141. Cic. *Q.F.* 1.2.15.

142. Cicero later alleged that Clodius played a part in the violence that prevented Gabinius's trial (*Sest.* 18). Not impossible, but it would be unsafe to attempt to make much of the claim.

143. Cf. Cic. *Sest.* 41, 67, 133.

144. Cic. *Q.F.* 1.2.16.

145. Dio 38.12.3.

146. Clodius's elder brother, Gaius, joined Caesar's staff at this time (Cic. *Sest.* 41), so Clodius was hardly out of step with his family in pursuing a connection with the coalition.

Chapter 5

1. Cic. *Pis.* 9; Asc. 8 (C). Sources: *MRR* 2:156.

2. These matters are discussed more fully in the first chapter.

3. Favory, "Classes dangereuses et crise de l'État," 139ff.; Flambard, "Clodius, les collèges, la plèbe et les esclaves," 126ff.; Nowak, *Der Einsatz Privater Garden*, 15ff.; Benner, *Die Politik des P. Clodius*, 155ff.; Rawson, *Roman Culture and Society*, 234ff.

4. Damio: Asc. 46f. (C); see Benner, *Die Politik des P. Clodius*, 158. C. Clodius: Cic. *Att.* 3.17.1; *Mil.* 46; Asc. 31 (C); he was perhaps a freedman: see Gruen, *Last Generation*, 339; Benner, *Die Politik des P. Clodius*, 166. P. Clodius: Cic. *Cael.* 27 (he was active in the prosecution of M. Caelius in 56); he was a client (so Gruen, *Last Generation*, 307) and perhaps a freedman (so Benner, *Die Politik des P. Clodius*, 166). T. Claudius: Cic. *Vat.* 3; see Gruen, *Last Generation*, 301.

5. Titius: Cic. *Dom.* 21; *Har. Resp.* 59; *Sest.* 80, 112. L. Gavius: *Att.* 6.3.6; cf. *Att.* 6.1.4;

Rawson, *Roman Culture and Society*, 235. T. Patina: Cic. *Mil.* 46. Scato (a financial operative for Clodius): Cic. *Dom.* 116; cf. *Att.* 4.4.2. Pola Servius: *Q.F.* 2.12(11).2; *Fam.* 8.12.2f.

6. For more detailed treatments of Sex. Cloelius, see Tatum, "Publius Clodius Pulcher and Tarracina," and Damon, "Sex. Cloelius, scriba" (whose conclusions are rather different from mine). That the name is Cloelius and not Clodius was proved by Shackleton Bailey, "Sex. Clodius–Sex. Cloelius," though Flambard, "Clodius, les collèges, la plèbe et les esclaves," 238f., and Vanderbroeck, *Popular Leadership*, 55, remain unconvinced, and Benner, *Die Politik des P. Clodius*, 156, is agnostic on the matter. Cloelius a *scriba*: Asc. 33 (C). On the status and influence of scribes, see Purcell, "The Apparitores," 129ff., and esp. Badian, "The *scribae* of the Roman Republic." Cloelius as drafter of *leges Clodiae*: Cic. *Dom.* 25, 47. Cloelius's prosecution *de vi*: Cic. *Mil.* 53, 90; Asc. 33, 35 (C). Cloelius's recall: Cic. *Att.* 14.13.6, 14.13A.2, 14.13B.3, 14.14.2, 14.19.2.

7. Decimus: Cic. *Dom.* 50; *Att.* 4.3.2; see Wiseman, *Cinna the Poet*, 152f., followed by Gruen, *Last Generation*, 296, and Benner, *Die Politik des P. Clodius*, 159. Antony: Cic. *Phil.* 2.48; Plut. *Ant.* 2.5 (Antony was, notoriously, young Curio's friend: Cic. *Phil.* 2.44f.). Gellius: Cic. *Har. Resp.* 59; *Sest.* 110ff.; *Vat.* 4; see Nicolet, *L'ordre équester*, 2:898ff.; Benner, *Die Politik des P. Clodius*, 160ff.

8. Gellius: Cic. *Att.* 4.3.2 (in 57); they were later reconciled (*Vat.* 4). Antony: Cic. *Mil.* 40; *Phil.* 2.21, 49; Dio 43.40.2; yet Antony was *subscriptor* in the prosecution of Milo for the death of Clodius, secured the recall of Sex. Cloelius in behalf of Clodius's son, and eventually married Fulvia.

9. Cic. *Sest.* 40; Schol. Bob. 130, 146 (St); Suet. *Iul.* 23.1; *Ner.* 2.2.

10. Clodius's lack of support among his fellow tribunes: Cic. *Q.F.* 1.2.16; *Sest.* 78.

11. Complete sources for Clodius's legislative program: *MRR* 2:196. The *quattuor leges* are here listed in an order different from that in Asconius.

12. See chapter 1, sections 4 and 5.

13. *Lex Manilia*: Asc. 45 (C); Dio 36.42; the law was later abrogated. Violence in 66: Cic. *Cat.* 1.15; Dio 36.44.3. On the political exploitation of *collegia* during the sixties, see (further) Benner, *Die Politik des P. Clodius*, 66f. (with ample bibliography).

14. Sources: Cic. *Red. Sen.* 33; *Red. Pop.* 13; *Sest.* 34, 55; *Pis.* 8; Asc. 6f., 75 ("Frequenter tum etiam coetus factiosorum hominum sine publica auctoritate malo publico fiebant") (C); Dio 38.13.2.

15. Demonstrated by Linderski, *Roman Questions*, 165ff. Linderski establishes the primacy of Asc. 7 (C) for recuperating the terms of the *senatus consultum* of 64. See Ausbüttel, *Untersuchungen zu den Vereinen*, 88ff., for a concise survey of modern scholarship.

16. Latte, *Römische Religion*, 90ff. Asc. 7 (C) makes it plain that the *senatus consultum* of 64 banned the celebration of the Ludi Compitalicii.

17. The sole attestation for the term is found in a third century A.D. inscription from Faesulae (*CIL* 11.1550), nor does this *collegium* correspond to Mommsen's conception of the *collegium compitalium* (Linderski, *Roman Questions*, 176). Mommsen's thesis need not detain us; for discussion see Linderski, *Roman Questions*, 168ff.; Flambard, "Collegia Compitalicia," 151ff.

18. Linderski, *Roman Questions*, 172ff.

19. Flambard, "Collegia Compitalicia," 151ff. (though with no reference to Linderski, *Roman Questions*, 165ff.); Flambard, "Les collèges et les élites locales," 78ff. This important matter deserves further detailed scrutiny.

20. Cic. *Pis.* 8; Asc. 7 (C).

21. Sources: Cic. *Red. Sen.* 33; *Dom.* 129; *Sest.* 34, 55; *Pis.* 9; *Att.* 3.15.4; Asc. 7f. (C); Dio 38.12.2.

22. Ausbüttel, *Untersuchungen zu den Vereinen*, 90f. This organization was normal for *collegia* and (despite the claims of some modern scholars) implies no paramilitary design in Clodius's law. The army, after all, provided the most accessible and reputable organizational scheme conceivable to the Romans.

23. Flambard, "Collegia Compitalicia," 154, 157, 165f.; Welwei, "Das Sklavenproblem," 66.

24. Treggiari, *Roman Freedmen*, 169.

25. Ibid., 256f.; Annequin and Létroublon, "Une approche des discours de Cicéron"; Favory, "Classes dangereuses et crise de l'État," 111ff.

26. Cicero's attitude toward the urban *plebs*: Brunt, *Fall of the Roman Republic*, 53f. Toward *Clodiani*: Favory, "Classes dangereuses et crise de l'État," 129ff.

27. Financial requirements of *collegia*: Ausbüttel, *Untersuchungen zu den Vereinen*, 43f.

28. Patronage of *collegia* is a well-attested imperial phenomenon: Clemente, "Il patronato nei collegia dell'impero romano."

29. See Flambard, "Collegia Compitalicia," 165f.

30. Garnsey, *Famine and Food Supply*, 3ff. The wretched living conditions of ordinary Romans: Scobie, "Slums, Sanitation and Mortality."

31. Rickman, *The Corn Supply of Ancient Rome*; Nicolet, *World of the Citizen*, 186ff.; Virlouvet, *Famines et émeutes*, 96ff.; Garnsey, *Famine and Food Supply*, 195ff.; Herz, *Studien*, 24ff.

32. Sources for Gaius's grain law: *MRR* 1:514. Its background: Garnsey and Rathbone, "The Background to the Grain Law of Gaius Gracchus"; Ungern-Sternberg, "Überlegungen zum Sozialprogramm der Gracchen."

33. Plut. *G. Gracch.* 6.2; Festus, 392L.

34. Additional costs: Garnsey, *Famine and Food Supply*, 213f. Nutritional limitations: Duncan-Jones, *The Economy of the Roman Empire*, 146f., who expresses proper caution regarding his calculations (caloric equivalence alone is in any event a misleading basis for nutritional comparison even if Duncan-Jones's figures should be valid).

35. M. H. Crawford, *Roman Republican Coinage*, 2:636, demonstrates the treasury's capacity to absorb the cost of the *frumentationes*.

36. Surveys of republican legislation concerning grain distributions: Schneider, *Wirtschaft und Politik*, 361ff.; Nicolet, *World of the Citizen*, 186ff.; Rickman, *The Corn Supply of Ancient Rome*, 161ff.; Nippel, *Aufruhr und Polizei*, 110f.

37. Rickman, *The Corn Supply of Ancient Rome*, 169f.; Fehrle, *Cato Uticensis*, 98ff.

38. Virlouvet, *Famines et émeutes*, 63; Garnsey, *Famine and Food Supply*, 206.

39. Cic. *Att.* 2.19.3 ("Rosciae legi, etiam frumentariae minitabantur"); Benner, *Die Politik des P. Clodius*, 56, oddly sees this as a cause of rather than a response to the dynasts' unpopularity. Virlouvet, *Famines et émeutes*, 111f., discusses the circumstances of 59. There is no basis for Schneider's conclusion, *Wirtschaft und Politik*, 383f., that Clodius's law was intended to follow Caesar's legislation as a sort of *popularis* package.

40. Sources: Cic. *Dom.* 25; *Sest.* 55; Asc. 8 (C); Plut. *Cic.* 30.1; Dio 38.13.1; *Schol. Bob.* 132 (St). The provision for those aged ten: Brunt, *Italian Manpower*, 382. It is worth

mentioning, as a possible precedent for Clodius, P. Claudius Pulcher (cos. 184), who in 189, as curule aedile, in conjunction with his colleague, Ser. Sulpicius Galba, set up twelve gilded shields to commemorate their punishment of unscrupulous grain merchants (Liv. 38.35.5).

41. Vanderbroeck, *Popular Leadership*, 95, rightly observes that *frumentationes* were valuable to *tabernarii* as well as the very poor (though one need not see matters solely in terms of patronage, as he tends to do). It is worth noting that, under the empire, membership in the *plebs frumentaria* became something of a distinction, a symbol of citizenship; no stigma was attached to this entitlement: Rickman, *The Corn Supply of Ancient Rome*, 182ff.

42. See chapter 1, section 3.

43. A nearly contemporary event serves as a healthy corrective: when Licinius Lucullus died in 57, there was a spontaneous demonstration by the *plebs* demanding that he receive his funeral on the Campus Martius, although Lucullus can hardly be described as a friend of the people (Plut. *Luc.* 43.2–3).

44. The position taken by Benner, *Die Politik des P. Clodius*, 59f., 71, stands in stark contrast to the one adopted here. *CIL* 6.14, Suppl. 1 (Ostia), 4707, indicates that the Porta Romana in Ostia was, at some point, renovated by a P. Clodius (or Claudius) Pulcher. Unfortunately, this Clodius/Claudius cannot be further identified owing to the very fragmentary condition of the inscription.

45. See the discussion in Rickman, *The Corn Supply of Ancient Rome*, 172. The annexation of Cyprus is examined below. Special coinage in 58: M. H. Crawford, *Roman Republican Coinage*, 1:446f.; M. Scaurus and P. Hypsaeus minted coins *ex s.c.*, indicating a separate issue (2:606ff.), the purpose of which is not specified. But Clodius's *lex frumentaria* represented the major (and unforeseen) expense of the year. There was little incentive for the aediles to advertise Clodius's coup. Rome minted coins in order to cover its expenses, not to regulate the economy; see M. H. Crawford, "Money and Exchange," 40.

46. See Rickman, *The Corn Supply of Ancient Rome*, 170f. Most recently on the statistics for the *frumentationes* of the late republic: Pelling, "Rowland and Cullens on Corn-Doles." All calculations are a fairly risky business, however, owing to the high degree of stylization in the Romans' reporting of figures: Scheidel, "Finances, Figures and Fiction."

47. Flambard, "Clodius, les collèges, la plèbe et les esclaves," 145ff., followed by Nicolet, "La *Lex Gabinia-Calpurnia*," 282ff. Cic. *Dom.* 25 is accepted as an accurate account of Cloelius's (formal) responsibilities by Schneider, *Wirtschaft und Politik*, 381f., 388; Rickman, *The Corn Supply of Ancient Rome*, 52ff., 173; Nicolet, *World of the Citizen*, 194; Virlouvet, *Famines et émeutes*, 15, 44f.; Benner, *Die Politik des P. Clodius*, 60, 100; Garnsey, *Famine and Food Supply*, 216.

48. PHI CD Rom 5.3 (Latin Texts; Bible Versions), compilation 1991, the Packard Humanities Institute, Los Altos, California.

49. Schol. Bob. 132 (St). See *TLL* 2:113f. Asconius was writing his commentaries ca. A.D. 54–57: Marshall, *A Historical Commentary on Asconius*, 28ff. On the *Schol. Bob.*, see Badian, "Marius' Villas."

50. See Seager, *Pompey*, 111f., for a brief narrative and sources. This incident is discussed more fully in chapter 7, section 2.

51. Senatorial derogation of scribes, despite their importance and influence: Pur-

cell, "The Apparitores," 132, 136. Admittedly Pompey's commission included a grant of *imperium*, but that was not the sole stimulus to criticism.

52. Compare the experience of Gaius Gracchus: Plut. *G. Gracch.* 6.3.

53. Clodius's dependency on Cloelius: *Dom.* 25, 47. For the general criticism of excessive reliance on subordinates, cf. Cic. *Q.F.* 1.1.17; *Verr.* 2.187. There existed a tradition of Claudian dependence on scribes: Ranouil, *Recherches sur le patriciat*, 168f. On Cicero's frequent and misleading abuse of Cloelius (often accepted at face value by modern scholars), see Tatum, "Publius Clodius Pulcher and Tarracina," 301ff.

54. Not until the empire would the Roman state become efficiently involved in the provisioning of the city: Garnsey, *Famine and Food Supply*, 218ff., esp. 231ff. Certainly the difficulties confronted by Pompey in 57 and subsequently discourage the conclusion that any significant state mechanisms were in place.

55. Nicolet et al., *Insula Sacra*, esp. 96ff., essentially repeated at Nicolet, "La *Lex Gabinia-Calpurnia*," 282ff. See also Nicolet, Moreau, Ferrary, and Crawford, "Lex Gabinia Calpurnia de insula Delo."

56. Rickman, *The Corn Supply of Ancient Rome*, 185ff.

57. Suet. *Iul.* 41.3; Plut. *Caes.* 55.3; Dio 43.21.4.

58. Livy 30.26.5–6 (*vicatim*); cf. Livy 31.4.6 (dispensement at Ludi Romani), 31.50.1, 33.42.8, for other distributions by aediles. Nicolet, *World of the Citizen*, 198, suspects that distribution by district constituted the normal practice.

59. Rickman, *The Corn Supply of Ancient Rome*, 174f., though Rickman does not recognize the Clodian practice advanced here.

60. Lintott, "P. Clodius Pulcher," 163; Flambard, "Clodius, les collèges, la plèbe et les esclaves," 148f. See also Nicolet, *World of the Citizen*, 195; Nippel, *Aufruhr und Polizei*, 111; Benner, *Die Politik des P. Clodius*, 70.

The involvement of *collegia* in the organization of the city's water supply has long been suspected; see Crook, "Lex 'Rivalicia,'" 48ff., for a review of the evidence, scholarship, and problems. So many cobweb claims leave scant room for certitude, but there is something attractive in Crook's own "fanciful thought" that it was Ap. Claudius who, in constructing his aqueduct, made some effort to integrate *collegia* into Rome's new water organization. If so, there would have existed a powerful family *exemplum* to instruct and to legitimate Clodius's exploitation of *collegia* in grain distributions.

61. Cic. *Dom.* 13, 89; see Benner, *Die Politik des P. Clodius*, 162f.

62. Dio 39.24.1; cf. Dion. Hal. *Ant. Rom.* 4.24.5; Suet. *Aug.* 42.2. That the scale of the these emancipations has been overstated is the view of Hopkins, *Conquerors and Slaves*, 128.

63. Sall. *Cat.* 37.4–7; Varro *R.R.* 2.3; App. *B. Civ.* 2.120; Suet. *Aug.* 42.3.

64. Sources: Cic. *Red. Sen.* 11; *Sest.* 33, 56; *Har. Resp.* 58; *Vat.* 18ff.; *Prov. Cons.* 45f.; *Pis.* 9f.; Asc. 8 (C); Dio 38.13.6. That Asconius and Dio do not constitute sources that are incontestably independent of Cicero is recognized by T. N. Mitchell, "The *Leges Clodiae*," 172 (an important departure from previous scholarship). That we have to do with a single Clodian law is indicated by *Sest.* 33, 56.

65. Mentioned only at Cic. *Sest.* 33 and *Prov. Cons.* 46.

66. The bibliography is daunting. Important are Valeton, "De iure obnuntiandi," (fundamental for the study of *obnuntiatio*); Sumner, "Lex Aelia, Lex Fufia"; Astin,

"Leges Aelia et Fufia"; Weinrib, "*Obnuntiatio*: Two Problems." Sumner's remains the most thorough examination of the two laws.

67. Cic. *Pis.* 10. See the discussions of Sumner, "Lex Aelia, Lex Fufia," 344ff., and Astin, "Leges Aelia et Fufia," 432ff. There is in my view much to recommend Sumner's suggestion that these laws be dated circa 132. Cf. Badian, "E.H.L.N.R.," for another (possible) attempt to prevent a repetition of the excesses of Gracchus's tribunate.

68. Schol. Bob. 148 (St). See Michels, *The Calendar of the Roman Republic*, 94ff., and the excellent treatment by Weinrib, "*Obnuntiatio*: Two Problems," 416ff. Astin, "Leges Aelia et Fufia," 438 n. 2, is right to observe that no source indicates that *promulgation* (as distinct from the carrying) of legislation was prohibited during this period.

69. Asc. 8 (C): "obnuntiatio enim qua perniciosis legibus resistebatur, quam Aelia lex confirmaverat." Cf. Cic. *Red. Sen.* 11; *Har. Resp.* 58; *Vat.* 18ff.; *Pis.* 9; *Att.* 2.9.1. The context of our sources for the *Leges Aelia et Fufia*: Astin, "Leges Aelia et Fufia," 423; Weinrib, "*Obnuntiatio*: Two Problems," 403.

70. Mommsen, *Römisches Staatsrecht*, 3:372f.; Weinrib, "*Obnuntiatio*: Two Problems," 416ff.

71. As Sumner judiciously observes ("Lex Aelia, Lex Fufia," 351), we cannot be sure that Clodius's law prescribed exactly this modification, but it must have contained a provision along these lines. Suspension of the *lex Fufia*: Dio 36.39.1; Cic. *Att.* 1.16.13. The prosecution of Cato: Sumner, "Lex Aelia, Lex Fufia," 338f.

72. Various explanations for the (presumably traditional) prohibition embodied in the *lex Fufia* have been proposed: see Astin, "Leges Aelia et Fufia," 437ff., and Weinrib, "*Obnuntiatio*: Two Problems," 416ff. The *lex Fufia* as a response to Ti. Gracchus: Sumner, "Lex Aelia, Lex Fufia," 349f., followed by Weinrib, "*Obnuntiatio*: Two Problems," 415. In view of the delays that plagued elections in 59 (on which see Linderski, *Roman Questions*, 72ff.), Clodius's reform may have carried more moment in 58 than is readily perceptible.

73. Linderski, "The Augural Law," is the best examination of Roman augury.

74. On *vitium*, see ibid., 2162ff., esp. 2163f. (magistrates) and 2165ff. (legislation).

75. See the explication of this construction by Nisbet, *M. Tulli Ciceronis De Domo Sua*, 202f.

76. On *obnuntiatio*, see Valeton, "De iure obnuntiandi," and de Libero, *Obstruktion*, 56ff.

77. According to Zonaras 7.19.2, *obnuntiatio* was extended to tribunes in 449, but see Weinrib, "*Obnuntiatio*: Two Problems," 410ff., for a likelier reconstruction of the circumstances leading to the establishment of tribunician *obnuntiatio*.

78. Disagreement exists over whether *obnuntiatio* was possible at electoral assemblies before 58. Most modern scholars, by my count, do not detect a distinction before 58, but one who does and who cannot be overlooked is Linderski, *Roman Questions*, 74 (with further bibliography).

79. Consuls against colleagues: e.g., Suet. *Iul.* 20.1; Gell. 13.15 implies that lower magistrates had similar rights; see Valeton, "De iure obnuntiandi," 87, 233, as well as the state of affairs desired by Cicero in *Leg.* 3.10, 3.27; tribunes against colleagues: Zonaras 7.19.1–2; tribunes against consuls: Cic. *Sest.* 79, 83; *Phil.* 2.99; *Q.F.* 3.3.2; *Att.* 4.3.3f., 4.17.4; tribunes against censors: *Att.* 4.9.1; Dio 37.8.4 (tribunes delay the *lectio senatus*, presumably by *obnuntiatio*).

80. Weinrib, "*Obnuntiatio*: Two Problems," 395ff.

81. Ibid., 402 n. 32, rightly rejects other evidence that has been brought to bear on this problem. Burckhardt, *Politische Strategien der Optimaten*, 183ff., advances new arguments against Weinrib's thesis.

82. Peterson, *M. Tulli Ciceronis Orationes*; Cousin, *Cicéron, Discours*; Maslowski, *M. Tullius Cicero scripta quae manserunt omnia*. Cf. Weinstock, "Clodius and the *Lex Aelia Fufia*," 219. One might, of course, argue for *tr. (pl.)*.

83. The subtle interpretation of *Sest.* 78 advanced by Sumner, "Lex Aelia, Lex Fufia," 353f.—though very clever—is unpersuasive. Taylor, "Forerunners of the Gracchi," 22ff., suggested that the *leges Aelia et Fufia* gave magistrates the right to obnuntiate against tribunes, though they had not before possessed the right.

84. Tatum, "Cicero's Opposition," 189.

85. Weinrib, "*Obnuntiatio*: Two Problems," 397ff. The role of tribunes in safeguarding the politics of the senatorial establishment: Bleicken, *Das Volkstribunat*; Thommen, *Das Volkstribunat*. Burckhardt, *Politische Strategien der Optimaten*, 188ff., examines the potential of *obnuntiatio* as an optimate mainstay but concludes that Cicero's claims (ergo Dio's claims) are exaggerated.

86. The near deposition of L. Trebellius in 67 (Asc. 72 [C]; Dio 38.30.1f.) is adduced as evidence for the vulnerability of tribunician intercession, but see Thommen, *Das Volkstribunat*, 216ff., and Badian, "The Case of the Cowardly Tribune," 78ff. It is important to bear in mind that both intercession and *obnuntiatio* were regarded as serious actions, not to be undertaken lightly, and that the increasing frequency with which both were employed in the late republic was symptomatic of the polarization of politics.

87. Bibulus's *obnuntiatio*: Suet. *Iul.* 20.1; Dio 38.6.1–5. According to Dio, Bibulus attempted to block Caesar's legislation by declaring a ἱερομηνία (*indictio feriarum*), which has been taken literally by Gelzer, *Caesar*, 74f., and Shackleton Bailey, *Cicero's Letters to Atticus*, 1:407. However, it is more likely (especially in view of Suetonius's explicit statements) that Dio has suffered a confusion; see Linderski, *Roman Questions*, 73; Lintott, *Violence*, 144. Bibulus informed his colleague of his action διὰ τῶν ὑπηρετῶν. The tribunes who supported Bibulus were Q. Ancharius, Cn. Domitius Calvinus, and C. Fannius; sources in *MRR* 2:189f.

88. Long recognized if not long appreciated: see Valeton, "De iure obnuntiandi," 82f., 101f.; Linderski, *Roman Questions*, 73f. The same conclusion was arrived at independently by Lintott, *Violence*, 144f.

89. Valeton, "De iure obnuntiandi," 103.

90. See Schol. Bob. 146 (St); Dio 38.13.5 (both admittedly likely to be derived ultimately from Cicero). On the nature of the *libri reconditi* mentioned by Cicero, see Linderski, *Roman Questions*, 496ff.

91. Valeton, "De iure obnuntiandi," 243; Astin, "Leges Aelia et Fufia," 431.

92. Weinstock, "Clodius and the *Lex Aelia Fufia*."

93. Balsdon, "Roman History, 58–56 B.C.: Three Ciceronian Problems," 15f., followed by Astin, "Leges Aelia et Fufia," 442.

94. Greenidge, "The Repeal of the *Lex Aelia Fufia*."

95. Valeton, "De iure obnuntiandi," 248ff.; Sumner, "Lex Aelia, Lex Fufia," 352.

96. McDonald, "Clodius and the *Lex Aelia Fufia*."

97. Cic. *Phil.* 1.25: "Quaero autem quid sit cur aut ego aut quisquam vestrum, patres conscripti, bonis tribunis plebis leges malas metuat. Paratos habemus qui

intercedant; paratos qui rem publicam religione defendant: vacui metu esse debemus." It is irrelevant that in 44 Nonius Asprenas did not resort to *obnuntiatio* in his attempt to block the passage of a bill granting Dolabella the province Syria (App. *B. Civ.* 3.7): his method was the *obnuntiatio* of *auspicia oblativa* (in this instance, *auspicia ementita*), which was rejected by the presiding magistrate, M. Antony. In view of what we learn from Cic. *Phil.* 1.31 and 2.83, Asprenas can hardly be faulted for having expected his strategem to succeed with Antony as the presiding official.

98. ἐσήνεγκε μηδένα τῶν ἀρχόντων ἐν ταῖς ἡμέραις ἐν αἷς ψηφίσασθαί τι τὸν δῆμον ἀναγκαῖον εἴη, τὰ ἐκ τοῦ οὐρανοῦ γιγνόμενα παρατηρεῖν (Dio 38.13.6).

99. Meier, *Res Publica Amissa*, 192 n. 437; T. N. Mitchell, "The *Leges Clodiae*," 175.

100. T. N. Mitchell, "The *Leges Clodiae*," 175f.; Tatum, "Cicero's Opposition," 189f. Cf. the sensible appraisal offered by Gruen, "Safeguards remained and abuse was checked. By voting the bill the Roman people had yielded not to demagoguery but to sound administrative reform" (*Last Generation*, 257). It should be clear by now that not all of Clodius's legislation can be pigeonholed as *popularis* or opportunistic; one clear example of this is his *lex de scribis quaestoriis*, which attempted, along the lines of Cato's earlier efforts, to curb the abuses of quaestorian scribes (see the appendix, section 3).

101. Sources: Cic. *Sest.* 55; *Pis.* 9f.; Asc. 7f. (C); Dio 38.13, 40.47; Schol. Bob. 132 (St). For a more detailed examination of this law (with references to earlier treatments), see Tatum, "The *Lex Clodia de Censoria Notione.*"

102. See Astin, "Regimen Morum," esp. 31ff., on censorial sanctions, several of which remain controversial.

103. One example is the defense of C. Gracchus before the censors; see Badian, "The Silence of Norbanus," 160ff.; for more examples, see Suolahti, *The Roman Censors*, 50.

104. Sources: *MRR* 1:158f. The controversies attending this law do not affect our purposes here, since the relevant point, the assignment of the *lectio* to the censors, is well established.

105. Tatum, "The *Lex Clodia de Censoria Notione,*" 37ff. (with detailed arguments).

106. Asc. 8(C): "ne quem censores in senatu legendo praeterirent, neve qua ignomina afficerent, nisi qui apud eos accusatus et utriusque censoris sententia damnatus esset." See also Dio 38.13, 40.57; Schol. Bob. 132 (St).

107. In fact, *iudicia* necessitated by Clodius's law were held in 54; see Cic. *Att.* 4.16.8 (adopting the certain correction of the corrupt phrase *lege Coctia*).

Another, though unlikely, innovation of Clodius's law has been suggested. Mommsen, *Römisches Staatsrecht*, 2:386f., believed that censors lacked initiative in conducting the *regimen morum*. Consequently, he maintained, when Clodius's law revised the *lectio senatus*, that limitation was imposed on that procedure as well. But, in fact, censors did not lack the right of initiative in exercising the *cura morum* within the census proper (Tatum, "The *Lex Clodia de Censoria Notione,*" 35f.). However, one just might construe the phrase *apud eos* in Asconius's explanation of the *lex Clodia* (Asc. 8 [C]), cited above) so closely with *accusatus* that one finds in the text the implication that a third party was required to lay an accusation. That would be something of a stretch, however, and it seems more likely that the phrase, coming as it does at the clause's beginning, is meant to stress the active participation required of both censors (a point emphasized in Dio's language as well: Dio 38.13).

108. Astin, "Censorships in the Late Republic," 181; Develin, "Sulla and the Senate."

109. Sources: *MRR* 2:126f.

110. Dio 37.8.4.

111. Dio 37.46.4.

112. The Sullan constitution, by rendering admission to the senate virtually auto-matic upon reaching the quaestorship, may actually have induced some senators to view their positions as entitlements; since the censors no longer granted the rank of senator, they should not have the power to take it away.

113. See Tatum, "The *Lex Clodia de Censoria Notione*," 39f., for a review (and criticism) of such views.

114. Crassus and *pedarii*: Ward, *Marcus Crassus*, 76ff.

115. The suggestion by Benner, *Die Politik des P. Clodius*, 51f., and T. N. Mitchell, *Cicero*, 129, that the law was an attempt to safeguard the senate's *populares* is too restrictive and in any case relies on a (false) assumption that there obtained some sort of party unity among *populares*.

116. Cic. *Sest.* 55; *Pis.* 9f.; cf. *Dom.* 130; *Har. Resp.* 58; *Prov. Cons.* 46. See Astin, "Cicero and the Censorship," for a discussion of Cicero's more philosophical ex-postulations on the role of the censors in Roman society.

117. Recognized by Dio 40.57.1–3.

118. Cic. *Att.* 4.16.8, 4.9.1; see Astin, "Censorships in the Late Republic," 188.

119. Dio 40.57.1–3. For a more detailed discussion of the law's failure, see Tatum, "The *Lex Clodia de Censoria Notione*," 42ff.

120. Dio 38.12.8; cf. Plut. *Cic.* 30.

121. Cic. *Sest.* 34, 55; *Red. Sen.* 33; *Dom.* 54; *Pis.* 8; Asc. 7(C). Since Clodius's legislation came before the people sometime between 3 and 7 January (*Pis.* 9; see Michels, *The Calander of the Roman Republic*, 205), the celebration of the *ludi* would be a very fresh memory indeed.

122. Cic. *Pis.* 8; Asc. 7(C).

123. Cic. *Pis.* 8.

124. On Ninnius, see Wiseman, *Roman Studies*, 12, 20, 373 (with further refer-ences). Ninnius's opposition (with Cicero) to Clodius's legislation is infrequently discussed; for more detail, see Tatum, "Cicero's Opposition."

125. Dio 38.14.1.

126. Asc. 7(C).

127. Dio 38.14.1–2.

128. Long recognized: Drumann and Groebe, *Geschichte Roms*, 2:203 (though it is there concluded that Cicero and Ninnius could not have opposed *any* of Clodius's laws).

129. A connection made already by Meyer, *Caesars Monarchie*, 97 n. 1, and Dru-mann and Groebe, *Geschichte Roms*, 2:208 n. 6.

130. Dio's attitude toward Cicero: Millar, *A Study in Cassius Dio*, 46ff.

131. Tatum, "Cicero's Opposition," 192f.

132. Suet. *Iul.* 23.

133. *Lex Memmia*: Val. Max. 3.7.9; Suet. *Iul.* 23.

134. A point made explicitly by Badian, "The Attempt to Try Caesar," 147.

135. See ibid. It is unnecessary to rehearse all of Badian's arguments here. Let it suffice to observe that his view is consistent with Suetonius's language and with the context of *Iul.* 23, which covers the period from the agitation of Memmius and Domitius at the start of 58 to Domitius's candidature in 56 (the opening of *Iul.* 24);

furthermore, Badian's reconstruction fits better our prosopographical evidence. The attempt to try Caesar is dated to 58 by Gruen, "Some Criminal Trials," 62ff., and T. N. Mitchell, *Cicero*, 130.

136. The incident is excluded from the valuable catalog of collective behavior in Vanderbroeck, *Popular Leadership*, 218ff.

137. Cic. *Vat.* 33f.; *Sest.* 135; Schol. Bob. 140, 150 (St). See Gruen, "Some Criminal Trials," 65ff.; Badian, "The Attempt to Try Caesar," 154ff.

138. Badian, "The Attempt to Try Caesar," 157.

139. Ibid., 164 n. 34.

140. Schol Bob. 150 (St).

141. Vatinius's failure: Broughton, *Candidates Defeated in Roman Elections*, 43.

142. Hence it is somewhat misleading for Gruen to write: "Clodius intervened—in characteristic fashion" ("Some Criminal Trials," 66).

143. Lintott, *Violence*, 76; Treggiari, *Roman Freedmen*, 173ff.; Nowak, *Der Einsatz Privater Garden*, 112, 114f.; Benner, *Die Politik des P. Clodius*, 68ff.; Nippel, *Aufruhr und Polizei*, 113f.

144. Yavetz, *Plebs and Princeps*, 38ff. See Val. Max. 3.5.3 (on Clodius's possession of *favor plebis*).

145. It hardly seems necessary to explain Clodius's familiarity with the workings of the *collegia* in terms of his youthful experiences in electioneering, which were, as we have seen, far from unique, *pace* Lintott, "P. Clodius Pulcher," 159; Benner, *Die Politik des P. Clodius*, 68.

146. The importance of a benefactor's social superiority: Saller, *Personal Patronage*, 38.

147. Cic. *Att.* 4.3.3; *Q.F.* 2.3.4; *Red. Sen.* 18; *Dom.* 14; *Sest.* 18.27.38; *Vat.* 40.

148. *Att.* 4.3.3.

149. Asc. 32, 33, 37, 38, 40 (C); cf. Cic. *Har. Resp.* 22.

150. Cic. *Sest.* 94.

151. Cic. *Red. Sen.* 32; *Sest.* 85.

152. See the detailed analysis of Cicero's description of Clodius's following by Favory, "Classes dangereuses et crise de l'État." A somewhat narrower (and less thoughtful) study of Cicero's terminology, with particular regard to Clodius's use of slaves, is Annequin and Létroublon, "Une approche des discours de Cicéron."

153. Cic. *Red. Quir.* 13; *Pis.* 11.

154. Cic. *Dom.* 61.

155. Cic. *Pis.* 23; cf. *Sest.* 42; *Pis.* 16; *Planc.* 35.

156. Favory, "Classes dangereuses et crise de l'État," 172.

157. Flambard, "Clodius, les collèges, la plèbe et les esclaves," 122ff.; Nippel, *Aufruhr und Polizei*, 113f.; Vanderbroeck, *Popular Leadership*, 87. Benner, *Die Politik des P. Clodius*, 78ff., underestimates the importance of *tabernarii* in Clodius's following.

158. See Cic. *Dom.* 54; cf. *Dom.* 89.

159. Benner, *Die Politik des P. Clodius*, 78ff., is right to recognize the significance of the *nova collegia* enrolled by Clodius, as does Nowak, *Der Einsatz Privater Garden*, 112, but they tend to exaggerate their significance over that of craftsmen and shopkeepers. In general, Clodius's following at a demonstration will have been a mingling of different lower-class groups, the precise admixture varying from occasion to occasion. But the role played by *tabernarii* cannot be ignored.

160. Clodius did not ordinarily rely on gladiators: Nowak, *Der Einsatz Privater Garden*, 118f.; Benner, *Die Politik des P. Clodius*, 81 (contra: Lintott, *Violence*, 77).

161. Weapons illegal: Aigner, "Zur Wichtigkeit der Waffenbeschaffung in der späten römischen Republik." Clodius's slave created a sensation on 11 August 58 when he dropped a dagger near a meeting of the senate (Cic. *Dom.* 129; *Sest.* 69; *Har. Resp.* 49; *Pis.* 28; *Mil.* 18; Asc. 46 [C]; Plut. *Pomp.* 49). Cf. Nippel, *Public Order in Ancient Rome*, 16ff.

162. Nippel, *Aufruhr und Polizei*, 242; Vanderbroeck, *Popular Leadership*, 123f.

163. Cic. *Att.* 1.14.5; *Red. Sen.* 32; *Dom.* 13, 58, 61, 72, 75, 92; *Sest.* 28, 42, 95; *Pis.* 11, 15f., 23; *Planc.* 35; *Mil.* 37.

164. Clodius during the Bona Dea scandal: Tatum, "Cicero and the *Bona Dea* Trial," 206ff. (with literature there cited). Cicero's characterization of Clodius was largely a reaction to the tactics of Clodius's supporters. The common outline for *popularis* figures: Vanderbroeck, *Popular Leadership*, 178ff.

165. A salubriously skeptical (even if not convincing in most respects) examination of the coherence of the Catilinarian conspiracy: Seager, "Iusta Catilinae." Trials stemming from the Catilinarian conspiracy: Gruen, *Last Generation*, 282ff.

166. Cic. *Mil.* 26 ("servos agrestes et barbaros") clearly refers to Clodius's personal retinue, as does *Mil.* 28 ("Graeci comites").

167. Clodius and Etruria: Cic. *Mil.* 26, 50ff., 74, 87, 98; *Phil.* 12.23; see Lewis, "Inscriptions of Amiternum," 36f. Caesar and Etruria: Rawson, *Roman Culture and Society*, 289ff.

168. Lewis, "Inscriptions of Amiternum," 31ff.—though some of the connections drawn by Lewis are (as he admits) tenuous.

169. L. Sergius: Cic. *Dom.* 13; Lewis, "Inscriptions of Amiternum," 37ff.

170. Cic. *Cael.* 14.

171. So rightly Lintott, "P. Clodius Pulcher," 169.

172. Favory, "Classes dangereuses et crise de l'État"; May, *Trials of Character*, 75f., 134ff., 153ff.; Havas, "Schemata und Wahrheit." Clodius and Antony were not the only victims of this characterization: Gabinius is depicted in Catilinarian terms at Cic. *Red. Sen.* 10, 12; *Dom.* 62; *Planc.* 87; *Pis.* 20; as for Piso, see Kubiak, "Piso's Madness."

173. Vanderbroeck, *Popular Leadership*, 142ff.

174. Yavetz, *Plebs and Princeps*, 39.

175. Lack of police: Nippel, "Policing Rome," and *Public Order in Ancient Rome*, 1ff. *Selbsthilfe*: Lintott, *Violence*, 22ff. Rural violence common: Frier, "Urban Praetors and Rural Violence." The Roman ideology of violence: Lintott, *Violence*, 6ff. (esp. 52ff.), dealing with the morality of violence; Nippel, *Public Order in Ancient Rome*, 47ff.

176. Lintott, *Violence*, 61ff., surveys Cicero's varying judgments.

177. See Nippel, *Public Order in Ancient Rome*, 73f. (with further citations). Lentidius: *Dom.* 89; *Sest.* 80. Lollius: *Dom.* 13f., 21, 89. Plaguleius: Cic. *Dom.* 89; *Att.* 10.8.3; Asc. 55(C). Sergius: *Dom.* 13, 89. In *Dom.* 13, Lollius and Sergius are to be understood as staunch defenders of Clodius, not as his hired bodyguards.

178. Firmidius: Cic. *Sest.* 112.

179. Pomponius: Asc. 31(C). Fidulius: Cic. *Dom.* 79f., 80, 82.

180. Brunt, *Fall of the Roman Republic*, 382ff. (esp. 431ff.).

181. Veyne, "La folklore à Rome."

182. So Nippel, "Policing Rome," 128f.

183. So Benner, *Die Politik des P. Clodius*, 71, 111ff.

184. A commonly expressed idea: Lintott, *Violence*, 82; Benner, *Die Politik des P. Clodius*, 58ff.

Chapter 6

1. Triumvirs impressed: Cic. *Prov. Cons.* 42; *Sest.* 39; *Pis.* 79.

2. The law was hardly likely, on its face, to draw support from Pompey, as T. N. Mitchell, *Cicero*, 133, supposes; cf. Seager, *Pompey*, 105f., who nonetheless does not sufficiently distinguish Clodius's two measures concerning Cyprus, the one annexing the kingdom and the other assigning the job to Cato (see below). Cicero, who is our principal source, tends to lump the two measures together: *Dom.* 129; *Har. Resp.* 28f.; 58; *Sest.* 56f.; *Mil.* 73.

3. Dio 38.30.5; App. *B. Civ.* 2.23.

4. Economic motive: Festus *Brev.* 13.1; Amm. Marc. 14.8.15.

5. Marcellus's mission: Badian, "M. Porcius Cato," 119f., shows that Clodius was aware of this action.

6. Cicero's daughter was married to C. Piso, a kinsman of the consul (*Pis.* 12).

7. Older accounts tend to view Clodius and the consuls strictly as instruments of the dynasts in this matter: Drumann and Groebe, *Geschichte Roms*, 2:101; Pocock, "Publius Clodius and the Acts of Caesar," 61; Marsh, "The Policy of Clodius," 32f. More recent accounts add nuance, but the basic framework remains the same: Seager, *Pompey*, 104; T. N. Mitchell, *Cicero*, 129ff. On the other hand, Clodius's "independence" in 58, rightly stressed by Gruen, "P. Clodius," Lintott, "P. Clodius Pulcher," and Rundell, "Cicero and Clodius," must not be taken to mean that the tribune was immune to the requirements of reciprocity that characterize all Roman politics.

8. Seager, *Pompey*, 104, adduces other reasons for Gabinius's opposition to Cicero in 58. T. N. Mitchell, *Cicero*, 131 n. 98, oddly discounts the attractiveness to the consuls of this measure, insisting instead on triumviral pressure for the consuls and tribune to intimidate Cicero.

9. Cic. *Sest.* 39–42 represents Cicero's most expansive version of the dynasts' attitudes. Ward, *Marcus Crassus*, 243f., makes a good case for Crassus's trying to remain on decent terms with Cicero while not offending Clodius. The evidence is exiguous, however. Cicero later claimed that Crassus referred his case to the authority of the consuls (*Sest.* 41).

10. Cic. *Red. Sen.* 32f.; *Dom.* 131; *Har. Resp.* 47; *Sest.* 39ff., 52; *Prov. Cons.* 18, 43; *Att.* 10.4.1, 3; Plut. *Cic.* 30.1–4; *Caes.* 14.9; Dio 38.17.1–2. Cicero remained convinced that Caesar wanted him exiled (*Att.* 3.15.3, 3.18.1, 10.4.1), but that is no proof that he in fact wished it so. Nor is Caesar's attitude toward Cicero once the orator was in exile a reliable guide to his intentions before Cicero retired from Rome.

11. Cic. *Sest.* 39–42, which stresses Pompey's continued fear of assassination as a factor (see also *Sest.* 69; *Har. Resp.* 49; *Mil.* 18, 65ff.; Asc. 36, 50 [C]) in his defection; cf. *Dom.* 28; *Pis.* 76; *Att.* 3.15.4; *Q.F.* 1.4.4. See the discussion in Seager, *Pompey*, 104f.

12. Plut. *Cic.* 31; Dio 38.17.3.

13. Cic. *Pis.* 79.

14. *Lex de provinciis*: Cic. *Dom.* 129; *Har. Resp.* 28f., 58; *Sest.* 56f.; *Mil.* 73. *Lex de capite civis Romani*: Cic. *Att.* 3.15.5; *Sest.* 25, 53f.; *Pis.* 16, 30; *Dom.* 50, 54, 62, 110; Vell.

2.45.1; Asc. 46 (C); Plut. *Cic.* 30f.; *Cat. Min.* 35.1; *Pomp.* 48.6; *Caes.* 14.9; App. *B. Civ.* 2.15; Dio 38.14– 17; Liv. *Per.* 103; Schol. Bob. 130, 147, 168 (St).

15. Wirszubski, *Libertas as a Political Idea*, 24ff.

16. Dio 38.14.5, 38.17.2.

17. As tribune, Metellus Nepos had attacked Cicero for his responsibility in the execution of *cives indemnati* (sources in *MRR* 2:174). From the start, then, criticism of Cicero's action was configured along the opposition of *provocatio* to magisterial abuse and *senatus auctoritas*, a line of interpretation that ignored other relevant aspects of Roman justice; see Nippel, *Public Order in Ancient Rome*, 60ff. Generally on *provocatio*, see Lintott, "Provocatio."

18. Cic. *Sest.* 39ff. See also *Red. Sen.* 32; *Har. Resp.* 47; *Prov. Cons.* 42; *Pis.* 70.

19. Pompey: Dio 38.16.6. Caesar: Dio 38.17.1–2. Plut. *Cic.* 30.4 represents Caesar's support for the law as unequivocal, but Dio's version rings truer.

20. Cic. *Red. Sen.* 32; *Dom.* 5, 131; *Har. Resp.* 47; *Sest.* 40ff.; 52; Suet. *Iul.* 23.1; Schol. Bob. 130, 146 (St); Plut. *Caes.* 14.

21. Cic. *Sest.* 39.

22. Support for Cicero: Cic. *Att.* 3.15.5; *Red. Sen.* 12; *Red. Quir.* 8, 13; *Sest.* 25f.; *Pis.* 77; *Planc.* 87; Plut. *Cic.* 30.5–31.1; Dio 38.16.2–6; App. *B. Civ.* 2.15.

23. Lucullus, Torquatus, and Lentulus lobbied Pompey to intervene on Cicero's behalf; he promised to follow the leadership of the consuls: Cic. *Sest.* 41; *Pis.* 77; Plut. *Cic.* 31; Schol. Bob. 122 (St).

24. Cic. *Red. Sen.* 12ff., 32; *Red. Quir.* 13; *Dom.* 91, 96, 131; *Sest.* 25ff.; *Pis.* 11, 13f., 17ff.; *Planc.* 86f.; Plut. *Cic.* 31.1; Dio 38.16.5–6.

25. Cic. *Sest.* 27; *Mil.* 37 (including the accusation that the senator C. Vibienius was manhandled so roughly by Clodius's thugs that he ultimately died from his injuries); Plut. *Cic.* 30.5.

26. Dio 38.16.5.

27. Sources: Cic. *Dom.* 129; *Har. Resp.* 28f., 58; *Sest.* 56f.; *Mil.* 73. Interpretation: Oost, "Cato Uticensis and the Annexation of Cyprus"; Balsdon, "Roman History, 65–50 B.C.: Five Problems," 135; Badian, "M. Porcius Cato," 110ff.; Rundell, "Cicero and Clodius," 301ff.; Tatum, "Cicero's Opposition," 193.

28. It is unlikely that Clodius saw in Cato a rival for popular support, as proposed by Benner, *Die Politik des P. Clodius*, 61f.; Clodius's *lex frumentaria* had easily and immediately eclipsed Cato's.

29. Rundell, "Cicero and Clodius," 315f.

30. Whether Caesar actually congratulated Clodius on this shrewd device (so Cic. *Dom.* 22) seems doubtful.

31. Compare the story of Ap. Claudius the Decemvir's vain appeal to the tribunes in Liv. 3.56.6.

32. Cic. *Red. Sen.* 17; *Red. Quir.* 13; *Sest.* 20, 42; *Pis.* 11ff.; *Q.F.* 1.3.10, 1.4.4, 1.12.16; *Att.* 3.7.2, 3.9.2, 3.15.2ff.; *Fam.* 1.19.13f.; Plut. *Cic.* 31.3–4; *Cat. Min.* 35.1; Dio 38.4. See T. N. Mitchell, *Cicero*, 137f.

33. Coincidence of legislation and departure: Cic. *Sest.* 53. The exact date has not been satisfactorily determined; see Shackleton Bailey, *Cicero's Letters to Atticus*, 2:227ff.

34. Cic. *Sest.* 53f.; *Red. Sen.* 18; *Dom.* 59, 62; *Pis.* 26; *Att.* 4.2.5, 7; *Fam.* 14.2.2; Asc. 10 (C); Plut. *Cic.* 33.1; Dio 38.17.6.

35. T. N. Mitchell, *Cicero*, 142f., collects the evidence in support of such a verdict.

36. The best and most detailed treatment of this law is Moreau, "La lex Clodia sur le bannissement de Cicéron." See also Moreau, "Lex Clodia." Other relevant discussions include Nippel, *Aufruhr und Polizei*, 118f., and Tatum, "The *Lex Papiria de Dedicationibus*," 326f.

37. Modification: Cic. *Att.* 3.2, 3.4; cf. Moreau, "La lex Clodia sur le bannissement de Cicéron," 470. Latinity: Nisbet, *M. Tulli Ciceronis De Domo Sua*, 204f.

38. Details in Moreau, "La lex Clodia sur le bannissement de Cicéron," 465ff. It has been proposed that the *interdictio* prescribed by the law sufficed to indicate a loss of property; see Grasmück, *Exilium*, 94 n. 205; Fuhrmann, *RE* 23:2595; Nippel, *Aufruhr und Polizei*, 119. The passages adduced in support of this view (Liv. 25.4.9; Dion. Hal. 5.13.4) fail to prove anything, however, nor can the case be made by strict logic. In addition to Cicero's Palatine property, his villas at Tusculum and Formiae were seized (*Att.* 4.2.3ff.).

39. See Liv. 25.4.9, 26.3.12.

40. *Privilegium* (a law directed against an individual or in special favor of an individual, forbidden by the Twelve Tables; see Cic. *Leg.* 3.11, 44): Cic. *Dom.* 26, 43ff., 57f., 62. Virtual proscription: *Dom.* 44, 48, 107, 116.

41. *Lex Caecilia et Didia*: sources in *MRR* 2:4. Cicero's criticism: Cic. *Dom.* 53. Sources for *lex Licinia*: *Dom.* 51 (which is Cicero's complaint regarding the *lex Clodia*); *Leg. Agr.* 21.

42. For instance, Cicero's misleading deployment of the *lex Papiria de dedicationibus*, see Tatum, "The *Lex Papiria de Dedicationibus*."

43. So Greenidge, *The Legal Procedure of Cicero's Time*, 364. Cf. Clodius's supervision of the grain dole, discussed in chapter 5, section 3. As Moreau ("La lex Clodia sur le bannissement de Cicéron," 476) observes, however, confiscated property seems often to have fallen beneath the purview of the urban praetor and quaestors, though one should hesitate before elevating that pattern to an actual rule. Moreau's own suggestion, that the law specified a *societas* of buyers, seems overly ingenious.

44. Cic. *Dom.* 106; see Moreau, "La lex Clodia sur le bannissement de Cicéron," 478f.; Tatum, "The *Lex Papiria de Dedicationibus*," 326f.

45. The *crimen regni* in general: Nippel, *Aufruhr und Polizei*, 80ff. Leveled by Clodius against Cicero: *Att.* 1.16.10 (aftermath of the Bona Dea trial); *Dom.* 7 (*hostis Capitolinus*), 10, 75 (*crudelis tyrannus*); *Har. Resp.* 17; *Sest.* 109. The charge came against Cicero from other quarters as well; see Allen, "Cicero's House and Libertas"; Lenaghan, *A Commentary on Cicero's Oration De Haruspicum Responso*, 103ff. Clodius's claim that Cicero identified himself with Jupiter (*Dom.* 92), perhaps based on the orator's poetry, was part and parcel of his depiction of Cicero as a would-be *rex*; Weinstock, *Divus Julius*, 302ff. The discussion of *rex* and related terms in political invective by Erskine, "Hellenistic Monarchy and Roman Political Invective," while it usefully points out inconsistencies in the Romans' attitude toward monarchy, tends to be overly schematic and exaggerates the role of Caesar's dictatorship in the construction of Roman attitudes. See also Rawson, *Roman Culture and Society*, 169ff.

46. Cassius: sources in *MRR* 1:20. Maelius: sources in *MRR* 1:56. Manlius Capitolinus: Cic. *Dom.* 101; *Phil.* 2.87, 114; see Crawford, *Roman Republican Coinage*, 1:455f.

47. Cic. *Dom.* 101f. Full sources in *MRR* 1:520.

48. Lintott, *Violence*, 8f.; Nippel, *Aufruhr und Polizei*, 116f.

49. Cic. *Red. Sen.* 18 (Piso and Gabinius); *Dom.* 62 (Piso); *Pis.* 26 (Piso); *Dom.* 116 (Scato and the Claudii).

50. Saller, *Patriarchy, Property and Death*, 80ff.

51. Ibid., 89f. This equation was by no means confined to the empire: see Cic. *Mil.* 38; Orr, "Roman Domestic Religion."

52. *Imagines*: Mommsen, *Römisches Staatsrecht*, 1:442f., 492 n. 3; Flower, *Ancestor Masks and Aristocratic Power*. Trophies: Saller, *Patriarchy, Property and Death*, 90ff.; Wiseman, "*Conspicui Postes*."

53. *Aedificatio* was a vice: Cic. *Pis.* 48; *Leg.* 3.30; Varro *R.R.* 1.13.6; Nepos *Att.* 13.1; Columella 1.4.8; Pliny *Pan.* 51.1; Tac. *Ann.* 3.37. At the same time, the necessity of ostentatious building was recognized: Cic. *Off.* 1.138f.; Tac. *Ann.* 3.55. See Wallace-Hadrill, "The Social Structure of the Roman House," 44ff.; Wallace-Hadrill, *Houses and Society*, 4f. Cicero explicitly accuses Clodius of *aedificatio* in *Mil.* 53, 74 (where Clodius's ambitious plans for developing villas and gardens constitute the climax in the list of his crimes), 85.

54. Coarelli, "Architettura sacra"; Wiseman, "*Conspicui Postes*"; Wallace-Hadrill, *Houses and Society*, 10ff., 17ff. The social function of the *domus* is examined in Schneider, *Wirtschaft und Politik*, 178ff.; Clarke, *The Houses of Roman Italy*, 1ff. The significance of Roman villas: Leen, "Cicero and the Rhetoric of Art."

55. Plut. *Pomp.* 40.5.

56. Tamm, *Auditorium and Palatium*, 42f.

57. Wallace-Hadrill, "The Social Structure of the Roman House," 58ff.

58. Wiseman, "*Conspicui Postes*," 395f.

59. Coarelli, "Architettura sacra," esp. 200ff.

60. Ibid., 199f. Africanus and Jupiter: Livy 26.19.6; Val. Max. 8.15.1; Dio 16.57.39. Discussion of Pompey's house: Gros, "Trois temples"; Gros, *Aurea Templa*, 124ff.; Coarelli, "Il Campo Marzio," 816. Caesar's *fastigium*: Weinstock, *Divus Julius*, 276ff. Numismatic evidence is also relevant: see M. H. Crawford, *Roman Republican Coinage*, 1:445ff., for examples contemporary with Clodius.

61. Cic. *Off.* 1.138.

62. *MRR* 1:2.

63. Cic. *Fam.* 5.6.2; *Att.* 1.12.1f., 1.13.6; cf. Gell. 12.12.

64. Cic. *Att.* 1.16.10. For other aspects of the criticism of Cicero, see [Sall.] *In Cic.* 2ff.; Nippel, *Aufruhr und Polizei*, 116f. Cicero's house brought him criticism even in 56, after its restoration: Cic. *Att.* 4.5.1–2.

65. Nisbet, *M. Tulli Ciceronis De Domo Sua*, 206ff.; Allen, "The Location of Cicero's House"; Tamm, *Auditorium and Palatium*, 28ff.; Coarelli, *Il foro romano* (esp. 25f., for the ancient extent of the Palatium; p. 263 offers a helpful schematic plan to those of us whose capacity for grasping space is more visual than verbal); Carandini, "*Domus* e *insulae*"; Royo, "Le quartier républicain du Palatin"; Wiseman, "*Conspicui Postes*." All of these contain abundant bibliography.

66. Via Sacra: Coarelli, *Il foro romano II*, 290ff.

67. Tamm, *Auditorium and Palatium*, 28ff.; Royo, "Le quartier républicain du Palatin," 91ff.; Richardson, *A New Topographical Dictionary*, 111ff.

68. Carandini, "*Domus* e *insulae*," 264.

69. Cic. *Fam.* 5.6.2; Gell. 12.12.

70. Early Claudian presence on the Palatine: Liv. 3.49.5 (possibly). Claudian con-

nections with the Palatine temple to Magna Mater: Cic. *Har. Resp.* 11.24; Liv. 29.37.1–2; Val. Max. 1.8.11; Tac. *Ann.* 4.64.

71. Clodius the builder: Cic. *Mil.* 53; Plin. *N.H.* 36.10.3.

72. Carandini, "*Domus* e *insulae.*" The house of Aemilius is of special interest in view of the possibility that recent excavations have uncovered its basement. If the identification is sound, then at least a part of what ultimately became Clodius's property has been unearthed.

73. Sources and discussion in Tamm, *Auditorium and Palatium*, 29ff.; Carandini, "*Domus* e *insulae,*" 266ff.; Royo, "Le quartier républicain du Palatin," 107. Cerutti, "The Location of the Houses of Cicero," adds little.

74. The visibility of Cicero's site: Cic. *Dom.* 101, 103, 116.

75. Seius: Nicolet, *L'ordre équestre*, 2:1017.

76. Cic. *Dom.* 115: "prope dimidio carius quam aestimabatur."

77. Moreau, "La lex Clodia sur le bannissement de Cicéron," 478ff.

78. Mommsen, *Römisches Staatsrecht*, 2:619ff., is fundamental. Important bibliography includes Strong, "The Administration of Public Building"; Morgan, "The Portico of Metellus"; Morgan, "Villa Publica and Magna Mater"; Morgan, "The Introduction of the Aqua Marcia"; Coarelli, "Public Building in Rome."

79. According to Pliny, *N.H.* 33.17, the controversial Cn. Flavius was tribune as well as aedile in 304, when he dedicated the temple of Concord over the objections of Scipio Barbatus, the pontifex maximus. But the bulk of the tradition favors the view that Flavius dedicated as aedile; see *MRR* 1:168. To be sure, tribunes could be involved in public works—see Mommsen, *Gesammelte Schriften*, 3:31f.—but one notes that even in this sphere their activity was sometimes accompanied by a distinct appointment: for instance, M. Flavius Flaccus, while tribune in 270, was elected *IIvir aequae perducendae* in the same year after the death of M'. Curius Dentatus (*MRR* 1:199).

80. The distinction between inaugurated *templa* and consecrated *aedes* or *ara*: Linderski, "The Augural Law," 2249 n. 407.

81. Porticoes: Strong, "The Administration of Public Building," 100; Morgan, "The Portico of Metellus," 499ff. Our ignorance as to the precise status of Catulus's portico: Moreau, "La lex Clodia sur le bannissement de Cicéron," 480. Rebuilding a temple—in whole or in part—required a new consecration and allowed for a new inscription: Bardon, "La naissance d'un temple," 178f. (see also *Res Gestae* 20.1, where Augustus ostentatiously surrenders his opportunity to replace the inscriptions posted by other families). The refitting of Catulus's portico as part of Clodius's shrine may be assumed to allow for similar treatment.

82. Cicero's lamentations: *Dom.* 113f., 137. Cicero's silence: Moreau, "La lex Clodia sur le bannissement de Cicéron," 480. The portico of Catulus was extensively altered, as demonstrated by the contracts let for its reconstruction following the pontiffs' ruling that the *aedes Libertatis* could safely be dismantled (Cic. *Att.* 4.2.5). The consul of 78 had been an object of *popularis* attack during his lifetime (Suet. *Iul* 15.1; Dio 37.44.1–2); he left two daughters, but otherwise the family vanishes after an early imperial inscription commemorating the premature death of the son of one of these daughters (Syme, *Augustan Aristocracy*, 194).

83. See chapter 7, section 3.

84. Stambaugh, "The Functions of Roman Temples," 566.

85. *Dom.* 134f. Ritual procedures for dedication: Mommsen, *Römisches Staatsrecht*, 2:618ff.; Wissowa, *Religion und Kultus*, 385ff.; Latte, *Römische Religionsgeschichte*, 199f.

86. *Dom.* 101, 103, 116.

87. Cic. *Dom.* 81. This statue was a private token of honor to Clodius. Cicero mentions it no doubt to highlight the private aspect of the *aedes*, though its presence in the shrine is better understood as another dimension of the mingling of public and private in this structure (after all, Clodius's benefaction to Menulla came in the form of a *plebiscitum*). On the distinction between public and private honorific statues, see Plin. *N.H.* 34.17; Lahusen, *Untersuchungen zur Ehrenstatue,* 92f. On the *lex de iniuriis publicis,* see the appendix, section 3.

88. Even Cicero recognized that only *part* of his site was used for Clodius's shrine: *Dom.* 116.

89. Picard, "L'aedes Libertatis."

90. Coarelli, "Architettura sacra," 191ff. Temple B: Coarelli, Kajanto, Nyberg, and Steinby, *L'area sacra,* 19ff., 37ff.

91. Picard's actual arguments from the text of *De Domo,* though advanced with confidence, are, to say the least, farfetched; see Picard, "L'aedes Libertatis."

92. The temple of Libertas: Liv. 34.16.19; cf. Kock, *RE* 13.1:101; Platner and Ashby, *Topographical Dictionary,* 296 (both with further references). The events at Beneventum and their record in the temple: Liv. 34.16.9–19. Generally on the divinity Libertas: Wissowa, *Religion und Kultus,* 138f.

93. See M. H. Crawford, *Roman Republican Coinage,* 1:290f., 293, 405f., 406, for examples.

94. Liv. 43.16.13, 45.15.5; Servius *Ad Aen.* 1.7126. Cf. Kock, *RE* 13.1:102f.; Kroll, *RE* 13.1:103f., with further references.

95. M. H. Crawford, *Roman Republican Coinage,* 1:290f., 452 (*leges tabellariae*; for their connection with *libertas,* see Wirzubski, *Libertas as a Political Idea,* 293).

96. Late republican thinking about *libertas*: Wirzubski, *Libertas as a Political Idea*; Stylow, *Libertas und Liberalitas,* 9ff.; Brunt, *Fall of the Roman Republic,* 281ff., esp. 330ff.

97. Strong, "The Administration of Public Building," 99f.; Morgan, "The Portico of Metellus," 480ff.; Morgan, "Villa Publica and Magna Mater," 227ff. Generally on the significance of public building, see Demandt, "Symbolfunktionen antiker Baukunst."

98. The Roman view that "bigger is better": Büchner, *Studien zur römischen Literatur,* 23ff. For the influence of Clodius on Pompey and Augustus, see Wiseman, "*Conspicui Postes,*" 406.

99. *Pace* Lintott, *Violence,* 166, and Seager, *Pompey,* 106. Pocock's thesis, "Publius Clodius and the Acts of Caesar," that Clodius's attacks on Pompey were intended to keep him loyal to the triumvirate, continues to find adherents: Briscoe, Review of Benner.

100. Clodius's overconfidence: Seager, *Pompey,* 107.

101. Cic. *Har. Resp.* 46, 50ff.; *Prov. Cons.* 44f., 47. See Seager, *Pompey,* 106.

102. Sources: Cic. *Dom.* 129; *Har. Resp.* 28f., 58; *Sest.* 56f.; *Mil.* 73. Date: Cic. *Att.* 3.8.3; Asc. 47 (C).

103. Deiotarus, Brogitarus, and the situation in Galatia: Magie, *Roman Rule in Asia Minor,* 1235ff. (with references); Sullivan, *Near Eastern Royalty and Rome,* 164ff. Friendly kings were sources of both prestige (Badian, *Foreign Clientela,* 163ff.) and profit (Braund, *Rome and the Friendly King,* 79ff.).

104. Cic. *Har. Resp.* 28.

105. Braund, *Rome and the Friendly King*, 58ff.

106. *Pace* T. N. Mitchell, *Cicero*, 145, who views Clodius's actions almost solely in these terms, to the extent that the break with Pompey becomes collateral damage in Clodius's drive "to use his tribunate to build his wealth and expand his family's eastern connections."

107. Braund, *Rome and the Friendly King*, 24.

108. Pompey's disposition of Armenia: Seager, *Pompey*, 47; Sullivan, *Near Eastern Royalty and Rome*, 284f.

109. Asc. 47 (C). See also Cic. *Dom.* 66; *Mil.* 18, 37; Plut. *Pomp.* 48; Dio 38.30.1–2; Schol. Bob. 118f. (St).

110. Cf. Cic. *Att.* 3.8.3, 3.10.1, 3.13.1; *Q.F.* 1.4.2.

111. Cic. *Har. Resp.* 46, 50; *Prov. Cons.* 44, 47.

112. Cic. *Red. Quir.* 14; *Dom.* 66, 124; *Pis.* 27f.; Dio 38.30.2.

113. The significance of *fasces* and their shattering: Nippel, *Public Order in Ancient Rome*, 12f. *Consecratio bonorum*: Mommsen, *Römisches Staatsrecht*, 1:14, 157f. Its use in the late republic: Thommen, *Das Volkstribunat*, 188f. It appears that *consecratio bonorum* ordinarily required a plebiscite, though not invariably (Plin. *N.H.* 7.144). The problems of sorting out the various senses of *consecratio* and their overlap with *dedicatio* are discussed by Nisbet, *M. Tulli Ciceronis De Domo Sua*, 210ff.

114. Ninnius's consecration of Clodius's property: Cic. *Dom.* 125.

115. Cic. *Sest.* 68; *Red. Sen.* 3; *Pis.* 29; *Att.* 3.24.2; Plut. *Cic.* 23; Dio 38.30.3.

116. Cic. *Att.* 3.8.3, 3.15.3, 6; *Red. Sen.* 3; *Sest.* 67f.; *Pis.* 27; Dio 38.30.

117. Cic. *Sest.* 69; *Att.* 3.12.1, 3.15.6.

118. Cic. *Att.* 3.12.1; cf. *Red. Sen.* 8.

119. Cic. *Q.F.* 1.3.9; *Att.* 3.8.3, 3.15.1, 3.18.1.

120. Cic. *Att.* 3.9.2.

121. Cic. *Att.* 3.15.1, 3, 3.18.1.

122. Cic. *Prov. Cons.* 46.

123. Seager, *Pompey*, 107. This episode has been much discussed (to various conclusions): see Ward, *Marcus Crassus*, 246ff.; Benner, *Die Politik des P. Clodius*, 133ff.; T. N. Mitchell, *Cicero*, 147ff., each with further bibliography.

124. Cic. *Dom.* 40; *Har. Resp.* 48.

125. It is hard to imagine Pompey's participation in these demonstrations. In any event, the augurs could, under such circumstances, reveal only their individual opinions; these were hardly formal *responsa* of the college.

126. Cic. *Dom.* 40, 42; *Har. Resp.* 48, 50; *Prov. Cons.* 45f.; *Fam.* 1.9.10; *Q.F.* 2.2.2f.

127. Cic. *Att.* 3.13.1; *Q.F.* 1.4.3; *Fam.* 14.2.2.

128. Cic. *Att.* 3.22.2.

129. Cic. *Att.* 3.23.4, 3.24.2, 3.25; *Q.F.* 1.4.3.; *Fam.* 14.1.2, 14.2.2, 14.3.3.

130. Cic. *Dom.* 129; *Sest.* 69; *Har. Resp.* 49; *Pis.* 28; *Mil.* 18; Asc. 46 (C); Plut. *Pomp.* 49.

131. Nisbet, *M. Tulli Ciceronis in L. Calpurnium Pisonem Oratio*, xiii; Seager, *Pompey*, 109.

132. Cic. *Red. Sen.* 4, 29; *Red. Quir.* 14; *Dom.* 67, 110; *Sest.* 69, 84; *Har. Resp.* 49, 58; *Pis.* 16, 29; *Mil.* 18f., 73; Asc. 46f. (C).

133. Asc. 47 (C).

134. Cic. *Har. Resp.* 49.

135. Bill of the eight tribunes: Cic. *Att.* 3.15.5, 3.19.1, 3.20.3, 3.23.1; *Red. Sen.* 4, 29; *Sest.* 69f.

136. Cic. *Sest.* 71.

Chapter 7

1. *Q.F.* 1.4.3.

2. Messius: However valid the claim of *Red. Sen.* 21 that Messius was motivated by *amicitia* for Cicero, his actions throughout 57 reveal his foremost loyalty; see Gruen, *Last Generation*, 109f. Spinther: Cic. *Att.* 3.22.2: "saepe enim tu ad me scripsisti eum [Spinther] totum esse in illius [Pompey] potestate." He also owed gratitude to Caesar (Caes. *B. Civ.* 1.22.4), though his actions at this time can hardly be deemed to be predicated on that relationship (as represented in Drumann and Groebe, *Geschichte Roms*, 2:243) in view of Cicero's letter. In any event, Spinther, an enemy of Clodius as early as the Bona Dea scandal (Dio 39.6.2), also had a will of his own.

3. T. N. Mitchell, *Cicero*, 152, argues that many *principes*, continuing to see in Clodius a foil to Pompey, remained noncommittal at this time; see also Ward, *Marcus Crassus*, 248 n. 53. This seems closer to the truth than Gruen, *Last Generation*, 294, who asserts that the senate and dynasts united to humble Clodius, a state of affairs that better describes the situation after the riot of 23 January 57 (see below). See also Drumann and Groebe, *Geschichte Roms*, 2:244, asserting that, after the meeting of 1 January, no one could have expected Clodius to succeed so long in blocking Cicero's repatriation. Benner's notion, *Die Politik des P. Clodius*, 136f., that the *principes* supported Cicero out of principle (viz. consuls should not be judged retrospectively by the urban *plebs* for executing decrees of the senate) seems unlikely.

4. Caesar: Cic. *Sest.* 71. Cf. *Att.* 3.23.5; *Fam.* 1.9.9; *Pis.* 80. The quotation is from M. Gelzer, *Caesar*, 113. Crassus: Ward, *Marcus Crassus*, 243ff., though one need not accept the motive for Crassus's conduct there advanced. But see T. N. Mitchell, *Cicero*, 150 n. 20, for the opinion that Crassus showed no support for Cicero. Crassus's movements during this period are more difficult to trace than those of a quark. Cicero, for one, was unsure of Crassus: *Fam.* 14.2.2. Atticus's lobbying of Metellus Nepos: Cic. *Att.* 3.22.2, 3.24.2. Cicero's efforts: *Fam.* 5.4.1–2. *Fam.* 5.4.1 reveals that Nepos's attitude was variable in December 58. On 1 January 57 Nepos publicly set aside his grudge against Cicero for the good of the republic. Dio 39.6 places Nepos's conversion too late in 57, explaining it as a reaction to the violence between Clodius and Milo. Ciaceri, *Cicerone e i suoi tempi*, 2:67, suggests that Nepos hoped to curry favor with Pompey.

5. Clodius must have been disappointed when M. Cispius (tr. pl. 57), whose family had been estranged from Cicero owing to differences in a private suit (Cic. *Red. Sen.* 21), elected not to oppose Cicero's restoration, a salutary reminder that not all Romans prosecuted their enmities to the utmost.

6. There is some confusion here. Only Messius is explicitly said to have promulgated a bill in Cicero's behalf (Cic. *Red. Sen.* 21); elsewhere it is claimed that most of the tribunes supported Cicero's return (e.g., *Sest.* 72)—in fact, even before entering office P. Sestius was drafting a bill to recall Cicero (*Att.* 3.20.3). But Messius's leadership was soon eclipsed by that of Q. Fabricius, who introduced a measure (presumably his own) on 23 January (*Sest.* 78). Fabricius is claimed by Cicero to have been

vigorous in his support (*Red. Sen.* 19–22), on account of which the orator refers to him as "princeps rogationis" (*Sest.* 75), though that is not equivalent to calling him the promulgator of the bill; cf. *Sest.* 70 ("princeps Lentulus . . . causam suscepit"); *Red. Sen.* 8.

7. Cic. *Sest.* 70.

8. Cic. *Sest.* 72. Sources for the tribunates of Serranus and Numerius: *MRR* 2:202f. As Numerius was a new man from Picenum (Gruen, *Last Generation*, 118), he might have been expected to side with Pompey and hence a basis for Cicero's slur. On Serranus, see Benner, *Die Politik des P. Clodius*, 172f. He was loyal to Clodius throughout 57.

9. Cic. *Att.* 3.24.1.

10. Cic. *Att.* 3.25.

11. Cic. *Prov. Cons.* 22.

12. Cic. *Red. Quir.* 11; *Red. Sen.* 5, 8f.; *Sest.* 72.

13. Cic. *Dom.* 68, 84; *Sest.* 73; *Leg.* 3.45.

14. *Dom.* 69; *Sest.* 74; *Leg.* 3.45. This had long been Cicero's position as well—cf. *Att.* 3.15.5; he worried over attacking Clodius's law on the grounds that "in qua popularia multa sunt."

15. Cic. *Att.* 4.2.4; *Red. Sen.* 12; *Sest.* 74f.

16. For the date, see Cic. *Sest.* 75.

17. Fabricius's posture is plain enough: Cic. *Sest.* 75; Drumann and Groebe, *Geschichte Roms*, 2:245; Vanderbroeck, *Popular Leadership*, 245; Nowak, *Der Einsatz Privater Garden*, 130f.; Loposzko, *Mouvements sociaux*, 40 (though there are some confusions in his overall account). Nippel, *Aufruhr und Polizei*, 121, maintains that Fabricius was prepared to ignore Appius's *obnuntiatio*, but this infers too much from *Sest.* 78.

18. Cic. *Red. Sen.* 5–9, 22; *Sest.* 75–78, 85, 126; Dio 39.7.2f.; Plut. *Cic.* 33.4. The presence of gladiators on Clodius's side should not eclipse the participation of the urban poor (see, for instance, *Sest.* 85). The details vary little in our sources, though Dio's account suggests that violence did not ensue immediately.

19. Loposzko, *Mouvements sociaux*, 43.

20. Cic. *Sest.* 85. Drumann and Groebe, *Geschichte Roms*, 2:257, unquestionably exaggerate in saying "Clodius, ein Privatmann, beherrschte die Stadt," but his continued clout, made all too evident by his successful violence against strong opposition, could only attract *invidia*.

21. Both possibilities were mentioned by Cicero at *Sest.* 78 as preferable to violence, even if unwelcome in themselves.

22. Nippel, *Aufruhr und Polizei*, 120f.

23. Nowak, *Der Einsatz Privater Garden*, 130f. Ciceronian despair: Cic. *Att.* 3.26, 3.27.

24. *Red. Sen.* 19; *Sest.* 85, 88–90; *Mil.* 35. It is unclear, owing to Cicero's understandable lack of precision, whether Milo's house was attacked early in 57, as it unquestionably was later in the year, though Cicero's references to Milo's restraint and his frustrated recourse to the courts (see the following note) in the aftermath of attempts on his *domus* imply that such assaults took place early on. The beginning of Clodius's hostility toward Milo: Drumann and Groebe, *Geschichte Roms*, 2:248. Maslowski, "Domus Milonis Oppugnata," argues persuasively that the attack on Milo's house

mentioned at *Sest.* 85 should, on the logic of Cicero's narrative to that point, be dated in the early part of 57. The attack on Milo's house would have provided a very sound basis on which to build a prosecution *de vi*.

25. Milo's first attempt to try Clodius *de vi*: Cic. *Att.* 4.3.2; *Fam.* 5.3.2; *Red. Sen.* 19; *Sest.* 87ff.; *Mil.* 35, 40; Plut. *Cic.* 33.4; Dio 39.7.4 (confused). On the *lex Plotia de vi* see Lintott, *Violence*, 107ff. The suppression of the courts, probably in February (when Nepos held the *fasces*), is best discussed in Meyer, *Caesars Monarchie*, 109 n. 3, supported by Brunt, "Iudicia Sublata." Brunt's ingenious argument (pp. 230f.) that the senate authorized a *iustitium* in early 57, based primarily on *Sest.* 95, is unpersuasive; T. N. Mitchell, *Cicero*, 153 n. 29, is probably right to look toward the executive powers of the higher magistrates (see Greenidge, *Roman Public Life*, 175).

26. Cic. *Red. Sen.* 19f.; *Sest.* 86, 127; *Mil.* 38.

27. Cic. *Q.F.* 2.3.6; *Red. Quir.* 14; *Red. Sen.* 7; *Dom.* 13; *Sest.* 79ff., 85; *Mil.* 38. The date of the assembly is unknown; it probably occurred early in the year: see Sumner, "Lex Aelia, Lex Fufia," 354, 356.

28. Nippel, *Aufruhr und Polizei*, 120, wrongly assumes that the assembly was called by Nepos in an effort to recall Cicero (because he fails to connect the events described by Cic. *Red. Quir.* 14 and *Red. Sen.* 7 with the assault on Sestius). The suggestion by Linderski that Sestius's *obnuntiatio* was intended to hinder Clodius's candidacy for the aedileship is appealing; see *Rzymskie zgromadzenia wyborcze od Sulli do Cezara* (Warsaw, 1966), 89f., reported in Loposzko, *Mouvements sociaux*, 150. However, this would require the incident to be dated quite late in the year inasmuch as Nepos's responsibility for aedilician elections (which he attempted to hold in November 57) only came about because Spinther (the consul who ought to have presided over the election of curule aediles) had by then departed for his province, on which state of affairs see Linderski, *Roman Questions*, 80.

29. Senatorial business suspended in 58: *Pis.* 29; *Att.* 3.24.2; Plut. *Cic.* 33. The situation in 57: *Red. Sen.* 6; *Sest.* 77, 85, 89; Brunt, "Iudicia Sublata," 230.

30. Lentidius was a *dux tabernariorum* (*Dom.* 89); see Benner, *Die Politik des P. Clodius*, 162. Titius was evidently a closer, certainly a more conspicuous, adherent of Clodius: Cic. *Dom.* 21; *Har. Resp.* 59; *Sest.* 80, 112; see Benner, *Die Politik des P. Clodius*, 114. Both men were modest citizens, very likely leaders of *collegia* (Benner, *Die Politik des P. Clodius*, 165).

31. On the problematic biography of Bestia, see most recently J. W. Crawford, *M. Tullius Cicero: The Lost and Unpublished Orations*, 144, and *MRR* 3:46, each with further references.

32. Cic. *Sest.* 82. Nowak, *Der Einsatz Privater Garden*, 132f. (countenanced by Benner, *Die Politik des P. Clodius*, 174f.), cannot be correct to suggest that Numerius spoke out against the attack on Sestius (hence the threats of the *Clodiani* against him); this fact Cicero would certainly have relayed. The destruction of consular *fasces* was also an extremely provocative action—with absolutely no (even symbolic) justification under the circumstances—which must have offended Nepos. On the symbolism of breaking *fasces*, see Nippel, *Aufruhr und Polizei*, 120.

33. The composition of Sestius's bands is made clear by the charges brought against him at his trial: Cic. *Sest.* 84: "homines emisti, coegisti, parasti," a point essentially admitted by Cicero at *Red. Sen.* 20 and *Sest.* 84ff.; cf. *Sest.* 78, 90ff. Sestius's activism clearly follows that of Milo (*Mil.* 38), which means that one may discount Loposzko's

argument that Sestius had already assembled his bands and was equally responsible for the violence in which he suffered his famous wounds; see *Mouvements sociaux*, 45ff. On Sestius's (peevish) nature, see Q.F. 2.4.1.

34. Senatorial contributions: *Red. Sen.* 22; *Mil.* 38. Pompey's role: Plut. *Pomp.* 49; *Cic.* 33. On the composition and organization of Milo's gangs, see Cic. *Q.F.* 2.5.3; *Vat.* 40; *Off.* 2.58; Asc. 31, 34f., 55 (C); Dio 39.8.1; Nowak, *Der Einsatz Privater Garden*, 147ff., esp. 149f.

35. Violence in the streets, in which Milo and Sestius tended to prevail: Cic. *Red. Quir.* 14f.; *Red. Sen.* 19f., 30; *Sest.* 77; Dio 39.8.1; Nippel, *Aufruhr und Polizei*, 114, 120; Benner, *Die Politik des P. Clodius*, 81. Cicero's justifications: Lintott, *Violence*, 60ff.

36. The year 57 may well represent the peak of organized violence in Rome, as observed by Nippel, *Aufruhr und Polizei*, 120.

37. Capua: Cic. *Fam.* 1.9.9, 12, 14; *Prov. Cons.* 43; *Pis.* 80; Dio 39.10.1. Tour of Italy: Cic. *Red. Sen.* 29; *Mil.* 39.

38. Cic. *Red. Quir.* 10; *Red. Sen.* 31; *Dom.* 30, 75; *Har. Resp.* 46; *Prov. Cons.* 43; *Pis.* 25, 80.

39. Cic. *Sest.* 126.

40. A point rightly made by Gruen, *Last Generation*, 297, though it hardly constitutes an exhaustive explanation.

41. Epstein, *Personal Enmity in Roman Politics*, 25ff. Cicero on Clodius's *crudelitas*: *Dom.* 60ff. One might consider the example of Marius, whose influence was such that it could survive his violent suppression of Saturninus but faltered when the hero from Arpinum pressed too far his *inimicitiae* in opposing the recall of Metellus Numidicus; see Badian, "The Death of Saturninus," 130ff., esp. 138.

42. Cic. *Red. Sen.* 24; *Dom.* 73, 85; *Planc.* 78; *Sest.* 50, 116, 120, 128; *Pis.* 34; App. *B. Civ.* 2.57. Cicero claimed that such a decree in regard to an individual citizen was unprecedented, a measure of the orator's strong support in the senate.

43. Cic. *Sest.* 116–23; *Planc.* 78; *Schol Bob.* 136, 166 (St). For the timing of these games see Grimal, *Études de chronologie cicéronienne*, 127f. (apparently not accepted by T. N. Mitchell, *Cicero*, 154f.).

44. Cic. *Sest.* 126. On Metellus Scipio's games: Cic. *Sest.* 124ff.; *Schol. Bob.* 137 (St); Grimal, *Études de chronologie cicéronienne*, 162; Ville, *La gladiature*, 62.

45. Despite our limited data regarding the typical political attitudes of spectators at popular entertainments during the republic, Cic. *Att.* 1.16.11 makes it clear that Cicero believed the shows the place to gauge his popularity with the lowest orders. The audiences described in the *Pro Sestio* were clearly unusual in their composition owing to the efforts of Pompey and others to import supporters from throughout Italy, a point long recognized (e.g., Drumann and Groebe, *Geschichte Roms*, 2:249) but sometimes missed (e.g., Gruen, *Last Generation*, 441). See Tatum, "Another Look," for a more extensive discussion of audiences at the spectacles during the republic, contra Vanderbroeck, *Popular Leadership*, 77ff., who maintains that audiences regularly displayed an anti-*popularis* bias.

46. Taylor, *Party Politics*, 61, and Martin, *Die Popularen*, 96, rightly stress Clodius's support among the urban *plebs* at this time.

47. Cic. *Dom.* 74; *Pis.* 41. On the influence of the *scribae* (and the gaps in our knowledge as to the organization of the other *apparitores*), see Badian, "The *scribae* of the Roman Republic." The zeal of the publicans represented a crucial shift in their position: Cic. *Q.F.* 1.4.4. It is unclear which *collegia* Cicero refers to: a very few *collegia*

included men wealthy enough to qualify as equestrians (Treggiari, *Roman Freedmen*, 196f.); Cicero may have enjoyed support from these, or perhaps they were *collegia* over which Cicero's supporters had influence.

48. Gruen, *Last Generation*, 440f., doubts that the *plebs urbana* had any real interest in Clodius's struggle against Cicero's restoration. This seems unlikely, and in any case the issue forced itself (often literally) on everyone. What mattered was not only the individual commoner's devotion to Clodius himself, but also his relationship to the influential men of his *vicus*, many of whom were clearly attached to Clodius—or to one of Clodius's intermediaries—after the events of 58. The variety of personal influences affecting each commoner (as well as the ideological incentives that came into play) must be borne in mind even if it is impossible to map them out in detail (see chapter 5, section 8). The important point is that Clodius's following was not simply a matter of popular devotion to the past patrician himself.

49. Ciaceri, *Cicerone e i suoi tempi*, 2:68, proposes that Pompey's industry and the demonstrations against Clodius in the theater were the key factors in Nepos's decision to side with Spinther against his own kinsman in subsequent senatorial deliberations.

50. Timing: T. N. Mitchell, *Cicero*, 155.

51. Sources: Cic. *Mil.* 38; Asc. 48 (C). Discussion: Nowak, *Der Einsatz Privater Garden*, 131f.; Benner, *Die Politik des P. Clodius*, 111ff.; Vanderbroeck, *Popular Leadership*, 247f. Marshall, *A Historical Commentary on Asconius*, 72, 200, errs in assuming that Asconius has created a doublet based on the riots at the Ludi Romani, which occurred later in 57.

52. Nicolet, *World of the Citizen*, 202ff.; Virlouvet, *Famines et émeutes*, 43ff.; Garnsey, *Famine and Food Supply*, 201.

53. Natural causes: Cic. *Dom.* 11. *Lex Clodia*: *Dom.* 25. Pompey and associates: *Dom.* 14; Plut. *Pomp.* 49.6ff.

54. Cic. *Fam.* 5.17.2; see Virlouvet, *Famines et émeutes*, 15, 46f. Sittius was condemned *in absentia*; on his fascinating career, see Shackleton Bailey, *Cicero: Epistulae ad Familiares*, 1:323. Speculation: Garnsey, *Famine and Food Supply*, 205f.

55. It is worth remembering that Cicero's widely accepted claim that Clodius created a virtual *cura annonae* for Sex. Cloelius was made in this tempestuous atmosphere of charged allegations (*Dom.* 25). The *lex Clodia* is held at least partially responsible by Berchem, *Les distributions de blé*, 16f., and Schneider, *Wirtschaft und Politik*, 384f.

56. A point made by Nicolet, *World of the Citizen*, 204, Virlouvet, *Famines et émeutes*, 43f., and Garnsey, *Famine and Food Supply*, 205, but worth repeating in view of the tendency to believe that Pompey engineered the shortage: see, e.g., Drumann and Groebe, *Geschichte Roms*, 2:257; Syme, *The Roman Revolution*, 37; Loposzko, *Mouvements sociaux*, 66ff.; Benner, *Die Politik des P. Clodius*, 119.

57. Virlouvet, *Famines et émeutes*, 63; Garnsey, *Famine and Food Supply*, 31.

58. Benner, *Die Politik des P. Clodius*, 111; Vanderbroeck, *Popular Leadership*, 247; Garnsey, *Famine and Food Supply*, 206. Nippel, *Aufruhr und Polizei*, 124, is more circumspect.

59. Role of the *praetor urbanus*: Asc. 59 (C); Nicolet, "La *Lex Gabinia-Calpurnia*," 283, and Benner, *Die Politik des P. Clodius*, 112. But cf. Nippel, *Aufruhr und Polizei*, 249f.

60. This is contrary to the view of Nippel, *Aufruhr und Polizei*, 125, 249f., and Benner, *Die Politik des P. Clodius*, 71, 113.

61. As observed by Vanderbroeck, *Popular Leadership*, 122, important in view of the inclination to see the grain crisis itself as damaging to Clodius's popularity: e.g., Loposzko, *Mouvements sociaux*, 72.

62. Cic. *Dom.* 14 claims that grain prices dropped suddenly upon the announcement of the senate's resolution in his favor (which occurred a few days after the riot). Now while it is true that grain merchants could lower prices temporarily in the hope of improved conditions (Virlouvet, *Famines et émeutes*, 48f.), nonetheless, one must beware of Cicero's tendency to interpret fluctuations in grain prices as if his own career were the sole variable (p. 45).

63. Cic. *Red. Sen.* 25f., 31; *Dom.* 30; *Sest.* 129f.; *Mil.* 39; *Pis.* 34ff.

64. Seager, *Pompey*, 110.

65. Cic. *Pis.* 35.

66. *Red. Quir.* 16f.; *Red. Sen.* 26; *Sest.* 107; *Pis.* 34, 80.

67. Cic. *Sest.* 108.

68. Cic. *Red. Sen.* 27; *Sest.* 129; *Pis.* 35.

69. Plut. *Cic.* 33.3; *Pomp.* 49.3.

70. See the narratives provided by Gelzer, *Cicero*, 149ff., and T. N. Mitchell, *Cicero*, 156f.

71. Sources: Cic. *Att.* 4.1.6–7; *Fam.* 5.17.2; *Dom.* 6–7, 10–16; Dio 39.9.2–3. The chronology here is that of Shackleton Bailey, *Cicero's Letters to Atticus*, 2:167, which is rejected by T. N. Mitchell, *Cicero*, 158 n. 50. A narrative quite different from the one provided here can be found in Loposzko, *Mouvements sociaux*, 58ff.

72. Cic. *Dom.* 11 (whence the quotation) and 12.

73. Cic. *Dom.* 14. Cf. *Att.* 4.1.6. The incident is discussed by Lintott, *Violence*, 10. More generally on Clodius's use of public defamation, see Benner, *Die Politik des P. Clodius*, 84f., and Nippel, *Public Order in Ancient Rome*, 76.

74. Cic. *Dom.* 13.

75. Nepos wounded: Cic. *Dom.* 12–14 (though Cicero probably exaggerates the nature of the rough treatment given the consul). *Clodiani* demonstrate: Cic. *Att.* 4.1.6; *Dom.* 14f. Cicero at home: Cic. *Dom.* 6.

76. Attendance: Cic. *Att.* 4.1.6; *Dom.* 6, 15. Support for Pompey: Cic. *Att.* 4.1.6 (wherein Cicero is clearly at pains to persuade Atticus that *boni* as well as *plebs* supported Pompey's appointment); *Dom.* 16. The demonstration was probably orchestrated by Pompey, though the possibility that it was unrehearsed cannot be excluded categorically. Nippel, *Aufruhr und Polizei*, 124, is quite right to observe how this event shows that Clodius did not hold a monopoly on the interpretation (or the manipulation) of the popular will. Pompey's intentions: Cic. *Att.* 4.1.6 ("idque ipse [Pompeius] cuperet").

77. This is the clear and long recognized implication of Cic. *Dom.* 9. See Stein, *Die Senatssitzungen*, 34; Ooteghem, *Pompée le Grand*, 362ff.

78. Plut. *Pomp.* 49.6ff.; see Benner, *Die Politik des P. Clodius*, 125.

79. Nothing in the methods employed by Pompey to secure Cicero's recall can have endeared Cicero to the urban populace. Pompey's *cura annonae*, though obviously unwelcome, was not a severe blow to Clodius's popularity, nor did it hamper his ability to organize popular demonstrations however much Pompey revised the system of grain distribution within the city (if he did so at all, since the main problem and the initial focus of Pompey's efforts was procurement). The threat was to his

dignity, since Pompey's *cura* would entail ever so much more prestige than Clodius's tribunician legislation. For a different interpretation of this matter, see Nippel, *Aufruhr und Polizei*, 125, and Benner, *Die Politik des P. Clodius*, 71, 113.

80. Cic. *Att.* 4.1.7.

81. Senatorial hostility toward Pompey's appointment: *Att.* 4.1.6f.; *Dom.* 15; Plut. *Pomp.* 49.4ff.; Dio 39.9.2–3. Intimidation: *Dom.* 5–8, 10, 12f.

82. Cic. *Dom.* 20.

83. Cic. *Att.* 4.1.8.

84. Watt, *M. Tulli Ciceronis Epistulae*.

85. Nisbet, Review of Shackleton Bailey, 240 (whence the quotation).

86. Messius's proposal: *Att.* 4.1.7 ("consulares duce Favonio fremunt" demonstrates its unpopularity in the senate); Dio 39.9.3; App. *B. Civ.* 2.18.67 (though misdated).

87. Shackleton Bailey, *Towards a Text of Cicero*, 15 (where he also cites predecessors in this view), though he was subsequently persuaded, wrongly in my view, by Nisbet, Review of Shackleton Bailey, 240; cf. Shackleton Bailey, *Cicero's Letters to Atticus*, 2:169. Nisbet's view, it must be said, reproduces that of Tyrrell, *The Correspondence of M. Tullius Cicero*, 2:6.

88. The Claudian *contio*: Cic. *Att.* 4.2.3. Senatorial curiosity: *Att.* 4.2.4.

89. Cic. *Dom.* 69.

90. Linderski, *Roman Questions*, 505f.; Linderski, "The Augural Law," 2161f.; Beard, "Priesthood in the Roman Republic," 32 n. 38. But this need not be considered invariable: see Morgan, "The Introduction of the Aqua Marcia," 48ff. (opinion of the *decimviri sacris faciundis* rejected by the senate).

91. Quint. 10.1.23: "Nam de domo Ciceronis dixit Calidius." I suspect, in view of Cicero's invective directed against Ap. Claudius (*Dom.* 111f.) and of Appius's subsequent actions in Clodius's behalf, that Appius also spoke for Clodius's cause—though there is no necessity to assume an equal number of pleaders on each side. Nor is it clear whether the tribunal met more than once or for more than one day; see Lenaghan, *A Commentary on Cicero's Oration De Haruspicum Responso*, 91f.

92. Cicero does not actually claim to provide an exhaustive list. Caesar's omission is obviously to be explained by his absence, but the orator had other reasons for excluding Pinarius, who presumably will have rejected Cicero's criticisms of his role in the consecration.

93. *MRR* 3:53f. See *Dom.* 127.

94. *Dom.* 118. This may reflect a claim actually made by Clodius in his speech, though sardonically reproduced here.

95. Pompey: *Dom.* 25; cf. *Har. Resp.* 13. Appeal to the prejudices of the elite: *Dom.* 13, 90.

96. Cic. *Dom.* 4, 11, 14, 18ff., 26, 31; Plut. *Pomp.* 49.

97. *Dom.* 92 suggests Clodius's complete gainsaying of Cicero's preferred reputation; see also *Dom.* 4: "'tune es ille,' inquit [Clodius], 'quo senatus carere non potuit.'" Cicero as *rex*: Cic. *Att.* 1.16.10 (Clodius); *Fam.* 7.24.1; *Dom.* 75 ("crudelis tyrannus"); *Sull.* 21ff.; *Planc.* 75; *Sest.* 109 (Clodius); *Vat.* 23; *Mil.* 12; [Sall.] *Inv. Cic.* 3.6, 4.7, 58; Cicero as *hostis*: cf. *Dom.* 7, 10.

98. *Dom.* 7. See Tatum, "*Hospitem* or *hostem*?"

99. Easily divined from *Dom.* 103–9, 137. Cf. *Dom.* 92, implying that Cicero's religiosity had been ridiculed.

100. Wardman, *Religion and Statecraft*; Price, *Rituals and Power*, 7ff.; North, "Religion and Politics"; Linderski, "The Augural Law"; Morgan, "Politics, Religion and the Games"; Beard, "Religion," each with extensive bibliography.

101. Morgan, "Politics, Religion and the Games," 30f.

102. Cic. *Har. Resp.* 26 indicates that Clodius was *quindecimvir sacris faciundis* by 57 and in view of his nobility he had probably obtained his priesthood long before that date: see Hahm, "Roman Nobility and the Three Major Priesthoods," and Szemler, *The Priests of the Roman Republic*, 165, 191f.

103. Cicero's ridicule of Clodius as *sacerdos*: *Dom.* 103, 105, 111, 116, 127; *Har. Resp.* 9, 12, 14, 22; *Sest.* 39, 66; *Pis.* 89; *Att.* 2.4. Cicero's invective against Ap. Claudius: *Dom.* 111f. Cicero's ridicule of Clodius's old-fashioned virtue: *Dom.* 105, 127; cf. *Har. Resp.* 9; Quint. 8.6.56; Schol. Bob. 88 (St).

104. Cic. *Dom.* 43f., 46f. Cf. *Red. Sen.* 48; *Sest.* 65, 133; *Pis.* 30.

105. See Tatum, "The *Lex Papiria de Dedicationibus*"; Tatum, "Ritual and Personal Morality" (each with extended discussion and further bibliography).

106. Cic. *Att.* 4.2.3.

107. Nippel, *Aufruhr und Polizei*, 122, notes that Clodius appears to have employed the language of *evocatio*, which summoned the citizenry to rescue the state.

108. Cic. *Att.* 4.2.3ff.

109. Cic. *Att.* 4.3.2ff. Cf. *Sest.* 85; *Cael.* 78; *Mil.* 38, 87; Dio 39.20.3. Discussion: Vanderbroeck, *Popular Leadership*, 251f.; Nowak, *Der Einsatz Privater Garden*, 135ff.

110. Decimus and Gellius: Cic. *Att.* 4.3.2: "[Clodius] desertus a suis vix iam Decimum dissignatorem, vix Gellium retinet, servorum consiliis utitur" (Watt's text). Two problems trouble this passage, the identity of Decimus and the significance of *dissignatorem*. Wiseman plausibly identifies Decimus with D. Iunius Brutus (cos. desig. 42), the tyrannicide (*Cinna the Poet*, 151ff.), a view rejected by Shackleton Bailey, *Two Studies*, 34 (cf. *Cicero's Letters to Atticus*, 2:174), though on insufficient grounds. Further discussion and bibliography can be found in Benner, *Die Politik des P. Clodius*, 159. Benner also records an ingenious explanation of Cicero's application of *dissignatorem* to Decimus. It should be noticed that the structure of Cicero's sentence requires that Decimus and Gellius (discussed in chapter 5, section 1) come from groups quite distinct from freedmen or the lower classes generally. Their role in November is misrepresented by Gruen, *Last Generation*, 296.

111. Clodius's isolation at this time is also mentioned by Cicero at *Att.* 4.3.5. Cicero, of course, had reason to emphasize this turn of events.

112. P. Sulla: Cic. *Att.* 4.3.3. Sulla (allegedly) lent his support to Catiline in the sixties; see Gruen, *Last Generation*, 284f., but see Berry, *Cicero: Pro P. Sulla Oratio*, 1ff. That the *familiarus* of Atticus referred to by Cicero was Hortensius is the likely proposition of Shackleton Bailey, *Cicero' Letters to Atticus*, 2:176; cf. T. N. Mitchell, *Cicero*, 161 n. 56.

113. *Fam.* 1.19.15; *Har. Resp.* 50; *Sest.* 85, 89, 95.

114. Badian, *Roman Imperialism*, 73f.; Shatzman, "The Egyptian Question," 364f.; Green, *Alexander to Actium*, 553ff. Plutarch reports (*Cat. Min.* 35) that Auletes, while making his way to Rome, visited M. Cato in Rhodes, where the severe Stoic (sitting at the latrine) lectured the king on the dangers of involving himself with corrupt politicians in Rome.

115. Shatzman, "The Egyptian Question."

116. Pompey's support of Auletes: Strabo 17.1.11; Dio 39.14.3; cf. Cic. *Rab. Post.* 6.

Auletes could not have been introduced to the senate before Cicero's fate had been determined (necessary to open the door to new business, the first of which would be foreign delegations). The decision by the senate in May to summon the citizenry to Rome might have been deemed sufficient to allow the senate to move on to other business. Since Spinther was suspected of supporting Pompey's *cura annonae* in July 57 in order to eliminate a rival for the assignment of restoring Auletes (Plut. *Pomp.* 49.5), Auletes' case must have been presented to the senate before Cicero's return and before the grain crisis attending it. See Stein, *Die Senatssitzungen*, 32f., 35 (though he draws slightly different conclusions).

117. Cic. *Cael.* 23ff., 51, 54; Dio 39.13.1ff. Cf. Cic. *Har. Resp.* 34; Strabo 17.1.11. There is no reason to date Dio's murder to 56, as does Wiseman, *Catullus and His World*, 61 n. 39.

118. Plut. *Pomp.* 49.5.

119. The senate's decree: The sources do not explicitly date the *senatus consultum* in Spinther's behalf; however, Dio 39.12.1 and Plut. *Pomp.* 49 suggest September as the likeliest month (see Stein, *Die Senatssitzungen*, 35). See also Cic. *Fam.* 1.1.1; *Q.F.* 2.2.3; *Cael.* 18; *Rab. Post.* 6. Spinther's departure: Cic. *Att.* 4.2.4–5; *Har. Resp.* 13; see Stein, *Die Senatssitzungen*, 35f.

120. Cic. *Fam.* 1.1.1–2; *Q.F.* 2.2.3. See Shatzman, "The Egyptian Question," 365ff.

121. Spinther had his own supporters in the financial community; for example, Q. Selicius (Cic. *Fam.* 1.5A.3–4); see Shatzman, "The Egyptian Question," 367f.

122. As Clodius was already a formal candidate by 14 November and elections were postponed for the first time on the 19th (*Att.* 4.3.3f.), the constitutional preliminaries must have taken place in October. See Earl, "Appian *B.C.* 1, 14 and 'Professio.'"

123. He had prosecuted Clodius at the Bona Dea trial: Schol. Bob. 85, 89 (St).

124. Cic. *Att.* 4.3.3f. Milo's indictment: Cic. *Sest.* 89; *Mil.* 40; Plut. *Cic.* 33; Dio 39.7.4.

125. Cic. *Att.* 4.3.4f. It is unwise to conclude (as does Gruen, *Last Generation*, 296), on the basis of *Mil.* 15, that the senate passed a decree condemning Clodius or insisting that Clodius be tried before the elections—which is far from what Cicero wrote to Atticus at the time.

126. Sources for the tribunates of Caninius and C. Cato are collected in *MRR* 2:209. For C. Cato see also *MRR* 3:169f. The tie between Clodius and C. Cato has been unduly minimized by Benner, *Die Politik des P. Clodius*, 175. Clodius also found support from another tribune, called Cassius at Cic. *Q.F.* 2.1.2; see Shackleton Bailey, *Two Studies*, 23, who suggests emending this otherwise unknown Cassius to Caninius apparently on the odd grounds that with the unemended reading we would be faced with the predicament of knowing the names of all ten tribunes for 56. In any case, Caninius does not seem to have been a Clodian ally, but rather a supporter of Pompey; see Seager, *Pompey*, 118.

127. Cic. *Q.F.* 2.1.2; the nature of Racilius's oration: *Q.F.* 2.1.3. Sources for Racilius's tribunate: *MRR* 2:209; cf. also *MRR* 3:181.

128. Dio 39.7.4.

129. Cic. *Q.F.* 2.1.3. The identity of L. Antistius Vetus: Badian, "Two Roman Non-Entities," 200ff.; Shackleton Bailey, *Two Studies*, 11f.; *MRR* 3:17f. Although the disturbance outside the senate was alarming, it was probably not a major riot: Nowak, *Der Einsatz Privater Garden*, 138.

130. Dio 39.7.4; Nepos's claim: Cic. *Fam.* 5.3. There is no necessity of assuming (along the lines of Shackleton Bailey, *Cicero: Epistulae ad Quintum Fratrem*, 172) that

Marcellinus's proposal was actually passed at a subsequent meeting of the senate (only to be quashed by the consul). It is more likely that Nepos's influence was adequate to prevent the senate's taking up the issue again. Perhaps a formal notice on Nepos's part was necessary to keep the urban praetor, Caecilius Rufus, who was no friend to Clodius, from exploiting the unprecedented circumstances so as to take matters into his own hands; Brunt, "Iudicia Sublata," 228. For the urban praetor's role in establishing courts *de vi*, see Mommsen *Römisches Staatsrecht*, 2:585 n. 5.

131. This is made clear by Cic. *Sest.* 95; *Fam.* 1.9.15, though T. N. Mitchell, *Cicero*, 162, is correct that one need not infer from *Sest.* 95 that there was a formal senatorial resolution. Still, such an inference is by no means impossible; see Stein, *Die Senatssitzungen*, 37 (followed by Gruen, *Last Generation*, 296).

132. Cic. *Q.F.* 2.2.2.

133. Long recognized: Cic. *Har. Resp.* 50; Drumann and Groebe, *Geschichte Roms*, 2:270. See Gruen, *Last Generation*, 295ff.; T. N. Mitchell, *Cicero*, 162. Mitchell, "Cicero before Luca," 315, stresses Clodius's *nobilitas* as a factor in his maintaining the senate's favor—important, but by no means an irrevocable guarantee of security (as Clodius well knew from his own experience).

134. Date: Cic. *Q.F.* 2.2.2; cf. also *Sest.* 95 and Dio 39.18.1. Dio says that Clodius was elected παρακελευστός, which could mean, as the Loeb editor translates it, "by a political combination" (Dio 53.21.7, where παρακέλευσις is used in this sense) but which could simply indicate that Clodius enjoyed splendid endorsements or ample popular acclaim (or both). To assert Clodius's continuing popularity with the *plebs* is not (it should be clear) to insist that he and he alone had influence over the populace or that his influence was all pervasive: Benner, *Die Politik des P. Clodius*, 88f., responding to Gruen, *Last Generation*, 446. The idea that Clodius was senior aedile derives from his presidency at the Ludi Megalenses: Wiseman, *Cinna the Poet*, 161.

135. Vanderbroeck, *Popular Leadership*, 127.

136. *Q.F.* 2.2.2. Cyrus was employed both by Cicero and by Clodius, and he honored both in his will: *Att.* 2.3.2; *Mil.* 46ff.

137. Caninius's bill: Cic. *Fam.* 1.2.1, 1.4.1, 1.7.3f.; *Q.F.* 2.2.3, 2.4.5; Plut. *Pomp.* 49.6; Dio 39.16.1. Ptolemy's letter: Dio 39.16.2. Pompey's detractors: Cic. *Fam.* 1.1.2; Dio 39.16.2. In fact the grain crisis remained acute in April; see *Q.F.* 2.6.1–2. Lightening: Dio 39.15.1.

138. Cic. *Fam.* 1.1.1; *Q.F.* 2.2.3; Dio 39.15.1ff. Quindecimvirs with augurs and pontiffs constituted the three major priestly colleges: Szemler, *The Priests of the Roman Republic*, 26ff. The Sibylline books: Parke, *Sibyls and Sibylline Prophecy*, 190ff.; Potter, *Prophecy and History*, 109ff. Supervision of *haruspices* by *quindecimviri*: Rawson, *Roman Culture and Society*, 303; see also Parke, *Sibyls and Sibylline Prophecy*, 203ff.

139. Thulin, *Die Etruskische Disciplin*, 12ff.

140. Szemler, *The Priests of the Roman Republic*, 164f., collects what little we know. Crassus as *quindecimvir*: Taylor, *Party Politics*, 215 n. 48, though this is admittedly her surmise from the politics of the Egyptian question itself.

141. Fenestella, fr. 21 (Peter); see Meyer, *Caesars Monarchie*, 129f.

142. *Fam.* 1.4.2, 1.7.4.

143. Parke, *Sibyls and Sibylline Prophecy*, 203f. The *libri Sibyllini* had been destroyed by fire in 83.

144. Ibid., 191.

145. Cic. *Fam.* 1.1.3. Hortensius and M. Lucullus opposed accepting the oracle's prohibition.

146. Contra: Brunt, *Fall of the Roman Republic*, 484f. Cic. *Fam.* 1.7.4–5 records the plan recommended to Spinther by Cicero and Pompey whereby the king could be restored without violating the Sibylline oracle. The fact that Spinther did not attempt it does not mean the plan, the combined product of Rome's finest general and most devious sophist, was unworkable.

147. Cic. *Q.F.* 2.2.3.

148. Cic. *Fam.* 1.1.3, 1.2.1f., 1.4.1f.; *Q.F.* 2.2.3.

149. Sources for Milo's trial: Cic. *Q.F.* 2.3.1–4 (the principal source), 2.6.4; *Fam.* 1.5B.1; *Sest.* 95; *Vat.* 40f.; Asc. 48 (C); Dio 39.18–19; Schol. Bob. 122, 151 (St).

150. Gruen's objections to the view that Milo was prosecuted in a *iudicium populi* (*Last Generation*, 298 n. 139) do not persuade. Cicero's language cannot imply speeches given at *contiones* preparatory to a trial (Lintott, Review of Gruen, 242), and Asconius, who had Tiro's account of the trial before him, makes it plain that the trial was *apud populum* (49 [C]). The right of aediles to conduct public trials is discussed (with further bibliography) by Bauman, "Criminal Prosecutions by the Aediles." The charge against Milo, designated *de vi* in the sources, centered on his disruptive use of gladiators while tribune: Cic. *Vat.* 40; Dio 39.18.1; Schol. Bob. 122, 151f. (St); see also Bauman, "Criminal Prosecutions by the Aediles," 251f.

151. Vatinius as witness: Cic. *Vat.* 40; Schol. Bob. 151f. (St). Clodius had saved Vatinius from trial in 58 (see chapter 5, section 7).

152. Cic. *Vat.* 13, 15, 38. How convincing are Cicero's protestations is another matter altogether.

153. M. Marcellus (cos. 51): Cic. *Q.F.* 2.3.1; he also defended Milo in 52 (Asc. 34, 39, 40 [C]). Pompey as *advocatus*: *Q.F.* 2.3.1.

154. The events that follow took place either on 7, 8, and 9 February or on 6, 7, and 8 February. The issue cannot be resolved; see Seager, *Pompey*, 118 n. 27.

155. Cic. *Q.F.* 2.3.2. A literary example of verse attacking Clodius and his sister is Catullus 79.

156. Dio 39.19.1f. A series of jibes different from the one in *Q.F.* 2.3.2 is recorded by Plut. *Pomp.* 48.7: " 'Who is the licentious general?' 'Who is the man who seeks another man' 'Who scratches his head with one finger?' " Cf. Plut. *Mor.* 89E. This technique was called *complexio* (*Rhet. Her.* 4.20).

157. Plut. *Pomp.* 48.7.

158. Cic. *Q.F.* 2.3.2: "is [Crassus] aderat tum, Miloni animo non amico." Shackleton Bailey, *Cicero: Epistulae ad Quintum Fratrem*, 176, argues unpersuasively for taking *Miloni* with *aderat*. The sentence is rightly construed by Ward, *Marcus Crassus*, 252 n. 66; Seager, *Pompey*, 119 n. 28; T. N. Mitchell, *Cicero*, 165 n. 65.

159. Plut. *Crass.* 7.9. See Gruen, *Last Generation*, 67f.

160. Cic. *Q.F.* 2.3.2. Cicero does not disguise the fact that the violence was initiated by Milo's supporters.

161. Cic. *Q.F.* 2.3.2. A convenient precis of the career of Servilius Isauricus (cos. I 48, cos. II 41) can be found in Shackleton Bailey, *Cicero's Letters to Atticus*, 1:340.

162. Cic. *Q.F.* 2.3.3. Despite Cicero's desperate protestations at Milo's trial in 52 (*Mil.* 12; cf. Quint. 5.2.1), such decrees were hardly neutral, and C. Cato's speech following the senate's resolution as well as Pompey's reaction to the whole affair (*Q.F.*

2.3.3f.) make it clear that Pompey was the object of the senate's disapproval. Gruen, *Last Generation*, 299, believes that the senate's decree was directed at Clodius (followed by J. W. Crawford, *M. Tullius Cicero: The Lost and Unpublished Orations*, 141, who also conflates the two distinct meetings of the senate on the 8th and 9th); this is at odds with the unmistakable force of Cicero's letter.

163. Cic. *Q.F.* 2.3.3. A similar tactic had been employed against Pompey by Crassus during the time of the Bona Dea scandal: Cic. *Att.*, 1.14.4.

164. Cic. *Q.F.* 2.3.3. Marshall, "Pompeius' Fear of Assassination," 126f., argues that this is another instance of Pompey insinuating that his life was in danger in order to underline for his contemporaries that he was indispensable; he seems to believe that there was a direct connection between Pompey's advertised fears for his life and the willingness of his fellow triumvirs to shore up their relationship at Luca, all of which strikes me as unlikely. Seager, *Pompey*, 109, is nearer the mark when he describes Pompey as "a man with his exaggerated fears of plots against his life."

165. Cic. *Q.F.* 2.3.4; *Fam.* 1.5B.1.

166. Cic. *Q.F.* 2.5.3 (2.4.5).

167. C. Cato's bill: *Q.F.* 2.3.1; *Fam.* 1.5A.2, 1.5B.2; *Sest.* 144. The nature of C. Cato's bill is misunderstood by Ward, *Marcus Crassus*, 251.

168. Cic. *Fam.* 1.5B.2 (Cicero hopeful); 1.7.3; *Q.F.* 2.3.4 (Pompey will resist C. Cato's bill).

169. Cic. *Q.F.* 2.3.4. C. Cato's bill directed against Milo may have dealt with the violent employment of *bestiarii*, but this is mere speculation; see *Q.F.* 2.5.3 (2.4.5) and Shackleton Bailey, *Cicero: Epistulae ad Quintum Fratrem*, 181.

170. Cic. *Q.F.* 2.5.2 (2.4.4).

171. Cic. *Fam.* 1.7.5–6.

172. Cic. *Q.F.* 2.6(5).4.

173. Tatum, "The Marriage of Pompey's Son." Gruen, *Last Generation*, 299, misrepresents Milo's escape: "The senate would not indulge Clodius further" (see also p. 303). Drumann and Groebe, *Geschichte Roms*, 2:274, believe that Clodius let Milo's prosecution drop because he was intimidated by Pompey's reinforcements, another view that ignores the significance of Luca. Cic. *Q.F.* 2.6(5).4 makes it clear that the prosecution of Milo was not dropped until *after* Luca.

174. Dio 39.18.2.

175. See Cicero's description of Pompey at *Q.F.* 2.5.3 (4.3.5): "et hercule non est idem; nam apud perditissimam illam atque infimam faecem populi propter Milonem suboffendit et boni multa ab eo desiderant, multa reprehendunt." Benner, *Die Politik des P. Clodius*, 126, believes that Clodius's opposition to Pompey's receiving the assignment to restore Ptolemy was based on his principled opposition to extraordinary commands, a view unlikely to persuade many.

176. Cicero's *dolor*: *Q.F.* 2.2.3, still manifestly felt in 55 when Cicero penned *Fam.* 1.1.8. But one should not overlook Cicero's feeling, on 12 February, that his authority was again on the rise (despite Pompey's misfortunes); see *Q.F.* 2.3.7.

177. Cic. *Q.F.* 2.3.5.

178. The issue of the decree's relationship to the *lex Licinia* attracts unnecessary controversy: see the detailed discussion by Linderski, *Roman Questions*, 204ff., as well as, more briefly, Lintott, "Electoral Bribery," 9 (without reference to Linderski).

179. Election reform in the late republic: Lintott, "Electoral Bribery," with literature there cited. *Sodalitates*: Linderski, *Roman Questions*, 208, 648f. (with further

references). *Decuriati*: Linderski, *Roman Questions*, 112f. Linderski is inclined to see in Cicero's use of *decuriati* an (at least possible) allusion to the *collegia*.

180. Long recognized, if lost in the midst of abundant scholarship: Mommsen, *De collegiis*, 60; Waltzing, *Étude historique sur les corporations professionnelles*, 1:111f. For the view, rejected here, that the *senatus consultum* of 56 affected *collegia* in retaliation for Clodius's conduct at Milo's trial, see De Robertis, *Il diritto associativo romano*, 100f.; Accame, "La legislazione romana intorno ai collegi," 32ff.; Treggiari, *Roman Freedmen*, 175f.; Taylor, *Party Politics*, 210.

181. Sources for Sestius's trial: Cic. *Sest.*; *Vat.*; *Fam.* 1.9.7, 2.3.5, 2.4.1; Quint. 11.1.73; Plut. *Cic.* 26.5; Schol. Bob. 125ff. (St).

182. Cn. Nerius is attested only at Cic. *Q.F.* 2.3.5 and was evidently quite obscure. M. Tullius was equally unnotable. P. Albinovanus, however, is probably to be identified with the *pontifex* mentioned at *Har. Resp.* 12; see Shackleton Bailey, *Two Studies*, 7, and *MRR* 3:14. T. Claudius, attested solely at *Vat.* 3, is no better known to us than Nerius.

183. See *MRR* 3:9.

184. Cic. *Vat.* 41. Cf. Schol Bob. 125 (St): "accusare de vi P. Clodius coepit." Clodius's role is taken for granted by Gruen, *Last Generation*, 300ff., whose detailed examination of the trial represents a standard view.

185. See Marshall, *Crassus*, 120; Ward, *Marcus Crassus*, 254. Gruen, "P. Clodius," 129 n. 49, rightly makes it part of his case for Clodius's political independence from Crassus, though it should not follow that Clodius and Crassus were incapable of cooperation—especially during this time.

186. This is essentially the view of Pocock, *A Commentary on Cicero In Vatinium*, 198f., who adds that Crassus's participation would also have served to deflate Pompey's recent complaints against him. Sestius's senatorial support: *Vat.* 10: "his principibus civitatis, qui adsunt P. Sestio."

187. A point vigorously made by Epstein, *Personal Enmity in Roman Politics*, 100ff.

188. T. N. Mitchell, *Cicero*, 174ff., recognizing the influence of Cic. *Fam.* 1.9 on subsequent interpretations of the events of 56 (which is not to say I share Mitchell's view of the precise nature of that influence).

189. Gruen's notion that Clodius hid in the background (an opinion which gives very little credit to the perceptive powers of the jurors) finds no support in his assertion that Clodius had alienated the nobles (*Last Generation*, 302). As we have seen, the contrary was true, as Pompey regretted.

190. Cic. *Sest.* 86f., 90, 135; *Vat.* 40.

191. Cic. *Vat.* 3, 41. See Pocock, *A Commentary on Cicero In Vatinium*, 134ff., who tends to believe Vatinius's charges (as does Seager, *Pompey*, 120).

192. Cic. *Q.F.* 2.4.1.

193. Albini, "L'orazione contre Vatinio"; T. N. Mitchell, "Cicero before Luca" (a view reasserted in T. N. Mitchell, *Cicero*, 175ff.).

194. *Supplicatio*: Caes. *B. Gall.* 2.35.4; Cic. *Prov. Cons.* 27; *Balb.* 61; *Pis.* 45, 59; Plut. *Caes.* 21.1f.; Dio 39.5.1. Generally on Caesar in late 57 and early 56, see Gelzer, *Caesar*, 116ff.

195. Cic. *Vat.* 38. Vatinius had been defeated 20 January 56—in the very elections in which Clodius was so successful.

196. Cic. *Q.F.* 2.5.2 (2.4.5).

197. Badian, "The Attempt to Try Caesar." That the attempt took place in 56 and

not in 58 hangs on the proper comprehension of *mox* at Suet. *Iul.* 23.1. The correctness of Badian's construal is abundantly established by the material collected in Rose, "Mox."

198. Suet. *Iul.* 24.1; Plut. *Cat. Min.* 41.3. Domitius Ahenobarbus ultimately became consul for 54.

199. Clodius's friendship with Caesar: Cic. *Sest.* 39f.; *Har. Resp.* 47; *Planc.* 86.

200. Gaius: Cic. *Sest.* 41. Appius was to be governor of Sardinia in 56 (Plut. *Caes.* 21.2); he was still with Caesar in March 56 (Cic. *Q.F.* 2.5.4 [2.4.6]).

201. Cic. *Planc.* 75ff.; Schol. Bob. 165 (St).

202. The suggestion of Gruen, *Last Generation*, 304, 321, followed by J. W. Crawford, *M. Tullius Cicero: The Lost and Unpublished Orations*, 170ff.

203. Cicero's poor relationship with Cispius before 57: Cic. *Har. Resp.* 21.

204. Sources: Cic. *Q.F.* 2.5.4 (2.4.6); *Cael.* 78.

205. Badian, "The *scribae* of the Roman Republic."

206. The remark is appended immediately to Cicero's recounting of Cloelius's acquittal: "sed hoc incommodum consolantur cottidianae damnationes inimicorum" (*Q.F.* 2.5.4 [2.4.6]).

207. So Gruen, *Last Generation*, 305. At *Q.F.* 2.5.4 (2.4.6) Cicero takes special glee in the forensic shipwreck of a certain Sevius, who is otherwise unknown. Even if *Servius* is to be read here, the man in question cannot be the Servius Pola who was among the supporters of the *gens Clodia* in 54 (*Q.F.* 2.12.2); see Shackleton Bailey, *Cicero: Epistulae ad Quintum Fratrem*, 182.

208. Sources: Cic. *Cael.*; Dio 39.14.3. Cf. Strabo 17.1.11; Quint. 4.2.27, 11.1.51, 11.1.68; Suet. *Gram.* 26.

209. *Tirocinium fori* with M. Crassus and Cicero: Cic. *Cael.* 9. Prosecution of Antonius: *Cael.* 73f.; Dio 39.40.2. For an excellent sketch of Caelius, see Wiseman, *Catullus and His World*, 62ff. (the year of Caelius's quaestorship is discussed on p. 66).

210. Sumner, "The Lex Annalis," 248 n. 11; Wiseman, *Catullus and His World*, 66.

211. Cic. *Cael.* 17.

212. Caelius *pater*'s African property: Cic. *Cael.* 73.

213. Wiseman, *Catullus and His World*, 67.

214. Epstein, *Personal Enmity in Roman Politics*, 118f.

215. Caelius's prosecutors: see Austin, *M. Tulli Orationis Pro M. Caelio Oratio*, 154ff. Caelius's treatment of Bestia: Wiseman, *Catullus and His World*, 67f.

216. *Paternae inimicitiae* and the courts: Thomas, "Se venger au forum"; Epstein, *Personal Enmity in Roman Politics*, 92ff. Cicero's treatment of Atratinus: Gotoff, "Cicero's Analysis."

217. Gruen, *Last Generation*, 307.

218. See the lively treatment by Wiseman, *Catullus and His World*, 69ff.

219. Heinze, "Ciceros Rede *Pro Caelio*"; Classen, "Ciceros Rede für Caelius"; Gruen, *Last Generation*, 305ff.; Stroh, *Taxis und Taktik*, 243ff.; Wiseman, *Catullus and His World*, 71ff. A valuable, but often overlooked, study is Geffcken, *Comedy in the Pro Caelio*.

220. Geffcken, *Comedy in the Pro Caelio*, 21ff.

221. The most influential political analysis is Gruen, *Last Generation*, 305ff.

222. See section 9 of this chapter.

223. Only the references to L. Lucceius, an associate of Pompey who had acted as Dio's host (Cic. *Cael.* 51–55), entangle Pompey in the charges against Caelius. But it is by no means clear that Lucceius came off badly in the prosecution's case, nor can this tenuous link bear so much weight as to define the central significance of the trial; see Epstein, *Personal Enmity in Roman Politics*, 118f.

224. Skinner, "Clodia Metelli"; Wiseman, *Catullus and His World*, 38ff.

225. Twice more the Claudii Pulchri would attempt to ruin Caelius: in 54 Servius Pola, in behalf of the Claudii, prepared to prosecute Caelius (Cic. *Q.F.* 2.12.2) and Ap. Claudius attempted to bring Caelius to trial in 50 (Cic. *Fam.* 8.12.1–3).

226. Skinner, "Clodia Metelli," 283f.

227. Cic. *Q.F.* 2.3.4.

228. Plut. *Pomp.* 48; Dio 39.19.1f.

229. Nicolet, "Le Temple des Nymphes," collects and evaluates the evidence for the importance of the temple in the grain distributions and for its destruction.

230. See Cic. *Cael.* 78; *Har. Resp.* 57; *Mil.* 73; *Parad. Stoic.* 4.31. See Benner, *Die Politik des P. Clodius*, 121 (who summarizes earlier attempts to explain Clodius's *strategy* in destroying the temple; scholars have tended to accept Cicero's allegations with remarkable credulity).

231. Sources: Cic. *Har. Resp.* 22–26; see Lenaghan, *A Commentary on Cicero's Oration De Haruspicum Responso*, 114ff.

232. Cicero on Clodius and slaves: Treggiari, *Roman Freedmen*, 265f.; Favory, "Classes dangereuses et crise de l'État," 129ff. Clodius's personal interest in producing successful games is made clear in his exertions to import lions from Macedonia: Cic. *Pis.* 89. Clodius suffered more than one setback: D. Laberius refused to provide the aedile with a mime (Macrob. *Sat.* 2.6.6).

233. Benner, *Die Politik des P. Clodius*, 111ff., collects earlier proposals.

234. Ibid., 114.

235. Cic. *Q.F.* 2.5.1.

236. Lenaghan, *A Commentary on Cicero's Oration De Haruspicum Responso*, 117. Cicero's departure: *Q.F.* 2.6.4.

237. Cic. *Q.F.* 2.6.4.

238. The law and its controversy: T. N. Mitchell, *Cicero*, 102, 105–7 (with full references). Cicero's proposal: Cic. *Q.F.* 2.6.1; *Fam.* 1.9.8. Lupus's proposal: Cic. *Q.F.* 2.1.1. Senatorial machinations: Cary, "Asinus Germanus"; Seager, *Pompey*, 114. Debate: Cic. *Fam.* 1.9.8.

239. Cic. *Q.F.* 2.6.2; *Fam.* 1.9.9ff.

240. Tatum, "The Marriage of Pompey's Son."

241. Cic. *Fam.* 1.9 is sufficient testimony to that.

Chapter 8

1. Plut. *Caes.* 21.2; *Pomp.* 51.3; App. *B. Civ.* 2.17.

2. The dynasts' (especially Pompey's) need for aristocratic support: Gruen, "Pompey," 8off.; Gruen, *Last Generation*, 146ff.

3. Clodius's family loyalty: Hillard, "The Claudii Pulchri," 290ff.

4. Benner, *Die Politik des P. Clodius*, 127ff., recognizes the necessity for Clodius to shore up support in the *comitia centuriata* at this stage in his career.

5. This despite the fact (more obvious in retrospect) that the dynasts were not invariably effectual at placing their candidates at elections; see Gruen, *Last Generation*, 146ff.; Seager, *Pompey*, 127ff.

6. Wiseman, *Cinna the Poet*, 163, has no basis for his proposal that Pompey and Clodius were negotiating before Luca. Cf. Seager, *Pompey*, 126.

7. Marriage tie: Tatum, "The Marriage of Pompey's Son." Clodius's reaction: Seager, *Pompey*, 126, alleges that Clodius's enthusiastic posture made its insincerity obvious to everyone, but this is to take too Ciceronian a line. Clodius's palinode: Schol. Bob. 170 (St). Dio 39.29.1 offers a motive for Clodius's support of Pompey that is banal and unhelpful. Benner, *Die Politik des P. Clodius*, 137ff., follows Stein and Gelzer in dating the *Har. Resp.* to September 56 (against which view see Lenaghan, *A Commentary on Cicero's Oration De Haruspicum Responso*, 22ff.), as a consequence of which he argues that Clodius's volte-face was not an immediate product of the conference at Luca but came rather later.

8. Milo's trial seems to have been dropped, however; Dio 39.20.2.

9. Clodius's good standing: Cic. *Fam.* 1.9.10, 19; *Q.F.* 2.3.4. Optimate resentment of Cicero: Cic. *Att.* 4.5.1–3; *Fam.* 1.7.7, 1.9.19. See T. N. Mitchell, *Cicero*, 181ff.; Meier, "Das Kompromiss-Angebot an Caesar."

10. Dio 39.20.1–2. Cf. Cic. *Har. Resp.* 20, 62.

11. The continuous text of the *responsum* has been culled by Wissowa, *Religion und Kultus*, 545 n. 4 (numerals in parentheses refer to the text of the *Har. Resp.*). The text presented here, which depends on Maslowski, *M. Tulli Ciceronis scripta quae manserunt omnia*, diverges from the one printed by Wissowa.

12. For the procedure, see Wissowa, *Religion und Kultus*, 544f. Further on the *haruspices*, see Thulin, *Die Etruskische Disciplin*; Rawson, *Roman Culture and Society*, 289ff.; MacBain, *Prodigy and Expiation*, 43ff.; North, "Diviners and Divination at Rome." This *responsum* is analyzed by Thulin, *Die Etruskische Disciplin*, 78f.

13. Rawson, *Roman Culture and Society*, 302ff. (p. 306 canvasses various possible political interpretations of the response, a survey which itself demonstrates the absence of any indisputable political reference).

14. North, "Diviners and Divination at Rome," 54f.

15. In June many in the senate still felt that Cicero should give up his Palatine home (no doubt for numerous reasons): *Att.* 4.5.2.

16. Record of the *contio*: Cic. *Har. Resp.* 8. It is uncertain whether there was another attack on Cicero's *domus* at this time, as Dio 39.20.3 asserts; cf. Cic. *Har. Resp.* 16; Wiseman, *Cinna the Poet*, 164; and Lenaghan, *A Commentary on Cicero's Oration De Haruspicum Responso*, 23f. In any case, Milo probably set up a guard over Cicero's property, and there was on Cicero's part genuine anxiety over its well-being: Cic. *Att.* 4.7.3 and *Har. Resp.* 15.

17. Authority of *quindecimviri sacris faciundis*: Torelli, *Elogia Tarquiniensia*, 105f.

18. Cic. *Har. Resp.* 55; cf. Dio's uncertain remarks about Clodius's blocking public business in connection with Milo's trial but set in his text as an introduction to Clodius's public attacks on Cicero in the immediate aftermath of the *haruspices'* response (39.19.3). Doubt regarding the whole matter is expressed by Lenaghan, *A Commentary on Cicero's Oration De Haruspicum Responso*, 184f.

19. Cic. *Fam.* 1.9.9–10; *Q.F.* 2.6.2.

20. The precise date of this meeting depends on the date of the *Har. Resp.*, itself an

issue freighted with difficulties. A date for the speech before 15 May seems likeliest: Lenaghan, *A Commentary on Cicero's Oration De Haruspicum Responso*, 22ff.

21. Cic. *Prov. Cons.* 10–12; *Pis.* 41; *Q.F.* 3.2.2; Dio 39.59.2. See Badian, *Publicans and Sinners*, 109; for a more charitable (but less plausible) assessment of Gabinius's governorship of Syria, see Williams, "*Rei Publicae Causa*," 25ff.

22. Clodius's Syrian interests: *In Clod. et Cur.*, frr. 7–11 (Crawford); Rawson, *Roman Culture and Society*, 119, 122 (where she takes this very episode as proof of Clodius's Syrian *clientela*). Appius also had Syrian connections; see Rawson, *Roman Culture and Society*, 115f. Clodius's concern will have been for the local Syrian aristocracy, which was of course Gabinius's interest as well (Badian, *Publicans and Sinners*, 115). The Claudii Pulchri, one should perhaps note, were not invariably hostile to the tax farmers: Cic. *Fam.* 3.3.4 and Rawson, *Roman Culture and Society*, 240f.

23. Servilius: Cic. *Har. Resp.* 2. Offense at Cicero's conduct: Cic. *Har. Resp.* 3. Opposition to *publicani*: Cic. *Att.* 1.17.9; Badian, *Publicans and Sinners*, 100f.

24. Often discussed, most recently by T. N. Mitchell, *Cicero*, 186ff. (with further literature).

25. Cic. *Prov. Cons.* 14; *Q.F.* 2.6.1; *Phil.* 14.24. Cicero does not actually relate the basis for Gabinius's claim, but presumably it was his defeat of Alexander and his general suppression of revolt in 57 (sources in *MRR* 2:203).

26. Cicero's palinode: Cic. *Att.* 4.5.1. The precise reference of Cicero's expression is irrecoverable (despite numerous proposals).

27. Cic. *Fam.* 1.7.10; *Prov. Cons.* 28; *Balb.* 61. Cicero's (fruitless) attack on Piso and Gabinius: *Prov. Cons.* 1ff., 17; Asc. 2 (C).

28. T. N. Mitchell, *Cicero*, 184ff.

29. Dio 39.21.1. The tribunes who joined Cicero are not actually named. That this law was the target of Cicero's expedition is made explicit by Dio. Antony attempted a similar action against the tablets of Dolabella in 47 (Dio 42.32.3).

30. Culham, "Archives and Alternatives," 105ff.

31. Dio 39.21.2.

32. Dio 39.21.2; Plut. *Cat. Min.* 40.1; *Cic.* 34.1. This episode is discussed by Gelzer, *Cicero*, 178; Fehrle, *Cato Uticensis*, 162ff.; Nippel, *Aufruhr und Polizei*, 248.

33. This is made clear by Plutarch's account: *Cat. Min.* 40.1; *Cic.* 34.1.

34. Dio 39.21.4; Plut. *Cat. Min.* 40.1; *Cic.* 34.1.

35. Dio 39.22.1; Plut. *Cat. Min.* 40.2; *Cic.* 34.2. Cato returned to Rome in late summer: Fehrle, *Cato Uticensis*, 153.

36. Various honors for Cato were mooted in the senate in the immediate aftermath of Cato's homecoming, all (characteristically) rejected by the stern Stoic. Cato's return and its importance to the *optimates* as a rallying point: Fehrle, *Cato Uticensis*, 159ff.

37. Schol Bob. 171 (St).

38. Cic. *Att.* 4.15.4; *Q.F.* 2.2.2, 2.15(14).2, 2.16(15).2, 3.4.2, 3.4.4, 3.6(8).1; *Fam.* 1.7.7, 1.7.10, 1.9.21, 2.6.4; *Planc.* 91ff. For discussion, see T. N. Mitchell, *Cicero*, 183f., 191.

39. Dio 39.22.4–39.23.2, correctly elucidated by Mommsen, *Römisches Staatsrecht*, 1:321 n. 6. There is no justification whatsoever for detecting in this passage a reference to freedmen, as do Eder, *Servitus Publica*, 24ff., and Benner, *Die Politik des P. Clodius*, 64f.

40. Dio 39.23.3–4. Fehrle, *Cato Uticensis*, 163f., regards the involvement of Caesar as an anachronism on Dio's part.

41. Dio 39.27; Plut. *Pomp.* 51; *Crass.* 14; *Caes.* 21; *Cat. Min.* 41; App. *B. Civ.* 2.17; Suet. *Iul.* 24; cf. Cic. *Att.* 4.8A.2.

42. Dio 39.27.3.

43. Dio 39.27.3–39.29.3; Val. Max. 6.2.6.

44. M. Nonnius Sufenas, another tribune of 56, also cooperated with C. Cato and with Clodius. Sufenas and Cato, with the support of the coalition, were elected praetors in 55 for 55; see Linderski, *Roman Questions*, 118ff.

45. Dio 39.31; Plut. *Pomp.* 52; *Crass.* 15; *Cat. Min.* 41; App. *B. Civ.* 2.17–18; cf. Vell. 2.46.

46. *Libertas* a slogan: Plut. *Pomp.* 52.

47. Aedilician elections: Dio 39.32.2; Plut. *Pomp.* 53.3; App. *B. Civ.* 2.17. Trebonian legislation: Dio 39.32.3–39.36.2; Plut. *Crass.* 15.5; *Cat. Min.* 43.

48. There is no reason to suppose, as does Benner, *Die Politik des P. Clodius*, 126f., 145, that the public attacks on Pompey's statues that followed the passage of the *lex Trebonia de provinciis consularibus* (Plut. *Cat. Min.* 43.4) were led by Clodius.

49. *Q.F.* 2.8(7).2. For speculation on the exact nature of the Ciceronian project, very possibly having to do with Cicero's commission to restore the temple of Tellus, see Shackleton Bailey, *Cicero: Epistulae ad Quintum Fratrem*, 189.

50. Mommsen, *Römisches Staatsrecht*, 2:690ff.

51. Cic. *Leg.* 3.8.18.

52. Cic. *Mil.* 50, 55, 74ff.; *Phil.* 12.23. In late 53, Clodius bought the Palatine house of M. Scaurus for HS 14,800,000, cf. Plin. *N.H.* 36.103.

53. Lenaghan, *A Commentary on Cicero's Oration De Haruspicum Responso*, 133; Benner, *Die Politik des P. Clodius*, 122 n. 503, 145.

54. Cic. *Att.* 4.6.4, 4.9.2, 4.10.2.

55. Cic. *Att.* 4.11.12. On the expression, see Shackleton Bailey, *Cicero's Letters to Atticus*, 2:197. Benner, *Die Politik des P. Clodius*, 145, exaggerates the significance of this passage.

56. Sources for the *lex Licinia*: Cic. *Planc.* 36ff.; *Fam.* 8.2.1; Dio 39.37.1; Schol. Bob. 152 (St). The *senatus consultum* of 10 February 56: see chapter 7, section 10. Electioneering became an issue immediately after the consular elections were over: Cic. *Q.F.* 2.9(7).3; Dio 39.37.2–4.

57. Apparently Hortensius, who also spoke on Plancius's behalf, dealt with the technical aspects of the accusation; see Cic. *Planc.* 37.

58. De Robertis, *Il diritto associativo romano*, 110f.; Accame, "La legislazione romana intorno ai collegi," 32ff.; Treggiari, *Roman Freedmen*, 176f.; Taylor, *Party Politics*, 210; Ausbüttel, *Untersuchungen zu den Vereinen*, 92. Even Linderski (the best and fullest examination of this measure), *Roman Questions*, 211f., is willing to accept a connection with *collegia*. The *lex Licinia* not concerned with *collegia*: Mommsen, *De collegiis*, 60; Waltzing, *Étude historique sur les corporations professionnelles*, 1:111f.; Lintott, "Electoral Bribery," 9.

59. See chapter 7, section 10.

60. Cic. *Planc.* 45 (*decuriatio tribulium—descriptio populi—suffragi largitione devincta—decuriasse—conscripsisse—sequestrem fuisse—pronuntiasse—divisisse*); 47 (*sequestrem fuisse—largitum esse—conscripsisse—tribules decuriavisse*).

61. *Collegia* in elections: *Comm. Pet.* 30. Cicero's exposition, such as it is, in *Pro Plancio* and especially the language of Dio 39.37.1 make it clear that the principal thrust of this law was to prevent candidates from securing office by offering bribes, Dio's explicit point being that bribery was every bit as objectionable as was violence,

certain forms of which were of course already illegal; see Nippel, *Public Order in Ancient Rome*, 53ff. The relationship between the *lex Licinia* and the *senatus consultum* of 56 is established beyond doubt by Linderski, *Roman Questions*, 204ff., 648.

62. See esp. Cic. *Planc.* 86ff. Ward, *Marcus Crassus*, 271f.; Seager, *Pompey*, 129; and Benner, *Die Politik des P. Clodius*, 145, view the *lex Licinia* as an action hostile to Clodius; they see Clodius's *legatio libera* as a ruse on the part of the consuls to remove Clodius from the scene.

63. Cic. *Mil.* 24; *De aere alieno Milonis*, fr. 16 (Crawford). Elections postponed: Plut. *Pomp.* 54; Dio 40.45.5.

64. E.g., Benner, *Die Politik des P. Clodius*, 146.

65. Badian, *Studies*, 150.

66. Cic. *Att.* 1.1.

67. Sources: *MRR* 2:215. Hearings in July 54: Cic. *Att.* 4.17.7.

68. Tac. *Ann.* 11.7; Tatum, "Cicero, the Elder Curio, and the Titinia Case," 369.

69. Cic. *Q.F.* 2.12(11).2.

70. Cic. *Att.* 4.15.4; *Q.F.* 3.4.2.

71. Safe from Clodius: *Q.F.* 2.15(14).2. C. Cato: Cic. *Att.* 14.6.5. Ap. Claudius: *Fam.* 1.9.4.

72. Detailed discussion in Linderski, *Roman Questions*, 115ff., 639ff. (with further bibliography).

73. Cic. *Att.* 4.16.5, 4.15.4; Sen. *Contr.* 7.4.7. The *lex Licinia Iunia*: *MRR* 3:173.

74. The relevant passage is Sen. *Contr.* 7.4.7, the Latin of which is admittedly susceptible to more than one interpretation: Münzer, *RE* 13:432; Marshall, *A Historical Commentary on Asconius*, 121; Alexander, *Trials in the Late Roman Republic*, 137f. The argument that Calvus spoke for the defense is made by Linderski, *Roman Questions*, 130ff.; Gruen, "Cicero and Licinius Calvus," 223f., 231f.

75. Sen. *Contr.* 7.4.7: "nec umquam postea Pollio a Catone advocatisque eius aut re aut verbo violatus est." The plural is significant. The word *advocatus* is not employed with such specificity that a possible reference to other *patroni* is excluded.

76. Cic. *Att.* 4.16.5, 4.15.4; Asc. 18, 19 (C); Sen. *Contr.* 7.4.7.

77. Cic. *Att.* 4.16.5: "de C. Catone . . . ego tibi nuntio absolutum iri, neque patronis suis tam libentibus quam accusatoribus."

78. Cic. *Att.* 4.15.4; Plin. *N.H.* 37.81; Dio 39.27.3.

79. The text cited here is that of Watt, *M. Tulli Ciceronis Epistulae*.

80. Shackleton Bailey, *Cicero's Letters to Atticus*, 2:208. But this is thoroughly refuted by Linderski, *Roman Questions*, 126ff.

81. Cicero's formulation of the reason behind Procilius's condemnation (*Att.* 4.15.4), that the court wanted to make plain its disapproval when a *paterfamilias* was cut down in his own *domus* ("patrem familias domi suae occidi nolle"), no doubt recollects the peroration of Clodius, on which Cicero goes on to comment. The actual charge against Procilius probably came under the *lex Cornelia de sicariis et veneficis*; see Alexander, *Trials in the Late Roman Republic*, 138.

82. Val. Max. 4.2.5.

83. Cic. *Att.* 4.16.6, 4.15.7, 4.17.2; *Q.F.* 2.15(14).4, 2.16(15).2f.; see Gruen, *Last Generation*, 148f.

84. Cic. *Scaur.* 31ff.; Schol Ambr. 275 (St).

85. Cic. *Q.F.* 2.13.5.

86. Cic. *Att.* 4.15.7.

87. The sources for Scaurus's trial are assembled in Alexander, *Trials in the Late Roman Republic*, 143f. The basic modern discussion remains Gruen, *Last Generation*, 332ff.

88. On this point, see Tatum, "The Marriage of Pompey's Son," 123.

89. Cic. *Scaur.* 36. There is no reason to believe (with Gruen, *Last Generation*, 33) that Q. and M. Pacuvius, who were among Scaurus's prosecutors, were clients of Appius (even if, as seems unlikely, the manuscripts are correct in reporting their cognomen as Claudius); cf. Courtney, "The Prosecution of Scaurus," 154; Rawson, *Roman Culture and Society*, 235f.

90. Cic. *Att.* 4.17.2; *Q.F.* 3.1.16.

91. Sources: Alexander, *Trials in the Late Roman Republic*, 141f.

92. Plut. *Pomp.* 52; *Cat. Min.* 42; Dio 39.32.1f.; Val. Max. 7.5.6.

93. Cic. *Q.F.* 2.15.3; *Fam.* 1.9.19.

94. Cic. *Fam.* 1.9.19.

95. Gruen, *Last Generation*, 332ff.

96. Cic. *Scaur.* 34.

97. Cic. *Scaur.* 37: "quamquam ea, quae dixi, non secus dixi, quam si eius frater essem, non is, qui et est et qui multa dixit, sed is, qui ego esse in meum consuevi." The passage does not say anything about the length of the whole of Clodius's speech but rather of Clodius's remarks on Appius, *pace* Gruen, *Last Generation*, 334.

98. Could Appius's recent behavior have been the subject of the letter written by Clodius to Caesar, which, to Cicero's satisfaction, Caesar had decided to leave unanswered (*Q.F.* 3.1.11)?

99. Cic. *Att.* 4.17.2f.; *Q.F.* 3.1.16.

100. Cic. *Att.* 4.17.2ff.; *Q.F.* 2.6(8).3, 3.3.2.

101. Cic. *Att.* 4.18.1; *Q.F.* 3.4.1, 3.6(8).4ff.

102. Cic. *Q.F.* 3.2.1; Dio 39.62.1. See Gruen, *Last Generation*, 322ff.; Seager, *Pompey*, 136ff.; Williams, "*Rei Publicae Causa.*"

103. Cic. *Q.F.* 3.2.3; Dio 39.60.3. Discussion: Tatum, "The Marriage of Pompey's Son," 124.

104. Gruen, *Last Generation*, 322ff.

105. Cic. *Att.* 4.18.3; *Q.F.* 3.2.1, 3.3.2.

106. Sources: Alexander, *Trials in the Late Roman Republic*, 145.

107. Cic. *Q.F.* 3.4.2. The violent image of having one's ear bitten off ("auriculam fortasse mordicus abstulisset") leads directly into Cicero's reference to Clodius.

108. Asc. 30 (C). Clodius's inevitable praetorship, and its danger to Rome, is a theme of Cicero's *Pro Milone*, see esp. *Mil.* 88ff. (where the likelihood of Clodius's consulship emerges).

109. Cic. *Q.F.* 3.6(8).6.

110. Asc. 35 (C); Cic. *Fam.* 1.1.3; *Flacc.* 20; Schol Bob. 100 (St).

111. See Gruen, *Last Generation*, 151f., and Linderski, "Q. Scipio Imperator."

112. Asc. 30, 48 (C). Clodius's role in the consular elections was a major one. One need not, however, accept Cicero's claim that he was the actual manager of Plautius's and Metellus Scipio's campaigns (*Mil.* 25) or that, if all went as planned, they would in effect be Clodius's consuls (*Mil.* 89), however great the debt they would, in that eventuality, owe him.

113. Cic. *Fam.* 2.6.3; *Q.F.* 3.7(9).2; *Mil.* 25, 34, 95f.; Asc. 31, 33, 53f. Cic. *Fam.* 2.6 illustrates the depth of Cicero's support.

114. Cic. *Mil.* 25. In addition to these activities, Cicero reports that Clodius "Collinam novam dilectu perditissimorum civium conscribebat," an unclear and possibly corrupt expression. Whether it specifically refers to the enrollment of a new *collegium* or the less formal acquisition of riffraff supporters from the Collina (for Plautius and Metellus Scipio, one hastens to observe) or something else altogether is beyond determination. In fact, whether any specific activity at all lies behind Cicero's phrase must itself be uncertain, since his point is to depict Clodius's electioneering as inept and ineffectual for all its industry, hence the orator's continuation: "quanto ille [Clodius] plura miscebat, tanto hic [Milo] magis in dies convalescebat." On various scholarly attempts to recuperate the exact sense of the reference, see Linderski, *Roman Questions*, 212f., 649, and Benner, *Die Politik des P. Clodius*, 128f. (each with further literature).

115. Cic. *Mil.* 25, 34, 43; Asc. 30, 48 (C); Plut. *Caes.* 28.3f.; *Cat. Min.* 47.1; Liv. *Per.* 107; Dio 40.46.3, 40.48.2; Schol. Bob. 169, 172 (St).

116. Schol. Bob. 169 (St).

117. Milo's munificence: Cic. *Q.F.* 3.6(8).6, 3.7(9).2; *Fam.* 2.6.3; *Mil.* 95. Milo's debts: Plin. *N.H.* 36.104; Schol. Bob. 169 (St). The political liability of excessive indebtedness: Frederiksen, "Caesar, Cicero and the Problem of Debt."

118. Schol. Bob. 169 (St). Cicero's speech was the *De aere alieno Milonis*; see J. W. Crawford, *M. Tullius Cicero: The Fragmentary Speeches*, 265ff.

119. Cic. *Q.F.* 3.6(8).6.

120. Dio 40.46.3; Schol. Bob. 172 (St).

121. Violence in Via Sacra: Asc. 48 (C). Violence at elections: Cic. *Mil.* 41, 43.

122. Cic. *Mil.* 40; *Phil.* 2.21, 49.

123. Elections postponed: Asc. 30f., 33 (C); Dio 40.46.1, 40.48.1; Schol. Bob. 169, 172 (St). Plancus's obstruction: Asc. 30f.; Plut. *Cat. Min.* 47.

124. Cic. *Mil.* 87; *De aere alieno Milonis*, frr. 17, 18 (Crawford); Asc. 52 (C); Schol. Bob. 173 (St).

125. Sources and thorough discussion in Treggiari, *Roman Freedmen*, 37ff. (esp. 49f. on *popularis* proposals).

126. Ap. Claudius Caecus: sources in *MRR* 1:160. C. Claudius Pulcher: sources in *MRR* 1:424.

127. Clodius's interest in *collegia* has a (possible) precedent in Caecus; see chapter 5, section 3, note 60.

128. Cic. *Mil.* 33.

129. The "multi homines urbani industrii, multi libertini in foro gratiosi" mentioned at *Comm. Pet.* 29 will, owing to their concentration in the four urban tribes, have dominated the centuries of the first class of those tribes (Brunt, *Fall of the Roman Republic*, 171 n. 95). However, once the wealthy *libertini*, at any rate those not dwelling in Rome, were redistributed, the *libertini* as a group may actually have proved a less potent electoral block in those tribes, a change that the unredistributed *libertini* might not have appreciated.

130. See chapter 1, section 2.

131. Loposzko, "Gesetzentwürfe betreffs der Sklaven"; Loposzko, *Mouvements sociaux*, 84ff. See also Benner, *Die Politik des P. Clodius*, 130ff., who tends to follow Loposzko and provides further bibliography.

132. Treggiari, *Roman Freedmen*, 29f.

133. Gaius 3.56.

134. Dio 40.47.1–2.

135. Cic. *Mil.* esp. 27ff.; Asc. 32f. (C); App. *B. Civ.* 2.21.75f.; Dio 40.48.2; Schol. Bob. 111f. (St); Liv. *Per.* 107. See Marshall, *A Historical Commentary on Asconius,* 159ff.

136. The exact chronology of the incident was controversial already in antiquity (Asc. 31 [C]); Asconius took pains to consult the *acta;* see Marshall, *A Historical Commentary on Asconius,* 55ff. Matters are helped by a letter from Cicero to Atticus written in 51 (*Att.* 5.13.1), at which time Cicero was still reckoning the number of days since Clodius's death.

137. Cic. *Mil.* 28; Asc. 31 (C). At *Mil.* 53, Cicero suggests that Clodius had installed a large number of men in the terraces of his villa, whose mission was to fall upon Milo when he appeared.

138. Asc. 31f. (C). The cult of Juno Sospes: Cic. *N. D.* 1.82; Liv. 8.14.2. M. Saufeius is called the *antesignanus* of Milo's slaves by Asconius (Asc. 32 [C]). He has been connected with a distinguished family from Praeneste; see Marshall, *A Historical Commentary on Asconius,* 209f. (with further literature); he was later prosecuted *de vi* for his role in Clodius's death, defended by Cicero and Caelius, and was narrowly acquitted (Asc. 55 [C]).

139. The presence of the Bona Dea's shrine: Cic. *Mil.* 86; Asc. 31 (C).

140. This is the motive adduced by Asc. 32 (C) and Dio 40.48.2.

141. That Saufeius was the actual enforcer is made clear at Asc. 55 (C).

142. Cic. *Mil.* 17.

Conclusion

1. Teidius: Asc. 32 (C). Events in Rome following Clodius's death: Cic. *Mil.* 12f., 31, 33, 61, 67f., 70, 91; Caes. *B. Gall.* 7.1; Asc. 32ff., 44, 46, 51f., 55 (C); Liv. *Per.* 107; Dio 40.49.5–50.1; App. *B. Civ.* 2.21.77f.; Schol. Bob. 116 (St).

2. See Seager, *Pompey,* 144ff., for sources and discussion.

3. Senatorial resolution: Cic. *Mil.* 12f., 31; Asc. 44 (C); Schol Bob. 116 (St). *Lex Pompeia: MRR* 2:234; see Gruen, *Last Generation,* 234ff.

4. Sources for Milo's trial are collected in Alexander, *Trials in the Late Roman Republic,* 151f.

5. See ibid., 159f., for sources and recent scholarship.

6. Cloelius's condemnation: Asc. 55f. (C). Cloelius's recall: Cic. *Att.* 14.13.6, 14.13A.2, 14.13B.3, 14.14.2, 14.19.2.

7. Val. Max. 3.5.3. His career: *CIL* 6.1282. Discussion: Wiseman, *Roman Studies,* 45ff.

8. Family relations among the Claudii Pulchri of this generation are not easy to disentangle: see Syme, *Augustan Aristocracy,* 149, and Wiseman, *Roman Studies,* 45ff.

9. Suet. *Aug.* 62.

10. Prosecution of Appius: Cic. *Fam.* 3.11.1–3; *Fam.* 8.6.1. Marriage with Tullia: Cic. *Att.* 5.4.1, 6.1.10, 5.5.1, 7.3.12; *Fam.* 2.15.2, 3.10.5, 8.6.2, 8.13.1. Dolabella's adrogation: Dio 42.29.1; see Shackleton Bailey, *Two Studies,* 29ff. His tribunate: sources in *MRR* 2:287.

11. Discussion, with sources, in T. N. Mitchell, *Cicero,* 263ff.

12. Sources in *MRR* 2:287. Caesar's legislation: sources in *MRR* 2:286.

13. That this state of affairs obtained in Rome has long been recognized and documented: Alföldi, "The Main Aspects of Political Propaganda."

14. Yavetz, *Plebs and Princeps*, 26, 92ff.

15. Eck, "Senatorial Self-Representation," 129ff.; Zanker, *The Power of Images*.

16. See Wardman, *Religion and Statecraft*, 75f.

17. Syme, *The Roman Revolution*, 284ff.; Dyson, *Community and Society*, 56ff.

18. Agrippa's aedileship: *MRR* 2:415.

The following bibliography, hardly exhaustive, assembles full references to all works cited in the notes, with the exclusion of *RE* articles. Abbreviations for the titles of journals follow standard practices.

Accame, S. "La legislazione romana intorno ai collegi nel I secolo a.c." *Bolletino del museo dell' impero romano* 13 (1942): 13–48.

Achard, G. *Pratique rhétorique et idéologie politique dans les discours "optimates" de Cicéron*. Leiden, 1981.

Afzelius, A. "Die politische Deutung des jüngeren Catos." *C&M* 4 (1941): 100–203.

Aigner, H. "Gab es im republikanischer Rom Wahlbestechungen für Proletarier?" *Gymnasium* 85 (1978): 228–38.

——. "Zur Wichtigkeit der Waffenbeschaffung in der späten römischen Republik." *GB* 5 (1976): 1–24.

Albini, U. "L'orazione contre Vatinio." *PP* 66 (1959): 172–84.

Alexander, M. C. "*Praemia* in the *Quaestiones* of the Late Republic." *CP* 80 (1985): 20–32.

——. *Trials in the Late Roman Republic, 149 BC–50 BC*. Toronto, 1990.

Alföldi, A. "The Main Aspects of Political Propaganda in the Coinage of the Roman Republic." In *Essays in Roman Coinage presented to Harold Mattingly*, edited by R. A. G. Carson and C. H. V. Sutherland, 63–95. Oxford, 1956.

Allen, W., Jr. "Cicero's House and Libertas." *TAPA* 75 (1944): 1–9.

——. "The Location of Cicero's House on the Palatine Hill." *CJ* 35 (1939–40): 134–43.

——. "Nisbet on the Question of the Location of Cicero's House." *CJ* 35 (1939–40): 291–95.

Annequin, J., and M. Létroublon. "Une approche des discours de Cicéron: Les niveaux d'intervention des esclaves dans la violence." *Actes du colloque sur l'esclavage 1972*, 211–48. Paris, 1974.

Astin, A. E. "Censorships in the Late Republic." *Historia* 34 (1985): 175–90.

——. "Cicero and the Censorship." *CP* 80 (1985): 233–39.

——. "Leges Aelia et Fufia." *Latomus* 23 (1964): 421–45.

——. "Regimen Morum." *JRS* 88 (1988): 14–34.

Ausbüttel, F. M. *Untersuchungen zu den Vereinen im Westen des römischen Reiches*. Kallmünz, 1982.

Austin, R. G. *M. Tulli Orationis Pro M. Caelio Oratio*. 3rd ed. Oxford, 1960.

Babcock, C. L. "The Early Career of Fulvia." *AJP* 86 (1965): 1–32.

Badian, E. "The Attempt to Try Caesar." In *Polis and Imperium: Studies in Honour of Edward Togo Salmon*, edited by J. A. S. Evans, 145–66. Toronto, 1974.

——. "The Case of the Cowardly Tribune: C.T.H.R.E. on E.H.L.N.R." *AHB* 3 (1989): 78–84.

——. "The Clever and the Wise: Two Roman *Cognomina* in Context." In *Vir Bonus Discendi Peritus: Studies in Celebration of Otto Skutsch's Eightieth Birthday*, edited by N. Horsfall, 6–12. London, 1988.

——. "The Death of Saturninus." *Chiron* 14 (1984): 101–47.

——. "E.H.L.N.R." *Museum Helveticum* 45 (1988): 203–18.

——. *Foreign Clientela (264–70 B.C.)*. Oxford, 1958.

——. "The House of the Servilii Gemini." *PBSR* 52 (1984): 49–71.

——. "M. Porcius Cato and the Annexation and Early Administration of Cyprus." *JRS* 55 (1965): 110–21.

——. "Marius' Villas: The Testimony of the Slave and the Knave." *JRS* 63 (1973): 121–32.

——. *Publicans and Sinners*. Ithaca, N.Y., 1972.

——. *Roman Imperialism in the Late Republic*. 2nd ed. Ithaca, N.Y., 1968.

——. "The *scribae* of the Roman Republic." *Klio* 71 (1989): 582–603.

——. "The Silence of Norbanus: A Note on Provincial Quaestors under the Republic." *AJP* 104 (1983): 156–71.

——. *Studies in Greek and Roman History*. New York, 1964.

——. "Tiberius Gracchus and the Beginnings of the Roman Revolution." In *Aufstieg und Niedergang der römischen Welt: Geschichte und Kultur Roms im Spiegel der neueren Forschung*, vol. 1, pt. 1, edited by H. Temporini and W. Haase, 668–731. Berlin and New York, 1972.

——. "*Tribuni plebis* and *Res Publica*." In *Imperium Sine Fine: T. Robert S. Broughton and the Roman Republic*, edited by J. Linderski, 187–213. Stuttgart, 1996.

——. "Two Roman Non-Entities." *CQ* 19 (1969): 198–204.

Balsdon, J. P. V. D. "Fabula Clodiana." *Historia* 15 (1966): 65–73.

——. "Panem et circenses." In *Hommages à M. Renard*, 2:57–60. Brussels, 1969.

——. "Roman History, 58–56 B.C.: Three Ciceronian Problems." *JRS* 47 (1957): 15–20.

——. "Roman History, 65–50 B.C.: Five Problems." *JRS* 52 (1962): 134–41.

Bardon, H. "La naissance d'un temple." *REL* 33 (1955): 166–82.

Bauman, R. A. *The Crimen Maiestatis in the Roman Republic and the Augustan Principate*. Johannesburg, 1967.

——. "Criminal Prosecutions by the Aediles." *Latomus* 33 (1974): 245–64.

Beard, M. "Cicero and Divination: The Formation of a Latin Discourse." *JRS* 76 (1986): 33–46.

——. "Priesthood in the Roman Republic." In *Pagan Priests: Religion and Power in the Ancient World*, edited by M. Beard and J. North, 17–48. London, 1990.

——. "Religion." In *The Cambridge Ancient History*, vol. 9, 2nd ed., edited by J. A. Crook, A. Lintott, and E. Rawson, 729–63. Cambridge, 1994.

Beard, M., and J. North, eds. *Pagan Priests: Religion and Power in the Ancient World*. London, 1990.

Bellinger, A. R. "The End of the Seleucids." *Transactions of the Connecticut Academy of Arts and Sciences* 38 (1949): 51–102.

Beloch, K. J. *Römische Geschichte*. Berlin, 1926.

Benabou, M. "Rome et la police des mers au 1er siècle avant J.C.: La répression de la piraterie cilicienne." In *L'homme méditerranéen et la mer*, edited by M. Galley and L. Ladjimi Sebai, 60–69. Paris, 1985.

Benner, H. *Die Politik des P. Clodius Pulcher*. Stuttgart, 1987.

Berchem, J. van. *Les distributions de blé et d'argent à la plèbe romaine sous l'empire*. Geneva, 1939.

Berry, D. H. *Cicero: Pro P. Sulla Oratio*. Cambridge, 1996.

Bleicken, J. *Lex Publica. Gesetz und Recht in der römischen Republik*. Berlin, 1975.

———. "Oberpontifex und Pontifikalkollegium, eine Studie zur römischen Sakralverfassung." *Hermes* 85 (1957): 345–66.

———. *Das Volkstribunat der klassischen Republik*. Munich, 1955.

Borghesi, B. *Oeuvres*. Vol. 4. Paris, 1865.

Bosworth, A. B. "History and Artifice in Plutarch's *Eumenes*." In *Plutarch and the Historical Tradition*, edited by P. A. Stadter, 56–89. London, 1992.

Botsford, G. W. *The Roman Assemblies*. New York, 1909.

Braund, D. *Rome and the Friendly King*. New York, 1984.

Briscoe, J. Review of H. Benner, *Die Politik des P. Clodius Pulcher*. *Gnomon* 60 (1988): 659–61.

Broughton, T. R. S. *Candidates Defeated in Roman Elections: Some Ancient Roman Also-Rans*. Philadelphia, 1991.

———. *The Magistrates of the Roman Republic*. Vols. 1–2. New York, 1951–52. Supplement. New York, 1960. Vol. 3. Atlanta, 1986.

Brouwer, H. H. *Bona Dea: The Sources and a Description of the Cult*. Leiden, 1989.

Brunt, P. A. *The Fall of the Roman Republic and Related Essays*. Oxford, 1988.

———. *Italian Manpower, 225 B.C.–A.D. 14*. Oxford, 1971; repr., 1987.

———. "Iudicia Sublata (58–57 B.C.)." *LCM* 6 (1981): 227–31.

———. "Nobilitas and Novitas." *JRS* 72 (1982): 1–18.

———. "Philosophy and Religion in the Late Republic." In *Philosophia Togata: Essays on Philosophy and Roman Society*, edited by M. Griffin and J. Barnes, 174–98. Oxford, 1989.

———. "The Roman Mob." *P&P* 35 (1966): 3–27.

Büchler-Isler, B. *Norm und Individualität in den Biographien Plutarchs*. Stuttgart, 1972.

Büchner, K. *Studien zur römischen Literatur III: Horaz*. Wiesbaden, 1962.

Burckhardt, L. A. "The Political Elite of the Roman Republic: Comments on Recent Discussions of the Concepts *Nobilitas* and *Homo Novus*." *Historia* 39 (1990): 89–98.

———. *Politischen Strategien der Optimaten in der späten römischen Republik*. Stuttgart, 1988.

Cameron, A. *Circus Factions*. Oxford, 1976.

Carandini, A. "*Domus* e *insulae* sulla pendice settentrionale del Palatino." *Bollettino della commissione archeologica communale di Roma* 91 (1986): 263–78.

Carcopino, J. *Jules Caesar*. 5th ed. Paris, 1968.

Cary, M. "Asinus Germanus." *CQ* 17 (1923): 103–7.

Cébeillac-Gervasoni, M., ed. *Les "Bourgeoisies" municipales italiennes aux IIe and Ier siècle av. J.-C*. Paris and Naples, 1983.

Cerutti, S. M. "The Location of the Houses of Cicero, Clodius and the Porticus Catuli on the Palatine Hill in Rome." *AJP* 118 (1997): 417–26.

Champlin, E. *Final Judgments: Duty and Emotion in Roman Wills, 200 B.C.–A.D. 250*. Berkeley, 1991.

Ciaceri, E. *Cicerone e i suoi tempi*. 2 vols. Milan, 1939–41.

Cicu, L. "Moechus Calvus." *Scandalion* 10–11 (1987–88): 83–89.

Clarke, J. R. *The Houses of Roman Italy, 100 B.C.–A.D. 250*. Berkeley: 1991.

Classen, C. J. "Ciceros Rede für Caelius." In *Aufstieg und Niedergang der römischen Welt: Geschichte und Kultur Roms im Spiegel der neueren Forschung*, vol. 1, pt. 3, edited by H. Temporini and W. Haase, 60–94. Berlin and New York, 1973.

Clemente, G. "Il patronato nei collegia dell'impero romano." *Studi Classici ed Orientali* 21 (1972): 142–229.

Coarelli, F. "Alessandro, i Licinii e Lanuvio." In *L'art décoratif à Rome à la fin de la république et au début du principat*, 229–84. Rome, 1981.

——. "Architettura sacra e architettura privata nella tarda repubblica." In *Architecture et société de l'archaïsme grec à la fin de la république romaine*, edited by P. Gros, 191–217. Paris and Rome, 1983.

——. "Il Campo Marzio occidentale. Storia e topographia." *MEFRA* 89 (1977): 807–46.

——. *Il foro romano: Periodo arcaico*. Rome, 1983.

——. *Il foro romano II: Periodo repubblicano e augusteo*. Rome, 1985.

——. "Public Building in Rome between the Second Punic War and Sulla." *PBSR* 45 (1977): 1–23.

Coarelli, F., I. Kajanto, U. Nyberg, and M. Steinby. *L'area sacra di Largo Argentina*. Rome, 1981.

Constans, L. A. *Un correspondant de Cicéron, Ap. Claudius Pulcher*. Paris, 1921.

Corbeill, A. *Controlling Laughter: Political Humor in the Late Roman Republic*. Princeton, 1996.

Cornell, T. J. *The Beginnings of Rome*. London, 1995.

——. "Some Observations on the *crimen incesti*." In *Le délit religieux dans la cité antique*, edited by J. Sheid, 26–37. Paris, 1981.

——. Review of T. P. Wiseman, *Clio's Cosmetics*. *JRS* 72 (1982): 203–6.

Courtney, E. "The Prosecution of Scaurus in 54 B.C." *Philologus* 105 (1961): 151–56.

Cousin, J. *Cicéron, Discours, Tome XIV (Pour Sestius, Contre Vatinius)*. Paris, 1965.

Cram, R. V. "The Roman Censors." *HSCP* 51 (1940): 71–110.

Crawford, J. W. *M. Tullius Cicero: The Fragmentary Speeches*. 2nd ed. Atlanta, 1994.

——. *M. Tullius Cicero: The Lost and Unpublished Orations*. Göttingen, 1984.

Crawford, M. H. "Money and Exchange in the Roman World." *JRS* 60 (1970): 40–48.

——. *Roman Republican Coinage*. 2 vols. Cambridge, 1974.

Cripiano, M. *Fas et Nefas*. Rome, 1978.

Crook, J. *Law and Life of Rome*. London, 1967.

——. "Lex 'Rivalicia' (FIRA I, NO. 5)." *Athenaeum* 64 (1986): 45–53.

Culham, P. "Archives and Alternatives in Republican Rome." *CP* 84 (1989): 100–115.

Dallo, D. *Ubi Venus Mutatur. Omosessualità e diritto nel mondo romano*. Milan, 1987.

Damon, C. "Sex. Cloelius, scriba." *HSCP* 94 (1992): 227–50.

David, J.-M. *Le patronat judiciaire au dernier siècle de la république romaine*. Rome, 1992.

David, J.-M., S. Demougin, E. Demougin, D. Ferey, J.-M. Flambard, and C. Nicolet. "Le 'Commentariolum Petitionis' de Quintus Cicéron. Etat de la question et étude prosopographique." In *Aufstieg und Niedergang der römischen Welt: Geschichte und Kultur Roms im Spiegel der neueren Forschung*, vol. 1, pt. 3, edited by H. Temporini and W. Haase, 239–77. Berlin and New York, 1973.

De Blois, L. *The Roman Army and Politics in the First Century B.C.* Amsterdam, 1987.

de Libero, L. *Obstruktion. Politische Praktiken im Senat und in der Volksversammlung der ausgehenden römischen Republik (70–49 v. Chr.).* Stuttgart, 1992.

Demandt, A. "Symbolfunktionen antiker Baukunst." In *Palast und Hütte. Beiträge zum Bauen und Wohnen im Altertum von Archäologen, Vor- and Frühgeschichtlern*, edited by D. Papenfull and V. M. Strocka, 49–62. Mainz am Rhein, 1982.

de Neeve, P. W. *Peasants in Peril: Location and Economy in Italy in the Second Century B.C.* Amsterdam, 1984.

De Robertis, F. M. *Il diritto associativo romano dai collegi della reppublica alle corporazione del basso impero.* Bari, 1938.

———. *Lavoro e lavoratori nel mondo romano.* Bari, 1967.

Deroux, C. "L'identité de Lesbie." In *Aufstieg und Niedergang der römischen Welt: Geschichte und Kultur Roms im Spiegel der neueren Forschung*, vol. 1, pt. 3, edited by H. Temporini and W. Haase, 390–416. Berlin and New York, 1973.

De Sanctis, G. *Storia dei Romani.* 4 vols. Turin, 1907.

Dettenhofer, M. H. *Perdita Iuventus. Zwischen den Generationen von Caesar und Augustus.* Munich, 1992.

Develin, R. "Sulla and the Senate." *AHB* 1 (1987): 130–34.

Dondin-Payne, M. "*Homo novus*: Un slogan de Caton à Cesar." *Historia* 30 (1981): 22–81.

Downey, G. *A History of Antioch in Syria.* Princeton, 1961.

———. "The Occupation of Syria by the Romans." *TAPA* 82 (1951): 149–63.

———. "Q. Marcius Rex at Antioch." *CP* 32 (1937): 144–51.

Drumann, K. W., and P. Groebe. *Geschichte Roms in seinem Übergang von der republikanischen zur monarchischen Verfassung.* Vol. 2. Berlin and Leipzig, 1902.

Drummond, A. "Early Roman *Clientes*." In *Patronage in Ancient Society*, edited by A. Wallace-Hadrill, 89–115. London, 1989.

———. *Law, Politics and Power: Sallust and the Execution of the Catilinarian Conspirators.* Stuttgart, 1995.

———. "Some Observations on the Order of the Consuls' Names." *Athenaeum* 66 (1978): 80–108.

Duncan-Jones, R. *The Economy of the Roman Empire.* 2nd ed. Cambridge, 1982.

———. *Structure and Scale in the Roman Economy.* Cambridge, 1990.

Dyson, S. L. *Community and Society in Roman Italy.* Baltimore, 1992.

Earl, D. C. "Appian *B.C.* 1, 14 and 'Professio.'" *Historia* 14 (1965): 325–32.

———. *The Moral and Political Tradition of Rome.* Ithaca, N.Y., 1967.

Eck, W. "Senatorial Self-Representation: Developments in the Augustan Period." In *Caesar Augustus: Seven Aspects*, edited by F. Millar and E. Segal, 129–68. Oxford, 1984.

Eckstein, A. M. *Senate and General: Individual Decision-Making and Roman Foreign Relations, 264–194 B.C.* Berkeley, 1987.

Eder, W. *Servitus Publica: Untersuchungen zur Entstehung, Entwicklung und Funktion der öffentlichen Sklaverei in Rom.* Wiesbaden, 1980.

Ellis, R. *A Commentary on Catullus.* 2nd ed. Oxford, 1889.

Epstein, D. F. "Cicero's Testimony at the *Bona Dea* Trial." *CP* 81 (1986): 229–35.
———. *Personal Enmity in Roman Politics, 218–43 B.C.* London, 1987.
Erskine, A. "Hellenistic Monarchy and Roman Political Invective." *CQ* 41 (1991): 106–20.
Evans, J. K. "Plebs rustica. The Peasantry of Classical Italy." *AJAH* 5 (1980): 19–47, 134–71.
Favory, F. "Classes dangereuses et crise de l'État dans le discours cicéronien d'après les écrits de Cicéron de 57 à 52." In *Texte, politique, idéologie: Ciceron*. Annales littéraires de l'Université de Besançon, no. 187, 109–233. Besançon, 1978–79.
Fehrle, R. *Cato Uticensis*. Darmstadt, 1983.
Flambard, J.-M. "Clodius, les collèges, la plèbe et les esclaves. Recherches sur la politique populaire au milieu du Ier siècle." *MEFR, Antiquité* 89 (1977): 115–56.
———. "Les collèges et les élites locales à l'époque républicaine d'après l'exemple de Capoue." In *Les "bourgeoises" municipales italiennes aux IIe et Ier siècles av. J.-C.*, edited by M. Cébeillac-Gervasoni, 75–90. Paris and Naples, 1983.
———. "Collegia Compitalicia: Phénomène associatif, cadres territoriaux et cadres civiques dans le monde romain à l'époque républicaine." *Ktema* 6 (1981): 143–66.
Flower, H. *Ancestor Masks and Aristocratic Power in Roman Culture*. Oxford, 1996.
Fordyce, C. J. *Catullus: A Commentary*. Oxford, 1961.
Frank, T. "Cicero and the Poetae Novi." *AJP* 40 (1919): 396–415.
Frederiksen, M. W. "Caesar, Cicero and the Problem of Debt." *JRS* 56 (1966): 128–41.
Frézouls, E. "La construction du *theatrum lapidum* et son contexte politique." In *Théâtre et Spectacles dans l'Antiquité. Actes du Colloque de Strasbourg 5–7 novembre 1981*, 193–214. Leiden, 1983.
Frier, B. W. *The Rise of the Roman Jurists*. Princeton, 1985.
———. "Urban Praetors and Rural Violence: The Legal Background to Cicero's *Pro Caecina*." *TAPA* 113 (1983): 221–41.
Gagé, J. *Matronalia*. Brussels, 1963.
Gallini, C. "Politica religiosa di Clodio." *SMSR* 33 (1962): 257–72.
Garnsey, P. D. A. "Independent Freedmen and the Economy of Roman Italy under the Principate." *Klio* 63 (1981): 359–71.
———. *Famine and Food Supply in the Graeco-Roman World*. Cambridge, 1988.
———. *Social Status and Legal Privilege in the Roman Empire*. Oxford, 1970.
Garnsey, P. D. A., and D. Rathbone. "The Background to the Grain Law of Gaius Gracchus." *JRS* 75 (1985): 20–25.
Garnsey, P. D. A., and G. Woolf. "Patronage of the Rural Poor in the Roman World." In *Patronage in Ancient Society*, edited by A. Wallace-Hadrill, 153–70. London, 1989.
Gasperini, L. "Due nuovi apporti epigrafici alla storia di Cirene romana." *Quaderni di Archelogia della Libia* 5 (1967): 53–64.
Geffcken, K. A. *Comedy in the Pro Caelio*. Leiden, 1973.
Gelzer, M. *Caesar: Politician and Statesman*. Translated by P. Needham. Oxford, 1968.
———. *Cicero, ein biographischer Versuch*. Wiesbaden, 1969.
Gill, C. "The Character-Personality Distinction." In *Characterization and Individuality in Greek Literature*, edited by C. B. R. Pelling, 1–31. Oxford, 1991.
Gonfroy, F. "Homosexualité et idéologie esclavagiste chez Cicéron." *Dialogues d'histoire ancienne* 4 (1978): 219–62.

Gotoff, H. C. "Cicero's Analysis of the Prosecution Speeches in the *Pro Caelio*: An Exercise in Practical Criticism." *CP* 18 (1986): 121–32.

Grasmück, E. L. *Exilium. Untersuchungen zur Verbannung in der Antike.* Paderborn, 1978.

Green, P. *Alexander to Actium.* Berkeley, 1990.

Greenhalgh, P. *Pompey: The Roman Alexander.* London, 1980.

Greenidge, A. H. J. *The Legal Procedure of Cicero's Time.* London, 1901.

———. "The Repeal of the *Lex Aelia Fufia*." *CR* 7 (1893): 158–61.

———. *Roman Public Life.* London, 1901.

Grimal, P. *Études de chronologie cicéronienne (années 58 et 57 av. J.-C.).* Paris, 1967.

Gros, P. *Aurea Templa.* Rome, 1976.

———. "Trois temples de la Fortune." *MEFR* 79 (1967): 503–66.

Gruen, E. S. "Cicero and Licinius Calvus." *HSCP* 71 (1966): 215–33.

———. *The Last Generation of the Roman Republic.* Berkeley, 1974.

———. "M. Antonius and the Trial of the Vestals." *RhM* 111 (1968): 59–63.

———. "P. Clodius: Instrument or Independent Agent?" *Phoenix* 20 (1966): 120–30.

———. "Pompey, the Roman Aristocracy and the Conference at Luca." *Historia* 18 (1969): 71–108.

———. Review of L. A. Burckhardt, *Politischen Strategien der Optimaten in der späten römischen Republik. Gnomon* 62 (1990): 179–81.

———. "Some Criminal Trials of the Late Republic: Political and Prosopographical Problems." *Athenaeum* 49 (1971): 54–69.

———. "The Trial of C. Antonius." *Latomus* 32 (1973): 301–10.

Habicht, C. *Cicero the Politician.* Baltimore, 1990.

Hahm, D. E. "Roman Nobility and the Three Major Priesthoods." *TAPA* 94 (1963): 73–85.

Hallett, J. P. *Fathers and Daughters in Roman Society.* Princeton, 1984.

Halliwell, S. "Traditional Greek Conceptions of Character." In *Character and Individuality in Greek Literature*, edited by C. B. R. Pelling, 32–59. Oxford, 1990.

Hamilton, M., and M. Hirszowicz. *Class and Inequality in Pre-Industrial, Capitalist and Communist Societies.* Sussex, 1987.

Hardy, E. G. "Three Questions as to Livius Drusus." *CR* 27 (1913): 261–62.

Harris, W. V. "On the Applicability of the Concept of Class in Roman History." In *Forms of Control and Subordination in Antiquity*, edited by T. Yuge and M. Doi, 598–610. Leiden, 1988.

———. *War and Imperialism in Republican Rome, 327–70 B.C.* Oxford, 1979.

Harvey, P. B. Review of D. R. Shackleton Bailey, *Two Studies in Roman Nomenclature. AJP* 101 (1986): 114–20.

Hathorn, R. Y. "Calvum ex Nanneianis: *Ad Atticum* I.16.5." *CJ* 50 (1954): 33–34.

———. "The Political Implications of the Trial of P. Clodius." Ph.D. diss., Columbia University, 1950.

Havas, L. "Schemata und Wahrheit in der Darstellung der spätrepublikanischen politischen Ereignisse." *Klio* 72 (1990): 216–24.

Heinze, R. "Ciceros Rede *Pro Caelio*." *Hermes* 60 (1925): 193–258.

Hejnic, J. "Clodius auctor. Ein Beitrag zur sog. Sallusts Invektive." *RhM* 99 (1956): 255–77.

Hellegouarc'h, J. *Le vocabulaire latin des relations et des partis sous la république.* Paris, 1963.

Herz, P. *Studien zur römischen Wirtschaftgesetzgebung*. Stuttgart, 1988.

Hillard, T. W. "The Claudii Pulchri 76–48: Studies in Their Political Cohesion." Ph.D. diss., Macquarie University, 1976.

——. "*In triclinio Coam, in cubiculo Nolam*: Lesbia and the Other Clodia." *LCM* 6 (1981): 149–54.

——. "P. Clodius Pulcher, 62–58 B.C.: Pompei Adfinis et Sodalis." *PBSR* 50 (1982): 34–44.

——. "Plutarch's Late-Republican Lives: Between the Lines." *Antichthon* 21 (1987): 19–48.

——. "The Sisters of Clodius Again." *Latomus* 32 (1973): 505–14.

Hillard, T. W., M. Taverne, and C. Zawawi. "Q. Caecilius Metellus (Claudianus)?" *AJAH* (forthcoming).

Hillman, T. P. "The Alleged *Inimicitiae* of Pompeius and Lucullus: 78–74." *CP* 86 (1991): 315–18.

Hollemann, A. W. J. "The First Claudian at Rome." *Historia* 35 (1986): 377–78.

Holmes, T. Rice. *The Roman Republic*. 3 vols. Oxford, 1923.

Holzapfel, L. *De transitione ad plebem*. Leipzig, 1877.

Hopkins, K. *Conquerors and Slaves*. Sociological Studies in Roman History, no. 1. Cambridge, 1978.

——. *Death and Renewal*. Sociological Studies in Roman History, no. 2. Cambridge, 1983.

Huttunen, P. *The Social Strata in the Imperial City of Rome*. Oulu, 1974.

Jackson, J. A., ed. *Social Stratification*. Cambridge, 1968.

Jehne, M., ed. *Demokratie in Rom? Die Rolle des Volkes in der Politik der römischen Republik*. Stuttgart, 1995.

Jocelyn, H. D. "The Roman Nobility and the Religion of the Roman State." *Journal of Religious History* 4 (1966–67): 89–104.

Keaney, A. M. "Three Sabine nomina: *Clausus, Consus, *Fisus*." *Glotta* 69 (1991): 202–14.

Keaveney, A. *Lucullus: A Life*. London, 1992.

Keil, J., and A. Wilhelm. *Monumenta Asiae Minoris Antiqua*. Vol. 3. Manchester, 1931.

Kierdorf, W. " 'Funus' und 'Consecratio'. Zu Terminologie und Ablauf der römischen Kaiserapotheose." *Chiron* 16 (1986): 43–70.

Konrad, C. F. "A Note on the Stemma of the Gabinii Capitones." *Klio* 66 (1984): 151–56.

Koster, S. *Die Invektive in der griechischen und römischen Literatur*. Meisenheim an Glan, 1980.

Kubiak, D. P. "Piso's Madness (Cic. *In Pis.* 21 and 47)." *AJP* 110 (1989): 237–45.

Kühnert, B. *Die Plebs Urbana der späten römischen Republik: Ihre ökonomische Situation und soziale Struktur*. Innsbruck, 1991.

Lacey, W. K. "Cicero and Clodius." *Antichthon* 8 (1974): 85–92.

Lacour-Gayet, G. *De P. Clodio Pulchro tr. pl.* Paris, 1888.

——. "P. Clodius Pulcher." *Revue Historique* 41 (1889): 1–37.

Lahusen, G. *Untersuchungen zur Ehrenstatue in Rom*. Rome, 1983.

Lange, L. *Römische Altertümer*. 3 vols. Berlin, 1876–79.

——. *Über die Transitio ad Plebem: Ein Beitrag zum römischen Gentilrecht und zu den Scheingeschäften des römischen Rechts*. Leipzig, 1864.

Latte, K. *Römische Religionsgeschichte*. Munich, 1960.

Lazenby, J. F. Review of L. De Blois, *The Roman Army and Politics in the First Century B.C. CR* 39 (1989): 150–51.

Leeman, A. D., H. Pinkster, and H. L. W. Nelson. *M. Tullius Cicero De Oratore Libri III.* 2 vols. Heidelberg, 1981–85.

Leen, A. "Cicero and the Rhetoric of Art." *AJP* 112 (1991): 229–45.

Lenaghan, J. O. *A Commentary on Cicero's Oration De Haruspicum Responso.* The Hague, 1969.

Leumann, M. *Lateinische Laut- und Formen-Lehre.* Munich, 1963.

Levick, B. "Morals, Politics, and the Fall of the Roman Republic." *G&R* 29 (1982): 53–62.

———. *Tiberius the Politician.* London, 1976.

Lewis, R. G. "Inscriptions of Amiternum and Catilina's Last Stand." *ZPE* 74 (1988): 31–42.

Liebenam, W. *Zur Geschichte und Organisation des römischen Vereinswesens.* Leipzig, 1890.

Liebeschuetz, J. H. W. G. *Continuity and Change in Roman Religion.* Oxford, 1979.

Liebmann-Frankfort, T. *La frontière orientale dans la politique extérieure de la république romaine.* Brussels, 1969.

Linderski, J. "The Augural Law." In *Aufstieg und Niedergang der römischen Welt: Geschichte und Kultur Roms im Spiegel der neueren Forschung,* vol. 2, pt. 16, fasc. 3, edited by H. Temporini and W. Haase, 2146–2312. Berlin and New York, 1986.

———. "Q. Scipio Imperator." In *Imperium Sine Fine: T. Robert S. Broughton and the Roman Republic,* edited by J. Linderski, 145–85. Stuttgart, 1996.

———. *Roman Questions.* Stuttgart, 1995.

Lindsay, W. M. *The Latin Language.* Oxford, 1894.

Ling, R. "A Stranger in Town: Finding the Way in an Ancient City." *G&R* 37 (1990): 204–14.

Lintott, A. W. "Electoral Bribery in the Roman Republic." *JRS* 80 (1990): 1–16.

———. "P. Clodius Pulcher—*Felix Catilina?*" *G&R* 14 (1967): 157–69.

———. "Provocatio: From the Struggle of the Orders to the Principate." In *Aufstieg und Niedergang der römischen Welt: Geschichte und Kultur Roms im Spiegel der neueren Forschung,* vol. 1, pt. 2, edited by H. Temporini and W. Haase, 226–67. Berlin and New York, 1972.

———. Review of F. M. Ausbüttel, *Untersuchungen zu den Vereinen im Westen des römischen Reiches. JRS* 78 (1988): 249–50.

———. Review of E. S. Gruen, *Last Generation of the Roman Republic. CR* 26 (1976): 241–43.

———. "Trinundinum." *CQ* 15 (1965): 281–85.

———. *Violence in Republican Rome.* Oxford, 1968.

Loposzko, T. "Die Bestechung der Richter im Proceß des Klodius im Jahre 61 v.u.Z." *Athenaeum* 56 (1978): 288–303.

———. "Gesetzentwürfe betreffs der Sklaven im Jahre 53 v.u.Z." *Index* 8 (1978–79): 158–66.

———. *Mouvements sociaux à Rome dans les années 57–52 av. J.-C.* Lublin, 1980.

MacBain, B. *Prodigy and Expiation: A Study in Religion and Politics in Republican Rome.* Brussels, 1982.

McDermott, W. C. "Curio Pater and Cicero." *AJP* 93 (1972): 381–411.

———. "Suetonius, *Iul.*, 74, 2." *Latomus* 6 (1947): 173–75.

——. "The Verrine Jury." *RhM* 120 (1977): 64–75.

——. "*Vettius ille, ille noster index.*" *TAPA* 80 (1949): 351–67.

McDonald, W. F. "Clodius and the *Lex Aelia Fufia.*" *JRS* 19 (1929): 164–79.

McGushin, P. *Sallust: The Histories.* Vol. 2. Oxford, 1994.

Mackie, N. "*Popularis* Ideology and Popular Politics at Rome in the First Century B.C." *RhM* 135 (1992): 49–73.

MacMullen, R. "How Many Romans Voted?" *Athenaeum* 58 (1980): 454–57.

——. *Roman Social Relations, 50 B.C. to A.D. 284.* New Haven, 1974.

Magie, D. *Roman Rule in Asia Minor.* Princeton, 1950.

Malcovati, E. *Oratorum Romanorum Fragmenta Liberae Rei Publicae.* 3rd ed. Rome, 1967.

Manfredini, A. D. "*Qui commutant cum feminis vestrem.*" *RIDA* 32 (1985): 257–71.

Marasco, G. "Roma e la pirateria cilicia." *RSI* 99 (1987): 122–46.

Marsh, F. B. "The Policy of Clodius." *CQ* 21 (1927): 30–35.

Marshall, B. A. "Catilina: Court Cases and Consular Candidature." *Scripta Classica Israelica* 3 (1976–77): 127–37.

——. *Crassus: A Political Biography.* Amsterdam, 1976.

——. *A Historical Commentary on Asconius.* Columbia, 1985.

——. "Pompeius' Fear of Assassination." *Chiron* 17 (1987): 119–33.

Martin, J. *Antike Rhetorik. Technik und Methode.* Munich, 1974.

——. *Die Popularen in der Geschichte der späten Republik.* Freiburg, 1965.

Maslakov, G. "Valerius Maximus and Roman Historiography: A Study of the *exempla* Tradition." In *Aufstieg und Niedergang der römischen Welt: Geschichte und Kultur Roms im Spiegel der neueren Forschung,* vol. 2, pt. 32, fasc. 1, edited by H. Temporini and W. Haase, 437–96. Berlin and New York, 1984.

Maslowsi, T. "Domus Milonis Oppugnata." *Eos* 64 (1976): 20–30.

——. *M. Tullius Cicero scripta quae manserunt omnia.* Fasc. 22. Leipzig, 1986.

Mattingly, H. B. "The Consilium of Cn. Pompeius Strabo in 89 B.C." *Athenaeum* 53 (1975): 262–66.

May, J. M. "Cicero and the Beasts." *Syllecta Classica* 7 (1996): 143–53.

——. *Trials of Character: The Eloquence of Ciceronian Ethos.* Chapel Hill, 1988.

Meier, C. *Caesar.* Berlin, 1982.

——. "Das Kompromiss-Angebot an Caesar i. J. 59 v. Chr., ein Beispiel senatorischer Verfassungspolitik." *Mus. Helv.* 32 (1975): 197–208.

——. "Pompeius' Rückkehr aus dem Mithridatischen Kriege und die Catilinarische Verschwörung." *Athenaeum* 40 (1962): 103–25.

——. *Res Publica Amissa.* 2nd ed. Wiesbaden, 1980.

——. "Zur Chronologie und Politik in Caesars ersten Konsulat." *Historia* 10 (1961): 68–98.

Messer, W. S. "Mutiny in the Roman Army: The Republic." *CP* 15 (1920): 158–75.

Meyer, E. *Caesars Monarchie und das Principat des Pompeius.* Stuttgart and Berlin, 1922.

Michels, A. K. *The Calendar of the Roman Republic.* Princeton, 1967.

Millar, F. "The Political Character of the Classical Roman Republic, 200–151 B.C." *JRS* 74 (1984): 1–19.

——. "Political Power in Mid-Republican Rome: Curia or Comitium?" *JRS* 79 (1989): 138–50.

——. "Politics, Persuasion and the People before the Social War (150–90 B.C.)." *JRS* 76 (1986): 1–11.

——. *A Study in Cassius Dio.* Oxford, 1964.

Mitchell, R. E. *Patricians and Plebeians.* Ithaca, N.Y., 1990.

Mitchell, T. N. "Cicero before Luca (September 57–April 56 B.C.)." *TAPA* 100 (1969): 295–320.

——. *Cicero: The Senior Statesman.* New Haven, 1991.

——. "The *Leges Clodiae* and *Obnuntiatio.*" *CQ* 36 (1986): 172–76.

Momigliano, A. "The Theological Efforts of the Roman Upper Classes in the First Century B.C." *CP* 79 (1984): 199–211.

Mommsen, T. *De collegiis et sodaliciis Romanorum.* Kiel, 1843.

——. *Die römische Chronologie bis auf Caesar.* 2nd ed. Berlin, 1859.

——. *Gesammelte Schriften.* 8 vols. Berlin, 1904; repr., 1965.

——. *Römische Forschungen.* Vol. 1. Berlin 1864; repr., 1962.

——. *Römisches Staatsrecht.* 3 vols. Leipzig, 1887.

——. *Römisches Strafrecht.* Leipzig, 1899.

Moreau, P. "Cicéron, Clodius et la publication du Pro Murena." *REL* 58 (1980): 220–37.

——. "Lex Clodia." In *Roman Statutes*, 2 vols., edited by M. H. Crawford, 773–76. London, 1996.

——. "La lex Clodia sur le bannissement de Cicéron." *Athenaeum* 75 (1987): 465–92.

——. *Clodiana Religio. Un procès politique en 61 av. J.-C.* Paris, 1982.

Morgan, M. G. "The Introduction of the Aqua Marcia into Rome, 144–140 B.C." *Philologus* 122 (1978): 25–58.

——. "Politics, Religion and the Games in Rome, 200–150 B.C." *Philologus* 134 (1990): 14–36.

——. "The Portico of Metellus: A Reconsideration." *Hermes* 99 (1971): 480–505.

——. "Villa Publica and Magna Mater: Two Notes on Manubial Building at the Close of the Second Century B.C." *Klio* 55 (1973): 215–46.

Morgan, M. G., and J. A. Walsh. "Tiberius Gracchus (tr. pl. 133 B.C.), the Numantine Affair and the Deposition of M. Octavius." *CP* 73 (1978): 200–210.

Moscovich, M. J. "Historical Compression in Cassius Dio's Account of the Second Century B.C." *Ancient World* 8 (1983): 137–43.

Mueller, H.-F. "Exempla Tuenda: Religion, Virtue and Politics in Valerius Maximus." Ph.D. diss., University of North Carolina, 1994.

Mulroy, D. "The Early Career of P. Clodius Pulcher: A Re-Examination of the Charges of Mutiny and Sacrilege." *TAPA* 118 (1988): 155–78.

Nardo, D. *Il Commentariolum Petitionis: La propaganda elettorale nella Ars di Quinto Cicerone.* Padova, 1970.

Nicolet, C. "La *Lex Gabinia-Calpurnia de insula Delo* et la loi 'annonaire' de Clodius (58 av. J.-C.)." *CRAI* (1980): 259–87.

——. *L'ordre équestre a l'époque républicaine (312–43 av. J.-C.).* 2 vols. Paris, 1966, 1974.

——. "Le Temple des Nymphes et les distributions frumentaires à Rome." *CRAI* (1976): 29–51.

——. *The World of the Citizen in Republican Rome.* Translated by P. S. Falla. London, 1980.

Nicolet, C., J.-C. Dumont, J.-L. Ferrary, and P. Moreau. *Insula Sacra. La loi Gabinia Calpurnia de Délos (58 av. J.-C.)*. Paris and Rome, 1980.

Nicolet, C., P. Moreau, J.-L. Ferrary, and M. H. Crawford. "Lex Gabinia de insula Delo." In *Roman Statutes*, 2 vols., edited by M. H. Crawford, 345–51. London, 1996.

Nippel, W. *Aufruhr und "Polizei" in der römischen Republik*. Stuttgart, 1988.

——. "Policing Rome." *JRS* 74 (1984): 20–29.

——. *Public Order in Ancient Rome*. Cambridge, 1995.

Nisbet, R. G. M. *Tulli Ciceronis De Domo Sua ad Pontifices Oratio*. Oxford, 1939.

Nisbet, R. G. M. *M. Tulli Ciceronis in L. Calpurnium Pisonem Oratio*. Oxford, 1961.

——. Review of D. R. Shackleton Bailey, *Towards a Text of Cicero "Ad Atticum."* *CR* 11 (1961): 238–40.

North, J. "Diviners and Divination at Rome." In *Pagan Priests: Religion and Power in the Ancient World*, edited by M. Beard and J. North, 49–71. London, 1990.

——. "Religion and Politics, from Republic to Principate." *JRS* 76 (1986): 251–58.

Nowak, K.-J. *Der Einsatz Privater Garden in der späten römischen Republik*. Munich, 1973.

Odelstierna, I. *Invidia, Invidiosus, and Invidiam Facere: A Semantic Investigation*. Uppsala Universitets Arrskrift, no. 10. Uppsala, 1949.

Ogilvie, R. M. *A Commentary on Livy, Books 1–5*. Oxford, 1965.

O'Gorman, F. "Campaign Rituals and Ceremonies: The Social Meaning of Elections in England 1780–1860." *P&P* 135 (1992): 79–115.

Omerod, H. A. *Piracy in the Ancient World*. London, 1924.

Oost, S. I. "Cato Uticensis and the Annexation of Cyprus." *CP* 1 (1955): 98–112.

Ooteghem, J. van. *Lucius Licinius Lucullus*. Brussels, 1959.

——. *Pompée le Grand*. Brussels, 1954.

Orr, G. G. "Roman Domestic Religion: The Evidence of the Household Shrines." In *Aufstieg und Niedergang der römischen Welt: Geschichte und Kultur Roms im Spiegel der neueren Forschung*, vol. 2, pt. 16, fasc. 2, edited by H. Temporini and W. Haase, 1557–91. Berlin and New York, 1978.

Palmer, R. E. *The Archaic Community of the Romans*. Cambridge, 1970.

Parke, H. W. *Sibyls and Sibylline Prophecy in Classical Antiquity*. London, 1988.

Parrish, E. P. "The Senate of 1 January 62 B.C." *CW* 65 (1972): 160–68.

Pelling, C. B. R. "Childhood and Personality in Greek Biography." In *Character and Individualization in Greek Literature*, edited by C. B. R. Pelling, 214–22. Oxford, 1990.

——. "Plutarch's Adaptation of His Source Material." *JHS* 100 (1980): 127–40.

——. "Plutarch's Method of Work in the Roman Lives." *JHS* 99 (1979): 74–96.

——. "Rowland and Cullens on Corn-Doles." *LCM* 14 (1989): 117–19.

Perelli, L. *Il movimento populare nell'ultimento secolo della repubblica*. Turin, 1982.

Peterson, W. *M. Tulli Ciceronis Orationes*. Vol. 5. Oxford, 1911.

Phillips, E. J. "Cicero, Ad Atticum I 2." *Philologus* 114 (1970): 291–94.

Picard, G. C. "L'aedes Libertatis de Clodius au Palatin." *REL* 43 (1965): 228–37.

Platner, S., and T. Ashby. *A Topographical Dictionary of Ancient Rome*. Oxford, 1929.

Pocock, L. G. *A Commentary on Cicero In Vatinium*. London, 1926.

——. "Publius Clodius and the Acts of Caesar." *CQ* 18 (1924): 59–64.

Pöschl, V. "Invidia nelle orazione di Cicerone." *Atti del 1 Congresso Internazionale di Studi Ciceroniani*, 2:119–25. Rome, 1961.

Potter, D. S. *Prophecy and History in the Crisis of the Roman Empire*. Oxford, 1990.

Price, S. R. F. *Rituals and Power: The Roman Imperial Cult in Asia Minor*. Cambridge, 1984.

Purcell, N. "The Apparitores: A Study in Social Mobility." *PBSR* 51 (1983): 125–73.

Raaflaub, K., ed. *Social Struggles in Archaic Rome: New Perspectives on the Conflict of the Orders*. Berkeley, 1986.

Ranouil, P. C. *Recherches sur le patriciat: 509–366 av. J.-C*. Paris, 1975.

Rathbone, D. "The Slave Mode of Production in Italy." *JRS* 73 (1983): 160–68.

Rawson, E. *Roman Culture and Society*. Oxford, 1991.

Reinach, T. *Mithridate Eupator, roi du Pont*. Paris, 1890.

Reinhold, M. *From Republic to Principate: An Historical Commentary on Cassius Dio's Roman History Books 49–52 (36–29 B.C.)*. Atlanta, 1988.

Richard, J.-C. *Les origines de la plèbe romaine: Essai sur la formation du dualisme patricio-plébéien*. Paris, 1978.

——. "Patricians and Plebeians: The Origin of a Social Dichotomy." In *Social Struggles in Archaic Rome*, edited by K. Raaflaub, 105–29. Berkeley, 1984.

Richardson, L., Jr. *A New Topographical Dictionary of Ancient Rome*. Baltimore, 1992.

Richlin, A. *The Garden of Priapus*. New Haven, 1984.

Rickman, G. *The Corn Supply of Ancient Rome*. Oxford, 1980.

Ridley, R. T. "*Falsi triumphi, plures consulatus*." *Latomus* 42 (1983): 372–82.

——. "Fastenkritik: A Stocktaking." *Athenaeum* 18 (1980): 264–98.

Rink, B. "Diskussionsbemerkungen zu dem Aufsatz 'Catilina und Clodius— Analogien und Differenzen' von T. Loposzko und H. Kowalski." *Klio* 72 (1990): 211–15.

Rose, H. J. "Mox." *CQ* 21 (1927): 57–66.

Rosenstein, N. *Imperatores Victi: Military Defeat and Aristocratic Competition in the Middle and Late Republic*. Berkeley, 1990.

Rostovtzeff, M. *The Social and Economic History of the Hellenistic World*. Oxford, 1941.

Rotondi, G. *Leges Publicae Populi Romani*. Milan, 1912.

Royden, H. L. *The Magistrates of the Roman Professional Collegia in Italy from the First to the Third Century A.D.* Pisa, 1988.

Royo, M. "Le quartier républicain du Palatin, nouvelles hypothèses de localisation." *REL* 65 (1987): 89–114.

Rudé, G. *Ideology and Popular Protest*. London, 1980.

Rundell, W. M. F. "Cicero and Clodius: The Question of Credibility." *Historia* 28 (1979): 301–28.

Saller, R. P. "Men's Age at Marriage and Its Consequences in the Roman Family." *CP* 82 (1987): 21–34.

——. *Patriarchy, Property and Death in the Roman Family*. Cambridge, 1994.

——. "Patronage and Friendship in Early Imperial Rome: Drawing the Distinction." In *Patronage in Ancient Society*, edited by A. Wallace-Hadrill, 49–62. London, 1989.

——. *Personal Patronage under the Early Roman Empire*. Cambridge, 1982.

Scheidel, W. "Finances, Figures and Fiction." *CQ* 46 (1996): 222–38.

Schneider, H. *Wirtschaft und Politik. Untersuchungen zur Geschichte der späten römischen Republik*. Erlangen, 1974.

Schofield, M. "Cicero for and against Divination." *JRS* 86 (1986): 47–65.

Schulz-Falkenthal, H. "Zur politischen Aktivität der römischen Handwerkerkollegien." *Wissenschaftliche Zeitschrift der Universität Halle* 21 (1972): 79–
99.

Scobie, A. "Slums, Sanitation and Mortality in the Roman World." *Klio* 68 (1986):
399–433.

Scullard, H. H. *The Festivals and Ceremonies of the Roman Republic.* Ithaca, N.Y.,
1981.

Seager, R. "Cicero and the Word *Popularis*." *CQ* 22 (1972): 328–38.

———. "Clodius, Pompeius and the Exile of Cicero." *Latomus* 24 (1965): 519–31.

———. "Iusta Catilinae." *Historia* 22 (1973): 240–48.

———. *Pompey: A Political Biography.* London, 1979.

———. " 'Populares' in Livy and the Livian Tradition." *CQ* 27 (1977): 377–90.

Shackleton Bailey, D. R. "Brothers or Cousins?" *AJAH* 2 (1977): 148–50.

———. *Cicero: Epistulae ad Familiares.* 2 vols. Cambridge, 1977.

———. *Cicero: Epistulae ad Quintum Fratrem et M. Brutum.* Cambridge, 1980.

———. *Cicero's Letters to Atticus.* 7 vols. Cambridge, 1965–70.

———. "*Nobiles* and *novi* Reconsidered." *AJP* 107 (1986): 255–60.

———. "On Cicero's Speeches." *HSCP* 83 (1979): 237–85.

———. "The Prosecution of Roman Magistrates-Elect." *Phoenix* 24 (1970): 162–65.

———. "Sex. Clodius–Sex. Cloelius." *CQ* 10 (1960): 41–42.

———. *Towards a Text of Cicero "Ad Atticum."* Cambridge, 1960.

———. *Two Studies in Roman Nomenclature.* State College, Pa., 1976.

Shatzman, I. "The Egyptian Question in Roman Politics (59–54 B.C.)." *Latomus* 30
(1971): 363–69.

———. "Patricians and Plebeians: The Case of the Veturii." *CQ* 23 (1973): 65–77.

Sheid, J. "Le délit religieux dans la Rome tardo-républicaine." In *Le délit religieux
dans la cité antique*, edited by J. Sheid, 117–71. Paris, 1981.

Sherwin-White, A. N. *Roman Foreign Policy in the East, 168 B.C. to A.D. 1.* Norman,
Okla., 1983.

Skinner, M. B. "Clodia Metelli." *TAPA* 113 (1983): 273–88.

———. "Pretty Lesbius." *TAPA* 112 (1982): 197–208.

Slagter, M. J. "Transitio ad Plebem: The Exchange of Patrician for Plebeian Status."
Ph.D. diss., Bryn Mawr College, 1993.

Stambaugh, J. E. "The Functions of Roman Temples." In *Aufstieg und Niedergang
der römischen Welt: Geschichte und Kultur Roms im Spiegel der neueren Forschung*,
vol. 2, pt. 16, fasc. 1, edited by H. Temporini and W. Haase, 554–608. Berlin and
New York, 1978.

Startevant, E. H. *The Pronunciation of Greek and Latin.* Chicago, 1920.

Staveley, E. S. *Greek and Roman Voting and Elections.* London, 1972.

———. "The Nature and Aims of the Patriciate." *Historia* 32 (1983): 24–57.

Stein, P. *Die Senatssitzungen der ciceronischen Zeit (68–43).* Münster, 1930.

Sternberg, T. "Zur sozialen Struktur der plebs urbana gegen Ende der römischen
Republik." *Wissenschaftliche Zeitschrift der Wilhelm-Pieck-Universität Rostock,
Gesellschaftswissenschaftliche Reihe* 31, 1–2 (1982): 101–4.

Stockton, D. *Cicero: A Political Biography.* Oxford, 1971.

———. *The Gracchi.* Oxford, 1979.

Stroh, W. *Taxis und Taktik*. Stuttgart, 1975.

Strong, D. E. "The Administration of Public Building in Rome during the Late Republic and Early Empire." *BICS* 15 (1968): 97–109.

Stylow, A. U. *Libertas und Liberalitas: Untersuchungen zur innenpolitischen Propaganda der Römer*. Munich, 1972.

Sullivan, R. D. *Near Eastern Royalty and Rome, 100–30 BC*. Toronto, 1995.

Sumner, G. V. "The Last Journey of L. Sergius Catilina." *CP* 58 (1963): 215–19.

——. "Lex Aelia, Lex Fufia." *AJP* 84 (1963): 337–58.

——. "The Lex Annalis under Caesar." *Phoenix* 25 (1971): 246–71, 357–71.

Suolahti, J. *The Junior Officers of the Roman Army in the Republican Period*. Helsinki, 1955.

——. *The Roman Censors: A Study in Social Structure*. Helsinki, 1963.

Süss, W. *Ethos: Studien zur älteren griechischen Rhetorik*. Leipzig, 1910.

Syme, R. *The Augustan Aristocracy*. Oxford, 1986.

——. *Roman Papers*. Vol. 1. Oxford, 1979.

——. *The Roman Revolution*. Oxford, 1939.

Szemler, G. J. *The Priests of the Roman Republic*. Brussels, 1972.

Tamm, B. *Auditorium and Palatium*. Lund, 1963.

Tatum, W. J. "Another Look at the Spectators at the Roman Games." *AHB* 4 (1990): 104–7.

——. "Catullus 79: Personal Invective or Political Discourse?" *PLLS* 7 (1993): 31–45.

——. "Cicero, *ad Att.* 1.14.5." *CQ* 36 (1986): 539–41.

——. "Cicero and the *Bona Dea* Trial." *CP* 85 (1990): 202–8.

——. "Cicero, the Elder Curio, and the Titinia Case." *Mnemosyne* 44 (1991): 364–71.

——. "Cicero's Opposition to the *Lex Clodia de Collegiis*." *CQ* 40 (1990): 187–94.

——. "The Epitaph of Publius Scipio Reconsidered." *CQ* 38 (1988): 253–58.

——. "*Hospitem* or *hostem*?" *RhM* 139 (1996): 358–60.

——. "The *Lex Clodia de Censoria Notione*." *CP* 85 (1990): 34–43.

——. "The *Lex Papiria de Dedicationibus*." *CP* 88 (1993): 319–28.

——. "Lucullus and Clodius at Nisibis (Plutarch, *Lucullus* 33–34)." *Athenaeum* 79 (1991): 569–79.

——. "The Marriage of Pompey's Son to the Daughter of Ap. Claudius Pulcher." *Klio* 73 (1991): 122–29.

——. "Military Defeat and Electoral Success in Republican Rome." *AHB* 5 (1991): 149–52.

——. "Military Defeat and Electoral Success—Two Corrections." *AHB* 6 (1992): 24.

——. "The Poverty of the Claudii Pulchri: Varro, *De Re Rustica* 3.16.1–2." *CQ* 42 (1992): 190–200.

——. "Publius Clodius Pulcher and Tarracina." *ZPE* 83 (1990): 299–304.

——. "Ritual and Personal Morality in Roman Religion." *Syllecta Classica* 4 (1993): 13–20.

Taylor, L. R. "Caesar's Colleagues in the Pontifical College." *AJP* 63 (1942): 385–412.

——. "The Date and Meaning of the Vettius Affair." *Historia* 1 (1950): 45–51.

——. "Forerunners of the Gracchi." *JRS* 52 (1962): 19–27.

——. *Party Politics in the Age of Caesar*. Berkeley, 1949.

——. *Roman Voting Assemblies from the Hannibalic War to the Dictatorship of Caesar*. Ann Arbor, 1966.

———. *The Voting Districts of the Roman Republic*. Rome, 1960.

Taylor, L. R., and T. R. S. Broughton. "The Order of the Two Consuls' Names in the Yearly Lists." *MAAR* 19 (1949): 3–14.

Thomas, Y. "Se venger au forum. Solidarité familiale et procès criminel à Rome (premier siècle av.–deuxième siècle ap. J.C.)." In *La vengeance: Études d'ethnologie, d'histoire et de philosophie*, vol. 3, edited by J.-P. Poly, 65–100. Paris, 1984.

Thommen, L. *Das Volkstribunat der späten römischen Republik*. Stuttgart, 1989.

Thulin, C. O. *Die Etruskische Disciplin*. Göteborg, 1905–9; repr., Darmstadt, 1968.

Todd, S. "*Lady Chatterly's Lover* and the Attic Orators: The Social Composition of the Athenian Jury." *JHS* 90 (1990): 146–73.

Torelli, M. *Elogia Tarquiniensia*. Florence, 1975.

Treggiari, S. *Roman Freedmen during the Late Republic*. Oxford, 1969.

———. *Roman Marriage*. Oxford, 1991.

———. "Urban Labour in Rome: *Mercennarii* and *Tabernarii*." In *Non-Slave Labour in the Greco-Roman World*, edited by P. D. A. Garnsey, 48–64. Cambridge, 1980.

Trencsény-Waldopfel, I. "Calvus ex Nanneianis." *Athenaeum* 43 (1965): 42–51.

Tumin, M. M. *Social Stratification: The Forms and Functions of Inequality*. Englewood Cliffs, N.J., 1967.

Twymann, B. "The Metelli, Pompeius, and Prosopography." In *Aufstieg und Niedergang der römischen Welt: Geschichte und Kultur Roms im Spiegel der neueren Forschung*, vol. 1, pt. 1, edited by H. Temporini and W. Haase, 816–74. Berlin and New York, 1972.

Tyrrell, R. Y. *The Correspondence of M. Tullius Cicero*. Vol. 1, 2nd ed. Dublin, 1885. Vol. 2. Dublin, 1886.

Tyrrell, R. Y., and L. C. Purser. *The Correspondence of M. Tullius Cicero*. 6 vols. Dublin, 1904–33.

Ungern-Sternberg, J. von. "The End of the Conflict of the Orders." In *Social Struggles in Archaic Rome: New Perspectives on the Conflict of the Orders*, edited by K. Raaflaub, 353–77. Berkeley, 1986.

———. "Überlegungen zum Sozialprogramm der Gracchen." In *Sozialmassnahmen und Fürsorge. Zur Eigenart antiker Sozialpolitik*, edited by H. Kloft, 167–85. Graz, 1988.

Valeton, I. M. J. "De iure obnuntiandi comitiis et conciliis." *Mnemosyne* 19 (1891): 75–113, 229–70.

Vanderbroeck, P. J. J. "Homo Novus Again." *Chiron* 16 (1986): 239–42.

———. *Popular Leadership and Collective Behavior in the Late Roman Republic (ca. 80–50)*. Amsterdam, 1987.

Vasaly, A. "Personality and Power: Livy's Depiction of the Appii Claudii in the First Pentad." *TAPA* 117 (1987): 203–26.

Vernacchia, J. "L'adopzione di Clodio." *Ciceroniana* 1 (1959): 197–213.

Veyne, P. "La folklore à Rome et les droits de la conscience publique sur la conduite individuelle." *Latomus* 42 (1983): 3–30.

———. *Le pain et le circque. Sociologie historique d'un pluralisme politique*. Paris, 1976.

Ville, G. *La gladiature en occident des origines à la mort de Domitien*. Rome, 1981.

Virlouvet, C. *Famines et émeutes à Rome des origines de la république à la mort de Néron*. Paris and Rome, 1984.

Vretska, K. *C. Sallustius Crispus: De Catilinae Coniuratione*. Heidelberg, 1976.

Walbank, F. W. *A Historical Commentary on Polybius.* 3 vols. Oxford, 1957–79.

Wallace-Hadrill, A. *Houses and Society in Pompeii and Herculaneum.* Princeton, 1994.

———. "Patronage in Roman Society: From Republic to Empire." In *Patronage in Ancient Society*, edited by A. Wallace-Hadrill, 63–88. London, 1989.

———. "The Social Structure of the Roman House." *PBSR* 56 (1988): 43–97.

———, ed. *Patronage in Ancient Society.* London, 1989.

Waltzing, J.-P. *Étude historique sur les corporations professionnelles chez les Romains depuis les origines jusqu'à la chute de l'Empire d'Occident.* 4 vols. Louvain, 1895–1900.

Ward, A. M. *Marcus Crassus and the Late Roman Republic.* Columbia, Mo., 1977.

Wardman, A. *Religion and Statecraft among the Romans.* London, 1982.

Watson, A. *The Law of Persons in the Late Roman Republic.* Oxford, 1967.

———. *Rome of the XII Tables.* Princeton, 1975.

Watson, G. R. *The Roman Soldier.* Ithaca, N.Y., 1969.

Watt, W. S. *M. Tulli Ciceronis Epistulae, Epistulae ad Atticum.* Oxford, 1965.

Weber, M. *Wirtschaft und Gesellschaft.* 3rd ed. Tübingen, 1947.

Weinrib, E. J. "*Obnuntiatio*: Two Problems." *ZSS* 87 (1970): 395–425.

———. "The Prosecution of Roman Magistrates." *Phoenix* 22 (1968): 32–56.

Weinstock, S. "Clodius and the *Lex Aelia Fufia.*" *JRS* 27 (1937): 215–22.

———. *Divus Julius.* Oxford, 1971.

Weische, A. *Studien zur politischen Sprache der römischen Republik.* Münster, 1966.

Welwei, K.-W. "Das Sklavenproblem als politische Faktor in der Krise der römischen Republik." In *Vom Elend der Handarbeit*, edited by H. Mommsen and W. Schulze, 50–69. Stuttgart, 1981.

Wickham, C. "Marx, Sherlock Holmes, and Late Roman Commerce." *JRS* 78 (1988): 183–93.

Willems, P. *Le sénat de la république romaine.* 2 vols. Louvain, 1878–83.

Williams, R. S. "The Appointment of Glabrio (cos. 67) to the Eastern Command." *Phoenix* 38 (1984): 221–34.

———. "*Rei Publicae Causa*: Gabinius' Defense of His Restoration of Ptolemy Auletes." *CJ* 81 (1985): 25–38.

Wirszubski, C. *Libertas as a Political Idea at Rome during the Late Republic and Early Principate.* Cambridge, 1950.

Wiseman, T. P. *Catullan Questions.* Leicester, 1969.

———. *Catullus and His World: A Reappraisal.* Cambridge, 1985.

———. "Celer and Nepos." *CQ* 21 (1971): 180–82.

———. *Cinna the Poet and Other Roman Essays.* Leicester, 1974.

———. *Clio's Cosmetics.* Leicester, 1979.

———. "*Conspicui Postes Tectaque Digna Deo*: The Public Image of Aristocratic and Imperial Houses in the Late Republic and Early Empire." In *L'urbs. Espace urbain et histoire (Ier siècle avant J.-C.–IIIe siècle après J.-C.)*, edited by C. Pietri, 393–413. Paris and Rome, 1987.

———. *New Men in the Roman Senate.* Oxford, 1971.

———. Review of P. A. Brunt, *The Fall of the Roman Republic and Related Essays. CR* 40 (1990): 106–7.

———. *Roman Studies.* Liverpool, 1987.

Wissowa, G. *Religion und Kultus der Römer*. Berlin, 1912.

Wlosok, A. "Nihil nisi ruborem—über die Rolle der Scham in der römischen Rechtskultur." *Grazer Beiträge* 9 (1980): 155–72.

Yakobson, A. "*Petitio et Largitio*: Popular Participation in the Centuriate Assembly of the Late Republic." *JRS* 82 (1992): 32–52.

Yavetz, Z. *Plebs and Princeps*. Oxford, 1969.

Zanker, P. *The Power of Images in the Age of Augustus*. Translated by A. Shapiro. Ann Arbor, 1988.

Capitol, Roman, 161, 220

Capua, 181

Cassius Dio (cos. suff. A.D. 205), 40;
on Clodius at Nisibis, 47–48; on
Clodius's *transitio ad plebem*, 99–102;
on Clodius's legislative program, 125,
131, 135–38; on Clodius's prosecution
of Milo, 204

Cassius Vecellinus, Sp. (cos. 502), 158

Catiline. *See* Sergius Catilina, L.

Cato. *See* Porcius Cato, M.

Catullus. *See* Valerius Catullus, C.

Causinius Schola, C., 81, 239

Census and censors, 16, 67, 106–7, 117,
124, 127, 131, 133–35, 165, 227, 236–37,
294 (n. 107), 295 (n. 112)

Centuriate assembly. *See* Assemblies:
centuriate

Centuries, 19, 24

Ceres, 171

Cicero. *See* Tullius Cicero, M.

Cilicia, 47–52, 153, 195, 204, 266 (n. 99)

Cispius, M. (tr. pl. 57), 178, 208

Claritas. See Ancestry

Claudia, 60, 242, 244, 248

Claudii Marcelli, 247

Claudii Pulchri, 23–36, 60, 68–71, 85,
106, 144, 158, 161, 169, 208–10, 213–15,
228, 231–34, 291 (n. 53), 321 (n. 22),
326 (n. 8)

Claudius, Ap. (decemvir 451), 32

Claudius, L., 190

Claudius, T., 115, 206

Claudius Aesopus, 182

Claudius Caecus, Ap. (cos. 307), 32, 210,
236–37, 291 (n. 60)

Claudius Marcellus, C. (cos. 50), 162

Claudius Pulcher, Ap. (cos. 143), 33, 35

Claudius Pulcher, Ap. (cos. 79), 33, 36,
39, 65, 135, 248

Claudius Pulcher, Ap. (son of pr. 56),
241

Claudius Pulcher, Ap. (cos. 54): origins
and family connections of, 33–36;
Appietas of, 39, 232; serves with
Lucullus, 44, 52, 266 (n. 99); cooper-
ates with Clodius, 81, 111, 164, 178–79,
181, 184, 189, 192, 196; praetorship of,

174, 179, 181–82; censorship of, 191;
and Caesar, 207–8, 214–15; and conference at Luca, 214–15; consulship
of, 224, 227, 231–34; and friendship
with Cicero, 228; prosecuted by
Dolabella, 242; perhaps called
Clodius, 247

Claudius Pulcher, Ap. (cos. 38), 241

Claudius Pulcher, Ap. (Julia's lover),
241–42

Claudius Pulcher, C. (cos. 177), 236

Claudius Pulcher, C. (cos. 92), 33, 247

Claudius Pulcher, C. (pr. 56), 33–36, 98,
207, 214–15, 220, 231–32, 247–48

Claudius Pulcher, P. (cos. 249), 32

Claudius Pulcher, P. (cos. 184), 290
(n. 40)

Claudius Pulcher, P. (aed. 56). *See*
Clodius Pulcher, P.

Claudius Pulcher, P. (pr. uncertain
date), 60–61, 241, 248

Claudius Pulcher, P. (cos. A.D. 21 or
22), 241

Claudius Nero, Ti., 32

Claudius Sabinus, Ap. (cos. 495), 32

Clausus, Attus. *See* Claudius
Sabinus, Ap.

Cleopatra Selene, 50

Clientela. See Client-patron
relationship

Client-patron relationship, 8, 23, 115–16,
180, 255 (n. 72), 257 (n. 112); and
friendship, 21, 24; nature and significance of, 21–22, 114–15; and *collegia*,
26, 118–19, 146; and *salutatio*, 27; and
provincials, 90, 169, 195, 199; not
threatened by grain distributions,
121, 148

Clodia Luculli, 34, 73–74, 81, 247

Clodia Metelli, 34–35, 43, 70–71, 84, 90,
108, 162, 202, 209–10, 228, 247–48

Clodiani, 115–16, 142–45, 180, 184–85,
193. *See also* Gangs

Clodia Tertia, 34, 247

Clodius, C., 115, 119

Clodius, P., 115, 209

Clodius Pulcher, P. (aed. 56), 5, 13;
proper name of, 33, 106, 247–48;

birth and childhood of, 33–36, 43–44, 248–49; and kinship with Metelli, 34–36, 69–70, 89, 97; demands of heritage, 38–39, 236–37; principal sources for, 39–40; and impediments to biography, 39–41; personality and character of, 40–43, 47–48, 61, 67, 74, 81, 85–86, 106, 138, 152, 167, 170, 243; eloquence and invective of, 41, 53, 79, 89, 158, 160, 167, 187, 190–91, 202, 227–31, 244, 278 (n. 127), 300 (n. 45), 311 (nn. 94, 97), 323 (n. 81); religious and rectitudinous posture of, 42, 132, 158, 173–74, 191, 215–19, 230–31, 300 (n. 45), 312 (n. 103), 323 (n. 81); appearance of, 43; and prosecution of Catiline, 44, 53–55, 59–60; and mutiny at Nisibis, 44–49, 52, 61, 73, 81; military service of, 44–53, 61, 218; assisted by status and family connections, 48, 52–52, 61, 68–71, 81, 87, 90, 106, 142, 164, 177, 179, 190, 198, 214–15, 221, 234; arrogance and sense of *dignitas* of, 48, 61, 67, 87–88, 90, 98–99, 167, 243; serves under Marcius Rex, 49–53, 218, 265 (n. 93); serves under Pompey, 50, 52–53, 69, 76, 265–66 (n. 99); assimilated to Catiline by Cicero, 54, 59, 78, 88, 96, 142–45, 277 (n. 117); and enmity with Lucullus, 56, 61, 73; and service and friendship with Murena, 56–61, 71, 268 (n. 142); implements Murena's bribery scheme, 58–59; conduct of, during Catilinarian conspiracy, 59–61, 63–64, 144; and Bona Dea scandal, 59–88 passim, 96, 108, 144, 145, 149; children of, 60–61; and marriage to Fulvia, 60–61; and orthodoxy of early career, 61; and enmity with Cicero, 62, 65, 79, 89–90, 95, 97–98, 102, 109, 111, 113, 138, 151–52, 181, 193, 215, 218, 235, 278 (n. 127); elected quaestor, 63–64, 68; and transvestism, 66, 85; *potentissimus homo* in the year 61, 68–71; political friendships and associates of, 69–71, 74, 89, 112, 114–16, 142–44,

146–47, 164, 174, 177, 181, 193–94, 209, 225; and enmity with Pompey, 70, 123, 143, 167–75, 181, 186–87, 201–4, 211–12, 243; and enemies in the senate, 73–74, 80–81, 87–88, 176, 190, 196, 231; use of gangs by, 79, 115–16, 141–44, 146–47, 170, 174, 176, 178–80, 193–94, 198, 202–4, 211–12, 287 (n. 142); property of, 81, 161–63, 218, 224–25, 244; financial difficulties of, 84, 87, 199, 224–25; deprived of service as quaestor in Syria, 87–88; and *dolor* as motive, 88, 98–99, 149; attacks Fabia, 89; and role in elections of 61, 89; and quaestorship in Sicily, 89–90, 95–96; in *deductio* with Cicero, 90; *transitio ad plebem*, 90–91, 95–102, 139, 142, 148, 283 (n. 55); adoption of, 101, 104–11, 173; and early friendship with Pompey, 102–3, 109, 111–13, 136, 138; anticipates tribunate, 108–11; and relationship with senate and with *optimates*, 108–11, 114, 116, 132–56 passim, 166–74, 179, 184–204 passim, 220–21, 232, 234, 237, 242–43, 283 (n. 55), 305 (n. 3); and relationship with First Triumvirate, 108–13, 116, 136, 138, 140–41, 150–55, 166, 168–69, 171–74, 204, 213–15, 222–23, 234; *inimicus Caesaris*, 109–10; elected tribune, 111; and friendship with Caesar, 112, 204, 207, 221, 284 (n. 79), 318 (n. 199); and role in Vettius affair, 112–13; and popularity with *plebs urbana*, 114, 118–19, 121, 125, 135–38, 141–50, 166–67, 173, 180, 182, 184, 193–94, 198, 211–12, 215, 222–23, 225–26, 234, 237, 241–45, 310 (n. 76), 314 (n. 134); and *Clodiani*, 115–16, 142–44, 180, 184–85, 193, 202, 211; and grain supply, 117, 119–24, 135, 137, 139, 141–42, 147, 150, 182–86, 190, 202, 211– 12, 242, 244, 290 (nn. 40, 44); legislates civic religion and assemblies, 117, 125–33, 135, 137; and census procedures, 117, 133–35, 137, 227, 294 (n. 107); and *collegia*, 117–19, 124–25, 135–48 passim, 193,

205, 211–12, 225–26, 244; *descriptio* of *collegia*, 118, 124–25; and annexation of Cyprus, 122, 124, 150–51, 155–56; attacks Pompey's *cura annonae*, 123, 186–87, 211–12; and balanced aspects of tribunician legislation, 132–33, 135–36, 138, 149, 243, 249; and purposes of initial legislative package, 135–36, 141–42, 145, 148, 243; employs popular ideology, 140–41, 148, 151–58, 165–67, 169–71, 174, 179, 192–93, 197, 201–2, 218, 222–23, 237, 243–45, 299 (n. 17), 300 (n. 45); lends *auxilium* to Vatinius, 140–41, 148–50, 155, 167; employs popular violence, 140–49, 155, 158, 162, 166–86 passim, 193–205 passim, 211–25 passim, 234–35, 244–45, 287 (n. 142); and slaves, 142, 174, 176, 193, 211–12, 221–22, 238–39, 296 (n. 152); and cooperation with Crassus, 143, 152, 177, 190, 202–4, 222–23; and Etruria, 144, 224; *felix Catilina*, 145; and exile of Cicero, 146, 151–58, 165, 243, 299 (n. 17), 300 (n. 45); and freedmen, 146–47, 174, 236–39; secures support of Piso and Gabinius, 152–53, 287 (n. 142); opposed by *equites*, 154–55, 172, 182, 218–19, 222–23; *aedes Libertatis*, 157–58, 162–67, 174, 186–92, 198–99, 215–19, 244; and house on Palatine, 161–66, 224; honorific statue of, 164; and interference in Pompey's eastern *acta*, 168–70; consecrates Gabinius's property, 171; attacks Caesar's *acta*, 173–74; attempts to assassinate Pompey, 174; resists Cicero's restoration, 176–85; and enmity with Milo, 178–80, 193–206 passim, 234–40, 320 (n. 8); and enmity with Sestius, 179–80, 193, 205–7; abused at games, 181–82; *quindecimvir sacris faciundis*, 191, 200, 218; condemns violence, 191–92; and restoration of Auletes, 194–204; is accused *de vi*, 196–98; as candidate for aedile, 196–98; and clients in east, 199; prosecutes Milo, 201–5, 320 (n. 8); and friendship and marriage

alliance with Pompey, 204, 214–15, 221; and trial of Sestius, 206–7; fails to prosecute Cispius, 208; and role in trial of Caelius, 210; and destruction of Temple of the Nymphs, 211–12; conducts Megalensian Games, 211–12, 319 (n. 232); opposes *publicani*, 218–19; and tablets recording tribunician legislation, 219–21; attacks Cato's administration of Cyprus, 221; and clash with Cato over Cypriot slaves, 221–22; seeks *legatio libera*, 223–25; described by Cicero as *illa populi Appuleia*, 225; as candidate for praetorship, 226–27, 234–39; and C. Cato's trial, 228–29; prosecutes Procilius, 229–30, 323 (n. 81); defends Scaurus, 232–33; attacks Milo's indebtedness, 235; and inspiration of Claudian ancestry, 236–37, 290 (n. 40), 291 (n. 60); and proposals for praetorian legislation, 236–39, 244; death of, 239–40; riots at death of, 241; proposal to erect honorific statue of, 242; historical significance of, 242–46; identity of mother of, 248–49; and possible appearance in Ostian inscription, 290 (n. 44); *Collinam novam*, 325 (n. 114)

Cloelius, Sex., 115, 119, 122–23, 136, 170, 208, 211, 237, 241, 309 (n. 55)

Collective identities. *See* Groups

Collegia: in elections, 19, 29, 226; nature and significance of, 25–26, 117–19, 136, 142, 147, 244; organization of, 26, 118, 205; patronage of, 26, 118–19, 146; and support for Clodius, 115, 118–19, 125, 136–37, 143, 145–48, 182, 193, 211–12, 244; suppressed by senate, 117–18, 136–37; new, 117–19, 139, 143; slaves in, 118; *descriptio* conducted by Clodius, 118, 124–25; employed by Clodius in grain distributions, 124–25, 184, 291 (n. 60); support Cicero's restoration, 182; not affected by senatorial decree of February 66, 205; not affected by *lex Licinia*, 225–26; and membership of elites, 258 (n. 125), 308–9 (n. 47);

and city water supply, 291 (n. 60). *See also* Local stratification; Lower classes

Collegia compitalicia, 25, 117

Collegia opificum, 25. See also *Opifices*

Comitia. See Assemblies

Commentariolum Petitionis, 15, 148, 256 (n. 99); as guide to group identities, 19; as guide to campaigning practices, 23–27, 30

Commoda populi, 11, 30, 120–21, 148, 150. See also *Beneficia; Iura populi;* Lower classes

Concilium plebis. See Assemblies

Concordia, 129

Conducticii, 18, 142–43

Conference at Luca, 204, 213–15, 218–22. *See also* First Triumvirate

Conflict of the Orders, 9–10

Conformity, 66–67, 86, 147

Consecratio bonorum, 171

Consulship, 23, 24, 37–38, 39, 98, 170–71

Contiones, 28–29, 76–77, 79–80, 89, 95–96, 110–11, 130, 143, 145, 154–55, 173, 184, 192, 196, 217–18. See also *Plebs contionalis*

Co-optation, 92–94, 100–101

Cornelii Lentuli, 74, 80–81

Cornelius Cethegus, C., 72

Cornelius Cinna, L. (cos. 87), 33, 236

Cornelius Dolabella, P. (cos. suff. 44), 93, 106, 242, 244–45

Cornelius Lentulus Crus, L. (cos. 49), 80–81, 154. *See also* Cornelii Lentuli

Cornelius Lentulus Marcellinus, Cn. (cos. 56), 81, 192–207 passim, 214, 222

Cornelius Lentulus Marcellinus, P. (q. 75), 150

Cornelius Lentulus Niger, L. (pr. by 61), 81

Cornelius Lentulus Spinther, P. (cos. 57), 81, 106, 174–84 passim, 190, 195–204, 232

Cornelius Lentulus Sura, P. (cos. 71), 88

Cornelius Sulla, L. (cos. 88), 33, 63, 84, 120, 236

Cornelius Sulla, P. (cos. desig. 65), 162, 193–94, 234

Cornelius Scipio, Cn., 38

Cornelius Scipio Africanus, P. (cos. 205), 160

Cornificius, Q. (pr. 67 or 66), 72–73

Cornificius, Q. (pr. 45), 72

Craftsmen. See *Opifices; Tabernarii*

Crudelitas, 41, 181

Cura annonae, 122–25, 186–88, 190, 195, 244, 309 (n. 55). *See also* Cloelius, Sex.; Grain subsidies and supply; Pompeius Magnus, Cn.

Cura morum. See Census and censors

Curatores (tribal), 24

Custom. See *Mos maiorum*

Cyprus, 122, 124, 150, 155–56, 195, 220–21

Cyrene, 122, 150

Damio, 115, 174

De caelo servasse, 125–33 passim

Decuriae, 26, 118, 143, 205, 225–26

Deductatores, 27–28, 90

Deference, 19, 21, 255 (n. 72)

Deiotarus, 168–69

Delictum. See Religion

Delos, 124

Demonstrations, 141, 143–48, 174, 182–86, 201–3, 205, 211–12, 245. *See also* Violence

Dies comitiales, 126, 132

Dies fasti, 125–26

Dies nefasti, 126

Dignitas: as legitimate aristocratic value, 8, 13, 37–39, 68, 134–35; and tension with patriotism, 8, 134; as motive for *popularis* career, 12–13; and *dolor*, 13, 38, 98–99; and popularity, 15, 37; and patronage, 21; and consulship, 37; and competition, 37–39, 78–79, 134, 234; and one's *domus*, 159–61. *See also* Prestige

Dio. See Cassius Dio

Dio of Alexandria, 195, 209

Di penates, 159–60

Divisores, 24, 26, 57–58, 59, 70, 89. See *also* Bribery

Dolor: as motive for *popularis* career, 13, 88, 98–99; and political competition,

38–39, 204; and Clodius, 88, 98–99, 149; and Cicero, 204

Domitius Ahenobarbus, Cn. (cos. 96), 13–14

Domitius Ahenobarbus, L. (cos. 54), 13, 15, 23, 112, 139, 172, 207, 222–23

Domitius Calvinus, Cn. (cos. 53), 231–33

Domus, 159–61, 166

Domus publica, 160

Egypt, 50, 51, 52, 108, 194–204 passim

Elections, 20; and campaigning practices, 22–30, 205, 225–26, 235; and bribery, 23, 57–58, 89, 205; and role of intermediaries, 24, 205, 225–26; and diversity of electorate, 24–27; and importance of ancestry, 37, 235; for the year 57, 174, 176; for the year 56, 196–98; for the year 55, 222–23; for the year 53, 226–27, 231–34; for the year 52, 234–39. *See also* Assemblies

Elite classes, 17; and attitudes toward occupations, 18, 115, 143; and patronage, 21–22; use of intermediaries by, 19, 23, 24, 26, 114–15; and advantages in assemblies, 20; religious sensibilities of, 66, 74, 86, 125–33, 160, 173, 191, 200–201; and attitudes toward *transitio ad plebem*, 91–95, 97–99; and attitudes toward lower classes, 118, 120–21, 190; and census, 133; and attitudes toward violence, 146. See also *Equites*; Nobility; Patricians; Senators

Enmities: importance of, to political stature, 53, 151–52, 228, 305 (n. 5), 308 (n. 41); in Bona Dea scandal, 73–74, 80–81; and *crudelitas*, 181, 305 (n. 5), 308 (n. 41); in Caelius's trials, 209–10, 227–28

Equestrian order. See *Equites*

Equites, 13, 16, 17, 19, 20, 55, 57, 76, 82, 182, 211, 281 (n. 2); and *populares*, 3–5, 115–16, 126, 154–155, 218–19; and role in elections, 23, 27–28; in *deductio*, 27–28; and Clodius's provincial service in Gaul, 56; and Cicero, 151,

154–55, 172; during the Catilinarian conspiracy, 154; and public building, 166; and Auletes, 195–96, 209; at Cloelius's trial, 208; and controversy over Syrian tax contracts, 218–19; and membership in *collegia*, 258 (n. 125), 308–9 (n. 47)

Etruria, 144, 224

Eudamus, 240

Extraordinary commands: for Cato in Cyprus, 6, 122, 155–56; *popularis* issue, 6, 150–51; Pompey's *cura annonae*, 122–24, 190; for Piso and Gabinius, 152–53

Fabia, 44, 89

Fabius Hadrianus, M., 45

Fabricius, Q. (tr. pl. 57), 128, 131, 177–79

Fadius Gallus, M. (tr. pl. 75), 162

Family connections, 8, 22–23, 32, 60–61, 63, 69–71, 87, 90, 110, 152, 177, 203–4, 214–15, 221, 223, 231–32, 248–49. *See also* Ancestry; Friendship

Famine. See Grain subsidies and supply

Fannius, C. (cos. 122), 30

Fannius, C. (tr. pl. 59; pr. uncertain date), 81, 112, 190

Fasces, 170–71, 180

Fasti, 91

Fausta, 240

Favonius, M. (pr. 49), 79, 203

Fenestella, 55

Fides, 3, 21, 195, 216

Fidulius, 146

Firmidius, 146

First Triumvirate, 103–4, 108–10, 112, 116, 121, 136, 138–41, 150–55, 169, 171–74, 201, 203–4, 213–15, 222–23, 231–34. *See also* Conference at Luca; Friendship; Julius Caesar, C.; Licinius Crassus, P.; Pompeius Magnus, Cn.

Flaccus, Q. See Fulvius Flaccus, Q.

Flagitatio, 185

Flaminius, C. (cos. 223), 10

Flavius, L. (pr. 58), 97, 102, 170

Food shortages. See Grain subsidies and supply

Fonteius, P., 70, 104–6

Fortuna Primagenia, 160
Forum: importance of, in political life, 27–29
Fratres, 34–35
Freeborn citizens (*ingenui*), 17; in various occupations, 18; in *collegia*, 25
Freedmen (*libertini*), 2, 17, 125, 180; in various occupations, 18, 115; disadvantages of, in tribal assemblies, 20, 117, 236–38; and relationships with former masters, 21, 114–15, 147; role of, in elections, 23; in *collegia*, 25, 118, 146–47, 244; and Ap. Claudius Caecus, 32, 236–37; active in politics, 115–16, 244; and *lex Manilia*, 117; described as slaves in hostile rhetoric, 118; and Jupiter Libertas, 165; and Clodius's proposal concerning registration in rural tribes, 236–38; and Clodius's proposal concerning informally manumitted slaves, 238–39; and Augustus, 244
Freedom. See *Libertas*
Friendship, 8, 14, 22, 53, 71, 115–16, 191, 223; in elections, 15, 23; *amicus inferior*, 21, 148; between senators and Italian aristocracy, 24, 144; and *sodalitates*, 27; and family connections, 60–61, 110, 214–15, 221; and formation of First Triumvirate, 103, 214–15; and wills, 265 (n. 90)
Frumentatio. See Grain subsidies and supply
Fufius Calenus, Q. (cos. 47), 70, 75–77, 79–80
Fulvia, 60–61, 70, 239, 241, 244
Fulvii Flacci, 161
Fulvius Bambalio, M., 60–61
Fulvius Flaccus, M. (cos. 125), 158
Fulvius Flaccus, Q., 193

Gabinius, A. (cos. 58), 48–49, 112–13, 116, 123–24, 143, 152–56, 158, 170–71, 218–19, 230, 233–34
Galatia, 169
Games, 15, 199, 257 (n. 104), 319 (n. 232); gauge of popularity of, 20, 181–82, 308 (n. 45); importance of, to candidates, 26, 235, 319 (n. 232); demonstrations and violence during, 182–85; religious significance of, 216–17
Gangs, 69–70, 79, 82, 115–16, 141–48, 170–85 passim, 192–93, 202–4, 273 (n. 54)
Gavius, L., 115
Gellius Publicola, Cn. (or Q.), 70, 115–16, 146, 193, 206–7
Gellius Publicola, L. (cos. 72), 70, 115
Gellius Publicola, L. (cos. 36), 70
Gladiators, 90, 145, 178, 180, 182, 201, 240
Gloria, 37–38
Gordyene, 44
Gracchi and Gracchan reforms, 3, 4, 12, 99, 141. *See also* Sempronius Gracchus, C.; Sempronius Gracchus, Ti.
Grain subsidies and supply, 3, 6, 117, 119–24, 135, 139, 145, 150, 182–87, 199, 202, 211–12, 242, 244, 290 (nn. 40, 44)
Gratia, 14, 19, 23, 27, 99, 121, 146, 148, 255 (n. 72). *See also* Local stratification; Prestige
Grex Catilinae, 78
Groups and group identities, 17–21, 148, 245; importance of, in political choices, 19, 30, 148, 256–57 (n. 101); in assemblies, 20. See also *Collegia*; *Equites*; *Opifices*; *Publicani*; Senators; *Tabernarii*

Habra, 67
Haruspices, 200, 216–19
Herennius, C. (tr. pl. 60), 70, 96–100
Herennius Balbus, L., 209
Honores, 15, 16; require popular favor, 20–21; competition for, 22–30, 38
Hortensius Hortalus, Q. (cos. 69), 74, 76, 79–80, 138, 154–56, 162, 201, 228–30

Incest, 42, 73, 74, 81, 90, 202, 206; with Vestal Virgins, 44, 72–75, 81
Indictio feriarum, 293 (n. 87)
Influence. See *Gratia*; Local stratification; Popularity
Instauratio, 67, 73

lower classes, 19, 29, 142, 146–48, 244, 309 (n. 48); and *collegia*, 25–26, 118–19, 142, 146–48, 244. See also *Gratia*; Prestige; Social stratification; Status

Lollius, 146, 185

Lower classes, 17–18; benefits for, 15, 24, 102, 118–24, 126, 136, 141–42, 147–48, 150, 198–99, 212, 235, 244–45, 255 (n. 72); attitude of, toward occupations, 18; resent being despised, 18; and importance of local stratification, 19, 118–19, 125, 141–42, 146–48, 244, 309 (n. 48); in assemblies, 20, 28, 29, 58, 244; and patronage, 21, 255 (n. 72); observe distinctions of status in *collegia*, 25–26, 118, 147; political ideology of, 30, 31, 141, 145–48, 151–55, 166, 179, 192, 245, 299 (n. 17), 309 (n. 48); fragmented character of, 31, 143, 256–57 (n. 101), 296 (n. 159); and importance of Ludi Compitalicii, 117–18, 136; resent suppression of *collegia*, 118, 136; attitude of, toward Catiline, 144; attitude of, toward violence, 145–46, 180, 211–12, 245, 297 (n. 175). See also *Collegia*; *Commoda populi*; Grain subsidies and supply; *Iura populi*; *Libertas*; *Populares*

Luca. *See* Conference at Luca

Lucullus, M. *See* Terentius Varro Lucullus, M.

Ludi: Compitalicii, 117–18, 136, 149; Florales, 181–82; Apollinares, 182–84; Romani, 185; Megalenses, 210–12

Lutatius Catulus, Q. (cos. 102), 159, 162–63

Lutatius Catulus, Q. (cos. 78), 54, 74, 76–77, 82–83, 87–88, 158, 162–63

Macedonia, 33, 153

Maelius, Sp., 92, 158

Magistri: importance of, in *collegia*, 25, 136, 142, 146–48; as political intermediaries, 26, 29, 125, 136, 142, 146–48; influence of, 29, 146–48; support Clodius, 115, 125, 136, 142, 146–48; and grain distributions, 125, 142, 147

Magna Mater, 169

Manilius, C. (tr. pl. 66), 117, 236

Manlius Capitolinus, M. (cos. 392), 158

Manlius Torquatus, 106

Manlius Torquatus, L. (cos. 65), 54, 55, 154

Marcius Philippus, L. (cos. 91), 115

Marcius Philippus, L. (cos. 56), 197

Marcius Rex, Q. (cos. 68), 34, 47–53, 60, 61, 69

Marius, C. (cos. 107), 28

Memmius, C. (pr. 58), 110, 139–40, 231–33

Memmius, C. (tr. pl. 54), 234

Menulla of Anagnia, 164, 249

Mercatores, 18

Mercenarii, 18, 29, 115, 143, 146

Messius, C. (tr. pl. 57), 176–79, 186, 189

Minucius Esquilinus Augurinus, L. (cos. or cos. suff. 458), 92–93, 100

Mithridates VI (king of Pontus), 44–50, 194

Montes, 25

Mos maiorum: and *populares*, 2, 10; and *optimates*, 3, 10; as political motive, 9, 99–100, 140; codified in law, 126–27, 134; and religion, 130, 164, 190

Motives: contradictory interpretations of, in sources, 1, 2, 12, 39–40; and *populares*, 6–7, 12–15; of Cicero, 8–9, 78–80; and Roman frankness, 9; in politics, 11–16, 23–24; and local stratification, 19, 146–48; revenge, 73, 80–81, 95, 97–98, 138, 150, 204, 209, 283 (n. 55); of senators in Bona Dea scandal, 73–74, 80–81; of Clodius in Bona Dea scandal, 85–86; and *dolor* of Clodius, 88, 98–99; for destruction of Temple of the Nymphs, 211

Mucia, 35, 63, 69, 110, 249

Mucius Scaevola, Q. (cos. 95), 105

Munatius Plancus, T. (tr. pl. 52), 236, 241

Municipalities, 2, 19, 24–25, 154, 181, 183, 185, 239, 245

Negotiatores, 18

Neighborhoods, 19, 23, 25, 29, 117–18, 124–25, 147–48, 184, 211, 256–57

48, 179, 182, 184, 212, 225, 234–45 passim; and food shortages, 119–21, 145, 182–86, 202, 211–12; and attitude toward Catiline, 144; collective identity of, 148, 245, 256–57 (n. 101); and shattering of *fasces*, 170–71, 180; and hostility to Pompey, 174; and violence after death of Clodius, 241, 245. *See also* Client-patron relationship; *Collegia*; Grain subsidies and supply; Lower classes; Neighborhoods; *Populares*; Popularity; Violence

Plinius Secundus, C., 92

Pliny the Elder. *See* Plinius Secundus, C.

Plutarch, 40, 55, 249; on mutiny at Nisibis, 45–48, 56; on Clodius and Catilinarian conspiracy, 60; represents Clodius as foil to Pompey, 102–3

Politics: fluid alliances in, 5, 27, 30, 145, 151, 194, 231–33, 243–44; focused on short-term objectives, 5, 243–44; conceptualized in personal not programmatic terms, 7, 23, 27, 30, 37–39, 73–80, 116, 151, 166, 191, 231–35, 243, 309 (n. 48); and competition, 7–8, 9, 37–39, 134, 187, 193–94, 198–99, 222–23, 231–34, 243–44; aristocratic conceptions of, 7–8, 37–39; elements of, 8; and *dignitas*, 8, 37–39; and *mos maiorum*, 9; aristocratic initiative in, 10; importance of popularity in, 10–11, 15–16, 20–21, 26–27, 29, 30, 68–69, 80, 99, 140–42, 145, 211–12, 235, 244–45; importance of neighborhood groups in, 19, 26, 29–30, 115, 118–19, 146–48, 244, 256–57 (n. 101), 309 (n. 48); and importance of *clientela*, 21–22; role of intermediaries in, 24, 26, 29, 30, 115, 146–48, 225, 239, 309 (n. 48); citizens active in, 28–30, 296 (n. 159); and local stratification, 29–30, 118–19, 146–48, 244; popular ideologies in, 30, 145–48, 151–55, 166, 179, 299 (n. 17); and importance of aristocratic *domus*, 159–61, 166, 188–93; and appropriation of cults, 160, 165; and military service, 263 (n. 63).

See also Elections; Family connections; Friendship; Lower classes; Popularity; Popular sovereignty

Pompeia, 64, 67, 71, 85

Pompeius Magnus, Cn. (cos. 70), 5, 9, 28, 32, 44, 47, 49, 52, 61; marries Mucia, 35; and Nisibis mutiny, 48; and war against pirates, 50; returns from the East, 62–64, 102; rebuffed by Cato, 63; divorces Mucia, 63, 69–70; and Bona Dea scandal, 69–70, 76–77, 85; as object of senatorial concern, 71, 102–4, 116, 139–41, 168–72, 176, 189–208 passim, 221, 241; and Afranius, 89, 102, 201; and Cicero, 102, 176–85; and early friendship with Clodius, 102–4, 136–38; and Caesar, 103, 110, 214–15, 241; and Clodius's adoption, 104–5, 108; and Vettius affair, 111–13, 153; *cura annonae* of, 122–25, 183, 186–88, 190, 195, 199–200, 211–12; house and theater complex of, 159–60, 166; Clodius attacks eastern settlement of, 168–70; home attacked by Clodian gangs, 174; assassination attempt against, 174, 203; and struggle with Clodius over Cicero's restoration, 176–85, 190; employs urban violence, 180, 184–87, 191, 203, 211, 222–23; accused by Clodius of causing grain shortage, 183, 186, 190; and restoration of Auletes, 194–209 passim; defends Milo, 202–4; and friendship and marriage alliance with Claudii Pulchri, 204, 214–15, 221; defends Sestius, 206; second consulship of 222–23; and return of Gabinius, 233–34; opposes Milo's candidacy for consulship, 234–35; created sole consul after death of Clodius, 241, 245. *See also* First Triumvirate

Pompeius Rufus, Q. (tr. pl. 52), 239, 241

Pompey the Great. *See* Pompeius Magnus, Cn.

Pomponius, P., 146, 239

Pomponius Atticus, T., 11, 15, 23, 54, 65, 67, 72, 77, 82, 84–85, 90, 102, 108–9,

137–38, 170, 172, 176–77, 188–89, 225, 228, 242

Pontifex Maximus, 13, 64, 67, 74, 104–5

Pontiffs, 13, 67, 72–74, 104–5, 107, 158, 163–64, 187–92, 217, 274 (n. 72)

Populares: Cicero's description of, 1–3, 13–14, 77, 297 (n. 164); consistent with *mos maiorum*, 2, 4, 7, 10–11, 13–15, 146, 153–54, 157–58, 237; and lower classes, 3, 5, 7, 9, 12–15, 77, 141–42, 146, 167, 236–38, 247; and *equites*, 3, 5, 154–55; typical issues of, 3–5, 76–77, 102, 141–42, 150–53, 236; not radical reformers, 4; and *iura populi*, 5, 9, 12, 76–77, 146, 148, 151–55, 167, 237, 243; brief careers of, 5, 12, 15–16, 121, 148, 176, 236–39, 243; and tribunate, 5, 13–14, 76–77, 151–52, 176, 223; not a political party, 5, 77, 116, 295 (n. 115); no affinity among, 5, 295 (n. 115); motives of, 6–7, 12, 14, 76–77; and *libertas*, 7, 9, 76, 141, 153, 167, 174, 192, 236–39, 243; and alienation from senate, 7, 13–14, 114, 146, 153–54, 194, 243; ideology of, 7–11, 13, 146, 150–53; and *furor*, 12; and *dignitas*, 12–13; and *dolor*, 13, 98–99; and aristocracy, 13–14; not egalitarian, 15, 142, 147, 247, 255 (n. 72); and *clientela*, 22; dichotomy with *optimates* too schematic, 31, 143–44, 153–54, 168–74, 194, 243; and politics in Bona Dea trial, 76–80; *levissimus*, 77; and Caesar's consulship, 103–4; and significance of grain distributions, 120–22, 150; and *obnuntiatio*, 128–29, 132; and shattering of *fasces*, 170–71, 180; and freedmen, 236–39. See also *Provocatio*

Popularity: importance of, in politics, 10–11, 15, 20–21, 80, 99, 140–42, 145, 214–15, 235, 244–45; inherited, 13, 68; at trials, 15, 140–41, 145; at games, 15, 145, 257 (n. 104), 308 (n. 45), 319 (n. 232); and consistency and fickleness of public, 15–16, 141–42, 148, 235, 310 (n. 76); and *clienta*, 21–22; and *collegia*, 26, 119; and *gloria*, 37;

and nobility, 68–69, 247; and grain supply, 121; constant benefactions unnecessary for, 121, 148; and importance of *domus*, 160, 166; and aedileship, 198–99. *See also* Grain subsidies and supply; *Gratia*; Lower classes; *Plebs urbana*

Popular sovereignty, 3, 10. *See also* Assemblies; *Libertas*

Porcius Cato, C. (tr. pl. 56), 70, 112, 126, 197, 200, 203–4, 214, 222–23, 228–30

Porcius Cato, M. (cos. 195), 107

Porcius Cato, M. (pr. 54), 12, 32, 203, 219, 243; tribunate of, 6, 120–21, 249; and excessive devotion to principle, 11–12; and *dolor*, 38; contrasted with Clodius in tradition, 40; and prosecution of Murena, 58; and Catilinarian conspiracy, 62; rebuffs Pompey, 63; and Bona Dea scandal, 74, 79, 81–82, 87–88, 281 (n. 2); defends Fabia from Clodius, 89; opposes Flavius, 102; opposes First Triumvirate, 103, 222–23; and annexation of Cyprus, 122, 155–56, 220; as Clodian intermediary, 138; defends legitimacy of Clodius's tribunate, 220–21; clashes with Clodius over Cypriot slaves, 221–22; fails to win praetorship, 232; family connections of, 249

Porta Romana at Ostia, 290 (n. 44)

Portico of Catulus, 159, 162–64, 192–93

Postumius Albinus, 106

Postumus, C., 58–59

Praefectus annonae, 123

Praeneste, 160

Prensatio, 23

Prestige, 17, 133; in neighborhoods, 19, 118–19, 125, 244; and importance of clients, 21–22; and foreign kings, 51, 169, 195, 199–201, 203–4, 265 (n. 96). *See also Auctoritas; Dignitas*; Local stratification; Popularity; Status

Procilius, 229–30, 323 (n. 81)

Prodigia, 73

Professio, 23, 54, 140, 227

Proletarii, 17, 20

Provocatio, 10, 30, 79, 146, 153–54, 158,
165, 167, 179, 182, 188, 243, 299 (n. 17).
See also *Iura populi; Libertas*
Proximate stratification. *See* Local
stratification
Ptolemy (king of Cyprus), 50, 150
Ptolemy X Alexander, 194–95
Ptolemy XII Auletes, 108, 194–204,
208–9, 233, 312–13 (n. 116)
Publicani, 2, 17–19, 170, 233, 321 (nn. 22,
23); role of, in elections, 23; as ene-
mies of Lucullus, 44; support Cicero,
154, 182; and controversy over Syrian
contracts, 218–19, 321 (nn. 22, 23)
Public building, 26, 163–66, 189,
198–99, 244, 302 (n. 79)
Publilius Syrus, 14
Pulchellus, 43
Pupius Piso, M. (cos. 61), 69, 71, 74–75,
79, 85, 87, 89, 96. See also *Rogatio*
Puteoli, 119

Quaestor Ostiensis, 119
Quinctius, L. (pr. 68), 47
Quindecimviri sacris faciundis, 191,
200–201, 218

Rabirius Postumus, C., 195
Racilius, L. (tr. pl. 56), 197–98, 220
Ravenna, 208
Regimen morum. See Census
Regnum, 14, 158, 300 (n. 45)
Religion, 3, 14; rites of Bona Dea,
64–65, 69; *delictum*, 65–67, 72–75,
81, 216–19; and sensibilities in late
republic, 66–67, 74, 86, 125–33, 160,
191–92, 200–201, 216–19, 274 (n. 73);
and role of senate, 71–75, 163, 188–93,
200–201, 216–19, 274 (n. 73); and
family *sacra*, 105–7, 159–60; and *execratio*, 110–11; and Ludii Compitalicii,
117–18, 136, 149; and augural law, 126–
32, 163, 173; vitiation in, 127, 129–30,
172–74, 189; and importance of
domus, 159–60; and political appropriation of cults, 160, 165; and *aedes
Libertatis*, 162–67, 187–92, 216–19;
consecration, 163–64, 187–92, 216–19,

304 (n. 113); cult of Magna Mater at
Pessinus, 169; and *consecratio bono-
rum*, 171; and authority of Roman
people, 192. See also *Haruspices;
Ludi; Obnuntiatio; Pax deorum;
Quindecimviri sacris faciundis;*
Sibylline oracles
Revenge. *See* Motives
Rights of the people. *See Iura populi*
Rogationes. See Legislative proposals
Rural poor, 3, 4. *See also* Lower classes;
Plebs rustica
Rutilius Lupus, P. (pr. 49), 201, 212

Sacrilegium, 72–73, 75
Sacrorum detestatio, 101–2, 105–6
Sallust. *See* Sallustius Crispus, C.
Sallustius Crispus, C. (pr. 46), 12,
240; on political motivations, 1–2;
class bias in writings of, 3; as source
for Clodius's life, 40; on events at
Nisibis, 45–46
Salutatores, 27–28
Sampsigeramus, 51–52
Sardinia, 119, 215, 231–32
Saufeius, M., 240
Scato, 115, 158
Scholia Bobiensia. See Bobbio Scholiast
Scribes, 115, 182, 208, 249, 291 (n. 53)
Scribonius Curio, C. (cos. 76), 69,
79–81, 88, 110, 112, 154–55, 172, 190,
203
Scribonius Curio, C. (tr. pl. suff. 50),
70, 78–80, 110, 112
Seius Postumus, Q., 161–62, 164
Sempronia, 60
Sempronii Atratini, 93
Sempronius Atratinus, L. (cos. suff. 34),
209–10, 282 (n. 35)
Sempronius Gracchus, C. (tr. pl. 123),
10, 13, 15, 28, 119–20, 122, 158. *See also*
Gracchi and Gracchan reforms
Sempronius Gracchus, Ti. (cos. 238),
165
Sempronius Gracchus, Ti. (cos. 215),
165
Sempronius Gracchus, Ti. (cos. 177),
236

Sempronius Gracchus, Ti. (tr. pl. 133), 1, 13, 22, 28, 33, 126. *See also* Gracchi and Gracchan reforms

Senate, Roman, 1, 13, 16, 17, 19, 30; principal members of (*principes*), 2, 7, 74, 150–58, 193–94, 206, 216, 305 (n. 3); conflicting demands on, 8, 116, 152, 194, 231–34, 243; and need to cultivate popularity, 20–21; and importance of clients, 21–22; and reliance on intermediaries, 24, 26–27; and Italian aristocracy, 24, 144, 154, 181–82, 239, 245; in *deductio*, 27; and religious matters, 71–73, 130, 160, 163, 173, 189–93, 200–201, 216–19, 274 (n. 73); relations with *equites*, 82, 154–55, 218–19, 281 (n. 2), 321 (nn. 22, 23); reacts to Clodius's acquittal in Bona Dea trial, 87–89, 281 (n. 2); hostile to First Triumvirate, 103–4, 109–11, 116, 139–41, 168, 214–19, 221–23, 231–34, 241; suppresses *collegia*, 117–18, 136–37; hostile to grain subsidies, 120–21, 150; and the census, 133–35, 294 (n. 107), 295 (n. 112); maximum capacity of, 134; and *pedarii*, 135, 227; and Cicero's exile, 151–58; responds to Clodian violence, 155, 171, 179–81, 184, 187, 191–94, 196, 297 (n. 175); and support of *boni* for Clodius, 168–74, 193–94, 196–98, 202–4, 218–21, 232, 234, 237, 305 (n. 3); and shattering of *fasces*, 170–71, 180; and recognition and restoration of Auletes, 194–204, 208–9; censures Pompey for urban violence, 203, 210; disbands *sodalitates* and *decuriati*, 205, 225–26; and hostility toward Caesar, 207–8; votes special funds for grain supply, 212; and conference at Luca, 214–15; responds to Clodius's death, 241; and military service, 263 (n. 63). *See also* Elections; Elite classes; *Invidia*; *Lectio senatus*; *Optimates*; Politics; *Senatus auctoritas*

Senatus auctoritas, 1, 10, 11, 13, 14, 31, 85, 134–35, 168, 243; and *populares*, 3, 7, 76–80, 96, 153–54, 168, 299 (n. 17);

and *optimates*, 3, 153–54; identified with Cicero, 77–80, 103, 151–55, 188, 299 (n. 17)

Senatus consultum ultimum, 63, 153, 241

Sequester, 26, 58, 84. *See also* Bribery

Sergius, L., 78, 144, 146, 185

Sergius Catilina, L. (pr. 68), 13, 38, 210; linked with Clodius in tradition, 40; prosecuted by Clodius in 65, 53–55, 59–60; electoral campaign in 63, 56–57, 145; conspiracy of, 58–60, 62–64, 72, 77–78, 88, 112, 117, 120, 145, 151, 154; as recurring element in Ciceronian vilification, 142–45, 277 (n. 117)

Serranus. *See* Atilius Serranus Gavianus, Sex.

Servilia, 248–49

Servilii, 32

Servilius, C. (pr. before 218), 93–94

Servilius, P. (cos. 252), 93

Servilius Ahala, C., 158

Servilius Caepio, Q. (cos. 106), 248–49

Servilius Geminus, C. (cos. 203), 93

Servilius Pulex Geminus, M. (cos. 202), 93

Servilius Rullus, P. (tr. pl. 63), 14

Servilius Vatia Isauricus, P. (cos. 79), 201, 203, 218, 227

Servilius Vatia Isauricus, P. (cos. 48), 203

Servius Pola, 115, 227

Sestius, P. (pr. 54), 1, 143, 174, 176, 179–80, 182, 196, 205–7

Shopkeepers. See *Opifices*; *Tabernarii*

Shrine of Liberty. See *Libertas*

Sibylline oracles, 200–201

Sicily, 89–90, 95–97, 99, 119

Sittius, P., 183

Slaves, 17, 75, 174, 180, 240; in elections, 18; in various occupations, 18; in *collegia*, 25, 117; and Catilinarian conspiracy, 63; in trials for *incestum*, 81; freed in response to Clodius's *lex frumentaria*, 125; in Clodius's following, 142, 193, 296 (n. 152); and Jupiter Libertas, 165; Clodius's proposal concerning informal manumission of, 238–39. *See also* Lower classes

Social stratification, 16–22. *See also* Local stratification

Social War, 4

Sodalitates, 19, 23, 26–27, 70, 205, 225–26. *See also* Bribery; Elections

Spectio. See Obnuntiatio

Spes, 30

Statues, 160, 164, 242, 303 (n. 87)

Status: based on wealth and character, 16–17, 133; and occupations, 18; among lower classes, 19, 25; in assemblies, 19–20; change from patrician to plebeian, 90–102, 104–8; and *domus,* 159–61, 166. *See also* Ancestry; Local stratification

Sulpicia, 94

Sulpicius Rufus, P. (tr. pl. 88), 13, 93–95, 97, 236

Sulpicius Rufus, P. (q. 69), 94

Sulpicius Rufus, P. (cens. 42[?]), 94

Sulpicius Rufus, Ser. (tr. mil. c. p. 388), 94

Sulpicius Rufus, Ser. (cos. 51), 56–58, 94, 101

Sulpicius Rufus, Ser. (son of cos. 51), 94

Syracuse, 89

Syria, 49–52, 87–88, 96, 153, 218–19

Tabernarii, 17, 198; not a single interest group, 18, 29; in *deductio,* 28; close shops, 29, 143, 199; support Clodius, 115, 143–48, 180, 185, 296 (n. 159). See also *Opifices*

Tarpeius Montanus Capitolinus, Sp. (cos. 454), 93

Teidius, Sex., 241

Temple of Castor, 142–43, 179

Temple of Juno Moneta, 158

Temple of Juno Sospita, 268 (n. 139)

Temple of Jupiter Libertas, 165

Temple of the Nymphs, 211–12

Temple of Venus Victrix, 159

Templum, 163

Tenues homines, 17, 118. *See also* Lower classes; *Plebs urbana*

Terentius Varro, M. (pr. uncertain date), 36, 172

Terentius Varro Lucullus, M. (cos. 73), 154, 201–2

Terracina, 115

Tettius Damio, 193

Theater. *See* Games; Ludi

Tigranes (king of Armenia), 44–47, 50–51, 109, 170

Tigranes (son of the king), 170

Tigranocerta, 44

Titius of Reate, 115, 180

Tradition. See *Mos maiorum*

Transalpine Gaul, 56

Transitio ad plebem, 90–102. *See also* Co-optation; *Sacrorum detestatio*

Transvestism, 66

Treasury. See *Aerarium*

Trebonius, C. (cos. 45), 223

Trials, 15; of M. Scaurus, 13; of Lentulus, 42, 230–31; of Catiline, 53–55; of Murena, 58–59; of Clodius, 80–85, 87–88, 144, 160, 190, 230–31, 239; of Antonius, 103–4, 109, 209; of C. Cato, 126, 228–29; hearings before censors, 133–35, 227; of Caesar's ex-quaestor, 139; of Vatinius, 140–41, 232; of Milo, 201–6, 212, 320 (n. 8); of Sestius, 205–7; of Cispius, 208; of Cloelius, 208, 211; of Plancius, 208, 225; of Caelius, 208–10, 227–28; of Bestia, 209; conference at Luca, 218–21; of Sufenas, 229; of Procilius, 229–30, 323 (n. 81); of Scaurus, 231–33; of Milo in 52, 241; of Munatius Plancus, 241; of Pompeius Rufus, 241

Tribal assembles. *See* Assemblies: tribal

Tribes, 19, 23–24, 26, 117, 235, 236–38, 249, 325 (n. 114)

Tribune of the *plebs,* 1; and *populares,* 3, 5, 148, 223; and Conflict of the Orders, 9; and *auxilium,* 9, 118, 140–41; as office of opposition, 9–10, 94, 96, 118, 151–55, 167; Cicero's hostility toward, 10–11; and *libertas,* 11, 151–55; and value of support in elections, 23; office useful for winning gratitude, 39, 99, 244; co-optation of, 92–94;

and *obnuntiatio*, 127–32; and interference with fellow tribunes, 129; and interference with census, 134; and public building, 164, 302 (n. 79); and *consecratio bonorum*, 171; and tablets recording legislation, 220; and Augustus, 245

Tribuni aerarii, 16–17, 55, 76, 82

Trinundinum (*Trinum Nundinum*), 23, 107

Tullio, P., 218

Tullius, M., 205–6

Tullius Cicero, M. (cos. 63): on *populares* and *optimates*, 1–3, 5, 12–14; class bias in orations of, 2–3, 118, 143, 190, 193, 212; usurps role of *popularis*, 6, 14; career of, 8–9; embodies optimate ideology, 9, 77–80, 103, 151–55; on popular sovereignty, 10; and hostility to tribunate, 10–11, 126; criticizes Cato, 11–12; on motives for *popularis* career, 12–13; on legitimate *popularis* legislation, 13–14; and popularity at games, 15, 20; represents interests of *collegia*, 19; on cultivating popularity, 20–21; and campaign for consulship, 23, 72; on splendor of Claudii, 32–33; on Scaurus's career, 37; as principal source for Clodius's life, 39–40, 97–98, 125, 140, 156, 219, 247–48; on Nisibis mutiny, 49; on Clodius's alleged collusion in Catiline's trial, 53–55, 59–60; assimilates Clodius to Catiline, 54, 59, 78, 88, 96, 142–45, 277 (n. 117); attacks Clodius's provincial service in Gaul, 56, 58–59; attacks Catiline, 56–57; defends Murena, 58–59; and role in Catilinarian conspiracy, 62, 77, 79; and role in Bona Dea scandal, 65–67, 74–85 passim; and Roman religion, 66, 125–32; *invidia Ciceronis*, 78–79, 103, 151–55, 176, 186–87, 191, 194, 215, 217; attacks Clodius after his acquittal, 83–85, 87–90; *In Clodium et Curionem*, 87–89, 95–96; denies *dolor* as Clodian motive, 88; attacks Clodius's role in elections of 61, 89; in *deductio* with

Clodius, 90; on inaccuracies in Roman history, 91; and Clodius's *transitio ad plebem*, 95, 97–98, 100–102, 107; and Pompey, 102, 136–38, 185–87, 219; and First Triumvirate, 103–4, 108–10, 138, 151–56, 171, 213–15, 219, 232; attacks legitimacy of Clodius's tribunate, 104–5, 220; on Clodius's adoption, 104–8; loses *domus*, 107, 156, 157–58, 162, 186–92, 217–20, 300 (n. 38); and role in Vettius affair, 112, 153; resists Clodius's legislation, 116, 136–38, 166; confounds freedmen with slaves in hostile rhetoric, 118, 193, 211–12, 238, 296 (n. 152); denounces *lex Clodia de agendo cum populo*, 125–26, 130–32; exile of, 129, 146, 151–58, 243; denounces *lex Clodia de censoria notione*, 135; relationship with *optimates*, 138, 171, 187, 191, 194, 215, 217–21, 232; attacks Clodius's popular following, 142–44, 146, 296 (n. 152); as symbol of tyranny, 165; and restoration from exile, 171–85, 187, 193, 208, 243; accused by Clodius of causing grain shortage, 183, 185, 190; attacked by Clodian gangs, 193; and restoration of Auletes, 194–204 passim, 208–9; defends Milo, 202–4, 241; defends Sestius, 206–7; attacks Caesar, 207; defends Caelius, 209–10; clashes with Clodius over *publicani*, 218–19; removes Clodian tablets from Capitol, 219–21; avoids conflicts in court for fear of Clodius, 228–30; defends Scaurus, 231–33; defends Vatinius, 232; return of Gabinius, 233–34; prosecutes Munatius Plancus and Pompeius Rufus, 241; and Dolabella, 242

Tullius Cicero, Q. (pr. 62), 148, 162, 178, 184, 193, 218, 228, 234, 256 (n. 99)

Tullius Decula, M. (cos. 81), 91

Tullius Longus, M'. (cos. 500), 91

Tullius, Servius, 92

Tullus, Attius, 92

Urban *plebs*. See *Plebs urbana*

Valerius Catullus, C., 41, 70, 248
Valerius Maximus, 94, 230, 241
Valerius Messalla, M. (cos. 61), 74, 77,
190, 227. See also *Rogatio*
Valerius Messalla Rufus, M. (cos. 53),
231–33
Valerius Publicola, P. (cos. suff. 509),
160
Vatinius, P. (cos. 47), 108, 130, 132, 140–
41, 143, 148, 155, 167, 202, 206–7, 230,
232
Vergilius Balbus, C. (pr. 62), 89–90
Vesta, 42, 231
Vestal Virgins, 64, 66–67, 74–75
Veterans, 18, 29, 57, 68–69, 102, 120
Veto, 79, 97, 102, 122, 128–29, 137, 153,
156, 169, 171, 177–78, 181, 192–93. See
also *Intercessio*
Vettius, L., 111–12
Vettius affair, 111–13, 153
Vettius Cyrus, 198–99
Veturius, L., 107
Vibullius Rufus, L., 218
Vicinitates, 19, 25, 117–18, 148, 184
Violence, 115, 117, 127–28, 137, 201; and
attempt to recall Pompey during
Catilinarian conspiracy, 63; and Bona
Dea scandal, 79, 82; and Caesar's
consulship, 103–4, 129–30; and
attempt to try Gabinius for *ambitus*,

112; and food riots, 120, 125, 145,
182–85, 211–12; at Vatinius's trial, 141,
149, 155, 167; Roman proprieties
regarding, 145–46, 297 (n. 175); and
events leading to Cicero's exile, 154–
55; directed at Cicero's property, 156,
158, 162, 193; in the Tigranes episode,
170; between Clodius and Gabinius,
170–71; and attempt to assassinate
Pompey, 174; between Clodius and
Milo, 178–80, 193, 196, 198; in Cicero's
restoration, 178–81, 191; by Auletes,
195, 209; and elections for the year
56, 196–97; at Milo's trial, 202–5; at
Megalensian Games, 211–12; as an
offense to the gods, 216; and Cicero's
removal of Clodian tablets from the
Capitol, 220; and elections for the
year 55, 222–23; at C. Cato's trial, 228;
during campaigns for magistracies
of 52, 235–40; incited by Clodius's
death, 241; and the political identity
of the *plebs urbana*, 245
Vipsanius Agrippa, M. (cos. 37), 245
Virtus, 7, 37
Volcacius Tullus, L. (cos. 66), 54, 201

War, 18, 37, 263 (n. 63)
Wealth, 3, 8; and status, 16–17; importance of, in assemblies, 19–20, 24;
expended in elections, 27
Weapons, 143

Made in United States
North Haven, CT
29 October 2021